The Book of the BSA BANTAM

Covering the Practical Maintenance of all 1948–1970 BSA Bantam Two-stroke Motor-cycles

W. C. Haycraft, F.R.S.A.

Revised by

A. G. Lupton, C.Eng, M.I.Mech.E.

INTRODUCTION

Welcome to the world of digital publishing ~ the book you now hold in your hand, while unchanged from the original edition, was printed using the latest state of the art digital technology. The advent of print-on-demand has forever changed the publishing process, never has information been so accessible and it is our hope that this book serves your informational needs for years to come. If this is your first exposure to digital publishing, we hope that you are pleased with the results. Many more titles of interest to the classic automobile and motorcycle enthusiast, collector and restorer are available via our website at www.VelocePress.com. We hope that you find this title as interesting as we do.

NOTE FROM THE PUBLISHER

The information presented is true and complete to the best of our knowledge. All recommendations are made without any guarantees on the part of the author or the publisher, who also disclaim all liability incurred with the use of this information.

TRADEMARKS

We recognize that some words, model names and designations, for example, mentioned herein are the property of the trademark holder. We use them for identification purposes only. This is not an official publication.

INFORMATION ON THE USE OF THIS PUBLICATION

This manual is an invaluable resource for the classic motorcycle enthusiast and a "must have" for owners interested in performing their own maintenance. However, in today's information age we are constantly subject to changes in common practice, new technology, availability of improved materials and increased awareness of chemical toxicity. As such, it is advised that the user consult with an experienced professional prior to undertaking any procedure described herein. While every care has been taken to ensure correctness of information, it is obviously not possible to guarantee complete freedom from errors or omissions or to accept liability arising from such errors or omissions. Therefore, any individual that uses the information contained within, or elects to perform or participate in do-it-yourself repairs or modifications acknowledges that there is a risk factor involved and that the publisher or its associates cannot be held responsible for personal injury or property damage resulting from the use of the information or the outcome of such procedures.

WARNING!

One final word of advice, this publication is intended to be used as a reference guide, and when in doubt the reader should consult with a qualified technician.

Preface

The two-stroke B.S.A. Bantam was introduced to the British public at the 1948 Motor Cycle Show. Since its introduction it has "caught on" in a truly remarkable manner. This is perhaps not surprising considering the Bantam's alluring looks, lightness (Model D7: 214 lb), and satisfying all-round performance.

The Bantam steers with precision, holds the road tenaciously and can cruise at around 40 m.p.h. almost indefinitely without "fuss." Fuel consumption is *extremely* low. As in the case of other renowned B.S.A. models, easy starting and thorough reliability are predominant characteristics.

With every motor-cycle, thorough reliability over a prolonged period depends, ultimately, on how the machine is maintained by its owner. The purpose of this handbook is to provide in a convenient and digestible form all essential instructions necessary for the efficient maintenance of *all* 1948–70 *Bantams*, so as to assist owners to obtain the maximum pleasure and mileage per gallon and per hour.

Note that instructions are included in this book for competition as well as touring models, and that all instructions for Model D7 apply also to the 1965–6 de luxe Model D7D/L which is almost identical. In August 1966 the Model 7 was replaced by a more powerful version known as the D10 (fitted with either a three or four-speed gearbox), which in turn was superseded for the 1968 season by the D14/4 (still more powerful, and incorporating the four-speed gearbox). In 1970 this model became known simply as the Bantam 175.

In conclusion I sincerely thank B.S.A. Motor Cycles Ltd. of Birmingham, 11, for valuable assistance in regard to technical data, and for according me permission to reproduce some B.S.A. copyright illustrations. I also thank Wico-Pacy Group Sales Ltd., Amal Ltd., and other firms for their helpful co-operation.

W. C. HAYCRAFT

Contents

1 Handling a Bantam

It is assumed that you are about to purchase or have just taken delivery of a new or second-hand 123 cm^3 or 174 cm^3 B.S.A. Bantam, a machine of which you will doubtless be proud and find easy to handle, even if you have had no previous experience.

Should you yourself be a complete novice, obtain, read, and thoroughly digest the *Highway code*. A full knowledge of this booklet is essential to ensure safe riding and compliance with the law. See that you have a crash helmet for use on long and short runs. Accident statistics show that motorcyclists are particularly prone to serious head injuries. Such injuries can have disastrous effects.

Various Preliminaries. Before you can legally ride a Bantam on the public highway you must comply with various essential preliminaries. In this book which is primarily concerned with Bantam maintenance it is only possible to deal with these preliminaries in the barest outline.

If you purchase a new or second-hand Bantam from a reputable dealer, you will almost invariably find him ready to assist you with most of the essential preliminaries (licensing, number plates, insurance, etc.), and it may only be necessary for you to settle financially with the dealer, either cash down or on hire-purchase terms, and then take personal delivery of your Bantam or have it delivered by the dealer to your address.

As regards the essential preliminaries, here is a brief outline of them. You must:

1. Insure against all third-party risks (injuries to persons other than yourself or a pillion passenger, if carried). If you purchase your machine on hire-purchase terms, the dealer concerned will insist on your taking out a full comprehensive insurance, which is always advisable in the case of a valuable new machine.

2. Obtain a "Certificate of Insurance" or a cover note (for a new machine) pending the issue of a certificate by your insurance company. Without either, you will be unable to obtain a registration licence.

3. Obtain a registration licence and registration book[1] (Form V.E. 1/2),

[1] On Form V.E. 1/2 you are required to state the engine and frame numbers. On 1948–52 Bantams the engine number is located at the front of the crankcase on the near side, between the engine fixing lugs. On 1953–70 models the engine number is on top of the crankcase, below the cylinder. On all 1948–70 Bantams the frame number is located on the bottom of the front down-tube (or at the top of the steering-head tube).

or renew the existing licence (Form V.E. 1/A) if expired. All B.S.A. 123 cm³, 148 cm³ and 174 cm³ Bantams are taxed at the rate of £5 per annum. If a sidecar is attached (not advised), no additional tax is necessary.

4. Fit the registration licence disc in the waterproof licence holder on the near side of the front forks.

5. See that the index letters and registration numbers allocated to your Bantam are painted correctly on the number plates.

Fig. 1. Cheap to run, easy to maintain, light and thoroughly reliable—the attractive 1968 174 cm³ Bantam (Model D14/4)

This popular general-purpose mount weighing only 214 lb has a de luxe finish in electric blue and black with chromium plated tank panels. The other 1968 B.S.A. lightweight, the 174 cm³ "Bantam Sports" (Model D14/45) is basically similar. Both these modern machines have a highly efficient two-stroke engine with built-in gearbox, a quickly detachable light-alloy cylinder head, petroil lubrication, coil ignition, battery lighting, a most comfortable dualseat, telescopic front forks, and swinging arm rear suspension

6. Mount "L" plates at the front and rear if you are a "learner."

7. Obtain a "Provisional" (six months) or "Qualified" (three-year) driving licence (Form D.L.1.), whichever is appropriate. You are *not* entitled to a full licence for Group G unless you are aged *sixteen* and have complied with one of these conditions:

(*a*) You have held a licence (other than a provisional or Visitor's licence), authorizing the driving of vehicles of the class or description applied for, within a period of ten years ending on the date of coming into force of the licence applied for.

(*b*) You have passed the prescribed driving test (a test passed when serving in H.M. Forces is valid) during the above period.

8. If you carry a pillion passenger while a "learner," see that he or she sits *astride* a proper pillion seat or dualseat securely *fixed* to the machine, and has a "qualified" driving licence (cost is £1).

9. Verify that the fork-mounted or headlamp-mounted speedometer *is* in proper working order. A Smith's speedometer (driven from the rear wheel) is fitted as standard. To comply with the law the speedometer must indicate within ±10 per cent accuracy when 30 m.p.h. is being exceeded, and be illuminated at night.

10. If the machine is second-hand, make sure it is thoroughly roadworthy. Check that *both* brakes are in proper working order, that the front and rear lights are functioning correctly (with *rear* number plate illuminated) and that the horn gives "audible warning of approach." A bulb horn is fitted to a.c. models, but an electric horn is available as an extra for 1951–65 Bantams with Wipac a.c. direct lighting, and is standard equipment on models having a Lucas or Wipac battery-lighting set.

11. If you own a Bantam registered for the first time after 1st July, 1953, you must use an "ignition-suppression" type sparking plug which does not interfere with radio and television sets.

12. If you are a "learner" and feel qualified to take a driving test, apply for one on Form D.L.26. The cost of a driving test is £1.75.

13. If your B.S.A. Bantam was first registered more than three years ago, obtain an MoT certificate (see page 15).

Vetting a Second-hand Bantam. Make sure that all accessories and equipment are securely mounted. With the appropriate spanners check over the external nuts for tightness, paying special attention to the wheel-spindle nuts and the external nuts on the engine and those securing it to the frame. See that there is no excessive "shake" in the wheel and steering-head bearings, that the saddle or dualseat is comfortable, that the rear chain and wheel sprocket are not badly worn, and that the tyres are in reasonably good condition. Above all, make sure that no excessive mechanical noise emanates from the engine when it is turned over or started up. Nothing should be taken for granted where a second-hand machine is concerned, though many examples (especially where there has been only one previous owner) are in first-rate condition and require little or no attention before taking the road (*see also* paragraph 10 above).

Handlebars Adjustable for Angle. Should the riding position not be the best obtainable, having regard to your own particular physique, you can vary the angle of the handlebars to some extent by loosening the four bolts on the top of the handlebar clamps and then turning the bars to the desired angle. On the 1954 Model D3 and many D3 and D5 models, slacken the four nuts clamping the handlebar bend to the aluminium cover. The nuts are situated below the bars, two in front and two at the rear. Having done this, you can then turn the bars to the required angle, Be sure that you afterwards retighten the bolts or nuts securely. On competition models the footrests are adjustable to six different positions. To adjust the angle of each footrest, first remove its securing nut and lightly tap the footrest off its hexagonal shaft. Then replace the footrest in the required position and tighten its securing nut.

THE BANTAM CONTROLS

If you have never before handled a Bantam, you should get quite familiar with the control layout before making any attempt to start up. Note the exact location of each control and consider what it is for and how it is operated. Also reflect on which controls are used in conjuction with each other. It is a sound idea to sit astride the saddle and twiddle the various controls while imagining what the effect would be were the engine running.

Three Control Groups. The Bantam controls (*see* Figs. 3–5) are mostly located on the handlebars, and for convenience may be divided into three groups: (1) engine controls, (2) motor-cycle controls, and (3) electrical controls.

1. The engine controls comprise: (*a*) the throttle twist-grip, (*b*) the carburettor strangler or (on 1966–70 models) the air control, (*c*) the ignition switch, on models with coil ignition, (*d*) the decompressor on competition models only, and (*e*) the kick-starter.
2. The motor-cycle controls are: (*a*) the clutch lever, (*b*) the foot gear-change pedal, (*c*) the front brake lever, and (*d*) the rear brake pedal.
3. The electrical controls are: (*a*) the lighting switch, (*b*) the dipper switch, and (*c*) the horn button.

The Throttle Twist-grip. This is mounted on the handlebar extremity on the right side. Turning the rubber-covered grip *inwards* (i.e. towards the rider) raises the throttle slide in the single-lever needle-jet Amal carburettor and admits more mixture, thus increasing engine speed. Turning the grip outwards closes the throttle and decreases engine speed. Full movement: about ¼ turn.

The Carburettor Strangler (1949–65 Models). No air lever is provided on the handlebars. Instead a strangler is embodied in the bell of the carburettor air-intake and controls the amount of air admitted to the carburettor. The strangler consists of a perforated plate the rotation of which masks or unmasks similar bell perforations.

Except when starting from cold, when the strangler should be *momentarily* closed (*see* page 12), the strangler should at all times be kept fully open. To close the strangler in order to provide a very rich mixture, *raise* the small lever on the right side of the carburettor.

The Carburettor Air Control (1966 Models). A shutter is not provided on the bell of the carburettor air-intake. Instead a carburettor air slide is included, and this is controlled by a spring-loaded plunger on top of the Amal instrument as shown in Fig. 2.

To close the air control in order to reduce the amount of air sucked into the carburettor and thereby enrich the air–petrol mixture, press down the plunger as far as possible and then rotate it until it is secured by the locking

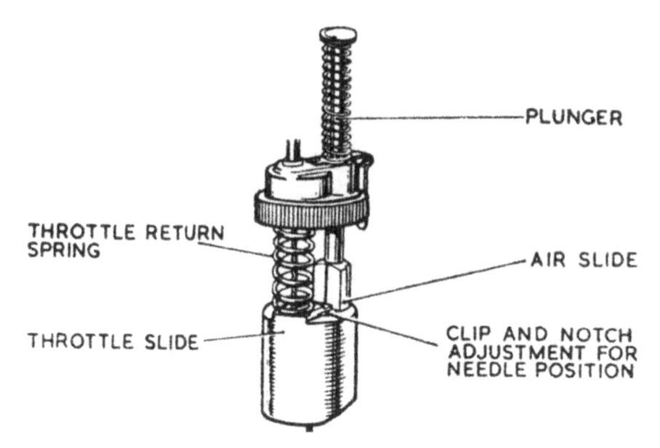

Fig. 2. Showing the air-control plunger and air slide fitted to the Amal "Monobloc" carburettor on all 1966 models

Depress the plunger only momentarily when difficulty is experienced in starting a cold engine

clip. Closing this control is recommended *if necessary* when starting up a *cold* engine. Immediately the engine fires, open it to obtain the normal air supply by further rotating the spring-loaded plunger until it is released from the locking clip.

Never ride with the air control closed and when using the control for starting, close it for a *brief* period only.

The Carburettor Air Control (1967–70 Models). An air slide is included in the specification of the Amal "Concentric" carburettor fitted to these models (*see* Fig. 16) and is controlled by a lever on the right handlebar. To close the air slide for cold starting purposes only, turn the lever in an anti-clockwise direction (away from the rider), but at all other times the lever should be kept in the fully clockwise position.

Special Note on Carburettors for All Models. It must be emphasized that excessive use of the strangler or air control, as the case may be, is likely to cause liquid petrol to enter the crankcase and render starting almost impossible until the petrol is drained off by removing the smaller of the two drain plugs beneath the crankcase.

The Ignition Switch (1950–3 Models). On Bantams equipped with Lucas coil-ignition and battery-lighting equipment, an ignition key is provided in the centre of the headlamp lighting switch. This does *not* apply to 1954–66 models with Wipac rectifier and battery lighting. The Lucas ignition key has three positions:

EMG—Emergency position for starting when the battery is fully discharged and it is necessary to switch the generator output direct into the ignition circuit by disconnecting the battery.

Fig. 3. The Model D1, D3 Bantam handlebar controls, speedometer, horn, etc.

Above is a pre-1958 Model D1 with Wico-Pacy flywheel generator and direct lighting. On the battery models an electric horn is fitted, and an ignition key is provided in the centre of the lighting switch (Lucas only). Competition models have a decompressor lever on the near side of the handlebars. A handlebar screen is available as an extra

1. *Combined filler cap and oil measure*
2. *Dipper switch*
3. *Clutch lever*
4. *Lighting switch*
5. *Smiths 55 m.p.h. speedometer*
6. *Front-brake lever*
7. *Throttle twist-grip*
8. *Bulb horn (direct lighting models)*

OFF—Ignition switched off. Battery and generator disconnected.

IGN—Ignition switched on. Battery passing L.T. current through the primary circuit (i.e. coil primary-winding and contact-breaker).

For all normal starting and riding, the ignition switch should be kept in the IGN position. Use the EMG position solely for an emergency start when the battery is badly run down. To obtain the maximum generator output, it may be necessary to move the lighting switch to the "pilot" (P) position. As soon as the engine fires, turn the ignition switch over to the IGN position, otherwise the battery will not be on charge. If the battery is completely "flat," you may have to run for a period with the ignition switch in the EMG position, but this period must never be excessive.

When you "cut" a Bantam engine with Lucas coil-ignition, always remember that you must switch off the ignition, otherwise there is a risk of the battery becoming discharged if the contacts of the contact-breaker happen to be closed. If the battery should be removed from the machine make no attempt to start up the engine (*see* note on page 10).

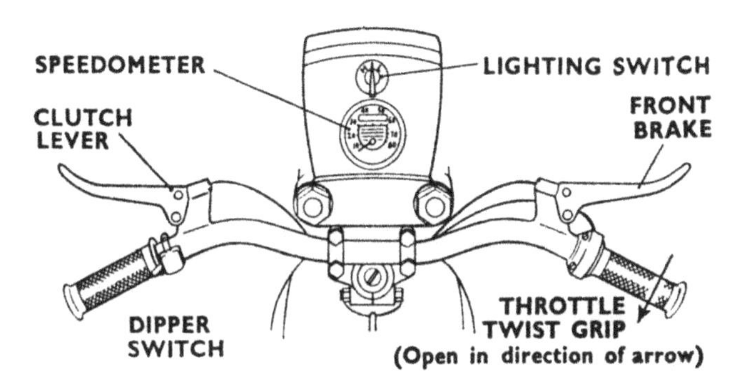

Fig. 4. The Model D5, D7 handlebar controls, lighting switch, etc. (Wipac direct lighting)

Applicable to 1958–65 Models

The Ignition Switch (1964–70 Models). On 1964–70 coil-ignition models with Wico-Pacy lighting-ignition equipment the ignition switch is separately located from the lighting switch on the offside of the headlamp nacelle. Its three positions are as below.

1. With the switch positioned straight ahead as shown in Fig. 5, the ignition is switched off. When a Bantam is left standing with the engine stopped the ignition should always be left switched off, otherwise after hours (overnight, for example) the battery may become badly discharged through leakage via the contact-breaker, if the contacts happen to be closed.
2. For normal starting procedure the ignition switch should be turned so that position "I" is straight ahead.
3. In the event of the battery being badly discharged for some reason, the ignition switch should be turned until position "E" lies straight ahead; the lighting switch turned to the "OFF" position, and an emergency start attempted. As soon as the engine fires, the ignition switch should be turned to the "I" position. Do not run the engine with the ignition switch in the emergency position for more than 15 minutes.

The Decompressor. On B.S.A. Bantam competition models the first of which was introduced in April, 1949, a decompressor unit (commonly called a compression-release valve) is screwed into the cylinder head and is actuated by a lever on the near side of the handlebars.

The Kick-starter Pedal. This is located on the off-side at the rear end of the engine and gearbox unit, and depressing the pedal turns the engine over. The kick-starter pedal is provided for starting purposes only (with the foot gear-change pedal in "neutral" and the clutch engaged). On Bantam competition models the pedal is of the positive spring-loaded folding type,

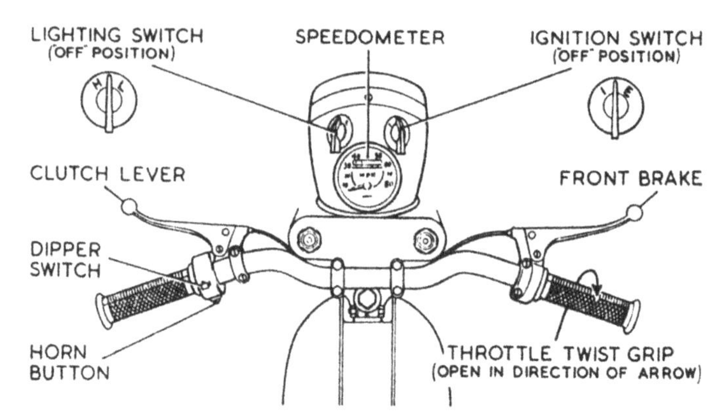

Fig. 5. Handlebar controls for Models D7, D10, D14, and Bantam 175 lighting switch, ignition switch, etc. (Lucas battery lighting)

The above switch arrangement applies to all 1964–70 Bantams with Wipac coil-ignition equipment. The only Lucas component used is the battery. On models D10 and D14 and Bantam 175, the right handlebar also carries the carburettor air control lever (not shown in the illustration) and the headlamp is an independent unit

the pedal automatically remaining in the folded or "action" position, as required.

The Clutch Lever. The handlebar lever for engaging or disengaging the clutch is positioned in front of the left-side handlebar grip. To disengage the clutch (i.e. to disconnect the drive from the engine to the rear wheel), it is necessary to "squeeze" the lever fully. On releasing the lever the clutch automatically becomes re-engaged.

It is necessary to disengage the clutch in order to engage first gear (from "neutral"), with the machine stationary, and when making each subsequent gear change (*see* page 13). No attempt must be made to control the speed of the machine by means of the clutch.

The Foot Gear-change Pedal. On the off-side of the engine and gearbox unit is the toe-operated positive-stop gear-change pedal. This, in conjunction with the clutch (see earlier paragraph), enables "neutral" and the three gear ratios (four on later models) to be obtained as required. It should be particularly noted that the gear-change pedal *always returns to the same position* after each gear change is effected.

To change to a higher gear, it is necessary to *raise* the foot gear-change pedal to its full extent with the toe. Similarly to change to a lower gear, the pedal must be *depressed* with the toe. To obtain first gear from "neutral," a downward movement of the gear-change pedal is required. A gear-change indicator (*see* Fig. 6) is provided on the secondary chain guard on early models.

The Front-brake Lever. This handlebar control lever is similar to the clutch lever, but is mounted on the right side. Observe that the front-brake lever has no connection with the operation of the rear brake, but both brakes should be operated simultaneously to obtain the maximum braking with the minimum wear of the brakes, tyres, and transmission.

The Rear-brake Pedal. Situated on the left side of the machine, this control needs no explaining other than to mention that the brake pedal should be applied progressively and simultaneously with the front-brake lever. Before using either brake, the throttle should always be closed.

The Lighting Switch. On 1948–51 Bantams having direct-lighting equipment, the lighting switch comprises a remote control lever (*see* Fig. 28) on the left side of the handlebars. Moving the switch lever in one direction obtains consecutively the following four positions—OFF, PARK, FULL, and DIP. The park position is intended solely for use when the machine is stationary (the parking bulb being lit by a dry battery behind the reflector).

On 1952–65 Bantams with direct lighting equipment, the lighting switch (January, 1952, onwards) is built into the headlamp, and has three positions —OFF, LOW, and HEAD (OFF, L, H). A dry battery (in the headlamp) is retained for the LOW position used for parking, but an essential difference from the earlier equipment is the provision of a dipper switch on the handlebars.

On Bantams fitted with Lucas (1950–3) or Wipac (1954–66) battery-lighting as an alternative to the Wipac direct-lighting set, the lighting switch, together with the ammeter, is mounted on top of the headlamp shell and also has three positions—OFF, P, H (Lucas) or OFF, L, H (Wipac). A parking bulb is lit with the switch in the P or L position. A double-filament main bulb is provided, and with the switch in the H position, a dipper switch switches over from the main driving beam to the dipped beam. With Wipac battery lighting, maximum generator output occurs with the lighting switch in the L position. If the battery is discharged, turn to position L.

The Dipper Switch. With the 1952–66 Wipac or the 1950–3 Lucas equipment referred to above, the dipper switch is mounted on the left side of the handlebars behind the clutch lever. It controls the switching from main to dipped beam. On all models with direct lighting it is a separate unit clipped to the handlebars.

On all models (except D3, D1) with battery lighting the dipper switch is combined with a horn button in a single housing adjacent to the handlebar grip.

Note that on 1951–2 models with direct-lighting equipment it is important to operate the dipper switch in a *positive* way from right to left, or vice versa. Be careful not to press the switch upwards or downwards, because this may cause a sharp rise in the voltage due to poor electrical contact, and thus a possible failure of the speedometer and tail lamp bulbs.

The Horn Button. On models having an electric horn instead of a bulb horn built into the steering stem (i.e. on Bantams with battery lighting equipment), the horn button is screwed into the front-brake lever bracket on the right side of the handlebars on Models D1, D3 and D5 but on Models D7, D10, D14, and Bantam 175, is combined with the dipper switch. (*See* Fig. 5.)

STARTING PROCEDURE

Use of Petrol Tap. The petrol (or more correctly "petroil") tap is conveniently located beneath the rear end of the tank. During 1948–66 two different designs of tap have been fitted to Bantams.

On 1948 to late 1951 models the tap fitted has two knobs, one being hexagonal in shape, and the other serrated. To *turn on* this type of tap, push in the *hexagon-shaped knob*. To turn off the tap, push in the serrated knob.

Late 1951 and subsequent Bantams have a button-type tap (*see* Fig. 6). In this instance, to turn on the tap, pull out the button and lock it in position by turning anti-clockwise. To turn off the tap, turn the button clockwise and then push it in. Some models have *two* petrol taps of the button type. Keep one tap closed to maintain a petrol reserve.

Battery Leads Disconnected (Lucas). On 1950–3 Bantams with the Lucas coil-ignition and battery-lighting equipment, it is very important never to attempt to start up the engine with the ignition switch in the IGN or EMG position and the battery disconnected.[1] Failure to observe this precaution will adversely affect the equipment, and if the lamps are switched on with the ignition switch in the IGN position, the bulb filaments will undoubtedly be burned out.

Battery Leads Disconnected (Wipac). Many 1954–64 Bantams have Wipac battery-lighting sets; should it be necessary to run the engine continuously with the Varley battery removed and the battery leads disconnected,[2] the *positive* lead must be connected to an earthed portion of the motor-cycle frame on early 1954 models (see page 77). On late 1954 and 1955–70 Bantams with the "positive earth" system, it is necessary to connect the *negative* lead to the frame. Unless this is done, the rectifier may be damaged. On 1956–70 machines, to avoid the risk of fusing all bulbs and burning out the rectifier, completely disconnect the rectifier at the snap connectors and insulate all leads from each other and from earth.

[1] Note that the battery leads must be reconnected with the battery *positive* terminal earthed. Damage to the rectifier will result from reversal of the battery leads.

[2] See that the battery leads are subsequently reconnected with the correct terminal of the battery earthed. Reversal of the battery leads will damage the rectifier. Do not rev. an engine with battery removed.

To Start Up the Engine. It is assumed that fuel and oil replenishment have been attended to, and that the tyre pressures have been checked and if necessary corrected (*see* page 104). To start up proceed as follows:

1. See that the foot gear-change lever is in the "O" or "neutral" position (between first and second gears), and verify that it *is* in this position by observing (where provided) the gear-change indicator (*see* Fig. 6) or by moving the machine freely backwards or forwards.

2. Turn on the petrol tap (*see* page 10), and if the engine is stone cold, momentarily depress the "tickler" on the float chamber of the carburettor.

Fig. 6. Left-side close-up view showing 1953 engine, clutch adjustment, gear-change indicator, rear-brake pedal, etc.

1. *Button type petrol tap*
2. *Gear-change indicator (positions front to rear: 1, 0, 2, 3)*
3. *Grease nipple for clutch withdrawal mechanism*
4. *Lock-nut for clutch adjusting-pin*
5. *Clutch adjusting-pin*
6. *Rear-brake pedal shaft*

If the engine is fairly warm, no flooding of the carburettor should be necessary. Avoid oscillating the "tickler" rapidly because this is liable to damage the rather vulnerable float.

3. Close the air strangler (if the engine is quite cold) by raising the small lever on the offside of the carburettor. Closing the strangler is rarely necessary when starting up after making a brief halt. If dealing with a *cold* 1966 engine which refuses to start, lower the air slide in the carburettor by depressing the air-control plunger (*see* Fig. 2) on top of the carburettor.

In the case of 1967–70 engines the slide is closed by means of a lever on the right handlebar (see page 5).

4. On a 1950–3 Bantam provided with Lucas coil-ignition and d.c. battery-lighting equipment, turn the ignition switch (*see* page 5) in the centre of the lighting switch to the IGN position (the EMG position if the battery is discharged). On a 1964–70 Bantam provided with Wipac coil-ignition and battery lighting, turn the ignition switch until the position marked "I" (*see* Fig. 5) is straight ahead. Unless this is done it will be quite impossible for the engine to fire. For emergency starting *with a discharged battery*, rotate the switch until position "E" is straight ahead. The lighting switch must be in the "OFF" position.

5. Open the throttle slightly by turning the twist-grip a small amount (about one-eighth to one-quarter of its total movement).

6. Turn the engine over slowly until resistance is felt and then smartly by applying a vigorous sweeping thrust on the starter pedal. The engine should fire at the first or second attempt. On a Competition model the starter pedal can be neatly folded as soon as the engine starts up.

7. Immediately the engine fires, open the air strangler or the air slide, according to model (*see* page 5). If very cold weather prevails, however, it may be necessary to run the engine for a brief period before opening the strangler or air slide. Note that either should normally be used only momentarily (*see* special note on page 5). If an emergency start was made, return the ignition switch to its normal position.

8. Should the engine fail to start up quickly, first verify that the petroil mixture is reaching the float chamber of the carburettor. Watch for petrol drips on depressing the "tickler" on the float-chamber lid. Avoid excessive flooding, however. If the fuel supply is in order, remove the sparking plug and inspect it carefully. If necessary, clean it thoroughly and reset the gap to between 0·018 in. and 0·020 in. (0·020–0·025 in., coil ignition).

HINTS ON RIDING

Even if you are absolutely "green," you will quickly master the handling of the machine on the road. The Bantam, besides being light and easy to man-handle, has excellent road manners, and the gear-change pedal is easy to operate. Confidence born of practice is soon acquired.

Practise moving off, gear changing, and stopping on a quiet road until you feel ready to venture forth upon a major road with normal traffic.

Before attempting to negotiate main road traffic it is essential to get so used to handling the Bantam that the operation of the controls becomes instinctive and your reactions immediate. So long as you have to premeditate what you are about to do, you are a road menace.

To Engage First Gear. It is assumed that the gear-change pedal is still in neutral. Now, to engage first gear, disengage the clutch, and with the toe of the foot *depress* the foot gear-change pedal to its *full* extent. Should it be found that first gear does not engage readily, do not attempt to exert force on the pedal, but rock the machine gently backwards and forwards while maintaining gentle foot pressure on the pedal until first gear is *felt* to engage.

Moving Off. Having engaged first gear, open the throttle slightly to avoid stalling the engine, by gently turning the twist-grip inwards, and gradually engage the clutch. Your Bantam will then move off. As it gathers momentum, progressively open the throttle still farther to maintain a steady increase in the speed of the engine and machine.

Changing Up into Second Gear. When your Bantam attains a road speed of 12–15 m.p.h. (10 m.p.h. on models with four-speed gearboxes), change up into second gear. Disengage the clutch, close the throttle slightly, pause a second, and *raise* the foot gear-change pedal *fully* (deliberately but without force) with the toe of the foot until second gear is felt to engage. Then engage the clutch, but do not remove the toe from the pedal until the clutch is *fully* engaged. Immediately afterwards open the throttle again to maintain speed.

Changing Up into Third Gear (and Fourth Gear on Later Models). Repeat the procedure used for obtaining second gear, but change up into top gear on 3-speed models when you attain a road speed of 20–25 m.p.h. For 4-speed models, change into third gear at about 20 m.p.h. and into top gear at about 25/30 m.p.h.

To Change Down. Throttle down until your Bantam is running at a speed normal for the gear to be selected. Now disengage the clutch, open the throttle slightly, pause a second, and *depress* the gear-change pedal to its *full* extent until the lower gear is *felt* to engage. Avoid the use of any force, but employ a smart action of the foot. As soon as the gear is felt to engage, gently let in the clutch, and remove your toe from the pedal. Then adjust the throttle opening according to the road speed required. Repeat this procedure for each downward gearchange.

Changing Down from Top to First Gear. Except when climbing a gradient it is not essential to complete each of the gear changes individually. You can instead use this procedure: first reduce your speed to a crawl by closing the throttle and applying the front and rear brakes; then disengage the clutch and depress the foot gear-change pedal to its full extent twice (three times on a four-speed gearbox) in quick succession, "blipping" the engine slightly prior to each movement of the pedal. This procedure sounds difficult but in practice is easily mastered. When first gear is felt to engage, engage the clutch, remove the toe from the gear-change pedal, and open the throttle as required.

To Stop in Neutral. Close the throttle almost completely, apply the front and rear brakes together, disengage the clutch and change down into first or second gear. Then with the machine stationary, the engine running slowly and the clutch disengaged, obtain neutral from first or second gear by *slightly* raising or depressing respectively the gear-change pedal.

To stop the engine itself, switch off the ignition by means of the ignition key or switch, according to model. Where an ignition switch is not provided it is necessary to close the throttle completely to stop the engine. Alternatively turn off the petrol tap. Do this before leaving the machine for an extended period so that the petroil mixture is thereby drained from the carburettor float chamber, thus obviating the risk of oil settling in the float chamber while the machine is left standing.

Technique of Good Gear Changing, Continue to practise gear changing until the changes can be effected silently, positively, and quickly. Avoid excessive noise, and remember that listening to the rise and fall in the exhaust note considerably facilitates good gear changing. Operate the throttle twist-grip, clutch, and gear-change pedal in one well co-ordinated movement keeping the eyes straight ahead when making each change.

During each gear change keep a steady pressure on the gear-change pedal until the clutch is *fully* engaged. To avoid undue wear and tear, do not let the engine labour in top gear. Always change down *before* the engine gets "bothered" and do not rev-up the engine excessively with a lower gear engaged. The Bantam gearbox is sturdy, but always treat it with some respect. You will then find that it will operate efficiently without any attention to its mechanism for a very big mileage. For information on gearbox lubrication, *see* page 18.

Steering Lock (1956–70 Models). Mounted beneath the bottom fork-yoke on 1956–9 Bantams, this has a key. To lock the steering, turn the forks to the *left* and then turn the key *anti-clockwise* in the lock to release the plunger. The machine is then safe from being wheeled or ridden away. Always keep the key on a chain ring to prevent loss. On 1960–70 models no plunger and key are provided and a padlock should be used for locking purposes. Turn the forks to the left until the hole in the special frame lug coincides with a corresponding hole in the bottom yoke lug. Then lock the two lugs together with a padlock.

Ministry of Transport Test Certificate. A MoT certificate for road worthiness must be obtained from an authorized garage, dealer or repair shop in respect of any motor-cycle used in the U.K. which was first registered *more than three years ago*. Subsequently the certificate must be renewed *annually*. It must be produced when applying for a registration licence in respect of renewal or change of ownership (Forms VE 1/A and VE 1/2 respectively), together with a valid *certificate of insurance* and the registration book.

The MoT certificate costs 87½p and it is legal to ride an *untaxed* motor-cycle to a suitable testing station after making an appointment for a test there. The required certificate is issued on the spot if the motor-cycle passes the statutory test for efficiency of the tyres, brakes, steering, lamps, horn, etc.

2 Bantam lubrication

ENGINE LUBRICATION

The basic purpose of all engine lubrication systems is to prevent friction (and consequent heat) between all moving surfaces by creating an oil film between these moving surfaces and thereby preventing damaging metal-to-metal contact. To ensure efficient lubrication it is necessary to:

1. Use a suitable brand and grade of engine oil.
2. See that the petroil mixture in the tank contains the correct proportions of oil and petrol.
3. Drain off occasionally any liquid oil accumulated in the crankcase. Do not coast downhill for long with the *throttle shut*.

The Petroil Lubrication System. This is the simplest form of two-stroke engine lubrication system, highly efficient and requiring the minimum of attention on the part of the owner rider. With this system the engine oil is mixed with the fuel in the tank in definite proportions (*see* later paragraph) and this petroil mixture is fed to the carburettor and sucked into the crankcase via the inlet port during each upward piston stroke. As the piston descends the petroil mixture is compressed in the crankcase and most of the oil is separated out as liquid oil which gets on the crankshaft assembly and splash-lubricates the various internal moving parts (assisted by a fan-type impeller, 1956–66).

The petrol and air components of the petroil mixture pass up through the transfer port into the combustion chamber. Surplus engine oil is carried by the transfer of fuel into the combustion chamber. Later D1, D5, D7, D7D/L engines (with caged roller big-end bearing) have a positive oil feed for the mainshaft bearings (*see* Fig. 10)

Suitable Engine Oils. It is most desirable always to purchase engine oil in sealed containers or from branded cabinets and never to buy an inferior or unsuitable oil, otherwise you may be landed with a worn or damaged cylinder, piston, bearings, etc. If you must economize, cut down on cigarettes, not engine oil. B.S.A. Motor Cycles Ltd. recommended the use of one of the following oils, for summer and winter use:

1. Castrol Two-stroke Oil.
2. Mobiloil Mobilix TT.

3. Esso Two-stroke (2T) Motor Oil.
4. Energol Two-stroke Oil.
5. Shell 2T Two-stroke Oil.
6. Regent Motor Oil 2T.

Self-mixing Engine Oils. The first five of the above oils are specially prepared for two-stroke engines and dissolve very quickly and completely with the petrol.

The Petroil Mixture. It is essential that the petroil mixture consists of the correct proportions of petrol and engine oil.

In 1967 the proportion of petrol and self-mixing oil was changed as a result of the development of improved oils for use in two-stroke engines and shortly afterwards the oil measure hitherto incorporated in the filler cap was discontinued.

Although all earlier Bantams were supplied with an oil measure, the dimensions of which varied according to model and various mixture strengths quoted for different purposes, the latest recommendations are suitable for all models. Hence cap markings can be ignored.

Recommended petroil mixture (by volume) using one of the specially prepared two-stroke engine oils quoted above, is as follows

1 part oil to 24 parts petrol (i.e. a 4 per cent mixture)

The majority of garage petroil dispensers are designed to give variable proportions, so make sure that the attendant has set the controls to give the correct ratio.

It is always important to ensure that during replenishment, the petrol and oil are thoroughly mixed. If the oil is not properly absorbed in the petrol, there is considerable risk of undiluted oil reaching the carburettor jet, with consequent difficulty in starting.

For those owners who prefer to mix their own petroil using "standard" oil, or are unable to obtain ready-mixed fuel containing the special two-stroke lubricating oil, an engine oil of SAE 40 grade must be used, the proportions of the mixture being 1 part oil to 32 parts petrol (or a 3 per cent mixture). In these circumstances, it is preferable to have the petrol in a separate container, add the right amount of engine oil, and shake thoroughly until the oil is completely dissolved in the petrol. Only then should the petroil be put into your Bantam tank. It will also be advisable before starting up, especially after standing overnight, to agitate the fuel in the tank by rocking the machine sideways. This will avoid the possibility of neat oil (which may have settled in the bottom of the tank) passing direct to the carburettor, making starting difficult, if not impossible. It must be emphasized that the manufacturers strongly recommend the use of the special two-stroke engine oils and every effort should be made to obtain these lubricants. Use the SAE 40 grade of engine oil only when the recommended engine oils cannot be obtained.

Suitable grades of SAE 40 engine oils are: Castrol XXL; Shell X100–40; Esso Motor Oil 40/50; Mobiloil "A"; Energol SAE 40; Havoline SAE 40.

Draining the Crankcase. It is seldom that any appreciable quantity of liquid engine oil accumulates in the crankcase, but when such oil is present it should be drained off. Do this preferably after a run, when the engine is warm and the oil flows freely, thus clearing any impurities or deposits within the crankcase. During the running-in period (1,500 miles) it is particularly important to drain the crankcase, as this eradicates any minute metallic particles collected therein and produced by the bedding down of bearings, piston rings, etc.

The makers of the Bantam strongly advise draining the crankcase of a new or reconditioned engine after covering approximately 250 miles (400 km) and again at 1,000 miles. Subsequently, draining at intervals of about 2,000 miles (3,200 km) should be quite sufficient. To drain the crankcase remove the *smaller* of the two screwed plugs from the base of the crankcase after placing a drip tray or dish beneath the engine, and allow all accumulated oil to drain off. When oil ceases to drip, replace the drain plug and washer, and make quite sure that the drain plug is tightened securely. Remember that on a two-stroke engine a crankcase leakage will result in loss of compression.

Draining the Gearbox. Although the engine and gearbox embody unit construction, and the gearbox is essentially a part of the power unit, the

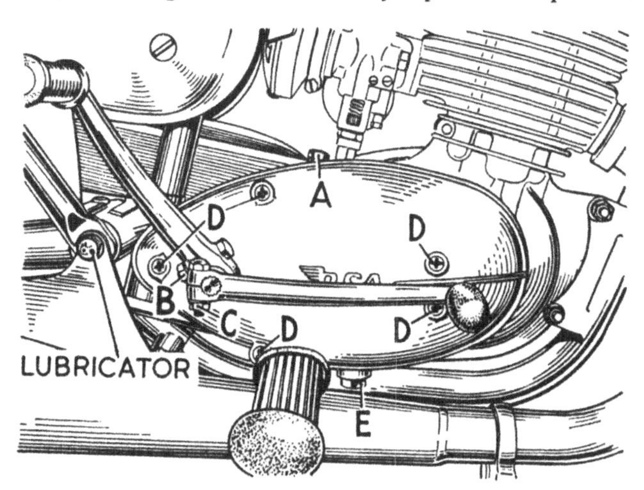

Fig. 7. The primary drive chain-case

A. *Gearbox filler plug*
B. *Nut securing kick-starter crank*
C. *Nut securing gear-change lever*
D. *Cheese-headed screws (five) securing primary drive chain-case cover*
E. *Gearbox drain plug*

gearbox is from a lubrication point of view entirely separate. It is advisable when draining the crankcase (*see* previous paragraph) also to drain and flush out the gearbox. Except during the running-in period, draining and flushing about every 2,000 miles is sufficient.

To drain the gearbox, remove the *larger* of the two plugs beneath the gearbox (the plug is shown at *E* in Fig. 7) and allow the whole of the old oil to drain off into a suitable receptacle. Then flush out the gearbox with a suitable flushing oil, and refill it with new oil (*see* below) to the level of the dipstick graduation (*see below*). The capacity of the gearbox is $\frac{3}{4}$ pint (425 cm^3), except for four-speed gearboxes, when the capacity is 1pint (570 cm^3).

Suitable Gearbox Oils. Self-mixing engine oils should *not* be used for gearbox lubrication. They should be of grade SAE 40. Six suitable oils to use (summer and winter) are:

1. Castrol XXL.
2. Mobiloil BB.
3. Esso Extra Motor Oil 40/50.
4. B.P. Energol SAE 40.
5. Shell X–100 SAE 40.
6. Regent Havoline SAE 40.

Top-up the Gearbox Every 1,000 Miles. Remove the filler plug, *A*, Fig. 7, and check the oil level in the gearbox. If necessary, top-up with one of the six engine oils mentioned above so that the level just reaches to the bottom of the dipstick attached to the filler plug, when the latter is *placed* in position over the filler-plug orifice. When the filler plug is screwed fully home, the oil level will then reach the graduation (showing the correct oil level) on the dipstick.

With the introduction of the four-speed gearbox, one of the chaincase cover drain screws *D*, Fig. 7 (coloured red) adjacent to the footrest is utilized to determine the oil level.

Remove the screw and filler plug *A*, adding oil until it flows from the level hole. Replace the screw as soon as surplus oil has drained away, and re-fit the filler plug.

Primary Chain Lubrication. The chain is enclosed within the chain-case on the off-side of the power unit (*see* Fig. 52), and provided that the gear-box is kept topped-up correctly, the chain as well as the gearbox contents is adequately lubricated. Both have a common oil supply. (*See* also Fig. 10.)

The Oil-dip Air Cleaner (1948–60). 1948–60 Bantams have an oil-dip type air cleaner built into the intake bell of the Amal carburettor. About every 1,000 miles (1,500 km) release the clip bolt and detach the bell. Allow it to soak thoroughly in petrol, dry it out, and then submerge in light engine oil for several minutes. Remove the bell, drain off all surplus oil, dry the bell externally, and finally replace it on the carburettor.

The Air Cleaner (1961–6). The air cleaner is built into the air intake bell of the carburettor and should be dismantled and cleaned about every 1,000 miles. Release the clip bolt and remove the bell. Soak it thoroughly in petrol, allow to dry, and reassemble.

The Air Cleaner (1967). The air cleaner is of the "pill-box" type and unscrews from the carburettor. Release the clip bolt, remove the perforated band and the filter element. Wash this thoroughly in petrol and dry thoroughly before replacing. Great care is necessary when screwing the air cleaner on to the carburettor because the threads are shallow and easily "crossed." This problem is aggravated by the comparatively soft material of which the carburettor is made.

The Air Cleaner (1968–70). The felt element is concealed by the right-side panel and is retained by a flexible strap. After removal, wash in petrol, allow to dry, and replace.

Special Note for Air Cleaners. Regular servicing is essential, otherwise the cleaner will become choked, resulting in heavy petrol consumption, poor performance, and excessive wear of the cylinder walls, due to an over-rich mixture at the carburettor.

Contact-breaker Lubrication. Where Wipac electrical equipment is provided, the contact-breaker requires little attention. Every 5,000 miles (4,500 km) remove the cam lubricating-pad (*see* Figs. 18, 19, 20 and 21) and smear it lightly with a little high-melting-point grease. On machines with Lucas electrical equipment (1950–3) smear a few drops of engine oil every 3,000 miles on the felt lubricator shown at *E* in Fig. 22. Also withdraw the contact-breaker rocker arm and smear a trace of grease or engine oil on the contact-breaker rocker arm pivot *C*.

THE MOTOR CYCLE PARTS

Although engine lubrication is of paramount importance, never neglect to lubricate the motor-cycle parts *regularly*. For most lubrication points a grease gun is required, but certain items need attention with an oil can.

Suitable Greases. Six suitable greases, recommended by B.S.A. Motor Cycles Ltd. are:

1. Castrolease L.M.
2. Shell Retinax A.
3. Esso Multi Purpose Grease H.
4. B.P. Energrease L2.
5. Mobilgrease MP.
6. Regent Marfak Multi purpose 2.

All the above greases possess excellent lubrication properties.

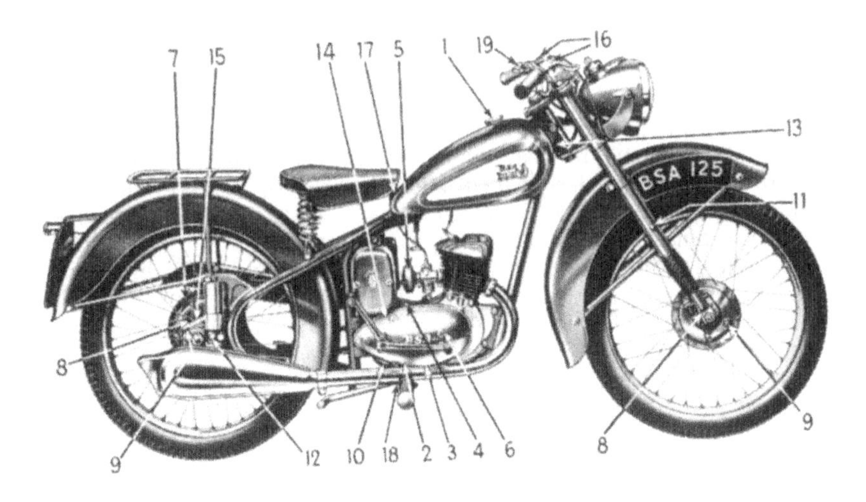

Fig. 8. When and where to lubricate your Bantam

A 1952 spring-frame Model D1 is shown above. With few exceptions, the lubrication points indicated are similar on all models.

1. Petroil tank. *Replenish with a 24 to 1 mixture of petrol and engine oil. The petrol and oil must be thoroughly mixed (see page 17)*
2. Crankcase. *Drain after the first 250 miles, at 1,000 miles, and subsequently at intervals of 2,000 miles (see page 18)*
3. Gearbox. *Drain, flush out, and replenish with new engine oil at 250 miles, 1,000 miles, and thereafter at 2,000 miles (see page 18)*
4. Gearbox. *Top-up every 1,000 miles with engine oil to the level indicated on the dipstick or level screw hole (see page 19)*
5. Air cleaner. *Every 1,000 miles remove and clean thoroughly (see page 20)*
6. Contact-breaker. *If Wico-Pacy, grease cam lubricating pad every 5,000 miles. If Lucas, oil felt cam-lubricator and rocker-arm pivot every 3,000 miles (see page 20)*
7. Secondary Chain. *Oil or grease chain regularly. Periodically remove, clean and immerse in mixture of grease and graphite (see page 22)*
8. Wheel hubs. *Grease every 1,000 miles where nipples are provided (see page 22). These were discontinued on later models.*
9. Brake-cam spindles. *Oil every 1,000 miles, grease every 2,000 miles (see page 23)*
10. Rear brake pedal. *Oil shaft weekly (see page 23)*
11. Front forks. *Grease both nipples where provided every 1,000 miles (see page 23). On D7, D10, D14, and Bantam 175 models renew oil in fork legs when necessary (see page 23)*
12. Plunger suspension units. *Grease both nipples every 1,000 miles (see page 24). On Models D7, D10, D14, and Bantam 175 grease swinging arm pivot nipples*
13. Steering head. *Apply grease gun to single nipple (where provided) every 1,000 miles (see page 24)*
14. Clutch withdrawal mechanism. *Grease nipple every 1,000 miles (see page 24)*
15. Speedometer drive. *Grease gearbox every 2,000 miles (see page 24)*
16. Control cables and levers. *Oil weekly (see page 25)*
17. Saddle-nose bolt. *Oil every 1,000 miles (see page 25) Early models only.*
18. Central stand. *Oil every 1,000 miles (see page 25)*
19. Dipper switch. *Oil every 5,000 miles (see page 9)*
20. Stop–tail lamp switch (not shown). *Oil occasionally*

Lubrication of Secondary Chain. No automatic lubrication of the secondary chain is provided, and whenever the chain appears to be running somewhat dry, apply an oil-can to the lower chain run while slowly turning the rear wheel by hand. Alternatively smear some grease on the chain with a stiff brush.

It is advisable periodically (say every 2,500–3,000 miles) to remove the chain and submerge it in a paraffin bath. Permit the chain to soak well, so that all dirt is removed, and then hang the chain up to dry. Afterwards thoroughly grease or oil the chain. Preferably it should be immersed for about five minutes in a suitable receptacle containing a warm mixture of grease and graphite. Then allow all surplus to drain off the chain. Finally fit the chain to the gearbox and rear-wheel sprockets. In doing this, make sure that the spring link is replaced with the open end facing *away from* the direction of chain movement.

Grease Hubs Every 1,000 Miles (D1, D3 and D5 Models). Apply the grease gun to the nipples on the front and rear hubs about every 1,000 miles (1,500 km), using three to four strokes. Be careful not to over-lubricate the hubs, or grease may penetrate to the brake linings and seriously reduce

Fig. 9. Showing rear hub speedometer drive

Grease the nipple shown at A about every 2,000 miles

braking efficiency. On no account use engine oil, this being too thin for the heavy duty roller bearings. On Models D7, D10, D14, and Bantam 175 the ball journal bearings are packed with grease during initial assembly and this should suffice until a complete overhaul is necessary.

Oil Brake-cam Spindles. At the same time as you lubricate the hubs (i.e. at 1,000 mile intervals), apply an oil-can to the brake-cam spindle lubricators. Only a few drops of oil are needed. On Models D5, D7, D10, D14, and Bantam 175, apply grease every 2,000 miles, using one stroke only of the grease gun. This is important, because excessive lubrication may cause the brake linings to become contaminated with grease, seriously reducing braking efficiency.

The Rear-brake Pedal. Weekly lubricate with a few drops of oil the rear-brake pedal shaft. Also oil the brake linkage.

Lubrication of Front Forks (Models D1, D3, D5). A grease nipple is provided on each telescopic front-fork leg for the lubrication of the sliding members, and it is advisable to apply the grease gun to it every 1,000 miles, giving a few strokes of the gun. Apart from the two grease nipples the forks have no other lubrication points requiring attention.

Lubrication of Front Forks (Models D7, D10, D14, and Bantam 175). No grease nipples are provided and the only lubrication necessary is renewal of the oil in the fork legs after a considerable mileage. The need for renewing the oil is indicated by excessive fork movement. Suitable oils to use are: Shell Motor Oil 101, Esso 10W/30, Mobil Super, Castrolite, B.P.

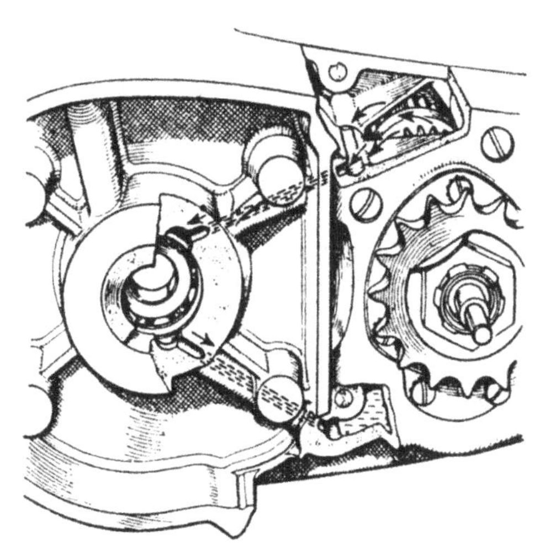

Fig. 10. On the 1958–9 Model D5 and the 1958–70 Models D1, D7, D10, D14, and Bantam 175, the gearbox and primary chain case oil automatically lubricates the crankshaft left- and right-side bearings respectively

Surplus oil drains back into the primary chain-case
(By courtesy of "Motor Cycle," London)

Energol 10W/40, and Regent Havoline 10W/30. Oil renewal for each leg should be effected in the following manner.

Prise out the cap on the top of each fork leg by means of the small hole provided, and with a tubular spanner unscrew the small nut exposed. Next remove the large nut which carried the cap. Then disconnect the mudguard stay and unscrew the stud which is also the lower mudguard connection. Allow all oil to drain out. Then apply the front brake and depress the forks a few times to drain out any remaining oil. Replace the drain stud and fibre washer and add $\frac{1}{8}$ pint of one of the above-mentioned oils to each fork leg. Finally replace the top nuts and cap.

The 1968 D14 Bantam Sports and all 1969–70 D14 models were fitted with new forks based on the design of those used on the larger machines. A drain screw is provided at the bottom of each leg and the oil can be renewed after unscrewing the large cap nut on top of the fork leg. When draining, remove the cap nut first and, after the drain plug has been taken out, apply the front brake and "pump" the forks up and down a few times to make sure the legs are quite empty. Replace the drain screw, refill with 175 cm^3 of oil from the above list, firmly tightening the cap nut afterwards. The quantity of oil quoted is a little less than $\frac{1}{3}$ pint.

Plunger Suspension Units (Models D1, D3). Each unit has one grease nipple. Apply the grease gun every 1,000 miles (a few strokes). It is important to lubricate the rear-suspension units regularly, as this gives maximum comfort and reduces any tendency for the lower tubular members to rust.

Rear Suspension (Models D5, D7, D10, D14, and Bantam 175). The two suspension units which are sealed during manufacture require no lubrication. The swinging arm pivot has lubricators (*see* Fig. 7) and the grease-gun should be applied every 1,000 miles.

Grease Steering Head Every 1,000 Miles (D1, D3 and D5 models). A few strokes of the grease gun to the nipple low down on the near side of the head is all that is necessary.

The Clutch Withdrawal Mechanism. To ensure smooth and positive operation of the clutch, it is important to apply the grease gun about every 1,000 miles (1,500 km) to the grease nipple on the near side just above the clutch-control adjustment (*see* Figs. 6 and 56).

Folding Kick-starter (Competition Models). Lubricate the pivot pin occasionally with engine oil.

The Speedometer Drive. The drive for the speedometer is taken off the rear hub, and a grease nipple for lubricating the speedometer gearbox on the off side is provided (*see* Fig. 9). Apply the grease gun about every 2,000 miles. Give a few strokes.

Oil Control Cables and Levers Weekly. Apply an oil-can (engine oil) to the handlebar levers, and do not omit to lubricate the ends of the operating cables which are subjected to considerable stresses. Also oil all external linkages to ensure free movement and reduce rusting. A few drops of oil are quite sufficient. Little and often is the best policy.

Saddle-nose Bolt. Apply every 1,000 miles a few drops of engine oil to the saddle-nose bolt (except where a dualseat is fitted).

The Central Stand. Apply a few drops of engine oil every 1,000 miles to the stand pivots.

The Steering Lock (1956–9 D3, D5, D7). Do not insert oil into the keyhole, for this is apt to clog the wards and disperse the specially prepared lubricant used during the initial assembly of the steering lock. It is permissible, however, after a big mileage and when riding continuously in wet weather to apply a few drops of *thin machine oil* to the periphery of the moving drum.

3 Correct carburation

The purpose of the carburettor is to supply the crankcase and the combustion chamber (via the transfer ports) with a correctly proportioned mixture (about 13 parts of air to 1 of petrol). The mixture on the Bantam also contains oil mist which is deposited in the crankcase during downward piston strokes.

Once the carburettor is correctly tuned it requires very little attention. The maker's settting is suitable for big temperature variations and road conditions, and it is rarely necessary to interfere with this setting. So long as the engine runs well it is best to leave the carburettor well alone, except for occcasional cleaning. Circumstances may, however, arise where it is desirable to alter the setting.

The Instrument Fitted. The carburettor fitted to the D1, D3 Bantams is a standard clip-fitted needle-controlled single-jet Amal instrument, and its official type number is 261/001D on the 1948–50 models. On the 1951–63 D1, D3 Bantams the carburettor number is 361/1 (223/7 on the 148 cm^3 models). The essential difference between the carburettor fitted to 1948–50 models and that specified on 1951–63 models is that in the former case the float-chamber cover screws into the chamber, whereas in the latter instance the the float-chamber cover is secured by two pins.

Twist-grip throttle control is provided and control of the carburettor air-strangler is by a small lever on the strangler itself. The carburettor has a semi-automatic action, and it is necessary to close the strangler or air slide (according to model) only when starting up from cold (*see* page 4). For comprehensive details of the "Monobloc" carburettor used on models D5 and D7 *see* page 32, and for details of the "Concentric" carburettor used on models D10, D14, and Bantam 175, *see* page 32.

STANDARD CARBURETTOR DETAILS

Before considering the actual tuning of the Amal carburettor, it is desirable to discuss briefly the various components which are directly concerned with tuning.

The Main Jet. The main jet (shown at (21) and *A* in Figs. 11, 12, respectively) does not affect the slow-running, or tick-over mixture, but it regulates the maximum supply of petroil from the *half to full throttle* positions. Every Amal main jet is carefully calibrated for fuel flow, and you will observe a number stamped on its hexagon. This is an indication of the volume of petroil which can flow through the main jet orifice in a given time. Note that the jet numbers are in multiples of five, e.g. 25, 30, 35, 40, 45, 50, 55, etc., and the higher the jet number, the greater is the flow capacity of the jet. When you buy a new jet, see that it has a seal attached. This seal guarantees that the size of the jet is in accordance with the number stamped on it. On no account attempt to ream out the jet orifice.

The Throttle Slide. The throttle valve or slide shown at (15) in Figs. 11, 11A is cable-controlled from the throttle twist-grip and from the fully closed to fully open position increases progressively the volume of gas sucked into the crankcase. Every throttle slide has a cut-away portion or slope as indicated at *J* in Fig. 11A. Throttle slides with different cut-aways are available and each particular cut-away has a number stamped at the base. Note that the bigger the cut-away and corresponding number, the weaker is the petroil mixture for slow-runnning (idling) and up to the half-throttle position. The same of course holds good for the half-throttle position to the slow-running position.

The Jet-needle. The needle shown at (19) in Figs. 11, 11A is secured to the throttle slide by the spring clip shown at (14) in Fig. 11 and therefore works up and down with the throttle slide. The tapered portion of the needle also moves similarly in the needle-jet shown at (18) in Fig. 11, and thereby regulates the admission of petrol vapour at different throttle openings. As may be seen in Fig. 11A, several grooves are provided on the needle, and the fitting of the clip (14) into different grooves will affect the mixture. Note that No. 1 groove is that near the end of the non-tapered part of the needle. No. 1 groove provides the lowest needle position and the weakest mixture. The effect of raising the needle by using groove No. 2, 3, or 4 is to enrich the mixture. In Fig. 11A, the spring clip is shown in groove position 2.

The Needle-jet. This is shown at (18) in Fig. 11. No marking is used on the standard size jet, but other size jets are obtainable and these are marked accordingly. Note that if the mixture becomes over-rich at half throttle after a very big mileage has been covered, it is probable that the bore of the needle-jet has worn, and the jet requires to be renewed. If the slow-running mixture is very weak, this may be corrected by fitting a larger bore needle-jet, if a smaller cut-away and raising of the needle do not effect a cure.

The Carburettor Strangler. As has been mentioned on page 4, the carburettor strangler is normally closed only when starting up the engine from cold. The effect of closing the strangler is to cut down the air supply and

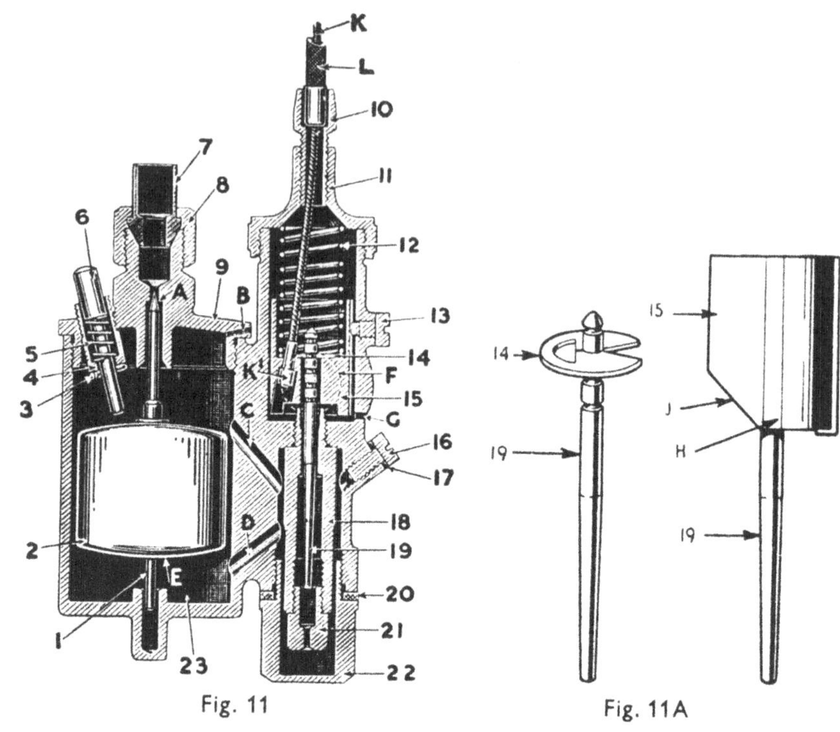

Fig. 11. Diagrammatic section through Amal standard type single-jet carburettor

Note that on type 361 carburettors a spring bow is fastened to the float at E and secures the float needle to the float. Type 261 carburettors have a one-piece float and needle as shown. The anchorage K¹ of the cable K is actually in front of the jet, not as shown

Fig. 11A. Amal throttle slide and jet-needle

A. *Float-needle seating*
B. *Float-chamber air vent*
C. *Air release duct*
D. *Petroil duct to main jet*
E. *Location for spring bow on type 361 carburettor*
F. *Choke bore*
G. *Mixing-chamber drain hole (to counteract flooding)*
H. *Throttle-slide guide groove*
J. *Throttle-slide cut-away*
K. *Throttle cable (to twist-grip)*
K¹. *Throttle-cable nipple*
L. *Cable casing*

1. *Float needle*
2. *Float*
3. *Cotter for tickler*
4. *Bush for tickler*
5. *Tickler return-spring*
6. *Tickler*
7. *Fuel-pipe union nipple*
8. *Fuel-pipe union nut*
9. *Float-chamber cover*
10. *Throttle-cable adjuster*
11. *Mixing-chamber cap*
12. *Throttle-spring*
13. *Locating screw for throttle slide*
14. *Spring clip securing tapered needle to throttle slide*
15. *Throttle slide*
16. *Feed-hole screw*
17. *Washer for feed-hole screw*
18. *Needle-jet*
19. *Tapered jet-needle*
20. *Washer for jet plug*
21. *Main jet*
22. *Jet plug*
23. *Float chamber*

increase the suction on the jet. When tuning the carburettor, however, it may be very helpful to close the strangler experimentally for a brief period in order to find out the effect of enriching the mixture.

ADJUSTMENT (STANDARD CARBURETTOR)

Permissible Adjustment. B.S.A. Motor Cycles Ltd. emphasize that no alteration to the carburettor setting should be made except for special requirements, and then preferably on expert advice. If the conditions of running are such that it is felt that greater economy of fuel can be obtained, try the effect of fitting a slightly smaller main jet *A* (Fig. 12). Alternatively lower the jet needle *B one notch*. Note that the fitting of a smaller size main jet will weaken the mixture slightly throughout the entire range of throttle openings, but the lowering of the jet-needle will weaken the mixture only on intermediate throttle openings. Full throttle openings will be unaffected.

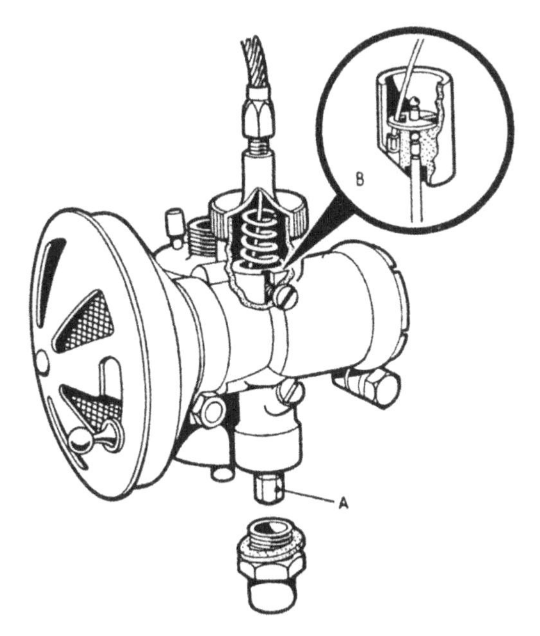

Fig. 12. Standard carburettor with jet plug removed

A. Main jet *B. Jet needle*

If the engine is running on an obviously weak mixture, you can try the effect of fitting a slightly larger main jet or raising the jet-needle *one notch*. The former adjustment will enrich the mixture throughout the entire throttle range, while the latter adjustment will affect intermediate throttle openings only.

Table I
STANDARD CARBURETTOR SETTINGS FOR 1948–63 TWO-STROKE BANTAMS (SEE ALSO PAGES 39 AND 42)

Bantam model	Carburettor type No.	Main jet	Throttle valve	Needle-jet	Needle position
D1 (1948–50)	261/001D	75	5	0·106	2
D1 (1951–63)	361/1	75	5	0·106	2
D3 (1954–7)	223/7	95	5	0·1075	2

MAINTENANCE (STANDARD CARBURETTOR)

Dismantling Carburettor. This is quite straightforward. To obtain access to the main jet and the needle-jet into which it is screwed, it is only necessary to unscrew the jet plug (as shown in Fig. 12) from the base of the mixing chamber. Both jets can then be removed.

To remove the throttle slide and the tapered needle attached to it, unscrew the mixing-chamber cap and withdraw the throttle slide and jet-needle. Note that the locating screw (13) (*see* Fig. 11) engages a groove in the throttle slide and guides the slide.

To release the throttle operating-cable, detach the cable from the slot in the throttle slide. To remove the float and attached needle from the float chamber, remove the float-chamber cover (*see* page 28) and withdraw them from the top of the float chamber. To remove the carburettor strangler from the air intake, slacken the clip securing-bolt and pull the assembly away.

Attention to Float Chamber. Impurities which collect in the float chamber are a frequent cause of persistent flooding, and it is therefore important to clean the float chamber every few months. Detach the petrol pipe from the float chamber cover, remove the cover, also the float, and carefully clean out all passages. Check that the needle, integral with the float or secured to it by a spring bow, is not bent. A bent needle will cause the float to stick and thereby cause flooding. Also shake the float to ascertain that no petrol has entered it as the result of a small puncture or a damaged seam.

If persistent flooding occurs in spite of the float chamber being clean, and the needle is not bent or the float punctured, it is probable that the float needle is not seating properly. Insert the tapered end of the needle in its seating and rotate it lightly backwards and forwards between the thumb and finger, as though grinding-in a valve. But never use any grinding compound. Should a deep groove be observed on the tapered end of the float needle, renewal of the needle (and float if integral) is called for.

Before replacing the float-chamber cover make sure that the tickler springs back and works freely. Check that the air vent in the rim of the cover is unobstructed. When replacing the float-chamber cover, first check that the blunt end of the float needle is located in the guide hole at the base of the float chamber, and then before securing the float-chamber cover, carefully guide the cover over the tapered end of the needle.

Wear of Throttle Slide and Needle-jet. After a very big mileage the throttle slide may become worn and a slack fit in the barrel of the mixing chamber. Such wear will cause air leaks and interfere with good slow-running, and the remedy, of course, is to renew the throttle slide.

Bear in mind that a badly worn throttle slide will permit lateral movement of the tapered needle in the needle-jet. The needle itself is of hardened steel and does not wear, but the lateral movement of the needle will gradually widen the bore of the needle jet, thus enriching the mixture and increasing the fuel consumption. The remedy is to lower the tapered jet-needle one notch in the throttle slide (*see* Fig. 11A), or better still, to renew the needle-jet.

Slackness of Air Strangler. Verify that the air strangler when fully opened does in fact *remain* fully open. If the perforated plate is inclined to be slack, slightly bend it so as to make its movement more stiff.

Fit of Carburettor on Inlet Pipe. After the carburettor has been removed from the inlet pipe, it is important when replacing it to make certain that the instrument is pushed fully home on the inlet pipe before spannering the nut which tightens the securing clip (D1, D3). The carburettor must always be a good push-fit on the inlet pipe and should be pushed home true with a screwing action after smearing some oil on the inlet pipe. Slackness or excessive tightness must always be avoided.

If the Mixture is Weak. The usual symptoms of a weak mixture are: erratic slow-running; poor acceleration; spitting back in the carburettor; overheating of the engine; a tendency for the engine to run poorly at full throttle openings; and greyness and dryness of the sparking plug points. If the engine ticks-over better after depressing the float tickler and delivers greater power with the air strangler partly closed, the mixture is undoubtedly weak.

Some possible causes of a weak mixture are: air leaks at the crankcase joint; a partial obstruction in the main jet or fuel supply; fuel accidently contaminated with water; a main jet which is too small; an incorrect jet-needle position (needle too low in throttle slide).

If the Mixture is Rich. The accompanying symptoms are generally as follows: a tendency for the engine to indulge in four-stroking; spraying of fuel from the carburettor; high fuel consumption; black (sooty) smoke issuing from the silencer; heavy "lumpy" running of the engine; and quick sooting-up of the sparking plug. If tick-over is better with the fuel tap shut temporarily, and spitting-back disappears on opening the throttle quickly (with the engine cold), the mixture is certainly rich.

Possible causes of a rich mixture include: sticking of the float tickler; a main jet which is too large or not screwed right home; a needle-jet whose bore has increased in size through wear; an incorrect jet-needle position (needle too high in throttle slide); flooding (*see* page 30).

"MONOBLOC" CARBURETTOR DETAILS

The Pilot Air-adjusting Screw. This adjusting screw, shown at (29) in Fig. 13, regulates the suction imposed on the pilot jet, shown at (9) in Fig. 14, by controlling the volume of air which mixes with the petrol. It controls the mixture strength for idling and also for initial throttle openings (up to one-eighth throttle).

The Throttle Stop. The throttle-stop screw, shown at (30) in Fig. 14, is normally adjusted to prop the throttle valve open sufficiently to enable the engine to tick-over nicely when the throttle twist-grip is fully closed. To obtain good slow running a combined adjustment of the throttle-stop screw and the pilot air-adjusting screw is required.

The Main Jet. This jet, shown at (13) in Fig. 14, controls the fuel supply at throttle openings exceeding three-quarters open. At smaller throttle openings the fuel supplied passes through the main jet, but the amount is decreased owing to the needle in the needle-jet, shown at (15)

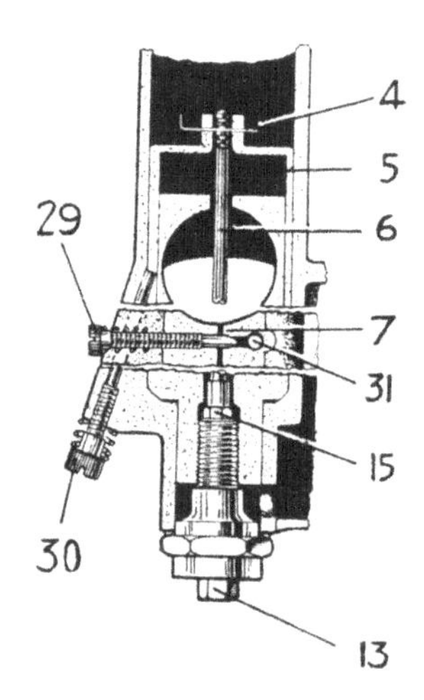

Fig. 13. Showing the throttle-stop and pilot air adjusting screw for slow-running adjustment

For key to numbered parts, see page 35

in Fig. 14 having a controlling effect. The main jet is screwed into the needle-jet and can readily be withdrawn after removing the main-jet cover nut shown at (12) in Fig. 14.

Each Amal main jet is numbered and calibrated so that its precise discharge is known. Thus it follows that any two main jets having the same number are identical in all respects. The larger the jet, the higher is its number. It is not advisable to use a main jet larger than the size recommended by B.S.A. Motor Cycles Ltd.

The Jet-needle and Needle-jet. The jet-needle, shown at (6) in Fig. 13 is attached to, and moves with, the throttle valve. Being tapered, it permits more or less fuel to pass through the needle-jet, shown at (15) in Fig. 13, as the throttle is opened or closed respectively. This applies throughout the range of throttle openings, except at full throttle and when idling. The needle-jet is of a specified size, and this should not be changed.

As may be seen in Fig. 13, the position of the jet-needle (6) relative to the throttle opening can be adjusted according to the mixture required by securing the needle to the throttle valve with the needle spring-clip (4) in a particular groove, five of which are provided. Position 3, for example, means the *third groove from the top*. At throttle openings from one-quarter to three-quarters open *raising* the needle *enriches* the mixture, while *lowering* the needle *weakens* it. The needle itself is made in one size only, and its position should not normally be changed.

MAINTENANCE ("MONOBLOC" CARBURETTOR)

Altering Slow-running Adjustment. The adjustment should be made with the engine already *warmed up*. If slow running is poor, screw home the pilot air-adjusting screw and then unscrew it (usually about *two* complete turns) until the engine idles at an excessive speed, with the throttle twist-grip closed and the throttle valve abutting the throttle-stop screw. The air strangler or air control (1966 models) should be fully open.

Referring to Fig. 13, unscrew the throttle-stop screw (30) until the engine slows up and begins to falter. Then screw the pilot air-adjusting screw (29) in or out as required to enable the engine to run regularly and faster. To *weaken* the mixture, screw the pilot air-adjusting screw *outwards*.

Slowly lower the throttle-stop screw until the engine again commences to falter. Then re-set the pilot air-adjusting screw to obtain the best slow running. If after making this second adjustment the engine ticks-over too fast, repeat the adjustment a third time. The combined adjustment sounds complicated, but in practice it is quite simple. It is important to avoid excessive richness of the slow-running mixture, especially if much riding is done on small throttle openings. If the mixture is too rich, considerable running on the pilot jet will occur while riding, with consequently a high fuel consumption.

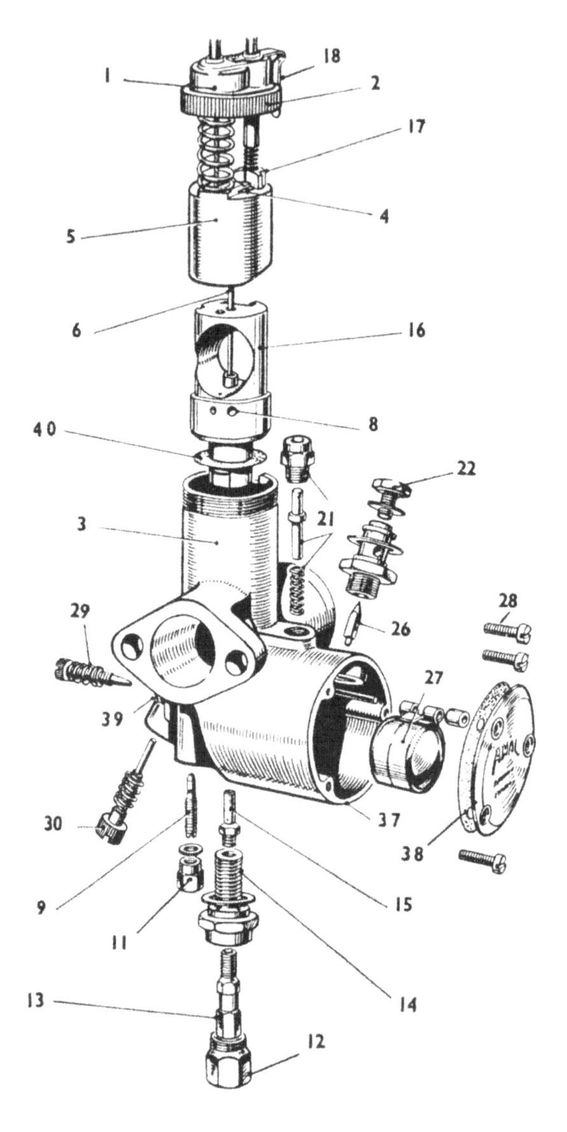

Fig. 14. Exploded view of Amal "Monobloc" Carburettor

A key to the numbered parts of the carburettor is given opposite. This carburettor is fitted to the 1958–66 Models D5, D7, D7D/L
(B.S.A. Motor Cycles Ltd.)

Aim at obtaining the best tick-over at a *moderate speed* with a mixture bordering on the weak side. The engine should be on the point of "spitting-back." Too slow a tick-over is not recommended as this can cause insufficient lubrication of the cylinder bore while the engine is hot. An excessively fast tick-over speed should be avoided as this causes overheating and excessive noise.

Persistent Poor Slow Running. If poor slow running continues after making a careful slow-running adjustment as previously described, the cause may be one or more of the following:

1. An obstructed pilot jet.
2. Air leaks caused through a poor joint between the carburettor flange and cylinder barrel face.
3. A sparking plug which has become dirty or oily or has an incorrect gap between the points.
4. An incorrect contact-breaker gap.
5. Incorrect ignition timing.

To Clear an Obstructed Pilot Jet. The pilot jet has a very narrow fuel passage and can easily become choked. Referring to Fig. 14, to remove the pilot jet (9), remove its cover nut (11) and then unscrew the jet itself. Clean it thoroughly and then blow through it, using the motor-cycle pump. It is also important to see that the air passage to the pilot jet is unobstructed. This should also be blown through. The same applies to the pilot outlet and pilot by-pass passages.

An Abnormally High Petrol Consumption. Sometimes petrol consumption remains high in spite of the carburettor being carefully tuned for

---

Key to Figs. 13–15

1. *Mixing-chamber cap*
2. *Mixing-chamber lock ring*
3. *Mixing chamber*
4. *Jet-needle clip*
5. *Throttle valve*
6. *Jet-needle (tapered)*
7. *Pilot outlet*
8. *Pilot by-pass*
9. *Pilot jet (detachable)*
10. *Feed to pilot jet*
11. *Pilot jet cover nut*
12. *Main jet cover nut*
13. *Main jet*
14. *Main-jet holder*
15. *Needle-jet*
16. *Jet block*
17. *Air valve*
18. *Locking spring for 2*
19. *Cable adjuster (air)*
20. *Cable adjuster (throttle)*
21. *Tickler assembly*
22. *Banjo bolt*
23. *Banjo*
24. *Nylon filter*
25. *Needle seating*
26. *Float-chamber needle*
27. *Float (hinged)*
28. *Float-chamber cover screws*
29. *Pilot air-adjusting screw*
30. *Throttle-stop screw*
31. *Air passage to pilot jet*
33. *"Bleed" holes in 15*
36. *Throttle-valve cut-away*
37. *Float chamber*
38. *Float-chamber cover*
39. *Locating screw for 16*
40. *Jet block fibre seal*

slow running. There are many possible causes. Some are: leakage from the carburettor due to sticking of the moulded-nylon float needle: a faulty float; a poor float-chamber cover joint; a slack main jet holder or main-jet cover nut; a loose pilot jet; a worn needle-jet; slack petrol pipe union nuts; poor engine compression caused by badly fitting piston rings; binding of the brake shoes on the brake drums; an excessively tight or dry secondary chain; or a slipping clutch. A careful investigation for the cause must be made.

Some less obvious reasons for a high petrol consumption are; air leaks due to a poor joint between the carburettor flange and cylinder barrel or late ignition timing.

Do not attempt to reduce petrol consumption by fitting a smaller size main jet. The size of this jet has no effect unless the motor cycle is being ridden with the throttle more than half open. Where the reason for a high petrol consumption is found difficult or impossible to detect, try lowering the tapered jet-needle attached to the throttle valve *one notch*. See that the jet-needle clip beds home properly in the needle groove.

Dismantling "Monobloc" Carburettor. First see that the petrol tap is closed and disconnect the petrol pipe from the float-chamber union by unscrewing the union nut. Referring to Fig. 14, remove both nuts which secure the carburettor to the cylinder barrel face and unscrew the knurled lock-ring (2) on top of the mixing chamber (3). Then withdraw the carburettor. While removing the carburettor pull the air valve (17), provided on 1966 models. and the throttle valve (5) from the mixing chamber and tie them up temporarily out of the way. Unless it is desired to inspect the slides closely it is not necessary to remove them from their cables. Check that the carburettor flange washer is in good condition.

Further dismantling of the carburettor for cleaning and inspection is straightforward. Again referring to Fig. 14, to remove the jet-needle (6), withdraw the jet-needle clip (4), on top of the throttle valve (5) and remove the needle. To obtain access to the float (27) remove the three screws (28) securing the float-chamber cover (38) to the float chamber (37). Lift out the hinged float (27) and withdraw the moulded-nylon needle (26). Lay both aside for cleaning. The float-chamber vent, by the way, is embodied in the tickler assembly (21), and the top-feed union houses a filter element of nylon which is readily accessible for cleaning. To remove the nylon filter (*see* Fig. 15) unscrew the banjo bolt (22), remove the steeel washer, the banjo (23), and then the nylon filter (24).

To remove the main jet (13), remove the main-jet cover nut (12) and unscrew the jet from the jet holder (14). Remove the jet block locating-screw (39) to the left of and slightly below the pilot air-adjusting screw (29). Then push or tap out the jet block (16) through the larger end of the mixing chamber body. To remove the pilot jet (9), remove the pilot-jet cover nut (11) and unscrew the jet.

Cleaning the Carburettor. Wash all the carburettor components thoroughly clean with petrol and blow through the various ducts and passages to ensure that they are quite clear. Do not use a fluffy rag for drying purposes. Pay special attention to the small pilot jet passages in the jetblock. Be sure to remove all impurities from the inside of the float chamber. Also do not forget to clean the detachable pilot jet and the nylon filter shown at (24) in Fig. 15.

Inspecting the Components. If the carburettor had been in continuous service for a considerable period inspect the various components after dismantling the carburettor. Note the following.

1. *The Float Chamber.* Check that the vent is unobstructed and that the float is in perfect condition. Clean the moulded-nylon needle very thoroughly, and be careful not to damage it. If it tends to stick in its seating, relieve its three bearing edges with a fine file. The needle seating shown at (25) in Fig. 15 must be absolutely clean. See that the small nylon filter (24) is undamaged and contains no obstructions. Check that the joint faces of the float-chamber cover and the float chamber are not damaged or bruised, and that the joint washer is in sound condition, otherwise some petrol leakage from the cover joint may occur.

2. *The Throttle Valve.* Check that the throttle valve slides in the mixing chamber without excessive play. If excessive play exists, renew the throttle valve immediately.

3. *The Jet-needle Clip.* The spring clip securing the tapered jet-needle to the throttle valve must grip the needle firmly, and free rotation of the needle must occur, otherwise the needle groove will will become worn and necessitate a new needle being fitted. When the carburettor is reassembled be sure to replace the jet-needle with the spring clip in the correct needle groove (*see* page 39).

4. *The Needle-jet.* Inspect its orifice for signs of wear which are generally present after a mileage of about 15,000 miles. The tapered jet-needle is made of hard stainless-steel and its tapered part does not wear.

5. *The Jet Block.* Before tapping this home in the mixing chamber verify by blowing that the pilot-jet ducts are unobstructed and see that the jet block fibre seal (shown at (40) in Fig. 14) is in good condition.

6. *The Carburettor Flange.* Examine this for truth with a straight-edge. Slight distortion sometimes occurs after a considerable mileage, and this may cause an air leak. See that the heat-resisting joint washer is in perfect condition. If it is not, renew it. If the face of the carburettor flange is slightly concave, file the face carefully and then rub the face on emery cloth laid on a surface plate until a straight-edge shows the face surface to be dead flat. Alternatively have the face machined dead flat by using a grinder at a service garage.

To Reassemble "Monobloc" Carburettor. Assemble the carburettor in the reverse order of dismantling. Referring to Fig. 14, screw home the pilot jet (9) and the pilot-jet cover nut (11), not omitting to replace its washer. Push or tap home the jet block (16) and fibre seal (40) through the large end of the mixing chamber (3). Check that the fibre seal fitted to the stub of the jet block is in sound condition. Then fit the jet block locating-screw (39). Screw the main-jet holder (14) into the jet block after checking that the washer for the holder is sound and that the needle-jet (15) is securely screwed into the top of the holder. Now screw home the main jet (13) into the base of the main-jet holder and replace the main-jet cover nut (12).

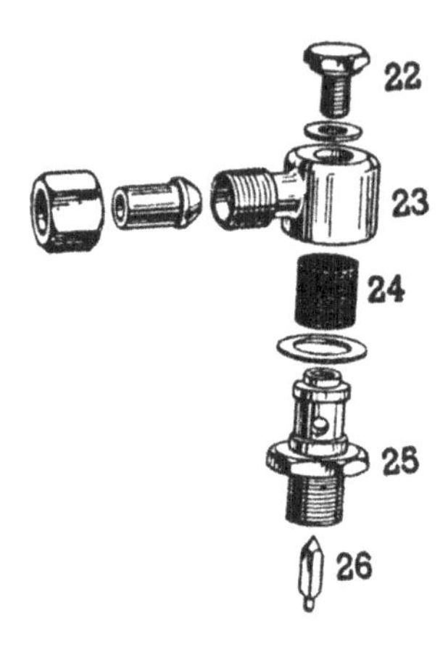

Fig. 15. Showing the nylon filter and adjacent parts

For key to numbered parts, see page 35
(The Enfield Cycle Co. Ltd.)

Replace the moulded-nylon needle (26) in the float chamber (37), and fit the hinged float (27) with the *narrow* side of the hinge uppermost. It must contact the nylon needle. Do not omit the short distance collar on the spindle. Afterwards fit the float-chamber cover (38) and replace the three securing screws (28). Be careful to tighten these three screws evenly. Before replacing the cover it is advisable to renew the washer and make sure that the float chamber and cover joint faces are absolutely clean. Replace items (22)–(24) shown in Fig. 15. Note that the small nylon filter (24) has longitudinal supports moulded in its sides. When replacing the filter see that these supports do not obstruct the feed holes in (25), otherwise some petrol starvation may result. Tighten the banjo bolt (22) securely when the petrol pipe is later connected to the banjo by the union nut.

If previously removed, attach the jet-needle (6) to the throttle valve (5) and secure with the jet-needle clip (4) (*see* Fig 14). Make sure that the clip enters the correct groove on the needle (*see* page 39).

Fit the heat-resisting washer to the face on the cylinder barrel. Renew it if not in perfect condition. Some models have a rubber "O" ring. Then smear a little oil on the outside of the throttle valve and ease the throttle valve (5) and the air valve (17), where fitted, down into the mixing chamber (3). When easing the throttle valve home make sure that the tapered jet-needle (6) really enters the hole in the jet block (16). Offer up the carburettor and secure its flange firmly to the cylinder barrel face and washer by means of the two nuts. It is important to tighten both nuts the same amount. Tighten down firmly the mixing-chamber knurled lock ring (2) so as to secure the mixing-chamber cap (1), and see that the throttle valve slides up and down freely when the cap is secured. Finally re-connect the petrol pipe and firmly tighten the union nut and the banjo bolt shown at (22) in Fig. 15.

The Correct Amal Carburettor (Settings 1958–66). All new 1958–66 Model D5, D7, D7D/L Bantam motor-cycles have the carburettor settings given below and the makers recommend that these settings should not be altered.

Main jet: 140.
Pilot jet: 25
Throttle valve: 375/3½.
Needle position: 2
Needle-jet: 0·1055.

CONCENTRIC CARBURETTOR DETAILS (1967–70)

This carburettor is a development of the "Monobloc" carburettor, dealt with in the previous pages, and the principles of operation, tuning, etc., are the same for both instruments. It is only the constructional details which differ, as will be seen by comparing Fig. 14 (Monobloc carburettor) with Fig. 16 (Concentric carburettor). It should be noted that the air slide, which is controlled by a spring-loaded plunger (Fig. 2) on the standard carburettor, is coupled by cable to a lever on the right handlebar for the Concentric carburettor. The latter is also fitted with a rubber sealing ring at the joint face with the cylinder barrel, to ensure an airtight connection. As already mentioned, most of the information provided for the Monobloc carburettor is suitable for both types, any essential differences being explained in the following notes.

The Pilot Air-adjusting Screw and the Throttle Stop. These are fitted with a rubber "O" ring, (*a*) to retain the screw adjustment, and (*b*) to prevent air leaks.

The Main Jet. This becomes accessible after the float chamber has been removed (retained by two screws). Reference to Fig. 16 shows that the main jet screws into the jet holder, which in turn screws into the carburettor body. On very late Bantam 175 models the float-chamber body incorporates a hollow drain plug which should be removed periodically and any sediment cleaned out. The aperture may also be used as an access point

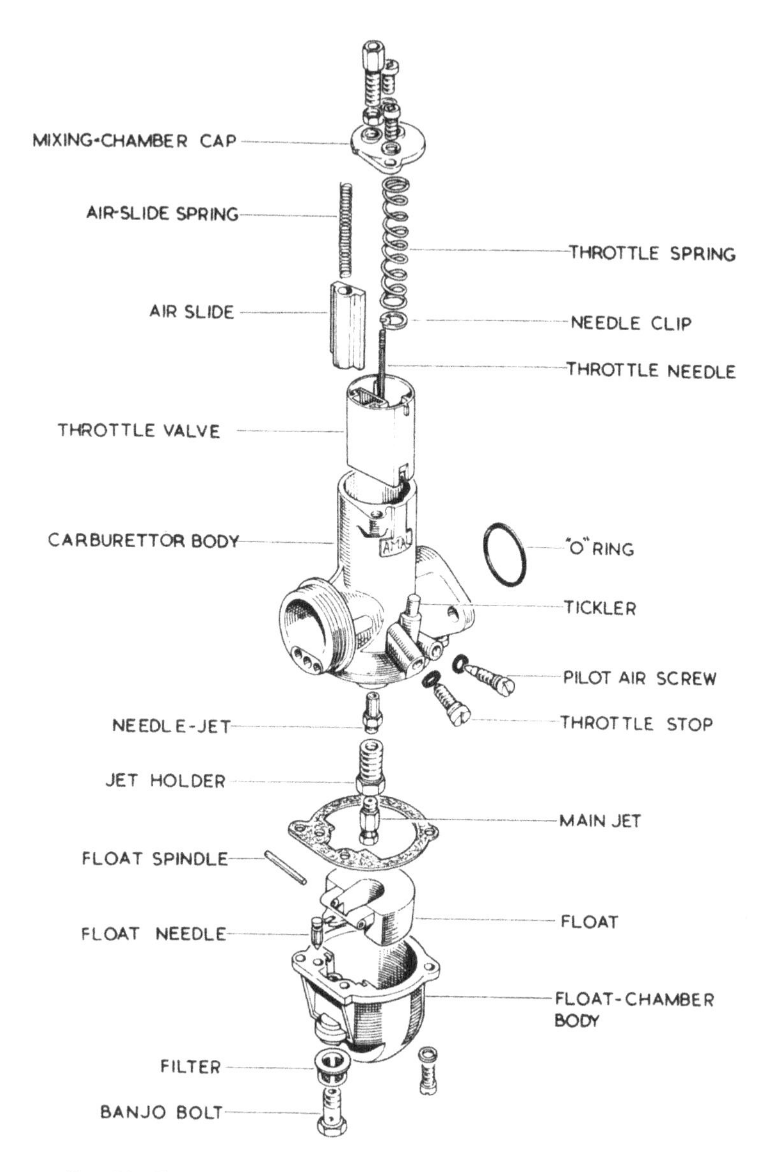

Fig. 16. Exploded view of Amal "Concentric" carburettor

for removal of the main jet. When this is replaced do not screw in too tightly, otherwise when unscrewing at a future date the jet holder may also be unscrewed.

The Jet-needle and Needle Jet. The notes given for the Monobloc carburettor apply here, except that the jet needle has four grooves only.

The Pilot Jet. As with the main jet, the pilot jet is accessible after removal of the float chamber and screws into the underside of the carburettor body (Fig. 16). It should be noted that, on most D14 and all Bantam 175 models, this jet is not detachable and in fact is not even visible (*see below*).

MAINTENANCE (CONCENTRIC CARBURETTOR)

Altering Slow-runnning Adjustment. The notes given for the Monobloc carburettor apply in this instance, except that the air slide is *opened* by means of the handlebar lever, which must be turned in a *clockwise* direction as far as possible.

To Clear an Obstructed Pilot Jet. Unscrew the pilot jet and clean as described on page 35. On most D14 and all Bantam 175 models, where this jet is not detachable, it must be cleared by the use of compressed air applied to the outer hole on the face of the carburettor intake. It will, of course, be necessary to disconnect the flexible pipe from the air cleaner, to expose this, and other, holes.

Dismantling the Concentric Carburettor. Turn off the petrol and unscrew the banjo bolt beneath the float chamber, thus releasing the petrol-pipe connection and also the smaller filter. Remove both nuts from the carburettor flange and draw the carburettor off its studs. Watch for the "O" ring inserted in the joint face.

Take off the carburettor top cover (using the correct type of screwdriver!), complete with the air-slide and throttle-valve assemblies. To remove the needle from the throttle slide, first compress the spring and then extract the needle clip. With the spring still compressed, the cable nipple can be released from the throttle valve. A similar procedure allows the cable to be released from the air slide.

Next, take off the float-chamber body, which is attached to the carburettor body by two screws, and take care not to damage the gasket during this operation. The float can then be lifted out of the chamber, and it should be noted at this stage that the needle groove fits into the forked tongue on the float and that the spindle is a tight fit in the float chamber slots.

If further dismantling is required, unscrew the main jet and then the jet holder from the base of the carburettor body. On many of the Concentric carburettors fitted to Bantam engines, the pilot jet can also be unscrewed, although on the later models the jet is not detachable and is fixed in position within the main body of the carburettor.

If required, the throttle stop and the pilot air screw may be taken out, in which case take good care of their "O" rings. The primer (or "tickler") may also be removed, but since this item is not in frequent use it is not likely to be worn sufficiently to require replacement.

Cleaning the Carburettor. See notes on page 37.

Inspecting the Carburettor. *See* notes for Monobloc carburettor, page 37. It will be noticed by comparison of Figs. 14 and 16 that the Concentric carburettor is not fitted with a "jet block."

Reassembling the Concentric Carburettor. Reassembly does not present any difficulties if Fig. 16 is carefully studied, but one or two points may require further comment.

Firstly, before assembly, all components must be absolutely clean and free from any foreign matter. The gasket between the float chamber and the carburettor must be in good order and if there is any doubt about this, renew the gasket. Similar remarks apply to the "O" rings fitted to the throttle stop and pilot air screws.

If possible use a torque spanner set to 120 lb in. to tighten the jet holder in position, while a torque of 50 lb in. is required for the main jet.

When the float and needle has been reassembled, check that the rise and fall of the float causes a corresponding movement of the needle. If there is any sign of wear on the tapered seat of the needle, a new one should be fitted, otherwise the petrol level will be affected.

Carburettor Settings (1967–70). The settings for the D10 and D14 Bantam engines are given below. Do not alter any of these items.

1967: D10	Main jet 150, pilot 25, throttle valve 3, needle position 2, needle jet 0·105
1968: D14	Main jet 160, pilot 25, throttle valve 3, needle position 3, needle jet 0·105
1969–70: D14 and Bantam 175	Main jet 180, pilot 622/107, throttle 3½, needle position 2, needle jet 0·105

4 Maintaining a good spark

By keeping the ignition system at maximum efficiency you will be assured of a "fat" spark occurring regularly at the sparking plug. This ensures rapid starting-up under all weather conditions, and guarantees complete and quick combustion of fuel in the combustion chamber, factors vital to good performance and minimum fuel consumption.

Six Bantam Ignition/Lighting Systems. On all 1948–66 Bantams an efficient flywheeel generator (which incorporates the contact-breaker) is provided for supplying the current required for ignition and lighting. For the years 1967–70 the flywheel type of generator was discontinued in favour of separate generator and contact-breaker units, the former being mounted on the left side of the crankshaft and the latter on the right side of the crankshaft within a special oil-tight housing, comprising part of the primary chaincase. This chapter, apart from a general introductory paragraph, deals only with those components concerned with ignition, the components of the lighting system being dealt with in detail in the next chapter. The ignition and lighting systems, although dealt with in separate chapters, cannot be regarded as independent systems. Below is a brief outline of the six ignition/lighting systems used on 1948–70 B.S.A. Bantams.

The 1948–50 direct ignition and lighting system (Model D1) where a Wipac (Wico-Pacy) a.c. flywheel "Geni-mag" supplies a.c. current direct to the sparking plug and a.c. current direct to the headlamp main bulb. A bicycle-type *dry* battery incorporated inside the headlamp supplies current for illuminating the pilot bulb and tail lamp.

2. *The 1951–65 direct ignition and lighting system* (Models D1, D3, D5, D7) where a Wipac a.c./d.c. flywheel generator (type S55/Mk. 8) supplies d.c. current direct to the sparking plug, and a.c. current direct to the headlamp main bulb. A bicycle-type *dry* battery inside the headlamp lights the pilot bulb and tail lamp.

3. *The 1950–3 coil-ignition and battery lighting system* (Model D1) where a Lucas a.c. flywheel generator (type 1A45) supplies current via a rectifier to a Lucas lead-acid battery from which d.c. current is drawn for coil ignition and illuminating *all* lamps.

4. *The 1954–64 battery lighting system* (Models D1, D3 and D5) where a Wipac a.c./d.c. flywheel generator (type S55/Mk. 8) feeds d.c. current to the

sparking plug and d.c. current via a rectifier to a Varley or Lucas lead-acid battery from which current is drawn for lighting *all* lamps.

5. *The 1964–6 coil ignition and battery lighting system* (Models D7, D7D/L) where a Wipac a.c./d.c. generator (type S55/Mk. 8) supplies a.c. current direct to the headlamp main bulb and trickle-charges d.c. current to a Lucas lead-acid battery responsible for coil ignition and lighting the headlamp pilot bulb and stop–tail lamp.

6. *The 1967–70 coil ignition and battery lighting system* (Models D10 and D14) where a Wipac alternator supplies current via a rectifier to the battery, the charge rate varying with the lighting switch positions. The battery is used as the source of all the electrical requirements, including coil ignition and head and parking lights. The system also accommodates a method for emergency starting with a discharged battery, when the lights must be extinguished and the ignition switch moved to a special position, thus diverting full generator (alternator) output to the battery. *This switch position must not be used for more than a quarter of an hour, because of the very high charging rate involved.*

NOTE: where system (1), (2) or (5) is utilized the headlamp main bulb cannot be illuminated *unless the engine is running*. On all Bantams the electric horn is operated by current from the dry battery or lead-acid battery according to which type is fitted.

THE SPARKING PLUG

On a two-stroke engine the sparking plug fires once every engine revolution and, as might be expected, the combustion chamber is an extremely hot place. It is therefore essential always to run on a reputable make of plug of the correct type.

Suitable Plugs for Bantams. All 1948 and subsequent Bantams require a 14 mm sparking plug with a 12·5 mm (½ in.) reach except for the years 1967–70 when "long-reach" plugs were fitted (¾ in). Three excellent makes of sparking plug are the Champion, the Lodge, and the K.L.G. Any of these plugs can be relied upon to give satisfactory results. N.G.K. plugs are also suitable.

B.S.A. Motor Cycles Ltd. have always fitted as official factory equipment Champion sparking plugs which in their opinion are well suited to the particular requirements of the B.S.A. power units.

CHAMPION. Always fit a single-point, non-detachable type L–10 to 1948–53 Bantams (cast-iron heads). On 1954–66 Models D1, D3, D5, D7 and D7D/L (alloy heads) fit a type L–7. For 1967–70 Models D10, D14, and Bantam 175, use type N4.

LODGE. Fit type CN on 1948–54 Model D1 Bantams (cast-iron heads), and an HN plug on 1955–66 Model 5 D1, D3, D5, D7 and D7D/L Bantams (light-alloy heads) For 1967–70 Models D10, D14, Bantam 175, fit type HLN.

K.L.G. Always fit a type F75 on 1955–66 models, but for all subsequent years (i.e. 1967–70) use FE75.

On 1948–54 models (cast-iron heads) fit an F50 plug.

Weatherproof Plug Terminal Covers. All-weather Bantam riders would do well to consider fitting a weatherproof plug terminal cover or (if the old plug requires to be renewed) a watertight plug. Excellent Champion, Lodge, and K.L.G. waterproof terminal covers are available which give complete plug protection by thorough shielding of the top insulation, and prevent the risk of a short circuit being caused by water, dirt, or oil getting on the insulator. They are quickly-detachable and will fit any standard type of plug, assuming that the covers and plugs are of the same make.

Symptoms of Faulty Plug. If no spark occurs between the plug electrodes, the engine will fail to start up, or if the engine has been running, will suddenly stop. Should the plug fire, but intermittently, the symptoms will be difficulty in starting up, misfiring, with perhaps some banging in the silencer, and erratic slow-running. All these symptoms are most annoying. If the plug is suspected to be faulty, test it immediately.

How to Test a Plug. The accepted and quite satisfactory method of testing a sparking plug for good sparking is to lay it on the cylinder head or other convenient metal part with the terminal (if unprotected by a moulded terminal cover) clear of the head; then smartly rotate the engine by means of the kick-starter and observe whether the plug sparks regularly and well. A spark should occur at every engine revolution. It should be distinctly visible in daylight, and it should be possible to hear a distinct "click" as the spark bridges the gap between the electrodes.

If only a weak spark occurs in spite of a good spark being obtainable at the end of the h.t. lead thoroughly inspect the sparking plug and, if still usable, service it.

Inspect the Sparking Plug Every 1,000 Miles. Remove the plug about every 1,000 miles for careful inspection. On a new engine inspect the plug after the first 500 miles. If the Amal carburettor is correctly tuned, the electrodes should remain clean for a long period. A rich mixture, however, will soon cause the points to acquire a sooty deposit, and this deposit will also adhere to the base of the plug before long. Note that a wrongly proportioned petroil mixture (*see* page 17) will result in fouling of the plug. Leaded fuels are also apt to cause grey-coloured deposits.

Before deciding that a sparking plug is no longer serviceable, examine it very closely. If inspection reveals that the electrodes are badly burned, put the plug in the nearest dustbin, not in the cylinder head. Where bad burning occurs within a short period, this indicates an incorrect mixture or too small a plug gap.

Light-coloured fuel deposits affect efficiency to a very small extent, except when accompanied by a bad condition of the plug or oiling-up. Nevertheless they should always be removed completely. Look for soft or hard carbon deposits which affect efficiency considerably, and especially when they collect inside the plug body. Such deposits can cause internal sparking and spoil engine performance, or even cause a complete stoppage. All carbon deposits must be completely removed by thoroughly cleaning the plug.

Carbon deposits are caused by mixture fouling, and by oil fouling. In the former instance the deposits are dull black and sooty, but in the latter case they are generally shiny black, hard, and moist. Should rapid fouling take place, you can often diagnose the origin of the trouble by carefully noting the precise nature of the deposits.

Oiling-up. Inspect for oiling-up which sometimes occurs together with the presence of carbon deposits. An oiled-up plug is generally dirty and wet with oil. Careful cleaning is called for. During the first 1,000 miles, i.e. when running-in the engine, there is sometimes a tendency for oiling-up to occur, but this tendency should gradually disappear. If oiling-up occurs after running-in, this is caused through using an incorrect petroil mixture, poorly fitted or worn piston rings, or a worn cylinder barrel and/or piston skirt.

Insulation of Plug. Check during the inspection of the plug that the insulation has not become damaged or cracked, and that it is externally clean.

Do Not Forget the Plug Washer. See that the washer located between the cylinder head and plug body is not damaged. Renew this washer if it has become badly flattened and hard (thereby reducing conductivity of heat); also renew it if its condition is likely to cause loss of compression or "blowing."

On Champion plugs, the washer is an integral part, and will last for the life of the plug.

Check the Plug Gap. When removing the sparking plug for inspection and cleaning, always check the gap between the electrodes (points). B.S.A. Motor Cycles Ltd. recommend a gap for all plugs of between 0·020 in. and 0·025 in. when used with coil-ignition systems or 0·018 in. with "direct" ignition. Difficult starting up, misfiring, and an indifferent engine performance are sometimes caused by an incorrect gap. An excessive gap tends to overheat the centre electrode and cause pre-ignition, while an insufficient gap obviously increases any latent tendency for oiling-up to occur.

The gap slowly but surely increases and it is therefore advisable about every 1,000 miles (when inspecting the sparking plug) to check the plug gap with a suitable feeler gauge which can be obtained from any large accessory firm.

After making sure that the plug points are quite clean, insert the appropriate blade of the feeler gauge between the earthed (outer) electrode(s) and the insulated (centre) electrode. Should you find that the plug gap is outside the limits 0·020–0·025 in., you should re-gap the plug immediately. An excellent tool for checking the gap and regapping the plug is the combined Champion regapping tool and feeler gauge. This is an inexpensive tool which is suited for any make of plug.

To Regap the Sparking Plug. An adjustment to correct the gap should always be made by bending the *earth* (outer) electrode(s). Never attempt to move the insulated (centre) electrode, or you will ruin the plug. Do not tap the electrode(s), but gently *press* towards the centre electrode, using the Champion tool as shown in Fig. 17; the tool is obtainable from any

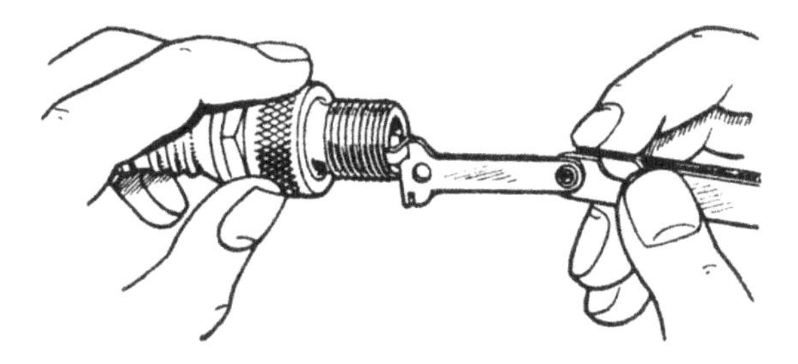

Fig. 17. Regapping sparking plug with Champion tool

The Champion tool shown includes suitable gauges

Champion plug stockist or from the plug makers. Continue to make an adjustment until the correct gap is obtained. Obviously, when regapping a plug it is best to adjust the points to the lower limit (0·020 in.) as the plug will then not require further regapping for a considerable period.

Cleaning the Plug Quickly. If an inspection of the sparking plug shows that it is not badly fouled, it is generally sufficient to brighten up the electrode points with some *fine* glass-paper, or to scrape them clean with the blade of a small pen-knife. Clean the outside of the plug with a cloth moistened with paraffin or petrol.

Note that the plugs recommended for Bantam engines are of the non-detachable type and cannot be dismantled for thorough cleaning.

To Clean Plugs Thoroughly. Visit a garage with an abrasive blast service unit installed. Within a few minutes the plug will then be automatically scoured of all deposits, washed, subjected to a high-pressure air line, and finally tested for good sparking at a pressure in excess of 100 lb per sq in. Renew the plug if it fails to pass this test satisfactorily. Any type of sparking plug can be cleaned and tested in this manner.

If no "air blast" service unit is conveniently available, remove the plug from the cylinder head, pour a little petrol down between the insulated central electrode and the plug body, and set fire to the plug.

Before screwing the plug back into the cylinder head, wipe the tip and outside of the insulation absolutely clean, and polish the electrode points with some *fine* glass-paper. Finally check the gap between the points (0·020–0·025 in.).

Replacing the Plug. Before screwing the plug into the cylinder head, clean the external threads (carbon is a poor conductor) with a wire brush, and check that the washer is in good condition (*see* page 46). Use only normal hand pressure on the plug spanner, and verify that the h.t. lead or terminal cover is firmly secured to the plug terminal.

THE WIPAC FLYWHEEL GENERATORS

On 1948–50 Model D1 Bantams (up to engine No. YDI–40660) provided with Wipac (Wico-Pacy) flywheel generators giving ignition and lighting, the equipment specified includes the Wipac 27-watt "Geni-mag" ignition and a.c. lighting unit.

On 1951–66 Models D1 (after engine No. YDI–40660), D3, D7, D5 with Wipac flywheel generators giving direct ignition and lighting, direct ignition and battery lighting, or coil-ignition and battery lighting, the equipment used includes the Wipac flywheel a.c./d.c. series S55/Mk. 8 generator.

Both the above types of flywheel generator comprise two assemblies: (*a*) the flywheel, and (*b*) the stator which carries the ignition coil, the lighting coils, the contact-breaker unit, and condenser. Ignition, except on models with coil-ignition and battery lighting, is direct from the flywheel generator, a desirable characteristic of which is its constant spark output over a wide timing range. The necessity for frequent contact-breaker adjustment is thereby avoided. The contact-breaker and other parts are, however, extremely accessible, and such maintenance as is required is simply effected.

On 1967–70 models D10, D14, and Bantam 175, the generator and contact-breaker are separate entities, situated at opposite ends of the crankshaft, the contact-breaker being housed within a separate compartment (cast integrally with the primary chaincase) and accessible after removal of the large cover. A special seal is used to keep the compartment free from oil contamination. The generator (in this case known as an alternator) is exposed when the left-side crankcase cover is removed and since there is an air gap between the rotor (rotating central portion) and the stator (fixed outer portion) wear cannot take place between these components and hence maintenance is unnecessary.

Check Contact-breaker Adjustment Every 5,000 Miles. About every 5,000 miles carefully check the gap between the contact-breaker points (studs with very hard metal faces ground flat). Remove the contact-breaker cover, secured by a spring clip or two fixing screws (August, 1949, onwards). Then turn the engine over slowly until the contacts are wide apart; slip a suitable feeler gauge between them. The correct gap is 0·015 in. (0·38 mm). If the gap varies appreciably from the specified gap, make a contact-breaker adjustment as described below.

Referring to Figs. 18, 19, and 20, with a small screwdriver slacken off the locking screw *E* above the contacts about one turn. Then in the case of the "Geni-mag" contact-breaker (1948–50) turn the eccentric adjuster-screw *F* (Fig. 18) clockwise or anti-clockwise as required until the contact-breaker gap is found to be correct. In the case of the Wipac a.c./d.c. series S55/Mk. 8 ignition/lighting generator (1951–66), after loosening the screw *E* (Figs. 19, 20), move the fixed contact plate[1] (with a suitable screwdriver engaged in the recess provided) up or down until the 0·015 in. blade of the feeler gauge just enters the gap without binding. Afterwards firmly retighten the locking screw *E*.

Referring to Fig. 21 for the 1967–70 models, slacken the locking screw *E*, rotate the eccentric pin *H* until the gap between the points is 0·012 in., and retighten screw *E*.

Cleaning the Contacts. Occasionally clean the contacts of the contact-breaker by inserting a smooth piece of cloth or paper between them and withdrawing the paper while the contacts are in the closed position. Always keep the contacts absolutely clean and free from oil, grease, and petrol, otherwise they will become blackened, burned, and perhaps pitted. If the contacts are discoloured or slightly pitted, polish them lightly with a small piece of smooth fine-grade emery cloth. Avoid rubbing the contacts excessively. When the contacts are closed, they must be tight and in line.

Renewing the Contacts. Note that the moving contact is integral with the contact-breaker rocker arm. Should either contact be in such a condition as to require renewal, see that the other contact is renewed simultaneously. The renewal of contacts individually is not practicable.

When assembling the moulded rocker arm, prime the pivot pin lightly with some oil or soft grease. The rocker arm on the "Geni-mag" is of the self-lubricating type, but on the later models (1951–70) it is beneficial to prime the pivot pin at occasional and regular intervals. When replacing the rocker arm, be careful to insert the correct number of thin spacing washers behind the rocker arm so as to align the contacts truly and to ensure proper insulation. Then anchor the end of the contact-breaker spring to the terminal post with the screw and shake-proof washer. Position one of the spring washers over the pivot on the outer side of the rocker arm and insert the spring clip in the groove or, in the case of the 1967–70 models, tighten the screw.

[1] On no account ever attempt to bend the fixed-contact plate.

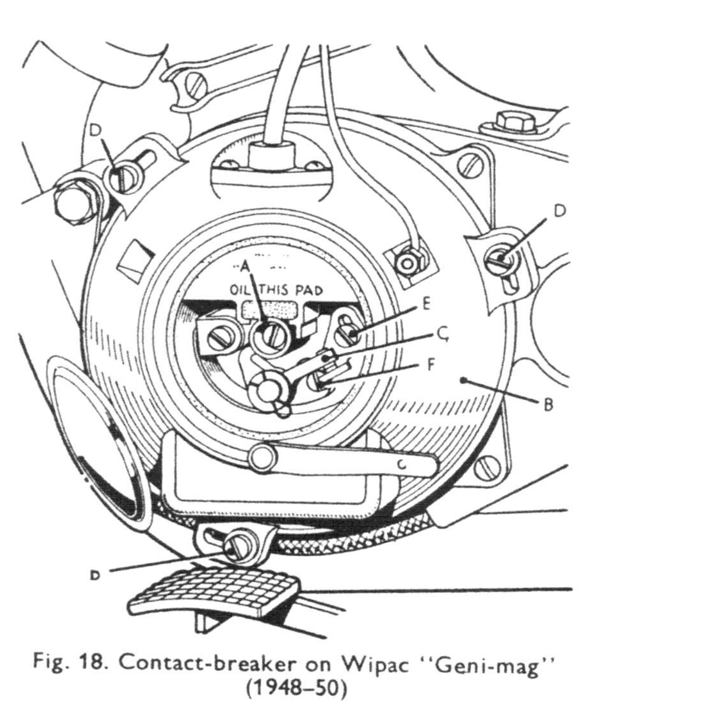

Fig. 18. Contact-breaker on Wipac "Geni-mag" (1948–50)

Applicable to direct ignition and lighting models

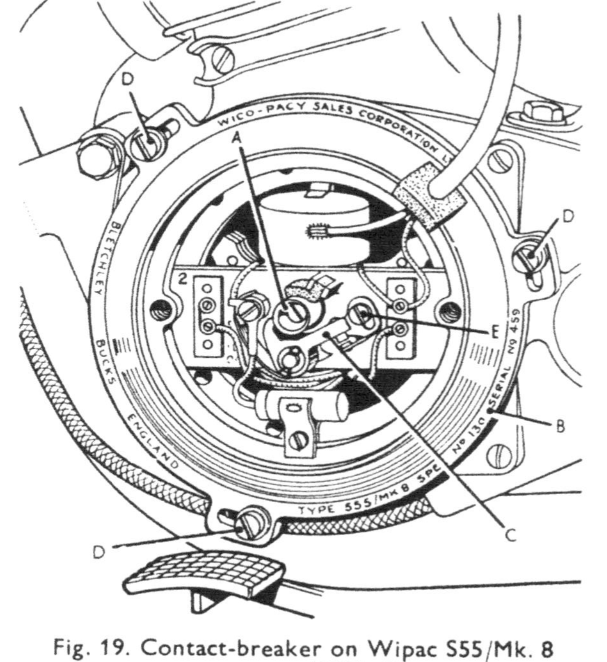

Fig. 19. Contact-breaker on Wipac S55/Mk. 8 generator (1951–63)

Applicable to Wipac direct ignition and lighting models, also Wipac battery-lighting models

Key to Figs. 18, 19, 20

A. *Contact-breaker cam*
B. *Contact-breaker housing*
C. *Rocker arm*
D. *Screw securing B*
E. *Screw securing fixed contact*
F. *Eccentric adjuster screw*

Wear of Rocker-arm Heel. When a flywheel generator (or contact-breaker unit on later models) has been in use for very many thousands of miles, some wear may occur on the rocker-arm heel. This is liable to cause loss of power and irregular running. If such symptoms develop and the rocker arm is suspect, inspect the heel and carefully scrutinize its edges which bear against the cam. If the heel is in good condition, the edges should be sharply defined. If they are rounded, considerable wear has obviously occurred, and the rocker arm must be renewed.

A Weak Condenser. If the condenser becomes weak, sparking occurs across the contacts of the contact-breaker, accompanied by burning of the contacts. An intense blue spark is a definite indication of a weak condenser whose function is to prevent excessive build-up of l.t. current. A weak condenser should be renewed immediately.

Wipac Generator Timing. This is accurately set to very close limits by the makers, and no ignition advance and retard lever is included on the handlebars because in practice manual control has been found to be entirely unnecessary. On all Wipac "Geni-mags" and Wipac a.c./d.c. flywheel generators the contact-breaker cam (shown at *A* in Figs. 18, 19, 20) is keyed to an extension of the flywheel main-shaft, and it is therefore obvious that its position relative to that of the piston is absolutely fixed (only one key is provided).

As may be seen in Figs. 18, 19, 20, the contact-breaker housing *B* has slotted lugs for the three housing-securing screws, and this enables a limited variation in the ignition timing to be made where required. After slackening the three securing screws *D*, the contact-breaker housing *B* can be rotated through a small angle. Afterwards the three securing screws must be firmly retightened.

From Fig. 21 it will be seen that the contact-breaker back plate *B* is slotted to accept the fixing screws *D*. When these are slackened the plate can be moved through a very limited arc.

Provided that the ignition timing has not been disturbed, it should *never* be necessary for the private owner to make an ignition timing adjustment. Experimental variation of the timing must *not* be made. The small adjustment provided is to facilitate the accurate setting of the ignition timing at the Bantam factory and is not designed for the use of "Bantamites." Note that the change over to premium grade fuels does not permit of an advance in the ignition timing where Bantams are concerned. Also note that to ensure correct ignition timing, as well as proper electrical functioning of the magneto portion of the flywheel generator, it is essential to maintain the correct gap between the contacts (wide open) of the contact-breaker (*see* page 49).

To Check Ignition Timing. Should you have good reason to doubt the accuracy of the ignition timing, you can readily check it. First verify that

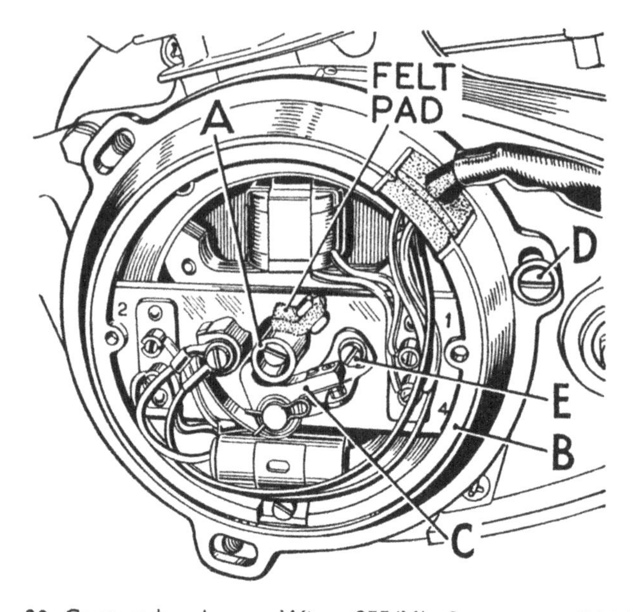

Fig. 20. Contact-breaker on Wipac S55/Mk. 8 generator (1964–6)

Applicable to all coil-ignition and battery lighting models. This also applies, except as regards the wiring layout, to all 1964–5 models with a direct ignition and lighting system

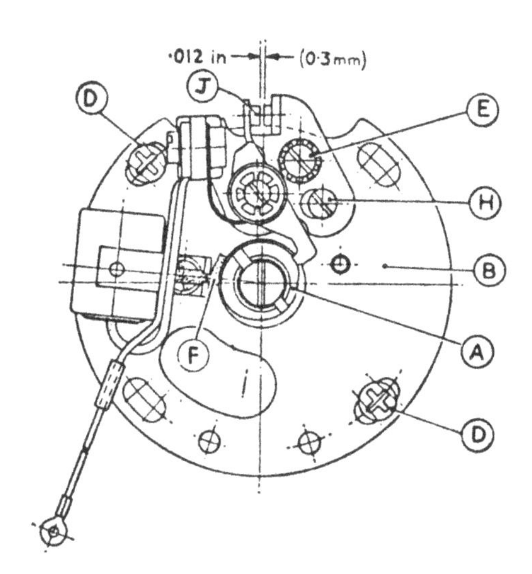

Fig. 21. Contact-breaker unit on 1967–70 models (D10, D14, and Bantam 175)

the contact-breaker gap is correct (*see* page 49). Next remove the sparking plug and rotate the engine slowly until the piston is exactly at top dead centre (T.D.C.). To find the true T.D.C. position, insert a suitable rod through the plug hole and "rock" the engine slowly with the piston right up. When the "rock" produces no piston movement, the piston is exactly at T.D.C. Now turn the engine back until the piston has descended $\frac{5}{32}$ in. ($\frac{1}{16}$ in., D5 and D7; 0·076 in., D10 and 0·057 in. for D14 and Bantam 175). Scratch a mark on the rod to indicate the precise descent of the piston, or alternatively remove the cylinder head and measure the piston descent with a steel rule. When the piston has been correctly positioned, the contact-breaker rocker arm should be just beginning to rise on the contact-breaker cam, and the contacts should have opened not more than 0·002 in. (0·05 mm). A larger opening indicates that the ignition is excessively advanced, whereas a smaller opening indicates that the ignition is excessively retarded. A small variation in the timing, however, will not adversely affect engine performance.

Removing Condenser (1948–50 "Geni-mag"). Should the condenser fail (causing rapid burning of the contacts), renew it immediately. To remove a faulty condenser, first detach the stator by unscrewing the three clamp nuts. You can then gently ease the stator off the three stator-plate studs. Be careful when doing this not to bend it, or you may break the lead connecting the lighting coils to the terminal on the stator. Now disconnect the lead from the terminal post and unscrew the clamp nut located on the securing-spring post of the contact-breaker cover.

When fitting a new condenser, see that its lead is pushed down as far as possible into the well formed by the stator housing otherwise the flywheel may rub, and possibly sever, the lead.[1] The flywheel rim also reaches to within about $\frac{1}{16}$ in. of the head of the insulated lighting-terminal stud, and this must be kept pushed down below this level.

Removing Condenser (1951–66 Wipac Generators). As may be seen in Figs. 19, 20, the condenser is extremely accessible. To withdraw it, remove the condenser-terminal nut and free the condenser lead. Then uncrew the condenser bracket fixing-screw and lift the condenser away. Observe the note at the foot of this page.[1]

Removing Condenser (1967–70 Wipac Contact-breakers). The screw securing the condenser bracket is located below the felt lubricating pad, which will also be released as the screw is withdrawn. Disconnect the condenser earth-lead at the screw which serves the purpose of retaining the moving contact spring and remove the condenser.

[1] It is extremely important that all stray loops of wire are kept bent in to behind the radius of the stator.

To Remove Contact-breaker and Stator Unit (Wipac S55/Mk. 8 Generator). Referring to Figs. 19, 20 remove the cover plate from the contact-breaker after removing the two-securing screws. Next remove the central screw securing cam *A* and pull the cam away; lift out the key which locates it on its shaft. Then remove the three screws *D* holding the contact-breaker housing, and lift off the housing, complete with contact-breaker and stator unit.

Important Warning (1948–66 Wipac Generators). In the case of "Geni-mags" and the later Wipac a.c./d.c. flywheel lighting-ignition generators it is extremely important to note that *under no circumstances should you attempt to remove either the generator flywheel or generator rotor from the engine near-side main shaft without using the special B.S.A. extractors supplied for the purpose.* If you attempt removal without using these extractors, you will almost certainly cause serious damage to the main shaft. It is advisable to entrust this type of work to a Bantam repair specialist or any competent dealer.

1967–70 Wipac Generators. The rotor is mounted on a parallel shaft and keyed in position. An extractor is not necessary for removal.

Flywheels Are Not Interchangeable. Note that the series S55/Mk. 8 a.c./d.c. ignition generator has more magnets in the flywheel than the 27-watt "Geni-mag" which is purely an a.c. unit. The two flywheels, although of similar appearance, are therefore not interchangeable.

The S55/Mk. 8 flywheel can be readily identified as it is clearly marked "WIPAC AC/DC." It is also essential that the correct stator plate is used in conjunction with the appropriate flywheel, otherwise trouble will occur.

Servicing Wipac Generators. Unless you happen to be an electrical expert (in which case refer to B.S.A. Service Sheets Nos. 810, 810A), you are not advised to tackle any servicing of "Gemi-mags" (1948–50) or S55/Mk. 8 ignition lighting generators (1951 onwards) other than normal maintenance, i.e. the lubrication (page 20), cleaning and adjustment of the contact-breaker, and the renewal where necessary of the contacts and the condenser.

Should the ignition coils, stator, flywheel rotor, etc., develop trouble and need any attention, ride or deliver the *complete machine* to the nearest authorized Wico-Pacy service station where the equipment will receive expert attention. The appropriate address can be obtained from Wipac Group Sales Ltd., Buckingham, Bucks.

LUCAS COIL-IGNITION

On many 1950–3 123 c.c. Model D1 Bantams, Lucas coil-ignition equipment (first fitted, December, 1949) is provided as an alternative to the

Wipac "Geni-mag" or a.c./d.c. S55/Mk. 8 flywheel generator, dealt with in previous sections.

The Lucas equipment differs fundamentally from the Wipac direct ignition (and lighting) equipment in that a 45-watt Lucas a.c. flywheel generator (type 1A45) supplies current to a 5 amp-hr Lucas type LVW5E lead-acid battery, a rectifier being incorporated to convert a.c. to d.c. for battery charging. Current stored in the battery is then drawn upon for lighting purposes and the coil-ignition system, which, of course, includes an ignition coil, a cam-operated contact-breaker (on the generator), and an ignition switch in the centre of the headlamp rotary-type lighting switch.

The Lucas a.c. Generator. Some details of the a.c. generator and notes concerning its output are given on page 61. Except so far as the contact-breaker is concerned, no maintenance is necessary.

Use of Ignition Switch. The EMG, OFF, and IGN positions of the three-way ignition switch in the centre of the lighting switch on the SSP575P Lucas headlamp are fully explained on page 6, and the correct use of the ignition switch is made clear from these instructions. The following important point concerning the ignition switch is emphasized.

Never attempt to start up your Bantam with the battery disconnected from the circuit and the ignition switch in either the IGN or EMG position. (*See* page 10.)

Servicing a.c. Generator. Except in the event of your being a genuine electrical expert (in which case refer to B.S.A. Service Sheets Nos. 812 and 812A) it is not advisable to undertake any servicing of the Lucas 1A45 generator (1950–3) other than normal maintenance, namely, the lubrication (page 20), cleaning, and adjustment of the contact-breaker, and the renewal, if required, of the contact points and the condenser.

In the event of the stator coils, stator, rotor, etc., developing a fault, send or ride the complete machine to the nearest authorized Lucas service station for expert attention. The appropriate address can be obtained from Joseph Lucas (Sales and Service) Ltd., Great Hampton Street, Birmingham, 19. In the London area the largest service station is at Dordrecht Road, Acton Vale, Acton, W.3.

Inspect the Contact-breaker Gap About Every 3,000 Miles. It is necessary occasionally (say about every 2,500–3,000 miles) to withdraw the contact-breaker cover by removing its two securing screws and then check the gap between the contacts. When the contacts require cleaning (*see* page 56), check the gap *after* cleaning. Provided that the contact-breaker is regularly cleaned, actual adjustment of the contacts is rarely necessary.

To check the gap, rotate the engine slowly until the contacts (*B*, Fig. 22) are observed to be wide open, and then insert a suitable feeler gauge (one is attached to the ignition screwdriver in the tool kit) between the contacts.

The correct gap is 0·010–0·012 in. (0·25–0·30 mm). If the gap differs appreciably from the correct gap, regap the points.

Maintain the engine in a position giving maximum opening of the contacts and loosen screws *D* securing the fixed contact plate (*see* Fig. 22). Then alter the position of this plate until the correct contact-breaker gap is obtained. Afterwards firmly retighten the plate-securing screws.

Cleaning the Contacts. Always inspect the contacts when checking the contact-breaker gap. Never permit the contact-breaker, and especially the contacts, to become oily, greasy, or dirty, otherwise they will rapidly become burned and pitted, and serious ignition trouble will probably occur. If cleaning is necessary, this should be effected *before* making a final gap adjustment. The contacts when in good condition should have a grey, frosted appearance, in which case they should not be interfered with.

To facilitate cleaning of the contacts, it is advisable to detach the moving contact and its spring arm (*see* Fig. 22) from its fixing. To do this, loosen the nuts on the terminal post *A* and lift off the spring which is slotted to assist removal. Then lift the rocker arm off its pivot *C*.

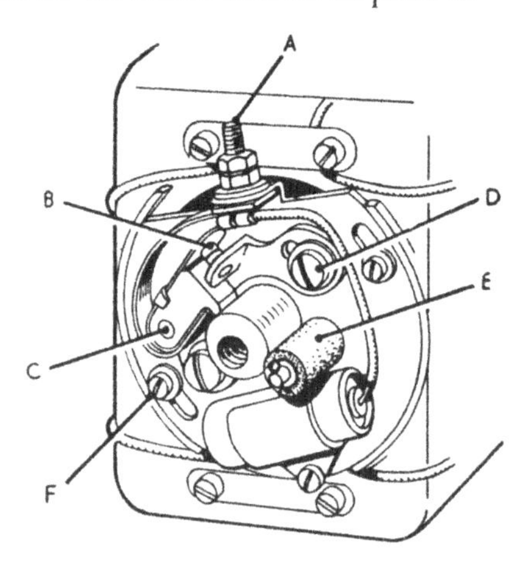

Fig. 22. Contact-breaker on Lucas A.C. generator (1950–3)

Applicable to all models with Lucas coil-ignition and battery lighting

A. *Terminal post*
B. *Contacts*
C. *Rocker-arm pivot*
D. *Screws securing fixed-contact plate*
E. *Felt lubricator*
F. *Screws securing timing-control plate*

If the contacts are not pitted, but merely slightly discoloured, it is generally satisfactory to wipe the contacts with a clean cloth moistened with petrol. But if the contacts are blackened, burned, or pitted, clean them up with a slip of fine carborundum stone, or if not available, some *very fine* emery cloth. During the cleaning and truing up of the contacts, be very careful not to remove more than the barest amount of contact metal to ensure brightness of the surfaces, that the two contacts are parallel, and that the two faces are absolutely smooth. Note that some new Lucas contact sets supplied by Joseph Lucas Ltd. have slightly *convex* faces, and obviously if such contacts are fitted, they should be cleaned only with very fine emery cloth.

After cleaning the contacts, replace the moving contact and spring arm, and check the gap between the contacts as described on page 48. Finally, replace the contact-breaker cover.

Contact-breaker Lubrication. *See* instructions on page 20.

To Remove the Contact-breaker. Remove the contact-breaker-base fixing screws, and then lift up the contact plate, complete with the condenser (*see* Fig. 22). Note the position of the contact-breaker base relative to the generator body and make a suitable mark to avoid the necessity for re-timing the ignition when it is assembled.

The Generator and Rectifier. It is not possible or necessary to make any adjustment to either the Lucas 1A45 generator or CTR1 rectifier.

To remove the generator (not advised except by experts), first remove the cover from the generator and disconnect all wires at the "snap" connectors beneath the forward end of the fuel tank. Next remove the bolt securing the rotor and insert in its place the special rotor extracting-bolt supplied with the machine, and withdraw the rotor until it is just free of the crankshaft. Then remove the nuts and spring washers from the studs passing through the generator body and crankcase, and withdraw the complete generator assembly. On no account remove the rotor from the generator body, or loss of magnetism will result.

Lucas a.c. Generator Timing. The timing ($\frac{5}{32}$ in. before T.D.C.) is accurately set by the makers and should not normally be interfered with; but if desired the timing can readily be checked as described on page 5 for the Wipac flywheel generator. Should it be necessary for some special reason to make a slight variation in the ignition timing, you can do this by slackening off the screws shown at *F* in Fig. 22 and turning the timing control plate a small amount in a clockwise or anti-clockwise direction, according to whether it is desired to advance or retard the spark respectively.

Care of Battery. For instructions on the maintenance of the Lucas lead-acid battery *see* pages 61–4.

The Ignition Coil. The Lucas-type ignition coil (below the fuel tank) must always be kept clean externally, especially between its terminals. The terminal connections must also always be kept tight. Apart from these two points, no maintenance is necessary.

To Remove High Tension Cable. Removal is necessary when the rubber insulation shows signs of perishing or cracking. Always use 7-mm rubber-covered ignition cable for renewal purposes. To connect the cable, thread the knurled moulded nut over the cable, bare the cable end for approximately ¼ in., thread the wire through the metal washer, and bend back the strands. Afterwards screw the nut into its terminal.

5 The lighting equipment

This chapter deals with the lighting components of the flywheel generator, the battery (where rectifier lighting is provided), the headlamp, and the tail lamp or stop–tail lamp. Some useful wiring diagrams are included at the end of the chapter.

Brief reference to various types of Wipac generators fitted to 1948–66 Bantams is made below. See page 61 for details of the Lucas generator on 1950–3 battery-lighting models with coil ignition.

THE FLYWHEEL GENERATOR

The Wipac and Lucas flywheel generators are all of very compact design, and of a type requiring the minimum attention. A few hints concerning their normal maintenance are included in this section.

The Wipac a.c. "Geni-mag" (1948–50 models)

Maintenance. No maintenance is normally required in respect of the magnetic units, lighting, coils, etc. (*See* remarks on page 54 concerning servicing in the event of trouble occurring.) Some ignition components of the flywheel generator do require periodical maintenance, and the appropriate instructions are given on pages 48–54.

The Wipac a.c./d.c. S55/Mk. 8 Generator. This flywheel generator superseded the "Geni-mag" (August, 1950) which is an a.c. unit. On 1951–65 123 cm^3, 148 cm^3, 174 cm^3 Bantams with Wipac direct ignition and lighting, the permanent-magnet generator produces alternating current direct into the lamp load. On 1954–64 models with Wipac battery-lighting equipment, the generator charges via a rectifier the battery from which current is taken for the lamps and horn.

The generator and rectifier maintain the battery well charged under all running conditions, a system of coil switching varying the generator output according to the prevailing load. The 6-volt a.c./d.c. unit has an output of 30 watts at about 2,800 rev/min. The flywheel comprises six cast magnets with laminated pole pieces. It is "self-keeping," and it is possible to separate the flywheel from the stator without the risk of any loss of magnetism occurring. The laminated stator has six salient poles. Of these, four are wound with coils of enamelled copper wire.

Where a battery is fitted to Model D5 or D7 an a.c./d.c. trickle charge is used. The stator plate has three lighting coils and the two outer coils are connected in series, with one end earthed, to provide a.c. current for the headlamp main bulb. Unless the engine is running the headlamp bulb does not light. The small centre coil is connected via a small full-wave rectifier to the battery and provides trickle charge current with the lighting switch in all positions. The trickle charge system provides battery current to operate the parking lights, stop light and horn.

It is possible for any Bantam owner to convert his a.c. direct lighting set into d.c. (Varley) battery lighting with (Sentercel) rectifier. A suitable Wipac conversion set is obtainable (1948–54). On new 1957–65 B.S.A. Bantams, Wipac direct lighting or battery lighting is specified as alternative equipment. On 1950–3 models, Lucas battery-lighting (*see* page 54) was the alternative equipment.

Maintenance. This is not necessary except in respect of the ignition components, the maintenance of which is dealt with on pages 48–54. Should the generator require any further attention other than the renewal of the contacts and condenser, send or take the complete machine to an authorized Wico-Pacy service station.

Wipac Conversion Kits. It is now possible for any Bantam owner to convert a direct-lighting set into rectifier lighting, with battery. Three types of "Convertakit" kits (requiring no special tools for fitting, and with full instructions) are obtainable from the Wipac Group Sales Ltd., London Road, Buckingham, Bucks., or through B.S.A. agents and accessory dealers. The kits are applicable to 1948–51 Bantams with remote-control lighting switch and to 1952–65 models with built-in rotary-type headlamp switch.

To Remove Wipac Contact-breaker and Stator Unit. First remove the two screws holding the contact-breaker cover plate in position and remove the cover plate. Next remove the central screw securing the cam *A* (*see* Figs. 18, 19 20). Pull the cam away and lift out its key. Now remove the three screws *D* which secure the contact-breaker housing. You can then lift off the whole unit, including the housing.

To Remove Wipac Contact-breaker (Models D10, D14, and Bantam 175, 1967–70). This is simply a matter of removing the two screws *D*, Fig. 21, securing the carrier plate and of uncoupling the earth lead at its snap connector or eyelet. The whole unit may then be withdrawn from its housing.

To Remove the Wipac Flywheel. Never attempt to do this unless you have available the appropriate B.S.A. service tool, namely the flywheel extractor, Part No. 61–3188. Any attempt to remove the flywheel without the extractor will damage the mainshaft.

Before extracting the flywheel, first verify that the cam key has been removed from its key-way. Remove the central nut and its shake-proof washer. Screw the B.S.A. extractor on to the exposed thread as far as it will go. Then with a suitable spanner turn the central extractor bolt until the flywheel is withdrawn from the taper on the mainshaft.

The Lucas a.c. 1A45 Generator. Fitted to many 1950–3 Model D1 Bantams with Lucas battery-lighting and coil ignition, the Lucas a.c. generator is of the inductor type.

When the lamps are switched on, the generator delivers maximum output, and during daylight running with the lighting switch in the OFF position a resistance is inserted into the circuit to reduce the generator output. Turning the headlamp lighting switch to the *H* position (*see* page 9) automatically effects a change-over from reduced to full generator output, the ammeter indicating the amount of current flowing out of or into the battery.

Maintenance. None is necessary except in regard to the ignition contact-breaker (*see* pages 55–7). As regards servicing, *see also* pages 20 and 35. Never attempt to remove the rotor from the stator assembly, otherwise a reduced generator output may ensue, necessitating remagnetizing of the assembly.

BATTERY MAINTENANCE

On Bantams with Lucas coil-ignition and battery-lighting equipment (provided on many 1950–3 models) as an alternative to direct ignition and lighting, the battery feeds current to the headlamp, the tail lamp, the electric horn, and to the ignition coil (except when the ignition switch is in the EMG position). Correct battery maintenance is vital. This section covers the Lucas 5 amp-hr and 9 amp-hr lead-acid batteries (fitted to 1950–3 and 1956–66 battery models respectively) and the Varly 9 amp-hr "dry" battery (used on 1954–5 battery models).

Topping-up a Lucas Battery. It is advisable to inspect the acid level about every *two weeks*, and more frequently in very warm climates. To inspect the level of the electrolyte it is preferable to take the battery right off. Slacken the battery clamping bolt, release the strap, and lift the battery out. On 1956–66 "swinging arm" Bantams unscrew the two nuts under the rear of the dual-seat and lift the latter off to the rear. Then remove the two small bolts securing the battery strap, unscrew the terminals, and withdraw the battery. Now remove the battery lid.

For D10, D14, and Bantam 175 models, it is first necessary to take off the left side panel to expose the battery and then to release the wire clamp retaining the battery to its platform. If the lid is taken off while the battery is still in position, the height of the battery is sufficiently reduced to allow it to be extracted through the aperture in the centre panel.

Unscrew the three filler plugs. Inspect the vent hole in each plug and make sure that it is not choked. See that each rubber washer (where fitted) is undamaged. On no account hold a naked light near the filler-plug holes.

If necessary add distilled water (obtainable from most garages and chemists) as required to bring the electrolyte level up to the top of the separators. *Never use tap water*. Top-up the battery just *before* a daylight run, as the agitation and gassing will mix the solution.

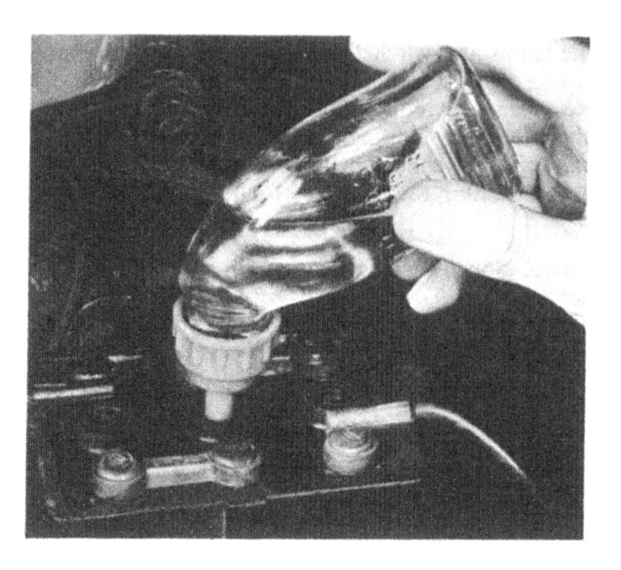

Fig. 23. Topping-up Lucas battery with Lucas battery filler

Before commencing to top-up, wipe the top of the battery clean with a rag to prevent the possibility of any dirt entering the cells. Destroy the rag afterwards as it will corrode any metal parts with which it comes into contact. The most convenient method of topping-up a Lucas battery is to use a Lucas battery filler. Insert the nozzle of the battery filler into each cell as shown in Fig. 23 until the nozzle rests on the separators. Hold the filler in this position until air bubbles cease to rise in the glass container. The cell is then topped-up to the correct level. When all three cells have been topped-up, wipe away all moisture from the top of the battery.

Replenishing the Lucas Battery Filler. When replenishing the Lucas battery filler with distilled water, see that the screw-on nozzle is correctly replaced. Be sure that the rubber washer is fitted over the valve with the small peg in the centre of the valve engaging the hole in the projecting boss of the washer.

Checking the Lucas Battery Condition. Occasionally it is advisable to check the condition of the battery by taking hydrometer readings (specific gravity values) of the solution in each of the cells. The method of doing this is shown in Fig. 24. The Lucas hydrometer contains a graduated float which indicates the specific gravity of the battery cell from which a sample of the electrolyte is taken.

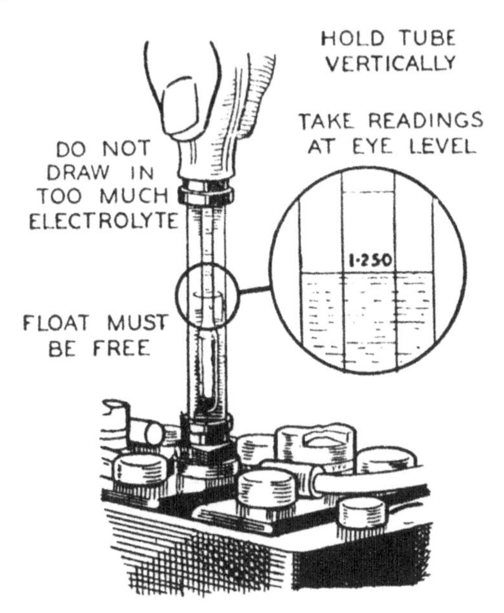

Fig. 24. Checking specific gravity of electrolyte in Lucas battery

After a sample has been taken and checked, it must, of course, be returned to the cell. The taking of specific gravity readings with a hydrometer is the most efficient way of ascertaining the state of charge of the battery. The specific gravity readings should be approximately the *same for all three cells*. Should the reading for one cell differ substantially from the readings for the others, probably some acid has been spilled or has leaked from the cell concerned. There is also a possibility of a short-circuit between the battery plates. In the latter case is will be necessary to return the battery to a Lucas service depot for attention.

Under no circumstances must the battery be permitted to remain in a discharged condition for long, or serious deterioration will occur. After checking the specific gravity readings and topping-up the cells, wipe the top of the battery and remove any spilled electrolyte or water; replace all the filler plugs and the battery lid. Then fit and tighten the battery clamping bolt.

Lucas Battery Connections. Keep the battery connections clean, free from corrosion, and tight, otherwise the ammeter readings will *not* indicate the true state of charge of the battery. To prevent corrosion both connections should be smeared with petroleum jelly. Note that a "positive earth" system is used and if the battery is removed, the terminals must be correctly reconnected. The coloured lead must be connected to the battery negative (—) terminal.

Specific Gravity. With Lucas batteries on B.S.A. Bantams, the specific gravity readings at an acid temperature of approximately 60°F should be: 1·280–1·300, battery fully charged; about 1·210 battery, about half discharged; about 1·110–1·150, battery fully discharged.

Never leave the battery in a discharged state for any appreciable period. A low state of charge is often caused through parking the machine for long periods with the lighting switch in the "L" position, unaccompanied by much daylight running. The remedy is, of course, to undertake more daylight running and to keep the switch in the OFF position as much as possible until the battery regains its normal state of charge.

Running Minus a Battery. On machines provided with a battery it is important to disconnect the rectifier completely at the snap connectors and to insulate all leads properly from each other and from earth, prior to running with the battery removed. Do not switch on the lights with the engine running, otherwise all bulbs will fuse and there is a risk of the rectifier being burnt out.

Storage. If Lucas equipment is laid by for some months, the battery must be given a small charge from a separate source of electrical energy about once a month, in order to obviate any permanent sulphation of the plates. In no circumstances must the electrolyte be removed from the battery and the plates allowed to dry, as certain chemical changes take place which result in permanent loss of capacity.

The Varley MC 5/9 Battery. This five-plate, 6-volt, 9 amp-hr battery is used on 1954–5 Bantams with Wipac battery-lighting (and on a.c. sets converted to d.c.). It is a "dry" lead-acid type and has some definite advantages over the "free acid" type. The whole of the necessary electrolyte is completely absorbed and held in suspension by the porous plates and separator material which together form a block completely filling all space in the battery container. The battery has no free acid to spill, is unaffected by vibration, corrodes very gradually, has a big useful life, and requires a negligible amount of maintenance.

Maintenance of the Varley Battery. Provided that the Bantam is taken out regularly for daylight runs, the generator will maintain the battery in a good state of charge. But *once a month* it is desirable to top-up the battery.

Always keep the battery connections clean and tight and the positive terminal earthed. See that the upper part of the battery (below the lid) is kept quite clean and dry. Make sure that all the filler plugs have their rubber washers intact and properly positioned. Also verify that the vent holes are unobstructed. Check the above points when topping-up the battery. If the battery is permitted to stand idle for a considerable period, you should give it a freshening charge about once a month.

To Top-up the Varley Battery. To maintain the plates and separators in a moist condition, top-up (monthly) the cells, using about a *teaspoonful* of distilled water per cell. Top-up *after*, and not before a run. After allowing the battery to stand for a quarter of an hour, remove all surplus liquid with a small syringe or by shaking out. This is most important.

Voltage and State of Charge. The following voltages shown by a moving coil voltmeter indicate the approximate state of charge of the Varley MC 5/9 battery:

Fully discharged: 5·7 volts or under
Partially discharged: 6·15 volts or under
Open circuit fully charged: 6·3 volts or over
On charge, fully charged: 7·8 volts or over

Bench Charging Varley Battery. Should bench charging be necessary, note that the normal charge rate is 1 amp. When the voltage reading on charge reaches 7·8 volts, continue to charge for a further three hours. Charging for twelve hours at 1 amp is normally sufficient.

If the battery becomes abnormally dry, top-up with distilled water before and during charging. Subsequently remove all surplus liquid.

If the capacity of the battery falls after the battery has been in use for a considerable time, it may be necessary to top-up with weak sulphuric *acid* (1·100 S.G.) instead of distilled water, for one or two bench charges.

THE RECTIFIER

In the case of Lucas (1950–3) and Wipac (1954–70) battery-lighting equipment, the rectifier itself is responsible for converting the alternating current produced by the generator into direct (unidirectional) current for battery charging. It is important to see that the rectifier always makes good contact with its support, the rectifier being cooled by surface contact.

Maintenance. Provided that the rectifier leads are securely attached to the rectifier, no maintenance of any kind is required, and the rectifier (attached to the toolbox bracket below the saddle or between the toolbox and battery) should not be interfered with. If any trouble occurs, return the complete unit to the nearest B.S.A. or Wipac agent. Avoid obstructing the air flow to the rectifier by fitting any additional accessories, or stowing personal belongings, beneath the saddle or dualseat.

Note particularly that the electrical equipment (and especially the rectifier) on the B.S.A. Bantam is specifically designed for use with the "positive earth" system, and the *positive* terminal of the battery must always be *earthed*. Therefore when it is necessary to remove the battery from the machine, it must always be replaced with the positive terminal properly earthed. Incorrect connecting up of the battery leads will immediately result in the complete burning out of the rectifier. The exception to this is certain D1 and D3 models where a "negative earth" system was employed (*see* page 77).

THE LAMPS

Lucas lamps are specified on 1950–3 Model D1 Bantams with battery lighting and coil ignition. On 1948–65 models with direct lighting and ignition, Wipac lamps are used exclusively; several different types of headlamp have been specified. The headlamp fitted to 1954–70 Bantams having battery lighting is also of Wipac design. Note that a Wipac stop–tail light is available only for Wipac battery-lighting models.

The Lucas SSP575P Headlamp (1950–3). This Lucas headlamp has a double-filament main bulb and a pilot bulb. The main bulb is a "pre-focus" type which requires *no focusing adjustment*, the filament being permanently positioned in focus relatively to the reflector. One filament of the double-filament main bulb is responsible for the main driving beam, while the other filament (controlled by a dipper switch on the handlebars) provides a dipped beam for riding in foggy weather and when passing oncoming vehicles.

The Lucas headlamp embodies a Lucas "light unit" comprising a combined reflector, bulb holder, and front lens assembly. On 1950–1 models (and up to March, 1952) the pilot bulb is mounted at the rear of the light unit (*see* Fig. 25) and shines through a transparent window in the reflector. The 1952–3 Lucas headlamp has an underslung pilot light, the bulb being mounted vertically downwards on a carrier plate at the base of the lamp shell (*F*, Fig. 26) and shining through an external window beneath the reflector.

Lighting Switch Positions on Lucas Headlamp. See the appropriate information given on page 9.

Warming Up of Lucas Headlamp Shell. Should the headlamp shell become warm while riding by day with the lamps off, do not suspect a fault in the wiring. The condition is quite normal and is caused through the reduced-charge resistance *G* (in headlamp shell) dispersing some of the energy from the generator in the form of heat, thus causing a rise in the temperature of the headlamp shell.

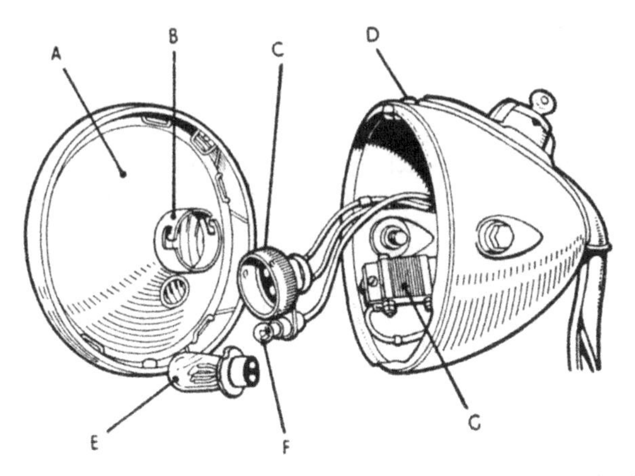

Fig. 25. Lucas "Pre-focus" type headlamp with pilot bulb fitted internally (1950–1)

The Lucas light-unit assembly is shown removed from the headlamp

Key to Figs. 25, 26

A. *Reflector of light unit*
B. *Bulb holder*
C. *Adapter*
D. *Lamp front securing-screw*
E. *Main bulb*
F. *Pilot bulb (carrier plate, Fig. 26)*
G. *Reduced charge resistance*

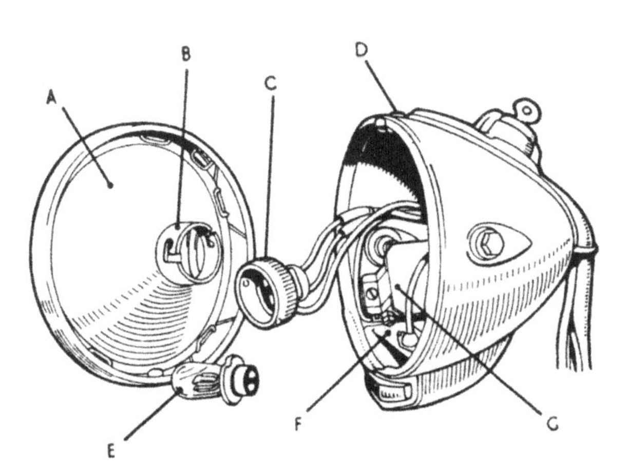

Fig. 26. Lucas "Pre-focus" headlamp with underslung pilot light (1952–3)

In this instance also, the light-unit assembly is shown removed

Aligning Lucas Headlamp. No focusing adjustment is called for as the headlamp is of the "pre-focus" type, but it is sometimes desirable to check the alignment of the lamp. Unless this is correct, the best illumination is unobtainable and some dazzle, annoying to other road users, may be caused.

The best method of checking the alignment is to stand your Bantam in its normal riding attitude facing a light-coloured wall at a distance of about 25 ft. Switch on the main driving light and observe whether the beam is projected straight ahead and parallel with the ground.

With a tape measure or a piece of string, take vertical measurements from the centre of the headlamp, and from the centre of the illuminated circular patch on the wall, to the ground. Both measurements should be the same. If they are unequal, obviously the headlamp is tilted and must be correctly aligned. Slacken both securing bolts which hold the headlamp between the brackets on the front-fork legs, and then move the headlamp up or down as required to obtain a beam centre truly parallel with the ground. Finally, retighten the two lamp securing bolts firmly.

To Remove Lucas Lamp Front. With a screwdriver slacken the small plated screw on top of the headlamp shell (*D*, Figs. 25 and 26), withdraw the rim, complete with light-unit assembly, outward from the top; as the light-unit *A* emerges, raise it slightly to free the lower metal tongue from the headlamp shell.

To replace the lamp front (light-unit assembly), locate the small metal tongue on the headlamp rim with the corresponding slot at the bottom of the lamp shell, and carefully press the lamp front home. Afterwards secure in position by tightening the small securing screw at the top of the rim.

The Lucas 480 Tail Lamp (1950–3). To remove the shell of the lamp carrying the red glass, push it in and turn *anti-clockwise*. It can then be withdrawn as shown in Fig. 27. As may be seen from the sketch, the bulb itself also has a bayonet type fixing. To replace the lamp shell, engage the bayonet fixing, push in, and then turn clockwise to secure the shell to the flanged body of the lamp.

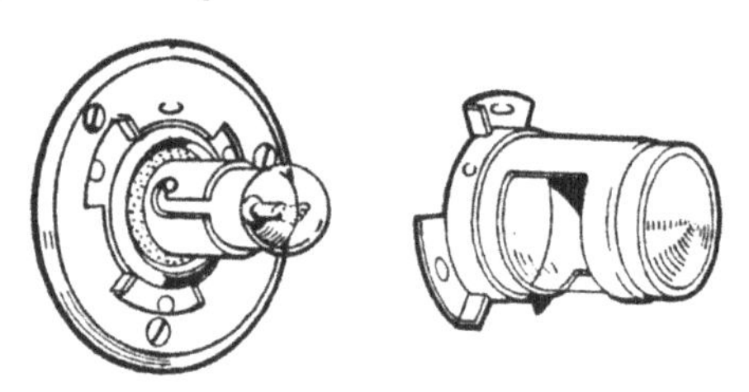

Fig. 27. The Lucas 480 tail lamp

Fitted to 1950–3 Bantams with Lucas battery-lighting

The Lucas Stop–Tail Lamp. Some 1952 and all 1953 Bantams with Lucas battery-lighting equipment have a Lucas stop–tail lamp provided instead of the ordinary tail lamp. To remove the red "Diacon"-plastic portion of the lamp and obtain access to the double-filament bulb, it is only necessary to remove the two securing screws.

Lucas Replacement Bulbs. It is preferable to renew bulbs after considerable service and before the filaments actually burn out, as this prevents deterioration of illumination caused through sagging of the filaments. Always use Lucas bulbs in Lucas lamps for which they are specially designed and tested. All Lucas bulbs have their metal caps marked with a number for identification, and when renewing a bulb see that the number on the cap (e.g. 200, 312, 988) is correct for the particular bulb concerned.

In a 1950–3 "pre-focus" Lucas headlamp use a 6-volt 30/24 watt, Lucas No. 312 double-filament main bulb. This has a broad locating flange on the cap and cannot be fitted wrongly, i.e. with the dipped-beam filament *below* the driving-light filament. A groove in the bulb flange engages a projection in the bulb holder.

In the case of the headlamp pilot light, fit a Lucas 6-volt, 3-watt, No. 988 bulb. In the tail lamp use a 6-volt, 6-watt, Lucas No. 205 bulb. The pilot and tail lamp bulbs have a bayonet type fixing. If a Lucas stop–tail lamp (similar in design to the tail lamp shown in Fig. 27) is specified, fit a 6-volt, 6/18-watt, Lucas No. 352 double-filament bulb which has offset securing pins to prevent incorrect fitting.

Fitting Bulbs to Lucas Headlamp. With the Lucas "pre-focus" type headlamp, to obtain access to the main and pilot bulbs for bulb renewal, remove the Lucas lamp front as described (page 68). Next, to remove the double-filament main bulb, turn the adaptor (*C*, Figs. 25, 26) *anti-clockwise* and pull it off. Then lift the "pre-focus" bulb *E* out of the bulb holder *B*. It is quite free once the adaptor has been removed.

On the 1950–1 headlamp, to remove the pilot bulb release the bayonet fixing securing the bulb (*F*, Fig. 25) to the holder on the adaptor. On the 1952–3 headlamp with underslung pilot light, slide the horizontal carrier plate (*F*, Fig. 26) inside the lamp out of its locating groove, and release the bayonet fixing of the bulb.

To renew a double-filament main bulb, fit the correct renewal bulb (*see* above) into the bulb holder (dipped-beam filament uppermost), engage the two projections on the inside of the adaptor with the slots in the bulb holder, press on, and secure by turning *clockwise*.

The Wipac 1–58 Headlamp (1948–51). This sturdy and thoroughly weatherproof headlamp has been fitted to Bantams with Wipac direct ignition and lighting up to January 1952. It has a double-filament main bulb supplied direct with current from the Wipac generator and pilot bulb above the main bulb for parking purposes; the pilot bulb is supplied with current from a bicycle-type dry battery inside the headlamp behind the reflector.

There is no focusing adjustment for the main bulb, the bulb being permanently in correct focus. But it is, of course, possible to align the headlamp in the front fork brackets. No external lighting switch is fitted to the headlamp, all switch components being totally enclosed inside the body of the lamp. The switch is therefore most unlikely to be affected by the weather. The switch (including the dipper circuit) is remote-controlled by a Bowden cable having its operating lever (*see* Fig. 28), conveniently mounted on the near side of the handlebars.

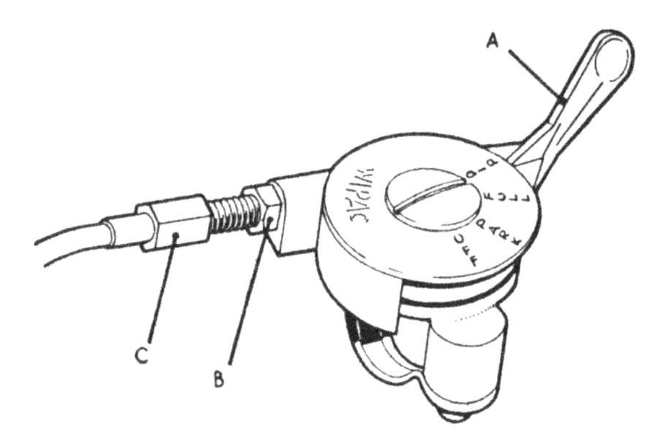

Fig. 28. Handlebar lighting switch for Wipac 1–58 headlamp (1948–51)

A. Switch lever *B. Lock-nut* *C. Adjuster for synchronizing*

Lighting Switch Positions for Wipac 1–58 Headlamp. The four consecutive lever positions of the remote-control switch lever fitted to 1948–51 Bantams are explained on page 9.

Adjustment of Remote-control Switch Lever. An adjustment of the remote-control switch lever for the Wipac 1–58 headlamp is seldom called for. But should the switch lever (shown at *A* in Fig. 28) ever need an adjustment to synchronize the lever movement with the action of the switch itself inside the headlamp, this can readily be effected as described below.

First check that the two lamp bulbs fitted are serviceable. Next place the Bantam on its central stand, start up the engine, and allow it to tick-over at a moderate speed. Move the lever *A* (Fig. 28) to the "FULL" position, and then slacken the lock-nut *B*, and while observing the headlamp, with a suitable spanner screw the adjuster *C* in or out as required to obtain the driving beam. Afterwards tighten the lock-nut *B* securely. If perfect synchronizing is obtained with the switch in the "FULL" position, the cable should be correctly aligned for the three remaining positions marked on the handlebar lever. It is, however, advisable to move the lever through *all* its positions and verify whether the headlamp switch responds.

Should no lighting occur with the lever in a certain position, leave the lever in this position, slacken the lock-nut *B* (Fig. 28) again, and with great care make a further adjustment with the adjuster *C* until the light appears. Retighten the lock-nut and move the lever back into the "FULL" position to confirm that the operating cable has not been moved too far from its initial setting. Should it have done so, once more repeat the adjustment, but turn the adjuster as required with the greatest caution.

Aligning Wipac 1–58 Headlamp. *See* page 68, "Aligning Lucas Headlamp."

To Remove Wipac 1–58 Lamp Front. The front rim of the headlamp houses the reflector and bulb-assembly bracket, and the parking battery is inside the lamp body at the rear. To obtain access to the bulbs and dry battery slacken the slotted screw at the base of the headlamp rim, and withdraw the lamp front outwards and upwards. On the 1948 headlamp the front has a hinge and spring clip, and the front can be gently pulled off.

The Wipac 1–59 Tail Lamp (1948–50). To remove the rim of the 1–59 tail lamp carrying the red glass, unscrew the small 6BA locking screw under the lamp and then turn the rim anti-clockwise and withdraw. The bulb holder has a bayonet type fixing for the bulb which can be instantly removed by the usual "push and-turn" method.

Note that the replacement for the 1–59 tail lamp fitted to 1948–50 Bantams has a 1½ in. diameter rear window and 6-watt bulb, to comply with 1955 rear light regulations. The Part No. of the modified tail lamp is 05160.

To Renew Parking Battery (Wipac 1–58 Headlamp). Remove the parking battery from inside the headlamp as soon as it is discharged. If it is permitted to remain in the lamp, it will corrode and spoil the body of the headlamp. Obtain a 3-volt twin-cell bicycle-lamp dry battery, type 800, and hold it so that the vertical contact strip faces towards the headlamp. Then locate the battery upside down in the support bracket so that the vertical contact connects with the metal battery holder at the rear of the headlamp. See that the horizontal contact-strip rests on top of the lower contact.

Wipac Replacement Bulbs. Renew bulbs before they burn right out (*see* page 69). With a.c. direct lighting equipment it is essential to fit bulbs of the correct wattage. For 1948–61 Wipac 1–58 and 1–58F headlamps, fit a 6-volt, 24/24-watt, double-filament main bulb, and a 2·5-volt, 0·25-amp parking bulb. Where a tail lamp is concerned, use a 6-volt, 6-watt, single-filament, double-contact bulb. For a pre-1954 stop–tail lamp, use a 6-volt,

6/18-watt bulb (*see also* page 75). The correct speedometer bulb is a 6·5-volt 0·3-amp, 1·95-watt type. The caps on all except pilot and speedometer bulbs (screw type) have a bayonet fixing.

Fitting Bulbs to Wipac 1–58 Headlamp (1948–51). To gain access to the headlamp bulbs, remove the lamp front as previously described. To remove the bulb-assembly bracket, bend downwards the small tabs which project from the base of the reflector. Then remove the bulb assembly bracket by turning it slightly anti-clockwise. The double-filament main bulb and the parking bulb are now readily accessible, and can be removed for inspection and renewal if necessary.

When fitting a new double-filament main bulb it is essential to check that the word "TOP" marked on the bulb is in fact at the top. Should the bulb be unmarked, you must fit it in accordance with the diagram shown in Fig. 29, i.e. with the offset (dip) filament uppermost.

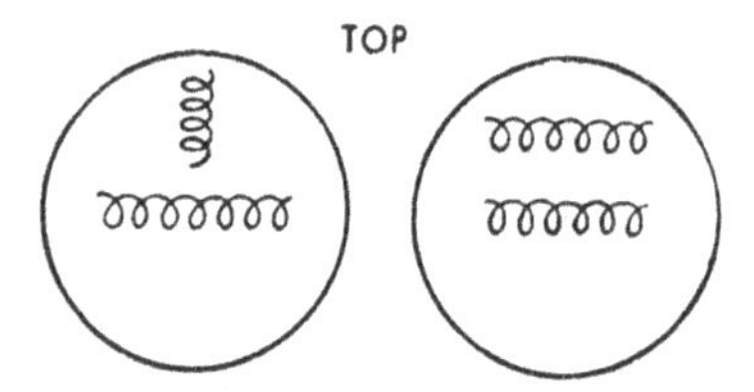

Fig. 29. Wipac main bulbs must always be fitted like this (1948–61 models)

The offset filament for dipping must be uppermost as indicated

The Wipac 1–58F Headlamp (1952–61). This type of a.c. headlamp (*see* Fig. 30) is specified on the 1952–61 Bantams provided with Wipac direct-lighting equipment. The rotary-type switch on top of the headlamp (introduced in January, 1952) is the main difference between this headlamp and the earlier (type 1–58) headlamp fitted to 1948–51 direct-lighting models with remote-control lighting switch on the handlebars. On this headlamp the pilot bulb is below the main bulb.

The 1–58 headlamp has a double-filament main bulb supplied with current direct from the lighting coils of the S55/Mk. 8 a.c./d.c. generator. A pilot bulb is fitted below the main bulb for parking purposes, and this is fed with current from a bicycle-type dry battery inside the headlamp behind the reflector.

There is no adjustment for main-bulb focus, but the headlamp can be tilted fore and aft for alignment, in the front-fork support brackets. The rotary-type lighting switch on top of the headlamp shell has three positions, namely OFF, L, H. When the switch is in the H position, the main driving beam can be dipped when required by means of a dipper switch on the handlebars.

To remove the lamp front see details for 1–58 lamp on page 71.

The Wipac 02143 Headlamp (1954–61). This d.c. headlamp on most 1954–61 Model D1, D3 Bantams with battery lighting is basically of similar design to the Wipac 1–58F headlamp already dealt with and illustrated in Fig. 30. The rotary lighting switch has the same three positions, and an ignition key is omitted because current for ignition is taken direct from the

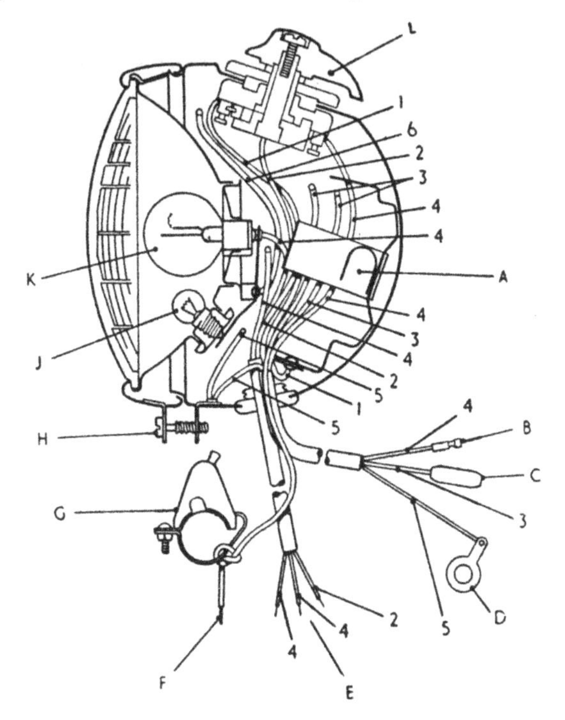

Fig. 30. Sectional drawing of a Wipac 1–58F headlamp (1952–61)

This headlamp is fitted to direct-lighting models. The rotary-type switch replaces the remote-control switch shown in Fig. 28, used in conjunction with the 1948–51 Wipac 1–58 headlamp.

A. *Parking battery (dry)*
B. *Generator lead*
C. *Tail lamp lead*
D. *Earth lead*
E. *Dipper-switch group*
F. *Speedometer lead*
G. *Dipper switch (handlebar fitting)*
H. *Lamp-front fixing screw*
J. *Parking bulb*
K. *Double-filament main bulb*
L. *Lighting switch*

1. *Green*
2. *Light red*
3. *Black*
4. *Dark red*
5. *Translucent*
6. *Blue*

S55/Mk. 8 generator (No. IG 1130 d.c.). The essential difference is in regard to the switch wiring, two leads being taken to the rectifier. Also the internal parking battery is omitted, the pilot bulb being fed direct from the battery.

1960–70 Wipac Headlamps. These are similar to earlier type Wipac headlamps but have pre-focus double-filament main bulbs. The main bulbs are 6-volt, 24/24 watt (30/24 watt from 1967 onwards.) No focusing adjustment is possible or necessary and a prefocus bulb cannot be fitted incorrectly. On machines with a direct lighting set fit a 2·5-volt, 0·25-amp parking bulb. On machines with battery equipment fit a 6-volt, 3-watt parking bulb.

The lamp front, together with the reflector and bulb assembly, is secured to the lamp casing by a slotted screw above or below the headlamp according to model. To remove a bulb it is therefore only necessary to loosen the slotted screw until you can withdraw the rim.

To replace the double-filament pre-focus main bulb, press the bulb retainer inwards and turn it slightly anti-clockwise. Then lift the retainer off and withdraw the bulb. Note that a new bulb automatically provides correct relationship of the two filaments.

To check that the headlamp beam is projected straight ahead and is parallel with the ground, position the Bantam, off its stand, about 25 feet away from a light-coloured wall. The height of the beam centre on the wall should be the same as the height of the headlamp centre. If it is not, move the lamp as required after slackening the bolts securing the headlamp. On models where the lamp front is secured to a nacelle (which replaces the lamp body) it is necessary to slacken two screws on the nacelle rim.

To Align Wipac 1–58F Headlamp (1948–61). Observe the instructions given on page 68 for the Lucas SSP575P headlamp.

To Renew Parking Battery (Wipac 1–58F Headlamp). Do this in accordance with the instructions given on page 71 for the 1–58 headlamp.

The Wipac 1–93 Tail Lamp (1951–3). To remove the half of the lamp carrying the red plastic, push in, turn anti-clockwise, and remove. This gives access to the bulb (single filament, a.c.; double filament, d.c.), which has the usual bayonet-type fixing and can instantly be withdrawn. When refitting the lamp half, engage the bayonet fixing, push in and turn clockwise.

The Wipac 1A–93 Stop–Tail Lamp (1950–3). Some 1950–3 D1's provided with Wipac battery lighting equipment[1] have a 1A–93 stop–tail lamp fitted instead of the 1–93 tail lamp. The Wipac 1A–93 stop–tail lamp is identical to the 1–93 tail lamp except that two wires and connectors are attached to the lamp, which has a single 6-volt, 6/18-watt double-filament bulb.

One filament, connected direct through the lighting switch, illuminates the red tail light, and the other one is illuminated only by the stop-light switch

[1] Wipac stop–tail lamps and switches are not designed or available for use on Bantams having a.c. flywheel generators giving direct lighting.

when the rear brake is applied. To remove the unit carrying the red glass, and to withdraw the double filament bulb, follow the instructions already given for the Wipac 1–93 tail lamp.

The Wipac 110 Stop–Tail Lamp (1954–62). Late 1954 Bantams (Models D1 and D3) with Wipac battery lighting, and all 1955–62 Bantams, are fitted with the Wipac 110 stop–tail lamp. On 1955–62 machines with direct lighting, the two stop-light bulbs are, of course, omitted. The 110 lamp can also be used as a replacement for the 1–93 and 1A–93 lamps.

The Wipac 110 stop–tail lamp comprises two parts, a back-plate and a red polystyrene plastic cover. As may be seen in Fig. 31, the back-plate has three bulbs. For the stop warning-lights (operated by the rear-brake pedal) two 6-volt, 3-watt screw-type bulbs are fitted on either side of a 6-volt, 6-watt bayonet fitting tail light bulb. With this bulb combination, renewal of the bulbs is much cheaper than is the case where a double-filament bulb is provided. The red polystyrene plastic cover has three "bull's eyes" located in line with the three bulbs, thereby giving penetrating illumination.

To remove the plastic cover from the 110 lamp, remove the two countersunk screws securing the cover to the back-plate. This exposes the three bulbs as shown in Fig. 31. To remove the 3-watt tail-lamp bulb, push the

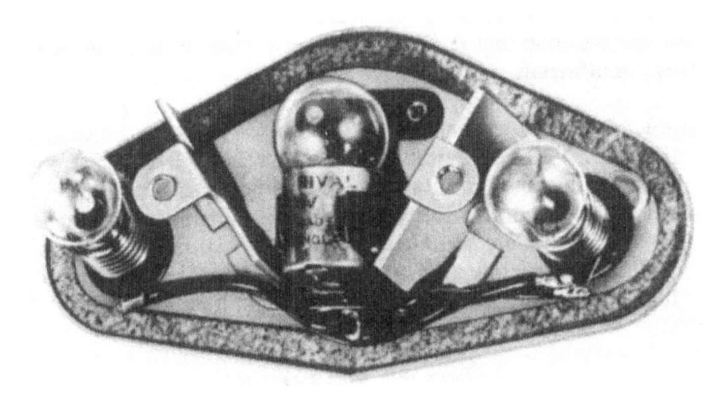

Fig. 31. The back-plate of the Wipac 110 stop–tail lamp (1954–62)

An unusual method of mounting the bulbs is used. On 1955–62 Bantams with direct lighting, the two stop-light bulbs are omitted

bulb sideways in its spring clip. To remove the 6-watt stop-light bulbs, unscrew the bulbs from the holders which are in the form of coil springs. These act as self locking devices when the bulbs are screwed home.

Wipac Stop–Tail Lamps (1963–6). On 1963–5 Bantams a Wipac 143 stop–tail lamp is fitted, very similar to the Wipac 110 lamp shown in Fig. 31.

On all except direct lighting models two 6-volt, 6-watt stop-light bulbs are fitted, one on each side of the 6-volt, 3-watt tail lamp bulb. On 1963–5 models with direct lighting the two stop-light bulbs are, of course, omitted. All 1966–70 Bantams have a Wipac 143B stop–tail lamp with a single 6-volt, 3/18-watt double-filament bulb. Access to the bulb or bulbs on all 1963–70 stop–tail lamps is obtained by unscrewing two countersunk screws and removing the transparent red plastic portion of the lamp.

Renewing Bulbs (Wipac 1–58F Headlamp, 1–93 Tail Lamp). The headlamp bulbs can be withdrawn without disturbing the reflector, and the whole of the instructions given on pages 72 and 74 apply. Be careful to fit the headlamp double-filament main bulb the correct way round (*see* Fig. 29). Bulb renewals as on page 72.

Alignment, Bulb Renewal, etc. (Wipac 02143 Headlamp.) Use the previous instructions given for the 1–58F headlamp disregarding all reference to the parking battery, and noting that a 6-volt, 3-watt pilot bulb is required instead of the 2·5-volt, 0·25-amp parking bulb referred to on page 74.

Care of Wipac Headlamps (1948–70). Very little attention is required. Occasionally verify that the wiring connectors are gripping the leads firmly, and check that the securing bolts on both sides of the headlamp body are firmly tightened. Always keep the glass front perfectly clean. If it is permitted to become dirty, the brilliance of the headlamp beam will necessarily be affected.

Improved Dipper Switch for 1951–2 Bantams. As has been mentioned on page 9, the series 1–102 dipper switch fitted to 1951–2 Bantams provided with direct lighting and ignition (and the S55/Mk. 8 generator) is rather sensitive to varying finger pressures which can cause momentary overloading of the lighting circuit. The trouble can be simply rectified by scrapping the series 1–102 dipper switch and fitting in its place the modified series 96 switch. This improved switch can be obtained from the Wipac Group Sales Ltd.

WIRING OF EQUIPMENT

It is rarely necessary to interfere with the wiring harness, and normally no attention is needed throughout the useful life of the motor-cycle, provided that the owner is not very careless or neglectful of the electrical components and does not leave the machine in the open unprotected.

Some useful wiring diagrams are included (Figs. 32–39) in this section for the benefit of those who may have to attend to the wiring at some time or other.

Keep All Connections Tight. Occasionally verify that all connections to the electrical components are tight and that all rubber shields, where provided, are pulled properly over the connections. The various connections can be readily identified by referring to the appropriate wiring diagram.

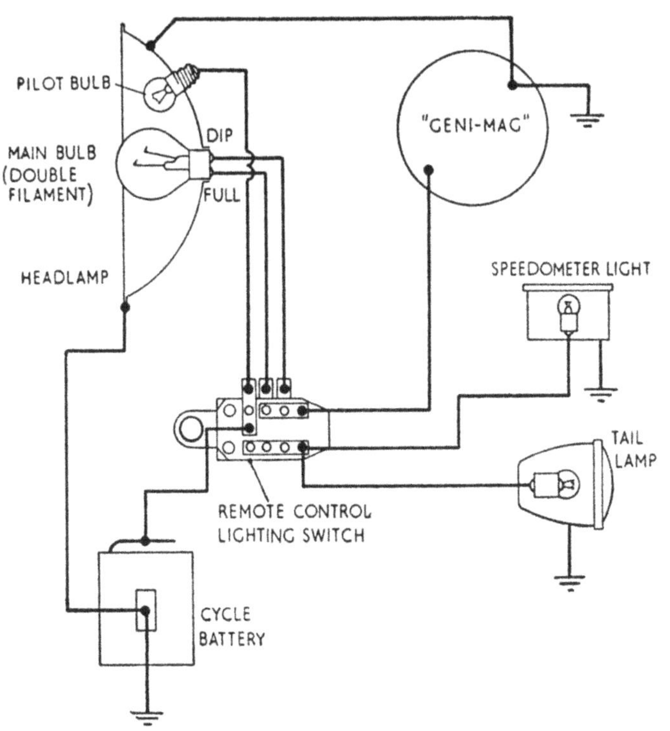

Fig. 32. Wiring diagram for 1948–50 Model D1 Bantams with Wipac a.c. "Geni-mag" and Wipac 1–58 headlamp with handlebar lighting switch

This diagram applies to 123 cm³ Bantams with Wipac direct lighting from 1948 up to August, 1950

Battery Leads on d.c. Equipment. It is important to note that on nearly all 1950–66 Bantams fitted with battery lighting, the *positive* terminal of the battery is earthed. If it is necessary for any reason to disconnect the battery leads, it is essential afterwards to reconnect them correctly, i.e. with the positive (+) to earth. As has been mentioned on page 10, the rectifier will suffer serious damage if the battery leads are accidentally reversed.

Where Wipac battery-lighting equipment is fitted to Models D1 and D3 Bantams prior to engine numbers DDB–101 and BD3B–5001 respectively, a multi-plate rectifier is used with a *negative* earth. On all later Wipac battery models the rectifier is of the enclosed single-unit "pancake" type, with the *positive* terminal earthed.

Attention to Lucas Wiring. Before making any alterations to the wiring on machines with Lucas equipment (or removing the panel housing the lighting switch), always disconnect the negative lead from the battery. This will prevent the danger of a short circuit occurring. This also applies to 1954–66 Wipac battery lighting equipment (*see* previous paragraphs).

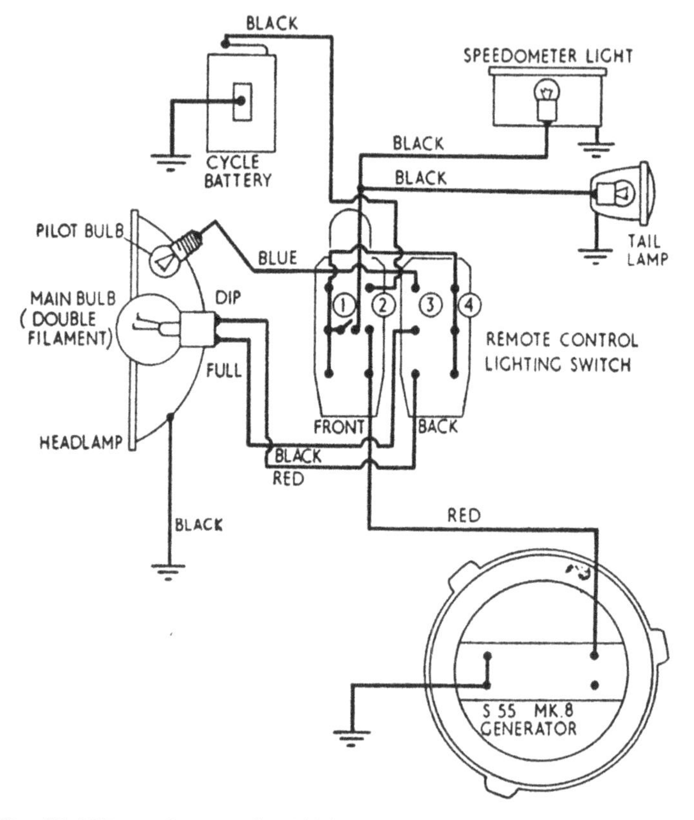

Fig. 33. Wiring diagram for 1950–1 Model D1 Bantams with Wipac a.c./d.c. S55/Mk. 8 generator and Wipac 1–58 headlamp with handlebar lighting switch

This diagram applies to 123 cm³ Bantams with Wipac direct lighting from August, 1950, to December, 1951, inclusive

The negative lead from the battery (approximately one foot in length) is connected to the lead from the lighting switch by a brass connector. A rubber shield insulates the connector which must never be permitted to touch the frame or other metal part of the machine. Should there be such contact, the battery will immediately be short-circuited. To unscrew the

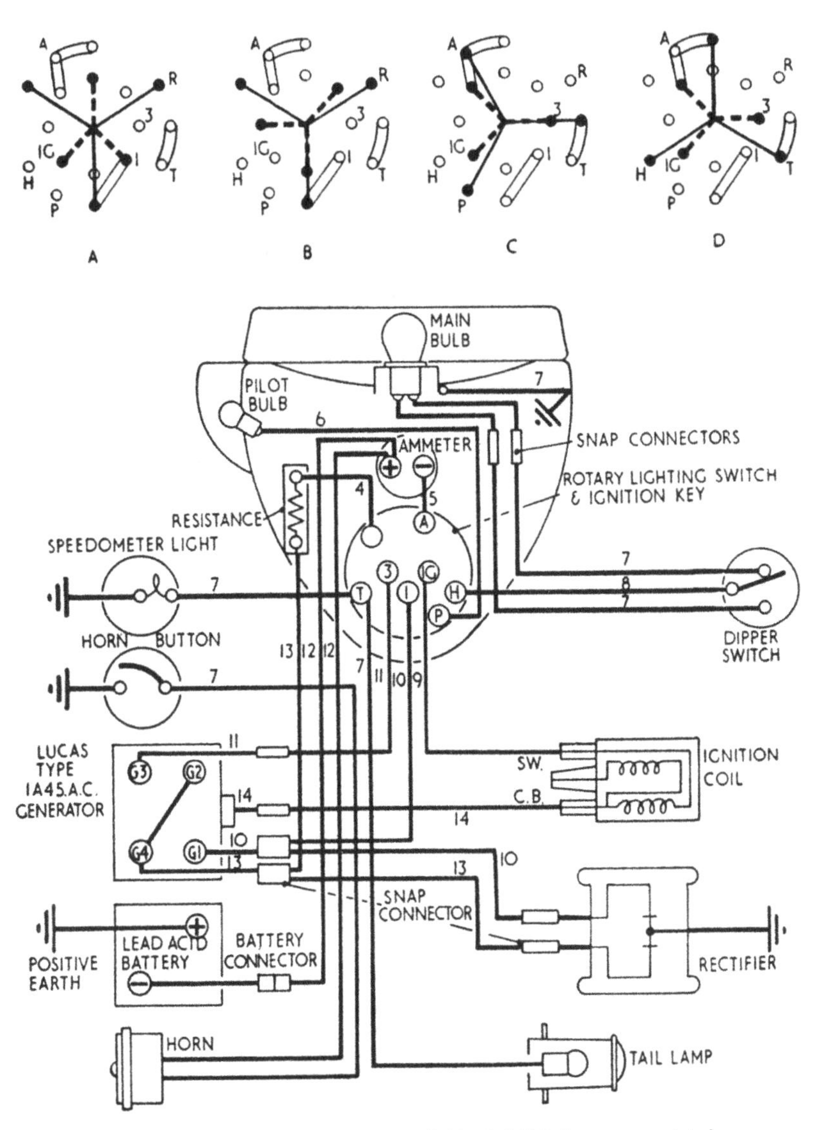

Fig. 34. Wiring diagram for 1950–3 Model D1 Bantams with Lucas a.c. generator and Lucas SSP575P headlamp with headlamp lighting switch

This diagram applies to 123 cm³ Bantams with Lucas battery-lighting (rectifier) and coil ignition, provided as an alternative to the Wipac direct-lighting equipment

4. *Brown and yellow*
5. *Brown and blue*
6. *Red and black*
7. *Black*
8. *Blue*
9. *White*
10. *Purple*
11. *Green*
12. *Brown*
13. *Yellow*
14. *White and black*

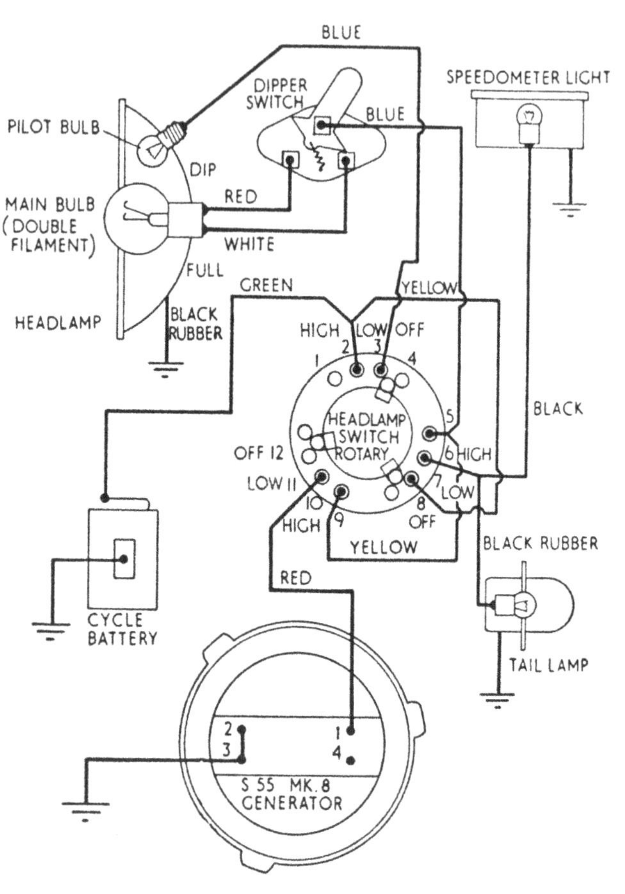

Fig. 35. Wiring diagram for 1952–61 Models D1 and D3 Bantams with Wipac a.c./d.c. S55/Mk. 8 generator and Wipac 1–58F headlamp with headlamp lighting switch

This diagram applies to 123 cm³ and 148 cm³ Bantams with Wipac direct lighting from January, 1952, to 1959 inclusive

brass connector it is, of course, necessary first to push back the rubber shield. After reconnecting the lead, make quite sure that the rubber shield is pulled well over the brass connector.

WIPAC ELECTRIC HORN

On Bantams having Wipac battery-lighting and direct-ignition equipment the electric horn is very carefully adjusted by the makers to give maximum performance, and it is rarely necessary to attend to the horn in any way until a very big mileage has been covered.

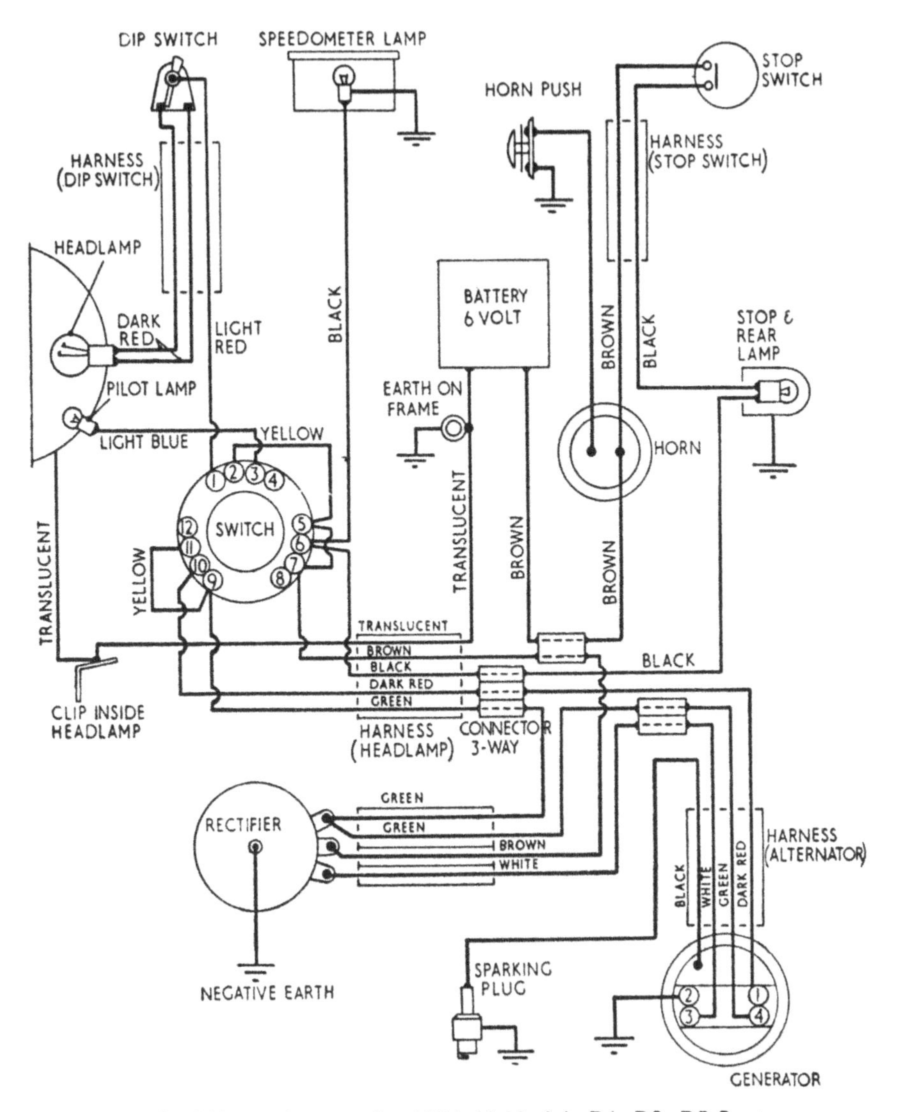

Fig. 36. Wiring diagram for 1954–61 Models D1, D3, D5 Bantams with Wipac 02143 headlamp and Wipac a.c./d.c. S55/Mk. 8 generator

On late 1954 and all 1955–61 battery lighting models the battery positive terminal is earthed and a three-bulb stop–tail lamp is fitted. On 1960–1 models the Wipac type 0213 headlamp was replaced by a Wipac type SO891 headlamp with a "pre-focus" main bulb. The above diagram, however, applies to all models

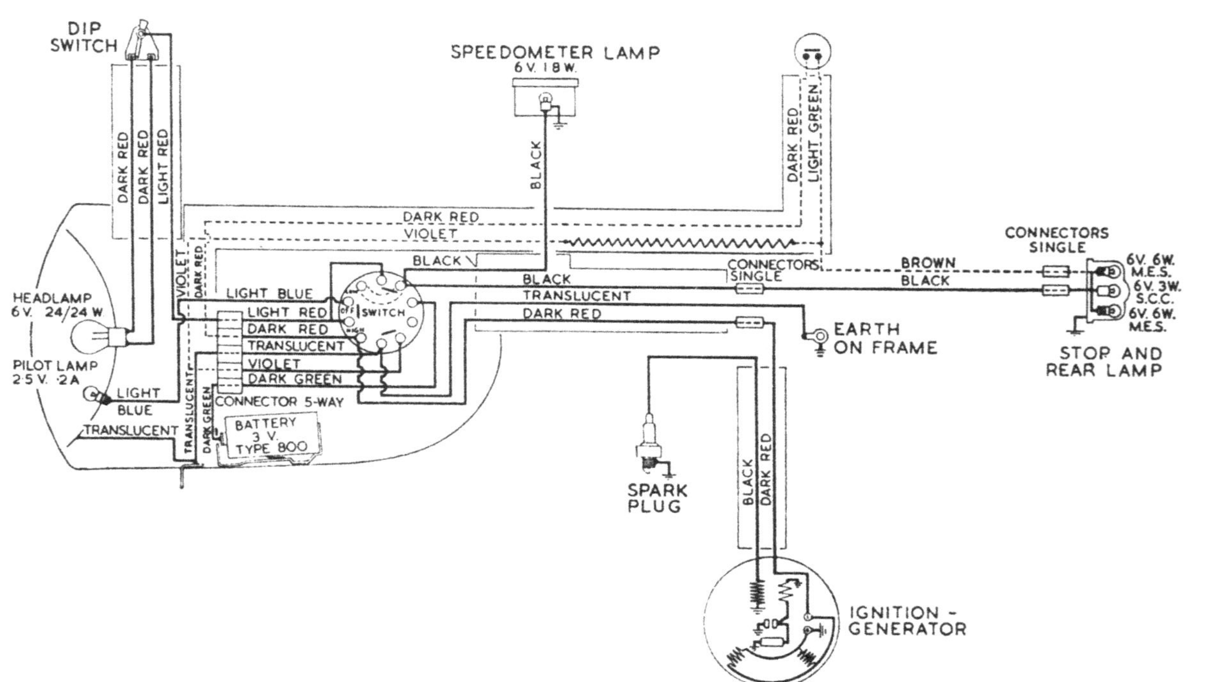

Fig. 37. Wiring diagram for 1962–5 direct lighting Models D7, D7D/L with Wipac a.c./d.c. S55/Mk. 8 generator and Wipac SO856 headlamp

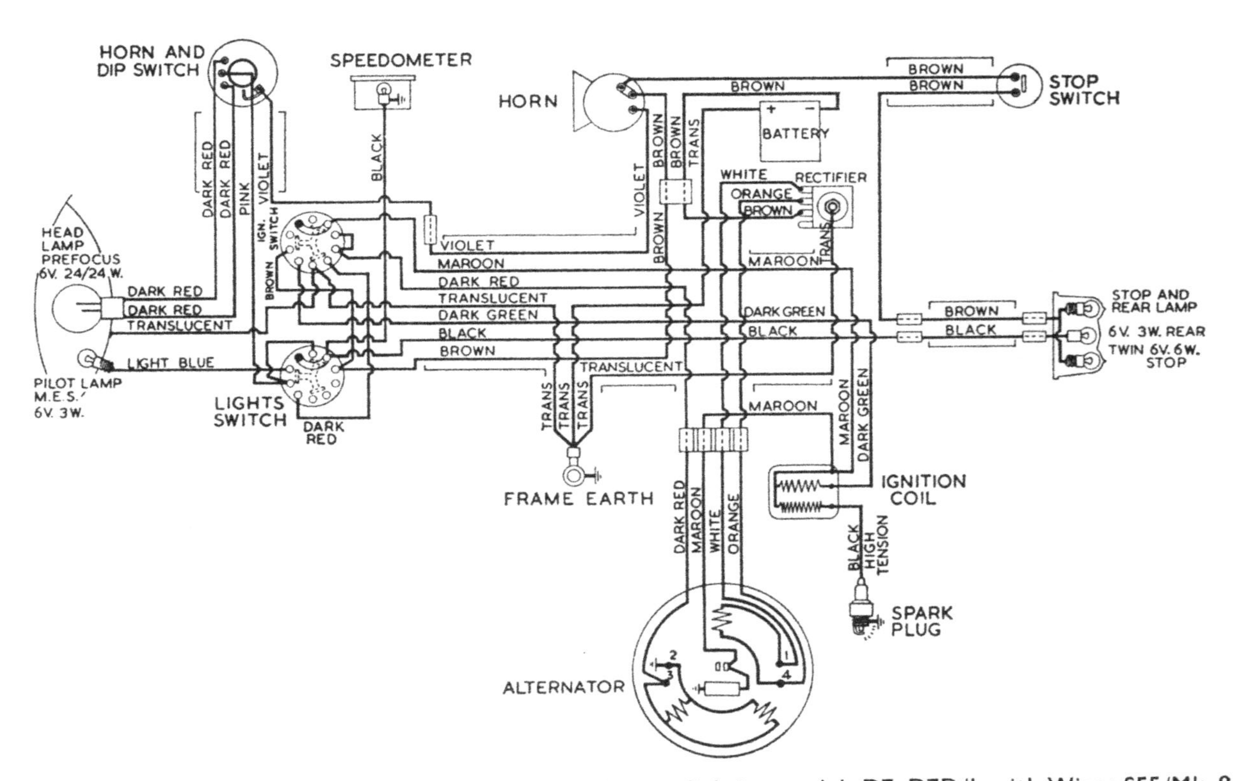

Fig. 38. Wiring diagram for 1962–6 coil ignition and battery lighting models D7, D7D/L with Wipac S55/Mk. 8 generator and Wipac SO891 headlamp

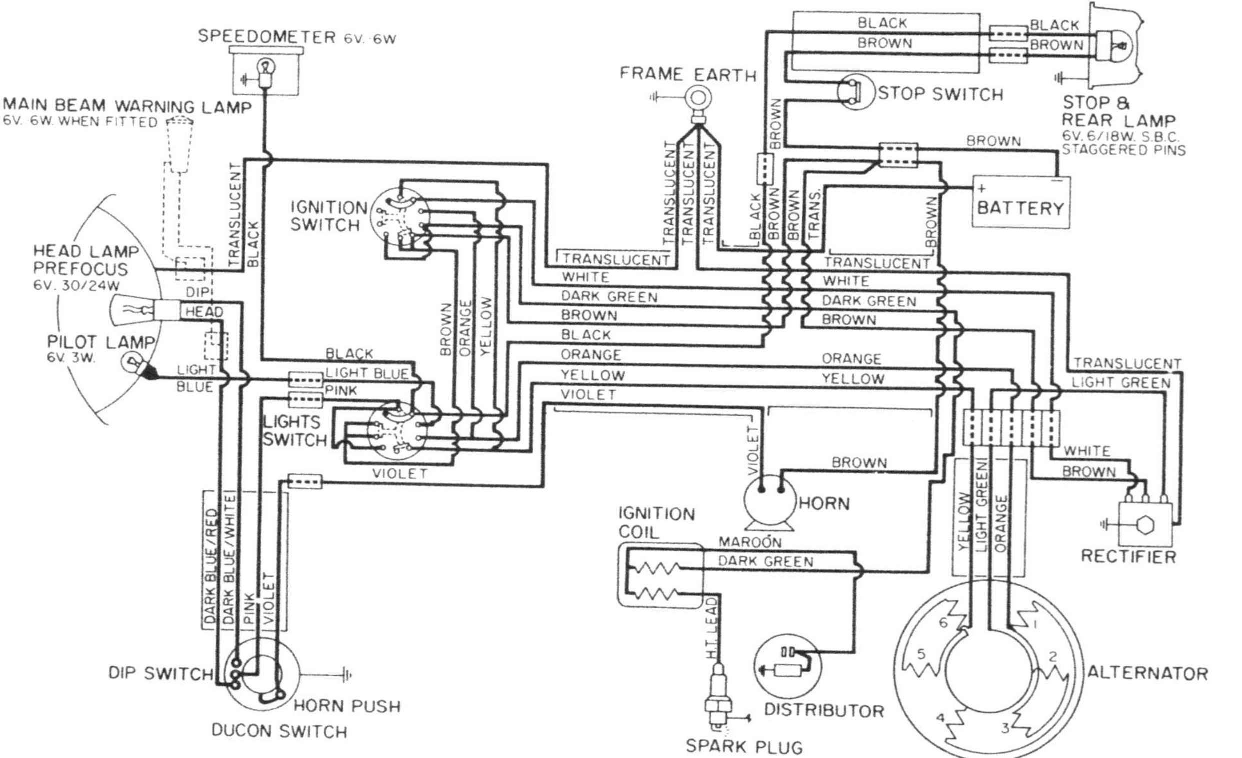

Fig. 39. Wiring diagram for 1967–70 coil-ignition and battery-lighting models D10, D14, and Bantam 175

Note that some cable colours (notably those from the generator) have changed from those on the preceding diagrams

If the Horn Becomes Ineffective. In the event of the horn becoming uncertain in action, failing to vibrate, or emitting only a choking sound, do not conclude immediately that the horn itself has failed. Verify that the horn trouble is not caused by some external source such as a loose connection, a short circuit in the wiring, or a discharged condition of the battery. Also check that the horn securing-bolt has not slackened off. This can interfere with the action of the horn.

To Adjust the Horn. Should it be found impossible to rectify poor horn action by checking the points mentioned in the previous paragraph, you can effect an adjustment of the horn in the following manner. First remove the rubber plug from the body of the horn. This exposes the adjuster screw. Then to make the required adjustment, turn the adjuster screw slightly clockwise or anti-clockwise while actuating the horn button, until an effective horn note is obtained. Afterwards replace the rubber plug in the horn body. If horn trouble persists in spite of all efforts to rectify it, return the complete horn to Wipac Group Sales Ltd., London Road, Buckingham, Bucks., or to one of their service stations for expert attention.

6 General maintenance

All essential instructions are given in this chapter concerning the normal maintenance, dismantling, and assembling required for 1948 and subsequent Bantams. Detailed reference is not made, however, to lubrication, carburation, the ignition system, and the lighting equipment, because these matters have already been fully covered in earlier chapters. This chapter has been subdivided into a number of main sections to enable the reader to refer quickly to any specific information.

Repairs and Spares. When it is necessary to forward or deliver parts to the makers (B.S.A. Motor Cycles Ltd., Service Dept., Armoury Road, Birmingham, 11), or to an appointed B.S.A. dealer, always remember to attach to each part a label bearing clearly your full name and address. Any correspondence about technical advice and repairs should always be written on *separate* sheets to ensure its being attended to with the minimum delay. To help identification, always quote the year of Bantam manufacture and model number. Also quote the corresponding engine or frame number (*see* footnote on page 1), accordingly.

A handy illustrated spares list is obtainable from any appointed B.S.A. spares stockist who keeps a comprehensive range of B.S.A. spares.

Items Needed for Maintenance. You *must* have handy in the garage or lock-up certain items besides those in the Bantam tool kit. They include: a can of paraffin for cleaning purposes; a stiff brush for scouring dirt off the crankcase and underneath the motor-cycle; a tin of suitable engine oil for the engine and gearbox (*see* page 20); a funnel for topping-up the gearbox; a canister of grease (*see* page 20); a receptacle for oil when draining the crankcase; a drip-tray; some dishes or jars in which to wash parts when dismantling; some non-fluffy rags; some fine emery cloth; a pair of new gudgeon-pin circlips.

A proprietary gudgeon-pin extractor may also prove useful, and it is desirable to obtain a small pair of snipe-nosed pliers for removing gudgeon-pin circlips; a small wire brush for cleaning plug threads, etc.; a Champion combined feeler gauge and plug regapping tool (*see* page 47); a suitable feeler gauge for checking the contact-breaker gap.

For the maintenance of the motor-cycle parts, you should obtain: a tyre-pressure gauge (*see* page 103); a tyre repair outfit; an extra tyre lever;

a box of spare chain links and a chain-rivet extractor; a Lucas battery filler (*see* page 62) or a small syringe for topping-up the battery on a Bantam fitted with a Lucas or Varley battery respectively; a chamois leather; a sponge and pail (if a hose is not available); some soft dusters (preferably of the Selvyt type): a tin of good wax or other proprietary polish for the enamelled parts; and last but not least, a tin of good hand cleanser.

Tools for Repair Work. In the event of your deciding to tackle as much repair work as possible besides normal routine maintenance, stripping-down, and assembly, it is advisable to rig up a suitable bench, complete with vice, and also to buy a steel rule and a few additional tools.

To commence with it is a good plan to purchase a good screwdriver; a medium-weight hammer, a small hand-drill, some twist drills, a hacksaw, some large and small (smooth and rough) files, and a reliable soldering outfit for repairing broken control cables. Major repair work necessitates considerable skill in the handling of tools, and some sound engineering knowledge. Without these you are not advised to attempt any major repair work on the power unit or machine.

If reconditioning of the engine and gearbox unit is undertaken, you will require some special service tools, among which may well be mentioned: No. 61–3188 for removing the generator flywheel (models prior to 1967); extractor No. 61–3796 for removing the engine sprocket; No. 61–3191 for removing the clutch plate circlip; No. 61–3256 for extracting the clutch hub; various other punches, reamers, etc.

Details of Bantam service tools, and helpful repair unstructions (such as how to part the flywheels and drive out the crankpin) are included in the B.S.A. service sheets Nos. 505, 506, 508, 509, etc., obtainable from B.S.A. spares stockists. Bantam repair work, is, of course, quite outside the scope of this maintenance handbook. One B.S.A. service tool likely to interest the average Bantam owner is No. 61–3191 (shown in use in Fig. 57) for compressing the clutch springs to enable the clutch-plate assembly to be withdrawn for inspection and the friction inserts and springs renewed if necessary.

Keep Your Bantam Clean. If bought new, it cost quite an appreciable sum, and it is well worth looking after carefully. If cleaned regularly and properly, it will run better, last longer, keep its good looks, and retain a good second-hand value in the event of your ever wishing to sell it. A dirty Bantam is an eyesore. Furthermore, dirt covers defects, accelerates rusting, and is a nuisance and a menace when dismantling. On no account leave your Bantam soaking wet overnight. If you cannot spare the time for cleaning the machine in wet weather, grease it all over before using it.

Cleaning the Power Unit. Always keep the cylinder barrel and light-alloy cylinder-head fins clean. If the barrel fins are rusted, clean them with a stiff brush dipped in paraffin and afterwards paint the fins with some proprietary cylinder black. Rusted cylinder-barrel fins, besides giving a shabby look to the engine, cause an appreciable loss in heat dispersion.

Scour off all filth from the lower part of the engine and gearbox unit with stiff brushes and paraffin. Thoroughly clean all aluminium alloy and bright surfaces with a rag damped in paraffin, helped by brushes where necessary.

To Clean the Enamel. Do not attempt to remove mud from the enamelled parts when dry and caked, as this is liable to scratch the surfaces. If available, use a hose carefully to soak the mud off. If a machine is very dirty, it may be advisable to paint the surfaces over with a cleaning compound such as "Gunk" before directing a jet of water on to the surfaces. Do not permit any water to get on to the wheel-hub bearings, brakes, and carburettor. Where a hose is not at hand, soak the mud and then disperse it with plenty of clean water, using a sponge and pail.

After removing all dirt or mud, dry the enamelled surfaces with a chamois leather and afterwards polish them with soft dusters and some good wax polish or a proprietary polish such as "Autobrite." I, myself, am more or less a "fine-weather" rider, mainly because I hate cleaning a muddy machine. I do manage to keep it in almost "showroom" condition merely by rubbing over all parts with a slightly paraffin-damped cloth and then polishing with a dry duster. If a machine is very dirty, this method of cleaning is, of course, quite useless.

The Chromium Plating. Do not use any liquid metal polish or paste for cleaning purposes, as this will rub down the thin chromium surface. It is permissible, however, to use some good chromium cleaning compound occasionally. The correct method of removing tarnish (salt deposits) is to wipe over the surfaces regularly with a damp chamois leather and then polish with soft dusters. "Belco" is a good cleaning compound.

How to Reduce Tarnishing. During the damp winter months is it a good plan occasionally to wipe over all surfaces with a cloth soaked in a proprietary anti-tarnish preparation such as "Tekall," obtainable from accessory firms in pint and half-pint tins.

Check Nuts Regularly for Tightness. Apply spanners regularly to the various external nuts and bolts to ensure tightness, paying particular attention to the engine nuts and bolts, the nuts on the engine-mounting bolts, and the pipe unions. After the running-in period is completed, check over the external nuts and bolts regularly, say every 2,000 miles. After decarbonizing, check over the cylinder-head retaining nuts after a brief mileage.

Bantam Lubrication. Detailed instructions for the correct lubrication of 1948 and subsequent Bantams are given in Chapter 2, and the lubrication chart on page 21 explains at a glance when and where to lubricate the power unit and machine.

Carburettor Tuning and Maintenance. For full information on the Amal carburettor fitted to all Bantams, refer to Chapter 3.

Maintenance of Ignition System. Chapter 4 contains all essential maintenance advice concerning Wipac and Lucas flywheel generators, sparking plugs, and other components of the ignition systems provided on the 1948–70 Bantams.

The Ignition Timing. No alteration to the timing is normally permissible, but if there is any doubt about the timing being correct, it can readily be checked as described on page 51.

Loss of Compression. Provided that you keep your Bantam tank replenished with the correct petroil mixture (*see* page 17), it is extremely unlikely that you will experience any loss of compression (and consequent decline in power output) until a very big mileage has been covered. Ultimately, of course, some loss of compression will occur because of cylinder barrel and piston ring wear. It should be noted, however, that on D1, D3 and other Competition Bantams some loss of compression may occur at intervals of 3,000–5,000 miles because of poor seating of the decompressor valve (omitted on touring models) screwed into the cylinder head.

It is advisable each time the above are decarbonized to examine and clean the decompressor valve. With a screwdriver applied to the valve head, rotate the valve backwards and forwards. Some paraffin will help to clean carbon deposits off the valve seating. If absolutely necessary, apply a smear of fine-grade grinding paste to the valve face and gently grind the valve on to its seat, lifting the valve every few oscillations to turn it to a new position. It should in practice rarely be necessary to grind-in a decompressor valve, as it is only used for starting and stopping purposes, and is in no way analogous to an exhaust valve on a four-stroke engine.

DECARBONIZING, ETC.

Carbon deposits form slowly but surely inside the engine (on the piston crown, the inside of the combustion chamber, and the exhaust port) because of: (*a*) incomplete combustion of fuel, (*b*) the burning of oil deposited by the petroil mixture, and (*c*) the burning of some road dust.

The formation of excessive carbon deposits inside the engine soon becomes apparent because of the disconcerting symptoms which accompany them. For instance, a Bantam begins to tire readily and lacks its former youthful liveliness and power; it begins to "pink" under slight provocation (particularly when there is a sudden increase in load); the two-stroke engine becomes noticeably "rough" and begins to run erratically, with excessive four- and eight-stroking.

A decline in power output is especially pronounced when carbon commences to foul the exhaust port. Such fouling obstructs the free escape of the exhaust gases, and prevents proper scavenging of the cylinder, an essential pre-condition for the efficient transfer of the combustible mixture from the crankcase.

Decarbonizing is an extremely simple operation to perform on the Bantam, and to obtain consequently smooth and "peppy" running, it is advisable to decarbonize at regular intervals of approximately 2,500–3,000 miles.

Cylinder Head Removal Normally Sufficient. It is normally unnecessary, and indeed undesirable, to remove the cylinder barrel at each "decoke." Most of the carbon deposits (except slight deposits under the piston crown) can readily be removed when the exhaust pipe and cylinder head are taken off. Therefore defer removing the cylinder barrel until such time as it is reasonably desirable to inspect the piston rings, the piston and the underneath of the piston crown. If compression is bad, remove the barrel after removing the cylinder head.

Petrol Tank Removal Unnecessary. If it is intended to remove the cylinder head, but not the barrel, you need not touch the fuel tank. However, should you wish to remove the cylinder head *and* the cylinder barrel, you should first raise the tank slightly. This greatly facilitates the removal of the cylinder barrel from the four long studs which retain the barrel and head to the crankcase.

To raise the tank at the rear, first loosen the two bolts securing the tank to the steering head, and remove completely the longer bolt securing the rear of the tank to the frame. This bolt, by the way, carries the earth lead of the electrical system. See that the fuel tap is turned off, disconnect the fuel pipe from the float chamber, and then raise the tank about one inch.

Note that on many Bantams a plastic-type petrol pipe is used, the upper end of the pipe being clipped to the petrol-tap union. It is not advisable to disturb this end of the petrol pipe unnecessarily. Normally it is quite sufficient to disconnect the pipe by unscrewing the union nut situated on top of the carburettor float-chamber.

To Remove the Cylinder Head from Barrel. First remove the air filter which is retained on the carburettor intake either by a clip bolt or by being screwed on (according to model). In the case of the 1968 and subsequent models, disconnect the air-hose clip.

Unscrew the mixing-chamber cap and release the clip bolt securing the carburettor to the induction stub, or, in the case of the 1958–70 D5, D7, D10 and D14 models, release the two nuts securing the carburettor flange to the rear of the cylinder. Withdraw the carburettor, and at the same time pull out the throttle slide and (on 1966–70 models) the air slide, together with the tapered jet-needle. Tie these up carefully out of the way. Place the carburettor in a box or on a sheet of clean paper. It is essential that no dirt is permitted to enter the instrument.

With a C spanner Part No. 68-9462 unscrew the union nut from the front of the cylinder barrel. If this nut should be difficult to turn, apply a few drops of penetrating oil to the threaded portion of the barrel immediately above the nut. Allow some time to elapse to enable the oil to penetrate around the threads before applying force with the C spanner. Now disconnect the exhaust pipe, or remove the pipe and silencer (two nuts).

Disconnect the high-tension lead from the 14 mm sparking plug, and with a box spanner, unscrew and remove the plug and its washer. On Competition models also disconnect the cable from the decompressor lever at the cylinder-head connection. Now with the appropriate spanner, unscrew evenly and in a diagonal order the four nuts securing the cylinder head and barrel, and withdraw the head (*see* Fig. 40) from the long crankcase studs. Never attempt to prise of the head which is of light alloy (1954–70) and is easily damaged. No gasket is used for the head joint, this being of the metal-to-metal type.

Withdrawing Cylinder Barrel. As has already been mentioned opposite, it is not necessary to remove the cylinder barrel each time the engine is decarbonized. Having taken off the cylinder head, to remove the barrel (in order to examine the piston and rings), turn the engine over so that the piston is well down on its stroke, and then with *both* hands carefully withdraw the barrel.

On the Bantam models there is ample room for the cylinder barrel to clear the tops of the four long crankcase-studs, without fouling the tank if it has already been raised slightly (*see* page 90).

As the piston emerges from the mouth of the cylinder barrel, steady it with one hand. The light alloy deflectorless-type piston must never be allowed to fall sharply against the side of the connecting-rod, as this may damage or distort the piston skirt. The slightest distortion (not necessarily visible to the naked eye) can have a most detrimental effect upon engine efficiency. The piston is perhaps the most vital part of the engine, but the most vulnerable when exposed. Therefore always treat it with the greatest respect.

After removing the cylinder barrel, inspect the compressed paper washer provided between the crankcase top face and the cylinder barrel. This must be in perfect condition. If it is in any way damaged, it must immediately be renewed, otherwise some loss of crankcase compression may occur during downward piston strokes.

As soon as possible after removing the cylinder barrel, wrap a non-fluffy rag or duster round the upper portion of the connecting-rod so as to cover completely the crankcase mouth. This will not only protect the piston and connecting-rod from swaying about and being damaged, but also eliminate the risk of some foreign body (such as a nut) or dirt entering the crankcase. If a nut does get into the crankcase, fishing it out can be a most tiresome business, especially on a sunny day! Lay the cylinder barrel and head in a safe position on the bench or floor, and have a look at the piston skirt and the piston rings. Examine the latter closely.

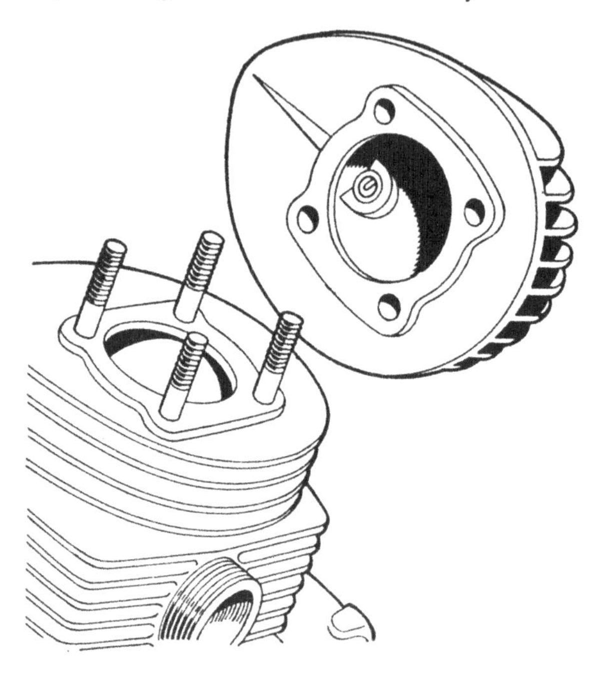

Fig. 40. Cylinder head removed

To Remove the Piston. The slightly domed die-cast piston, which, according to model, has either two or three plain rings, is secured to the small end of the connecting-rod by means of a fully-floating hollow gudgeon-pin secured in position by a pair of steel circlips (*see* Fig. 41).

It is seldom actually necessary to remove the piston from the connecting-rod, but when it is desired to make a close bench examination of the piston

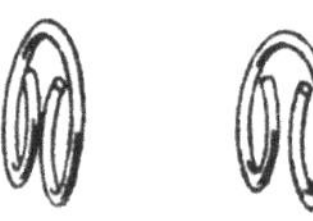

Fig. 41.
The circlips

and rings, it is obviously advisable to remove the gudgeon-pin and take off the piston.

To remove the gudgeon-pin, first remove with a small pair of snipe-nosed pliers, or other suitable implement, the two steel circlips from the grooves in the piston bosses. After removal, scrap the circlips, as they may be distorted or have lost springiness. Now, holding the piston firmly with one hand (to prevent any bending stresses on the connecting-rod), tap out the gudgeon-pin from the opposite side.

The gudgeon-pin is a somewhat close fit in the piston bosses, and if it cannot readily be tapped out while holding the piston with one hand, the safest course is first to warm the piston by means of a rag soaked in hot water and wrung out. Alternatively, apply a hot electric iron to the top of the piston crown. This will cause the aluminium-alloy piston to expand more than the steel gudgeon-pin. It should then be possible to push or tap out the pin quite readily. Alternatively, press out the gudgeon-pin with a proprietary gudgeon-pin removal tool. On 1962–70 D7, D10, D14, and Bantam 175 engines be careful not to damage the needle rollers in the small-end bearing. As the gudgeon-pin emerges, note its position relatively to the piston bosses. Mark one end as it is desirable always to replace it in the same running position. Lay the piston on the bench, or other safe place, and cover up the crankcase mouth.

Mark the Piston. Immediately you remove the piston, it is advisable to scratch an "R" mark on the inside of the skirt to indicate which is the rear. There is no deflector (used on most earlier two-stroke engines) on the piston crown which can be utilized for identification purposes. The piston must always be replaced in exactly the same position as originally fitted, because: (*a*) it laps out the cylinder bore in a specific manner, depending upon various factors such as thrust, lubrication, etc.; (*b*) the arrangement of the piston rings and ports is designed for one piston only (*see* page 99).

Examining the Piston Rings. If you go to the trouble of removing the piston, consider also removing the piston rings. The rings are responsible for maintaining compression and must therefore be full of springiness and in good condition. Before removing the rings, however, make a careful visual inspection of the rings which are located in their grooves and prevented from rotating (and thus possibly fouling the ports) by means of pegs which engage the rings at the piston ring gaps.

If the rings have a uniformly smooth metallic surface over their entire peripheries and have ample springiness, as evidenced by the fact that their "free" gap is considerably greater than their closed gap (*see* page 97), the rings are doubtless in sound condition and are functioning well. The state of engine compression is generally a reliable guide to the condition of the rings.

Should the piston rings on visual examination show signs of having been subjected to excessive heat, as indicated by brown or dark patches, they must be removed and renewed. The same applies if the rings have become stuck in their grooves, causing gas leakage. In this case it is likely that the piston ring lands and skirt are also scorched. Gummed-up rings must, of course, be removed, and substantial carbon deposits must be scraped from both the rings and their grooves.

If the piston rings appear to be in thoroughly good condition and carbon deposits are not appreciable, it is generally best not to disturb the rings. To remove them unnecessarily is bad practice and can cause temporary loss of compression without achieving any positive results. But if the condition of the rings is genuinely in doubt, remove them so that they and their grooves in the piston can be closely inspected.

Note that on the Bantam two-stroke engine excessive piston ring wear is most likely to be accompanied by a definite rise in petroil consumption, and if the wear is very pronounced some piston slap will probably be noticed, and possibly a peculiar sound known as "two-stroke rattle."

To Remove the Piston Rings. The compression rings fitted to the Bantam engine are made of cast iron and are of small section. They are therefore very brittle and easily broken if care is not taken during ring removal. The safest and most convenient method of removing (and fitting) the piston rings is indicated in Fig. 42. Insert three strips of sheet metal about 2 in. long and about $\frac{3}{8}$ in. wide under the rings. Then gently ease the compression rings off, starting with the top ring. Before commencing to ease each ring

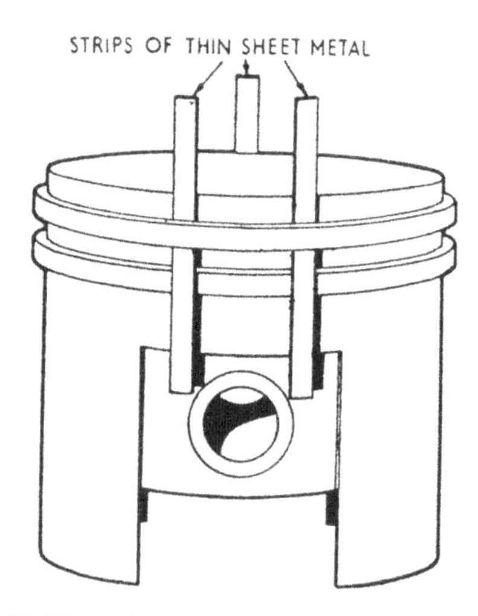

Fig. 42. The safest way to remove piston rings

It is advisable to employ this method also when fitting new rings or replacing the old ones. The two-stroke piston has no deflector, and the two plain compression rings are pegged. Recent D7 and D10 engines have three piston rings fitted, including a scraper ring, but the D14 and Bantam 175 engines reverted to two compression rings

off, see that its ends are clear of the locating peg in the piston groove. It is desirable, though not essential, to replace a serviceable ring in its original groove. Therefore lay the rings aside in such a manner that they can be identified on assembly.

When removing the rings, be particularly careful to avoid scratching or otherwise damaging the land between the rings and the land above the top ring. Any scoring here is most detrimental to engine efficiency. Should the rings be badly gummed-up by sticky carbon deposits, it is advisable to immerse the piston in a paraffin bath for about 20 minutes in order to soften the carbon. In extreme cases it may be necessary to remove the piston rings with a proprietary removal tool, or perhaps even to snap the rings off.

Should a slight piston seizure ever occur (generally caused by driving the engine too hard under unfavourable circumstances), it is probable that some smearing of the aluminium alloy at the edges of the lands will prevent the rings from springing out and thereby cause serious loss of engine compression. If the smearing is very bad, accompanied by scoring, the piston will have to be scrapped. If, on the other hand, the smearing is very slight, an expert mechanic can remove the barest amount of smeared metal with a very fine file and restore the piston and rings to serviceable condition.

Removing the Carbon Deposits. For scraping off carbon deposits from the piston, cylinder head, etc., it is advisable to use a blunt screwdriver or a proprietary scraper. For cleaning piston-ring grooves you can make up a suitable scraper by fitting a handle to a broken piece of piston ring ground at one end; alternatively you can obtain a proprietary piston-ring groove scraper.

Thorough decarbonizing is always worthwhile because carbon forms more slowly on smooth, clean surfaces. Where carbon deposits are found to be heavy, the application of a little paraffin will generally facilitate decarbonizing.

If removal of the cylinder head only has been effected, thoroughly scrape all carbon deposits from the piston crown, the combustion chamber walls, and the exhaust port of the cylinder barrel.

When removing carbon from the piston crown, be careful not to scratch deeply the aluminium-alloy surface and (except where the piston has been removed) do not use any abrasive such as emery cloth. If any abrasive particles get between the piston and the cylinder bore, they can cause most serious scoring of the highly polished cylinder barrel, and perhaps ruin the barrel. After decarbonizing the piston crown, wipe it with an oily rag to remove all loose particles.

Lay the cylinder head on the bench and chip off all carbon deposits from the combustion-chamber walls. The Bantam cylinder head (1954–70 models) is of aluminium alloy, and great care must be taken not to scratch it deeply with the decarbonizing tool. Do not forget to clean up the sparking plug hole, and when you have thoroughly decarbonized the combustion chamber wipe it clean with an oily rag.

The heaviest carbon deposits generally accumulate in the exhaust port and it is these deposits which cause considerable loss of power and a tendency for four-stroking to occur. When the exhaust pipe has been removed it is a simple matter to scrape off all carbon deposits from the port, but be very careful not to allow the scraper to slip inside the cylinder barrel and damage the bore surfaces.

If the cylinder barrel is removed as well as the cylinder head, also inspect closely the single inlet and twin tangential transfer ports for signs of carbon deposits. Until a considerable mileage has been covered, however, these deposits are unlikely to be heavy. But remove all existing deposits and afterwards wipe the cylinder bore and the inlet, exhaust, and transfer ports absolutely clean.

Where the piston has been removed and the rings taken off as previously described, remove any slight carbon deposits which may be present on the inside of the piston, but on no account touch the outside of the piston skirt. Clean the ring grooves very thoroughly, but be careful not to damage the sides of the grooves or the locating pegs. On a three-ring piston see that all carbon is removed from the slot at the bottom of the scraper ring groove. Also clean the backs of the piston rings and remove all carbon from the ends of each ring.

Cleaning the Silencer. If the silencer becomes badly choked up with carbon, some overheating, loss or power, and four stroking may occur due to excessive back pressure. On 1954–66 Model D1, D3, D7 and D7D/L Bantams the silencer has a detachable end cap and baffle, and the silencer can readily be taken apart and thoroughly cleaned. On 1948–53 models however, the silencer cannot be dismantled, and the best way to clean it effectively is to immerse the silencer in a caustic-soda solution of moderate strength. The caustic soda is, of course, corrosive, so keep it away from your hands and the chromium plating. Afterwards swill out the silencer thoroughly with water.

The 1954–63 silencer with detachable end-cap secured by a single central nut inside the exhaust opening can be dismantled as follows. Remove the nut and take off the cap and the internal baffle for thorough cleaning. When replacing the baffle unit, see that the copper sealing-ring is positioned before replacing the end cap. Replace the two plain washers and one spring washer on the stud before you tighten the central locking nut (1, Fig. 43).

The 1964–7 D7, D10 Bantams have a silencer provided with a detachable end-cap different from that shown in Fig. 43 and the internal baffles are not detachable. To clean the silencer remove the single nut and withdraw the end-cap. Then remove all carbon deposits from the cap and the baffles. To dissolve the carbon, if found difficult to remove, use a caustic soda solution. Before fitting the end-cap see that the copper sealing ring is replaced. Before replacing and tightening the nut securing the end-cap do

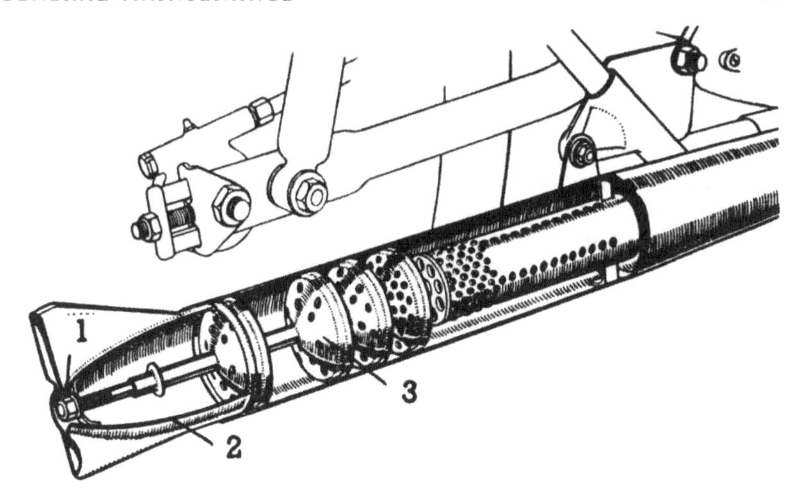

Fig. 43. The Bantam silencer with detachable end-cap and baffle (1954–63)

After removing the nut 1, the end-cap 2 can be removed and the baffle 3 withdrawn for cleaning

(*By courtesy of "Motor Cycling"*)

not forget to replace the plain washer and spring washer on the locating stud.

The 1968–70 D14 silencers are of different internal construction, those for the 1968 models containing spiral disc baffles mounted on a central tube, which can be withdrawn for cleaning purposes. Later models were of tubular construction and can be completely dismantled in the same way. Cleaning notes are as for the D7 models.

Fitting the Piston Rings. Indications that piston-ring renewal is called for have already been described on page 93. It is assumed that the piston-ring grooves have been thoroughly cleaned, the old rings also if these are found to be in serviceable condition and their gaps are within the permissible limits (*see* below). To replace the piston rings, use the method shown in Fig. 42, after first smearing a little engine oil on the rings and grooves. Fit the *bottom* ring first.

If the old rings are no longer serviceable, but the piston itself shows no signs of abnormal wear and is in sound condition, fit a new set of genuine B.S.A. Bantam rings. Piston rings of genuine B.S.A. manufacture are correctly gapped for use and have ample clearance for the locating pegs. Such may not be the case, however, if rings other than those of B.S.A. manufacture are used, and here it is essential to check the ring gaps, the fit of the rings in their grooves, and the clearances for the locating pegs.

To check the working gap of each piston ring, first insert the ring into the bore of the cylinder barrel and push it forward by pressing on it with the base of the piston skirt (or a bar of suitable diameter). This will ensure that the ring is absolutely square with the bore when the ring gap is checked with a suitable feeler gauge. To obtain efficient running on a Bantam engine, the piston ring gap (for both rings) must not be less than 0·009 in. (0·2 mm) and should not exceed 0·013 in. (0·3 mm). If the piston-ring gap is too small, remove a little metal from one end of the ring with a file, so as to increase the gap to 0·009 in. The gap, of course, gradually increases as wear of the ring and cylinder bore occurs, and it is therefore advisable to set the gap to the lowest permissible limit.

After checking that the piston-ring gap is correct, insert the ring in the piston-ring groove and verify that it is free to move without there being any appreciable up and down play. If the ring is a tight fit, rub down carefully *one* side of the ring on a sheet of fine emery cloth which must be laid on an absolutely flat surface. To ensure a uniform pressure being exerted on the piston ring during rubbing down, it is advisable to employ a rotary motion of the arm. As soon as the ring becomes a nice working fit in its groove (0·002 in.), clean the ring prior to fitting it.

It is essential to see that sufficient clearance exists between the inner portion of the piston-ring gap and the small locating peg in the piston ring groove. With finger pressure applied to the ring, fitted in its groove, close up the ring until the gap is reduced to nil, in which case there is obviously sufficient clearance at the peg. If it is impossible to reduce the gap to nil, the steps of the ring must be fouling the peg, and it is necessary to file the steps very carefully and lightly, using a very smooth file.

Testing the Connecting-rod Bearings. When you have occasion to withdraw both the cylinder head and the cylinder barrel, it is worth while taking the opportunity of checking the connecting-rod bearings for excessive wear. If very considerable wear has occurred you will probably have already noted in the case of the small-end bearing, a metallic "tinkling" noise or, in the case of the big-end bearing, a dull knock or rattling sound. The Bantam connecting-rod bearings (*see* Fig. 44), however, are of the heavy duty type and of generous proportions.

Provided that you are reasonably careful in handling your Bantam and are not neglectful in regard to petroil lubrication, you will find it possible to cover a very big mileage without having to renew either of the connecting rod bearings. Bearing renewal is a job which should be entrusted only to a really competent repairer or agent, as it requires considerable skill and special facilities, including the use of certain B.S.A. service tools. If the big-end bearing is in poor shape, the renewal of the roller bearing will involve the splitting of the flywheel assembly, an operation not likely to be undertaken with success by the inexperienced.

A convenient method of checking the small-end bearing for wear is to replace the gudgeon-pin in the small end bush and feel its fit by attempting to "rock" it in the bush. Although the gudgeon-pin must be able to rotate with perfect freedom, there should be no appreciable "rock" present.

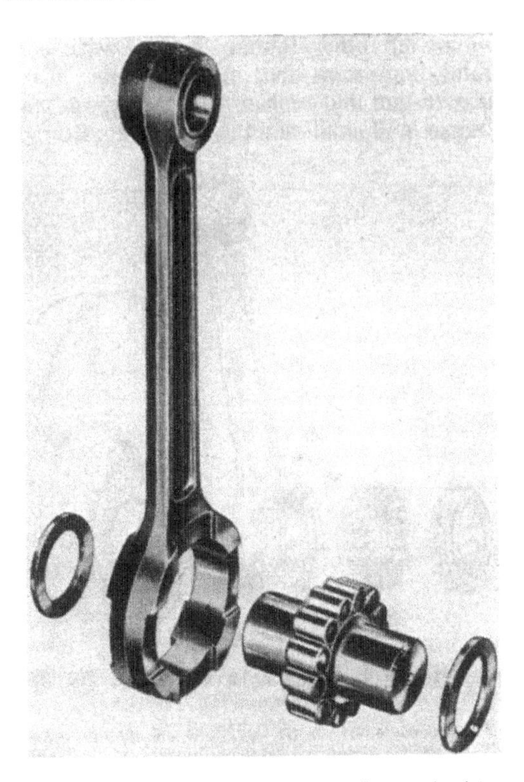

Fig. 44. The Bantam connecting-rod and sturdy big-end roller bearing (Models D1, D3)

To check the big-end bearing for wear, rotate the Bantam engine so that the single-row roller bearing is at the top of its movement, i.e. at T.D.C. (top dead centre), and then by gripping the connecting-rod with both hands and trying gently but firmly to pull and push the connecting-rod vertically, note whether there is any appreciable play present. None should exist, but some end movement is permissible and necessary. Be careful not to confuse end play with vertical play. If you do detect some vertical play but are not sufficiently experienced to determine whether it is sufficient to justify bearing renewal, it is best to obtain the opinion of an expert mechanic.

To Replace the Piston. It is assumed that the piston rings have been fitted, and that the piston itself is thoroughly clean internally and externally. Now offer up the piston to the small-end of the connecting-rod. When doing this make absolutely sure that the piston is replaced the correct way round (*see* page 93), with the two ring gaps to the *rear* in the case of Model D1 engines and to the *front* on all other Bantam engines with extra wide ports; it is hence vitally important that the ring gaps face to the front. Next oil the gudgeon-pin and replace it in its *original position*. Insert it into the piston bosses and small-end bush after first fitting one of the two *new* circlips.

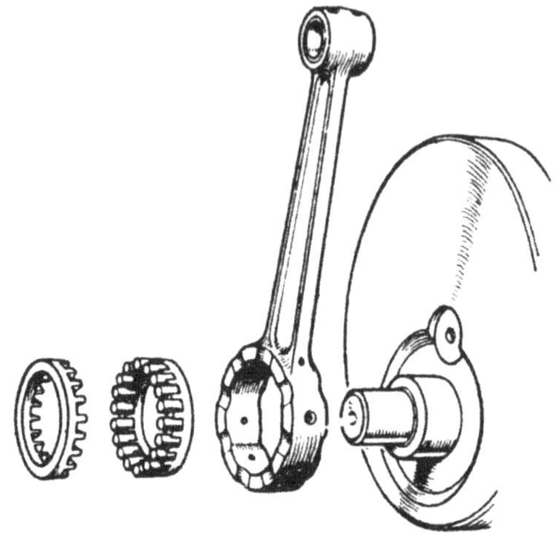

Fig. 45. Connecting-rod, caged rollers (Models D5, D7, D10, and Bantam 175)

Applies also to 1959–63 Model D1. On D7, D10, D14, and Bantam 175 engines a needle roller race is provided instead of a phosphor bronze bush for the small-end
(By courtesy of "Motor Cycle," London)

When tapping the gudgeon-pin home with a soft-metal drift and hammer, be very careful to support the piston firmly on the opposite side; if the pin is a very obstinate fit, first warm the piston by immersing it in hot water or by wrapping round it a rag soaked in hot water and wrung out. Alternatively, press the gudgeon-pin home with a suitable proprietary gudgeon-pin removal tool. See that the crankcase mouth is covered.

After tapping or pressing the gudgeon-pin until it abuts the circlip already fitted, carefully fit the second *new* circlip. When fitting it with a small pair of snipe-nosed pliers, squeeze the circlip ends together and employ a rotary motion of the hand to ensure that the circlip beds down snugly into the piston-boss groove. Remember that should a circlip spring out while the engine is running, the cylinder bore may easily be spoiled beyond repair; deep scores may be caused.

Pending the replacement of the cylinder barrel and cylinder head, cover up the piston as well as the crankcase mouth with a clean cloth.

Replacing the Cylinder Barrel and Head. Before replacing the cylinder barrel, wipe the cylinder bore thoroughly clean with a soft rag and some clean paraffin, and be very careful not to scratch its glossy surface. Check that the cylinder barrel spigot for the crankcase face, and the crankcase face itself, are absolutely clean. Also verify that the cylinder-base washer is in perfect condition. Should this compressed-paper washer be in any way damaged, renew it immediately and make sure that the washer referred to is correctly positioned. It is a good plan to smear some grease on both sides of the washer before fitting it to the crankcase face.

Smear some clean engine oil liberally on the outside of the piston and the inside of the cylinder barrel (i.e. the bore) and turn the engine over slowly until the piston is at or near the bottom of its stroke. Now replace the cylinder barrel over the piston and the four crankcase studs, carefully easing the piston rings with the fingers into the mouth of the cylinder barrel as the latter descends. Both rings must enter the bore readily without the necessity for using any force. It will be of considerable assistance in making a satisfactory job of this operation if a "slipper"—B.S.A. Service Tool 61-5051—is used to compress the rings while the piston is entering the cylinder bore. It is also important when lowering the cylinder barrel to make sure that it beds down properly on to the cylinder-base washer.

As soon as you have replaced the cylinder barrel, fit the head on the upper face of the barrel. No gasket is required, but the two contacting faces must be absolutely clean. Then replace the washers and nuts on the four holding-down studs. To avoid any risk of distorting the cylinder head, be most careful to tighten the four nuts evenly and in a diagonal order.

Final Assembly. Do this in the reverse order of dismantling. Replace the sparking plug (assumed to have been thoroughly cleaned and checked for gap), including the washer which must be in perfect condition and not flattened. Tighten the plug finger-tight first, and then firmly with a box-spanner. Reconnect the HT lead to the plug and make sure that its terminal connection is secure. On Competition models also reconnect the decompressor-valve operating cable to the decompressor unit screwed into the cylinder head.

Reposition the exhaust pipe and silencer (if previously completely removed), and with a mallet tap the exhaust pipe so that its end goes home into the exhaust port. Do not omit the gas-sealing ring. When doing this it is advisable to interpose a rag to prevent the risk of denting the pipe, and to apply the taps at several different points. On some engines a sharp blow with the closed fist may push the pipe home. Then with the C spanner securely tighten the union ring-nut which secures the pipe to the exhaust port of the cylinder barrel. The clip which secures the rear end of the pipe (and the silencer) can now be tightened down.

Replace the carburettor on the induction stub or flange (according to model). Before tightening the clip, check that the mixture chamber is truly vertical. Now insert the throttle slide, air slide (1966–70) and the tapered jet-needle. Afterwards replace the mixing-chamber cap, and with the twist-grip check that the throttle slide works freely.

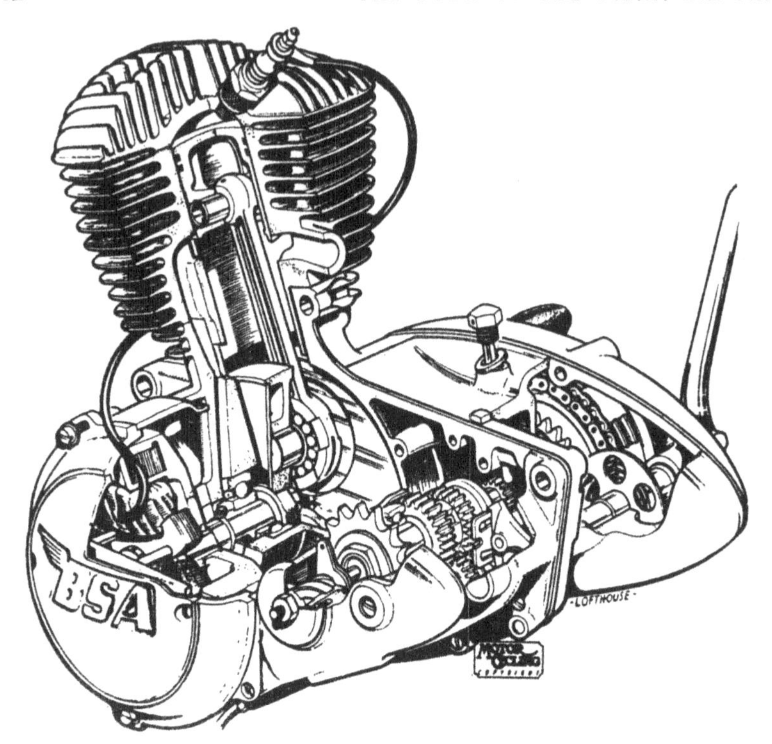

Fig. 46. Partly cut-away and sectioned view of assembled 148 cm^3 "Bantam Major" power unit

The engine shown has Wipac direct-ignition. Apart from the bore being increased from 52 mm to 57 mm, and the use of a light-alloy cylinder head and deeper cylinder finning, this engine is almost identical to the 123 cm^3 Bantam engines which have a stroke of 58 mm.

(By courtesy of "Motor Cycling")

If you have previously removed the cylinder barrel as well as the cylinder head, lower the petrol tank into its normal position at the rear and fit the long bolt securing this part of the tank to the frame. Before inserting this bolt, pass it through the earth connection tag attached to the electrical-system harness. To ensure good electrical contact, make certain that the tag is not dirty or corroded. Finally, with the appropriate spanners, firmly tighten the long rear bolt and the two shorter bolts securing the forward end of the tank to the steering head. Also reconnect the fuel pipe to the tank union. When tightening the fuel pipe union-nut, do not omit to hold the top hexagon with a spanner, otherwise you may strain the joint at the tank.

To Remove the Bantam Power Unit. Complete removal of the power unit is advisable for all work other than normal maintenance, including decarbonizing. The Bantam unit can readily be taken out of the loop frame. To do this this, remove the air filter and then the carburettor as explained on page 90, and then the decompressor cable (on Competition models), and the clutch cable. Also disconnect the fuel pipe, and the electrical lead from the flywheel generator. Next, with the "C" spanner unscrew the exhaust pipe union-nut (*see* page 91) and disconnect the exhaust pipe from the exhaust port. Remove the pipe and silencer together.

Disconnect the secondary chain and remove the chain and its guard. Now remove the nuts from the four bolts (two at the front of the crank-case, and two at the rear, one of these being below the engine) which secure the power unit to the frame members. Pull the bolts away, or if necessary tap them out with a suitable drift. Then carefully withdraw the complete Bantam power unit from the frame.

MAINTENANCE OF MOTOR-CYCLE PARTS

Do not be very conscientious in regard to engine maintenance, and at the same time neglect the motor-cycle parts. Proper and regular maintenance of the motor-cycle itself is really most important, and this applies particularly to the transmission, responsible for transmitting power from the engine to the road wheels. It always pays to keep down friction and wear of *all* moving parts to the absolute minimum, and to preserve that "showroom" appearance for as long as possible.

Items Needed for Maintenance. These are all included in the appropriate section on page 26. It is a simple matter to pick out those items not concerned with engine maintenance.

Tools Required. A comprehensive tool kit, plus a chain rivet extractor (not often needed), plus the B.S.A. service tool shown in Fig. 57, is normally sufficient for all routine maintenance, stripping-down, and assembly. If you wish to undertake repair work as well as maintenance, you will require a bench and some additional tools (*see* page 87).

Riding Tactics and Tyre Wear. These are very closely associated. Some riders are constantly paying heavy bills for tyres. Others obtain phenomenal mileages before tyre renewal becomes necessary. Above all, see that the tyre pressures are always maintained correctly and that the wheels are in true alignment.

Check the Tyre Pressures Weekly. It is just not good enough to use the old method of testing pressures by kicking the tyres before a run! Over-inflation causes discomfort, a tendency for skidding, vibration, strains the covers, and can result in a sudden concussion burst if a road irregularity is hit at speed. Under-inflation induces a proneness for tyre creep, rolling, instability of steering, and eventual cracking of the covers. Always check the tyre pressures weekly[1] with a suitable pressure gauge such as the Dunlop pencil-type No. 6, the Romac, the Holdtite, or the Schrader No. 7750 gauge. Keep the valve caps screwed down firmly, as slight leakage often occurs at the valves. Remove the valve "inners" annually.

The correct tyre-inflation pressures for 1948–70 solo Bantam models are given in Table II and these recommendations should be strictly adhered to,

Table II

CORRECT TYRE PRESSURES (IN LB PER SQ IN.) FOR 1948–70 B.S.A. BANTAMS (SOLO)

Model	D1	D3, D5	D7, D10, D14, Bantam 175
Front	16	16	17
Rear (Touring)	22	24	22
Rear (Competition)	16	16	—

except when a pillion passenger or heavy luggage is carried, in which case the pressure for the *rear* tyre should be increased by 5–10 lb per sq in., according to the extra load carried. Most riders increase the rear-tyre pressure by about 7 lb per sq in. when a medium-weight pillion passenger is carried.

Note that the tyre pressure recommendations given in Table II are correct for a solo rider weighing not more than 140 lb (10 stone). Should you be heavier than 140 lb, or carry a pillion passenger and/or heavy luggage, strictly speaking, the tyre pressures should be increased by one lb per sq in. for every 28 lb increase (front tyre), or 14 lb increase (rear tyre); or in accordance with Table III.

Table III

MINIMUM TYRE PRESSURES FOR SPECIFIC LOADS

Nominal tyre section (in.)	Inflation Pressures (lb per sq in.)					
	16	18	20	24	28	32
	Load per Tyre (lb)					
2·75	140	160	180	210	250	280
3·25	200	240	280	350	400	440
3·00	160	180	200	240	300	350

[1] Natural rubber tubes are porous, and a loss in pressure of 2–4 lb per sq in. weekly is normal (whether a machine is ridden or left standing). With the "Butyl" tubes (now supplied by the Dunlop Co. Ltd.) there is little porosity and the tyre pressures remain constant for an appreciable time.

Where an abnormal load is carried, the technically correct method of deciding the appropriate inflation pressures is to ride your Bantam to the nearest weighbridge (provided at most large railway stations and transport depots) and check individually the fully laden weight (with pillion passenger *seated*) on the front and rear tyre. Then for the appropriate inflation pressures, consult Table III.

Removing Inner Tube. On the Bantam the mudguards are somewhat heavily valanced and if a puncture occurs (even if its exact position is known), it is generally advisable to remove the wheel to avoid the risk of dirtying or damaging the tube when removing it from the cover. Wheel removal is described on pages 115, 116.

To remove one side of the cover prior to complete or partial withdrawal of the tube, first unscrew the valve cap and remove the valve core to ensure complete deflation of the tyre. Lay these two parts on the bench or table so that no dirt or grit can enter them.

Next press *both* wire beads off their seats. Insert a tyre lever *close to the valve stem*, and while pulling on this tyre lever, press the bead diametrically opposite into the well of the rim. Now insert a second tyre lever close to the first one, and lever the bead over the flange of the rim. When doing this, hold the removed portion of the bead with the first lever. Then remove one tyre lever and reinsert it a little farther away from the first one. Continue right round the bead in stages (about three inches apart) until the whole of the bead is removed. You can now push in the valve stem and withdraw the tube.

Repairing a Puncture. If the precise position of the puncture is unknown, submerge the inflated tube in water and watch for tell-tale air bubbles. Clean the tube in the vicinity of the puncture with some fine sand-paper and rub off all dust.

Select a suitable patch (not too small), preferably of the autovulcanizing type such as the "Vulcafix," and remove its linen backing. If rubber solution is not used, rub the prepared face of the patch with a cloth moistened in petrol and transfer the brown deposit on the cloth to the tube, around the puncture. Repeat this operation and allow the patch and transferred deposit to dry for one minute. If solution is used, apply it *to the tube only* and allow it to become "tacky." Now affix the patch, using slight pressure, particularly at the edges, and apply a little french chalk.

Replacing Tube and Cover. Before replacing the tube in the cover, inflate the tube just enough to round it out without causing it to stretch. This will reduce any tendency for twisting or for the tube to be nipped during the application of the tyre levers.

Fit the tube (see that it is not twisted and beds down snugly) and insert the valve stem through the hole in the wheel rim. At this stage screw down the knurled ring-nut only about half an inch. It is assumed that the wheel is horizontal; push the lower bead well down into the well of the rim *close to the valve*. Now start to press the upper bead home with the hands, commencing diametrically opposite to the valve. Use hand pressure except for the last portion of the cover (close to the valve), where the use of tyre levers (*see* Fig. 47) is generally called for. Push the valve stem into the

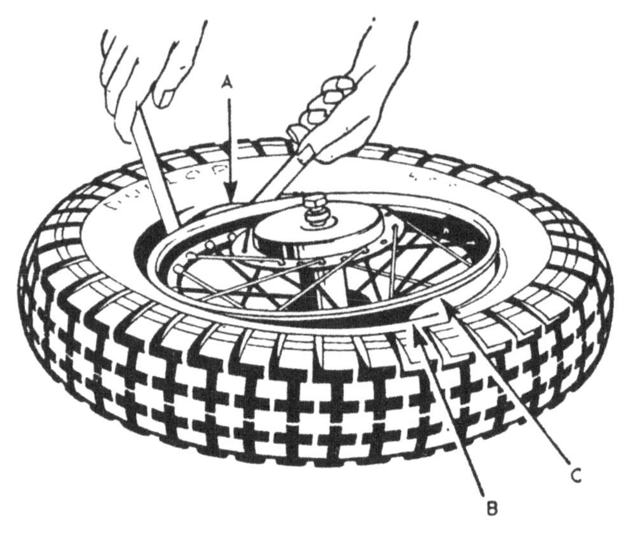

Fig. 47. Completing replacement of one side of the cover after inserting the inner tube

Always remember that wired-type beads cannot stretch. Therefore before attempting to lever the cover at A *over the wheel rim, you must push the cover bead at* B *off the shoulder* C *down into the well of the rim*

cover and then pull it down firmly by tightening the knurled ring-nut. Replace the valve core and pump up the tyre to the correct inflation pressure (*see* page 104), "thumbing" the cover at intervals to ensure that the beads are seating squarely all round. Finally, screw home the valve cap and replace the front or rear wheel in the motor-cycle (*see* page 116).

Correct Tyre Sizes. 2·75 × 19 tyres are required for the front and rear wheels of all Touring Bantams (Models D1 and D3), and for the *front* wheel of all Competition Bantams (Models D1 and D3). With 1958–70 Models D5, D7, D10, D14, and Bantam 175, however, the correct tyre size for the front and rear wheel is 3·00 × 18.

The Lighting Equipment. For full maintenance instructions concerning the Wipac and Lucas flywheel generators, batteries, and lamps, *see* Chapter 5. Wiring diagrams are given on pages 77–84 for the various Bantam models fitted with different types of lighting equipment.

Cleaning the Machine. For advice on cleaning the enamelled and chromium-plated motor-cycle parts, *see* page 88.

Bantam Lubrication. The correct lubrication of the various motor-cycle parts (excluding engine lubrication), is dealt with in detail on pages 20–5 in Chapter 2. Carefully observe items, 3, 4 and 7–20 on the lubrication chart given on page 21.

Check Nuts and Bolts for Tightness. After completing about 250 miles on a new machine, and subsequently about every 2,000 miles, check over the various nuts and bolts for tightness, paying special attention to the wheel-spindle nuts and the nuts and bolts on the forks. Do not overlook (on battery-lighting models) the battery-strap securing-bolt. Occasionally this slackens off, causing the battery to move about on the battery carrier. The battey should not be able to move, but avoid over-tightening the strap securing-bolt (two bolts fitted on D3, D5, D7 and D7D/L). On D10, D14, and Bantam 175 models (1967–70), the battery is retained by a "toggle-action" wire clamp which must be released before the battery can be removed.

The Front Forks (D1, D3, D5). Besides an occasional check for tightness of the nuts and bolts, and the weekly application of the grease gun to the fork nipples (*see* page 23), no maintenance is necessary. The forks have internal compression springs and (on 1951–9 Competition models) rubber shock-absorbers fitted inside the springs. No hydraulic damping, requiring topping-up of the fork legs, and no adjustment are provided.

Concertina-type rubber or plastic (March, 1952, onwards) gaiters (*A*, Fig. 50) are fitted to the lower ends of the fork legs to prevent the entry of dust or dirt into the moving parts. It is a good plan about every 3,000 miles, or when decarbonizing, to remove both gaiters and carefully clean and grease the sliding members of the fork legs. Never allow them to become dry or rusty. To remove 1948–53 gaiters it is first necessary to detach the spring-wire circlips which secure their upper and lower ends to the fork legs. The gaiters can then be taken off the legs. Be careful to fit all four circlips properly when replacing the gaiters. If a gaiter becomes cracked or damaged, it is advisable to renew it at the first opportunity. On 1954–63 Bantams the protective gaiters are a *push fit* on the tubes of the front fork.

It is rare for the maximum fork travel (normally 3¾ in.) to become increased because of weakening of the internal springs. But if fork movement becomes excessive, the forks should be stripped-down and the springs and oil seals examined and if necessary renewed. At the same time the phosphor-bronze bushes inside the fork legs should be inspected. If worn, the bushes should also be renewed. Note that on Bantams of vintage prior to May, 1951, the bushes are *fixed* to the outer fork-legs and the outer legs complete must be renewed if serious bush wear has occurred. Trouble with the telescopic front forks, however, is so infrequent and develops so slowly that I do not feel justified in including in this maintenance handbook detailed instructions for stripping-down the forks and reassembling them. If you do have occasion to undertake this work, I would refer you to B.S.A. Service Sheet No. 509 which contains the appropriate instructions.

The Front Forks (Models D7, D10, D14, and Bantam 175). No grease nipples are provided on the telescopic fork legs. The only maintenance normally necessary is the occasional renewal of the oil, the necessity for which is indicated by excessive fork movement. The procedure for renewing the oil and suitable types of oil to use are dealt with on page 23.

Rear Suspension Units. Rear suspension was introduced on B.S.A. Bantams as extra equipment in September, 1949. No maintenance of D1 and D3 units is required except 1,000 mile application of the grease gun to the nipples provided for lubrication (*see* page 24), and no adjustment is provided. If after very many thousands of miles, the maximum movement of the plungers (normally 2¼ in.) becomes excessive (although this is rare) because of weakening of the internal springs, it is advisable to dismantle each rear-suspension unit as described on page 121 and renew the two springs. The bushes in the sliding member should also be inspected at the same time for wear. Should they require to be renewed, you will have to replace the tube and bushes.

On Models D5, D7, D10, D14, and Bantam 175 swinging-arm type rear suspension is provided. The two suspension units each comprise a telescopic damper unit and a completely enclosed coil spring (exposed on later models). The hydraulic dampers are sealed during manufacture and require no maintenance. If trouble occurs, the damper units should be removed and renewed. Removal from the frame entails only the withdrawal of the upper pivot bolts and the bottom retaining nuts. The swinging arm pivot has grease nipples and these should not be overlooked (*see* page 24).

Steering Head Adjustment (Preliminaries). First raise the front wheel of your Bantam well clear of the ground. Place the machine on its central stand and then apply some weight to the saddle or dualseat so as to tilt the front wheel upwards. If play is felt on attempting to push the fork legs to and fro, adjust the steering head. First lessen the pinch bolt nut *C* (Fig. 48). Where a bulb horn is fitted, unscrew the horn and remove the steering-head dust cover so as to expose the lock-nut and the adjuster nut. If a bulb horn is not provided, unscrew the central plug, and on 1948–63 models remove the washer and dust cover.

To Adjust Steering Head (Model D1). After attending to the above preliminaries, loosen the small nut on the clip stud on each front-fork leg. Both of these nuts are readily accessible. On more recent models slacken the clip bolt on each fork leg below the lamp. You must, of course, first loosen the outer nuts securing the headlamp brackets, except on 1954–63 models

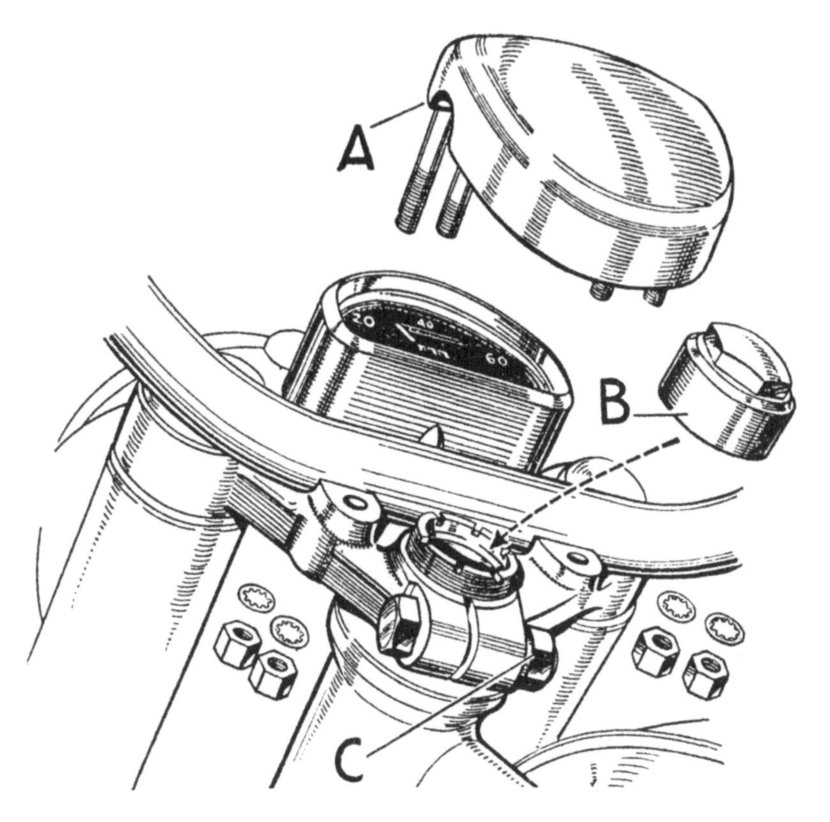

Fig. 48. Steering-head adjustment (Models D3, D5)
(By courtesy of "Motor Cycle," London)

having the headlamp brackets integral with the forks. The bottom yokes are now free to take up new positions when the head adjustment is made.

Slacken the lock-nut and tighten the adjuster nut situated beneath it until all steering head slackness has been eliminated. But avoid over-tightening the adjuster, otherwise the steering will become stiff and damage may be caused to the ball races. After the correct adjustment is obtained, tighten the lock-nut firmly, and also retighten the pinch-bolt nut *C* and the two clip nuts.

In the event of your removing both the lock-nut and the adjuster nut beneath it, make sure that on replacement the *thicker* adjuster nut is fitted first with its *recess downwards*.

To Adjust the Steering Head (Models D3, D5). Referring to Fig. 48, having dealt with the preliminaries (*see* page 108), remove the aluminium cover *A* which holds the handlebar bend in position, by unscrewing the four nuts beneath. This exposes the steering head lock-nut *B*; remove this nut. Now with a flat piece of metal applied to the adjuster-sleeve slots (the sleeve is below the lock-nut), turn the adjuster sleeve until all steering head slackness disappears. To prevent steering stiffness or damage to the ball races be careful not to over-tighten the sleeve. After the adjustment is made, retighten the nut *C* on the pinch-bolt, tighten the lock-nut above the adjuster sleeve, and replace the aluminium cover, being careful to align the handlebar bend properly.

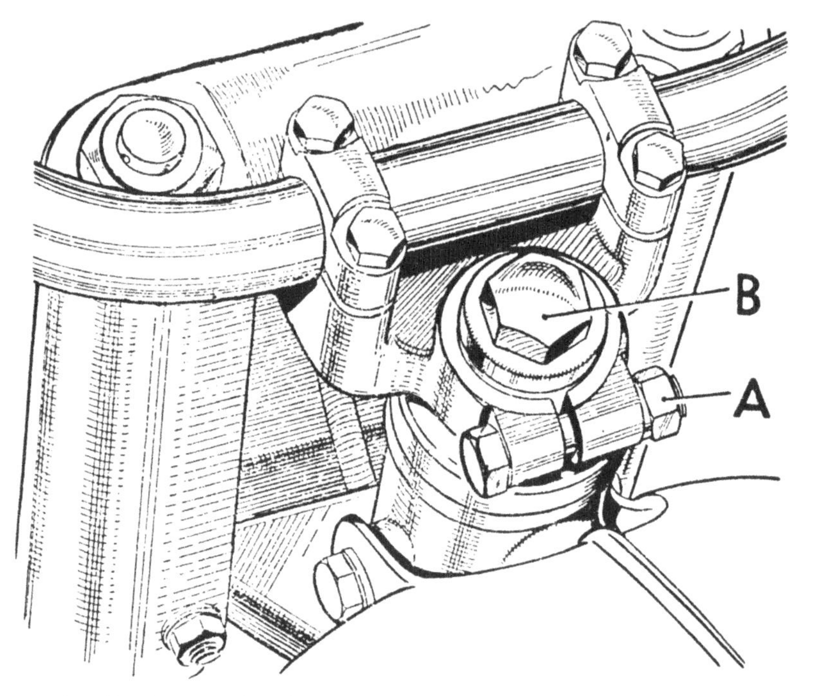

Fig. 49. Steering head adjustment (Models D7, D10, D14, and Bantam 175)

Steering Head Adjustment (Models D7, D10, D14, and Bantam 175). To take up any existing play first slacken the clip bolt on each fork leg below the headlamp or lamp nacelle (1964 onwards) to enable the bottom yoke to be free to take up a new position. Then, referring to Fig. 49, slacken the nut *A* on the steering head clip bolt and tighten the adjuster nut *B* until all slackness is taken up. Be careful not to over-tighten nut *B*, otherwise stiffness in the steering will occur and this may damage the ball races. Finally, firmly tighten nut *A* and the clip bolt on each fork leg so as to secure the bottom yoke.

Handlebars, Footrests. The footrests are adjustable only on Competition, D7 models (*see* page 4). Handlebars: *see* page 3.

Keep the Brakes Effective. To obtain powerful braking, it is desirable to keep both brakes adjusted so that with the brake pedal and lever released, the brake shoe linings almost make contact with the insides of the brake-drums. But both wheels must always be able to spin freely without any brake friction when the brakes are off.

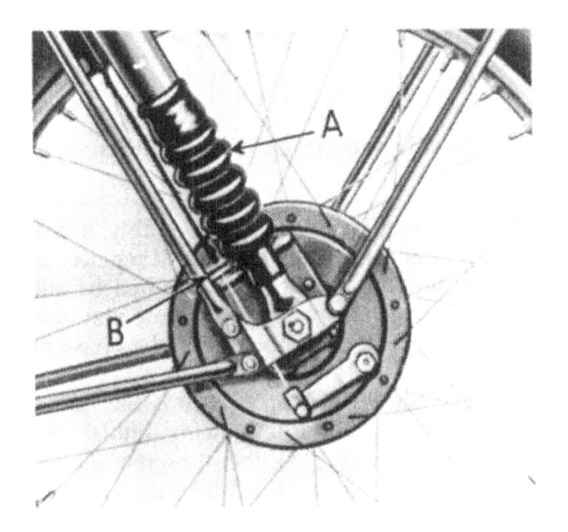

Fig. 50. Showing finger adjustment of front brake, and the fork gaiters (D1, D3, D5)

The friction linings riveted to the brake shoes gradually wear, thereby reducing the effective brake leverage, and a compensating adjustment must therefore occasionally be made by taking up slackness in the hand or foot control. On all 1948 and subsequent Bantams, finger adjustment is provided for both brakes.

To effect an adjustment of the front brake, turn as required the knurled adjuster-nut located at the cable stop as shown at *B* in Fig. 50. To adjust the rear brake, screw the knurled adjuster-nut shown at *C* in Fig. 53 along the rear-brake rod as required.

The Brake Linings. When repeated finger-adjustments have been made to both brakes, the brake cam-operating levers eventually assume positions where their leverage is poor. In such circumstances the only satisfactory course to take is to remove the brake shoes for replacement. If you wish to reline the shoes yourself, you are referred to B.S.A. Service Sheet No. 611.

If excessive lubrication of the wheel hubs causes grease to get on the

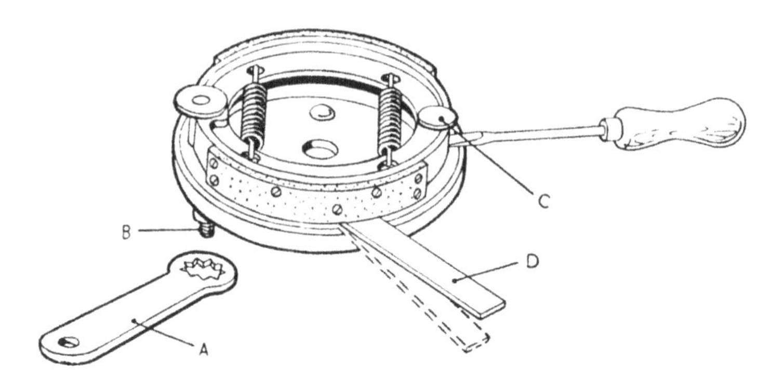

Fig. 51. Removing the brake shoes

brake linings and reduces stopping power, appreciably, it is wise to remove the brake shoes immediately and reline them or fit replacement shoes.

Harshness in brake action can often be remedied by filing down each brake lining for about one inch from each end. Note that new brake linings have rivet holes already drilled. The shoes themselves have no adjustment.

To Remove the Brake Shoes. The procedure is the same for front and rear brakes, the cover plates and shoes being similar in construction. First remove the wheel (*see* page 115), then unscrew the lock-nut on the wheel spindle, and the nut retaining the brake drum cover-plate. Withdraw the cover-plate and inspect the two shoes. Unless the brake linings are seriously worn and require to be renewed, it is not advisable to disturb the brake shoes.

Referring to Fig. 51, to remove the shoes from the brake cover-plate, first remove the brake operating-lever *A* from the serrations on the cam shaft *B*, and gently tap in the shaft until the cam plate clears the shoes. Now insert a screwdriver as shown between the shoe ends adjacent to the fulcrum pin *C*, and turn the screwdriver. Then place a small lever *D* between one shoe and the cover-plate, and prise the brake shoe upwards until you release the spring pressure. You can now withdraw the two shoes from the cover-plate.

The Non-adjustable Primary Chain. The primary chain (*see* Fig. 52) is sturdy ($\frac{3}{8}$ in. pitch) and it runs in short fixed centres in an oil-bath. Thus wear occurs very slowly indeed, and re-tensioning is neither necessary nor provided for. Only at very long intervals is chain renewal called for. It is, however, advisable to inspect the chain after covering many thousands of miles.

To inspect the primary chain, you must first take off the chaincase cover (*see* Fig. 7) after removing the foot gear-change and kick-starter levers.

Fig. 52. Showing the non-adjustable primary chain, and the clutch

The Bantam is one of the few machines with the primary transmission on the off side

These two levers are both located on their shafts by means of splines and secured by the pinch-bolts *C* and *B* (Fig. 7). Now remove the five cheese-headed screws *D* (Fig. 7) securing the cover, and carefully ease the cover off the primary drive chain-case. Do not attempt to prise it off. Then with the fingers check the tension of the primary chain in the centre of the lower chain run, with the chain in its tightest position. The total whip should be approximately $\frac{3}{8}$ in. (1 cm), and the maximum permissible up-and-down movement is about $\frac{3}{4}$ in. (2 cm). When the total movement reaches the specified maximum limit, it is generally time to remove the connecting link, take off the chain, and fit a new one. Make sure that the spring link is correctly replaced (*see* page 114).

To Re-tension the Secondary Chain. The $\frac{1}{2}$ in. pitch secondary chain, being of considerable length and protected only by a top run chain-guard instead of an oil-bath, naturally stretches far more quickly than does the primary chain. It is therefore advisable to check its tension at regular intervals, say about every 1,000 miles, and to retension the chain if necessary. Chain stretch depends, of course, to a considerable extent on whether or not the rider attends to its proper lubrication.

To check the tension of the secondary chain, first place the Bantam on its central stand (on spring-frame models the rear wheel *must* be in its *lowest* position). Then verify the chain whip (total up-and-down movement)

by applying pressure with the fingers to the bottom chain run about midway between the gear-box sprocket and the rear wheel sprocket. With the foot gear-change lever in neutral, turn over the rear wheel and verify the whip with the chain in a number of different positions. The whip with the chain in its tightest positon, should be ¾ in. (2 cm) on rigid frame models; ½ in. (1·27 cm) on Bantams with plunger springing; and ¾ in. on "swinging arm" models.

The adjustment of the secondary chain is effected by means of two draw-bolts (similar to those used on bicycles) in the rear-fork ends. Referring to Fig. 53, to re-tension the chain, slacken the rear-brake knurled adjuster-nut *C*, and both rear-wheel spindle nuts *A;* and then turn each adjuster nut *B* with a small spanner clockwise or anti-clockwise, as required, to tighten or slacken the chain respectively. When checking the tension after making an adjustment, be sure to push the wheel hard forward so that the spindle is hard up against the eyes of the draw-bolts. Be sure to tighten both adjuster nuts exactly the same amount so as to maintain the front and rear wheels in true alignment as described opposite. Having satisfied yourself that chain tension and wheel alignment are correct, firmly re-tighten both rear-wheel spindle nuts *A*.

Fitting the Spring Link. When replacing the old chain, or fitting a new one, always be extremely careful to fit the spring link so that its open end faces *away from* the direction of chain movement. Should a spring link come adrift when the chain is moving fast, a bad accident can be caused when the chain flies off the sprockets. Make absolutely sure that the spring link has not become distorted through careless removal, and that it beds down properly.

Checking Wheel Alignment. After removing the rear wheel and/or re-tensioning the secondary chain, it is advisable to check the alignment of the front and rear wheels in case the draw-bolt adjuster-nuts on each side of the rear wheel (*see* Fig. 53) have not been uniformly tightened. Misalignment of the wheels will cause uneven wear of the tyre treads, a tendency for skidding when the brakes are applied sharply, and imperfect steering when the hands are resting lightly on the handlebars.

To check that the alignment of the wheels is correct, set the front wheel so that it is pointing straight ahead, and then while standing at one end of the machine some distance away, glance along the line of the wheels. Any appreciable lack of alignment should at once be detected, assuming that you have good eyesight.

A more reliable and accurate method of checking the alignment, however, is to place a long straight-edge, the edge of a board, or a taut piece of string (tied to a peg in the ground at one end) so that it contacts the tyres of both wheels on one side of the Bantam. If the wheels are truly aligned, the straight-edge or string should contact simultaneously the front and rear walls of each tyre. But where a Bantam Competition model is

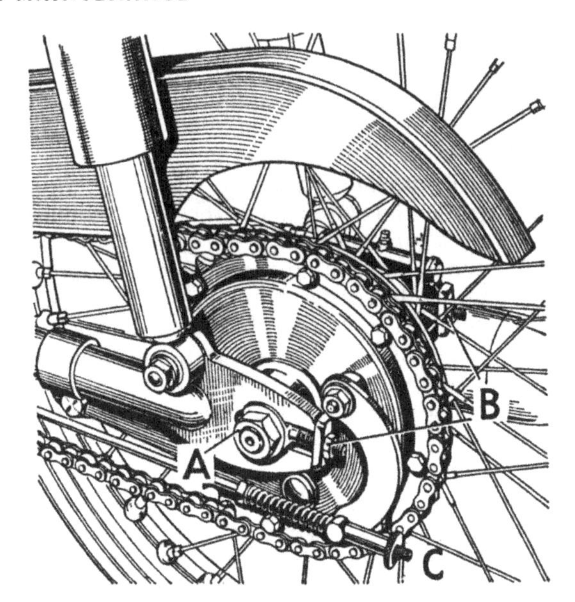

Fig. 53. The secondary chain and rear brake adjustments

concerned, it is necessary to take into account the fact that the rear tyre is of larger section than the front one.

If the wheels are found to be out of alignment, loosen the rear wheel-spindle nuts and adjust the position of the rear wheel in the fork ends by means of the draw-bolt adjuster-nuts shown at *B* in Fig. 53. Afterwards do not forget to check that the chain tension is correct (*see* page 113) and that the rear-wheel spindle-nuts *A* are firmly retightened.

To Remove the Front Wheel (Models D1, D3). Disconnect the brake operating cable at the lever on the brake cover-plate and unscrew its adjuster from the anchor-plate. Remove the two nuts from the wheel spindle. Next undo the three mudguard-stay bolts on the near side and raise the near-side fork leg sufficiently to enable the front wheel to drop out at an angle. It is necessary to do this to avoid fouling by the fork anchor-plate on the brake cover-plate.

To Remove Front Wheel (D5, D7, D7D/L). Disconnect the brake cable at the lever on the brake cover-plate and unscrew its adjuster from the anchor plate. Remove the nut which secures the cover-plate to the fork leg, and then the two caps from the bottom of the fork legs. When doing this support the front wheel. Then withdraw the wheel. Note that when the front wheel is subsequently replaced the spindle ends must be level with the end faces of the two caps.

To Remove Front Wheel (1968 (D14 Sports only) to 1970). Instructions for this operation are as those for models D7, except that the cover-plate carries a slotted arm which engages with a tongue on the fork leg. This avoids the use of a fixing nut.

To Remove the Rear Wheel. First disconnect the speedometer drive cable from the speedometer gearbox and remove the knurled adjuster nut from the rear-brake rod. Disconnect the secondary chain by removing its spring link, and unwinding the chain from the rear-wheel sprocket. It is best not to remove the chain from the gearbox sprocket. On Models D7, D10, D14, and Bantam 175 release the brake plate arm at the swinging arm. Afterwards loosen the rear-wheel spindle nuts sufficiently to enable the rear wheel to be withdrawn from the fork ends. During reassembly securely tighten the brake plate bolt at the swinging arm and check that the chain adjusters are firmly against the lug ends.

Replacing a Wheel. Be careful to locate the brake cover-plate anchorage properly, and make sure that it is secure. Before reconnecting the speedometer gearbox cable (rear wheel) first verify that the speedometer gearbox and cable casing are in proper alignment, because any sharp bends in the cable casing will probably result in a fracture of the cable itself.

Reconnect the front-brake cable or the rear-brake rod, the secondary chain (if dealing with a rear wheel), adjust the wheel spindle carefully in the fork ends, tighten the spindle lock-nuts securely (see that the chain adjusters abut the lugs), and finally check the brake adjustment (*see* page 111) for maximum efficiency.

Non-adjustable Wheel Bearings (Touring Models). The front and rear wheels on all Bantams have non-adjustable ball journal-bearing hubs. Provided that the ball bearings are greased regularly (*see* page 22), they should remain serviceable for the whole of the Bantam's operational life.

Gearbox Maintenance. On the Bantam the gearbox is, of course, in unit construction with the engine. Maintenance is confined to topping-up the gearbox and periodically changing the oil (*see* pages 18, 19).

In the unlikely event of some internal gearbox trouble developing, it is advisable for the average Bantam owner to entrust the dismantling, repair, and assembly of the gearbox to an authorized B.S.A. repair specialist.

Some Play in the Clutch Control is Essential. It is absolutely essential to the proper functioning of the clutch always to maintain a slight amount of play (say, $\frac{1}{32}$ in. to $\frac{1}{16}$ in.) in the clutch cable at the handlebar lever end, or in the clutch-operating mechanism (Fig. 55) comprising the slotted adjuster-pin (screwed into a quick-thread sleeve), the steel ball, and the clutch-operating rod (not shown in Fig. 55). Only by maintaining some play can

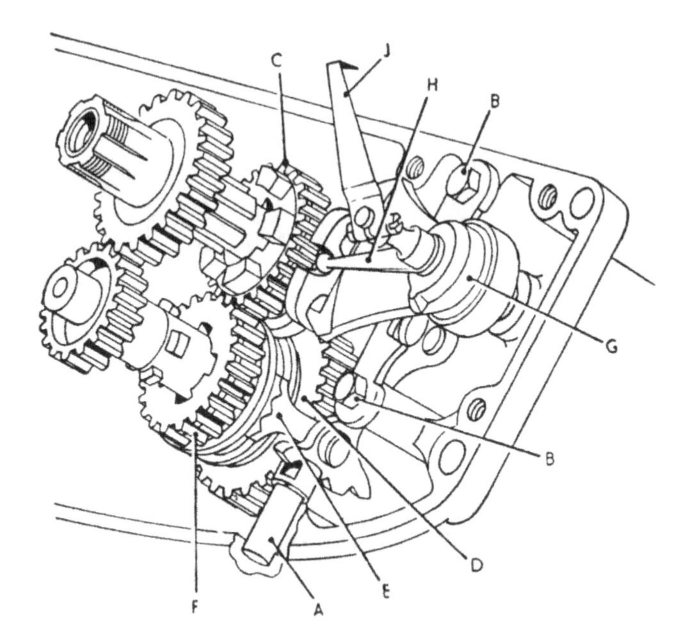

Fig. 54. The gear train in the B.S.A. three-speed gearbox

A. *Spring-loaded plunger*
B. *Bolts securing selector-mechanism*
C. *Mainshaft sliding gear*
D. *Layshaft first gear*
E. *Gear-selector arm*
F. *Layshaft second gear*
G. *Foot gear-change pedal shaft and spring-loaded claw assembly*
H. *Gear-position indicator lever*

you be sure that the clutch springs will exert full pressure on the plates and transmit the full power of the engine to the rear wheel.

Insufficient play causes a tendency for persistent clutch slip which is most irritating, and damaging to the friction inserts. Excessive play, on the other hand, while not being injurious to the friction-insert plates, renders gear changing somewhat uncertain and difficult. In either case an immediate adjustment is called for.

To Adjust the Clutch Control. Fig. 56 shows the very accessible external clutch adjustment on the near-side end of the gearbox mainshaft. The slotted adjuster-pin *C* is screwed into the clutch withdrawal quick-thread sleeve (*see* Fig. 55), and the lock nut *B* (Fig. 56) secures it firmly in position. The adjuster pin *C* presses against the long internal clutch-operating rod, and a steel ball is interposed between the pin and the rod.

Referring to Fig. 56 to adjust the clutch control, first slacken the lock-nut *B* with a suitable spanner. While holding the lock-nut, with a screwdriver turn the adjuster pin *C anti-clockwise* so that it is unscrewed one or two turns. Now, while still holding the lock-nut with a spanner, screw in the

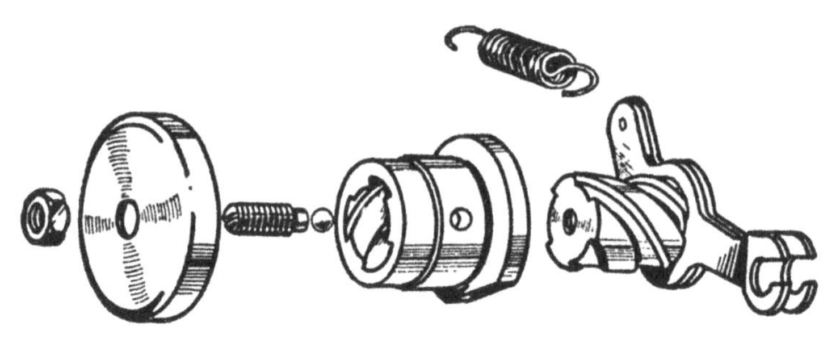

Fig. 55. Exploded view of clutch-operating mechanism
The long steel thrust-rod is not shown

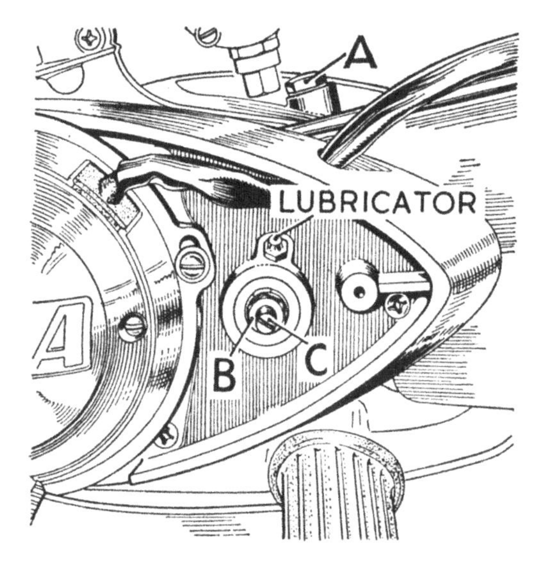

Fig. 56. The clutch-control adjustment on the near-side of the power unit

adjuster pin gently until it is felt to meet resistance. Then unscrew the adjuster pin *half a turn* and, while preventing it from turning, retighten the lock-nut *B*. If the foregoing instructions are followed, the clutch control adjustment should be correct. But check the adjustment to make quite sure.

Dismantling the Bantam Clutch. To obtain access to the multiplate clutch it is, of course, necessary to remove the die-cast aluminium cover from the primary drive chain-case. Referring to Fig. 7, pull or tap the foot gear-change lever from its splined shaft after unscrewing and removing the pinch-bolt *C*. Also similarly remove the kick-starter lever from its shaft splines after taking out the pinch bolt *B*. Next unscrew the five cheese-headed screws *D*. To ensure correct replacement of the screws, note that there are three screws at the rear, and two *longer* ones at the *front* of the chain-case cover. If it is stiff, tap it gently with a mallet, but make no attempt to prise it off. Examine the compressed-paper washer fitted between the cover and case. If this is in any way damaged, it must be renewed.

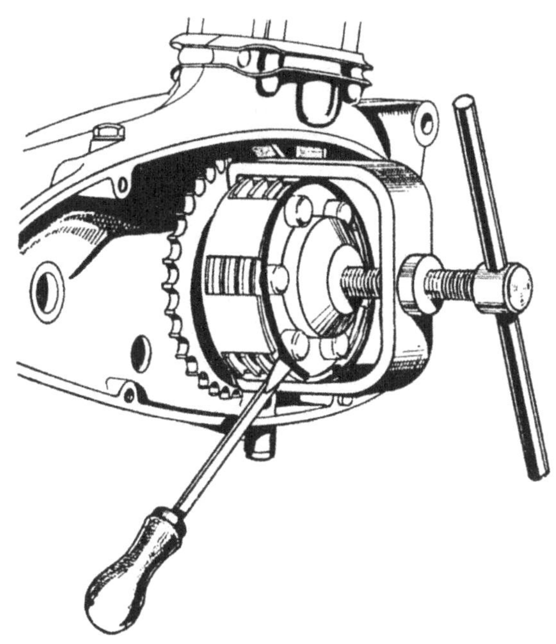

Fig. 57. Removing the steel circlip before dismantling the B.S.A. clutch

The springs have been compressed with the B.S.A. service tool and the circlip is shown partly prised out with a screwdriver

Removal of the primary chain-case cover exposes to view (*see* Fig. 52) the entire clutch assembly, the engine sprocket, the non-adjustable primary chain, the kick-starter quadrant, and the clock-type return spring for the kick-starter.

Should it be desired to dismantle the clutch plate assembly in order to have some new inserts fitted, first remove the primary chain by releasing the spring link. On 1950–70 models remove the steel cover-plate (the outer one) held by three set-screws to the spring-cup plate. Now fit the B.S.A. service tool No. 61–3191 over the clutch assembly in the manner illustrated in Fig. 57 and slowly turn the tommy-bar until the six helical compression

Fig. 58. The clutch plates removed

The correct reassembly order is 8–2. Plate (8) goes next to the plain sprocket plate (not shown). The six spring cups (also not shown) fit into the holes in plate (2), and the inner ends of the springs press against the outside of the pressure plate (3) the dished inside of which contacts the mushroom head of the clutch-operating thrust rod. On 1950–7 models a cover plate is fitted outside the retaining circlip and is secured by three set-screws. On the 1958–66 Models D5, D7 and D7D/L the clutch has three solid friction-plates bonded with Neolangite segments

1. *Steel circlip*
2. *Spring-cup plate*
3. *Pressure plate (dished)*
4. *Cork-insert plate*
5. *Plain steel-plate*
6. *Cork-insert plate*
7. *Plain steel-plate*
8. *Cork-insert plate*

springs are compressed sufficiently to enable you to prise off with a screw-driver, as shown in Fig. 57, the large steel circlip shown at (1) in Fig. 58. Referring to Fig. 58, removal of the circlip (and the service tool) permits of the spring-cup plate (2), the six spring cups (not shown), the six helical springs (not shown), the pressure plate (3), and the plain steel and friction-insert (later models friction pads) plates (4)–(8) being withdrawn for inspection in this order from the clutch body. For 1967–70 models, an additional friction-pad plate is fitted, increasing the quantity of these plates to four, with a corresponding increase in the width of the clutch. Also remove the mushroom-headed steel thrust rod from the drilled main-shaft.

For the purpose of fitting new inserts to the clutch plates, it is not necessary to remove the clutch sprocket-plate (which has no inserts), nor the clutch hub from the splined mainshaft. The reassembly of the clutch plates should be effected in the reverse order of dismantling.

Fit alternately the plain steel-plates, friction insert/pad plates. The correct assembly order is shown in Fig. 58 for the three friction-plate clutches. There will, or course, be an extra one of each of the plain and friction plates on models for 1967–70. Do not forget to replace the mushroom-headed steel thrust-rod before the pressure plate is replaced. Oil the rod before inserting it. To replace the steel circlip, you must first compress the six helical springs with the service tool as shown in Fig. 57. See that the circlip beds home snugly into the groove provided. On 1950–70 Bantams replace the outer cover and secure it to the spring-cup plate by means of the three set-screws.

When reconnecting the non-adjustable primary chain, make sure that its spring link is fitted with the closed end facing the direction of chain movement. After replacing the primary drive chain-case cover and compressed-paper washer (grease it on both sides), fit the kick-starter and the foot gear-change levers, and see that their pinch-bolts are firmly retightened.

Plunger Suspension Units (Models D1, D3). If as the result of an accident involving damage to the units, or in the very unlikely event of excessive

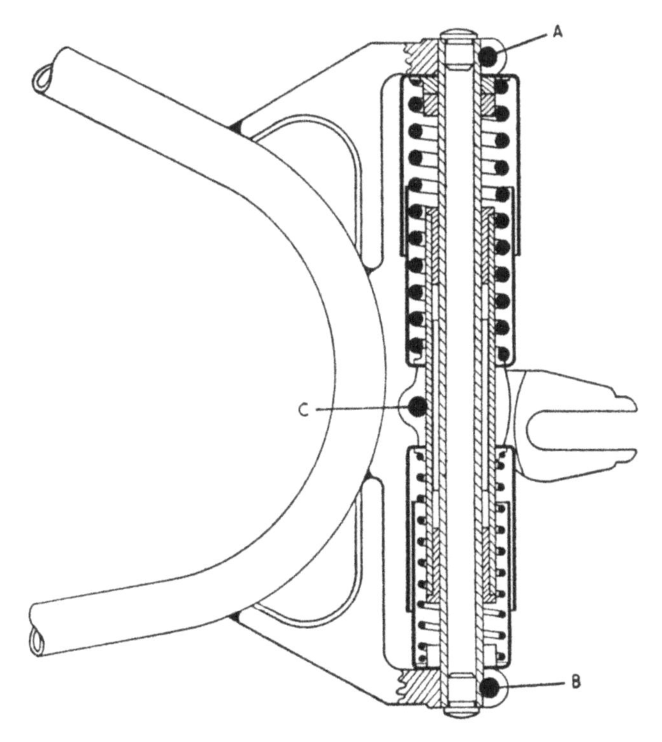

Fig. 59. Sectional view showing details of plunger suspension unit (Models D1, D3)

Pinch-bolts are fitted at A, B, and C

plunger movement (*see* page 108) occurring, it is necessary to dismantle each rear-suspension unit; do this as described below.

First remove the rear wheel (*see* page 116) and also the silencer. To remove the silencer, slacken the nut on the clip securing the silencer to the exhaust pipe, and remove the nut on the pinch-bolt *B* (Fig. 59) securing the silencer lug to the off-side rear-suspension unit.

Referring to Fig. 59, remove the pinch-bolts *A* and *B*. Next tap out the central column of each rear-suspension unit from below, and withdraw the column through the top lug. Having done this, slide off sideways from the bottom lug the remaining components of each suspension unit. Lay them on a clean sheet of paper ready for complete stripping-down. Note the relative and exact positions of the various components to ensure correct reassembly.

To separate the spring plunger (comprising the wheel-spindle bracket and attached bearing sleeve) from the bearing sleeve, it is only necessary to tap out the pinch-bolt *C*. Observe that this pinch-bolt engages a notch in the bearing sleeve, and that the pinch bolts at *A* and *B* similarly engage in notches in the central column (removed). When reassembling each suspension unit, it is vitally important to pay due attention to these notches and to be certain that they are correctly aligned.

Rear Suspension (D5, D7, D10, D14, and Bantam 175). Both suspension units are sealed and require no maintenance whatever. The "swinging arm" pivot, however, requires occasional greasing (*see* page 24).

Should the rear suspension units be damaged or become inefficient after a very big mileage, remove them and fit new ones. To withdraw the units from the Bantam frame, remove the pivot bolts at the top and the retaining nuts at the bottom.

Index

OTHER MOTORCYCLE MANUALS AVAILABLE IN THIS SERIES

AJS (BOOK OF) ALL MODELS 1955-1965:
350cc & 500cc Singles ~ Models 16,16S,18, 18S

ARIEL (BOOK OF) 1932-1939:
LF3, LF4, LG, NF3, NF4, NG, OG, VA, VA3, VA4, VB, VF3, VF4, VG, Red Hunter LH, NH, OH, VH & Square Four 4F, 4G, 4H

ARIEL WORKSHOP MANUAL 1933-1951:
All single, twin & 4 cylinder models

ARIEL (BOOK OF) 1939-1960:
OG, OH, VA, VG, NG, VB, LH (Colt) & Red Hunter NH, VH & VHA

BMW FACTORY WORKSHOP MANUAL R27, R28:
English, German, French and Spanish text

BMW FACTORY WORKSHOP MANUAL R50, R50S, R60, R69S:
Also includes a supplement for the USA models: R50US, R60US, R69US.
English, German, French and Spanish text

BSA BANTAM (BOOK OF) 1948-1970:
D7, D7D/L, D10, D14/4 & Bantam 175

BSA PRE-WAR SINGLES & TWINS (BOOK OF) 1936-1939:
All Pre-War single & twin cylinder SV & OHV models through 1939
150cc, 250cc, 350cc, 500cc, 600cc, 750cc & 1,000cc

BSA SINGLES (BOOK OF) 1945-1954:
OHV & SV 250cc, 350cc, 500cc & 600cc, Groups B, C & M

BSA SINGLES (BOOK OF) 1955-1967:
B31, B32, B33, B34 and "Star" B40 & SS90

BSA 250cc SINGLES (BOOK OF) 1954-1970:
B31, B32, B33, B34 and "Star" B40 & SS90

BSA TWINS (BOOK OF) 1948-1962:
All 650cc & 500cc twins

BSA TWINS (SECOND BOOK OF) 1962-1969:
All 650cc & 500cc, A50 & A65 OHV unit construction twins

DUCATI OHC FACTORY WORKSHOP MANUAL:
160 Junior Monza, 250 Monza, 250 GT, 250 Mark 3, 250 Mach 1, 250 SCR & 350 Sebring

HONDA 250 & 305cc FACTORY WORKSHOP MANUAL:
C.72 C.77 CS.72, CS.77, CB.72, CB.77 [HAWK]

HONDA 125 & 150cc FACTORY WORKSHOP MANUAL:
C.92, CS.92, CB.92, C.95 & CA.95

HONDA 90 (BOOK OF) ALL MODELS UP TO 1966:
All 90cc variations including the S90, CM90, C200, S65, Trail 90 & C65 models

HONDA 50cc FACTORY WORKSHOP MANUAL: C.100

HONDA 50cc FACTORY WORKSHOP MANUAL: C.110

HONDA (BOOK OF) ALL MODELS) 1960-1966:
50cc C.100, C.102, C.110 & C.114 ~ 125cc C.92 & CB.92
250cc C.72 & CB.72 ~ 305cc CB.77

LAMBRETTA (BOOK OF) MAINTENANCE & REPAIR:
125 & 150cc, all models up to 1958, except model "48".

LAMBRETTA (SECOND BOOK OF) MAINTENANCE & REPAIR:
125, 150, 175 & 200cc, all Li & TV models and derivates from 1958 to 1970.

MATCHLESS SINGLES (BOOK OF) 1945-1956:
350 & 500cc OHV Touring Singles G3L, G80, G3LS & G80S

MATCHLESS SINGLES (BOOK OF) 1955-1966:
350 & 500cc OHV Touring Singles G3LS, G3S, G3, G80S, G80, Mercury, Mercury Sports, Major & Major Sports

NORTON DOMINATOR TWINS (BOOK OF) 1955-1965
500, 600 & 650cc Dominator Twins and 750cc Atlas

NORTON FACTORY TWIN CYLINDER WORKSHOP MANUAL:
1957-1970: *Lightweight Twins:* 250cc Jubilee, 350cc Navigator and 400cc Electra and the *Heavyweight Twins:* Model 77, 88, 88SS, 99, 99SS, Sports Special, Manxman, Mercury, Atlas, G15, P11, N15, Ranger (P11A).

NORTON (BOOK OF) 1932-1939:
All SV & OHV models: 16H, 1, 50, 55, 18, 20, ES2, 19R & 19S

NORTON (BOOK OF) 1938-1956:
All Pre-War SV, OHV and OHC models: 16H, 16I, 18, 19, 20, 50, 55, ES2, CJ, CSI, International 30 & 40

SUZUKI 50cc & 80cc (BOOK OF) UP TO 1966:
M12, M15, M15D, M30 (SUZY), K10 & K11

SUZUKI 200 & 250cc FACTORY WORKSHOP MANUAL:
250cc T20 [X-6 Hustler] ~ 200cc T200 [X-5 Invader & Sting Ray Scrambler]

TRIUMPH (BOOK OF) MAINTENANCE & REPAIR 1935-1939:
All Pre-War single & twin cylinder models: L2/1, 2/1, 2/5, 3/1, 3/2, 3/5, 5/1, 5/2, 5/3, 5/4, 5/5, 5/10, 6/1, Tiger 70, 80, 90 & 2H. Tiger 70C, 3S & 3H, Tiger 80C & 5H, Tiger 90C, 6S, 2HC & 3SC, 5T & 5S and T100

TRIUMPH TWINS (BOOK OF) PRE-UNIT & UNIT 1956-1969:
3TA, T90, 5T, 5TA, T100, T100A, T100S/S, 6T, TR5, TR6, TR6S/S, T110 & T120

TRIUMPH 1937-1951 WORKSHOP MANUAL (A. St. J. Masters):
Covers rigid frame and sprung hub single cylinder SV & OHV and twin cylinder OHV pre-war, military, and post-war models

TRIUMPH 1945-1955 FACTORY WORKSHOP MANUAL NO.11:
Covers pre-unit, twin-cylinder rigid frame, sprung hub, swing-arm and 350cc, 500cc & 650cc.

VELOCETTE (BOOK OF) MAINTENANCE & REPAIR:
Covers LE Mk. I, II, & III, Valiant, Vogue, MOV, MAC, KSS, KTS, Viper, Venom & Thruxton. Includes some limited material on the Viceory scooter

VESPA (BOOK OF) MAINTENANCE & REPAIR 1946-1959:
All 125cc & 150cc models including 42/L2 & Gran Sport

VINCENT WORKSHOP MANUAL 1935-1955:
All Series A, B & C Models

COMING SOON IN THIS SAME SERIES:

BRIDGESTONE FACTORY WORKSHOP MANUAL:
50 Sport, 60 Sport, 90 De Luxe, 90 Trail, 90 Mountain, 90 Sport, 175 Dual Twin & Hurricane

BRITISH MILITARY MAINTENANCE & REPAIR MANUAL:
Service & Repair data for all British WD motorcycles

BRITISH MOTORCYCLE ENGINES: By the staff of "The Motor Cycle"

CEZETTA 175cc MODEL 501 SCOOTER MANUAL & PARTS BOOK

VILLIERS ENGINE WORKSHOP MANUAL: All Villiers engines through 1947

HONDA 50 (BOOK OF):
C100, C102, C110, C114, P50, PC50, PF50, C50 (Also applicable to C100 Series Monkey Bike and CE105H Trail Bike

Please check our website at
www.VelocePress.com
For our most up-to-date listing

Lightning Source UK Ltd.
Milton Keynes UK
UKOW07f1806010315

247092UK00005B/335/P

The International Law of Belli

Belligerent occupations existed in both World Wars and have occurred more recently in all parts of the world (including Iraq, Afghanistan, the former Yugoslavia, Congo, Northern Cyprus, Nagorno-Karabakh, Georgia, Eritrea and Ethiopia). Owing to its special length – exceeding half a century and still in progress – and the unprecedented flow of judicial decisions, a special focus is called for as regards the occupation of Palestinian territories by Israel.

International law addresses the subject of belligerent occupation in some detail. This second, revised, edition updates the text (originally published in 2009) in terms of both State practice and doctrinal discourse. The emphasis is put on decisions of the Security Council; legislation adopted by the Coalition Provisional Authority in Iraq; and predominantly case law: international (Judgments of the International Court of Justice, the International Criminal Tribunal for the Former Yugoslavia and the European Court of Human Rights; Advisory Opinions and Arbitral Awards) as well as domestic courts.

YORAM DINSTEIN is Professor Emeritus at Tel Aviv University. He is a former President of the University, as well as former Rector and former Dean of the Faculty of Law. He served twice as the Charles H. Stockton Professor of International Law at the US Naval War College in Newport, RI. He was also a Humboldt Fellow at the Max Planck Institute of International Law in Heidelberg, Germany, a Meltzer Visiting Professor of Law at New York University, and a visiting Professor of Law at the University of Toronto. Professor Dinstein has written extensively on subjects relating to international law, human rights and the law of armed conflict, including: *War, Aggression and Self-Defence* (6th edn, 2017), *The Conduct of Hostilities under the Law of International Armed Conflict* (3rd edn, 2016) and *Non-International Armed Conflicts in International Law* (2014).

The International Law of Belligerent Occupation

Second Edition

YORAM DINSTEIN

CAMBRIDGE
UNIVERSITY PRESS

University Printing House, Cambridge CB2 8BS, United Kingdom

One Liberty Plaza, 20th Floor, New York, NY 10006, USA

477 Williamstown Road, Port Melbourne, VIC 3207, Australia

314–321, 3rd Floor, Plot 3, Splendor Forum, Jasola District Centre,
New Delhi – 110025, India

79 Anson Road, #06-04/06, Singapore 079906

Cambridge University Press is part of the University of Cambridge.

It furthers the University's mission by disseminating knowledge in the pursuit of education, learning, and research at the highest international levels of excellence.

www.cambridge.org
Information on this title: www.cambridge.org/9781108497978
DOI: 10.1017/9781108671477

First published 2009
Second edition 2019

Printed and bound in Great Britain by Clays Ltd, Elcograf S.p.A.

A catalogue record for this publication is available from the British Library.

Library of Congress Cataloging-in-Publication Data
Names: Dinstein, Yoram, author.
Title: The international law of belligerent occupation / Yoram Dinstein.
Description: Second edition. | Cambridge [UK]; New York, NY:
Cambridge University Press, 2019. |
Includes bibliographical references and index.
Identifiers: LCCN 2018048987 | ISBN 9781108497978 (hardback) |
ISBN 9781108709354 (paperback)
Subjects: LCSH: Military occupation. | War (International law) |
BISAC: LAW / International.
Classification: LCC KZ6429.D56 2019 | DDC 341.6/6–dc23
LC record available at https://lccn.loc.gov/2018048987

ISBN 978-1-108-49797-8 Hardback
ISBN 978-1-108-70935-4 Paperback

Contents

Preface

This revised edition is a companion to three other volumes dealing with international and non-international armed conflicts published by Cambridge University Press: *War, Aggression and Self-Defence* (6th edn, 2017), *The Conduct of Hostilities under the Law of International Armed Conflict* (3rd edn, 2016) and *Non-International Armed Conflicts in International Law* (2014). The new edition updates the text (originally published in 2009), especially in terms of State practice, case law and doctrinal discourse.

It is occasionally suggested that belligerent occupation is an anomalous phenomenon and a side-issue in the present-day environment of international armed conflicts. But in reality quite a few contemporary occupations have cropped up in far-flung quarters of the world. They stretch from Israel to Iraq, from Northern Cyprus to the former Yugoslavia, from Afghanistan to Eritrea and Ethiopia, from Nagorno-Karabakh to Georgia, from Congo to Crimea.

This new edition goes in greater detail into some aspects of these occupations. In particular, there are extensive references to legislation adopted by the Coalition Provisional Authority during the short formal occupation of Iraq (in 2003–4). But, owing to its special length (exceeding half a century and still in progress) and the unprecedented flow of judicial decisions – dissecting a rich profusion of legal disputes in real time (while the occupation is ongoing) – it is only natural that much of the examination remains focused on the occupation of Palestinian territories by Israel. In the course of this prolonged occupation, numerous unique problems have surfaced. The practical experience acquired (for better or worse) as a result of the Israeli occupation has been of critical significance in assessing the interface between the theory and practice of belligerent occupation.

The author has the benefit of linguistic access to the Judgments of the Supreme Court of Israel, many of which are available only in Hebrew (although they have generally been excerpted in English in the *Israel Yearbook on Human Rights* and, in the more celebrated cases, have been translated in full and reproduced in other periodicals). The sheer mass of these Judgments, and even more so the compelling issues that they probe, invite serious consideration. Whether one agrees or disagrees with the interpretation of international law offered by the Israel Supreme Court, its Judgments have become nonpareil signposts that no future decision-maker can afford to ignore. The new edition strives to bring up to date the analysis of these Judgments.

The international legal regime of belligerent occupation constitutes a segment of the *jus in bello*, complementing the compendium of norms governing the conduct of hostilities. The book addresses some fundamental quandaries concomitant of the regime of belligerent occupation. These pertain to the interrelationship between the Occupying Power, the displaced sovereign and the civilian population. But the text equally deals with more commonplace questions with which this *materia* is riddled. How does belligerent occupation commence; how is it maintained; and how is it terminated? What is the rudimentary distinction between belligerent and other types of occupation? Who are the persons protected under belligerent occupation, and what is the scope of their protection? What is the interaction between the law of belligerent occupation and the law of human rights? What jurisdiction does the Occupying Power wield in the legislative, judicial and executive spheres? What specific legal safeguards are offered to the civilian population under occupation from capital punishment, collective penalties, deportations, detention, compulsory work, destruction or seizure of property, and other measures curtailing ordinary freedoms? Conversely, what measures can an Occupying Power lawfully resort to when encountering forcible resistance – and direct participation in hostilities – by embittered inhabitants of an occupied territory?

The study of the law of belligerent occupation cannot be confined to lawyers. It is noteworthy that recent military manuals of the law of armed conflict devote full attention to the topic of belligerent occupation. This is how it should be: armed forces must prepare themselves for the task of coming to grips with the administration of an occupied territory in wartime. The only way to be mentally geared up for this daunting – and often unexpected – challenge is for military personnel to prepare themselves in peacetime for the possible eventuality. Primarily, officers must be trained for the sort of mission accomplishment that has little in common with ordinary military feats, but is indispensable for a successful and law-abiding government of an occupied territory. It is to be hoped that this new edition will assist in such preparation and training, not only by identifying points of discord but also by suggesting modes of action that can be engaged in without supererogatory controversy.

Two important caveats:

(a) Although the book deals with the entitlement of an Occupying Power to resort to internment of protected persons as a security measure, it does not address the question of how persons under detention ought to be treated. The treatment topic calls for a comparative exegesis of the international legal rules governing the different categories of civilian detainees in occupied territories; civilian detainees in general (i.e. in non-occupied territories) both in wartime and in peacetime; and prisoners of war.

(b) While the book is replete with references to war crimes and to trials of war criminals, this is done only with a view to confirming the existence of – or shedding light on – the norms governing belligerent occupation. No attempt is made here to go into the intricate themes of individual penal accountability (or, for that matter, State responsibility for wrongful acts in the form of reparations).

To facilitate syntax, generic pronouns relating to individuals are usually drawn in masculine form. This must not be viewed as gender specific.

Table of Cases

A. International Courts and Tribunals

1. International Court of Justice

2. International Criminal Court

3. International Criminal Tribunal for the Former Yugoslavia (ICTY)

8. Inter-American Commission on Human Rights

9. Special Court for Sierra Leone

10. Eritrea Ethiopia Claims Commission

11. Other Arbitral Awards

B. National Courts and Tribunals

1. 'Subsequent Proceedings' at Nuremberg (US Military Tribunals)

2. *Austria*

3. *France*

4. *Germany*

5. *Israel*

6. *Italy*

7. *Netherlands*

8. *Norway*

9. *Singapore*

10. *United Kingdom*

11. *West Bank*

Table of Treaties

Table of Resolutions

A. Security Council

B. General Assembly

Abbreviations

ADRPILC	Annual Digest and Reports of Public International Law Cases
AFDI	Annuaire Français de Droit International
AJIL	American Journal of International Law
AYIL	African Yearbook of International Law
As.JIL	Asian Journal of International Law
BFSP	British and Foreign State Papers
BYBIL	British Year Book of International Law
Ber.JIL	Berkeley Journal of International Law
Brook.JIL	Brooklyn Journal of International Law
CFH	Criminal Further Hearing
CHRLR	Columbia Human Rights Law Review
CJICL	Cambridge Journal of International and Comparative Law
CLQ	Cornell Law Quarterly
CWC	Chemical Weapons Convention
CYIL	Canadian Yearbook of International Law
Cal.LR	California Law Review
Car.JICL	Cardozo Journal of International and Comparative Law
Car.LR	Cardozo Law Review
Chi.JIL	Chicago Journal of International Law
Col.LR	Columbia Law Review
Cre.LR	Creighton Law Review
DJILP	Denver Journal of International Law and Policy
ECHRJD	Judgments and Decisions of the European Court of Human Rights
EHRR	European Human Rights Reports
EJIL	European Journal of International Law
GJIL	Georgia Journal of International Law
GWILR	George Washington International Law Review
GYIL	German Yearbook of International Law
HCJ	High Court of Justice
HJLPP	Harvard Journal of Law and Public Policy

HLR	Harvard Law Review
Har.ILJ	Harvard International Law Journal
Heid.JIL	Heidelberg Journal of International Law
Hous.JIL	Houston Journal of International Law
IACHRJO	Judgments and Opinions of the Inter-American Court of Human Rights
ICJ Rep.	Reports of the International Court of Justice
IDF	Israel Defence Force
ICLQ	International and Comparative Law Quarterly
ICLR	International Community Law Review
ICRC	International Committee of the Red Cross
ICTY	International Criminal Tribunal for the Former Yugoslavia
IHL	International Humanitarian Law
IJIL	Indian Journal of International Law
ILM	International Legal Materials
ILR	International Law Reports
ILS	International Law Studies
IRRC	International Review of the Red Cross
IYHR	Israel Yearbook on Human Rights
Int.Leg.	*International Legislation* (M.O. Hudson ed., 1931–50)
Is.LR	Israel Law Review
JCSL	Journal of Conflict and Security Law
JICJ	Journal of International Criminal Justice
JIHLS	Journal of International Humanitarian Legal Studies
JILE	Journal of International Law and Economics
JSAL	Journal of South African Law
KH	Kovets Hatakanot [Secondary Legislation of the State of Israel [in Hebrew])
LLAICLR	Loyola of Los Angeles International and Comparative Law Review
LQR	Law Quarterly Review
LRTWC	Law Reports of Trials of War Criminals
LSI	Laws of the State of Israel [in English]
LSR	Law and Society Review
MPEPIL	The Max Planck Encyclopedia of Public International Law (R. Wolfrum ed., 2012)
MPYUNL	Max Planck Yearbook of United Nations Law
McG.LJ	McGill Law Journal
Mich.JIL	Michigan Journal of International Law
Mich.LR	Michigan Law Review
Mil.LR	Military Law Review
Minn.JIL	Minnesota Journal of International Law

Minn.LR	Minnesota Law Review
NILR	Netherlands International Law Review
NTIR	Nordisk Tidsskrift for International Ret
NYULR	New York University Law Review
PD	Piskei Din (Reports of the Israel Supreme Court [in Hebrew])
PG	Palestine Gazette
PSILR	Penn State International Law Review
RBDI	Revue Belge de Droit International
RCADI	Recueil des Cours de l'Académie de Droit International
RHDI	Revue Hellénique de Droit International
RIAA	Reports of International Arbitral Awards
RGDIP	Revue Générale de Droit International Public
SCL	Santa Clara Lawyer
SDLR	San Diego Law Review
SH	Sefer Hahukim [Primary Legislation of the State of Israel (in Hebrew)]
SJIL	Stanford Journal of International Law
SLR	Stanford Law Review
Supp.	Supplement
TAULR	Tel Aviv University Law Review [in Hebrew]
TGS	Transactions of the Grotius Society
TIPH	Temporary International Presence in Hebron
TLCP	Transnational Law and Contemporary Problems
ULR	Utrecht Law Review
UN	United Nations
UNBLJ	University of New Brunswick Law Journal
UNESCO	United Nations Educational, Scientific and Cultural Organization
UNJY	United Nations Juridical Yearbook
UNTS	United Nations Treaty Series
VAC	Various Applications, Criminal
VAT	Value Added Tax
VJTL	Vanderbilt Journal of Transnational Law
WWI	First World War
WWII	Second World War
YIHL	Yearbook of International Humanitarian Law
YJIL	Yale Journal of International Law
YLJ	Yale Law Journal

1 The General Framework

I. Belligerent Occupation as a Natural Phenomenon in War

1. A study of the legal regime of belligerent occupation must begin with the observation that it is frequently misconstrued or misunderstood, to a degree that shrouds it in many a myth. The most persistent myth is that the occurrence of belligerent occupation is an anomaly or even an aberration. In reality, when an international armed conflict breaks out, armies tend to be on the move on the ground whenever they have an opportunity to do so. Each Belligerent Party usually spares no effort to penetrate, and if possible take possession of, the territory of the enemy. Sometimes both sides in an international armed conflict do that simultaneously, in opposite directions, in diverse sectors of the front. Once combat stabilizes along fixed lines, not coinciding with the original international frontiers, the cross-border areas seized and effectively controlled by a Belligerent Party are deemed to be subject to belligerent occupation. As discerned by the 2015 US Department of Defense Law of War Manual, belligerent occupation 'involves a complicated, trilateral set of legal relations between the Occupying Power, the temporarily ousted sovereign authority, and the inhabitants of occupied territory'.[1]

2. Belligerent occupation ordinarily covers only a fraction of the overall territory of the enemy, so that the displaced sovereign loses only a part (or parts) of its land while continuing to exercise full control in the remaining area. Yet, if the armed forces of a Belligerent Party are singularly successful, they may overrun the entire enemy country: this is what happened in much of Nazi-occupied Europe during WWII (the Second World War) and in Iraq in 2003.

3. Even the total occupation of the territory of State *A* by State *B* does not by itself mean that the war between these Belligerent Parties is over. Territorial conquest by State *B* does not preclude the emergence of a Government-in-Exile acting as the 'depositary' of the sovereignty of State *A*.[2] As long as the

[1] US Department of Defense, *Law of War Manual* 771 (2015, updated 2016).

[2] S. Talmon, 'Who Is a Legitimate Government in Exile? Towards Normative Criteria for Governmental Legitimacy in International Law', *The Reality of International Law: Essays in Honour of Ian Brownlie* 499, 501–3 (G.S. Goodwin-Gill and S. Talmon eds., 1999).

war continues to be prosecuted by the armed forces of the Government-in-Exile of State *A* or its allies (States *C, D*, etc.), the armed conflict goes on and the status of belligerent occupation of the total territory of State *A* remains in effect.

4. However, complete military victory of State *B* may bring about a disintegration of State *A* through *debellatio*.[3] 'The principle that enemy territory occupied by a belligerent in the course of war remains the territory of the state against which the war is directed, can apply only as long as this community still exists as a state within the meaning of international law'.[4] If State *A* completely collapses as a result of utter military defeat, its *debellatio* puts an end to the war and to the legal regime of belligerent occupation.

5. That said, one must not rush to the conclusion that an enemy State has disappeared. The International Military Tribunal at Nuremberg – trying the major Nazi war criminals – bluntly proclaimed in its Judgment of 1946 that the doctrine of the subjugation (and dissolution) of an enemy State 'was never considered to be applicable so long as there was an army in the field attempting to restore the occupied countries to their true owners', as was the case in the struggle against the Nazis during WWII.[5]

II. Belligerent Occupation and the Legality of War

6. A second (by no means secondary) myth surrounding the legal regime of belligerent occupation is that it is, or becomes in time, inherently illegal under international law.[6] In truth, international law – far from stigmatizing belligerent occupation with illegality – recognizes its frequency and regulates its application in great detail. It is of more than passing interest that Resolution 1483 (2003) of the UN Security Council makes a matter-of-fact reference to the takeover of Iraq by 'occupying powers' (accompanied by a call to 'all concerned' to comply fully with their international legal obligations under the Hague Regulations and Geneva Conventions).[7] In and of itself, this text 'refuted the claim that occupation, as such, is illegal'.[8] In its Advisory Opinion of 2004 on the *Wall*, the International Court of Justice took Israel to task for multiple breaches of the law of belligerent occupation (see *infra* 769 *et seq*.),

[3] On the meaning of *debellatio*, see Y. Dinstein, *War, Aggression and Self-Defence* 52–3 (6th edn, 2017).
[4] H. Kelsen, *Principles of International Law* 75 (1st edn, 1952).
[5] International Military Tribunal (Nuremberg), 1946, 41 *AJIL* 172, 249 (1947).
[6] See, e.g., O. Ben-Naftali, A.M. Gross and K. Michaeli, 'Illegal Occupation: Framing the Occupied Palestinian Territories', 23 *Ber.JIL* 551, 609–12 (2005).
[7] Security Council Resolution 1483, 42 *ILM* 1016, 1017 (2003) (Preamble and para. 5).
[8] E. Benvenisti and G. Keinan, 'The Occupation of Iraq: A Reassessment', 86 *ILS* 263, 277 (R.A.P. Pedrozo ed., 2010).

but it conspicuously 'refrained from characterizing the Israeli occupation as "illegal"'.[9]

7. The Occupying Power may be waging a war of aggression or it may be the victim of aggression (militarily advancing in pursuit of a successful war of self-defence). The contemporary *jus ad bellum* is predicated on a striking contrast between wars of aggression – amounting to crimes – and wars of self-defence.[10] However, as an American Military Tribunal pronounced in the 1948 Judgment in the *Hostages* trial (part of the so-called 'Subsequent Proceedings' at Nuremberg):

> International Law makes no distinction between a lawful and an unlawful occupant in dealing with the respective duties of occupant and population in occupied territory. There is no reciprocal connection between the manner of the military occupation of territory and the rights and duties of the occupant and population to each other after the relationship has in fact been established. Whether the invasion was lawful or criminal is not an important factor in the consideration of this subject.[11]

Similarly, a Dutch Special Court stated in the 1948 *Christiansen* trial:

> The rules of international law, in so far as they regulate the methods of warfare and the occupation of enemy territory, make no distinction between wars which have been started legally and those which have been started illegally.[12]

8. The law of belligerent occupation is a branch of the *jus in bello*, otherwise known as law of international armed conflict or 'international humanitarian law' (IHL).[13] Obligations derived from the *jus in bello* apply equally to all Belligerent Parties, notwithstanding their unequal standing in the eyes of the *jus ad bellum*.[14] By the same token, the rights and obligations of an Occupying Power remain exactly the same, regardless of the chain of events in which the belligerent occupation was brought about (consisting of a war of aggression or a war of self-defence).[15]

9. In the *Demopoulos* case of 2010, the Grand Chamber of the European Court of Human Rights made the following remark about the Turkish occupation of Northern Cyprus (commencing in 1974): 'the mere fact that there

[9] R. Sabel, 'Book Review', 42 *Is.LR* 628, 631 (2009).

[10] See Dinstein, *supra* note 3, at 132–8, 279–88.

[11] *Hostages* trial (*List* et al.) (US Military Tribunal, Nuremberg, 1948), 8 *LRTWC* 34, 59.

[12] *Re Christiansen* (Netherlands, Special Court, 1948), 15 *ILR* 412, 413.

[13] The expression 'international humanitarian law' was once perceived as covering 'Geneva Law' (*infra* 17). It is now understood to cover both 'Geneva Law' and 'Hague Law' (*infra* 13). See the Advisory Opinion of the International Court of Justice on the *Legality of the Threat or Use of Nuclear Weapons*, [1996] *ICJ Rep.* 226, 256.

[14] See Y. Dinstein, *The Conduct of Hostilities under the Law of International Armed Conflict* 4–6 (3rd edn, 2016).

[15] See A. Gerson, 'War, Conquered Territory, and Military Occupation in the Contemporary International Legal System', 18 *Har.ILJ* 525, 539–42 (1976–7).

is an illegal occupation does not deprive all administrative or putative legal or judicial acts therein of any relevance under the [European] Convention'.[16] This language may appear to endorse the wrong assertion that a distinction should be made between legal and illegal occupations.[17] It would have been more accurate in the passage quoted (as in other, similar, texts) to have adverted to an illegal use of force generating occupation rather than to an illegal occupation. The crux of the matter is that, whether the use of force on which it is predicated is lawful or unlawful under the *jus ad bellum*, belligerent occupation is the font of the same body of law under the *jus in bello*.

III. The Strata of the International Law of Belligerent Occupation

10. The legal norms governing belligerent occupation are embodied in several strata[18] of international law. We shall address here customary international law and the leading treaties (additional treaties will be mentioned in specific contexts in other sections of the book).

A. *Customary International Law*

11. The definition of international custom, as formulated in Article 38(1)(b) of the Statute of the International Court of Justice, is 'general practice accepted as law'.[19] The customary layer of the law of belligerent occupation – as of any other branch of international law – has the downside of being *jus non scriptum* (incrementally consolidated in the general conduct of States), but this is counterweighed by the upside of being binding on all States (even if they never took part in the process leading to the custom's creation).[20]

12. The difficulty with custom is verifying the existence of a general practice of States accepted as law. On a host of issues, the practice of States in the domain of belligerent occupation is desultory. One may therefore question whether it lays sufficient ground for the development of customary international law. While the phrase 'general practice' is broad enough to cover domestic legislation, military manuals and the like,[21] these texts rarely address in depth

[16] *Demopoulos* et al. *v. Turkey* (European Court of Human Rights, Grand Chamber, 2010), para. 94.

[17] For such an assertion, see A. Zemach, 'Can Occupation Resulting from a War of Self-Defense Become Illegal?', 24 *Minn.JIL* 313–50 (2015).

[18] For the use of the term 'strata' (rather than 'sources'), see Y. Dinstein, 'The Interaction between Customary International Law and Treaties', 322 *RCADI* 243, 260–1 (2006).

[19] Statute of the International Court of Justice, Annexed to Charter of the United Nations, 1945, 9 *Int.Leg.* 327, 510, 522 (1950).

[20] See Dinstein, *supra* note 18, at 282–3, 313.

[21] See *ibid.*, 272–3.

the minutiae of daily interaction between the Occupying Power and the civilian population of an occupied territory. An important ingestion of meaningful practice into the body of customary law has occurred in Iraq, but the occupation (by the United States and the United Kingdom) was limited in duration. The only extensive contemporary practice, spread over more than fifty years of belligerent occupation, is that of Israel in the Palestinian territories. Regrettably (as will be shown in this study), the practice of the Occupying Powers – either in Iraq or in the Palestinian territories – has not always been in harmony with what is commonly perceived as the customary *lex lata*.

B. The Hague Regulations

13. A series of Hague Conventions was concluded by the Peace Conferences held in 1899 and 1907. Belligerent occupation is the cynosure of Section III (Articles 42 through 56) of the Regulations Respecting the Laws and Customs of War on Land, first composed as an annex to Hague Convention (II) of 1899 and then revised and attached as an annex to Hague Convention (IV) of 1907.[22] In the present volume, references and quotes – unless otherwise indicated – will be made to and from the more recent, and modified, 1907 version.

14. Originally innovative, the Hague Regulations have gradually acquired a declaratory status as a reflection of customary international law (solidified post-1907 through the general practice of States accepted as law). This was first acknowledged in the Nuremberg Judgment of the International Military Tribunal:

> The rules of land warfare expressed in the [Hague] Convention undoubtedly represented an advance over existing international law at the time of their adoption. But ... by 1939 these rules laid down in the Convention were recognized by all civilized nations, and were regarded as being declaratory of the laws and customs of war.[23]

The International Military Tribunal for the Far East, sitting in Tokyo for the trial of the major Japanese war criminals, echoed the Nuremberg dictum in its majority Judgment of 1948.[24] Both International Military Tribunals delivered their decisions on the subject in a generic fashion, relating to the *jus in bello* as a whole. Steering in the particular direction of belligerent occupation, the International Court of Justice twice gave its *imprimatur* to the same

[22] Hague Regulations Respecting the Laws and Customs of War on Land, Annexed to Hague Convention (II), 1899, and Hague Convention (IV), 1907, *The Hague Peace Conferences and Other International Conferences Concerning the Laws and Usages of War: Texts of Conventions with Commentaries* 206–7, 218–19, 244–53 (A.P. Higgins ed., 1909).

[23] International Military Tribunal (Nuremberg), *supra* note 5, at 248–9.

[24] International Military Tribunal for the Far East (Tokyo), 1948, 15 *ILR* 356, 365–6.

finding: first in the 2004 Advisory Opinion on the *Wall*,[25] and then in the 2005 Judgment in the *Armed Activities* case (Congo v. Uganda).[26]

15. The repercussions of the evolution in the standing of the Hague Regulations in the sphere of belligerent occupation are of tremendous import. Once the Regulations have acquired their declaratory nature, their provisions – as a mirror-image of customary law – have become binding on all States, whether or not they are Contracting Parties to the Hague Convention to which the Regulations are annexed.[27]

16. More than a century after their final revision, Hague Regulations 42 through 56 continue to form the keystone of the law of belligerent occupation. All the same, it cannot be forgotten that they were formulated prior to the two World Wars. The protection that they afford to the inhabitants of occupied territories is of fundamental value, but – as we shall see when we analyse these provisions in detail – their focus is property rights.[28] Although the life and liberty of the inhabitants are also safeguarded in the Hague Regulations, this is done in a more abstract manner. Tragically, the missing specifics proved to be of colossal significance in WWII, and the Holocaust (the systematic extermination by the Nazis of six million Jews in occupied Europe) demonstrated that the Hague Regulations are of little relevance to a savage occupation.

C. Geneva Convention (IV)

17. In 1949, four Conventions for the Protection of War Victims were adopted in Geneva. The first three Conventions recast earlier texts, but the fourth was new. Geneva Convention (IV) Relative to the Protection of Civilian Persons in Time of War[29] contains a section confined to the treatment of aliens in the territory of a Belligerent Party in an armed conflict. However, the bulk of the instrument lends protection – either exclusively or *inter alia* – to the civilian population of occupied territories. The paramount purpose of the Convention was to provide this population with enhanced protection, as compared to the stipulations of the Hague Regulations, in order to make sure that the calamitous events of WWII would not repeat themselves.

[25] Advisory Opinion on *Legal Consequences of the Construction of a Wall in the Occupied Palestinian Territory*, [2004] *ICJ Rep*. 136, 172.

[26] *Case Concerning Armed Activities on the Territory of the Congo* (Congo v. Uganda), [2005] *ICJ Rep*. 168, 243.

[27] See *ibid*.

[28] See H.A. Smith, 'The Government of Occupied Territory', 21 *BYBIL* 151, *id*. (1944).

[29] Geneva Convention (IV) Relative to the Protection of Civilian Persons in Time of War, 1949, *The Laws of Armed Conflicts: A Collection of Conventions, Resolutions and Other Documents* 575 (4th edn, D. Schindler and J. Toman eds., 2004).

18. As Article 154 of Geneva Convention (IV) sets forth, the Convention is 'supplementary' to the Hague Regulations.[30] In other words, the Convention builds on the Hague Regulations – either by extending their scope or by fleshing out their somewhat vague strictures – without superseding them. Admittedly, the ICRC (International Committee of the Red Cross) Commentary on the Convention goes as far as suggesting, for instance, that – in light of Article 31 of the Convention (quoted *infra* 178) – Hague Regulation 44 (quoted *infra* 176) 'no longer has any point'.[31] Contrary to that opinion, the present author believes that there is no escape from the conclusion that Regulation 44 remains in force today, side by side with Article 31 of the Convention. This is equally true of other Hague Regulations, even when they may seem to be redundant or 'very much out-of-date' when looked at from the angle of the Geneva Convention.[32]

19. At the time of writing, all four Geneva Conventions of 1949 are universal in their application, inasmuch as all States – bar none – have expressed their consent to be bound by them. Nevertheless, (i) this was not the case only a few years ago, and (ii) a State may come into being in the future without rushing to accede to the Conventions. Moreover, (iii) the question whether concrete provisions of Geneva Convention (IV) reflect customary international law may be of tangible consequence when they are applied by domestic courts on the domestic plane (see *infra* 89–90).

D. *Additional Protocol I*

20. In 1977, an Additional Protocol Relating to the Protection of Victims of International Armed Conflicts (Protocol I) was appended to the Geneva Conventions[33] (jointly with Protocol II, which is devoted to non-international armed conflicts[34]). Some of the clauses of Additional Protocol I deal with occupied territories. As a rule of thumb, the Protocol does not supersede the Geneva Conventions (including Convention (IV)), and the new text merely complements them. But, occasionally, the Protocol explicitly overrides earlier Geneva norms. For examples in which Geneva provisions relevant to

[30] *Ibid.*, 625–6.
[31] *Commentary, IV Geneva Convention* 618 (ICRC, O.M. Uhler and H. Coursier eds., 1958).
[32] *Ibid.*, 619.
[33] Protocol Additional to the Geneva Conventions of 12 August 1949, and Relating to the Protection of Victims of International Armed Conflicts (Additional Protocol I), 1977, *The Laws of Armed Conflicts*, *supra* note 29, at 711.
[34] Protocol Additional to the Geneva Conventions of 12 August 1949, and Relating to the Protection of Victims of Non-International Armed Conflicts (Additional Protocol II), 1977, *The Laws of Armed Conflicts*, *supra* note 29, at 775.

belligerent occupation are clearly amended or abrogated by the Protocol, see *infra* 209, 213, 296, 551 and 865.

21. Unlike the Geneva Conventions themselves, Additional Protocol I is not universally accepted. Whereas a large majority of States has ratified or adhered to the Protocol, a determined minority – led by the US and including Israel – has utterly rejected crucial portions of it. Since the US issued a formal announcement in 1987 that it will not ratify the Protocol – due to the fact that it is 'fundamentally and irreconcilably flawed'[35] – the international community has been riven by what the present writer calls a 'Great Schism'.[36] Still, even the US does not deny that there are 'certain meritorious elements' in the Protocol.[37] As for Israel, the Supreme Court has expressly acknowledged that several of the Protocol's provisions enshrine customary international law. This happened in the *Targeted Killings* case (per President A. Barak),[38] in the *Fuel and Electricity* case (per President D. Beinisch),[39] and in other instances (see, e.g., *infra* 327). In 2005, the ICRC produced a massive three-volume Study of Customary International Humanitarian Law, which (*inter alia*) attempts to establish chapter-and-verse what components of the Protocol are declaratory of existing law.[40] Unfortunately, the Study has failed to assuage concerns by the US[41] and others.[42]

IV. A Brief Historical Outline

A. The Past

22. The germination of the international legal regime of belligerent occupation in the modern sense occurred only after the Napoleonic Wars, in the first half of the nineteenth century.[43] Embryonic normative measures were crafted in

[35] Message from the President of the United States to the Senate, 1987, 26 *ILM* 561, 562 (1987).

[36] See Y. Dinstein, 'International Humanitarian Law and Modern Warfare', *International Expert Conference on Computer Network Attacks and the Applicability of International Humanitarian Law* 17, 18–19 (K. Byström ed., 2005).

[37] Message from the President, *supra* note 35, at 562.

[38] HCJ 769/02, *Public Committee against Torture in Israel* et al. *v. Government of Israel* et al., 62(1) *PD* 507, 560. (The Judgment is excerpted in English in 37 *IYHR* 305 (2007). A full translation is available in 46 *ILM* 375 (2007)).

[39] HCJ 9132/07, *Albassiouni* et al. *v. Prime Minister* et al., paras. 13–14. (The Judgment is excerpted in English in 38 *IYHR* 324 (2008)).

[40] *Customary International Humanitarian Law* (ICRC, J.-M. Henckaerts and L. Doswald-Beck eds, 2005).

[41] See Joint Letter by the Legal Adviser of the US Department of State and the General Counsel of the Department of Defense to the President of the ICRC, 2006, 46 *ILM* 511 (2007).

[42] See Y. Dinstein, 'The ICRC Customary International Humanitarian Law Study', 36 *IYHR* 1–15 (2006).

[43] See N. Bhuta, 'The Antinomies of Transformative Occupation', 16 *EJIL* 721, 725 (2005).

the 1863 'Lieber Code' (a set of instructions for the US armed forces, prepared by F. Lieber and promulgated as General Orders).[44] The Code was followed by a section on military authority over hostile territory, incorporated in a Project (draft) of an International Declaration prepared in Brussels in 1874.[45] This text was the precursor of the Hague Regulations of 1899/1907 in which the law of belligerent occupation acquired the lineaments of positive international law (see *supra* 13–14).

23. Subsequent to the conclusion of the Hague Regulations, there were a number of instances of belligerent occupation, e.g., the occupation by Italy in 1912 of the Dodecanese Islands from the Ottoman Empire.[46] The occupation lasted for more than a decade until Turkey formally ceded the Islands to Italy in the 1923 Lausanne Treaty of Peace[47] (forming part of a series of treaties concluding the First World War (WWI)). Between 1945 and 1947, the Dodecanese Islands were subject to a second round of belligerent occupation in the aftermath of WWII, this time by the British.[48] In the Paris Treaty of Peace of 1947, Italy ceded the Islands to Greece.[49]

24. Of particular note were the occupations related to WWI. In the course of the hostilities, large tracts of land were occupied by a number of Belligerent Parties (mostly Germany). The best known occupation was that of almost the entire territory of Belgium by Germany, from the outset of WWI in 1914 to its end in 1918. In the legal literature, a whole slew of the policies and practices of the German Occupying Power in Belgium were put to the test of the Hague Regulations and found wanting.[50] Of course, there were other occupations as well, including some by Allied States. Those that stand out were carried out by Britain in segments of the Ottoman Empire – parts of Iraq from 1914[51] and of Palestine from 1917[52] – dragging on for years after the general close of hostilities in November 1918.

[44] Instructions for the Government of Armies of the United States in the Field, 1863, *The Laws of Armed Conflicts, supra* note 29, at 3, 7–9 (Articles 31–47).

[45] Brussels Project of an International Declaration Concerning the Laws and Customs of War, 1874, *The Laws of Armed Conflicts, supra* note 29, at 21, 23–4.

[46] See J.G. Gregoriades, 'The Status of the Dodecanese 1912–1923, 1923–1945', 2 *RHDI* 237, 237–41 (1949).

[47] Lausanne Treaty of Peace with Turkey, 1923, IV *Major Peace Treaties of Modern History 1648–1967* 2301, 2309 (F.L. Israel ed., 1967) (Article 15).

[48] See T.L. Chrysanthopoulos, 'The British and Greek Military Occupations of the Dodecanese 1945–1948', 2 *RHDI* 227, 227–30 (1949).

[49] Paris Treaty of Peace with Italy, 1947, IV *Major Peace Treaties of Modern History 1648–1967, supra* note 47, at 2421, 2429 (Article 14).

[50] See E. Benvenisti, *The International Law of Occupation* 108–20 (2nd edn, 2012).

[51] See A. Wilson, 'The Laws of War in Occupied Territory', 18 *TGS* 17–39 (1932).

[52] See N. Bentwich, 'The Legal Administration of Palestine under the British Military Occupation', 1 *BYBIL* 139–48 (1920–1).

25. During WWII, there were some occupations conducted by and large on the basis of the Hague Regulations (for example, the occupation of Libya by Britain from 1942 until well after the end of the War).[53] But WWII will always be remembered because of the barbarous occupations of vast swathes of Europe, Asia, North Africa, East Asia and the Pacific by Nazi Germany and Imperial Japan. The hallmark of the Axis occupations was the systematic perpetration of gruesome atrocities, culminating in the Holocaust inflicted by the Nazis on European Jewry. As put forth by an American Military Tribunal in the 1947 *Justice* trial (part of the 'Subsequent Proceedings' at Nuremberg), '[t]he undisputed evidence in this case shows that Germany violated during the recent war every principle of the law of military occupation'.[54]

26. Dismal memories of the outrages of WWII spurred the adoption, in 1949, of Geneva Convention (IV), which rewrote, expanded and transformed the law of belligerent occupation in the interest of humanitarianism (see *supra* 17–18). But war crimes trials, held in the wake of WWII, showed that – even prior to the entry into force of the Geneva Convention, and merely on the ground of customary international law – some of the heinous acts of the German and Imperial Japanese Occupying Powers were manifestly unlawful and carried criminal accountability.

B. Recent Decades

27. Following WWII there has been a considerable reluctance by States to admit that they were Occupying Powers. This may be due to the odium that the label of an Occupying Power seemed to imply against the background of the appalling Nazi and Imperial Japanese record. But it was also due to a reluctance to be 'saddled with the burdens of full compliance' with the law of belligerent occupation.[55]

28. Excuses have frequently been put forward by States that their cross-border coercive territorial expansion fell short of belligerent occupation. Thus, in 1950, China justified the dispatch of troops to Tibet by relying on an old suzerain-vassal feudal relationship which had led it to liquidate Tibet's independence.[56] The military takeover of Goa in 1961 was excused on the ground that the enclave was a part of India.[57] Most of Western Sahara was annexed by

[53] See G.T. Watts, 'The British Military Occupation of Cyrenaica, 1942–1949', 37 *TGS* 69–81 (1951).

[54] *Justice* trial (*Altstötter* et al.) (US Military Tribunal, Nuremberg, 1947), 6 *LRTWC* 1, 59.

[55] K.E. Boon, 'Obligations of the New Occupier: The Contours of a *Jus Post Bellum*', 31 *LLAICLR* 57, 65 (2009).

[56] See C.H. Alexandrowicz-Alexander, 'The Legal Position of Tibet', 48 *AJIL* 265–74 (1954). *Per contra*, see T.-T. Li, 'The Legal Position of Tibet', 50 *AJIL* 394–404 (1956).

[57] See Q. Wright, 'The Goa Incident', 56 *AJIL* 617–32 (1962).

Morocco in 1975 in light of historical legal ties.[58] Likewise, invading countries – Argentina in 1982 (in the case of the Falkland Islands) and Iraq in 1990 (as regards Kuwait) – based their action on the recovery of lands deemed part of their respective patrimonial heritage.

29. The status of belligerent occupation has also been denied by States contending, sometimes in rather dubious circumstances, that they were acting consensually (see *infra* 106). In these instances, troops were deployed abroad in ostensible response to an invitation by another State, lending support to an incumbent Government embroiled in an internal convulsion. Prominent illustrations are the Vietnamese intervention in Cambodia (1978); the Soviet intervention in Afghanistan (1979); and the American interventions in either Grenada (1983) or Panama (1989).[59]

30. Until the end of the 'Cold War', the incessant inter-bloc rivalry precluded the possibility of eliciting a legally binding decision from the Security Council – in accordance with the mandate conferred on it by the United Nation Charter concerning the maintenance or restoration of international peace – as to the subjection of foreign territory to belligerent occupation. But the situation changed drastically upon the implosion of the Soviet Union.

31. The political and legal watershed was the invasion of Kuwait by Iraq in 1990. The Security Council constantly demanded that the Iraqi occupation of Kuwait be brought to an end (as happened eventually by virtue of a successful military action taken by a US-led coalition-of-the-willing in 1991).[60] In Resolution 674 (1990) – a binding Chapter VII text – the Security Council condemned the actions of Iraqi 'occupying forces' in Kuwait, in violation of Geneva Convention (IV).[61] The wheel turned full circle in 2003, when the land of the former Occupying Power – Iraq – became an occupied territory. The Occupying Powers of Iraq, as determined by the Security Council, were the US and the UK (see *infra* 36 *et seq.*).

32. The existence of belligerent occupation has been acknowledged unequivocally on several occasions in the contemporary jurisprudence of international courts and tribunals. The International Court of Justice affirmed the status of belligerent occupation of the West Bank by Israel in the 2004 Advisory Opinion on the *Wall*.[62] It also pronounced, in the *Armed Activities*

[58] In the *Western Sahara* Advisory Opinion of 1975, the International Court of Justice recognized the existence of these historical ties but did not find them of such a nature as affecting the right of self-determination of the people of the territory. [1975] *ICJ Rep.* 12, 68.

[59] See Benvenisti, *supra* note 50, at 177–87.

[60] See, e.g., Security Council Resolution 662 (1990), *Resolutions and Statements of the United Nations Security Council (1946–1992)* 529, *id.* (2nd edn, K.C. Wellens ed., 1993) (Preamble).

[61] Security Council Resolution 674 (1990), *ibid.*, 536, 537 (Preamble).

[62] Advisory Opinion on *Legal Consequences of the Construction of a Wall in the Occupied Palestinian Territory*, *supra* note 25, at 167.

case of 2005, that Uganda had been an Occupying Power in the Ituri region of Congo between 1999 and 2003 (see quotation *infra* 146). The status of Uganda as an Occupying Power in that region was also recognized by a Pre-Trial Chamber of the International Criminal Court, in the *Lubanga* case of 2007.[63] The ICTY (International Criminal Tribunal for the Former Yugoslavia) has registered the existence of belligerent occupation in some locations, in diverse time-frames, in the course of the fighting across the former Yugoslavia.[64] The Eritrea Ethiopia Claims Commission found in 2004–5 that there had been belligerent occupation in certain sectors of the front[65] (cf. *infra* 127). Earlier, in the *Loizidou* case of 1996, the European Court of Human Rights referred to 'the occupation of the northern part of Cyprus by Turkish troops', which took place 'as a consequence of a military action' and ended in 'effective control' of the area.[66] Another important decision on Northern Cyprus was rendered by the Grand Chamber of the European Court of Human Rights in the *Demopoulos* case of 2010 (*supra* 9). The Grand Chamber also determined, in its two concurrent Judgments of 2015 in the *Chiragov* and *Sargsyan* cases, that there was effective control through military action and occupation of Nagorno-Karabakh and surrounding Azerbaijani districts by Armenia.[67]

33. The Afghanistan War against the Taliban deserves a closer look:

(a) Between October and December 2001, there was patently an international armed conflict between the US and Taliban-led Afghanistan. To the extent that there were American 'boots on the ground', in effective control of Afghan territory, the US could be regarded as an Occupying Power of that territory.

(b) In December 2001, the Security Council endorsed provisional arrangements for the establishment of a new Afghan Government in Kabul (Resolution 1383)[68] and authorized the establishment of an International Security Assistance Force to assist the Afghan Interim Authority in the maintenance of security (Resolution 1386).[69] Hostilities in Afghanistan

[63] See *Prosecutor v. Lubanga Dyilo* (International Criminal Court, Pre-Trial Chamber, 2007), 101 *AJIL* 841, 843 (2007).

[64] See, e.g., *Prosecutor v. Rajić* (Rule 61) (ICTY, Trial Chamber, 1996), paras. 38–42; *Prosecutor v. Blaškić* (ICTY, Trial Chamber, 2000), paras. 149–50; *Prosecutor v. Naletilić* et al. (ICTY, Trial Chamber, 2003), para. 587.

[65] Eritrea Ethiopia Claims Commission, Partial Award (Central Front), Ethiopia's Claim 2, 2004, 43 *ILM* 1275, 1282 (2004).

[66] *Loizidou v. Turkey* (Merits) (European Court of Human Rights, 1996), 36 *ILM* 440, 453–4 (1997).

[67] *Chiragov* et al. *v. Armenia* (Merits) (European Court of Human Rights, Grand Chamber, 2015), 54 *ILM* 965, 1008–11 (2015); *Sargsyan v. Azerbaijan* (European Court of Human Rights, Grand Chamber, 2015), para. 224.

[68] Security Council Resolution 1383 (2001) (para. 1).

[69] Security Council Resolution 1386 (2001) (para. 1).

did not cease: in fact, they persist even at the time of writing. Arguably, for several years, the armed conflict in Afghanistan – between the international coalition (crafted around US forces) and the Taliban – retained its international character. If so, the US and its allies could be regarded as Occupying Powers of any territory over which they exercised effective control. However, once the armed conflict in Afghanistan transformed its character from international to non-international (with the foreign forces engaged in fighting the Taliban only with the consent and at the invitation of the new Kabul Government), any form of belligerent occupation automatically came to an end (inasmuch as there is no belligerent occupation in a non-international armed conflict; see *infra* 102).

34. There is every reason to consider the annexation of Crimea by Russia in 2014 as amounting to belligerent occupation.[70] The occupation was not militarily resisted by Ukraine from which Crimea was wrested. But, as we shall see, *infra* 69, an unresisted forcible occupation qualifies as belligerent occupation.

35. The situation in Georgia is more complex. Georgia contends that South Ossetia and Abkhazia (which had seceded from Georgia at the time of the dissolution of the USSR and have been recognized by Russia as independent States) are Russian-occupied territories. The 2009 Report of the Independent International Fact-Finding Mission on the Conflict in Georgia 'was hesitant to tackle' this 'challenging question'.[71] However, it can be clearly inferred from the Report that certain 'buffer zones' created by Russia during the August 2008 hostilities with Georgia, and retained for several months, were subject to belligerent occupation.[72]

V. The Occupation of Iraq

36. Iraq provides a clear-cut case in which the mantle of Occupying Powers was explicitly acknowledged by both States concerned – the US and the UK – within a matter of weeks of the launching of their offensive against Saddam Hossein's Iraq (on 19 March 2003). The status of the two Occupying Powers was formally proclaimed by the UN Security Council (in which the US and the UK serve as Permanent Members with veto power, so that the texts of resolutions had to be approved by them).

[70] See R. Heinsch, 'Conflict Classification in Ukraine: The Return of the "Proxy War"?', 91 *ILS* 323, 354 (2015). See also R. Geiss, 'Russia's Annexation of Crimea: The Mills of International Law Grind Slowly but They Do Grind', *ibid.*, 425, 443

[71] See Benvenisti, *supra* note 50, at 196.

[72] II *Report of the Independent International Fact-Finding Mission on the Conflict in Georgia* 304–12 (2009).

37. As early as 28 March, the Security Council – in Resolution 1472 – referred to the duty of an as-yet unidentified 'Occupying Power' (under Article 55 of Geneva Convention IV quoted *infra* 457) to ensure food and medical supplies to the population of Iraq.[73] April – the month that Baghdad fell – was, in many respects, an uncertain period of transition (see also *infra* 644). But on 8 May, the Permanent Representatives of the US and the UK sent a joint letter to the President of the Security Council accepting the role of Occupying Powers.[74] Resolution 1483, adopted on 22 May, referred to these two States as 'occupying powers under unified command'.[75] The status of other Coalition members is less clear:[76] the position of the ICRC was that, if these States had troops on the ground and were assigned responsibility over sections (however small) of territory, they were also Occupying Powers.[77] But cf. *infra* 160.

38. Starting on 16 May 2003 (that is, even before the adoption of Resolution 1483), the Coalition Provisional Authority – set up by the Occupying Powers, in order to 'exercise powers of government temporarily' in Iraq – promulgated its first Regulation.[78] Within a brief stretch of time, there followed a prodigious amount of other Regulations, Orders and implementing acts, legal memoranda and public notices, introducing sweeping legal reforms in Iraq.[79]

39. It is true that Resolution 1483 gave the Occupying Powers some leeway by allowing them to work towards 'the creation of conditions in which the Iraqi people can freely determine their own political future'.[80] Many scholars assume that, in using this formulation, the Security Council (drawing upon the powers vested in it by the UN Charter; see *infra* 836) modified the general law of belligerent occupation in the special case of Iraq.[81] As we shall see (*ibid.*), there are those contesting the entitlement of the Council to derogate from substantive provisions of occupation law. This view appears to the present author (and others) to be irreconcilable with the UN Charter. Be this as it

73 Security Council Resolution 1472, 42 *ILM* 767, *id.* (2003) (Preamble).

74 [2003] *Digest of United States Practice in International Law* 980 (S.J. Cummins and D.J. Stewart eds.).

75 Security Council Resolution 1483, *supra* note 7, at 1017 (Preamble).

76 See D. Thürer and M. MacLaren, 'Ius Post Bellum in Iraq: A Challenge to the Applicability and Relevance of International Humanitarian Law?', *Weltinnenrecht: Festschrift für Jost Delbrück* 753, 760–1 (K. Dickel *et al.* eds., 2005).

77 See K. Dörmann and L. Colassis, 'International Humanitarian Law in the Iraq Conflict', 47 *GYIL* 293, 304 (2004).

78 Coalition Provisional Authority Regulation Number 1, II *The Occupation of Iraq: The Official Documents of the Coalition Provisional Authority and the Iraqi Government Council* 3 (S. Talmon ed., 2013).

79 See *ibid.*, 4–759.

80 Security Council Resolution 1483, *supra* note 7, at 1017 (para. 4).

81 See R. Wolfrum, 'Iraq – From Belligerent Occupation to Iraqi Exercise of Sovereignty: Foreign Power versus International Community Interference', 9 *MPYUNL* 1, 16–17 (2005).

may, a careful reading of Resolution 1483 does not suggest that the Coalition Provisional Authority was free of any restrictions.[82]

40. The Coalition Provisional Authority pursued an omnibus legislative agenda, basing its Orders both on 'relevant U.N. Security Council resolutions' and on 'the laws and usages of war'.[83] The general perspective was palpably 'transformative' in nature – consonant with long-term objectives for a reconstructed Iraq – and the legislation did not always comport with the ordinary norms of belligerent occupation.[84] In fact, the Coalition Provisional Authority embarked on 'a series of invasive legislative reforms which repealed many of Iraq's corporate and economic laws'.[85] Moreover, it went so far as to establish a 'New Iraqi Army'[86] and lay down an 'Electoral Law' for the post-occupation period[87] (a 'Law of Administration for the State of Iraq for the Transitional Period' pending elections was also set out[88]). No wonder that – given the constraints of belligerent occupation – some of the Authority's enactments were critiqued by commentators as going too far.[89] It has also been asserted that customary international law governing the scope of legislation in occupied territories has been altered by the experience in Iraq.[90] But this is decidedly a minority view.

41. Largely due to a desire to be relieved of any applicable constraints, the Occupying Powers saw to it that the formal occupation in Iraq would last less than fourteen months. In Resolution 1546 – adopted on 8 June 2004 – the Security Council welcomed the end of occupation by 30 June when 'the occupation will end and the Coalition Provisional Authority will cease to exist', so that 'Iraq will reassert its full sovereignty'.[91] In the event, the occupation came to an end on 28 June.[92] Admittedly, the arbitrary cut-off date did not fully

[82] See K.H. Kaikobad, 'Problems of Belligerent Occupation: The Scope of Powers Exercised by the Coalition Provisional Authority in Iraq, April/May 2003-June 2004', 54 *ICLQ* 253, 254–5 (2005).

[83] For instance, Coalition Provisional Authority Order Number 1, II *The Occupation of Iraq: The Official Documents, supra* note 78, at 53, *id.*

[84] See D.J. Scheffer, 'Beyond Occupation Law', 97 *AJIL* 842, 847–53 (2003).

[85] See S. Power, 'The 2003–2004 Occupation of Iraq: Between Social Transformation and Transformative Belligerent Occupation', 19 *JCSL* 341, 349 (2014).

[86] Coalition Provisional Authority Order Number 22, II *The Occupation of Iraq: The Official Documents, supra* note 78, at 147, 149.

[87] Coalition Provisional Authority Order Number 96, *ibid.*, 650.

[88] Coalition Provisional Authority Document 511, *ibid.*, 1249.

[89] See G.H. Fox, 'The Occupation of Iraq', 36 *GJIL* 195, 240–5 (2004–5).

[90] See N.F. Lancaster, 'Occupation Law, Sovereignty, and Political Transformation: Should the Hague Regulations and the Fourth Geneva Convention Still Be Considered Customary International Law?', 189 *Mil.LR* 51, 90 (2006).

[91] Security Council Resolution 1546, 43 *ILM* 1459, 1460 (2004) (para. 2).

[92] Letter Concerning the End of Occupation (28 June 2004), II *The Occupation of Iraq: The Official Documents, supra* note 78, at 1111.

match the actual situation on the ground: for more on the end of the occupation in Iraq, see *infra* 834.

42. In many respects, the case of Iraq was *sui generis*. The Ba'athist Government was utterly defeated, the entire territory of Iraq was occupied and no standing army remained in the field. Thus, the belligerent occupation regime that emerged extended over the whole country rather than a fraction of it. Indeed, an argument has been made that '[t]he conflict in Iraq fulfilled the factual requirements of *debellatio*'[93] (see *supra* 4). But this was not the case, inasmuch as the continued existence of the State of Iraq – albeit thoroughly reconstructed – was taken for granted by the victorious coalition and by the international community as a whole.[94]

VI. The Case of Israel

43. If the formal occupation of Iraq was relatively short (less than fourteen months), the occupation of Arab territories by Israel – which started in 1967 and is still lasting (in part) after more than fifty years – is almost without parallel (see *infra* 357). The importance of the Israeli occupation, although related to its length, goes far beyond the marking of time. Never before has an occupation raised so many legal issues, drawing such intense international attention, or provided so much domestic jurisprudence as raw material for the law of belligerent occupation.

44. It all began in six days of hostilities in June 1967 during which the IDF (Israel Defence Force) captured (i) the Sinai Peninsula and the Gaza Strip from Egypt; (ii) the West Bank (including East Jerusalem) from Jordan; and (iii) the Golan Heights from Syria. The occupation of the Sinai Peninsula has been terminated (in stages) after two and a half decades. But elsewhere the occupation has persevered, although its form has undergone several incarnations over the decades (as will be shown).

45. The State of Israel was born in 1948, upon the demise of the British Mandate over Palestine. Independence was achieved in the throes of a multipartite war fought against invading armed forces of Egypt, Trans-Jordan, Syria, Lebanon and Iraq.[95] The War of Independence ended with Armistice

[93] M. Patterson, 'Who's Got Title? Or, the Remnants of Debellatio in Post-Invasion Iraq', 47 *Har. ILJ* 467, 480 (2006).

[94] It has also been suggested that a modern form of *debellatio* has evolved, based on 'a temporary abolition of any form of effective government of the defeated State', while the State's continuity as a subject of international law continues (W. Heintschel von Heinegg, 'Factors in War to Peace Transitions', 27 *HJLPP* 843, 851 (2004)). But the suggestion is not in line with the *lex lata*.

[95] On the British Mandate and the transition to the War of Independence, see Y. Dinstein, 'The Arab-Israeli Conflict from the Perspective of International Law', 43 *UNBLJ* 301, 303–9 (1994).

Agreements, signed in 1949 with four of the five adversaries[96] (all but Iraq). The former Mandated territory was partitioned three ways: (i) Israel (including West Jerusalem); (ii) the West Bank of the Jordan River (including East Jerusalem) occupied by Trans-Jordan; and (iii) the Gaza Strip occupied by Egypt. The Armistice Demarcation Lines between Israel, the West Bank and the Gaza Strip came to be known popularly as the 'Green Line'. In its Advisory Opinion on the *Wall*, the International Court of Justice took the Green Line for granted as the border between Israel and the West Bank[97] (although, curiously enough, it never mentioned the Jordanian rule in the West Bank prior to 1967[98]).

A. *The Sinai Peninsula and the Gaza Strip*

46. Albeit occupied together by Israel from Egypt in June 1967 (*supra* 44), the Sinai Peninsula and the Gaza Strip were two distinct territorial units. Sinai was an inseparable part of Egypt, but the Gaza Strip (as just noted) had been part of the British Mandate over Palestine and was occupied by Egypt in 1948. Egypt never annexed the Gaza Strip and it treated the area as a disconnected enclave subject to its military control.[99] The international frontier between the Gaza Strip and Egypt was maintained (with its import tariffs barrier) intact.[100] There was no freedom of movement between Egypt and Gaza, and Egyptian nationality was not offered to the local Palestinian population.

47. In 1979, Egypt and Israel concluded a Treaty of Peace, whereby Israel undertook to withdraw from the Sinai Peninsula over a period of three years.[101] The withdrawal, including the razing of Israeli settlements and military facilities in Sinai, was completed (as undertaken) in 1982. However, there were points of friction regarding the precise demarcation of certain portions of the international frontier, principally in the Taba area. The dissension led to an Arbitration Compromis in 1987,[102] and an Arbitral Award was rendered in 1988.[103] In March 1989, Israel withdrew behind the recognized international

[96] Israel-Egypt, General Armistice Agreement, 1949, 42 *UNTS* 251; Israel-Lebanon, General Armistice Agreement, 1949, *ibid.*, 287; Israel-Jordan, General Armistice Agreement, 1949, *ibid.*, 303; Israel-Syria, General Armistice Agreement, 1949, *ibid.*, 327.

[97] Advisory Opinion on *Legal Consequences of the Construction of a Wall in the Occupied Palestinian Territory*, *supra* note 25, at 166–7.

[98] This omission was noted by Judge P.H. Koojimnas in his Separate Opinion, *ibid.*, 221–2.

[99] See C. Farhi, 'On the Legal Status of the Gaza Strip', I *Military Government in the Territories Administered by Israel 1967–1980: The Legal Aspects* 61, 74–80 (M. Shamgar ed., 1982).

[100] See *ibid.*, 76.

[101] Israel-Egypt, Treaty of Peace, 1979, 18 *ILM* 362, 363 (1979) (Article I).

[102] Israel-Egypt, Arbitration Compromis, 1987, 26 *ILM* 2 (1987).

[103] *Case Concerning the Location of Boundary Markers in Taba between Egypt and Israel*, 1988, 20 *RIAA* 3.

boundary on the basis of additional agreements relating to the implementation of the Award.[104]

48. In stark contrast to the Sinai Peninsula, Israel was not obligated in the 1979 Treaty of Peace with Egypt to withdraw from the Gaza Strip. The Treaty prescribed that '[t]he permanent boundary between Egypt and Israel is the recognized international boundary between Egypt and the former mandated territory of Palestine ... without prejudice to the issue of the status of the Gaza Strip'.[105] Earlier, the 1978 Camp David Framework Agreements for Peace in the Middle East – laying the ground for the Treaty of Peace – stipulated a transition period (of five years) of self-governing autonomy in the West Bank and the Gaza Strip, accompanied by composite negotiations 'on the resolution of the Palestinian problem in all its aspects'.[106] Whereas the Camp David timeframe proved utterly illusory, and the occupation of the Gaza Strip went on as before, the Framework Agreements themselves must be regarded as a landmark. Not only did they pave the road to peace between Israel and Egypt, but they were instrumental in leading to an assumption by the Palestinians of ultimate responsibility for peace negotiations with Israel.

49. As an off-shoot of the 'Oslo Accords' (see *infra* 54), Israel pulled out its military forces consensually from much of the Gaza Strip. In September 2005, Israel withdrew unilaterally (that is, not acting in conformity with any agreement) from the remainder, dismantling all settlements and military installations. Israel has claimed that its belligerent occupation in the Gaza Strip thereby came to a close. But, as we shall see (*infra* 846 *et seq.*), the withdrawal – while impinging upon manifold practical aspects of the administration of the area – did not put paid to the overall occupation.

50. Notwithstanding Israel's unilateral withdrawal from the Gaza Strip, military clashes between the Gaza Strip and Israel have gone on. In most instances, this resulted from recurrent firing from Gaza into Israel of missiles, rockets, mortar shells and other explosive projectiles or incendiary devices. The use of such cross-border flying objects began even before the turbulent takeover of Gaza by Hamas in June 2007, but it escalated thereafter. Ordinarily, Israel responded by aerial targeting of selected military objectives in Gaza. Yet, on three occasions – in 2008/9, 2012 and 2014 – there were significant combined operations (on land, by sea and from the air), set in motion by Israel against Hamas on a large scale. These went on for weeks at a time, entailing severe loss of life and vast destruction of property. Many casualties were also caused in 2018 when Hamas tried to organize massive breaches of the fence surrounding

[104] Israel-Egypt, Agreements on Taba, 1989, 23 *Is.LR* 111, *id.* (1989).

[105] Israel-Egypt, Treaty of Peace, *supra* note 101, at 363 (Article II).

[106] Israel-Egypt, Camp David Agreements: A Framework for Peace in the Middle East, 1978, 17 *ILM* 1466, 1467–8 (1978).

the Gaza Strip. Regardless of exchanges of fire, the Gaza Strip (which has been declared by Israel in September 2007 as a 'hostile territory') is subjected by the IDF to a regime of relative 'closure' imposing strict regulation on ingress and egress of persons and goods. For more details, see *infra* 851 *et seq.*

B. The West Bank

51. When occupied by Israel in 1967, the West Bank (Judea and Samaria for Israelis) was part of the Kingdom of Jordan. Trans-Jordan (as the Kingdom was originally called) had occupied the West Bank in 1948, at the same time as the Egyptian occupation of the Gaza Strip. The West Bank consists of the area lying east of the Green Line, agreed upon between Israel and Jordan in the Armistice Agreement of 1949 (see *supra* 45). The fusion of the East and the West Banks of the Jordan River into a single State – renamed the Hashemite Kingdom of Jordan – was accomplished in April 1950, directly after elections serving as a referendum on the subject.[107] The Palestinians living in the Kingdom became Jordanian citizens. However, in 1988, in a formal Address to the Nation, King Hussein announced Jordan's decision to sever the legal and administrative bonds between the two Banks of the River, recognizing the Palestinians' aspiration to secede from Jordan and to create an independent State in the exercise of their right to self-determination (see *infra* 170).[108]

52. In 1994, Israel and Jordan concluded a Treaty of Peace, whereby the international boundary between the two countries was drawn along the Jordan River – i.e. splitting the two Banks of the River – although the frontier delimitation was done 'without prejudice to the status of any territories that came under Israeli military government control in 1967'.[109] This oblique reference to the West Bank was intended to give Israel and the Palestinians a free hand to press ahead with bilateral negotiations concerning the final status of the area,[110] in the spirit of the 'Oslo Accords' (*infra* 54) that preceded the Israeli-Jordanian Treaty of Peace.

C. The 'Oslo Process' Accords

53. As early as 1988, encouraged by Jordan's acceptance of their right to self-determination – and in response to the first *intifada* (uprising) in the

107 II *Digest of International Law* 1165–6 (M.M. Whiteman ed., 1963).

108 Jordan, Statement Concerning Disengagement from the West Bank and Palestinian Self-Determination, 1988, 27 *ILM* 1637, 1640–2 (1988).

109 Israel–Jordan, Treaty of Peace, 1994, 34 *ILM* 43, 47, 54 (1995) (Article 3(1)–(2); Annex I(a), Article 1).

110 See Y.Z. Blum, 'From Camp David to Oslo', 28 *Is.LR* 211, 216, 223 (1994).

occupied territories (which erupted in 1987 and petered out by 1992) – the Palestinian leadership, then based in Tunis, declared the creation of the State of Palestine.[111] The declaration was surrealistic, floating purely on wishful thinking.[112] Its futility is implicit in the so-called 'Oslo Process', which is supposed to lead to the establishment of a State of Palestine only in the indefinite future.

54. In 1993, after negotiations embarked upon by Israel and the Palestinians in Oslo, a Declaration of Principles on Self-Government Arrangements was signed in Washington.[113] Further negotiations produced a whole tier of accords between Israel and the Palestine Liberation Organization (PLO) in the 1990s (as part of the 'Oslo Process'), the main ones signed in Cairo (1994),[114] Erez (1994),[115] Washington (1995),[116] Jerusalem (1997),[117] Wye River (1998),[118] and Sharm el-Sheikh (1999).[119]

55. It was agreed by Israel and the PLO that the West Bank and the Gaza Strip would be divided into three areas (designated alphabetically as A, B and C), with different degrees of responsibility and power entrusted to a Palestinian Council and Authority (maximal in A, minimal in C).[120] Israel 'redeployed'[121] its military forces, removing them first from most of the Gaza Strip as well as Jericho, then gradually from other towns and densely populated areas in the West Bank. As a result of the 'Oslo Accords', the Palestinians attained a large

111 Palestine National Council, Political Communique and Declaration of Independence, 1988, 27 *ILM* 1660, 1670 (1988).

112 On the legal status of Palestine, see J. Crawford, *The Creation of States in International Law* 434–48 (2nd edn, 2006).

113 Israel-Palestine Liberation Organization, Declaration of Principles on Interim Self-Government Arrangements, 1993, 32 *ILM* 1525 (1993).

114 Israel-Palestine Liberation Organization, Agreement on the Gaza Strip and the Jericho Area, 1994, 33 *ILM* 622 (1994).

115 Israel-Palestine Liberation Organization, Agreement on Preparatory Powers and Responsibilities, 1994, 34 *ILM* 455 (1995).

116 Israel-Palestine Liberation Organization, Interim Agreement on the West Bank and the Gaza Strip, 1995, 36 *ILM* 551 (1997).

117 Israel-Palestine Liberation Organization, Protocol Concerning the Redeployment in Hebron, 1997, 36 *ILM* 650 (1997).

118 Israel-Palestine Liberation Organization, Wye River Memorandum, 1998, 37 *ILM* 1251 (1998).

119 Sharm el-Sheikh Memorandum on Implementation Timeline of Outstanding Commitments of Agreements Signed and the Resumption of Permanent Status Negotiations, 1999, 38 *ILM* 1465 (1999).

120 For an explanation of the agreed formula, see J. Singer, 'The Oslo Peace Process – A View from Within', *New Political Entities in Public and Private International Law with Special Reference to the Palestinian Entity* 17, 63–4 (A. Shapira and M. Tabory eds., 1999). For a brief summary, see Tables 1–3 in D. Reisner, 'Unraveling the Knot: Negotiating Civil Autonomy amidst Security and Political Uncertainty', *ibid.*, 71, 111–13.

121 On this phrase, see K. Calvo Goller, 'Legal Analysis of the Security Arrangements between Israel and the PLO', 28 *Is.LR* 236, 251 (1994).

measure of autonomy, although they remained subject to overall Israeli belligerent occupation.[122]

56. The net result of the 'Oslo Accords' – and of the stand-aside posture first of Egypt (*supra* 48) and then of Jordan (*supra* 52) – is that the Palestinian Authority can be considered, de facto if not exactly *de jure*, as having assumed (by some form of subrogation) the rights of these two countries respectively over the West Bank and the Gaza Strip. What this means is that any final status agreement arrived at (at some indeterminate future point) between Israel and the Palestinian Authority will be accepted by the international community as the equivalent of a treaty of peace terminating the armed conflict.

57. The trouble is that all attempts to bring about such a final status agreement have, so far, failed again and again. Consequent upon one crucial round of unsuccessful negotiations, in Camp David in 2000, a second *intifada* shattered any semblance of a rapport between Israel and the Palestinian Authority. The second *intifada* (which had subsided by 2005) was principally characterized by a wave of 'suicide bombers' launched into Israel, killing civilians indiscriminately. This served as a catalyst to fierce fighting and a temporary reoccupation by the IDF of all the densely populated areas of the West Bank (and the Gaza Strip), accompanied by a reassertion of Israeli military authority. Israel does not deny that it is still the Occupying Power in the West Bank (although it takes a different position as regards the Gaza Strip since the unilateral withdrawal of 2005; see *supra* 49).

58. The peace process between Israel and the Palestinians, caught in the slipstream of the second *intifada*, has not fully recovered thereafter. Direct negotiations have broken down for lengthy periods of time, and – despite several efforts made to overcome the impasse (for instance, in Annapolis, in 2007) – there has been little progress. Israel has committed itself in principle to the ultimate creation of a Palestinian State, but this is contingent on a number of conditions such as the latter's demilitarization. The basic understanding in the negotiations has been that there will be some exchange of territories between Israel and the future Palestinian State, in order to enable the main blocs of settlements in the West Bank to be retained by Israel. Yet, there has been no harmonization of views on specifics, and quite a few central issues (such as the future of Jerusalem; see *infra* 63–4) have not yet been seriously addressed. The US Government, which has played a dominant role in all previous stages of the peace process, tried more than once to jump-start its stalling engine. But at the time of writing these efforts have not yet come to fruition.

[122] See E. Benvenisti, 'The Status of the Palestinian Authority', *The Arab-Israeli Accords: Legal Perspectives* 47, 58–60 (E. Cotran and C. Mallat eds., 1996).

59. In view of the failure of the 'Oslo Accords' to bring about actual peace between Israel and the Palestinians, it has been argued occasionally that their continued validity is 'very much in doubt'.[123] But, despite the fact that numerous agreed-upon stipulations have been disregarded and even materially breached, neither the Parties to the 'Oslo Accords' nor the international community are willing to consider them defunct.

D. *East Jerusalem*

60. Under Jordanian reign, East Jerusalem was part of the West Bank. Shortly after the Israeli occupation in 1967, the Knesset enacted a Law amending a 1948 Ordinance, whereby the 'law, jurisdiction and administration' of the State will be extended to any area of Palestine designated by an Order issued by the Government.[124] For its part, the Government then passed an Order making such a designation regarding East Jerusalem.[125] The phrase 'law, jurisdiction and administration' per se need not be construed as an outright annexation. Indeed, in the context of Jerusalem – a single city, divided by Israel's War of Independence in 1948 and reintegrated as an outcome of the Israeli victory in 1967 – an 'administrative union of East and West Jerusalem' made pragmatic sense.[126] But this was not the end of the road.

61. In 1979, the Knesset enacted 'Basic Law: Jerusalem, Capital of Israel', which (eschewing the term annexation) expressly proclaims that 'Jerusalem, complete and united, is the capital of Israel'.[127] Given that the entire city – 'complete and united' – is declared to be the capital of Israel, there cannot be a shred of doubt that the Knesset considered East Jerusalem annexed. Subsequent Knesset legislation entrenched the Jerusalem Basic Law, requiring approval by a special majority (and even a referendum) if any transfer of jurisdiction is contemplated in the future.[128]

62. The view that East Jerusalem was annexed has been upheld by the Supreme Court of Israel, both before[129] and after[130] the adoption of the Basic Law. In the *Rabah* case, the Court openly asserted (per Justice

[123] Y. Shany, 'Faraway, So Close: The Legal Status of Gaza after Israel's Disengagement', 8 *YIHL* 369, 381 (2005).

[124] Law and Administration Ordinance (Amendment No. 11), 1967, 21 *LSI* 75, *id.* (1966–7).

[125] [1966–7] *KH* 2690.

[126] N. Feinberg, *Studies in International Law with Special Reference to the Arab-Israeli Conflict* 511–12 (1979).

[127] Basic Law: Jerusalem, Capital of Israel, 34 *LSI* 209 (1979–80) (Section 1).

[128] See R. Lapidoth, 'Jerusalem', VI *MPEPIL* 452, 456.

[129] HCJ 283/69, *Ravidi* et al. *v. The Military Court, Hebron Zone* et al., 24(2) *PD* 419, 422–4 (per Justice Kahan).

[130] HCJ 282/88, *M. Awad v. Prime Minister* et al., 42(2) *PD* 424, 429 (per Justice Barak).

T. Strasberg-Cohen) that – even if the Knesset enactment on the subject is incompatible with international law (notwithstanding a presumption of correspondence between the two legal systems; see *infra* 88) – the Court must abide by domestic legislation.[131]

63. From the standpoint of international law, the purported unilateral annexation of East Jerusalem (like any other part of an occupied territory; see *infra* 164) is bereft of any legal effect. The Security Council, on a number of occasions – starting with Resolution 252 (1968) – made no bones about it: 'all legislative and administrative measures and actions taken by Israel ... which tend to change the legal status of Jerusalem are invalid and cannot change that status'.[132] In Resolution 478 (1980), the Council censured 'in the strongest terms' the enactment of the Basic Law, and determined that any measures seeking to alter the status of Jerusalem are 'null and void'.[133] See also the text of Resolution 2334 (2016) quoted *infra* 736, 742. The International Court of Justice, in its Advisory Opinion on the *Wall* – after citing Security Council Resolution 478 and previous resolutions – gave a ringing affirmation to the proposition that the measures taken (and it specifically referred to the Basic Law on Jerusalem) have not converted Israel's status as an Occupying Power.[134]

64. The final status of East Jerusalem is a major hurdle that has yet to be surmounted in future political negotiations between Israel and the Palestinians. But it is necessary to distinguish between East and West Jerusalem. In 2018, US President D. Trump officially recognized Jerusalem as the capital of Israel while taking no position on boundaries or borders.[135]

E. The Golan Heights

65. In June 1967, Israel also occupied from Syria the Golan Heights (see *supra* 44). More than fifty years later, there is still no treaty of peace between Israel and Syria. Peace negotiations commenced but were not crowned with success. Following the outbreak of widespread insurgency in Syria in 2011, the prospect of the termination of the state of war only receded. As long as the state

131 HCJ 256/01, *Rabah* et al. *v. Jerusalem Court for Local Matters* et al., 56(2) *PD* 930, 934–5. (The Judgment is excerpted in English in 32 *IYHR* 356 (2002)).

132 Security Council Resolution 252 (1968), *Resolutions and Statements of the United Nations Security Council, supra* note 60, at 671, *id.*

133 Security Council Resolution 478 (1980), *Resolutions and Statements of the United Nations Security Council, supra* note 60, at 725, *id.*

134 Advisory Opinion on *Legal Consequences of the Construction of a Wall in the Occupied Palestinian Territory, supra* note 25, at 167.

135 See K. Daugirdas and J.D. Mortenson, 'Contemporary Practice of the United States Relating to International Law', 112 *AJIL* 295, 306 (2018).

of war between Israel and Syria is not ended, the Golan Heights remain under Israeli belligerent occupation.

66. Since few Syrian inhabitants remained in 1967 in the Golan Heights, Israel applied there its 'law, jurisdiction and administration' (a reiteration of the phrase first gaining fame with respect to East Jerusalem). In 1981, this formula was affirmed by the Knesset in the Golan Heights Law.[136] Although the Law does not employ the word annexation, there are those who consider the Heights annexed in consequence of it.[137] Others (including the present writer) disagree with that approach.[138] But, even if the annexationist interpretation of the Israeli domestic legislation is correct, this would have no impact on the status of the Golan Heights from the standpoint of international law.[139] In Resolution 497 (1981), the Security Council determined that 'the Israeli decision to impose its laws, jurisdiction and administration in the occupied Syrian Golan heights is null and void and without international legal effect'.[140]

F. The General Applicability of Geneva Convention (IV)

67. Israel was the first country in the world – since 1949 – called upon by the international community to implement the provisions of Geneva Convention (IV) in respect of occupied territories. Israel ratified all four Geneva Conventions as early as 1951, and is fully bound by them. Nevertheless, at the commencement of the occupation in 1967, Israel remonstrated with the international community that the legal status of the West Bank and the Gaza Strip, as parts of the former British Mandate over Palestine, was *sui generis* – bearing in mind that both Jordan and Egypt had themselves been only Occupying Powers there between 1948 and 1967 – and Geneva Convention (IV) was not *de jure* applicable.[141]

68. Article 2 (first and second paragraphs) of the Convention promulgates:

> In addition to the provisions which shall be implemented in peacetime, the present Convention shall apply to all cases of declared war or of any other armed conflict which

[136] Golan Heights Law, 1981, 36 *LSI* 7 (1981–2).

[137] See A. Maoz, 'Application of Israeli Law to the Golan Heights Is Annexation', 20 *Brook.JIL* 355, 368–83 (1994).

[138] See L. Sheleff, 'Application of Israeli Law to the Golan Heights Is Not Annexation', 20 *Brook. JIL* 333, 335–50 (1994).

[139] See V. Coussirat-Coustere, 'Israël et le Golan: Problèmes Juridiques Résultant de la Loi du 14 Décembre 1981', 28 *AFDI* 185, 188–93 (1982).

[140] Security Council Resolution 497 (1981), *Resolutions and Statements of the United Nations Security Council, supra* note 60, at 726, *id.*

[141] See M. Shamgar, 'The Observance of International Law in the Administered Territories', 1 *IYHR* 262, 263–5 (1971).

may arise between two or more of the High Contracting Parties, even if the state of war is not recognized by one of them.

The Convention shall also apply to all cases of partial or total occupation of the territory of a High Contracting Party, even if the said occupation meets with no armed resistance.[142]

The kernel of the Israeli contention was that the West Bank and the Gaza Strip did not come within the compass of the phrase 'territory of a High Contracting Party' appearing in the second paragraph.[143]

69. The Israeli argument along these lines was manifestly sterile, inasmuch as the second paragraph of Article 2 (hinging on the words 'shall also apply') comes on the heels of the opening paragraph. The general rule is stated in the first paragraph (which does not include the words 'territory of a High Contracting Party'), and the second paragraph (which does) relates only to the exceptional scenario of an occupation that meets with no armed resistance.[144] The historical genesis of the second paragraph can be traced back to the occupation of Denmark by Nazi Germany in 1940, when Denmark put up virtually no resistance to the occupation owing to the preponderant superiority of the Germans (see *infra* 96).[145] As the ICRC Commentary emphasizes, the second paragraph does not refer to cases in which an occupation meets with armed resistance, because in such circumstances 'the Convention will have been in force since the outbreak of hostilities or since the time war was declared' (as per the first paragraph).[146]

70. Even the leading exponent of the Israeli position – the IDF Military Advocate General in 1967, M. Shamgar (who later became successively Attorney-General, Supreme Court Justice and President of the Court) – could not deny the logic of attributing to the second paragraph of Article 2 what he called a complementary meaning, viz., one that is reconcilable with the applicability of the first paragraph 'to every armed conflict and all its resulting military developments including occupation'; although personally Shamgar was inclined to the view that a disjunctive interpretation of Article 2 was more plausible.[147]

[142] Geneva Convention (IV), *supra* note 29, at 580.

[143] See M. Shamgar, 'Legal Concepts and Problems of the Israeli Military Government – The Initial Stage', I *Military Government in the Territories Administered by Israel 1967–1980*, *supra* note 99, at 13, 39.

[144] The same formula is reiterated in Article 18(2) of the Hague Convention for the Protection of Cultural Property in the Event of Armed Conflict, 1954, *The Laws of Armed Conflicts*, *supra* note 29, at 999, 1007.

[145] See D. Schindler, 'The Different Types of Armed Conflicts according to the Geneva Conventions and Protocols', 163 *RCADI* 117, 132 (1979).

[146] *Commentary, IV Geneva Convention*, *supra* note 31, at 21.

[147] Shamgar, *supra* note 143, at 38–40.

71. The disjunctive interpretation of Article 2 has gained some rare support from commentators,[148] but has usually been rejected.[149] In any event, it was repudiated unreservedly by the International Court of Justice in its Advisory Opinion on the *Wall*:

> The object of the second paragraph of Article 2 is not to restrict the scope of application of the Convention, as defined by the first paragraph, by excluding therefrom territories not falling under the sovereignty of one of the contracting parties. It is directed simply to making it clear that, even if occupation effected during the conflict met with no armed resistance, the Convention is still applicable.[150]

72. Beside the fact that the disjunctive interpretation of Article 2 is distorted, one cannot ignore the thrust of Article 4 (first paragraph) of the Convention:

> Persons protected by the Convention are those who, at a given moment and in any manner whatsoever, find themselves, in case of a conflict or occupation, in the hands of a Party to the conflict or Occupying Power of which they are not nationals.[151]

The ICRC Commentary explains that the pivotal expression 'in the hands of' (an Occupying Power) 'is used in an extremely general sense': a protected person need not be physically in the hands of the Occupying Power – as a prisoner or a detainee – and the mere fact of being present in an occupied territory connotes that he is 'in the hands of' the Occupying Power.[152] This expansive construction of the phrase 'in the hands of' was quoted with approval by a Trial Chamber of the ICTY, in the *Tadić* Judgment of 1997, which went on to say that 'those persons who found themselves in territory effectively occupied by a party to the conflict can be considered to have been in the hands of the party'.[153] When Article 4 (first paragraph) is read carefully, there is no escape from the conclusion arrived at by T. Meron:

> It must be remembered that, as a humanitarian convention *par excellence*, the Fourth Geneva Convention is concerned primarily with people, rather than territory; with human rights, rather than with legal questions pertaining to territorial status.[154]

[148] See D.J. Ball, 'Toss the *Travaux*? Application of the Fourth Geneva Convention to the Middle East Conflict – A Modern (Re)assessment', 79 *NYULR* 990, 1024–8 (2004).

[149] See, e.g., Y. Arai-Takahashi, *The Law of Occupation: Continuity and Change of International Humanitarian Law, and Its Interaction with International Human Rights Law* 50–1 (2009).

[150] Advisory Opinion on *Legal Consequences of the Construction of a Wall in the Occupied Palestinian Territory*, *supra* note 25, at 175.

[151] Geneva Convention (IV), *supra* note 29, at 581.

[152] *Commentary, IV Geneva Convention, supra* note 31, at 47.

[153] *Prosecutor v. Tadić* (ICTY, Trial Chamber, 1997), 36 *ILM* 908, 924 (1997). There was a Dissenting Opinion here, but not on the point in question.

[154] T. Meron, 'West Bank and Gaza: Human Rights and Humanitarian Law in the Period of Transition', 9 *IYHR* 106, 109 (1979).

73. Article 4 of Additional Protocol I (quoted *infra* 164) – to which Israel, admittedly, is not a Party – underscores that the application of the Geneva Conventions and the Protocol itself does not affect the legal status of a territory under occupation. The Eritrea Ethiopia Claims Commission held, in 2004, that the language of the Convention and the Protocol does not sustain the idea that 'only territory the title to which is clear and uncontested can be occupied territory'.[155]

74. The Israeli line of reasoning regarding the applicability of the Convention was never germane to territories occupied outside the boundaries of Mandated Palestine, viz., the Sinai Peninsula and the Golan Heights.[156] But, even as regards the West Bank and the Gaza Strip, it is noteworthy that – despite its formally articulated stance – Israel disclosed its ambivalence by retaining there, in principle, the local law in force on the eve of the occupation (consonant with the law of belligerent occupation; see *infra* 330). Despite considerable political pressures brought to bear internally, no Government of Israel has ever sought to annex either the West Bank (with the exception of East Jerusalem) or the Gaza Strip.

75. For its part, the Israel Supreme Court has consistently diagnosed the status of the West Bank and the Gaza Strip (until the unilateral withdrawal of 2005; see *supra* 49) as territories subject to the application of the law of belligerent occupation. This is what the Court (per Justice[157] Barak) said about the West Bank in the *Jamait Askan* case:

> In the Six-Day War, 'East' Jerusalem, Judea and Samaria were occupied by the Israel Defence Force. In 'East' Jerusalem, 'the law, jurisdiction and administration of the State' were applied ... The approach concerning Judea and Samaria was different. The law, jurisdiction and administration of Israel were not applied in Judea and Samaria ... Judea and Samaria are held by Israel by way of military occupation or 'belligerent occupation'. In the area, a military government was established, headed by a military commander. The powers and authority of the military commander are nourished by the rules of public international law concerning belligerent occupation.[158]

The attitude of the Court was similar with respect to the Gaza Strip (until the 2005 withdrawal).[159]

[155] Eritrea Ethiopia Claims Commission, Partial Award (Central Front), Ethiopia's Claim 2, *supra* note 65, at 1282.

[156] See S.M. Boyd, 'The Applicability of International Law to the Occupied Territories', 1 *IYHR* 258, 260 (1971).

[157] Here and elsewhere in this volume, references to members of the Supreme Court by title – Justice, Deputy President and President – relate to the time-frame in which a specific Judgment was rendered.

[158] HCJ 393/82, *Jamait Askan* et al. *v. IDF Commander of Judea and Samaria* et al., 37(4) *PD* 785, 792. (The Judgment is excerpted in English in 14 *IYHR* 301 (1984)).

[159] See, especially, HCJ 1661/05 etc., *Gaza Coast Local Council* et al. *v. The Knesset* et al., 59(2) *PD* 481, 558–9. (The Judgment is excerpted in English in 37 *IYHR* 358 (2007)).

76. Since Israel forthrightly applied in the West Bank and Gaza the norms of customary international law governing belligerent occupation (including the Hague Regulations; see *infra* 90), the specific issue narrowed down in practical terms to the applicability of the Geneva Convention. Within a relatively short while after the beginning of the occupation of the West Bank and the Gaza Strip, the Government of Israel – fully cognizant of the frailty of its official policy concerning the Convention (see *supra* 67 *et seq.*) – decided to attenuate it. In 1971, in a Symposium convened at Tel Aviv University, Shamgar, by then the Attorney-General of Israel, officially announced that the Government committed itself (without prejudice to its fundamental legal position on the applicability of the Convention) 'to act *de facto* in accordance with the humanitarian provisions of the Convention'.[160] This policy articulation was the provenance of Israeli diplomacy for the next several decades, and it was frequently cited by the Supreme Court (especially when Shamgar became its President).[161]

77. At a cursory glance, the Shamgar announcement appears to be curtailed in its scope. But, in fact, its expanse is conterminous with the entire Convention, since – *ex hypothesi* – every clause in the instrument constitutes an integral part of what is usually called 'international humanitarian law' (see *supra* 8). Thus, Israel undertook to comply de facto with the whole gamut of the Convention, notwithstanding the fact that – in some nebulous and cryptic fashion – it retained its original *de jure* posture. This interpretation of the Government's position has been confirmed by the Supreme Court in the *Alfei Menashe* case (see *infra* 784).

78. It should be added that the fact that the other side to the armed conflict with Israel (in the West Bank and the Gaza Strip) is currently a non-State entity – namely, the Palestinian people (see *supra* 56) – is immaterial. The Convention handles this problem in Article 2 (third paragraph):

> Although one of the Powers in conflict may not be a party to the present Convention, the Powers who are parties thereto shall remain bound by it in their mutual relations. They shall furthermore be bound by the Convention in relation to the said Power, if the latter accepts and applies the provisions thereof.[162]

The International Court of Justice noted, in the Advisory Opinion on the *Wall*, that the Palestinians had given a unilateral undertaking to apply the Convention.[163]

[160] See Shamgar, *supra* note 141, at 266.

[161] See, e.g., HCJ 13/86 etc., *Shaeen* et al. *v. IDF Commander of Judea and Samaria*, 41(1) *PD* 197, 206–7. (The Judgment is excerpted in English in 18 *IYHR* 241 (1988)).

[162] Geneva Convention (IV), *supra* note 29, at 580.

[163] See Advisory Opinion on *Legal Consequences of the Construction of a Wall in the Occupied Palestinian Territory*, *supra* note 25, at 173.

G. *Judicial Review by the Supreme Court Sitting as a High Court of Justice*

79. Inhabitants of the Israeli occupied territories – as well as anyone acting on their behalf – can appear before the Supreme Court in Jerusalem, sitting as a first-instance High Court of Justice, in order to challenge any act of the Government of Israel or one of its organs (although cf. *infra* 83). The assumption of supervisory power by the Court over the military government in the occupied territories (like all governmental authorities at home) rests on Section 15 of the 'Basic Law: Judicature', under which all State and local officials are subject to judicial review by the High Court of Justice in respect of the lawful exercise of their functions.[164] The Court treats all acts of State officials in the occupied territories, including legislative acts, as subject to this provision.

80. In the seminal *Pithat Rafiah* case, there was a minority opinion – verbalized by Justice A. Witkon – to the effect that the Court should not exercise judicial review over the legislative acts of military commanders in the occupied territories, because they are injusticiable.[165] But the majority (Justices M. Landau and I. Kister) leaned in a different direction: the way they saw it, military commanders in the occupied territories are part of the IDF hierarchy and, being State officials, are subject to judicial review.[166] Justice Witkon's dissent 'received no support' in subsequent case law (in fact, it has not noticeably affected his own stand in later decisions), and the majority opinion in the *Pithat Rafiah* case became deeply ingrained as a legal truism.[167] Hence, even though a military commander may be perched at the top of the 'legal pyramid' in the occupied territories (see *infra* 184), he is just another State official when facing the High Court of Justice.[168]

81. The judicial review process is conducted by the Supreme Court within the ambit of both Israeli constitutional-administrative law and norms of international law incorporated into the Israeli legal system. This is a unique trait of the Israeli occupation (having no antecedents in any other instance of belligerent occupation),[169] and it has triggered an avalanche of petitions from the occupied territories to the Court. The imprint left by the Court's supervisory

164 Basic Law: Judicature, 38 *LSI* 101, 104 (1983–4).

165 HCJ 302/72 etc., *Abu Hilu* et al. *v. Government of Israel* et al., 27(2) *PD* 169, 180–2. (The Judgment is excerpted in English in 5 *IYHR* 384 (1975)).

166 *Ibid.*, 176–7, 183–4.

167 D. Kretzmer, *The Occupation of Justice: The Supreme Court of Israel and the Occupied Territories* 28 (2002).

168 A. Pach, 'Human Rights in West Bank Military Courts', 7 *IYHR* 222, 227–8 (1977).

169 See E. Nathan, 'The Power of Supervision of the High Court of Justice over Military Government', I *Military Government in the Territories Administered by Israel 1967–1980*, *supra* note 99, at 109, 110.

power on the acts of the military government has been indelible. The number of cases in which petitioners openly prevailed in court may not be impressive. But the statistical score-pad of in-court wins versus losses is highly misleading. A detailed study of hundreds of cases over a ten-year period (1986–95) reveals that, if one counts out-of-court settlements (often prodded by the Court), the majority of Palestinian petitioners actually obtained at least partial redress by filing a petition.[170] There is scarcely any doubt that a similar behavioural pattern permeates more recent proceedings before the Court. It must also be taken into account that often the mere threat of petitioning the Court has had a chilling effect on the military government, which has then either revoked or revised its original scheme of action.

82. By any standard, the record of the Supreme Court relating to the occupied territories is extraordinary. Apart from the astounding volume of the case law, the Court has generally – albeit not invariably – shown a skilful familiarity with international law (far beyond the average standard of domestic courts in general). For all that, the Court has not always construed the law of belligerent occupation in a manner that can be deemed satisfactory. While a plethora of dicta made by the Court on this topic are above reproach, the Court has championed positions on some critical issues that are indefensible, e.g., with regard to deportations (see *infra* 492–3) or demolition of houses as an administrative sanction (see *infra* 619 *et seq.*).

83. It will not be remiss to highlight some core aspects of the proceedings before the Court. First, being the judicial forum of last resort in Israel, the Court hears criminal, civil and administrative appeals – as well as other motions – where it occasionally adverts to questions of belligerent occupation. In 2018, the Knesset enacted a new law that channelled many petitions from the West Bank to the District Court of Jerusalem (sitting as a Court for Administrative Affairs) with a right of appeal to the Supreme Court. Whatever the practical impact of this law will be in the years ahead, it is a matter of record that – for more than half a century – the Supreme Court's supervisory jurisdiction as regards the occupied territories was exercised in most cases sitting as a first-instance High Court of Justice. A direct avenue to the High Court of Justice means that there is no possibility of appeal against its ultimate decision. Judicial review has been exercised (over petitions lodged by the inhabitants themselves or by NGOs acting in their interests) in a timely manner, that is to say, (i) in relatively fast response to 'planned or ongoing actions or policies',[171]

[170] See Y. Dotan, 'Judicial Rhetoric, Government Lawyers, and Human Rights: The Case of the Israeli High Court of Justice during the *Intifada*', 33 *LSR* 319, 332–6 (1999).

[171] See D. Kretzmer, 'The Supreme Court of Israel: Judicial Review during Armed Conflict', 47 *GYIL* 392, 394–5 (2004).

and (ii) where some delay was inevitable, interim injunctions – freezing imminent actions – have often been issued almost instantaneously.

84. The second point is that the Supreme Court – which, at the moment of writing, has an establishment of fifteen slots – sits in panels consisting of odd numbers of Justices. The ordinary size of a panel is three Justices, but there are larger benches in important cases or in reviews of earlier decisions. We shall see numerous examples of extraordinary panels, extending from five to eleven Justices.

85. Thirdly, the High Court of Justice does not exercise jurisdiction over the inhabitants of the occupied territories as such. The inhabitants are petitioners who freely opt to turn to the Court for relief against the military government. The only direct subjects of the Court's supervisory jurisdiction are the respondents (who are Israeli State officials, typically the Minister of Defence and IDF commanders).[172]

86. Fourthly, the High Court of Justice does not put itself in the shoes of the respondents and does not try to outguess them. In the *Ajuri* case, a special panel of nine Justices (per President Barak) defined the Court's supervisory role as follows:

> The Supreme Court, sitting as High Court of Justice, exercises judicial review of the legality of the exercise of the discretion of the military commander. The point of departure guiding this Court is that the military commander and his subordinates are public officials who fulfil a public task in accordance with the law. ... In this judicial review, we do not purport to be experts in security matters. We do not supplant the security consideration of the military commander by our security consideration. We do not take any position as to the management of security matters. ... Our task is safeguarding the boundaries and ensuring the conditions limiting the discretion of the military commander.[173]

H. The Domestic Applicability of Geneva Convention (IV)

87. The major premise of Israel's decision to apply de facto Geneva Convention (IV), plus the minor premise of the availability of a unique (and very effective) supervisory mechanism in the Supreme Court sitting as a High Court of Justice, do not lead – as they might seem to do – to an ineluctable syllogistic conclusion that the application of the Convention necessarily falls within the compass of judicial review. The fracture in the logical progression is

[172] See E. Nathan, 'Israeli Civil Jurisdiction in the Administered Territories', 13 *IYHR* 90, 114 n. 72 (1983).

[173] HCJ 7015/02 etc., *Ajuri* et al. *v. IDF Commander of the West Bank* et al., 56(6) *PD* 352, 375. (The Judgment is excerpted in English in 33 *IYHR* 249 (2003)).

due to the fact that Israel follows the UK constitutional model in respect of the reception of international law into the domestic legal system.[174]

88. In conformity with this model, the position in Israel is that customary international law is automatically received into the domestic law, as long as there is no head-on collision between the customary norms and statutes enacted by the Knesset; although there is a presumption of correspondence between domestic statutes and international customary norms.

89. Conversely, as far as treaties in force are concerned – without detracting from their legal effect on the international plane – they cannot be relied upon in proceedings before Israeli courts unless there exists explicit legislation incorporating them into the domestic law; always recalling that declaratory treaty provisions (reflecting customary international law) are automatically part of the law of the land *qua* custom.[175] An attempt to impugn these general norms was unswervingly and unanimously rejected by a special panel of five Justices of the Supreme Court in the *Afu* case; the panel was divided on another issue (see *infra* 493), but not on this.[176]

90. No legislation has been enacted by the Knesset incorporating the Geneva Conventions into Israeli domestic law. The Supreme Court held early on, by a special panel of five Justices in the *Beth El* case, that, in substance, Convention (IV) is constitutive in nature and – in the absence of legislation receiving it into the law of the land – it could not be invoked by petitioners.[177] By contrast, in the same case (after previous reluctance to do so), the Supreme Court recognized the declaratory attribute of the Hague Regulations and applied them as an embodiment of customary international law.[178]

91. In some instances, given the construct that the Geneva Convention could not be applied directly by the Court (in the absence of reception through domestic legislation), prominent Judgments revolved exclusively around clauses of the Hague Regulations (as a faithful picture of customary international law). Thus,

174 On the UK model of 'dualism', see A. Aust, *Modern Treaty Law and Practice* 168–72 (3rd edn, 2013).

175 The best authority for these legal propositions in the context of belligerent occupation can be found in the Judgment rendered by the Israel Supreme Court (per Deputy President Shamgar) in the *VAT* case: HCJ 69/81 etc., *Abu Aita* et al. *v. Commander of Judea and Samaria* et al., 37(2) *PD* 197, 233–4. (The Judgment is excerpted in English in 13 *IYHR* 348 (1983)).

176 HCJ 785/87 etc., *Afu* et al. *v. Commander of the IDF Forces in the West Bank* et al., 42(2) *PD* 4, 33–48 (per President Shamgar) 76–7 (per Justice Bach). (The Judgment is excerpted in English in 23 *IYHR* 277 (1993). A full translation is available in 29 *ILM* 140 (1990)).

177 HCJ 606/78 etc., *Ayub* et al. *v. Minister of Defence* et al., 33(2) *PD* 113, 120–2 (per Justice Witkon), 127–8 (per Deputy President Landau). (The Judgment is excerpted in English in 9 *IYHR* 337 (1979). A full translation is available in I *Military Government in the Territories Administered by Israel 1967–1980*, *supra* note 99, at 371).

178 *Ibid.*, 120 (per Justice Witkon). Justice Witkon corrected here an earlier (mistaken) stand, relying on Y. Dinstein, 'The Judgment in the Pithat Rafiha Case', 3 *TAULR* 934, 938–9 (1973–4).

the landmark pair of decisions of the Court on the legality of settlements in the West Bank (rendered by the same panel of five Justices) – the *Beth El* case (ruling in favour of the Occupying Power) and the *Elon Moreh* case (ruling in favour of the petitioners)[179] – were predicated on customary law concerning the requisition of private property, as mirrored in the Hague Regulations (see *infra* 748). This may appear to be an exercise in judicial sophistry when the matter at hand is the legality of settlements, inasmuch as the Hague Regulations are germane only tangentially (grappling with the topic in terms of requisition of property), whereas the heart of the problem is a Geneva prohibition of transfer of people to the occupied territory (see *infra* 734). Still, as the case law shows, the legal tactics of indirect approach – challenging the legality of acts of the military government on the somewhat opaque rationale of property rights, in keeping with the Hague Regulations – actually proved to be quite productive in multiple sets of circumstances.

92. Over the years, as a result of the confluence of two separate trends, the Geneva Convention managed nevertheless to leave a deep indentation on the case law of the Supreme Court:

(a) In a steadily increasing number of petitions brought before the Court, counsel for the respondents (i.e. the Government of Israel and its instrumentalities in the occupied territories), although technically able to turn a cold shoulder to the Convention, expressly gave their consent for the Court to scrutinize official acts *ad hoc* in light of concrete Geneva provisions.[180]

(b) The Court itself progressively developed a tendency to consult and analyse relevant clauses of the Convention – if only by way of lengthy *obiter dicta* – in order to show that, even had the treaty text been directly applicable, the result of the proceedings would have been the same.[181]

93. Governmental *ad hoc* acceptance of the Convention has been proffered so routinely that, in time, the Court has begun to take the consent for granted without necessarily going through the motions of eliciting it in so many

[179] HCJ 390/79, *Dweikat* et al. *v. Government of Israel* et al., 34(1) *PD* 1, 16–17 (per Deputy President Landau). (The Judgment is excerpted in English in 9 *IYHR* 345 (1979). A full translation is available in I *Military Government in the Territories Administered by Israel 1967–1980*, *supra* note 99, at 404).

[180] This consensual trend had started already in HCJ 337/71, *Christian Association for the Holy Places v. Minister of Defence* et al., 26(1) *PD* 574, 580. (The Judgment is excerpted in English in 2 *IYHR* 354 (1972)). For a more recent case, see the *Ajuri* case: HCJ 7015/02, *supra* note 173, at 364.

[181] The best illustration is the *Afu* case: HCJ 785/87 etc., *supra* note 176, at 21–33. Here the majority of the Court (per President Shamgar) chose to undertake a lengthy disquisition into the interpretation of Article 49 of the Convention on the topic of deportations (*infra* 493), despite the fact that it first clearly reiterated the position that the Convention was inapplicable (*ibid.*, 12).

words.[182] Actually, after more than five decades of occupation, the applicability of the Convention is no longer contested by the Government. At the present juncture, the Convention can be regarded not only as fully binding on Israel in the West Bank *de jure* but also (and most significantly) as fully subject to judicial review by the Court de facto.

[182] See, e.g., HCJ 5591/02, *Yassin* et al. *v. Commander of Ketziot Detention Facility* et al., 57(1) *PD* 403, 413 (per President Barak). (The Judgment is excerpted in English in 34 *IYHR* 300 (2004)).

2 The Legal Nature and Basic Principles of Belligerent Occupation

94. The term 'occupation' is used in several branches of international law, and it is therefore necessary to pay heed to the unique features of 'belligerent occupation' (a translation into English of the Latin term *occupatio bellica*). In particular, 'belligerent occupation' differs markedly from 'occupation' as a mode of acquisition of territory by States. The only territory which can be the object of occupation as a mode of acquisition is that 'which does not already belong to any state'.[183] Conversely, belligerent occupation is intrinsically linked to the capture of territory from an enemy State in the course of an international armed conflict.

I. Prerequisite Conditions for Belligerent Occupation

A. *Belligerent Occupation and Inter-State Armed Conflicts*

(a) ***The Linkage of Belligerent Occupation to War***

95. As the appellation 'belligerent occupation' suggests, there is an inextricable tie between this species of occupation and inter-State war (*bellum*). Even prior to the conclusion of Geneva Convention (IV), the logical presupposition was that an inter-State war may lead to belligerent occupation. Remarkably, the Convention shows that the war-occupation sequence can be turned on its head. Article 6 (first paragraph) prescribes that the Convention 'shall apply from the outset of any conflict or occupation mentioned in Article 2'.[184] Article 2 (second paragraph) sets forth that the Convention applies to 'all cases of partial or total occupation of the territory of a High Contracting Party, even if the said occupation meets with no armed resistance' (*supra* 68). The last words imply that belligerent occupation may be carried out without any hostilities either

[183] I Oppenheim's *International Law* 687 (9th edn, R. Jennings and A. Watts eds., 1992).
[184] Geneva Convention (IV), *supra* note 29, at 582.

preceding or following it.[185] Consequently, just as belligerent occupation may be fomented by war, war can be ignited by belligerent occupation.

96. What this amounts to is that belligerent occupation may constitute the sole manifestation of a state of war between State *A* and State *B*. Once a territory belonging to State *A* is coercively seized by State *B*, there is automatically a state of war in the material sense between these two Parties, even if State *A* remains completely passive and offers no resistance to the occupation. The archetypical example is that of the German takeover of Denmark in 1940 (see *supra* 69). An alternative scenario arises if armed forces of State *B* – originally stationed by consent within the territory of State *A* – adamantly remain in their positions, notwithstanding the fact that consent has been withdrawn, wielding power around them without a clash of arms.[186]

(b) Occupation Following Unconditional Surrender

97. Belligerent occupation may not only occur in the absence of hostilities: it may also outlast the cessation of hostilities (see *infra* 863). However, if war ends with an unconditional surrender – and the enemy completely collapses, ceasing to function as a State – occupation of its territory is not reckoned any more as belligerent. The template is the occupation of Germany and Japan following their unconditional surrenders in 1945. By dint of those unconditional surrenders, which brought WWII to a close, Allied occupations of the two principal Axis countries were not seen as belligerent occupations within the purview of the Hague Regulations.[187]

98. As far as Germany was concerned, the position was recapitulated in the Judgment of the American Military Tribunal in the *Justice* trial:

> It is this fact of the complete disintegration of the government in Germany, followed by unconditional surrender and by occupation of the territory, which explains and justifies the assumption and exercise of supreme governmental power by the Allies. The same fact distinguishes the present occupation of Germany from the type of occupation which occurs when, in the course of actual warfare, an invading army enters and occupies the territory of another State, whose government is still in existence and is in receipt of international recognition, and whose armies, with those of its Allies, are still in the field. In the latter case the occupying power is subject to the limitations imposed upon it by the Hague Convention and by the laws and customs of war. In the former case (the occupation of Germany) the Allied Powers were not subject to those limitations.[188]

185 *Commentary, IV Geneva Convention*, *supra* note 31, at 21, 60.

186 See R. Kolb and R. Hyde, *An Introduction to the International Law of Armed Conflicts* 230 (2008).

187 See R.Y. Jennings, 'Government in Commission', 23 *BYBIL* 112, 140 (1946).

188 *Justice* trial, *supra* note 54, at 29.

99. The status of Germany resembled that of *debellatio*[189] (see *supra* 4), although the victorious Allies did not choose to annex the occupied land. Diverse legal explanations have been offered to account for the exceptional policy adopted for occupied Germany.[190] But, whatever legal theory is subscribed to, the facts speak for themselves: the victors introduced in occupied Germany sweeping institutional changes that were incompatible with the law of belligerent occupation as enunciated in the Hague Regulations. The overtly stated goal was to eradicate all vestiges of the Nazi regime, introducing profound and far-reaching reforms affecting the whole spectrum of 'the economic, political, and social set-up of the country'.[191]

100. By the same token, the Allied (in practice, American) occupation of Japan was intended to purge militarism and ultra-nationalism, dissolve ruling cliques and usher in land reform.[192] The radical measures taken – which metamorphosed 'the entire social structure of Japan' – were unabashedly inconsistent with the Hague Regulations.[193]

101. To use a current popular idiom (cf. *supra* 40), the post-surrender occupations of Germany and Japan were 'transformative' in their nature.[194] The precedent value of these occupations – as salient departures from the law of belligerent occupation – may nevertheless be limited, in view of the subsequent adoption of Article 2 of Geneva Convention (IV) (quoted *supra* 68).[195]

(c) Non-International Armed Conflicts

102. The war to which belligerent occupation is inseparably linked must have an international texture: two or more States must be pitted against each other in an armed conflict. This means that the law of belligerent occupation is inapplicable to non-international armed conflicts.[196] 'It is of the essence of belligerent occupation that it should be exercised over foreign, enemy territory'.[197] In a non-international armed conflict, neither territory seized by insurgents nor

[189] See M. Virally, *L'Administration Internationale de l'Allemagne* 19–24 (1948).
[190] See B. Kempen, 'Germany, Occupation after World War II', IV *MPEPIL* 444, 446.
[191] P.B. Potter, 'Legal Bases and Character of Military Occupation in Germany and Japan', 43 *AJIL* 323, 324 (1949).
[192] See N. Ando, *Surrender, Occupation, and Private Property in International Law: An Evaluation of US Practice in Japan* 13–22 (1991).
[193] *Ibid.*, 105–6.
[194] See A. Roberts, 'Transformative Military Occupation: Applying the Laws of War and Human Rights', *International Law and Armed Conflict: Exploring the Faultlines, Essays in Honour of Yoram Dinstein* 439, 467–70 (M. Schmitt and J. Pejic eds., 2007).
[195] See *ibid.*, 470; A. Roberts, 'What Is Military Occupation?', 55 *BYBIL* 249, 267–71 (1984).
[196] See H.-P. Gasser and K. Dörmann, 'Protection of the Civilian Population', *The Handbook of International Humanitarian Law* 231, 267 (3rd edn, D. Fleck ed., 2013).
[197] See R.R. Baxter, 'Ius in Bello Interno: The Present and Future Law', *Law and Civil War in the Modern World* 518, 531 (J.N. Moore ed., 1974).

that retained or regained by the incumbent Government can be tagged as subject to belligerent occupation.[198] It is therefore misleading to claim that the destruction in March 2001 of the famous Buddha statues in Bamiyan (carried out by the Taliban regime in Afghanistan in the course of a non-international armed conflict) constituted an 'act of an occupying power'.[199]

103. Two comments should hedge this general statement of the law. One is that, under Article 1(4) of Additional Protocol I, armed conflicts in the exercise of the right of self-determination (see *infra* 170) are subject to the application of the Protocol and the Geneva Conventions, although they do not involve two States.[200] Obviously, this controversial provision does not bind non-Contracting Parties to the Protocol.

104. The other comment is that, if insurgents obtain from the incumbent Government 'recognition of belligerency', the armed conflict (albeit non-international in substance) will assume an international complexion, and the Geneva Conventions (including Convention (IV)) will apply *in toto*.[201] It is occasionally alleged that recognition of belligerency has fallen into disuse and that, even if it were to occur, only 'common Article 3 and not the [Geneva] Conventions as a whole will apply to the conflict'.[202] But this is an erroneous approach. Common Article 3 applies to any 'armed conflict not of an international character occurring in the territory of one of the High Contracting Parties',[203] and such application is not contingent on recognition of belligerency. Should recognition of belligerency be granted, it would undoubtedly signal that the conflict has to be treated as if it were an international armed conflict and that all the norms of the *jus in bello* (including the law of belligerent occupation) will consequently become applicable.

B. The Non-Consensual Nature of Belligerent Occupation

(a) Coercion as the Key to Belligerent Occupation

105. If occupation of the territory of State *A* (in whole or in part) by State *B* is suffused with coercion, the occupation is belligerent and the relationship between States *A* and *B* shifts from peace to war (even in the absence of hostilities; see *supra* 95–6). Moreover, as pointed out by the International Court of Justice in the *Armed Activities* case (*infra* 146), a justification given by an Occupying Power for the coercive occupation of a foreign territory is of no

[198] See Y. Dinstein, *Non-International Armed Conflicts in International Law* 222 (2014).
[199] See R. O'Keefe, *The Protection of Cultural Property in Armed Conflict* 98 (2006).
[200] Additional Protocol I, *supra* note 33, at 715.
[201] See L. Oppenheim, II *International Law* 211–12 (7th edn, H. Lauterpacht ed., 1952).
[202] L. Moir, *The Law of Internal Armed Conflict* 41–2 (2002).
[203] Geneva Convention (IV), *supra* note 29, at 580–1.

consequence. The fact that the Occupying Power pretends to 'liberate' the inhabitants of an occupied territory does not alter the legal taxonomy, as long as the occupation does not take place consensually.

106. The non-consensual trait of belligerent occupation sets it apart from 'pacific' (the antonym of 'belligerent') occupation. '*Occupatio pacifica* rests on consent'.[204] There can be a consensual, non-belligerent, occupation of a certain territory even during and because of war (for instance, the American occupation of the newly independent Iceland – following a brief British occupation – during WWII[205]). But the crux of belligerent occupation is that, at odds with pacific occupation, it is coercive by nature: no coercive occupation can be regarded as pacific.

107. Even if belligerent occupation proceeds benignly over a long period of time, its immanently coercive nature must not be forgotten. The authority of an Occupying Power is not derived from the will of the people, and democracy is not of any functional relevance to the running of an occupied territory. Belligerent occupation is not designed to win the hearts and minds of the local inhabitants: it has military – or security – objectives, and its foundation is the 'power of the bayonet'. The jurisdictional rights of the military government in an occupied territory (see *infra* 153) stem from effective control alone. The *jus in bello* offers the inhabitants of the territory vital safeguards against possible maltreatment by the Occupying Power. But belligerent occupation must be acknowledged for what it is and for what it is not.

108. It is wrong to suggest, as is done – perhaps wistfully – by some commentators, that an Occupying Power can or should administer an occupied territory as a 'trustee'.[206] A position of a trustee postulates trust, which is conspicuously missing from the relations between enemies in wartime. An occupied territory is not entrusted in the hands of the Occupying Power. The latter wrests control over the land from the displaced sovereign and wields power in it – as a war-related measure – energized by the military capability to do so. When the Occupying Power looks after the welfare of the inhabitants, its good will is generally spawned by (i) obligations imposed by the law of belligerent occupation, as well as the law of human rights (see Chapter 3); and (ii) a natural desire to hold sway in the territory under occupation with maximum tranquility and minimum friction with the civilian population.

[204] See G. Schwarzenberger, *The Law of Armed Conflict* (2 *International Law as Applied by International Courts and Tribunals*) 184 (1968).

[205] See Iceland-United States, Correspondence Concerning Defense of Iceland by United States Forces, 1941, 35 *AJIL*, Supp., 194 *et seq.* (1941).

[206] See, especially, A. Gerson, 'Trustee-Occupant: The Legal Status of Israel's Presence in the West Bank', 14 *Har.ILJ* 1, 39–46 (1973).

(b) Occupation Based on Agreement Following War

109. At times, occupation of a territory emanates from an agreement following war. By virtue of the agreement, the occupation – being consensual – cannot be classified as belligerent in character. The best illustration is that of the Rhineland in Germany (the left bank of the Rhine plus important 'bridgeheads' to the east of the river). The occupation – by the Allied Powers – was undertaken pursuant to the specific terms of the Armistice of 11 November 1918 concluded with Germany.[207] The continued occupation of the Rhineland, in theory for a period of fifteen years but actually ending much sooner, was confirmed in Article 428 of the 1919 Versailles Treaty of Peace (as a guarantee for the implementation of the instrument by Germany).[208] Surely, the post-Versailles occupation was a pacific occupation.[209] As for the initial post-Armistice occupation, opinions are divided. Still, given the consensual nature of the occupation (the Armistice agreement), the better view is that it too constituted a pacific (non-belligerent) occupation.[210]

(c) Consensual Occupation of Allied Territory during War

110. Towards the end of WWII, there were a number of instances of occupations for short duration of some Allied territories (e.g., France, Belgium, the Netherlands or Greece) by the armed forces of other Allied States (pre-eminently, the US and the UK) in the process of a genuine liberation from the Nazi yoke in 1944–5.[211] These occupations were carried out by consent of the Governments-in-Exile of the sovereigns displaced by the common enemy (Nazi Germany). Being consensual, they did not qualify as belligerent occupations, and accordingly the Hague Regulations were not applied (Geneva Convention (IV) was not yet formulated).[212]

111. It must be perceived that, should the presence of co-belligerent troops outlast the consent of the territorial sovereign, the situation would alter dramatically. Thus, during WWII, German troops were stationed in (Fascist) Italy with the consent of the Mussolini Government. Then, in September 1943, following the overthrow of that Government, Italy switched sides and declared war on Germany. When German troops remained on Italian soil – without the consent of the new (Badoglio) Italian Government – the provinces in which

[207] Conditions of an Armistice with Germany, 11 November 1918, I *A History of the Peace Conference of Paris* 459, 460 (H.W.V. Temperley ed., 1920).

[208] Versailles Treaty of Peace, 1919, *ibid.*, vol. III, 99, 329.

[209] See M.J. Kelly, 'Non-Belligerent Occupation', 28 *IYHR* 17, 24 (1998).

[210] See E. Fraenkel, *Military Occupation and the Rule of Law: Occupation Government in the Rhineland, 1918–1923* 183–6 (1944).

[211] See Starke's *International Law* 511 n. 16 (11th edn, I.A. Shearer ed., 1994).

[212] See Roberts, *supra* note 195, at 263–4.

they exercised effective control became subject to belligerent occupation[213] (cf. *infra* 116).

(d) Occupation by United Nations Forces

112. United Nations peacekeeping forces are sometimes engaged in the administration of a territory, exercising comprehensive governmental powers of legislation and management.[214] Notwithstanding some apparent dissent,[215] this type of control over territory can scarcely be viewed as belligerent occupation.[216] Withal, the presupposition here is that the territorial control is carried out temporarily by the peacekeeping force (based on a mandate set out by the UN Security Council) without coercion of the host country. For that reason, UN governance of territories such as Kosovo in 1999 – in the aftermath of an inter-State armed conflict[217] – goes beyond the scope of the present volume.[218]

113. UN consensual administration of territory is not to be confused with a state of affairs in which territorial control is engendered by force: either as a result of a straightforward enforcement action or even when a peacekeeping operation strays off course and gets entangled in an international armed conflict.[219] If the UN becomes a Belligerent Party to an armed conflict with a State, coercive territorial control by UN troops does not appreciably differ from any other instance of belligerent occupation.

114. In 1999, the UN Secretary-General promulgated a Bulletin on the Observance by United Nations Forces of International Humanitarian Law, in which he formally conceded that UN forces – if actually engaged as combatants in situations of armed conflicts – must comply with the norms of international humanitarian law.[220] The Bulletin does not expressly mention belligerent occupation.[221] Still, there is no reason to exclude that setting from the general rule[222]

[213] See *Re Lepore* (Italy, Supreme Military Tribunal, 1946), 13 *ILR* 354, 356.

[214] See M. Bothe, 'Peacekeeping Forces', VIII *MPEPIL* 225, 232.

[215] See S. Wills, 'Occupation Law and Multi-National Operations: Problems and Perspectives', 77 *BYBIL* 256, 321–2 (2006).

[216] See D. Shraga, 'The United Nations as an Actor Bound by International Humanitarian Law', *The United Nations and International Humanitarian Law* 317, 327–8 (L. Condorelli, A.-M. La Rosa and S. Scherrer eds., (1996).

[217] See M.J. Matheson, 'United Nations Governance of Postconflict Societies', 95 *AJIL* 76, 78–81 (2001).

[218] This is in response to a comment by M.J. Matheson, 'Book Review' [of the first edition of this book], 104 *AJIL* 701, 703 (2010).

[219] See Roberts, *supra* note 195, at 290.

[220] UN Secretary-General's Bulletin on the Observance by United Nations Forces of International Humanitarian Law, 1999, *The Laws of Armed Conflicts*, *supra* note 29, at 1229, 1230.

[221] See G.T. Harris, 'The Era of Multilateral Occupation', 24 *Ber.JIL* 1, 31 (2006).

[222] See D. Shraga, 'The Secretary-General's Bulletin on the Observance by United Nations Forces of International Humanitarian Law: A Decade Later', 39 *IHYR* 357, 374 (2009).

(provided that the Security Council does not say otherwise in a binding decision; see *infra* 836).

II. The Establishment of Belligerent Occupation

A. *The Origins of Belligerent Occupation*

115. Belligerent Occupation usually follows a successful invasion of territory by the enemy in wartime. The invasion will commonly lead to hostilities, but exceptionally there may be little or no resistance by the invaded State. As indicated (*supra* 96), the absence of resistance does not affect the nature of an occupation as belligerent, provided that it is coercive (namely, non-consensual).

116. Invasion is not the only plausible precursor of belligerent occupation. Sometimes, armed forces of State *B* are stationed in the territory of State *A* by consent. If – following the expiration of that consent – the forces of State *B* remain in the territory of State *A*, exercising effective control over a surrounding area, their unwelcome stay will qualify as belligerent occupation (see *supra ibid.*). Withdrawal of consent to the presence of Ugandan troops on Congolese soil lay at the root of the Judgment of the International Court of Justice in the *Armed Activities* case, where it was held that Uganda became an Occupying Power in the Ituri region of Congo (see *infra* 146).[223]

B. *Hague Regulation 42*

117. Hague Regulation 42 proclaims in its non-binding English translation:

> Territory is considered to be occupied when it is actually placed under the authority of the hostile army.
>
> The occupation extends only to the territories where such authority has been established, and can be exercised.[224]

The authentic (and binding) French text prescribes:

> Un territoire est considéré comme occupé lorsqu'il se trouve placé de fait sous l'autorité de l'armée ennemie.
>
> L'occupation ne s'étend qu'aux territoires où cette autorité est établie et en mesure de s'exercer.[225]

[223] *Case Concerning Armed Activities on the Territory of the Congo* (Congo v. Uganda), *supra* note 26, at 229–31.

[224] Hague Regulations, *supra* note 22, at 245.

[225] *Ibid.*, 244.

118. It is clear from the first paragraph of Hague Regulation 42 that whether or not an occupation occurs is a matter of fact ('placé de fait' in French). Thus, belligerent occupation cannot be fictitious, and it is not solely a matter of intention or notification.[226] There cannot be a 'paper occupation'.[227] The expression 'hostile army' has to be understood as embracing both regular and irregular military units of the enemy.[228]

119. It can be deduced from the second paragraph of Regulation 42 that there are two cumulative conditions for belligerent occupation: (i) the authority by the Occupying Power must be established; and (ii) the Occupying Power must be able to ('can') exercise that authority. In other words, belligerent occupation pertains only to that area in which the Occupying Power is actually exercising its authority and is capable of doing so.

C. Belligerent Occupation and Invasion

120. An occupation is to be distinguished from a mere hit-and-run raid or the passage of flying columns of troops on a reconnaissance mission.[229] In the words of the 2004 UK Manual of the Law of Armed Conflict, '[p]atrols, commando, and similar units, which move on or withdraw after carrying out their mission, do not normally occupy territory since they are not there long enough to set up an administration'.[230]

121. As mentioned (*supra* 115), belligerent occupation generally follows a successful invasion. However, '[t]he law of belligerent occupation generally does not apply to ... mere invasion'.[231] Invading troops may sweep hurriedly in a blitz campaign through a region, seeking distant prizes, without leaving adequate forces behind them for belligerent occupation.[232] An invasion constitutes a prelude to a regime of belligerent occupation only when the invading army (or some of its units) solidly seize a given territory from which the sovereign is displaced. As a rule, belligerent occupation 'is invasion plus taking firm possession of enemy territory for the purpose of holding it'.[233]

226 See O. Debbasch, *L'Occupation Militaire: Pouvoirs Reconnus aux Forces Armées Hors de Leur Territoire National* 324–5 (1962).
227 Schwarzenberger, *supra* note 204, at 194.
228 See V. Koutroulis, *Le Début et la Fin de l'Application du Droit de l'Occupation* 30–1 (2010).
229 See Roberts, *supra* note 195, at 256.
230 UK Ministry of Defence, *UK Manual of the Law of Armed Conflict* 276 (2004).
231 US Department of Defense, *Law of War Manual*, *supra* note 1, at 759.
232 See J.M. Spaight, *War Rights on Land* 327 (1911).
233 US Department of the Army, *Field Manual: The Law of Land Warfare* 138 (1956).

122. In the Judgment in the *Hostages* trial, the American Military Tribunal summed up the legal state of affairs:

Whether an invasion has developed into an occupation is a question of fact. The term invasion implies a military operation while an occupation indicates the exercise of governmental authority to the exclusion of the established government. This presupposes the destruction of organized resistance and the establishment of an administration to preserve law and order. To the extent that the occupant's control is maintained and that of the civil government eliminated, the area will be said to be occupied.[234]

123. The primary rule, as stated by the ICTY Trial Chamber in the *Tadić* Judgment of 1997, is that the protection of persons under the Geneva Convention is actuated by their falling into the hands of occupying forces, and '[t]he exact moment when a person or area falls into the hands of a party to a conflict depends on whether that party has effective control over an area' (quoting G. Schwarzenberger,[235] who emphasized that this does not include an invaded territory which has not yet been effectively occupied).[236] As long as hostilities are going on between the invading troops and opposing forces trying to repel the invasion, it is premature to talk of belligerent occupation in the contact zone.[237]

124. As early as 1961, M.S. McDougal and F.P. Feliciano had this to say while upholding the basic distinction between invasion and occupation:

It is of course rarely practicable to point to any particular degree of control as marking a precise dividing line between invasion and occupation. It is commonly more accurate to speak of a gradual settling of the corresponding expectations on the part of the inhabitants; the continuum ranges from initial attack to a fully functioning occupation government.[238]

In 2009, the same observation was made by R. Kolb and S. Vité when contesting the basic distinction between the two phases of invasion and occupation:

Du point de vue pratique, cette approche risque de ne pas tenir compte des zones grises entre invasion et occupation. La transition d'une étape a l'autre n'est pas nette en pratique. La transformation d'une invasion en occupation est un processus progressif et la distinction entre les deux situations est souvent affaire de nuance.[239]

[234] *Hostages* trial, *supra* note 11, at 55–6.
[235] Schwarzenberger, *supra* note 204, at 174, 176.
[236] *Prosecutor v. Tadić, supra* note 153, at 925.
[237] See J.E. Parkerson, Jr., 'United States Compliance with Humanitarian Law Respecting Civilians during Operation Just Cause', 133 *Mil.LR* 31, 75 (1991).
[238] M.S. McDougal and F.P. Feliciano, *Law, and Minimum World Public Order: Transnational Coercion and World Public Order* 734 (1961).
[239] R. Kolb and S. Vité, *Le Droit de l'Occupation Militaire: Prespectives Historiques et Enjeux Juridiques Actuels* 140 (2009).

But the presence of intermediate grey zones between polar extremes of black and white does not sap the vitality of the legal distinction between invasion and occupation. Without denying the reality of borderline cases, it is necessary to recognize that – generally speaking – the situation at an invasion stage 'is as yet fluid and unsettled, reflecting the uncertainty of the outcome of the invading belligerent's efforts'; and only effective control of the territory lays a solid foundation for belligerent occupation.[240]

125. The ICRC Commentary on Geneva Convention (IV) argues that '[s]o far as individuals are concerned, the application of the Fourth Convention does not depend upon the existence of a state of occupation within the meaning of' Hague Regulation 42; and it further contends that even a patrol (penetrating enemy territory without staying there) must respect Article 49 of the Convention (quoted *infra* 487) that prohibits deportations.[241] This thesis has attracted some enthusiastic doctrinal support on humanitarian grounds.[242] However, it has also engendered unflinching opposition anchored in State practice.[243] The very reliance of the Commentary on the deportations example is self-defeating, inasmuch as Article 49 (first paragraph) expressly refers to 'occupied territory'. The ICRC Commentary itself notes that many stipulations of the Convention 'presuppose the presence of the occupation authorities for a fairly long period'.[244] In consequence, supporters of the ICRC Commentary's thesis are driven to the assertion that the beginning of occupation is 'functional' (so that it cannot be determined holistically for all purposes).[245]

126. The ICTY Trial Chamber in the *Naletilić* case, in 2003, held that the Geneva provisions concerning unlawful compulsory work (see *infra* 538) apply from the moment that protected persons fall into the hands of the enemy, regardless of the question whether a belligerent occupation actually exists at the critical moment in the relevant location.[246] Yet, the Chamber was forced to admit that the protection of property is contingent on the advent of a regime of belligerent occupation.[247] Surely, the better view is that 'the same criteria apply for establishing an occupation for the purpose of the protection of persons and property'.[248]

[240] McDougal and Feliciano, *supra* note 238, at 733–4.
[241] *Commentary, IV Geneva Convention*, *supra* note 31, at 60.
[242] See M. Sassòli, 'A Plea in Defence of Pictet and the Inhabitants of Territories under Invasion: The Case for the Applicability of the Fourth Geneva Convention during the Invasion Phase', 885 *IRRC* 42–50 (2012).
[243] See M. Zwanenburg, 'Challenging the Pictet Theory', 885 *IRRC* 30–6 (2012).
[244] *Commentary, IV Geneva Convention*, *supra* note 31, at 60.
[245] See M. Siegrist, *The Functional Beginning of Belligerent Occupation*, *passim* (2011).
[246] *Prosecutor v. Naletilić* et al., *supra* note 64, at para. 222.
[247] *Ibid.*
[248] M. Zwanenburg, 'The Law of Occupation Revisited: The Beginning of an Occupation', 7 *YIHL* 99, 121 (2010).

D. *The Time Element*

127. There is no hard and fast rule as to a minimal length of time intervening prior to the advent of belligerent occupation. In the *Issa* case of 2004, the European Court of Human Rights was prepared to acknowledge that a military operation – conducted by Turkish forces in northern Iraq in 1995 for a few weeks only – entailed the exercise of effective control in the area.[249] The Eritrea Ethiopia Claims Commission (also in 2004) expressed a more extreme view, reducing the minimal period to a few days:

> On the one hand, clearly an area where combat is ongoing and the attacking forces have not yet established control cannot normally be considered occupied within the meaning of the Geneva Conventions of 1949. On the other hand, where combat is not occurring in an area controlled for just a few days by the armed forces of a hostile Power, the Commission believes that the legal rules applicable to occupied territory should apply.[250]

Having gone out on a limb, the Claims Commission had to admit in 2005:

> The Commission also recognizes that not all of the obligations of Section III of Part III of the Geneva Convention IV (the section that deals with occupied territories) can reasonably be applied to an armed force anticipating combat and present in an area for only a few days.[251]

When both passages are read jointly, it is by no means clear what the practical implications of the Claims Commission's position are.[252]

128. The reference in the first passage to 'just a few days' (which is apparently accepted by the ICRC[253]) is enigmatic, since an evanescent belligerent occupation is an oxymoron. It is hard to envision genuine belligerent occupation with a duration of less than several weeks. If the seizure of some territory by the enemy in wartime is so episodic that it lasts just a few days, one would be hard put to envision the incident as a true state of belligerent occupation.[254] Such an occupation does not end precipitately: it simply fails to begin *ex tunc*.

E. *An Interval between Invasion and Belligerent Occupation*

129. The real question is whether belligerent occupation that in itself lasts several weeks (perhaps months or even years) can begin instantly or whether

[249] *Issa v. Turkey* (European Court of Human Rights, 2004), 41 *EHRR* 567, 588.

[250] Eritrea Ethiopia Claims Commission, Partial Award (Central Front), Eritrea's Claims 2, 4, 6, 7, 8 & 22, 2004, 43 *ILM* 1249, 1260 (2004).

[251] Eritrea Ethiopia Claims Commission, Partial Award (Western Front), Aerial Bombardment and Related Claims, Eritrea's Claims 1, 3, 5, 9–13, 14, 21, 25 & 26, 2005, 45 *ILM* 396, 403 (2006).

[252] See A. Gioia, 'The Belligerent Occupation of Territory', *The 1998–2000 War between Eritrea and Ethiopia: An International Legal Perspective* 351, 359–60 (A. de Guttry, H.H.G. Post and G. Venturini eds., 2009).

[253] See T. Ferraro and L. Cameron, 'Article 2: Application of the Convention', *Commentary on the First Geneva Convention* 113 (ICRC, J.-M. Henckaerts *et al.* eds., 2016).

[254] See Gioia, *supra* note 252, at 361.

there must be an interval of a minimal period required for some stabilization. The answer depends on the circumstances of the case. An interval is uncalled for if the occupation encounters no resistance (see *supra* 96) and there is no impediment to the immediate exercise of effective control by the Occupying Power.

130. However, under ordinary circumstances – when an occupation follows invasion and hostilities (see *supra* 120 *et seq.*) – an interval is unavoidable. The reason is that there is no belligerent occupation unless and until a measure of stability is achieved in the occupied territory. In the language of the German Law of Armed Conflict Manual: 'Occupied territory does not include *battle areas*, i.e., areas that are still contested and not subject to permanent occupational authority'.[255] The term 'permanent' must be understood here in a relative sense: stable would have been a better choice of word.

131. Even prior to the beginning of occupation, the civilian population will benefit from some safeguards under the *jus in bello* pertaining to the conduct of hostilities. Yet, a more rigorous protective regime of protection of the civilian population will only become applicable once belligerent occupation is in effect. Many provisions of the law of belligerent occupation (e.g., with respect to allowing humanitarian relief from the outside; see *infra* 582) simply cannot be reconciled with a premature date of application.[256]

132. The ICRC Commentary on Geneva Convention (IV) avers: 'There is no intermediate period between what might be termed the invasion phase and the inauguration of a stable regime of occupation'.[257] This proposition does not correspond to general State practice, although it was quoted with approval by a Trial Chamber of the ICTY in the *Rajić* case of 1996.[258]

133. The proceedings in the *Rajić* case related to the wanton destruction of a Bosnian village at the very point of being overrun by Croat forces. The Trial Chamber determined that, notwithstanding the fact that the destruction occurred at the time of entry into the village, the property was already protected by Article 53 of the Convention (quoted *infra* 598), which relates to occupied territories.[259] As a matter of fact, there was no compelling reason for the Trial Chamber to rely on the special prohibition of wanton destruction of property by an Occupying Power under Article 53. After all, the general interdiction of such destruction pursuant to Hague Regulation 23(g) (quoted *infra*

255 *German Law of Armed Conflict Manual* 85 (German Federal Ministry of Defence, 2013).
256 See E.E. Kuijt, *Humanitarian Assistance and State Sovereignty in International Law: Towards a Comprehensive Framework* 84 (2015).
257 *Commentary, IV Geneva Convention*, *supra* note 31, at 60.
258 *Prosecutor v. Rajić*, *supra* note 64, at para. 41.
259 *Ibid.*, para. 42.

595) – which is applicable in all circumstances of conduct of hostilities (irrespective of occupation) – would have led to the same conclusion. The issue of an intermediate period between invasion and occupation was therefore irrelevant to the decision. The singular features of the case greatly diminish its value as a precedent.[260]

134. Quite frequently, there is an unavoidable hiatus between an incipient invasion stage and the subsequent achievement of stability in the territory. This was clearly recognized by the Grand Chamber of the European Court of Human Rights, in 2014, in the *Hassan* case: the Judgment dealt with events in Iraq in the course of April and early May 2003 'before the United Kingdom and its coalition partners had declared that the active hostilities phase of the conflict had ended and that they were in occupation'.[261]

135. The lapse of time preceding stability (and belligerent occupation) cannot be too long, Stability is not contingent on setting up an elaborate apparatus of administration of the occupied territory.[262] What it does mean is that the Occupying Power has successfully attained effective control over the occupied territory.

III. Effective Control

A. *The Substitution of Authority*

136. As Hague Regulation 42 (quoted *supra* 117) emphasizes, belligerent occupation means that territory is 'actually placed under the authority of the hostile army'. There are two elements here: one explicit and the other implicit. What is explicit is that the authority of enemy armed forces is actually established. What is implicit is the correlative dissolution of the authority of the displaced sovereign.

137. Assumption of authority in the sense of Regulation 42 means effective control over the territory.[263] Effective control is a *conditio sine qua non* of belligerent occupation. The key to the portals of the law of belligerent occupation is the substitution of the effective control (authority) of the displaced sovereign by that of the Occupying Power. This is confirmed by the International Court

[260] See C. Greenwood, 'The Development of International Humanitarian Law by the International Criminal Tribunal for the Former Yugoslavia', 2 *MPYUNL* 97, 126 (1998).

[261] *Hassan v. United Kingdom* (European Court of Human Rights, Grand Chamber, 2014), para. 75.

[262] See M. Bothe, 'Effective Control during Invasion: A Practical View on the Application Threshold of the Law of Occupation', 885 *IRRC* 37, 40 (2012).

[263] See T. Ferraro, 'Determining the Beginning and End of an Occupation under International Humanitarian Law', 885 *IRRC* 133, 140 (2012). See also Ferraro and Cameron, *supra* note 253, at 108–9.

of Justice in the *Armed Activities* case (see full quotation *infra* 146) and by the ICTY in the *Naletilić* case (see *infra* 144).

B. *Variations of Effective Control*

(a) ***The Degree of Effective Control***

138. Defining the exact amount of 'control' deemed objectively 'effective' in belligerent occupation is an imponderable problem.[264] In particular, the optimal size of the army of occupation and the manner of its deployment cannot be determined *a priori*. Circumstances vary from one occupied territory to another, and the degree of effective control required may depend on the terrain, the density of the population and a variety of other considerations.[265] Additionally, it is at least arguable that – if the original control by the displaced sovereign was imperfect – the demands of supplanting it may be less rigorous than in other situations.[266]

139. It is unrealistic to expect an Occupying Power to be able to field troops everywhere within an occupied territory. Effective control 'does not imply the extension of military control to every nook and corner of the disputed territory'.[267] In the *Naletilić* case, the Trial Chamber of the ICTY pronounced that the Occupying Power must have 'a sufficient force present, or the capacity to send troops within a reasonable time to make the authority of the occupying power felt'.[268] This is based on a statement in the US Army Field Manual of 1956 that a belligerent occupation does not require 'fixed garrisons'.[269] The 2015 US Department of Defense Law of War Manual states:

> It is sufficient that the occupying force can, within a reasonable time, send detachments of forces to enforce its authority within the occupied district. Military occupation does not require the presence of military forces in every populated area, although the occupying force must, inter alia, control the most important places.[270]

The question of what is 'a reasonable time' in this context does not always lend itself to an easy determination.[271]

[264] See D.A. Graber, *The Development of the Law of Belligerent Occupation 1863–1914: A Historical Survey* 69 (1949).

[265] See US Department of Defense, *Law of War Manual*, *supra* note 1, at 765.

[266] See HCJ 102/82 etc., *Tsemel* et al. *v. Minister of Defence* et al., 37(3) *PD* 365, 373 (per Deputy President Shamgar). (The Judgment is excerpted in English in 13 *IYHR* 360 (1983)).

[267] See A. Gerson, 'Off-Shore Oil Exploration by a Belligerent Occupying Power: The Gulf of Suez Dispute', 71 *AJIL* 725, 728 (1977).

[268] *Prosecutor v. Naletilić* et al., *supra* note 64, at para. 217.

[269] US Department of the Army, *Field Manual: The Law of Land Warfare*, *supra* note 233, at 139.

[270] US Department of Defense, *Law of War Manual*, *supra* note 1, at 764.

[271] See H. Cuyckens, 'Is Israel Still an Occupying Power in Gaza?', 63 *NILR* 275, 285 (2016).

140. Although effective control allows for remote control in peripheral areas, the Occupying Power must establish a military presence – through the deployment of some 'boots on the ground' – in the occupied territory.[272] The Grand Chamber of the European Court of Human Rights, in its two concurrent Judgments in the *Chiragov* and *Sargsyan* cases of 2015, referred to the physical presence of troops as a *sine qua non* requirement of occupation, adding that 'occupation is not conceivable without "boots on the ground"'.[273] It follows that a mere 'ability to project military power from a position beyond the boundaries' of the occupied territory does not suffice.[274] In the same vein, belligerent occupation cannot rest solely on either naval power or air power, however formidable that may be.[275] 'Supremacy in the air alone does not meet the requirement of effective control'.[276]

(b) *Effective Control 'by Proxy'*

141. Effective control may also be exercised 'by proxy' – through surrogate militias, rather than regular troops – as long as these militias are subordinated to the authority of the Occupying Power. The International Court of Justice made it abundantly clear – in the *Armed Activities* case – that, if an armed group is not 'under the control' of an Occupying Power, it does not administer a territory on its behalf.[277] At bottom, there is a double requirement of effective control relating to auxiliary forces: the militias must be in effective control of the territory, and the Occupying Power has to be in effective control of the militias.[278] There is some debate, in the case law as well as in the legal literature, with respect to the degree of effective control required over militias both in general[279] and in the specific context of occupied territories.[280] However, *in fine*, the question is whether the militias can be regarded as the de facto organs of the Occupying Power.

[272] In the first edition of this book it was stated that the presence of 'boots on the ground' is required 'in or near' the occupied territory. The words 'or near' were not meant to exclude such presence altogether. But, to avoid a misunderstanding (cf. Cuyckens, *ibid.*, 281), they have been deleted.

[273] *Chiragov* et al. *v. Armenia*, *supra* note 67, at 989; *Sargsyan v. Azerbaijan*, *ibid.*, para. 94.

[274] Ferraro, *supra* note 263, at 143–4.

[275] D. Wolf, 'Transitional Post-Occupation Obligations under the Law of Belligerent Occupation', 27 *Minn.JIL* 5, 16 (2018).

[276] Gasser and Dörmann, *supra* note 196, at 269.

[277] *Case Concerning Armed Activities on the Territory of the Congo* (Congo v. Uganda), *supra* note 26, at 231.

[278] See Ferraro, *supra* note 263, at 158. See also Ferraro and Cameron, *supra* note 253, at 116.

[279] See Dinstein, *supra* note 3, at 235–41.

[280] See A. Gilder, 'Bringing Occupation into the 21st Century: The Effective Implementation of Occupation by Proxy', 13 *ULR* 60, 63–5 (2017).

142. In the *Tadić* case, the Trial Chamber of the ICTY held that the armed forces of the *Republika Sprska* acted as de facto organs of former Yugoslavia (Serbia and Montengro) and their acts could be imputed to the latter.[281] The Judgment added:

the relationship of de facto organs or agents to the foreign Power includes those circumstances in which the foreign Power 'occupies' or operates in certain territory solely through the acts of local de facto organs or agents.[282]

Since their acts are imputed to the State, de facto organs are State actors. It is therefore wrong to consider the law of belligerent occupation as extending, through their activities, to non-State actors.[283]

(c) Control and Stability

143. Belligerent occupation posits a modicum of stabilization in the affected area (see *supra* 130). It is not enough to have 'a vacuum of authority' caused by the front lines moving back and forth.[284] When the front lines are constantly shifting – each side trying to dislodge the other from the zone of operations – it is impossible to tell who is ensconced in power, and the *jus in bello* norms applicable are those governing the conduct of hostilities rather than belligerent occupation. As already pointed out (*supra ibid.*), and as phrased by the Trial Chamber of the ICTY in the *Naletilić* case, 'battle areas may not be considered as occupied territory'.[285] But once it is established, belligerent occupation is not negated by mere 'sporadic local resistance'.[286] Certain isolated enclaves may even remain in the hands of forces loyal to the displaced sovereign: if successfully contained, belligerent occupation may robustly exist elsewhere.[287]

144. It does not suffice to keep the displaced sovereign at bay beyond a certain buffer zone, denying it the ability to exercise its dominion in the intervening area (thereby creating a vacuum of authority). As expounded by the Trial Chamber of the ICTY in the *Naletilić* case, an Occupying Power 'must be in a position to substitute its own authority for that of the occupied authorities, which must have been rendered incapable of functioning publicly'.[288] Ergo, there are two rudimentary requirements for belligerent occupation: (i) the displaced sovereign's forces must 'have surrendered, been defeated or withdrawn'[289] (or

[281] *Prosecutor v. Tadić, supra* note 153, at 926.
[282] *Ibid.*, 926–7.
[283] As argued by T. Gal, 'Unexplored Outcomes of *Tadiç*: Applicability of the Law Occupation to War by Proxy', 12 *JICJ* 59, 80 (2014).
[284] F. Mini, 'Liberation and Occupation: A Commander's Perspective', 35 *IYHR* 71, 86 (2005).
[285] *Prosecutor v. Naletilić* et al., *supra* note 64, at para. 217.
[286] *Ibid.*
[287] See L.C. Green, *The Contemporary Law of Armed Conflict* 258 (2nd edn, 2000).
[288] *Prosecutor v. Naletilić* et al., *supra* note 64, at para. 217.
[289] *Ibid.*

contained in isolated enclaves); and (ii) the displaced sovereign's mastery of the area is supplanted by that of the Occupying Power.

(d) Territory and Population

145. The gravamen of effective control, under Hague Regulation 42, is territory. Of course, in every occupied territory there is usually some population, which is the primary beneficiary – or victim – of the exercise of authority by the Occupying Power. As E. Benvenisti points out, '[b]y assuming control over the land the occupant assumes responsibility over the population situated on that land'.[290]

146. The Judgment of the International Court of Justice in the *Armed Activities* case clearly stated:

> In order to reach a conclusion as to whether a State, the military forces of which are present on the territory of another State as a result of an intervention, is an 'occupying Power' in the meaning of the term as understood in the *jus in bello*, the Court must examine whether there is sufficient evidence to demonstrate that the said authority [referred to in Regulation 42] was in fact established and exercised by the intervening State in the areas in question. In the present case the Court will need to satisfy itself that the Ugandan armed forces in the DRC [Democratic Republic of the Congo] were not only stationed in particular locations but also that they had substituted their own authority for that of the Congolese Government. In that event, any justification given by Uganda for its occupation would be of no relevance; nor would it be relevant whether or not Uganda had established a structured military administration of the territory occupied.[291]

The Court found that, whereas Ugandan troops were in actual control of the Ituri region – and, therefore, Uganda was the Occupying Power there – the presence of Ugandan troops in certain other locations in the Congo did not qualify as occupation in the sense of Hague Regulations 42.[292]

147. The formulation used by the Court as regards the substitution of authority has led to doctrinal criticism. The Judgment's support for the view that authority must be effected on the ground – and that mere potential ability to exercise it is not sufficient – has been contested by several scholars[293] (relying on the UK Manual of the Law of Armed Conflict, which suggests that it is

[290] Benvenisti, *supra* note 50, at 50.

[291] *Case Concerning Armed Activities on the Territory of the Congo* (Congo v. Uganda), *supra* note 26, at 230.

[292] See *ibid.*, 230–1.

[293] See V. Koutroulis, 'L'Affaire des *Activités Armées sur le Territoire du Congo* (Congo c. Ouganda): Une Lecture Restrictive du Droit de l'Occupation?', 39 *RBDI* 703, 710–15 (2006); T. Ruys and S. Verhoeven, 'DRC v. Uganda: The Applicability of International Humanitarian Law and Human Rights Law in Occupied Territories', *International Humanitarian Law and Human Rights Law: Towards a New Merger in International Law* 155, 167 (R. Arnold and N. Quénivet eds., 2008).

enough if the 'occupying power is in a position to substitute its own authority for that of the former government'[294]). It has even been argued that the Court's dictum 'does not reflect *lex lata*'.[295] But, in fact, the Court's statement of the law is entirely in keeping with Hague Regulation 42. A careful reading of the Regulation's text shows that the actual and the potential establishment of authority are cumulative ('and can be exercised'; in French, 'et en mesure de s'exercer'), and it is not enough to satisfy only one part of the equation. A theoretical capability to exercise authority does not suffice for purposes of effective control if in actuality no exercise of authority is demonstrated.

148. The quoted passage from the *Armed Activities* Judgment is important in shedding light on the geographic extent of belligerent occupation. The existence of effective control somewhere in the territory of a foreign State does not necessarily denote the consolidation of belligerent occupation in adjacent areas. There have to be clear indications that the effective control radiates into the environs, replacing the authority of the displaced sovereign.

(e) Maintaining Effective Control

149. Belligerent occupation 'once acquired must be maintained'.[296] There is a prerequisite of staying power as a building-block of continued effective control over an occupied territory. Even after a territory has been securely occupied, there is a distinct possibility of trouble brewing. If renewed hostilities flare up, they may reduce the degree of effective control exercised by the Occupying Power over some sections of an occupied territory some of the time. Yet – given staying power – a 'momentarily triumphant rebellion' does not signify that effective control has been dissipated, and by itself will not suffice to terminate the belligerent occupation.[297] The principal proviso is that the authority of the displaced sovereign is not effectively reestablished.[298]

150. In the *Hostages* Judgment of 1948, the American Military Tribunal had this to say:

> It is clear that the German Armed Forces were able to maintain control of Greece and Yugoslavia until they evacuated them in the fall of 1944. While it is true that the partisans were able to control sections of these countries at various times, it is established that the Germans could at any time they desired assume physical control of any part of the country. The control of the resistance movements was temporary only and not such as would deprive the German Armed Forces of its [*sic*] status of an occupant.[299]

[294] *UK Manual of the Law of Armed Conflict*, *supra* note 230, at 275.

[295] Ferraro, *supra* note 263, at 150.

[296] C.C. Hyde, III *International Law Chiefly as Interpreted and Applied by the United States* 1881 (2nd edn, 1945).

[297] See D.A. Graber, *supra* note 264, at 56.

[298] See Gasser and Dörmann, *supra* note 196, at 273.

[299] *Hostages* trial, *supra* note 11, at 56.

The test, then, is the capability of the Occupying Power to ultimately exercise its effective control, even in the face of significant resistance.[300] The Occupying Power does not lose effective control if it manages to display resilience in the face of temporary adversity. The matrix is the Israeli occupation of the West Bank, which has successfully survived two tidal waves of uprisings (*intifadas*) by the local inhabitants. For more about hostilities within occupied territories, see *infra* 307 *et seq.*

(f) Fluctuations of Effective Control

151. Should the Occupying Power be expelled from – or lose its grip over – an occupied territory, in whole or in part, the occupation in the area concerned is terminated (see *infra* 831, 843). Over time, the territory subject to the effective control of an Occupying Power is likely to grow or shrink in size, and the fluctuations may be egregious. Belligerent occupation may crumble and then (in consequence of a military rally) be resumed *de novo*, meaning that it is liable to be visited upon the same locale more than once in the course of the same war. Each time, the occupation must be distinguished from a passing incursion, and the conclusive test will be effective control.

152. The ebb and flow in the extent of the territory subject to belligerent occupation may be the direct outcome of battlefield victories or defeats. Spatial permutations may also result from agreements between the Belligerent Parties. Thus, by virtue of the 1979 Treaty of Peace between Israel and Egypt, Israel withdrew from the Sinai Peninsula but stayed on in the Gaza Strip (see *supra* 47–8).

IV. Some Ancillary Comments

A. Jurisdictional Rights

153. It used to be alleged that an Occupying Power has no jurisdictional rights in an occupied territory,[301] but this is a fallacy. On the contrary, as we shall see in Chapters 4–6, an Occupying Power – within the constraints imposed by the *jus in bello* – has jurisdiction to prescribe (i.e. to legislate or regulate), jurisdiction to adjudicate (viz., to subject the inhabitants to the process of courts or tribunals), and jurisdiction to enforce (to wit, to compel compliance) in an occupied territory.[302]

300 See N. Melzer, *Targeted Killing in International Law* 157 (2008).
301 See C. Rousseau, *Le Droit des Conflits Armés* 139 (1983).
302 On the three conceptual aspects of jurisdiction in general terms (unrelated to belligerent occupation), see I *Restatement of the Law: The Foreign Relations Law of the United States* 232 (American Law Institute, 3rd edn, 1987).

154. By itself, jurisdiction only means competence. Thus, the Occupying Power is not obliged to exercise the jurisdiction to prescribe or to adjudicate in an occupied territory. Especially if the belligerent occupation is short-termed, the Occupying Power may prefer to refrain from flexing its legislative muscles and it may abstain from any judicial proceedings. The Trial Chamber of the ICTY, in the *Naletilić* case, seems to have been under the impression that the Occupying Power must issue and enforce directives to the civilian population.[303] However, the issuance of edicts to the civilian population in an occupied territory (in exercise of the jurisdiction to prescribe) – much as it is a commonplace spectacle in almost every occupation and an unavoidable step in a prolonged one – is a prerogative of the Occupying Power and not, strictly speaking, an absolute requirement. In the event that the Occupying Power elects not to exercise its jurisdiction to prescribe or to adjudge – leaving the existing legal tissue in pristine condition – nobody can deprecate the act of omission. The sole duty of the Occupying Power to take action, whether or not it wishes to do so, relates to the jurisdiction to enforce. As we shall see (*infra* 278 *et seq.*), this jurisdiction flows from the Occupying Power's overall obligation to do its utmost to maintain law and order in the occupied territory, a responsibility that it cannot shirk.

B. Outlying Land Areas

155. Belligerent occupation does not extend to land areas cut off from the occupied territory and not subject to the effective control of the Occupying Power. Inaccessible islands are the best example. Shortly after the German occupation of Denmark in WWII, Iceland (heretofore in union with Denmark) declared its full independence, and was subsequently occupied consensually by the US (see *supra* 106). In Greenland too – still under Danish sovereignty – the US stationed forces and established military facilities by agreement.[304] Although the validity of the latter agreement has been contested,[305] the point to keep in mind is that – notwithstanding the unresisted German occupation of the entire Danish homeland – the Occupying Power's effective control did not spread to far-away islands, in the absence of German capability to land troops there.

[303] *Prosecutor v. Naletilić* et al., *supra* note 64, at para. 217.

[304] Denmark-United States, Agreement Relating to the Defense of Greenland and Exchange of Notes, 1941, 35 *AJIL*, Supp., 129 *et seq.* (1941).

[305] See H.W. Briggs, 'The Validity of the Greenland Agreement', 35 *AJIL* 506–13 (1941).

C. *Maritime Areas and Air Space*

156. Belligerent occupation is forged by effective control in land areas (cf. *supra* 140). When effective control is established on land, it attaches itself also to any abutting maritime areas and to the superjacent air space. As regards internal and territorial waters, this is settled in Article 88 of the 1913 Oxford Manual of Naval War, adopted by the *Institut de Droit International*:

> Occupation of maritime territory, that is of gulfs, bays, roadsteads, ports, and territorial waters, exists only when there is at the same time an occupation of continental territory, by either a naval or a military force. The occupation, in that case, is subject to the laws and usages of war on land.[306]

The implicit reference at the end of the text is to Hague Regulations 42 through 56.[307]

157. The Oxford Manual's exposition of the law should also apply to maritime areas not mentioned in the text, especially the continental shelf (in which no sovereign rights of the coastal State were recognized in 1913). After all, the continental shelf is 'the natural prolongation' of the land territory.[308] Accordingly, during the belligerent occupation of the Sinai Peninsula, Israel drilled for oil in its continental shelf in the Gulf of Suez (see *infra* 665). Granted, if oil installations in the continental shelf of an occupied territory are located at a great distance from the coastline, it is plausible that the displaced sovereign (or its co-belligerents) will actually prevent their use by the Occupying Power.

158. The airspace above the land and maritime territory of a country must be seen as an appurtenance of the latter. Consequently, belligerent occupation of the airspace is inconceivable independently of effective control over the subjacent land.[309] This is a corollary of the proposition that air supremacy alone does not qualify as effective control (see *supra* 140).

D. *Proclamation*

159. To remove doubts as to the existence of belligerent occupation, the Occupying Power may issue a proclamation in which notice is given to the inhabitants of the occupied territory about the new legal regime.[310] However,

[306] *Oxford Manual of Naval War*, Adopted by the Institute of International Law, 1913, *The Laws of Armed Conflicts*, *supra* note 29, at 1123, 1135.

[307] See P. Verri, 'Commentary on the 1913 Oxford Manual of Naval War', *The Law of Naval Warfare: a Collection of Agreements and Documents with Commentaries* 329, 337 (N. Ronzitti ed., 1988).

[308] Article 76(1) of the United Nations Convention on the Law of the Sea, 1982, *Official Text* 49.

[309] See M. Sassòli, 'The Concept and the Beginning of Occupation', *The 1949 Geneva Conventions: A Commentary* 1389, 1396 (A. Clapham, P. Gaeta and M. Sassòli eds., 2015).

[310] For an example, see the Proclamations issued by the Regional Commanders of the IDF in each of the territories occupied in June 1967, 1 *IYHR* 419 (1971).

the proclamation is declaratory rather than constitutive. It is not the legal backbone of the occupation, but merely reflects (and disseminates) the fact that the Occupying Power has assumed effective control over a particular territory.[311] In consequence, the occupation does not reach beyond the area over which the Occupying Power has actually acquired effective control, even if the proclamation professes to do so.[312]

E. Several Occupying Powers

160. As a rule, references in this volume are made to an Occupying Power in the singular. Of course, this is not necessarily what happens on the ground. Actually, there are four possible scenarios:

(a) Portions of the territory of a Belligerent Party (like Poland in September 1939) may be occupied by two or more States acting separately. There will then be two or more occupied areas carving up the territory of the displaced sovereign between the respective Occupying Powers. Each Occupying Power would wield effective control independently and exclusively in its own occupied area.

(b) A number of Occupying Powers may act together as a coalition governing a single occupied territory[313] (as happened in Iraq in 2003–4; see *supra* 36). These Occupying Powers will then bear the brunt of joint responsibility for what is happening within the area subject to their combined effective control.[314]

(c) When one or more members of the coalition 'relinquishes operational command or control over its troops' to another member of the coalition, the latter State will be regarded as the sole Occupying Power.[315]

(d) The existence of a coalition does not preclude its partners from opting to divide an occupied territory into discrete zones of occupation with little or no overlap of authority. In the absence of a central coordination body, each Occupying Power would then administer its own zone separately (as in the first scenario), assuming sole responsibility commensurate with the actual extent of its effective control.[316]

[311] See Shamgar, *supra* note 143, at 14. See also Civ.A 54/82, *Levi* et al. *v. Abu-Sharif Estate* et al., 40(1) *PD* 374, 388–9 (per Deputy President Ben Porat).

[312] See E. Colby, 'Occupation under the Laws of War, I', 25 *Col.LR* 904, 910 (1925).

[313] *UK Manual of the Law of Armed Conflict*, *supra* note 230, at 274–5.

[314] See K.E. Boon, 'The Future of the Law of Occupation', 46 *CYIL* 107, 121 (2008).

[315] See Ferraro and Cameron, *supra* note 253, at 119.

[316] See R.R. Baxter, 'Constitutional Forms and Some Legal Problems of International Military Command', 29 *BYBIL* 325, 355 (1952).

V. Sovereignty and Belligerent Occupation

A. Sovereignty and Non-Annexation

161. The main pillar of the law of belligerent occupation is embedded in the maxim that the occupation does not affect sovereignty. The displaced sovereign loses possession of the occupied territory de facto but it retains title *de jure*. For its part, the Occupying Power acquires possession – with jurisdictional rights (see *supra* 153) – but not title.

162. Since the de facto possession acquired by the Occupying Power cannot outlast the armed conflict with the displaced sovereign (and may end even earlier; see *supra* 151), belligerent occupation is in principle temporary in character. Any measure taken or arrangement made within the ambit of the occupation will equally be temporary (even if it is the product of an agreement[317]). However, since the armed conflict may continue for a long span of time, the Occupying Power's possession may be prolonged as is the Israeli occupation (see *infra* 357). Prolongation of the occupation does not affect its innately temporary nature. Some scholars cavil at the phenomenon of long-lasting occupations,[318] but that does not alter the law: the occupation may endure as long as the armed conflict is not terminated. Indeed, Article 6 (third paragraph) of Geneva Convention (IV) – quoted *infra* 864 – has expressly recognized the possibility of a prolonged occupation.[319]

163. Undeniably, divested of possession (more or less temporarily), 'the title of the territorial sovereign is considerably weakened and reduced to a naked title'.[320] Nevertheless, 'precarious' as it is,[321] the sovereignty of the displaced sovereign over the occupied territory is not terminated. As a matter of fact, it is not even 'suspended' (as inaccurately asserted by some commentators[322] and

[317] Pursuant to Article VII(10) of Protocol Concerning Redeployment and Security Arrangements, Annex I to Israel-Palestine Liberation Organization, Interim Agreement on the West Bank and the Gaza Strip (*supra* note 116, at 579), a 'Temporary International Presence in Hebron (TIPH)' was set up in 1997. The TIPH is a multinational observer unit (headed by Norway), which – as indicated in its designation – was envisioned as a temporary measure. Yet, it still operates after more than two decades.

[318] See O. Ben-Naftali, 'PathoLAWgical Occupation: Normalizing the Exceptional Case of the Occupied Palestinian Territory and Other Legal Pathologies', *International Humanitarian Law and International Human Rights Law: Pas de Deux* 129, 149–58 (O. Ben-Naftali, ed., 2011).

[319] See A. Roberts, 'Prolonged Military Occupation: The Israeli-Occupied Territories since 1967', 84 *AJIL* 44, 57 (1990).

[320] G. Schwarzenberger, 'The Law of Belligerent Occupation: Basic Issues', 30 *NTIR* 10, 17 (1960).

[321] See P.M.R. Stirk, *The Politics of Military Occupation* 168, 230 (2009).

[322] See Gasser and Dörmann, *supra* note 196, at 275.

military manuals[323]). In the words of L. Oppenheim, '[t]here is not an atom of sovereignty in the authority of the Occupying Power'.[324]

164. In the *Affaire de la Dette Publique Ottomane* of 1925, the Arbitrator E. Borel stated:

> Quels que soient les effets de l'occupation d'un territoire par l'adversaire avant le rétablissement de la paix, il est certain qu'à elle seule cette occupation ne pouvait opérer juridiquement le transfert de souveraineté.[325]

Article 47 of Geneva Convention (IV) (quoted *infra* 373) states that an Occupying Power cannot deprive the civilian population of an occupied territory of its protection through an (alleged) annexation. Article 4 of Additional Protocol I is more categorical:

> The application of the Conventions and of this Protocol, as well as the conclusion of agreements provided for therein, shall not affect the legal status of the Parties to the conflict. Neither the occupation of a territory nor the application of the Conventions and this Protocol shall affect the legal status of the territory in question.[326]

This is now an 'uncontested principle of international law'.[327] The long and the short of it is that any unilateral annexation by the Occupying Power of an occupied territory – in whole or in part – would be legally stillborn. The contingency of *debellatio* (see *supra* 4) forms an exception to the rule, but then the right to self-determination of the local people (see *infra* 170) has to be taken into account.

165. A limpid pronouncement on the issue of ostensible annexation appears in Security Council Resolution 662 (1990), dealing with occupied Kuwait:

> *Decides* that annexation of Kuwait by Iraq under any form and whatever pretext has no legal validity, and is considered null and void.[328]

Along the same lines, the International Court of Justice – in the Advisory Opinion on the *Wall* – concluded that events unfolding in the territories occupied by Israel (especially as regards East Jerusalem) have done nothing to alter Israel's status as an Occupying Power (see *supra* 63). The Court relied on relevant Security Council resolutions, in particular Resolution 478 (1980), which declared null and void any attempts by Israel to alter the status of Jerusalem

[323] *German Law of Armed Conflict Manual*, *supra* note 255, at 85.

[324] L. Oppenheim, 'The Legal Relations between an Occupying Power and the Inhabitants', 33 *LQR* 363, 364 (1917).

[325] *Affaire de la Dette Publique Ottomane* (Bulgaria, Irak, Palestine, Transjordan, Greece, Italy and Turkey), 1925, 1 *RIAA* 529, 555.

[326] Additional Protocol I, *supra* note 33, at 716.

[327] B. Zimmermann, 'Article 4', *Commentary on the Additional Protocols of 8 June 1977 to the Geneva Conventions of 12 August 1949* 71, 73 (ICRC, Y. Sandoz *et al.* eds., 1987).

[328] Security Council Resolution 662 (1990), *supra* note 60, at 530.

(see *supra ibid.*). The Security Council also took a parallel stand in Resolution 497 (1981) concerning the Golan Heights (see *supra* 66).

166. The special cases of East Jerusalem and the Golan Heights apart, it is important to accentuate that the Israel Supreme Court expressly acknowledged (per Justice E. Rivlin) – in the *Yinon* case – that belligerent occupation does not as such serve as a basis for acquisition of title by the Occupying Power.[329] Furthermore, the Court (per Justice Strasberg-Cohen) held, in the *Hamada* case, that the law prevailing in the occupied territories – even when enacted by the Israeli military government – must be viewed as foreign law from the vantage point of the Israeli (domestic) legal system.[330]

167. The principle of non-annexation has no bearing on the right of Belligerent Parties to consider a territory occupied by the adversary as enemy territory – and property belonging to the inhabitants as enemy property – for purposes of capture at sea and prize law.[331] An occupied territory may also be subject to a maritime blockade by the co-belligerents of the displaced sovereign (*à la* blockade of occupied Europe during WWII).[332]

B. *Transfer of Title over an Occupied Territory*

168. Transfer of title over an occupied territory from the displaced sovereign to the Occupying Power may be accomplished in a valid way, but this can be done only if the transfer is made in favour of the victim of aggression (see *infra* 826). A transfer of title to a third State is a different matter: the displaced sovereign may freely cede title over the occupied territory to a third State even *durante bello*.[333] Such a cession may unleash political and military complications for the Occupying Power, although its possession of the occupied territory will not be diminished.

169. Given the basic legal adage *nemo dat quod non habet*, the Occupying Power cannot transfer to a third State a valid title – one that it does not have – over the occupied territory. For similar reasons, the Occupying Power cannot successfully hatch up within the occupied territory new puppet States, as vainly attempted by the Axis Powers during WWII in Czechoslovakia and in Yugoslavia.[334]

329 Civ.A 1432/03, *Yinon Production and Marketing of Food Products Ltd. v. Qaraan* et al., 59(1) *PD* 345, 355–6.

330 Civ.A 6860/01, *Hamada v. Israeli Combine for Vehicle Insurance* et al., 57(3) *PD* 8, 16–17.

331 See C.J. Colombos, *The International Law of the Sea* 557 (6th edn, 1967).

332 See Article 1 of the London Declaration Concerning the Laws of Naval War, 1909, *The Laws of Armed Conflicts*, *supra* note 29, at 1111, 1113.

333 See Schwarzenberger, *supra* note 320, at 17.

334 See Talmon, *supra* note 2, at 503–4.

170. An extraordinary situation relating to transfer of title over an occupied territory concerns the invocation of the right of self-determination. This is a collective human right granted to all peoples, allowing them to freely determine their political status. Its anchor is common Article 1(1) of the twin International Human Rights Covenants of 1966.[335] Nowadays, as proclaimed by the International Court of Justice in the *East Timor* case of 1996, self-determination is deemed 'one of the essential principles of contemporary international law'.[336] The exercise of the right of self-determination is usually prorogued by belligerent occupation. Yet, the people living in an occupied territory may be given an opportunity to exercise some form of self-determination even while belligerent occupation is still under way.

171. The most striking illustration of self-determination being invoked and (to a limited extent) exercised in the midst of belligerent occupation is that of the Palestinian Authority representing the Palestinian people in the territories occupied by Israel. As noted (see *supra* 52), in its Treaty of Peace with Israel – concluded in 1994 – Jordan left the final status negotiations over the West Bank to Israel and the Palestinians. Egypt had already done the same, in the 1978 Camp David Framework Agreements for Peace in the Middle East, as regards the Gaza Strip (*supra* 48). Thereby, 'both Jordan and Egypt have renounced any claims to the territories in favour of the Palestinian people's right to self-determination'.[337]

172. The transfer of rights from Egypt and Jordan to the Palestinians has had unforeseen ramifications, inasmuch as the latter (non-State actors) subsequently assumed not merely the role of negotiators for the full implementation of their right of self-determination (with a view to the ultimate creation of an independent Palestinian State), but also the role of a successor adversary of Israel. Instead of bringing the 'Oslo Accords' (*supra* 54) to their logical conclusion (i.e. lasting peace), the Palestinians have opted to wage hostilities against Israel in the West Bank and the Gaza Strip. They thereby revived the armed conflict with Israel that appeared to be coming to an end. Instead of grinding to a finish, the state of belligerent occupation has thus been prolonged for many years (with no end in sight).

335 International Covenant on Civil and Political Rights, 1966, *Raoul Wallenberg Compilation of Human Rights Instruments* 43, *id.* (G. Melander and G. Alfredsson eds., 1997); International Covenant on Economic, Social and Cultural Rights, 1966, *ibid.*, 33, *id.*

336 *Case Concerning East Timor* (Portugal, Australia), [1995] *ICJ Rep.* 90, 102.

337 M. Milanovic, 'Lessons for Human Rights and Humanitarian Law in the War on Terror: Comparing *Hamdan* and the Israeli *Targeted Killings* Case', 866 *IRRC* 373, 383 (2007).

C. Nationality and Allegiance

173. The relations between the Occupying Power and the civilian population in an occupied territory are determined by the special circumstances of effective control without title. Since title to the occupied territory remains in the hands of the displaced sovereign, two interlaced conclusions ensue for the civilian population of the occupied territory.

174. The first conclusion is that inhabitants do not lose their nationality. Article 67 (second sentence) of Geneva Convention (IV) expressly states that military courts of the Occupying Power (to be dealt with *infra* 419 *et seq.*) 'shall take into consideration the fact that the accused is not a national of the Occupying Power'.[338] Those persons who were nationals of the displaced sovereign prior to the occupation, or acquire such nationality subsequently, cling to that nationality.[339]

175. A complementary inference is that inhabitants retain their allegiance to the displaced sovereign and do not owe allegiance to the Occupying Power. Article 68 (third paragraph) of the Convention – in connection with the imposition of the death penalty (see *infra* 441) – requires drawing the attention of the military court 'to the fact that since the accused is not a national of the Occupying Power, he is not bound to it by any duty of allegiance'.[340]

176. Hague Regulation 45 promulgates:

> Any compulsion on the population of occupied territory to take the oath [of allegiance] to the hostile Power is forbidden.[341]

Thus, allegiance to the displaced sovereign is not only retained but it cannot be altered by duress. Regulation 44 is cast in the same conceptual mould:

> Any compulsion on the population of occupied territory to furnish information about the army of the other belligerent, or about his means of defence is forbidden.[342]

177. The texts quoted from the Hague Regulations are the 1907 versions. The original 1899 language of Regulation 44 interdicted '[a]ny compulsion on the population of occupied territory to take part in military operations against its own country'.[343] The words excised in 1907 from the 1899 formulation of Regulation 44 were effectively reintroduced in the second paragraph of Regulation 23(h) of the 1907 text:

338 Geneva Convention (IV), *supra* note 29, at 599.
339 See G. von Glahn, *The Occupation of Enemy Territory: A Commentary on the Law and Practice of Belligerent Occupation* 60 (1957).
340 Geneva Convention (IV), *supra* note 29, at 600.
341 Hague Regulations, *supra* note 22, at 244–5.
342 *Ibid.*
343 *Ibid.*

A belligerent is likewise forbidden to compel the nationals of the adverse party to take part in the operations of war directed against their country, even when they have been in his service before the commencement of the war.[344]

178. The 1907 variant of Regulation 44 has been expanded in Article 31 of Geneva Convention (IV):

No physical or moral coercion shall be exercised against protected persons, in particular to obtain information from them or from third parties.[345]

Article 51 (first paragraph) of the Convention declares further:

The Occupying Power may not compel protected persons to serve in its armed or auxiliary forces. No pressure or propaganda which aims at securing voluntary enlistment is permitted.[346]

It ought to be noted that service in 'the occupied territory's civilian police force whose duty is to maintain public order' is excluded from the reach of this provision (see *infra* 195).[347]

179. During WWII, Alsatians of the German 'race' were subjected to compulsory military service in the German armed forces (occupied Alsace having been unilaterally annexed by Germany). In the *Wagner* trial, this was adjudged to be a war crime.[348] Compelling a protected person to serve in the forces of a hostile Power constitutes a grave breach of the Geneva Convention under Article 147,[349] and, as such, a war crime pursuant to Article 8(2)(a)(v) of the 1998 Rome Statute of the International Criminal Court.[350] Article 8(2)(b)(xv) of the Rome Statute[351] – following in the footsteps of the second paragraph of Regulation 23(h) of the 1907 Hague text – also brands as a war crime the compulsion of enemy nationals to take part in operations of war directed against their own country (even if they were in the service of the Belligerent Party before the war).[352]

344 *Ibid.*, 235.
345 Geneva Convention (IV), *supra* note 29, at 590.
346 *Ibid.*, 595.
347 Gasser and Dörmann, *supra* note 196, at 287.
348 See *Wagner* et al. trial (Permanent Military Tribunal, Strasbourg, 1946), 3 *LRTWC* 23, 28–9, 40, 45.
349 Geneva Convention (IV), *supra* note 29, at 624.
350 Rome Statute of the International Criminal Court, 1998, *The Laws of Armed Conflicts*, *supra* note 29, at 1309, 1317.
351 *Ibid.*, 1318.
352 Article 8(2)(a) of the Rome Statute sets out as war crimes the grave breaches enumerated in Article 147, when committed against protected persons; conversely, the victims of war crimes listed in Article 8(2)(b) do not have to be protected persons. See W.A. Schabas, *An Introduction to the International Criminal Court* 135 (4th edn, 2011).

180. It is necessary to differentiate here between two unlawful strands of duress that are inter-related but not identical:

(a) Compulsion to take part in operations of war against a protected person's own country – in violation of his duty of allegiance to it (see *supra* 175) – 'whether or not as part of military forces'.[353] An example would be 'the impressment of guides from the local inhabitants' of an occupied territory.[354]

(b) Forced conscription into the armed forces of the Occupying Power: such compulsory service is prohibited even when it does not entail fighting against the country of nationality (combat may take place against, e.g., an allied State).[355]

181. The prohibition of compulsory military service does not comprise 'genuine voluntary enlistment', although 'this will almost certainly be equivalent to treason under the municipal law' of the displaced sovereign.[356] The legality of unpressured enlistment of volunteers (as distinct from coerced conscription) to the Waffen SS – fighting against their own country – was confirmed by an American Military Tribunal in the *Ministries* trial (part of the 'Subsequent Proceedings' at Nuremberg) in 1949.[357]

VI. The Military Nature of the Government in an Occupied Territory

A. *The Administration of an Occupied Territory*

182. In exerting effective control over an occupied territory, the Occupying Power is not compelled to create any special structure of administration for running the area. It is true that the Trial Chamber of the ICTY, in the *Naletilić* case, advanced the view that one of the guidelines – determining whether the authority of an occupying power has been actually established – is that 'a temporary administration has been established over the territory' by the Occupying Power.[358] Yet, this dictum runs counter to the last words in the extract quoted from the Judgment of the International Court of Justice in the *Armed Activities*

[353] R. Cryer, H. Friman, D. Robinson and E. Wilmshurst, *An Introduction to International Criminal Law and Procedure* 295 (2nd edn, 2010).

[354] US Department of the Army, *Field Manual: The Law of Land Warfare*, *supra* note 233, at 107.

[355] K. Dörmann, *Elements of War Crimes under the Rome Statute of the International Criminal Court: Sources and Commentary* 97 (ICRC, 2003).

[356] H. McCoubrey and N.D. White, *International Law and Armed Conflict* 290 (1992).

[357] *Ministries* trial (*Weizsaecker* et al.) (US Military Tribunal, Nuremberg, 1949), 16 *ILR* 344, 357.

[358] *Prosecutor v. Naletilić* et al., *supra* note 64, at para. 217.

case (*supra* 146). The position of the International Court is better entrenched in State practice. Establishing a special structure of administration is a sensible step, but failure to do so cannot alter the reality of belligerent occupation. Much depends on the nature and expanse of the occupied territory (which may be too small or sparsely populated to require the setting up of a special administrative structure) and on the fact that the occupation may be expected to be brief (see *supra* 127). When the small scale or the short time-frame makes it feasible, the Occupying Power may prefer to exercise its authority in the occupied territory through ordinary military units.[359] Conversely, when the occupation stretches out over densely populated zones of some size, the creation of a special administrative structure may be well-nigh inescapable (especially if the occupation is anticipated to endure for some time).

183. With or without a structured administration, the government of an occupied territory is military *per definitionem*. Not in vain does Hague Regulation 42 (quoted *supra* 117) refer to 'the authority of the hostile army'. If the occupation lasts for a while, civilian affairs experts with acumen and skill are usually recruited, with a view to assisting the military in the performance of the manifold tasks that lubricate the gears of day-to-day occupation.[360] The Occupying Power may even create a 'civil administration' – as Israel did in 1981 – but only as a subdivision of the military government, and not as a separate body.[361] Such an administration has to be regarded as an arm of the military government handling civil (as distinct from security) affairs, rather than a separate apparatus run by civilians.[362]

184. Whatever *modus operandi* is chosen by the military government, the top military commander – placed in charge by the Occupying Power – is the pinnacle of authority in the occupied territory, and all functionaries in the administration (whether military or civilian, including officials enlisted locally) must answer to him.[363] The authority of the lower levels of the military government bureaucracy thus trickles down top-to-bottom.

185. For his part, the military commander in charge of an occupied territory does not act in a vacuum. The Israel Supreme Court has repeatedly propounded – e.g., in the *Beth El* case (per Deputy President Landau) – that the military commander is not his own master: he reports to higher echelons in the military hierarchy and he is executing the policy of the Government of the

359 See HCJ 102/82 etc., *supra* note 266, at 373.

360 See J. Singer, 'The Establishment of a Civil Administration in the Areas Administered by Israel', 12 *IYHR* 259, 263 (1982).

361 See *ibid.*, 265.

362 See Y. Butovsky, 'Law of Belligerent Occupation: Israeli Practice and Judicial Decisions Affecting the West Bank', 21 *CYIL* 217, 230 (1983).

363 See Wilson, *supra* note 51, at 18.

Occupying Power.[364] In the *Kiryat Arba* case, the Court (per Justice Shamgar) stated that, 'had it not been for this thesis, a democratic State would not have been able to establish a military government' in an occupied territory.[365]

B. *The Overall Responsibility of the Occupying Power*

186. Under Article 29 of Geneva Convention (IV):

> The Party to the conflict in whose hands protected persons may be, is responsible for the treatment accorded to them by its agents, irrespective of any individual responsibility which may be incurred.[366]

As indicated (see *supra* 72), any protected person present in an occupied territory may be regarded as someone in the hands of the Occupying Power. The ICRC Commentary also construes the term 'agents' in the broadest possible way, 'embracing everyone who is in the service of a Contracting Party, no matter in what way or in what capacity' (including soldiers, civil servants and judges, as well as locally recruited officials), even when the agents exceed their power.[367] The Commentary adds that there is no State responsibility for illicit private acts of nationals of the Occupying Power, unless there is lack of due diligence on the part of the military government in preventing or punishing these acts.[368] This is all in keeping with the fundamental principle that an internationally wrongful act must be attributable to the State, namely, it must be the conduct of the State's organs – acting in whatever function, even in excess of authority – and not that of private individuals (unless they are in fact acting under the direction or control of the State).[369]

C. *Self-Government*

187. In almost every instance of belligerent occupation, some measure of administrative self-government by the inhabitants of the occupied territory is countenanced by the Occupying Power.[370] At the very least, the military government of an occupied territory would be eager to avail itself of the

[364] HCJ 606/78 etc., *supra* note 177, at 126.
[365] HCJ 663/78, *Kiryat Arba Administration* et al. *v. National Labour Tribunal* et al., 33(2) *PD* 398, 403.
[366] Geneva Convention (IV), *supra* note 29, at 589.
[367] *Commentary, IV Geneva Convention*, *supra* note 31, at 211–12.
[368] *Ibid.*, 212–13.
[369] International Law Commission, Draft Articles on Responsibility of States for Internationally Wrongful Acts, Report of the 53rd Session, [2001] II (2) *Yearbook of the International Law Commission* 32–54 (Articles 1–11 and Commentary).
[370] See HCJ 102/82 etc., *supra* note 266, at 374.

continued services of low-level local officials deputized to handle peripheral (e.g., municipal or rural) affairs. The reason is prosaic: it is a matter of expediency and conservation of resources. Evidently, the Occupying Power will bear responsibility for the acts of the local officials who are acting subject to its overall supervision. As the European Court of Human Rights pointed out in the *Loizidou* case, it does not matter whether effective control of an occupied territory is maintained directly by the armed forces or is exercised 'through a subordinate local administration'.[371]

188. The degree of self-government in an occupied territory may be a lot more than nominal. As the case of Denmark during WWII shows, the Occupying Power may even enable the incumbent Government to remain in office under its tutelage.[372] The fact that the performance of some or most of the normal functions of government is left to those who used to be running the country prior to the occupation is not inconsistent with a regime of belligerent occupation, provided that these local authorities (at whatever level of power) are acting 'subject to the paramount authority of the Occupying Power'.[373]

189. The Occupying Power may equally allow a new local central authority – with a wide array of powers – to be installed during the occupation. The prototype of this scenario is the inauguration of the Palestinian Authority in the West Bank and the Gaza Strip following the 'Oslo Accords' (see *supra* 54). Naturally, the degree of the autonomy conferred on the new authority will be modulated. As long as the occupation lingers, the autonomous body cannot exercise the whole panoply of powers of a fully independent Government.

190. Article I(1) of the Israel-PLO Interim Agreement of 1995 prescribes that Israel 'shall transfer powers and responsibilities as specified in this Agreement' to the Palestinian Council (and Authority), yet 'Israel shall continue to exercise powers and responsibilities not so transferred'.[374] Conspicuously, (i) Israel is the source of those powers and responsibilities that are actually transferred to the Palestinians, and (ii) Israel retains residual powers in all spheres where no such transfer has been effected.[375] This is an extraordinary agreement, for the general principle underlying autonomy arrangements is that powers are bestowed on a self-governing entity by the sovereign State and residual powers inhere in the latter.[376] Here, exceptionally, Israel – as an Occupying Power

[371] *Loizidou v. Turkey* (Merits), *supra* note 66, at 453.

[372] See C. Bjørn, 'Denmark', *The Oxford Companion to World War II* 293, *id.* (I.C.B. Dear ed., 1995).

[373] US Department of Defense, *Law of War Manual*, *supra* note 1, at 766.

[374] Israel-Palestine Liberation Organization, Interim Agreement on the West Bank and the Gaza Strip, *supra* note 116, at 558.

[375] See Singer, *supra* note 120, at 47–8.

[376] See. Y. Dinstein, 'Autonomy', *Models of Autonomy* 291, 299 (Y. Dinstein ed., 1981).

(thus, not the sovereign) – is the fount of authority and the retainer of residual powers.

D. *The Employment of Local Officials*

191. The relationship between the Occupying Power and local public officials in an occupied territory is multi-layered, as thrashed out in Article 54 of Geneva Convention (IV). The second paragraph (second sentence) gives the Occupying Power leave to dismiss from their posts local public officials.[377] The decision is not likely to take place *en bloc*: usually, removal of officials will result from individual vetting.

192. Freedom of choice in this respect cuts both ways. Under Article 54 (first paragraph), if the Occupying Power wishes to keep in its employ local public officials – who, for their part, are disinclined to serve the military government for reasons of conscience – no coercive measures can be taken against them.[378]

193. Under Article 54 (second paragraph, first sentence), the provision of the first paragraph does not prejudice the application of Article 51 (second paragraph) regarding compulsory work (see *infra* 538).[379] What it boils down to is that the military government may compel some local public officials to stay on, working on its behalf. As explained in the ICRC Commentary, this saving clause is particularly relevant to 'public utility services' – such as water, gas, electricity, transport and health services – 'the function of which would be seriously compromised by a general withdrawal of the officials employed in them'.[380] The resignation of local public officials engaged in essential services may consequently be overridden by the Occupying Power.[381]

194. Where services of indigenous public officials are retained, the Occupying Power must assume responsibility for payment of their salaries, although it may defray the cost out of tax revenues raised from the occupied territory.[382] The Occupying Power does not have to foot the bill of unpaid salaries and pensions accruing from the pre-occupation period and owed by the displaced sovereign.[383]

195. The ICRC Commentary brings into relief the special case of local police officers whose predicament is derived from the prohibition – encapsulated in Article 51 (second paragraph) (see *infra ibid.*), in which there is an express

[377] Geneva Convention (IV), *supra* note 29, at 596.
[378] *Ibid.*
[379] *Ibid.*
[380] *Commentary, IV Geneva Convention*, *supra* note 31, at 306.
[381] See *ibid.*
[382] See A. Gerson, *Israel, the West Bank and International Law* 128 (1978).
[383] See M. Greenspan, *The Modern Law of Land Warfare* 229 (1959).

cross-reference to Article 54 (second paragraph) – of compelling protected persons 'to undertake any work which would involve them in the obligation of taking part in military operations'.[384] The Commentary elucidates that police officers 'cannot under any circumstances be required to participate in measures aimed at opposing legitimate belligerent acts, whether committed by armed forces hostile to the Occupying Power, by corps of volunteers or by organized resistance movements'.[385] Nonetheless, the Commentary sustains the right of the Occupying Power to demand that the local police take part in activities related to the maintenance of law and order in the occupied territory.[386]

VII. Protected Persons in Occupied Territories

196. There is a discrepancy between the span of protection afforded to the civilian population in occupied territories by Geneva Convention (IV) and by the Hague Regulations. The Hague Regulations employ the term 'inhabitants' of an occupied territory (see, e.g., Hague Regulations 44–5 quoted *supra* 176). The Geneva Convention does not follow suit: in some respects it is more restrictive in scope, but in others it is less so.

A. *Geneva Exclusions*

(a) Nationals of the Occupying Power

197. Article 4 (first paragraph) of Geneva Convention (IV) (quoted *supra* 72) – by using the words 'in the hands of a Party to the conflict or Occupying Power of which they are not nationals' – excludes from the protection of the Convention nationals of the Occupying Power, even if they live in the occupied territory. As we shall see (*infra* 544 *et seq.*), there is one deviation from the rule in the case of pre-war refugees. Otherwise, the Convention reflects the outdated principle that international law 'does not interfere in a State's relations with its own nationals'.[387] Modern human rights law goes in an opposite direction, and its consequences for nationals of the Occupying Power will be traced *infra* 259.

(b) Nationals of Neutral and Co-Belligerent States

198. The second sentence of Article 4 (second paragraph) reads:

> Nationals of a neutral State who find themselves in the territory of a belligerent State, and nationals of a co-belligerent State, shall not be regarded as protected persons while

[384] Geneva Convention (IV), *supra* note 29, at 595.
[385] *Commentary, IV Geneva Convention*, *supra* note 31, at 307.
[386] *Ibid.*
[387] *Ibid.*, 46.

the State of which they are nationals has normal diplomatic representation in the State in whose hands they are.[388]

The rather convoluted language used in this sentence creates a distinction between nationals of a neutral State and nationals of a co-belligerent (allied) State whose Government maintains normal diplomatic relations with the Occupying Power.

199. The correct interpretation of the text, as held by the UK Supreme Court in the *Rahmatullah* case of 2012, is that – insofar as nationals of a neutral State are concerned – the absence of normal diplomatic relations is relevant only within the territory of a Belligerent Party itself but not in an occupied territory (where the protection vouchsafed to them is impervious to the existence or non-existence of normal diplomatic relations).[389] Contrarily, as regards nationals of a co-belligerent (allied) State, if normal diplomatic relations are maintained between their country and the Occupying Power, they will not be protected either within the territory of a Belligerent Party or in an occupied territory.[390]

200. The explanation offered by the ICRC Commentary for the non-protection of the latter category of persons is that '[i]t is assumed in this provision that the nationals of co-belligerent States, that is to say, of allies, do not need protection under the Convention'.[391] The assumption is not necessarily corroborated by experience. The existence of normal diplomatic relations does not always guarantee that diplomatic protection will actually be available to all those who need it.[392] In the 2000 *Blaškić* case, a Trial Chamber of the ICTY expressed the opinion that – when individuals do not actually 'enjoy the normal diplomatic protection of their State' – 'they should be accorded the status of protected person[s]'.[393]

201. As early as 1931, in the *Chevreau* case, the Arbitrator – F.V.N. Beichmann – saw nothing wrong in the detention and deportation of a French national by British occupying forces in Persia (present-day Iran) during WWI, fought by the UK and France jointly as close allies.[394] Although the Arbitral Award preceded the Geneva Convention, the legal position has not been modified, bearing in mind the normal diplomatic relations that were well established at the time between the UK and France.

388 Geneva Convention (IV), *supra* note 29, at 581.

389 *Secretary of State for Foreign and Commonwealth Affairs* et al. v. *Rahmatullah* (UK Supreme Court, 2012), paras. 29–32 (Lord Kerr).

390 See *Commentary, IV Geneva Convention*, *supra* note 31, at 48–9.

391 *Ibid.*, 49.

392 See E. Salmón, 'Who Is a Protected Civilian?', *The 1949 Geneva Conventions: A Commentary*, *supra* note 309, at 1135, 1146.

393 *Prosecutor v. Blaškić*, *supra* note 64, at para. 145.

394 *Affaire Chevreau* (France, UK), 1931, 2 *RIAA* 1113, 1123.

(c) *Nationals of Non-Contracting Parties*

202. The first sentence of Article 4 (second paragraph) keeps out of the circle of protection '[n]ationals of a State which is not bound by the Convention'.[395] At the time of writing, this is an empty set.

(d) *Persons Protected by the other Geneva Conventions*

203. Article 4 (fourth paragraph)[396] removes from the scope of the Convention's protection persons who are protected by Geneva Conventions (I) to (III).[397] These Conventions deal mainly with members of the armed forces who are *hors de combat* (wounded, sick, shipwrecked and prisoners of war) or serve as medical or religious personnel.

B. *Geneva Inclusions*

204. Although the catalogue of protected persons in Geneva Convention (IV) does not cover all the inhabitants of an occupied territory, the compass of protected persons under the Convention also goes beyond the pale of inhabitants. This results from the reference – in Article 4 (first paragraph) (quoted *supra* 72) – to all persons who, 'in any manner whatsoever', happen to 'find themselves' in the hands of an Occupying Power. Since the formula used does not differentiate between domiciled residents and visitors or tourists who are only temporarily present in an occupied territory (arriving subsequent to the beginning of the occupation), the latter category is also covered.[398] For more on this subject, see *infra* 503–5.

205. It can be surmised from the exclusion of persons of certain nationalities (*supra* 197–8) that stateless persons in occupied territories (viz. those not having any nationality) remain under the umbrella of protected persons under the Convention.[399] To eliminate doubts, Article 73 of Additional Protocol I (quoted *infra* 550) 'reaffirms explicitly and unambiguously the status of stateless persons as protected persons as defined in Art. 4 of the Fourth

[395] Geneva Convention (IV), *supra* note 29, at 581.

[396] *Ibid.*

[397] Geneva Convention (I) for the Amelioration of the Condition of the Wounded and Sick in Armed Forces in the Field, 1949, *The Laws of Armed Conflicts*, *supra* note 29, at 459; Geneva Convention (II) for the Amelioration of the Condition of Wounded, Sick and Shipwrecked Members of Armed Forces at Sea, 1949, *ibid.*, 485; Geneva Convention (III) Relative to the Treatment of Prisoners of War, 1949, *ibid.*, 507.

[398] See *Commentary, IV Geneva Convention*, *supra* note 31, at 47.

[399] See C.F. Wenger, 'Article 73', *Commentary on the Additional Protocols*, *supra* note 327, at 845, 846. See also *Prosecutor v. Tadić* (ICTY, Appeals Chamber, 1999), 38 *ILM* 1518, 1550 (1999).

Convention'.[400] Article 73 does seem to exclude from protection persons who became stateless after the outbreak of hostilities, but this 'is probably inadvertent and may not be construed to diminish the protected status of stateless persons which they clearly have under any reasonable construction of Art. 4 of the Fourth Convention'.[401] The issue of statelessness is of more than passing interest in the context of the Gaza Strip (see *supra* 46).[402]

C. The Treatment of Saboteurs

206. Article 5 of Geneva Convention (IV) (captioned 'Derogations') sets forth in its second paragraph:

> Where in occupied territory an individual protected person is detained as a spy or saboteur, or as a person under definite suspicion of activity hostile to the security of the Occupying Power, such person shall, in those cases where absolute military security so requires, be regarded as having forfeited rights of communication under the present Convention.[403]

The term 'saboteur' is a somewhat outmoded equivalent of expressions like 'terrorist' or 'guerrilla' that are more popular today, but – this being the language of the Convention – it will be used also throughout the present volume.

207. The rights forfeited under the second paragraph of Article 5 pertain solely to communication. The third paragraph of Article 5 proceeds to say:

> In each case, such persons shall nevertheless be treated with humanity, and in case of trial, shall not be deprived of the rights of fair and regular trial prescribed by the present Convention.[404]

This clause emphasizes that the loss of the rights to communication does not imply any erosion of protection from violence and torture – bequeathed in Articles 27 (first paragraph) and 32 (quoted *infra* 250, 460) – or, should the saboteur be prosecuted, the right to a fair and regular trial featured in Articles 71 *et seq.* (see *infra* 435 *et seq.*).[405]

208. Rights of communication are spelt out in Article 30 (first paragraph) of the Convention:

[400] W.A. Solf, 'Article 73', *New Rules for Victims of Armed Conflicts: Commentary on the Two 1977 Protocols Additional to the Geneva Conventions of 1949* 501, 502 (M. Bothe, K.J. Partsch and W.A. Solf eds., 2nd edn, 2013).

[401] *Ibid.*, 504.

[402] See A. Zimmermann, 'The Nationality of the Inhabitants of the Palestinian Autonomous Territories', *New Political Entities in Public and Private International Law with Special Reference to the Palestinian Entity, supra* note 120, at 231, 244–5.

[403] Geneva Convention (IV), *supra* note 29, at 581.

[404] *Ibid.*, 582.

[405] See K. Dörmann, 'The Legal Situation of "Unlawful/Unprivileged Combatants"', 849 *IRRC* 45, 66 (2003).

Protected persons shall have every facility for making application to the Protecting Powers, the International Committee of the Red Cross, the National Red Cross (Red Crescent, Red Lion and Sun) Society of the country where they may be, as well as to any organization that might assist them.[406]

The forfeiture of rights of communication in occupied territories is linked to the rule that spies and saboteurs may be interned, as long as absolute military security so requires (on internment, see *infra* 519 *et seq.*).[407] However, as a special panel of five Justices of the Israel Supreme Court decided (per President Barak), in the *Obeid* case, reliance on security considerations for the denial of contacts with the representatives of the ICRC cannot be open-ended: after lapse of time, it is subject to the restrictive condition of reasonableness.[408]

209. For Contracting Parties to Additional Protocol I, the legal position is altered by Article 45(3) of that instrument:

Any person who has taken part in hostilities, who is not entitled to prisoner-of-war status and who does not benefit from more favourable treatment in accordance with the Fourth Convention shall have the right at all times to the protection of Article 75 of this Protocol. In occupied territory, any such person, unless he is held as a spy, shall also be entitled, notwithstanding Article 5 of the Fourth Convention, to his rights of communication under that Convention.[409]

The first sentence, which adduces Article 75 of the Protocol (granting fundamental guarantees; see *infra* 438), is an extrapolation and an extension of Article 5 (third paragraph) of the Convention. That is not the case with the second sentence – applicable directly to occupied territories – which amounts to an 'abrogation' of Article 5 (second paragraph) of the Convention, insofar as the rights of communication of saboteurs (albeit not spies) are concerned.[410]

VIII. Protecting Powers

A. *The Theory*

210. Article 9 (first paragraph) of Geneva Convention (IV) lays down that the Convention 'shall be applied with the cooperation and under the scrutiny of the Protecting Powers whose duty it is to safeguard the interests of the Parties to the conflict'.[411] Even stronger language is used in Article 5 of Additional

[406] Geneva Convention (IV), *supra* note 29, at 589.
[407] See G.I.A.D. Draper, 'The Geneva Conventions of 1949', 114 *RCADI* 63, 131 (1965).
[408] HCJ 794/98, *Obeid* et al. *v. Minister of Defence* et al., 55(5) *PD* 769, 772–3. (The Judgment is excerpted in English in 32 *IYHR* 351 (2002)).
[409] Additional Protocol I, *supra* note 33, at 734.
[410] J. de Preux, 'Article 45', *Commentary on the Additional Protocols, supra* note 327, at 543, 559.
[411] Geneva Convention (IV), *supra* note 29, at 582.

Protocol I.[412] A Protecting Power is defined in Article 2(c) of the Protocol as 'a neutral or other State not a Party to the conflict which has been designated by a Party to the conflict and accepted by the adverse Party and has agreed to carry out the functions assigned to a Protecting Power under the Convention and this Protocol'.[413]

211. The English term 'scrutiny', employed in Article 9 (first paragraph) of the Geneva Convention, was adopted – after lengthy discussions – as a translation of the French term 'contrôle'.[414] While it is not easy to gauge the precise measure of monitoring implied here, it must be taken into account that numerous clauses of the Convention require keeping the Protecting Power in the loop with up-to-date information about the discharge of the duties of the Occupying Power. Thus, Article 49 (fourth paragraph) ordains that the Protecting Power must be informed of any transfers and evacuations as soon as they have taken place;[415] Article 59 (fourth paragraph) (referred to *infra* 588) allots to it a task in the passage of relief consignments to occupied territories; and Article 74 (second paragraph) (cited *infra* 443) decrees that any sentence of death will be communicated to it as rapidly as possible.

212. Article 11 (second paragraph) of the Convention provides that, when protected persons do not benefit from the activities of a Protecting Power, the 'Detaining' (to wit, Occupying) Power 'shall' request a neutral State or an organization offering all the guarantees of impartiality and efficacy to undertake the functions of a Protecting Power.[416] This appointment of what is usually known as a 'substitute' to a Protecting Power is different from the procedure envisaged in Article 9 in that only a dual – in lieu of a triple – consent is demanded: that of the 'Detaining' Power and that of the substitute (neutral State or organization).[417] Alternatively, under the third paragraph of Article 11, the services of a humanitarian organization (such as the ICRC) may be offered to the 'Detaining' Power, with a view to performing the humanitarian functions of a Protecting Power.[418] Humanitarian functions are only a fragment of the overall mission of a Protecting Power whose tasks in practice include communications between the Belligerent Parties and even rendering consular services.[419]

412 Additional Protocol I, *supra* note 33, at 716–17.
413 *Ibid.*, 716.
414 See *Commentary, IV Geneva Convention, supra* note 31, at 85.
415 Geneva Convention (IV), *supra* note 29, at 594.
416 *Ibid.*, 583.
417 *Commentary, IV Geneva Convention, supra* note 31, at 107–8.
418 Geneva Convention (IV), *supra* note 29, at 583.
419 See H.-J. Heintze, 'Protecting Power', VIII *MPEPIL* 545, 548.

213. The procedure envisaged in Article 11 has drawn withering criticisms on the ground that the consent of the 'Power of origin' (the displaced sovereign) is dispensed with.[420] Article 5(4) of Additional Protocol I accordingly makes the functioning of a substitute contingent on the consent of the Parties to the conflict, thus reverting to the requirement of triple consent and repudiating the possibility of dual consent opened up by the Convention.[421]

B. *The Practice*

214. Although the institution of Protecting Powers is long-standing, it is scarcely in use nowadays.[422] The root of the problem is that, in spite of the mandatory language in which both Article 9 of Geneva Convention (IV)[423] and Article 5 of Additional Protocol I[424] are couched, the appointment of a Protecting Power is conditioned on the consent of all three States concerned: both Belligerent Parties (i.e. in circumstances of belligerent occupation, the Occupying Power and the displaced sovereign) and the neutral State.[425] The goal of attaining such triple consent tends to be elusive in practice, especially in recent times.[426] Various additional reasons have been cited for the decline of the institution of the Protecting Power,[427] but what ultimately counts is the dissatisfactory outcome.

215. As for substitutes, neither the second nor the third paragraph of Article 11 of the Convention has ever been galvanized into action. In the early seventies, the ICRC offered its services in the role of an official substitute to all the Belligerent Parties in the Arab-Israeli conflict, but '[t]here was no clearly affirmative response to the ICRC from any party'.[428]

216. In the de facto absence of a Protecting Power or even an official substitute, what is left is ordinary humanitarian assistance to protected persons

[420] See B. Zimmermann, 'Article 5', *Commentary on the Additional Protocols, supra* note 327, at 75, 85.
[421] See *ibid.*, 86–7.
[422] On the use of Protecting Powers subsequent to 1949, see G.A.B. Peirce, 'Humanitarian Protection for the Victims of War: The System of Protecting Powers and the Role of the ICRC', 90 *Mil.LR* 89, 123–5 (1980).
[423] See *Commentary, IV Geneva Convention, supra* note 31, at 86.
[424] See Zimmermann, *supra* note 420, at 79.
[425] See B. Zimmermann, 'Article 2', *Commentary on the Additional Protocols, supra* note 327, at 57, 61–2.
[426] See D.P. Forsythe, 'Who Guards the Guardians: Third Parties and the Law of Armed Conflict', 70 *AJIL* 41, 46–7 (1976).
[427] See R. Kolb, 'Protecting Powers', *The 1949 Geneva Conventions: A Commentary, supra* note 309, at 549, 557.
[428] Forsythe, *supra* note 426, at 48.

tendered by the ICRC and other impartial humanitarian organizations. Article 10 of the Convention sees no obstacle to the humanitarian activities of the ICRC or any other impartial humanitarian organization, but this is subject to the consent of the Parties to the conflict.[429] The consent condition 'is obviously harsh but it might almost be said to be self-evident'.[430]

[429] Geneva Convention (IV), *supra* note 29, at 583.
[430] *Commentary, IV Geneva Convention*, *supra* note 31, at 98.

3 Human Rights and Belligerent Occupation

217. One of the most contentious issues is the degree of synergy that exists between the law of belligerent occupation and the law of human rights. The doctrinal debate is confounded by two countervailing linguistic snags. On the one hand, there is an etymological affinity between the cognate terms 'humanitarian' – central to the expression 'international humanitarian law' (as a synonym for the *jus in bello*) – and 'human' in 'human rights'. On the other hand, the jargon of human rights scholars and the argot used by *jus in bello* experts often sound like two different dialects.[431] Even the staple phrase 'effective control' may have a different connotation in the *jus in bello* and in human rights law.[432] The disharmony in the use of the phrase caught the limelight in the UK House of Lords' decision in the *Al-Skeini* case of 2007.[433]

I. The International Law of Human Rights

218. Before getting into the substance of the interaction between human rights and the *jus in bello*, a compact *aperçu* of the law of human rights is in order. This law (which establishes corresponding obligations for States) is of quite recent origins in international law, having developed largely in the post-WWII era. Yet, by now, there exists a rich normative tapestry of international human rights. The interwoven threads consist of both customary *jus non scriptum* (obligating all States) and *jus scriptum*. The written law is mostly treaty law (see *infra* 219), but the seminal instrument is the Universal Declaration of Human Rights, adopted by the UN General Assembly in 1948.[434] At its inception, the Universal Declaration 'was not intended to impose legal obligations

[431] See N. Lubell, 'Challenges in Applying Human Rights Law to Armed Conflict', 860 *IRRC* 737, 745 (2005).
[432] See Wills, *supra* note 215, at 266–7.
[433] *Al-Skeini* et al. *v. Secretary of State for Defence* (UK House of Lords, 2007), 46 *ILM* 778, 799 (Lord Rodger), 808 (Lord Brown) (2007).
[434] Universal Declaration of Human Rights, UN General Assembly Resolution 217(III), 10 December 1948, *Raoul Wallenberg Compilation of Human Rights Instruments*, *supra* note 335, at 27.

on States, but rather to establish goals for States to work towards'.[435] Over the years since 1948, the position of the Universal Declaration has changed drastically.[436] '[T]here would seem to be little argument that many provisions of the Declaration today do reflect customary international law'.[437]

219. The principal human rights treaties are the two International Covenants that were opened for signature by the General Assembly, in 1966, as a sequel to the Universal Declaration. Together, the three instruments are often referred to as an International Bill of Rights. The Covenants (see *supra* 170) are devoted to (i) Civil and Political Rights, and (ii) Economic, Social and Cultural Rights.

220. On the regional level, the three most important treaties are the 1950 European Convention for the Protection of Human Rights and Fundamental Freedoms,[438] the 1969 American Convention on Human Rights,[439] and the 1981 African Charter on Human and Peoples' Rights.[440] We shall focus in this chapter on the European and the American Conventions, inasmuch as the African Charter – although the latest in date – is also the least effective and the most polemical.[441]

221. Apart from general human rights treaties – concluded either on the global or on the regional plane – there are international agreements galore dealing with select human rights (such as freedom from torture[442]), the special protection of vulnerable groups of persons (e.g., children[443]), and the prohibition of discrimination in diverse illicit forms (for instance, racial discrimination[444]).

222. The existing network of human rights treaties – global and regional – covers virtually the entire international community. At times, there are even strains of *embarras de richesse*: competing instruments intersect, raising both practical and theoretical problems relating to their simultaneous operation.[445]

435 A.H. Robertson and J.G. Merrills, *Human Rights in the World: An Introduction to the Study of the International Protection of Human Rights* 28 (4th edn, 1996).

436 See T. Meron, *Human Rights and Humanitarian Norms as Customary Law* 82–4 (1989).

437 Committee on the Enforcement of Human Rights Law, Final Report on the Status of the Universal Declaration of Human Rights in National and International Law, *International Law Association, 66th Conference* 525, 544 (Buenos Aires, 1994).

438 European Convention for the Protection of Human Rights and Fundamental Freedoms, 1950, *Raoul Wallenberg Compilation of Human Rights Instruments, supra* note 335, at 81.

439 American Convention on Human Rights, 1969, *Raoul Wallenberg Compilation of Human Rights Instruments, supra* note 335, at 155.

440 African Charter on Human and Peoples' Rights, 1981, *Raoul Wallenberg Compilation of Human Rights Instruments, supra* note 335, at 191.

441 See H.J. Steiner, P. Alston and R. Goodman, *International Human Rights in Context: Law, Politics, Morals: Text and Materials* 504 (3rd edn, 2008).

442 Convention against Torture and Other Cruel, Inhuman or Degrading Treatment or Punishment, 1984, *Raoul Wallenberg Compilation of Human Rights Instruments, supra* note 335, at 549.

443 Convention on the Rights of the Child, 1989, *Raoul Wallenberg Compilation of Human Rights Instruments, supra* note 335, at 279.

444 International Convention on the Elimination of All Forms of Racial Discrimination, 1965, *Raoul Wallenberg Compilation of Human Rights Instruments, supra* note 335, at 255.

445 See Robertson and Merrills, *supra* note 435, at 270.

But States are not on an equal footing in this regard, inasmuch as they are bound by different regional treaties and do not always adhere to the global treaties. The preliminary question in every case of belligerent occupation is whether the Occupying Power is a Contracting Party to a concrete treaty (relied upon by anyone contesting the legality of the State's conduct).

II. The Application of Human Rights Law in Occupied Territories

223. In the words of the Inter-American Commission on Human Rights, in the *Coard* case of 1999, 'while international humanitarian law pertains primarily in times of war and the international law of human rights applies most fully in times of peace, the potential application of one does not necessarily exclude or displace the other'.[446] There can be no doubt about the applicability of human rights law in wartime, subject to derogation (see *infra* 229) and to any built-in limitations (*infra* 241). As the International Court of Justice phrased it, in its Advisory Opinion on *Nuclear Weapons*:

> the protection of the International Covenant of Civil and Political Rights does not cease in times of war, except by operation of Article 4 of the Covenant whereby certain provisions may be derogated from in a time of national emergency.[447]

In the Advisory Opinion on the *Wall,* the Court covered the same ground:

> the Court considers that the protection offered by human rights conventions does not cease in case of armed conflict, save through the effect of provisions for derogation of the kind to be found in Article 4 of the International Covenant on Civil and Political Rights.[448]

The very fact that derogation is required to suspend the operation of given stipulations of the Covenant in wartime attests that – when no permissible derogation is in effect – human rights continue to be in force.

224. Article 72 of Additional Protocol I declares that its provisions relating to the treatment of persons in the power of a Party to a conflict (most of which are apposite to occupied territories) are additional 'to other applicable rules of international law relating to the protection of fundamental human rights during international armed conflict'.[449] The 'fundamental' human rights alluded to are probably those that are considered non-derogable (*infra* 238).[450] But, whatever

[446] *Coard* et al. *v. United States* (Inter-American Commission on Human Rights, 1999), para. 39.

[447] Advisory Opinion on the *Legality of the Threat or Use of Nuclear Weapons*, *supra* note 13, at 240.

[448] Advisory Opinion on *Legal Consequences of the Construction of a Wall in the Occupied Palestinian Territory*, *supra* note 25, at 178.

[449] Additional Protocol I, *supra* note 33, at 748.

[450] See C. Pilloud and J. Pictet, 'Article 72', *Commentary on the Additional Protocols, supra* note 327, at 841, 843.

the range of these human rights, they are deemed complementary to the *jus in bello*.[451]

225. Article 2(1) of the Civil and Political Rights Covenant enunciates:

> Each State Party to the present Covenant undertakes to respect and to ensure to all individuals within its territory and subject to its jurisdiction the rights recognized in the present Covenant, without distinction of any kind, such as race, colour, sex, language, religion, political or other opinion, national or social origin, property, birth or other status.[452]

The key phrase here is: 'within its territory and subject to its jurisdiction'. It is hard to gainsay that, 'on the basis of the plain and ordinary meaning of its text, this article establishes, in the conjunctive, that every state party is required to ensure the rights in the Covenant only to individuals who are both *within* its territory *and* subject to its sovereign authority'.[453] For this reason, the US takes the firm position that the Covenant does not apply abroad.[454]

226. In the Advisory Opinion on the *Wall*, the International Court of Justice – making short shrift of a contradictory position advocated by the Government of Israel (similar to that of the US) – held that the correct interpretation of the Covenant is that it is equally applicable 'in respect of acts done by a State in the exercise of its jurisdiction outside its own territory', including occupied territories.[455] Interestingly, in the *Alfei Menashe* case, the Israel Supreme Court did not disagree with the International Court's view that human rights treaties (such as the Covenant) apply in occupied territories (see *infra* 784).

227. The Grand Chamber of the European Court of Human Rights decided – in the 2001 *Banković* case – that, although the notion of jurisdiction is 'essentially territorial', some extra-territorial acts can exceptionally 'constitute an exercise of jurisdiction'.[456] An outstanding example is 'the effective control of the relevant territory and its inhabitants abroad as a consequence of military occupation' (illustrated by the *Loizidou* case; see *supra* 32).[457]

228. As treaty laws, the Covenant and the European Convention (whatever the correct interpretation of their texts) are, of course, limited in application to Contracting Parties. But it is necessary to pay heed to the customary law of

[451] See H.-J. Heintze, 'On the Relationship between Human Rights Law Protection and International Humanitarian Law', 856 *IRRC* 789, 798 (2004).

[452] International Covenant on Civil and Political Rights, *supra* note 335, at 44.

[453] M.J. Dennis, 'Application of Human Rights Treaties Extraterritorially in Times of Armed Conflict and Military Occupation', 99 *AJIL* 119, 122 (2005). Emphasis in the original.

[454] US Department of Defense, *Law of War Manual*, *supra* note 1, at 24.

[455] Advisory Opinion on *Legal Consequences of the Construction of a Wall in the Occupied Palestinian Territory*, *supra* note 25, at 179–80.

[456] *Banković v. Belgium* (Admissibility) (European Court of Human Rights, 2001), 41 *ILM* 517, 527 (2002).

[457] *Ibid.*, 528.

human rights, which is frequently reflected in the substantive clauses of these instruments. Customary human rights are conferred on human beings wherever they are. Irrefutably, the inhabitants of occupied territories are in principle entitled to benefit from the customary *corpus* of human rights that coexists with the law of belligerent occupation. The International Court of Justice observed, in the *Armed Activities* case, that 'both branches of international law, namely international human rights law and international humanitarian law, would have to be taken into consideration' in occupied territories.[458]

III. Derogations from Obligations to Respect Human Rights

A. *Derogations and War*

229. Article 4(1) of the Civil and Political Rights Covenant stipulates:

> In time of public emergency which threatens the life of the nation and the existence of which is officially proclaimed, the States Parties to the present Covenant may take measures derogating from their obligations under the present Covenant to the extent strictly required by the exigencies of the situation, provided that such measures are not inconsistent with their other obligations under international law and do not involve discrimination solely on the ground of race, colour, sex, language, religion or social origin.[459]

War is not mentioned here explicitly. At the same time,

> the omission of specific reference to war was surely not intended to deny the right of derogation in wartime; war is the most dramatic example of a public emergency which might 'threaten the life of the nation'.[460]

230. There is general recognition that war 'represents the prototype of a public emergency that threatens the life of the nation'.[461] The *travaux préparatoires* of the Covenant unambiguously divulge that war was uppermost in the minds of the framers of the derogation clause.[462] The drafters avoided the coinage 'war' only because they did not wish to create the impression that they were contemplating this calamity as a likely eventuality.[463]

[458] *Case Concerning Armed Activities on the Territory of the Congo* (Congo v. Uganda), *supra* note 26, at 243.

[459] International Covenant on Civil and Political Rights, *supra* note 335, at 44.

[460] T. Buergenthal, 'To Respect and to Ensure: State Obligations and Permissible Derogations', *The International Bill of Rights: The Covenant on Civil and Political Rights* 72, 79 (L. Henkin ed., 1981).

[461] M. Nowak, *U.N. Covenant on Civil and Political Rights: CCPR Commentary* 78 (1993).

[462] See A.-L. Svensson-McCarthy, *The International Law of Human Rights and States of Exception with Special Reference to the* Travaux Préparatoires *and Case-Law of the International Monitoring Organs* 214 (1998).

[463] See Buergenthal, *supra* note 460, at 79.

231. It is noteworthy that the reference to war is made *expressis verbis* in the derogation clauses of the European and the American Conventions: Article 15(1) of the European Convention speaks about a 'time of war or other public emergency threatening the life of the nation';[464] and Article 27(1) of the American Convention employs the formula: 'time of war, public danger, or other emergency that threatens the independence or security of a State Party'.[465]

232. A Contracting Party to the Covenant or a regional human rights treaty may decide to activate a derogation clause just within the confines of an occupied territory (and nowhere else). The International Law Association's 1984 Paris Minimum Standards of Human Rights Norms in a State of Emergency elucidate that '[t]he declaration of a state of emergency may cover the entire territory of the state or any part thereof, depending upon the areas actually affected by the circumstances motivating the declaration'.[466] The rationale applies even more vigorously to occupied territories (as completely separate entities) than to parts of the territory of a Belligerent Party.

B. Procedural and Substantive Requirements

233. When recourse is made to derogation of human rights by a Contracting Party, Article 4(3) of the Covenant enjoins that all the other Contracting Parties be immediately notified of the provisions derogated from and the reasons for the derogation (another communication must follow the termination of the derogation).[467] A similar duty is incorporated in Article 4(3) of the European Convention[468] and in Article 27(3) of the American Convention.[469] Notification has to be coupled with a public proclamation: this is explicitly adverted to in Article 4(1) of the Covenant and is implicit in the other texts.[470]

234. In addition to these procedural conditions, the exercise of derogation – under Article 4(1) (quoted *supra* 229) and its counterparts – is contingent on the fulfilment of certain substantive requirements. The first condition is that the measures taken must be strictly demanded by the exigencies of the situation. In the *Ireland v. United Kingdom* case of 1978, the European Court of Human

464 European Convention for the Protection of Human Rights and Fundamental Freedoms, *supra* note 438, at 85.

465 American Convention on Human Rights, *supra* note 439, at 163.

466 Paris Minimum Standards of Human Rights Norms in a State of Emergency, *International Law Association, Report of the 61st Conference* 1, 58 (Paris, 1984) (Section A, 4).

467 International Covenant on Civil and Political Rights, *supra* note 335, at 45.

468 European Convention for the Protection of Human Rights and Fundamental Freedoms, *supra* note 438, at 86.

469 American Convention on Human Rights, *supra* note 439, at 164.

470 See Jacobs and White, *The European Convention on Human Rights* 448–9 (4th edn, C. Ovey and R.C.A. White eds., 2006).

Rights held that States 'do not enjoy an unlimited power', even though they do have a considerable 'margin of appreciation' in determining the need for derogation.[471]

235. Moreover, the measures resorted to must not involve discrimination solely on grounds of race, colour, sex, language, religion or social origin. It is easy to gather from this condition – which is missing from the European Convention – that discrimination is not precluded on other grounds, e.g., national origin or political opinion, which are of special consequence in wartime.[472] Attention must also be drawn to the adverb 'solely'. It follows that derogation would be permissible – despite the fact that it affects a particular racial, religious or linguistic group more than others – if the discrimination is not the intended goal (for instance, when the derogation has a geographically limited range of application and the group happens to be concentrated within that area).[473]

236. The measures employed must not be inconsistent with supplementary obligations incurred under international law. This condition is linked to the strictures of other human rights instruments in force,[474] as well as to obligations devolving on States in wartime under the Geneva Conventions or kindred *jus in bello* instruments.[475]

237. The fact that derogation can validly be made does not mean that a Belligerent Party will inevitably feel compelled to avail itself of the privilege in a specific armed conflict: this is a matter of discretion and judgment. Even when the derogation clause is actually invoked, the proclamation may cover only specific derogable human rights and not the rest of them. Thus, Israel has made a derogation from Article 9 of the Covenant (referred to *infra* 257), and, in the Advisory Opinion on the *Wall*, the International Court of Justice pointed out that other derogable clauses of the Covenant have been left untouched.[476]

IV. Non-Derogable Human Rights

238. Not all human rights are derogable in wartime (or in any other public emergency). Article 4(2) of the Covenant forbids any derogation from itemized human rights,[477] as do Article 15(2) of the European

[471] *Ireland v. United Kingdom* (European Court of Human Rights, 1978), 25 *ECHRJD* 5, 79.
[472] See A. Siehr, 'Derogation Measures under Article 4 ICCPR, with Special Consideration of the "War against International Terrorism"', 47 *GYIL* 545, 567–8 (2004).
[473] See Nowak, *supra* note 461, at 86.
[474] See R. Higgins, 'Derogations under Human Rights Treaties', 48 *BYBIL* 281, 306 (1976–7).
[475] See D.J. Harris, M. O'Boyle and C. Warbrick, *Law of the European Convention on Human Rights* 502 (1995).
[476] Advisory Opinion on *Legal Consequences of the Construction of a Wall in the Occupied Palestinian Territory*, *supra* note 25, at 187–8, 192.
[477] International Covenant on Civil and Political Rights, *supra* note 335, at 45.

Convention[478] and Article 27(2) of the American Convention.[479] The lists of non-derogable human rights appearing in the three instruments coincide in part but they are not conterminous. These lists can be dissected as follows:

(a) Human rights that are non-derogable according to all three texts:
  (i) The right to life.
  (ii) Freedom from torture or cruel, inhuman or degrading treatment or punishment (extended in the American Convention to a broader right to humane treatment).[480]
  (iii) Freedom from slavery or servitude.
  (iv) Freedom from being held guilty of any act or omission, which did not constitute a criminal offence at the time of its commission or is subject to a heavier penalty than the one applicable at that time.

(b) Human rights that are non-derogable according to the Covenant and the American Convention (but not the European Convention):
  (v) Freedom of conscience and religion (extended by the Covenant to freedom of thought).
  (vi) The right to recognition as a person before the law.

(c) A human right that is non-derogable only according to the Covenant:
  (vii) Freedom from imprisonment on the ground of inability to fulfil a contractual obligation.

(d) Human rights that are non-derogable only according to the American Convention:
  (viii) Rights of the family (especially, the right to marriage).
  (ix) Right to a name.
  (x) Rights of the child.
  (xi) Right to a nationality.
  (xii) Right to participate in government.
  (xiii) Judicial guarantees essential for the protection of non-derogable rights.

(e) A human right that is non-derogable according to various Protocols to the Covenant and to the European Convention:
  (xiv) The abolition of the death penalty.[481]

[478] European Convention for the Protection of Human Rights and Fundamental Freedoms, *supra* note 438, at 86.

[479] American Convention on Human Rights, *supra* note 439, at 164.

[480] It should be added that, under Article 2(2) of the Convention against Torture and Other Cruel, Inhuman or Degrading Treatment or Punishment (*supra* note 442, at 550), no exceptional circumstances – not even 'a state of war' – may be invoked as a justification of torture.

[481] Second Optional Protocol to the International Covenant on Civil and Political Rights, 1989, *Raoul Wallenberg Compilation of Human Rights Instruments*, *supra* note 335, at 65, 66

(f) A human right that is non-derogable according to another Protocol to the European Convention:

(xv) Freedom from double jeopardy (the principle of *ne bis in idem*) in proceedings taking place within the same State.[482]

239. Some of these non-derogable rights have no special resonance in wartime, as showcased by the freedom from imprisonment on the ground of inability to fulfil a contractual obligation. The right to life is directly germane to wartime, but it does not lend protection from the ordinary consequences of hostilities, despite the catastrophic losses that these can entail. An exception to the non-derogation clause 'in respect of deaths resulting from lawful acts of war' is openly made in Article 15(2) of the European Convention.[483] The reference is not to any acts of war but only to acts that are lawful. Clearly, even from the perspective of human rights law, the lawfulness of acts causing death in wartime has to be looked for elsewhere (i.e. in the *jus in bello*).[484]

240. It is surprising that the human right to judicial guarantees of fair trial – enshrined in all the instruments[485] – is not included in the list of non-derogable rights. Only the American Convention enumerates as non-derogable those judicial guarantees that are essential to the protection of other non-derogable rights. This loose end was deftly used by the Inter-American Court of Human Rights – in two Advisory Opinions delivered on the subject in 1987 – to extrapolate that judicial remedies like the writs of *habeas corpus* and *amparo* can never be derogated, and they can therefore be used to exercise control also over the suspension of derogable rights.[486] More radically, the Human Rights Committee expressed the non-binding view – in General Comment No. 29 of

(Article 6(2)); Protocol No. 6 to the European Convention for the Protection of Human Rights and Fundamental Freedoms Concerning the Abolition of the Death Penalty, 1983, *ibid.*, 105, *id.* (Article 3); Protocol No. 13 to the European Convention for the Protection of Human Rights and Fundamental Freedoms Concerning the Abolition of the Death Penalty in All Circumstances, 2002, 41 *ILM* 515, *id.* (2002) (Article 2).

482 Protocol No. 7 to the European Convention for the Protection of Human Rights and Fundamental Freedoms, 1988, *Raoul Wallenberg Compilation of Human Rights Instruments*, *supra* note 335, at 109, 110 (Article 4(3)).

483 European Convention for the Protection of Human Rights and Fundamental Freedoms, *supra* note 438, at 86.

484 See R. Provost, *International Human Rights and Humanitarian Law* 275 (2002).

485 Universal Declaration of Human Rights, *supra* note 434, at 29 (Articles 10–11); International Covenant on Civil and Political Rights, *supra* note 335, at 47–8 (Article 14); European Convention for the Protection of Human Rights and Fundamental Freedoms, *supra* note 438, at 83–4 (Article 6); American Convention on Human Rights, *supra* note 439, at 158–9, 163 (Articles 8, 25).

486 Advisory Opinion on *Habeas Corpus in Emergency Situations* (Arts. 27(2), 25(1) and 7(6) American Convention on Human Rights), 8 *IACHRJO* 27, 35–48 (1987); Advisory Opinion on *Judicial Guarantees in States of Emergency* (Arts. 27(2), 25 and 8 American Convention on Human Rights), 9 *ibid.*, 23, 29–40 (1987).

2001 – that the list of non-derogable rights (as it appears in Article 4(2) of the Covenant) is not exhaustive, and that there can be no derogation (in particular) from judicial guarantees.[487]

V. Built-In Limitations of Human Rights

A. *Explicit Limitations*

241. Virtually all human rights, whether derogable or non-derogable, are subject to some limitations. This can be visible in the textual demeanour of the respective right. Thus, Article 21 of the Civil and Political Rights Covenant crafts freedom of assembly (a derogable right) in the following way:

> The right of peaceful assembly shall be recognized. No restrictions may be placed on the exercise of this right other than those imposed in conformity with the law and which are necessary in a democratic society in the interests of national security or public safety, public order (*ordre public*), the protection of public health or morals or the protection of the rights and freedoms of others.[488]

Beside the qualifying adjective 'peaceful', which perceptibly excludes riots, the specific mention of national security or public safety means that – even if freedom of assembly is not derogated – its implementation in wartime (especially under conditions of belligerent occupation) may be considerably circumscribed.[489] Thus, a demonstration calling for violent resistance against the military government of an occupied territory may be banned; and, if it takes place in brazen defiance of the prohibition, it may be forcibly broken up.[490]

242. The limitation of national security is attached in the Covenant not only to freedom of assembly but also to freedom of movement (Article 12(3)), freedom from expulsion (Article 13), judicial guarantees (Article 14(1)), freedom of expression (Article 19(3)(b)), and freedom of association (Article 22(2)).[491] Similar restrictions appear in the European and American Conventions. Such built-in limitations are occasionally referred to, in a somewhat overstated fashion, as 'escape clauses'.[492] Although built-in limitations

[487] Human Rights Committee, General Comment No. 29, Doc. CCPR/C/21/Rev.1/Add.11 (2001), paras. 13–15.

[488] International Covenant on Civil and Political Rights, *supra* note 335, at 50.

[489] On the interpretation of these terms in the Covenant, see A.C. Kiss, 'Permissible Limitations on Rights', *The International Bill of Rights*, *supra* note 460, at 290, 295–8.

[490] This is the general norm, irrespective of belligerent occupation. See Nowak, *supra* note 461, at 380.

[491] International Covenant on Civil and Political Rights, *supra* note 335, at 47–8, 50.

[492] K. Drzewicki, 'Pluralism and Freedom of Association: The Case of Trade Unionism', *The Strength of Diversity: Human Rights and Pluralist Democracy* 71, 74 (A. Rosas and J. Helgesen eds., 1992).

have a function comparable to that of derogations 'in the sense that both provide legal avenues for states to break free of obligations that would ordinarily constrain their actions', limitation clauses apply not only in exceptional situations or as stopgap measures.[493]

B. *Implicit Limitations*

243. The exercise of some human rights – preeminently freedom from torture – appears at first sight to be completely shorn of limitations, since none are explicitly incorporated in the text. But this is an optical illusion. Even torture has to be defined, and no definition is possible without abridgement of range. The first sentence of Article 7 of the Civil and Political Rights Covenant succinctly states that '[n]o one shall be subjected to torture or to cruel, inhuman or degrading treatment or punishment'.[494] Comparable language is employed in the Universal Declaration,[495] the European Convention,[496] and the American Convention.[497] What must be grasped, first off, is that (in the words of the European Court of Human Rights, in the *Ireland v. United Kingdom* case) 'ill-treatment must attain a minimum level of severity if it is to fall within the scope' of the prohibited forms of behaviour, and '[t]he assessment of this minimum is, in the nature of things, relative'.[498] Already, 'a certain qualification is introduced in a norm formulated in absolute terms'.[499] But there is more than one crossbar to vault. To fit the standards of the similarly sounding yet diverse modes of proscribed conduct (torture; cruel, inhuman or degrading treatment or punishment) – listed in a descending order of malignity – it is necessary to tell them apart. The European Court of Human Rights distinguished torture from other patterns of ill-treatment by 'the intensity of the suffering inflicted'.[500]

244. Article 1(1) of the 1984 Convention against Torture and Other Cruel, Inhuman or Degrading Treatment or Punishment states that '[f]or the purposes of this Convention, the term "torture" means any act by which severe pain or suffering, whether physical or mental, is intentionally inflicted on a person' in circumstances and for purposes detailed in the text.[501] Although Article 1(1)

[493] Steiner, Alston and Goodman, *supra* note 441, at 385.
[494] International Covenant on Civil and Political Rights, *supra* note 335, at 46.
[495] Universal Declaration of Human Rights, *supra* note 434, at 28 (Article 5).
[496] European Convention for the Protection of Human Rights and Fundamental Freedoms, *supra* note 438, at 82 (Article 3).
[497] American Convention on Human Rights, *supra* note 439, at 157 (Article 5(2)).
[498] *Ireland v. United Kingdom, supra* note 471, at 65.
[499] P. van Dijk and G.J.H. van Hoof, *Theory and Practice of the European Convention on Human Rights* 312 (3rd edn, 1998).
[500] *Ireland v. United Kingdom, supra* note 471, at 66.
[501] Convention against Torture and Other Cruel, Inhuman or Degrading Treatment or Punishment, *supra* note 442, at 549–50.

deliberately limits its application '[f]or the purposes of this Convention', a Trial Chamber of the ICTY opined – in the *Furundžija* case of 1998 – that the main elements of the definition have by now gained general acceptance.[502] The trouble is that the operative words 'severe pain or suffering' are somewhat amorphous.[503] New interrogation techniques (such as 'waterboarding'[504]) crop up as a constant reminder that the prohibition of torture is in danger of being outflanked. To prevent this, there is no escape from adding amplification to a rather vapid formulation.

245. The challenge of applying the phrase 'severe pain or suffering' to real-life scenarios beset for a while the Israel Supreme Court. Finally, in the *Torture* case, a special panel of nine Justices (per President Barak) ruled that interrogation techniques supposedly based on 'moderate physical pressure' – such as 'shaking' and sleep deprivation – are illegal.[505]

VI. Balance between Competing Human Rights

246. Human rights law must weigh not only the special interests of individuals and groups as against the heterogeneous societal interests of the State, but also conflicting interests (offsetting each other) of sundry individuals and groups. The reason is simple. The exercise of a certain human right by a given person or group may be irreconcilable with the invocation of the same – or a separate – human right by another individual or group. The clash may stir up a bitter and sanguinary dispute, like the one between Jews and Arabs, both relying on the collective human right of self-determination of peoples (*supra* 170) in the same territory between the Mediterranean and the River Jordan.

247. The requisite to 'secure due recognition and respect for the rights and freedoms of others' is emblazoned, as a limitation imposed on human rights across the board, in Article 29(2) of the Universal Declaration of Human Rights.[506] The Covenant avoids generalizations like this. Instead, the admonition to take into account 'the rights and freedoms of others' is embedded in the definitions of specific human rights, such as freedom of assembly (see Article 21 quoted *supra* 241). The same particularistic

[502] *Prosecutor v. Furundžija* (ICTY, Trial Chamber, 1998), 38 *ILM* 317, 350–1 (1999).

[503] See J.H. Burgers and H. Danelius, *The United Nations Convention against Torture: A Handbook on the Convention against Torture and Other Cruel, Inhuman or Degrading Treatment or Punishment* 122 (1988).

[504] See J.R. Crook, 'Contemporary Practice of the United States Relating to International Law', 102 *AJIL* 346, 359–61 (2008).

[505] HCJ 5100/94 etc., *Public Committee against Torture in Israel* et al. *v. Government of Israel* et al., 53(4) *PD* 817, 830, 846. (The Judgment is excerpted in English in 30 *IYHR* 352 (2000)).

[506] Universal Declaration of Human Rights, *supra* note 434, at 32.

drafting mode is used by the European Convention. Quite frequently, the European Court of Human Rights has in fact struck a balance between competing human rights. Thus, the Court decided to subordinate the freedom of expression of one person to the need to respect the religious beliefs of others.[507]

248. A collision between human rights can and does transpire also in an occupied territory. On some occasions, it is the very same right that is asserted by several contenders in a mutually exclusive rivalry. Preeminently, this is true of freedom of religion when a single shrine (like the Patriarchs' Tomb in the Machpela Cave in Hebron) is sacred to members of more than a single religious group. Confrontations and litigations also result from competition between multiple human rights. This is what happened in the *Rachel's Tomb* case, resolved by the Israel Supreme Court.[508] A petition was submitted to the Court by the municipality of Bethlehem, trying to block construction by the military government of a wall, designed to protect from attack people praying in Rachel's Tomb (a Jewish holy site). The Court (per Justice Beinisch) searched for a proper equipoise between freedom of movement (of the Palestinian inhabitants) and freedom of religious worship (of Jewish visitors), holding both human rights to be evenly matched.[509] Having considered the geographic range and intensity of the restriction of movement, as well as its duration, the Court was amenable to a compromise solution (hammered out in the course of the proceedings) that would enable proper respect for the two freedoms concurrently.[510]

VII. The Interaction between the Law of Belligerent Occupation and the Law of Human Rights

249. The interaction between the *jus in bello* and the law of human rights in occupied territories is a matter of cardinal import. It must be gleaned that the approaches taken by these two branches of international law may converge but they may also diverge. On rare occasions, there is a collision between the two (which cannot be syncretized through skilful interpretation), and then there is no alternative to pursuing an either/or choice between them. But usually there is enough room for a symbiotic relationship between the two systems.

[507] See Jacobs and White, *supra* note 470, at 230.

[508] HCJ 1890/03, *Betlehem Municipality* et al. *v. State of Israel, Ministry of De*fence et al., 59(4) *PD* 736. (The Judgment is excerpted in English in 36 *IYHR* 321 (2006)).

[509] *Ibid.*, 755–6.

[510] *Ibid.*, 757–65.

A. *Convergence, Divergence and Complementarity*

(a) ***Convergence***

250. The paradigmatic illustration of convergence between the law of human rights and the law of belligerent occupation is freedom from torture. This freedom is not only a non-derogable human right (see *supra* 238). Torture is also proscribed expressly in *jus in bello* treaties, both in general[511] and in the specific setting of belligerent occupation. Article 32 of Geneva Convention (IV) prohibits 'murder, torture, corporal punishment, mutilation and medical or scientific experiments not necessitated by the medical treatment of a protected person', as well as 'any other measure of brutality'.[512] Article 31 (quoted *supra* 178) forbids 'physical or moral coercion' against protected persons, 'in particular to obtain information'. Article 147 brands 'torture or inhuman treatment, including biological experiments' (when committed against protected persons) as a grave breach of the Convention.[513] As such, it is a war crime under Article 8(2)(a)(ii) of the Rome Statute of the International Criminal Court.[514] Subjecting a protected person to medical or scientific experiments that are not carried out in his interest, resulting in death or endangering his health, is also a war crime in accordance with Article 8(2)(b)(x) of the Statute.[515] The ICTY Trial Chamber in the *Furundžija* case pronounced that the *jus in bello* prohibition of torture constitutes a peremptory norm of customary international law (*jus cogens*).[516] Thus, where torture is concerned, whether the conduit to the prohibition is human rights law or the *jus in bello*, the outcome is the same.

251. Convergence of human rights law and the law of belligerent occupation may be brought about not only through reiteration of freedoms but also by consequence of their limitations. It is necessary to recall (see *supra* 241) that all human rights are subject to some limitations, and these can come to the fore under conditions of belligerent occupation. A perfect example is that of the limitations attached to freedom of movement. In the *Beit Sira* case of 2009, the Israel Supreme Court addressed freedom of movement in the setting of a banning of all local traffic on a major highway in the West Bank (see *infra* 397). President Beinisch (in a Separate Opinion) stated categorically that freedom of movement is a fundamental human right and that every effort must be made to uphold it even under belligerent occupation.[517]

[511] Additional Protocol I, *supra* note 33, at 748 (Article 75(2)(a)(ii)).
[512] Geneva Convention (IV), *supra* note 29, at 590.
[513] *Ibid.*, 624.
[514] Rome Statute of the International Criminal Court, *supra* note 350, at 1317.
[515] *Ibid.*, 1318.
[516] *Prosecutor v. Furundžija*, *supra* note 502, at 349–50.
[517] HCJ 2150/07, *Beit Sira* et al. *v. Minister of Defence* et al., 63(3) *PD* 331, 382. (The Judgment is excerpted in English in 41 *IYHR* 298 (2011)).

That said, freedom of movement is subject to admissible limitations, and these include the need to ensure public safety and order in an occupied territory.[518] The range of application of admissible limitations must be assessed on the merits of the concrete case: much depends on the degree of harm caused by the relevant limitation in the particular context.[519] In the specific circumstances, the Court rejected an absolute ban of local traffic on the road while allowing less severe limitations on freedom of movement (see *supra* 241). In another Judgment, rendered in the same year – in the *Dir Samet* case – the Court (per President Beinisch) overturned altogether an order for the closure of a rural road, pronouncing that the harm to the fabric of life of the local inhabitants far outweighed the pertinent security reasons and was therefore disproportionate.[520]

(b) Divergence

252. Divergence between the law of human rights and the law of belligerent occupation is equally a matter of record. It might perhaps be surmised that non-derogable human rights and *jus in bello* provisions would always be fully in harmony with each other. Yet, that is not invariably the case. For instance, the second sentence of Article 7 of the Civil and Political Rights Covenant declares that 'no one shall be subjected without his free consent to medical or scientific experimentation'.[521] The prohibition of exposure to scientific experimentation is a non-derogable human right (adjoined to freedom of torture), but it is subject to a significant built-in limitation: free consent. This used to be the *jus in bello* rule as well. In the *Medical* trial of 1947 (part of the 'Subsequent Proceedings' at Nuremberg), an American Military Tribunal held that human experimentation must satisfy certain basic requirements, above all voluntary consent.[522] The fly in the ointment is that, since protected persons are in a precarious position, there is a high potential of engineering of consent. To forestall abuse, Article 32 of Geneva Convention (IV) (quoted *supra* 250) permits experimentation only when required for the medical treatment of a protected person. Article 11(2) of Additional Protocol I bans any medical or scientific experiments on protected persons 'even with their consent' (save in some exceptional circumstances).[523] As a result, protected persons in occupied territories – unlike other persons who are safeguarded only by human rights

518 *Ibid.*, 383.
519 *Ibid.*
520 HCJ 3969/06, *Dir Samet* et al. *v. Minister of Defence* et al., paras. 34–5. (The Judgment is excerpted in English in 41 *IYHR* 287 (2011)).
521 International Covenant on Civil and Political Rights, *supra* note 335, at 46.
522 *Medical* trial (*Brandt* et al.) (US Military Tribunal, Nuremberg, 1947), 14 *ILR* 296, 297.
523 Additional Protocol I, *supra* note 33, at 720.

law – become the beneficiaries of a more airtight *jus in bello* prohibition of experimentation (eliminating the loophole of consent).[524]

(c) Complementarity

253. An undeniable divergence between the law of human rights and the law of belligerent occupation is not necessarily conclusive of the matter, inasmuch as human rights law may impact on the *jus in bello* in a complementary manner. This came to light in the decision of the Grand Chamber of the European Court of Human Rights in the *Al-Skeini* case of 2011,[525] which related to a number of incidents of shooting of civilians by British troops during the occupation of Iraq. The Grand Chamber did not contest the application of international humanitarian law to belligerent occupation.[526] However, it pronounced that '[t]he general legal prohibition of arbitrary killing by agents of the State would be ineffective in practice if there existed no procedure for reviewing the lawfulness of the use of lethal force by State authorities'.[527] These procedural obligations – concerning an effective investigation leading to a determination of whether the force used was justified in the circumstances – were held by the Grand Chamber to be applicable, even during an armed conflict, in consequence of human rights law.[528]

B. The Advantages of the Law of Belligerent Occupation

254. Derogable human rights may be suspended in wartime (see *supra* 229). When an Occupying Power issues the prerequisite proclamation – meeting all the designated conditions of derogation – protected persons become exclusively dependent on the law of belligerent occupation. The great advantage of the *jus in bello* over human rights law is that it cannot be suspended in wartime: every right established by the law of belligerent occupation is non-derogable.[529] This is a critical feature of the *jus in bello* that should be thoroughly cherished. Rights and duties created by the *jus in bello* come into play upon the onset of war – including belligerent occupation – and they remain unabated despite (indeed, because of) the prosecution of war. *Jus in bello* rights and obligations (which are usually in a sort of hibernation in peacetime) come

[524] On the application of Article 11 to occupied territories, see Y. Sandoz, 'Article 11', *Commentary on the Additional Protocols, supra* note 327, at 149, 153.

[525] *Al-Skeini* et al. *v. United Kingdom* (European Court of Human Rights, Grand Chamber, 2011), 50 *ILM* 995 (2011).

[526] *Ibid.*, 1022–5.

[527] *Ibid.*, 1039.

[528] *Ibid.*, 1040–1.

[529] See R. Arnold, 'Human Rights in Times of Terrorism', 66 *Heid.JIL* 297, 304 (2006).

into their own in wartime, inasmuch as they are directly shaped by and for the special demands of armed conflict.

255. Article 7 (first paragraph) of Geneva Convention (IV) does not permit Contracting Parties to conclude special agreements that 'adversely affect the situation of protected persons'[530] (a special agreement may thus devise more rights for protected persons, but not fewer rights).[531] Article 47 (quoted *infra* 373) incapacitates even the Occupying Power and the displaced sovereign – acting jointly – by disqualifying any agreement between them to deprive protected persons of the benefits of the Convention. Article 8 takes another step in the same direction by stressing that '[p]rotected persons may in no circumstances renounce in part or in entirety the rights secured to them by the present Convention'.[532] Some derogation of rights of protected persons in the course of belligerent occupation is possible in exceptional circumstances under Article 5 (second paragraph) of the Convention (quoted *supra* 206), but its implications are rather minor (see *supra* 208). It follows that, when derogation from general human rights occurs, *jus in bello* rights are called in to fill the vacant space.

256. The inherent advantage of the non-derogability of the norms of belligerent occupation bursts into view in more than one context. For example, Article 8(3) of the Civil and Political Rights Covenant creates a derogable freedom from forced labour (with several exceptions).[533] Nevertheless, in occupied territories – even if derogation from Article 8(3) is duly proclaimed – compulsory work can only take place subject to a series of cumulative and rather stringent conditions laid down by the Geneva Convention (see *infra* 538).

257. Another illustration relates to internment. When one compares Article 78 (first paragraph) of the Convention (quoted *infra* 519) with human rights provisions – such as Article 9 of the Covenant[534] or Article 5 of the European Convention[535] (both of which in effect forbid administrative detention altogether) – the Geneva solution (in giving leave to intern protected persons) seems to be 'more draconian'.[536] However, both human rights stipulations are subject to derogation. In the very first Judgment delivered by the European Court of Human Rights, in the *Lawless* case of 1961, the Court determined that – although, in general, administrative detentions are incompatible with the European Convention – Ireland, the detaining State in the proceedings, had

530 Geneva Convention (IV), *supra* note 29, at 582.

531 See R. Kolb, *Jus in Bello: Le Droit International des Conflits Armés* 180–1 (2003).

532 Geneva Convention (IV), *supra* note 29, at 582.

533 International Covenant on Civil and Political Rights, *supra* note 335, at 46.

534 *Ibid.*, 46–7.

535 European Convention for the Protection of Human Rights and Fundamental Freedoms, *supra* note 438, at 82–3.

536 Roberts, *supra* note 194, at 456.

acted legally (in a peacetime emergency) by virtue of a valid derogation.[537] It is when the law of human rights is eclipsed that one can observe the boon built into the Geneva system. After all, Article 78 of the Geneva Convention includes not only the first paragraph (permitting internment of protected persons) but also the second paragraph (see *infra* 526), whereby the Occupying Power must establish a regular procedure of appeal and periodic review (if possible, every six months) by a competent body. Hence, Article 78 actually provides a better protection to internees under belligerent occupation.

C. *The Advantages of Human Rights Law*

258. Since the temporal application of human rights law is more extensive than that of the law of belligerent occupation, this may be of practical relevance during an invasion of enemy territory. In other words, as long as effective control has not fully congealed to the point of emergence of a legal regime of belligerent occupation (see *supra* 121–3), human rights law may be of relevance in some contexts.

259. Human rights law may also fill a gap in an occupied territory, when the norms governing belligerent occupation are silent or incomplete. It must not be forgotten that the Geneva Convention does not extend its protection to everybody in an occupied territory. As noted (*supra* 197–8), the definition of protected persons excludes nationals of the Occupying Power and of co-belligerent States maintaining normal diplomatic relations with it. Since human rights law ('at a minimum its non-derogable core') applies to everybody in occupied territories, it can fill any gap in protection.[538] The point was made the most of by the Israel Supreme Court as regards settlers and other nationals of the Occupying Power who are present in the area under occupation (see *infra* 394–5).

260. When both alternative paths of human rights law and the law of belligerent occupation are open to a protected person whose rights have been infringed in an occupied territory, there may be a practical advantage in exploring the former, since an international mechanism may be readily available, enabling the injured party to seek and obtain effective redress. Proof positive can be found in the Judgment in the *Loizidou* case, where private property belonging to a Greek Cypriot was seized without compensation by the Turkish authorities in occupied Northern Cyprus (apparently in order to house displaced Turkish Cypriot refugees). This was considered by the European Court to be

537 *Lawless* case (Merits) (European Court of Human Rights, 1961), 3 *ECHRJD* 27, 54–62.
538 T. Meron, *The Humanization of International Law* 47 (2006).

a breach of a human right[539] guaranteed in Article 1 of Protocol No. 1 to the European Convention.[540] Pecuniary damages were subsequently awarded.[541]

D. *The* Lex Specialis *Rule*

261. There are settings in which human rights law and the law of belligerent occupation are both applicable (either because the relevant human right is non-derogable or because no valid derogation has been proclaimed), yet they point in diverse – perhaps contradictory – directions. If the two discordant legal regimes cannot be reconciled, the question arises as to which one of them ought to prevail. The answer is incisive: the special law of belligerent occupation trumps the general law of human rights on the ground of *lex specialis derogat lex generali*. However, as the International Law Commission pointed out in its 2001 Draft Articles on State Responsibility: 'For the *lex specialis* principle to apply it is not enough that the same subject matter is dealt with by two provisions; there must be some actual inconsistency between them'.[542]

262. The term *derogat* in the expression *lex specialis derogat lex generali* must not be construed as a total exclusion of the law of human rights.[543] The law of belligerent occupation is favoured with the standing of *lex specialis* in the sense that it serves as a prism filtering human rights law during armed conflict. Obligations under human rights treaties and custom continue to apply under belligerent occupation, yet 'the specific rules of the Fourth Geneva Convention take precedence regarding specific measures which are justified on the basis of these provisions'.[544] A Trial Chamber of the ICTY, in the *Kunarac* case of 2001, cautioned that 'notions developed in the field of human rights can be transposed in international humanitarian law only if they take into consideration the specificities of the latter body of law'.[545]

263. The *lex specialis* construct of the *jus in bello* was upheld by the International Court of Justice, in its Advisory Opinion on *Nuclear Weapons*. The question arising in these proceedings was the interaction between the *jus*

539 *Loizidou v. Turkey* (Merits), *supra* note 66, at 456.

540 Protocol No. 1 to the European Convention for the Protection of Human Rights and Fundamental Freedoms, 1954, *Raoul Wallenberg Compilation of Human Rights Instruments, supra* note 335, at 97, *id.*

541 See L.G. Loucaides, 'The Protection of the Right to Property in Occupied Territories', 53 *ICLQ* 677, 684–5 (2004).

542 International Law Commission, Draft Articles on Responsibility of States for Internationally Wrongful Acts, *supra* note 369, at 140.

543 See G. Gaggioli and R. Kolb, 'A Right to Life in Armed Conflicts? The Contribution of the European Court of Human Rights', 37 *IYHR* 115, 120 (2007).

544 J. A. Frowein, 'The Relationship between Human Rights Regimes and Regimes of Belligerent Occupation', 28 *IYHR* 1, 11 (1998).

545 *Prosecutor v. Kunarac* et al. (ICTY, Trial Chamber, 2001), para. 471.

in bello and Article 6(1) of the Civil and Political Rights Covenant, whereby '[n]o one shall be arbitrarily deprived of his life'.[546] The Court analysed the mutual influence of the two legal systems as follows:

In principle, the right not arbitrarily to be deprived of one's life applies also in hostilities. The test of what is an arbitrary deprivation of life, however, then falls to be determined by the applicable *lex specialis*, namely, the law applicable in armed conflict which is designed to regulate the conduct of hostilities. Thus whether a particular loss of life, through the use of a certain weapon in warfare, is to be considered an arbitrary deprivation of life contrary to Article 6 of the Covenant, can only be decided by reference to the law applicable in armed conflict and not deduced from the terms of the Covenant itself.[547]

Differently put, during an armed conflict it is the *jus in bello* as *lex specialis* that determines which acts amount to an arbitrary deprivation of the human right to life. A manifest example of arbitrary deprivation of life in wartime will be the execution of hostages (see *infra* 462).[548]

264. In its Advisory Opinion on the *Wall*, the International Court of Justice reaffirmed the *lex specialis* status of the *jus in bello* in the specific context of belligerent occupation:

As regards the relationship between international humanitarian law and human rights law, there are thus three possible situations: some rights may be exclusively matters of international humanitarian law; others may be exclusively matters of human rights law; yet others may be matters of both these branches of international law. In order to answer the question put to it, the Court will have to take into consideration both these branches of international law, namely human rights law and, as *lex specialis*, international humanitarian law.[549]

265. The first sentence in the Court's dictum – enumerating the three logical possibilities – is didactically correct, albeit not materially helpful in the absence of further elaboration. One observer has described it (with some embellishment) as an 'almost comically uninformative statement'.[550] Manifestly, the most pregnant words appear in the second sentence concerning the standing of IHL as *lex specialis*. Regrettably, the Court 'did not offer specific guidance' as to when exactly the *lex specialis* status applies.[551] What is worse, when it came to turning theory into practice, the Court stated flatly that Israel had impeded,

546 International Covenant on Civil and Political Rights, *supra* note 335, at 45.

547 Advisory Opinion on the *Legality of the Threat or Use of Nuclear Weapons*, *supra* note 13, at 240.

548 See Robertson and Merrills, *supra* note 435, at 312.

549 Advisory Opinion on *Legal Consequences of the Construction of a Wall in the Occupied Palestinian Territory*, *supra* note 25, at 178.

550 R. O'Keefe, 'Legal Consequences of the Construction of a Wall in the Occupied Palestinian Territory: A Commentary', 37 *RBDI* 92, 135 (2004).

551 See Dennis, *supra* note 453, at 133.

e.g., the freedom of movement of the inhabitants of the West Bank.[552] It relied on Article 12(1) of the Civil and Political Rights Covenant,[553] but declined (on the ground of lack of proportionality) to apply the extensive limitations built into this freedom in paragraph (3) of the same provision (see *supra* 242).[554] Having paid lip service to the abstract notion of *lex specialis,* the Court thus stumbled when it came to translating it into concrete form. A genuine *lex specialis* approach militates in favour of the conclusion that freedom of movement in occupied territories is actually subject to stringent restrictions or even suspension by an Occupying Power.[555]

266. It would be wrong to read the extract from the Court's Advisory Opinion as proof that IHL and human rights law 'are two different sides of the same coin'.[556] There is no way to ignore the reality that, '[w]hile the respective rules of humanitarian law and human rights law can mostly be interpreted in the light of one another, some of them are contradictory, and it has to be decided which one prevails'.[557] In other words, the two branches of international law can and do take divergent approaches to the parsing of legal problems, and the solutions that they offer may clash with one another. In such situations, the *jus in bello* – as the *lex specialis* – prevails over human rights law.

267. The screening of human rights by the *jus in bello* – as the *lex specialis* – must be carried out on a right-by-right basis, rather than in a wholesale manner. This attitude may perhaps find notional support in what the International Court of Justice said in the *Armed Activities* case:

> The Court thus concludes that Uganda is internationally responsible for violations of international human rights law and international humanitarian law committed by the UPDF [Uganda Peoples' Defence Forces] and by its members in the territory of the DRC and for failing to comply with its obligations as an occupying Power in Ituri in respect of violations of international human rights law and international humanitarian law in the occupied territory.[558]

[552] Advisory Opinion on *Legal Consequences of the Construction of a Wall in the Occupied Palestinian Territory*, *supra* note 25, at 191.

[553] International Covenant on Civil and Political Rights, *supra* note 335, at 47.

[554] Advisory Opinion on *Legal Consequences of the Construction of a Wall in the Occupied Palestinian Territory*, *supra* note 25, at 192.

[555] See *Commentary, IV Geneva Convention*, *supra* note 31, at 202; B.A. Feinstein and J.R. Weiner, 'Israel's Security Barrier: An International Comparative Analysis and Legal Evaluation', 37 *GWILR* 309, 429–31, 435, 437 (2005).

[556] S.R.S. Bedi, *The Development of Human Rights Law by the Judges of the International Court of Justice* 343 (2007).

[557] C. Droege, 'Elective Affinities? Human Rights and Humanitarian Law', 871 *IRRC* 501, 524 (2008).

[558] *Case Concerning Armed Activities on the Territory of the Congo* (Congo v. Uganda), *supra* note 26, at 245.

The passage is not easy to interpret.[559] But, assuming that the apparent duplication between the two parts of the sentence is not inadvertent, the Court may have wished to indicate that – even though IHL and human rights law apply both in and out of occupied territories (in the Ituri region and in the rest of the Congo) – they may apply differently. Since IHL (the *jus in bello*) distinguishes between the conduct of hostilities and belligerent occupation, human rights obligations for States may also not be the same everywhere in wartime: they depend on the specific *jus in bello* provision applicable in context. *Lex specialis*, thus, truly brings about specialization.

268. The *lex specialis* outlook on the law of belligerent occupation has also been endorsed by the Israel Supreme Court, notably in the *Ajuri* case[560] (sitting in a special panel of nine Justices) and in the *Targeted Killings* case[561] (both per President Barak). The position of the European Court of Human Rights is more ambivalent. In the *Al-Jedda* Judgment of 2011, the Grand Chamber of the Court ignored altogether the *lex specialis* standing of the law of belligerent occupation where internments are concerned, apparently on the curious ground that recourse to internments is not obligatory for the Occupying Power (see *infra* 521).[562] In the *Hassan* case of 2014, the Grand Chamber modified this stance by pronouncing that the relevant provision of the European Convention 'must also be interpreted in a manner which takes into account the context and the applicable rules of international humanitarian law'.[563] Yet, the Judgment refrained from expressly invoking the *lex specialis* maxim.[564]

[559] See J. Cerone, 'Human Dignity in the Line of Fire: The Application of International Human Rights Law during Armed Conflict, Occupation, and Peace Operations', 39 *VJTL* 1447, 1477 (2006).

[560] HCJ 7015/02, *supra* note 173, at 367.

[561] HCJ 769/02, *supra* note 38, at 546.

[562] See J. Pejic, 'The European Court of Human Rights' *Al-Jedda* Judgment: The Oversight of International Humanitarian Law', 883 *IRRC* 837, 849–50 (2011).

[563] *Hassan v. United Kingdom*, *supra* note 261, at para. 106.

[564] See C. Landais and L. Bass, 'Reconciling the Rules of International Humanitarian Law with the Rules of European Human Rights Law', 900 *IRRC* 1295, 1307 (2015).

4 The Maintenance of Law and Order in Occupied Territories

I. Hague Regulation 43

269. Hague Regulation 43, in its common non-binding English translation (1907 version), reads:

> The authority of the legitimate power having actually passed into the hands of the occupant, the latter shall take all steps in his power to re-establish and insure, as far as possible, public order and safety, while respecting, unless absolutely prevented, the laws in force in the country.[565]

The authentic (and binding) French text of Regulation 43 is:

> L'autorité du pouvoir légal ayant passé de fait entre les mains de l'occupant, celui-ci prendra toutes les mesures qui dépendent de lui en vue de rétablir et d'assurer, autant qu'il est possible, l'ordre et la vie publics en respectant, sauf empêchemant absolu, les lois en vigueur dans le pays.[566]

270. The juxtaposition of the English and French versions of Regulation 43 reveals remarkable discrepancies between them. The most blatant mistranslation relates to the first part of the provision where the phrase 'l'ordre et la vie publics' (i.e. public order and life) is rendered in English as 'public order and safety'. Safety, which is not even mentioned in French, thus becomes the focal point in English. This peculiar slip in the translation – left uncorrected for more than a century – cannot be easily explained, considering that only the French text is authentic. It has been conceded long ago that '[t]he word 'safety' does not precisely express the significance of the original words quoted above, which imply also the entire social and commercial life of the community'[567] (see further *infra* 278).

[565] Hague Regulations, *supra* note 22, at 245.
[566] *Ibid.*, 244.
[567] C. Phillipson, *International Law and the Great War* 219 (1915).

II. The Structure and Scope of Regulation 43

271. When one consults the *travaux préparatoires* of Regulation 43, it becomes apparent that – as initially drafted in Articles II and III of the 1874 Brussels Project of an International Declaration on the Laws and Customs of War – the provision consisted of two separate clauses:

II. L'autorité du pouvoir légal étant suspendue et ayant passée de fait entre les mains de l'occupant, celui-ci prendra toutes les mesures qui dépendent de lui en vue de rétablir et d'assurer, autant qu'il est possible, l'ordre et la vie publique.

III. A cet effet, il maintiendra les lois qui étaient en vigueur dans le pays en temps de paix, et ne les modifiera, ne les suspendra ou ne les remplacera que s'il y a nécessité.[568]

A corresponding structure of two consecutive stipulations characterized also the counterpart Articles 43–4 of the Oxford Manual of the Laws of War on Land, adopted by the *Institut de Droit International* in 1880.[569]

272. The two separate Brussels (and Oxford) provisions were patched up and condensed into a single text in Hague Regulation 43. That happened in response to a poignant anxiety, voiced in the course of the Hague Conference of 1899, that Brussels Article III – when standing alone – might be construed as conceding to the Occupying Power far-reaching legislative powers.[570] Still, the ensuing syntactic amalgamation of Brussels Articles II and III into a single Hague Regulation 43 was not designed to disrupt the substantive duality of the concepts involved.

273. In essence, two discrete obligations are imposed on the Occupying Power by Hague Regulation 43: (i) to reestablish and ensure, as far as possible, public order and life in the occupied territory; and (ii) to respect the laws in force in the occupied territory unless an 'empêchement absolu' exists. The two obligations have to be read independently of each other.

274. If the military government of the Occupying Power is considered (like other governments) as a three-pronged structure, it is obvious that different organs bear the onus of compliance with the obligations. The directive to reestablish and ensure public order and life has to be abided primarily by the executive branch of the military government (and secondarily by the judicial branch). Conversely, the mandate to respect the laws in force devolves on the legislative branch of that government.

568 Projet d'une Declaration Internationale Concernant les Lois et Coutumes de la Guerre, 1874, 65 *BFSP* 1059, 1059–60.

569 *Oxford Manual of the Laws of War on Land*, Adopted by the Institute of International Law, 1880, *The Laws of Armed Conflicts, supra* note 29, at 29, 35–6.

570 See E.H. Schwenk, 'Legislative Power of the Military Occupying Power under Article 43, Hague Regulations', 54 *YLJ* 393, 396–7 (1944–5).

275. The obligation to reestablish and ensure public order and life chiefly relates to acts of commission: the Occupying Power must take affirmative measures, as is necessary and proper, in order to carry out its duties. By contrast, the obligation to respect the laws in force calls for acts of omission: avoiding the suspension or modification of existing laws, except in cases of 'empêchement absolu'.

276. Neither obligation imposed on the Occupying Power by Regulation 43 is absolute, but each is subject to a divergent saving phrase which fine-tunes the general rule and allows deviation from it. The obligation to reestablish and ensure public order and life applies 'autant qu'il est possible (as far as possible)'. The obligation to respect the laws in force is subject to the proviso of 'empêchement absolu'. These two limitative limbs of the disparate obligations must not be superimposed on each other.

277. In this chapter, we shall deal with the Occupying Power's duty to reestablish and ensure law and order. The next chapter will concentrate on legislation.

III. Reestablishing and Ensuring Public Order and Life under Regulation 43

A. *The General Obligation*

278. The phrase 'l'ordre et la vie publics' has two components, which (as explained in the course of the Brussels Conference) do not replicate each other: public order denotes 'security or general safety', while public life betokens 'social functions [and] ordinary transactions which constitute daily life'.[571]

279. The two verbs 'rétablir' and 'assurer' are not synonymous. As the Israel Supreme Court (per Justice Barak) observed in the *Jamait Askan* case, there are two separate strands here: reestablishing public order and life, if disrupted ('rétablir'); and ensuring the continued existence of public order and life, if not ('assurer').[572] Indeed, one can go further: 'assurer' means that public order and life must be ensured even if order did not prevail in the territory prior to its occupation.[573]

280. The obligation to reestablish and ensure public order and life in an occupied territory has a relative rather than categorical character: it has to be implemented only 'autant qu'il est possible'. Two conclusions must be

571 See *ibid.*, 398.
572 HCJ 393/82, *supra* note 158, at 803–4.
573 See D.P. Goodman, 'The Need for Fundamental Change in the Law of Belligerent Occupation', 37 *SLR* 1573, 1578 (1984–5).

drawn: (i) factually, public life does not necessarily mean the *status quo ante*, although it does mean normal life;[574] and (ii) jurisprudentially, although bound to reestablish and ensure public order and life, the Occupying Power incurs an obligation not of result but of conduct. The Occupying Power must pursue the goal prescribed, yet nobody can cavil if (despite its best efforts) the measures taken will not be completely successful.[575]

B. Safety from Violence

281. The purpose of the first part of Hague Regulation 43 (viz., Brussels Article II) is to protect the civilian population from all acts of violence. As the International Court of Justice underscored in the *Armed Activities* case, the duty of the Occupying Power goes beyond not inflicting acts of violence on the inhabitants of the occupied territory: the Occupying Power must also not 'tolerate such violence by any third party'.[576]

282. Not tolerating violence by third parties (who are not subordinated to the Occupying Power) may be essential to the maintenance of security in the occupied territory.[577] It is possible to contemplate a state of affairs in which some segments of the civilian population are ravaged by roving bands of marauders who act circumspectly where the military government itself is concerned. In such circumstances, the Occupying Power may have no direct incentive to commit its military units to the fray. The commander in charge may be tempted to feel that – as long as the installations and units of the military government do not come under attack and the sole victims are local inhabitants – it is better to avoid the allocation of valuable resources to the suppression of criminal elements. The first part of Regulation 43 enjoins the Occupying Power not to sit idly by when law and order in the occupied territory are in jeopardy, even if its personnel are not at risk and its facilities are not encroached upon.

283. The duty with which the Occupying Power is saddled under the first part of Regulation 43 – to reestablish and ensure public order and safety as far as possible – goes far beyond the issue of a crime wave in an occupied territory. The framers of the Hague Regulations were afraid that the Occupying Power might tolerate pervasive turmoil and turbulence, not lifting a finger to prevent rampant anarchy from paralysing the life of the civilian population. Such

[574] See S. Vité. 'L'Applicabilité du Droit International de l'Occupation Militaire aux Activités des Organisations Internationales', 853 *IRRC* 9, 17 (2004).

[575] See M. Sassòli, 'Legislation and Maintenance of Public Order and Civil Life by Occupying Powers', 16 *EJIL* 661, 664 (2005).

[576] *Case Concerning Armed Activities on the Territory of the Congo* (Congo v. Uganda), *supra* note 26, at 231.

[577] See G.H. Fox, 'Transformative Occupation and the Unilateralist Impulse', 885 *IRRC* 237, 259–60 (2012).

inaction would surely amount to a breach of Regulation 43. There is a dictum pregnant with meaning – in a Judgment delivered by the Israel Supreme Court (per Justice D. Levin) in the *Taha* case – that, at the time of the first *intifada*, the military government had a *duty* (the word is underlined in the original) to cope with a major upheaval in the occupied territories.[578]

284. The danger to the safety of the civilian population may emanate not only from inside an occupied territory but also from the outside. In 1991, when Israel was attacked by Iraqi Scud missiles, and there was an apprehension that chemical warheads might be used, gas masks were distributed to the entire population of the country. Yet, the distribution did not embrace the Palestinians in the West Bank and the Gaza Strip. In the *Murkos* case, the Supreme Court (per Justice Barak) held that, under Regulation 43, the Occupying Power is required (as far as possible) to look after the security needs of all the inhabitants of the occupied territories, and, since gas masks were handed out to Israeli settlers, they had to be provided without discrimination to the Palestinians as well.[579]

285. The first part of Regulation 43 creates an obligation for the Occupying Power to take proper (and feasible) steps to protect the civilian population. The obligation is crystal clear, but there can be no responsibility without power. The Occupying Power cannot be denied a commensurate authority enabling the proper discharge of its duties. The first part of Regulation 43 must be read as an empowerment to do what is necessary to carry out the allotted tasks of maintaining law and order in the occupied territory.

286. This is corroborated by Article 27 (fourth paragraph) of Geneva Convention (IV):

> However, the Parties to the conflict may take such measures of control and security in regard to protected persons as may be necessary as a result of the war.[580]

The ICRC Commentary observes that '[t]he various security measures which states might take are not specified; the Article merely lays down a general provision'.[581] The choice of means deemed necessary to contend with the problems of control and security – as per Article 27 (fourth paragraph) – is left to the Occupying Power, subject of course to express limitations laid down in other provisions of the Geneva Convention or the Hague Regulations.

[578] HCJ 591/88, *Taha (minor)* et al. *v. Minister of Defence* et al., 45(2) *PD* 45, 63. (The Judgment is excerpted in English in 23 *IYHR* 300 (1993)).

[579] HCJ 168/91, *Murkos v. Minister of Defence* et al., 45(1) *PD* 467, 470–1. (The Judgment is excerpted in English in 23 *IYHR* 339 (1993)).

[580] Geneva Convention (IV), *supra* note 29, at 589.

[581] *Commentary, IV Geneva Convention*, *supra* note 31, at 207.

C. *Economic and Social Order*

287. It is not enough for the Occupying Power to conscientiously protect life and limb in the occupied territory. The military government cannot observe with equanimity an economy in shambles under occupation or a social breakdown causing distress to the civilian population.[582] This is important to bear in mind, inasmuch as the inhabitants of an occupied territory are enemy nationals, and the Occupying Power is liable to show callous indifference to any hardships (unrelated to safety and security) that befall them. That is why, under the first part of Regulation 43, a duty is imposed on the Occupying Power to ensure public life – and not only public order – in the occupied territory.

288. In lockstep with its empowerment in the domain of security, the Occupying Power must also be enabled to take the measures necessary to foster the social and economic dimensions of public life in the occupied territory. In the *Jamait Askan* case, the Israel Supreme Court (per Justice Barak) inferred from the first part of Regulation 43 an authority for the Occupying Power to promote the interests of the civilian population in the occupied territory.[583] The overall objective must be to ensure stability and continuity in the economic and social life of the inhabitants.[584] More on this *infra* 360 *et seq.*, in connection with prolonged occupation.

289. The Occupying Power can minister to the economy by introducing into circulation its own currency or creating a new currency valid only in the occupied territory.[585] In the Israeli occupied territories, the Israeli currency (Shekel) is the main legal tender. In Iraq, the Coalition Provisional Authority ordered the issuance of new Iraqi Dinar banknotes.[586]

290. If the Occupying Power chooses to introduce new legal tender in the occupied territory, potential problems of manipulation – i.e. fixing the rate of exchange to other currencies – arise.[587] Since the value of the occupation legal tender may depreciate over time as a result of the pressure of market forces, it is noteworthy that the military government is not permitted to increase extraordinarily the quantity of paper-money circulated (thereby causing rapid inflation and eroding the currency).[588]

[582] See C. Greenwood, 'The Administration of Occupied Territory in International Law', *International Law and the Administration of Occupied Territories: Two Decades of Israeli Occupation of the West Bank and Gaza Strip* 241, 246 (E. Playfair ed., 1992).
[583] HCJ 393/82, *supra* note 158, at 803–7.
[584] See Mann *On the Legal Aspect of Money* 563 (7th edn, C. Proctor ed., 2012).
[585] See *ibid.*, 562–5.
[586] Coalition Provisional Authority Order Number 43, II *The Occupation of Iraq: The Official Documents*, *supra* note 78, at 212, 213.
[587] See D. Carreau, 'Military Occupation Currency', 19 *SDLR* 233, 256 (1981–2).
[588] See Mann, *supra* note 584, at 566–7.

291. The administration of an occupied territory may have consequences vis-à-vis neighbouring countries – for instance, as a result of trans-border pollution where shared water resources are concerned – and the Occupying Power must bear international legal responsibility for any wrongful acts that relate to effective control of the occupied territory.[589] The question whether the Occupying Power can also, e.g., negotiate agreements allocating water resources with other riparian countries is more complicated in the absence of State practice.[590]

IV. Violent Resistance to Occupation

A. *Occupation and Violent Resistance*

292. Belligerent occupation tends to stimulate acts of violent struggle by the occupied population against the Occupying Power. Violence need not rage in an equal measure in the entire occupied territory: while some areas may remain relatively calm, others may be hotbeds of overt resistance to the occupation both by individuals and by organized armed groups.[591]

293. There is a widespread conviction that the civilian population in an occupied territory has a right to forcibly resist the Occupying Power.[592] This is a misconception that must be dispelled. In reality, the *jus in bello* allows civilians 'neither to violently resist occupation of their territory by the enemy nor to try to liberate that territory by violent means'.[593] Indeed, in the words of the US Department of Defense Law of War Manual:

> Subject to the restrictions imposed by international law, the Occupying Power may demand and enforce from the inhabitants of occupied territory such obedience as may be necessary for the security of its forces, for the maintenance of law and order, and for the proper administration of the country.[594]

As a Netherlands Special Court pronounced in the 1948 *Christiansen* trial:

> the civilian population, if it considers itself justified in committing acts of resistance, must know that, in general, counter-measures within the limits set by international law may be taken against them with impunity'.[595]

[589] See M. Bothe, 'The Administration of Occupied Territory', *The 1949 Geneva Conventions: A Commentary*, *supra* note 309, at 1455, 1478.

[590] See E. Benvenisti, 'Water Conflicts during the Occupation of Iraq', 97 *AJIL* 860, 870–1 (2003).

[591] See K. Watkin, 'Use of Force during Occupation: Law Enforcement and Conduct of Hostilities', 885 *IRRC* 267, 286 (2012).

[592] See, e.g., R.A. Falk and B.H. Weston, 'The Relevance of International Law to Palestinian Rights in the West Bank and Gaza: In Legal Defense of the Intifada', 32 *Har.ILJ* 129, 155 (1991).

[593] See M. Sassòli and A.A Bouvier, I *How Does Law Protect in War?* 231 (ICRC, 3rd edn, 2011).

[594] US Department of Defense, *Law of War Manual*, *supra* note 1, at 777.

[595] *Christiansen* trial (Netherlands, Special Court, 1948), 14 *LRTWC* 128, *id*. See also *supra* note 12 (the two reports of the Judgment are selective and do not match).

B. *Saboteurs and Prisoners of War*

294. When individual civilians in an occupied territory resist the occupation, their acts were once styled 'war treason'.[596] This is an infelicitous expression, since ordinary treason is based on the premise of betrayal of allegiance, whereas the inhabitants of an occupied territory do not owe allegiance to the Occupying Power (see *supra* 175). Nevertheless, the salient point (which remains cogent, irrespective of nomenclature) is that acts of violence in resistance to the occupation are generally labelled as crimes. It is for the Occupying Power to determine – through security legislation – what specific acts are punishable when committed in the occupied territory (see *infra* 343).[597] International law, as such, does not penalize these acts.[598] But it refrains from shielding perpetrators from the sanctions imposed on them by the security legislation of the Occupying Power: saboteurs (for the use of the expression, see *supra* 206) are not entitled to the privileged status of prisoners of war.[599]

295. As for enemy prisoners of war – viz. lawful (or privileged) combatants captured in the course of hostilities – Geneva Convention (III) of 1949 prescribes that, if released by the Occupying Power but then taken back into custody (in particular where an attempt has been made by them to rejoin their armed forces) while hostilities are going on outside the occupied territory, they must be treated once again as prisoners of war.[600] In other words, the status of prisoners of war is not lost as a result of an earlier release and recapture (although at the moment of recapture they are no longer serving in the armed forces of the enemy).[601]

C. Levée en Masse

296. Hague Regulation 1 sets out four cumulative conditions that must be fulfilled by those who lay claim to the status of prisoners of war:

1. That of being commanded by a person responsible for his subordinates;
2. That of having a distinctive emblem fixed and recognizable at a distance;
3. That of carrying arms openly; and

[596] On the origin of the expression 'war treason,' see L. Oppenheim, 'On War Treason', 33 *LQR* 266, 281–3 (1917).
[597] See R.R. Baxter, 'The Duty of Obedience to the Belligerent Occupant', 27 *BYBIL* 235, 266 (1950).
[598] See R.R. Baxter, 'So-Called "Unprivileged Belligerency": Spies, Guerrillas, and Saboteurs', 28 *BYBIL* 323, 337 (1951).
[599] See *ibid.*, 338.
[600] Geneva Convention (III), *supra* note 397, at 514 (Article 4(B)(1)).
[601] See H.S. Levie, *Prisoners of War in International Armed Conflict* 67 (59 *ILS*, 1978).

4. That of conducting their operations in accordance with the laws and customs of war.[602]

Article 4(A)(2) of Geneva Convention (III) retains the Hague formula,[603] making it even more stringent[604] (although Additional Protocol I, in Articles 43–4, utterly changes the legal position for Contracting Parties[605]). The evolution of the law in this regard will not be traced here, as it does not have a direct bearing on the matter at hand. Suffice it to point out that, as a rule, individuals who violently resist occupation do not meet the Hague conditions. Their clandestine activity will usually preempt the possibility of carrying arms openly and a distinctive sign; there may not be any subordination to responsible commanders; and they are not prone to submitting to the norms of the *jus in bello*.

297. An exception to the need to apply all four Hague conditions comes into play at the nascent phase of an invasion leading to occupation, when the *jus in bello* recognizes the special situation of a *levée en masse*. Hague Regulation 2 (1907 version) wrestles with this turn of events:

> The population of a territory which has not been occupied who, on the approach of the enemy, spontaneously take up arms to resist the invading troops without having had time to organize themselves in accordance with Article 1, shall be regarded as belligerents if they carry arms openly and if they respect the laws and customs of war.[606]

Similarly, Article 4(A)(6) of Geneva Convention (III) confers the status of prisoners of war on:

> Inhabitants of a non-occupied territory, who on the approach of the enemy spontaneously take up arms to resist the invading forces, without having had time to form themselves into regular armed units, provided they carry arms openly and respect the laws and customs of war.[607]

298. These provisions expressly apply only to inhabitants of non-occupied territories, and they therefore do not apply to the civilian population in 'the portion of the country which is occupied'.[608] A French Tribunal in the *Bauer* trial of 1945 pushed the envelope of *levée en masse* a little, to include a contested occupied area from which the enemy has been driven out but it is trying to retake.[609] In any event, the basic idea of *levée en masse* – originating

[602] Hague Regulations, *supra* note 22, at 218–19.
[603] Geneva Convention (III), *supra* note 397, at 513.
[604] See Dinstein, *supra* note 14, at 48–56.
[605] Additional Protocol I, *supra* note 33, at 732–3.
[606] Hague Regulations, *supra* note 22, at 220–1.
[607] Geneva Convention (III), *supra* note 397, at 514.
[608] In *re von Lewinski (called von Manstein)* trial (British Military Court, Hamburg, 1949), [1949] *ADRPILC* 509, 515.
[609] *Bauer* et al. trial (Permanent Military Tribunal, Dijon, 1945), 8 *LRTWC* 15, 18.

in the French Revolution[610] – is settled. When facing invasion, and in an attempt to stave off occupation, the civilian population (not having an opportunity to organize) is permitted to take up arms spontaneously. This is an extraordinary situation in which, for a short while and during an interim phase in the fighting, there is no need to meet all four Hague conditions. Only two cumulative conditions are indispensable: carrying arms openly and respect for the *jus in bello* (Hague conditions (3) and (4)). It follows that there is no need to meet the two other Hague conditions of subordination to a responsible commander and using a fixed distinctive emblem (conditions (1) and (2)).[611]

299. A *levée en masse* lapses *ex hypothesi* after a relatively short time. Thus, in the *Orić* Judgment of 2006, the ICTY Trial Chamber came to the conclusion that 'while the situation in Srebrenica may be characterised as a *levée en masse* at the time of the Serb take over and immediately thereafter in April and early May 1992, the concept by definition excludes its application to long-term situations'.[612]

300. The trajectory of subsequent events will go in one of three different directions: either (i) the territory is occupied (despite the *levée en masse*); or (ii) the invading force is repulsed (thanks to the *levée en masse* or to the arrival of reinforcements); or else (iii) the battle of defence stabilizes, and then there is ample opportunity for organization and meeting all four Hague conditions.

301. Assuming that a *levée en masse* has failed and that an occupation of the territory in question has taken place, those members of the civilian population who go on forcibly resisting the occupation will be regarded as saboteurs (see *supra* 206). Although entitled to the privileged status of prisoners of war if captured by the enemy while a *levée en masse* is in progress, civilians who persist in engaging the Occupying Power thereafter lose that prerogative.[613]

V. Riot Control

302. Riots may occur anywhere, but they are endemic in occupied territories. Under Article 2(2)(c) of the European Convention on Human Rights, deprivation of life is not regarded as inflicted in contravention of the human right to life if it results from use of force which is no more than absolutely necessary 'in action lawfully taken for the purpose of quelling a riot or insurrection'.[614]

[610] On the origins of the institution, see W.G. Rabus, 'A New Definition of the "Levée en Masse"', 24 *NILR* 232, *id.* (1977).

[611] In particular, as accentuated in the *Bauer* et al. trial, this means that '[i]t is immaterial whether they wear civilian clothes or any other kind of dress', *supra* note 609, at 18.

[612] *Prosecutor v. Orić* (ICTY, Trial Chamber, 2006), para. 136.

[613] See F. Kalshoven, *Reflections on the Law of War: Collected Essays* 551 (2007).

[614] European Convention for the Protection of Human Rights and Fundamental Freedoms, *supra* note 438, at 82.

The practical interpretation of this provision is that soldiers are not obligated to retreat when an agitated riot develops: fatalities and injuries may then be impossible to avoid (although caution must be exercised when dealing with intractable crowds before matters get out of control).[615] This is true both in general and in the special context of occupied territories.

303. Broadly speaking, provided that no hostilities are going on, quelling a riot in an occupied territory is not dissimilar to parallel law enforcement action in a domestic environment.[616] In other words, as long as full governmental functions can be effected in the area by the Occupying Power, the reestablishment of public order through riot control should be undertaken – whenever feasible – with minimum blood-letting. Usually, this would entail recourse to special means of subduing unruly crowds (like water cannons) and certain types of non-lethal ammunition (such as plastic bullets). As stated by the Israel Supreme Court (per President Shamgar), in the *League for Human and Civil Rights* case – denying a petition to disqualify the employment of plastic bullets – 'the legality of the use of firearms must be examined in accordance with the concrete circumstances of the time and space, as well as the operational and safety conditions' (bearing in mind that there is a difference between, e.g., using light versus heavy weapons and firing a single shot or automatic fire).[617]

304. Interestingly, the use of non-lethal weapons for the purposes of riot control in occupied territories may involve means that have been excluded from warfare (i.e. the conduct of hostilities) by the *jus in bello*. The leading example is that of non-lethal chemical weapons, mainly tear gas.

305. The general employment and even possession of any chemical weapons is interdicted in Article I of the 1993 Convention on the Prohibition of the Development, Production, Stockpiling and Use of Chemical Weapons and on Their Destruction (CWC),[618] which is well on its way to universality. The basic treaty prohibition of gas warfare goes back to the 1925 Geneva Protocol for the Prohibition of the Use in War of Asphyxiating, Poisonous or Other Gases, and of Bacteriological Methods of Warfare.[619] Since then, the injunction has consolidated as customary international law.[620] Indeed, '[e]mploying

615 See Harris, O'Boyle and Warbrick, *supra* note 475, at 53–4.

616 See W.H. Boothby, *Weapons and the Law of Armed Conflict* 122–3 (2nd edn. 2016).

617 HCJ 66/89, *League for Human and Civil Rights in Israel v. Minister of Defence*, 44(2) *PD* 221, 222. (The Judgment is excerpted in English in 25 *IYHR* 323 (1995)).

618 Convention on the Prohibition of the Development, Production, Stockpiling and Use of Chemical Weapons and on Their Destruction, 1993, *The Laws of Armed Conflicts*, *supra* note 29, at 239, 241–2.

619 Geneva Protocol for the Prohibition of the Use in War of Asphyxiating, Poisonous or Other Gases, and of Bacteriological Methods of Warfare, 1925, *The Laws of Armed Conflicts*, *supra* note 29, at 105, 107.

620 I *Customary International Humanitarian Law*, *supra* note 40, at 259–60.

asphyxiating, poisonous or other gases, and all analogous liquids, materials or devices' is now a war crime pursuant to Article 8(2)(b)(xviii) of the 1998 Rome Statute of the International Criminal Court.[621]

306. The term 'chemical weapons' is defined in Article II of the CWC: the mainstay of the definition (in paragraph 2) is that the chemical is toxic, namely, that 'its chemical action on life processes can cause death, temporary incapacitation or permanent harm to humans or animals'.[622] Non-lethal chemical agents, causing 'temporary incapacitation' to humans – such as tear gas – are thus clearly included in the definition of chemical weapons. In Article I(5) of the CWC, States Parties even undertake 'not to use riot control agents as a method of warfare'. However, Article II(9)(d) explicitly allows the employment of chemicals for '[l]aw enforcement including domestic riot control purposes'.[623] The net outcome is that resorting to tear gas and other riot control chemicals is permissible in non-combat law enforcement situations. This is true even in wartime, e.g., 'in prisoners-of-war camps or military prisons';[624] and there should be no hindrance to the use of tear gas and other riot control agents in an occupied territory.[625]

VI. Hostilities in Occupied Territories

A. *The Duality of Hostilities and Occupation*

307. The fact that a territory is under belligerent occupation does not exclude the possibility that fully fledged hostilities – in contradistinction to mere riots – will be rekindled in at least some sections of the occupied territory (see *supra* 149). Inexplicably, in the Advisory Opinion on the *Wall*, the International Court of Justice seemed to be oblivious to the actuality of hostilities raging in occupied territories (see *infra* 779). Yet, it is impossible to overlook a persistent reality.

308. Hostilities inside an occupied territory consist of actual combat conducted against the Occupying Power either by enemy regular troops (including rearguard units entrenched in fortified enclaves) or by locally organized insurgents. Whatever its form, combat is governed by the standard

621 Rome Statute of the International Criminal Court, *supra* note 350, at 1318.

622 Convention on the Prohibition of the Development, Production, Stockpiling and Use of Chemical Weapons and on Their Destruction, *supra* note 618, at 242.

623 *Ibid.*, 242, 244.

624 See W. Krutzsch and R. Trapp, *A Commentary on the Chemical Weapons Convention* 42 (1994).

625 See S. Longuet, 'Permitted for Law Enforcement Purposes but Prohibited in the Conduct of Hostilities: The Case of Riot Control Agents and Expanding Bullets', 901 *IRRC* 249, 266–7 (2016).

norms of the *jus in bello*. The present author cannot accept the argument submitted by some scholars that – in certain sets of circumstances – hostilities in occupied territories are governed by the law of non-international armed conflicts.[626] The fact that some fighting is waged against the Occupying Power by non-State actors does not affect the status of the overall armed conflict (within which the belligerent occupation is going on) as international. The applicability of the *jus in bello* to such fighting was recognized on more than one occasion by the Israel Supreme Court, particularly in the *Targeted Killings* case (per President Barak).[627]

309. Hostilities in occupied territories may escalate to such a point that the Occupying Power may practically have to reinvade and resubdue an insurgent area. In the Israeli case, this is what happened in the West Bank as a result of the second *intifada* in 2002. In Iraq, the protracted battle of Fallujah in 2004 reached high levels of fighting not witnessed hitherto.[628]

310. During hostilities, whether waged in an occupied territory or elsewhere, large-scale destruction or damage may be caused to private property (see *infra* 595). Demolition of private property by military authorities as a sanction in an occupied territory (see *infra* 619) is not to be mistaken for the destruction of property caused by combat operations. Even the Israel Supreme Court – which frequently blended the two concepts (see *infra* 628) – knew when to draw the line. In one of several *Jenin* cases, the Court (*per curiam*) refused to intervene in circumstances of heavy fighting (inflicting massive damage on residential buildings, used as bunkers and nests for snipers) in a refugee camp in the West Bank, at the peak of the second *intifada,* in 2002.[629]

311. When hostilities go on in an occupied territory, the law of belligerent occupation does not disappear. It has to be applied simultaneously with *jus in bello* norms relating to combat. This means that the Occupying Power will have to adjust itself to compliance with two different legal regimes. Vis-à-vis enemy soldiers or civilians who are taking a direct part in hostilities (at such time as they do so; see *infra* 315 *et seq.*), the governing norms will be those pertaining to the conduct of hostilities. But vis-à-vis the civilian population at large in the occupied territory – as long as it remains under its effective control – the military government must continue to obey the law of belligerent occupation.

[626] See, e.g., Arai-Takahashi, *supra* note 149, at 301–4.
[627] HCJ 769/02, *supra* note 38, at 544–50.
[628] See Watkin, *supra* note 591, at 282.
[629] See HCJ 2977/02, *Adallah – Legal Centre for Arab Minority Rights in Israel* et al. *v. IDF Commander of Judea and Samaria*, 56(3) *PD*, 6, 8. (The Judgment is excerpted in English in 32 *IYHR* 362 (2002)).

312. In the *Rafiah* case, the Supreme Court (per President Barak) pronounced that – even when fighting is in progress – the Occupying Power (i) must refrain from action that harms innocent civilians; and (ii) must ensure supplies of food – especially water – and medications to the civilian population, as well as the operation of medical services (in accordance with Articles 55–6 of Geneva Convention (IV); see *infra* 457, 567).[630] In the *Operation Cast Lead* case, the Supreme Court (per President Beinisch) held in 2009 – in the course of major fighting in the Gaza Strip – that (irrespective of the law of belligerent occupation) hostilities brought about obligations of care for the civilian population, protection of medical services and facilities (unless misused for the commission of acts outside their humanitarian duties), and more in the same vein.[631]

313. In the Israeli occupied territories, serious problems were encountered by the military government as a result of the abuse of ambulances (which were loaded with explosives) and medical facilities (in which saboteurs found refuge) in the course of combat. The Supreme Court held (per Justice D. Dorner), in two *Association of Physicians for Human Rights* cases (related to the second *intifada*), that – although the protection conferred on medical personnel and facilities would cease if they commit or are used to commit acts outside their humanitarian tasks – this abuse would not by itself justify a sweeping counter-measure by the Occupying Power ignoring the humanitarian norms mandating treatment of the wounded and respect for medical personnel.[632]

314. When combat is waged in an occupied territory, the status of *hors de combat* fighters must be respected.[633] Moreover, it must be borne in mind that innocent protected persons are liable to get into the crossfire and feasible precautions must be taken in order to minimize 'collateral damage' to them. The employment of certain weapons may be particularly hazardous to innocent civilians who happen to be present nearby. In another *Association of Physicians for Human Rights* case, the Court (per Justice E. Matza) underscored the duty of the military to proceed with caution but refused to forbid outright the use

[630] HCJ 4764/04, *Physicians for Human Rights* et al. *v. IDF Commander of Gaza*, 58(5) *PD* 385, 394–5. (The Judgment is excerpted in English in 35 *IYHR* 327 (2005)).

[631] HCJ 201/09 etc., *Physicians for Human Rights* et al. *v. Prime Minister* et al., 63(1) *PD* 521, 535–40. (The Judgment is excerpted in English in 39 *IYHR* 406 (2009)).

[632] HCJ 2396/02 etc., *Association of Physicians for Human Rights* et al. *v. IDF Commander of the West Bank*, 56(3) *PD* 3, 4–5; HCJ 2117/02, *Association of Physicians for Human Rights v. IDF Commander of the West Bank* et al., *ibid.*, 26, 28–9. (The two Judgments are excerpted in English in 32 *IYHR* 360, 371 (2002)).

[633] Cf. the 2017 Judgment of the Israeli Military Court of Appeals in the case of *Chief Military Prosecutor v. Azaria*, excerpted in English in 48 *IYHR* 360 (2018).

of any weapon that is not banned by the *jus in bello*, in this instance flechette shells (fired by tanks).[634]

B. Direct Participation in Hostilities

315. The principal issue during combat in occupied territories concerns civilians who choose to directly participate in the hostilities. Such behaviour leads to loss of protection from attack. The prescript of Article 51(3) of Additional Protocol I is that civilians enjoy a general protection against dangers arising from military operations, 'unless and for such time as they take a direct part in hostilities'.[635] Occasionally, the reference in *jus in bello* texts is to 'active' (instead of 'direct') participation in hostilities,[636] and at times either adjective is deleted.[637] The bottom line is essentially the same:[638] a person who takes part in hostilities loses his mantle of protection. No doubt, as pointed out by the Israel Supreme Court (per President Barak), in the *Targeted Killings* case, this provision reflects customary international law.[639]

316. There is virtually a consensus that a civilian can be targeted when he is taking a direct part in hostilities.[640] But this is limited temporally by the words 'for such time', appearing in Article 51(3). Not surprisingly, these words raise serious queries as to their scope.[641] The Government of Israel used to adhere to the view that the phrase 'for such time' does not reflect customary international law, but the Supreme Court summarily rejected that contention.[642] President Barak made it plain that a civilian who only sporadically takes a direct part in hostilities does not lose protection from attack on a permanent basis: if and when he disconnects himself from these activities, he regains his civilian protection from attack[643] (naturally, he may still be interned or prosecuted

[634] HCJ 8990/02, *Association of Physicians for Human Rights* et al. *v. Commander of Southern Region* et al., 57(4) *PD* 193, 195–6. (The Judgment is excerpted in English in 34 *IYHR* 319 (2004)).
[635] Additional Protocol I, *supra* note 33, at 736.
[636] See, e.g., Article 3(1) of Geneva Convention (IV), *supra* note 29, at 580.
[637] See, e.g., Article 8(a) of Additional Protocol I, *supra* note 33, at 718.
[638] Cf. *Prosecutor v. Akayesu* (International Criminal Tribunal for Rwanda, Trial Chamber, 1998), para. 629.
[639] HCJ 769/02, *supra* note 38, at 561.
[640] *Ibid.*, 562.
[641] See K. Watkin, 'Humans in the Cross-Hairs: Targeting and Assassination in Contemporary Armed Conflict', *New Wars, New Laws? Applying the Laws of War in 21st Century Conflicts* 137, 154–7 (D. Wippman and M. Evangelista eds., 2005).
[642] HCJ 769/02, *supra* note 38, at 563, 570.
[643] *Ibid.*, 570.

for any crime that he may have committed during his direct participation in hostilities[644]).

317. The desire to confine the exposure of civilians who directly participate in hostilities to a finite space of time makes a lot of sense. It is worthwhile keeping in mind that the armed forces of the Occupying Power may also incorporate units of reservists who are called up for a prescribed period and are then released from service. *Au fond*, a reservist is a civilian who dons the uniform of a combatant but only for a limited time. While in service, he is deemed a combatant with all the risks that this status implies. When the term of service ends, he doffs the uniform and returns to civilian life as well as to protection from attack. The same analysis should apply *grosso modo* to other types of civilians who directly participate in hostilities against the Occupying Power.

318. There are two significant riders that ought to be tagged on to the general proposition relating to direct participation in hostilities. The first is that the cycle of direct participation in hostilities commences at an early stage of preparation and deployment, continuing – throughout the engagement itself – to cover also the disengagement and withdrawal phase.[645] Although there are those who maintain that the expression 'for such time' should be construed narrowly as encompassing only the engagement itself, this claim is generally rejected.[646] The present writer's view is that, in demarcating the spell of time during which a person is actually taking part in hostilities, it is permissible to go as far as is reasonably necessary both 'upstream' and 'downstream' from the actual engagement.

319. The second rider is that, while a person directly participating in hostilities may still revert to a civilian status, this cannot be brought off when the hostile activities happen on a steadily recurrent basis with brief intermediate pauses (the so-called 'revolving door' phenomenon).[647] Those attempting to be 'farmers by day and fighters by night' lose protection from attack even in the interludes punctuating military operations. The same rationale applies if an individual becomes a member of an organized armed group (which collectively takes a direct part in the hostilities): he would lose civilian protection for as long as that membership lasts. In the locution of the Judgment in the *Targeted Killings* case, an organized armed group becomes the 'home' of the person concerned for whom a respite – interposing between acts of hostilities – merely means preparation for the next round.[648] In practical terms, the individual in

[644] See C. Pilloud and J. Pictet, 'Article 51', *Commentary on the Additional Protocols, supra* note 327, at 613, 619.

[645] HCJ 769/02, *supra* note 38, at 566.

[646] See K. Watkin, 'Controlling the Use of Force: A Role for Human Rights Norms in Contemporary Armed Conflict', 98 *AJIL* 1, 17 (2004).

[647] HCJ 769/02, *supra* note 38, at 571.

[648] *Ibid.*, 570.

question may be targeted even when not personally associated with any specific hostile act, simply due to his membership in such a group, provided that the affiliation is in evidence and it does not lapse.

320. Undisputedly, the concept of direct participation in hostilities is not open-ended, and it is far more restricted in scope than making a contribution to the war effort.[649] Still, activities of many hues can be identified as examples of direct participation in hostilities. As the *Targeted Killings* Judgment expounded, these include not only employing firearms or gathering intelligence, but also driving an ammunition truck to a place where it will be used for fighting purposes, acting as a guide to combatants, and, most pointedly, masterminding such activities through recruitment or planning (in contradistinction to, e.g., merely donating monetary contributions or selling supplies to combatants: the latter activities do not come within the bounds of direct participation in hostilities).[650]

321. Pursuant to Article 50(1) of Additional Protocol I, '[i]n case of doubt whether a person is a civilian, that person shall be considered to be a civilian'.[651] The provision is particularly germane to the issue of direct participation in hostilities. It is imperative to ensure that military units tasked with the mission of winnowing out civilians who engage in hostilities will not treat all civilians as targetable, 'shooting first and asking questions later'.[652] Additionally, the presence of civilians directly participating in hostilities among the civilian population does not deprive the general population of the protection from attack to which it is entitled.[653]

322. Hague Regulation 23(b) forbids the treacherous killing or wounding of enemy individuals,[654] and Article 8(2)(b)(xi) of the Rome Statute of the International Criminal Court brands that as a war crime.[655] Article 37(1) of Additional Protocol I prohibits killing an adversary by resort to perfidy (defined as an act inviting the confidence of an adversary to lead him to believe that he is entitled to – or is obliged to accord – protection under the *jus in bello*, with an intent to betray that confidence).[656] However, absent perfidy, a targeted killing per se is not unlawful.[657]

323. In an occupied territory (and only in an occupied territory), there is an additional question whether the Occupying Power is capable of taking

[649] See F. Kalshoven and L. Zegveld, *Constraints on the Waging of War* 102 (4th edn, 2011).
[650] HCJ 769/02, *supra* note 38, at 567–9.
[651] Additional Protocol I, *supra* note 33, at 735.
[652] Kalshoven, *supra* note 613, at 73–4, 214.
[653] Cf. Additional Protocol I, *supra* note 33, at 736 (Article 50(3)).
[654] Hague Regulations, *supra* note 22, at 234–5.
[655] Rome Statute of the International Criminal Court, *supra* note 350, at 1318.
[656] Additional Protocol I, *supra* note 33, at 730.
[657] See HCJ 769/02, *supra* note 38, at 552.

effective law enforcement measures against civilians who directly participate in hostilities, in lieu of using deadly force. As President Barak underlined, an arrest by the Occupying Power of a person directly participating in hostilities is the preferred step (if feasible).[658] But when an arrest is not a viable option, it must be recognized that a civilian taking a direct part in hostilities risks his life (like any combatant) and is exposed to a lethal attack.[659] Consequently, a strike targeting such a person – and slaying him – is permissible when non-lethal measures are either unavailable or deemed ineffective.[660]

324. A targeted killing (in or out of an occupied territory) must be carried out with due regard to the safety of genuine civilians – that is, civilians not participating in hostilities – who happen to be in the vicinity. President Barak was adamant that, whenever innocent civilians are present near the targeted individual and they are likely to be injured, the principle of proportionality must be applied.[661]

C. 'Human Shields'

325. An immensely important problem in hostilities taking place in occupied territories relates to the use of civilians as 'human shields'. Pursuant to Article 28 of Geneva Convention (IV), '[t]he presence of a protected person may not be used to render certain points or areas immune from military operations'.[662] For its part, Article 51(7) of Additional Protocol I reads:

> The presence or movements of the civilian population or individual civilians shall not be used to render certain points or areas immune from military operations, in particular in attempts to shield military objectives from attacks or to shield, favour or impede military operations.[663]

Irrefutably, the prohibition of the use of civilians as 'human shields' reflects customary international law.[664] Utilizing the presence of civilians or other protected persons to render certain points, areas or military forces immune from military operations is recognized as a war crime by Article 8(2)(b)(xxiii) of the Rome Statute of the International Criminal Court.[665]

326. If persons directly participating in hostilities in an occupied territory intermingle with innocent civilians – in order to hide among them or use them

658 *Ibid.*, 572.
659 *Ibid.*, 576–7.
660 *Ibid.*, 586–7.
661 *Ibid.*, 574–7.
662 Geneva Convention (IV), *supra* note 29, at 589.
663 Additional Protocol I, *supra* note 33, at 736.
664 See I *Customary International Humanitarian Law*, *supra* note 40, at 337.
665 Rome Statute of the International Criminal Court, *supra* note 350, at 1319.

as a screen impeding military operations – this is a breach of the *jus in bello*. Still, it is necessary to distinguish between voluntary and involuntary 'human shields'. As the Israel Supreme Court (per President Barak) established in the *Targeted Killings* case, whereas involuntary 'human shields' are victims, voluntary 'human shields' are to be deemed civilians who take a direct part in hostilities.[666] That being the case, voluntary 'human shields' – as highlighted in the legal literature[667] – are targetable (although, as a rule, that simply means that they will fail in their effort to render non-targetable a military objective which they are trying to shield). In case of doubt, 'human shields' must be regarded as involuntary.

327. The prohibition of placing civilians as 'human shields' around a military objective applies equally to all sides in the hostilities. Much as this has become a *modus operandi* symptomatic of those resisting an Occupying Power, the military government may be tempted to employ analogous tactics to facilitate its own operations. The issue arose in the *Early Warning* case, in which the Israel Supreme Court (per President Barak) had to determine the legality of a procedure (adopted by the IDF), whereby – when a saboteur has been cornered and besieged – a local resident would be encouraged to volunteer (on condition that no harm to the messenger was anticipated), in order to relay a warning and a call to surrender, so as to avoid unnecessary bloodshed.[668] The procedure was discredited by outside observers,[669] and it was invalidated by the Court.[670] Relying on Article 28 of the Convention and on Article 51(7) of Additional Protocol I (quoted *supra* 325), President Barak held that the *jus in bello* does not allow the use of protected persons as 'human shields' and that, therefore, the assistance of a local inhabitant can certainly not be required coercively.[671]

328. What about assistance of a local inhabitant given voluntarily, in circumstances where the person providing the assistance is not expected to be at hazard (as per the contested procedure)? President Barak ruled against the procedure on four grounds: (i) protected persons must not be used as part of the military effort of the Occupying Power (see *supra* 177–8); (ii) everything must be done to separate the civilian population from combat operations; (iii)

666 HCJ 769/02, *supra* note 38, at 569.

667 M.N. Schmitt, 'War, Technology and the Law of Armed Conflict', *The Law of War in the 21st Century: Weaponry and the Use of Force* 137, 177 (82 *International Law Studies*, A.M. Helm ed., 2006).

668 HCJ 3799/02, *Adallah – Legal Centre for Arab Minority Rights in Israel* et al. *v. Commander of the Central Region* et al., paras. 5–7. (The Judgment is excerpted in English in 37 *IYHR* 320 (2007)).

669 See R. Otto, 'Neighbours as Human Shields? The Israel Defense Forces' "Early Warning Procedure" and International Humanitarian Law', 856 *IRRC* 771–86 (2004).

670 HCJ 3799/02, *supra* note 668, at para. 25.

671 *Ibid.*, paras. 21–2.

voluntary consent in these circumstances is often suspect; and (iv) it is not possible to tell confidently in advance whether the activity of the person lending the assistance puts him in danger.[672]

329. *En principe*, President Barak's reasoning is persuasive. Yet, he did not explain why assistance cannot be offered by a close relative – especially, a mother or a father – of a saboteur besieged in a building that is about to be stormed (with the likelihood of death in action of the saboteur) when the initiative is taken by the parent who begs to be given a chance to persuade the son to surrender and save his life.[673] In such exceptional circumstances, there is little if any danger to the life of the father or mother, and humanitarian considerations actually tip the scales in favour of allowing the requested intercession to take place.

[672] *Ibid.*, para 24.

[673] The possibility was raised by Deputy President Cheshin in para. 3 of his Separate Opinion, *ibid.*

5 Legislation by the Occupying Power

I. The Meaning of the Phrase 'les lois en vigueur'

330. In accordance with the second part of Hague Regulation 43 (quoted *supra* 269), there is no legislative *tabula rasa* in case of belligerent occupation. The Occupying Power must respect 'les lois en vigueur (the laws in force)' in the occupied territory, unless there is an 'empêchement absolu'. Respect – as spelt out in the Brussels Project (*supra* 271) – means that the Occupying Power has to maintain the laws in force and not modify, suspend or replace them with its own legislation (subject to the saving clause).

331. In French, the term 'les lois' (i.e. promulgated 'laws') is narrower than 'le Droit' ('the Law' in an all-embracing sense). Promulgated laws embrace basic as well as trivial laws; whether national or municipal; either civil or criminal; substantive or procedural; but they are restricted to *jus scriptum*. All the same, there is no indication that the authors of the Hague Regulations really wished to exclude from the orbit of Regulation 43 *jus non scriptum* in the form of 'common law', domestic customary law, tribal law (particularly of indigenous and nomadic people), etc.

332. As for the phrase 'en vigueur', once again the Brussels Project is more precise in adverting to 'les lois qui étaient en vigueur dans le pays en temps de paix' (*supra ibid.*). No doubt, Regulation 43 equally pertains 'only to those laws which were "in force" in the occupied territory at the time of the commencement of the occupation'.[674] It must be discerned that the displaced sovereign has the full right to continue to legislate for the occupied territory even after the occupation begins.[675] However, for its part, the Occupying Power is not bound to respect any laws enacted by the displaced sovereign during the occupation.[676]

[674] E. Stein, 'Application of the Law of the Absent Sovereign in Territory under Belligerent Occupation: The Schio Massacre', 46 *Mich.LR* 341, 349 (1947–8).

[675] See E. Schwelb, 'Legislation for Enemy-Occupied Territory in the British Empire', 20 *TGS* 239, 258–9 (1944).

[676] See Hyde, *supra* note 296, at 1886.

333. Two caveats are in order in this connection. The first is that, sometimes, there may be a concordance of interests on the part of the displaced sovereign and the Occupying Power in having specific new legislation in force in the occupied territory. Should this come to pass, the Occupying Power (for reasons of political expediency) may choose to give effect in the occupied territory to a statute engraved in the law books by the displaced sovereign subsequent to the start of the occupation.[677]

334. The second caveat is that Regulation 43 does not purport to have any impact on the relations between the displaced sovereign and its own nationals living under occupation. The duty of allegiance of these nationals to their State is not corroded by the occupation (see *supra* 175). The Supreme Court of Norway, in the *Haaland* case of 1945, enunciated that – notwithstanding its absence from the occupied territory – the displaced sovereign is authorized to enact criminal measures pertaining to the conduct of its nationals during the occupation (especially where treason is concerned), although such legislative effusions will generally have no practical meaning until the end of the occupation.[678]

II. The Meaning of the Phrase 'empêchement absolu'

335. Since, in accordance with the second part of Regulation 43, the duty of the Occupying Power to respect the laws in force in the occupied territory (predating the occupation) is subject to an 'empêchement absolu', it is manifest that these laws are not immutable. The crucial question is: when does an 'empêchement absolu' occur? Despite the fact that the phrase sounds extremely restrictive, there is almost a consensus in the legal literature that 'empêchement absolu' is not as categorical as it sounds. Indeed, '[t]he term "absolutely prevented" has never been interpreted literally'.[679] The common interpretation of Regulation 43 is that 'empêchement absolu' is the equivalent of 'necessité' (the original language of Brussels Article III quoted *supra* 271). Necessity in this context is not circumscribed to military necessity, and its scope is a matter of reasonable assessment. Within the limits of sound judgment, the Occupying Power is allowed 'to legislate in almost all aspects of life in the occupied territory'.[680] Of course, any new legislation enacted by the Occupying Power can modify the laws in force in the occupied territory only for the duration of the occupation.

[677] See Stein, *supra* note 674, at 362.
[678] *Public Prosecutor v. Haaland* (Norway, Supreme Court, 1945), 12 *ILR* 444, 445.
[679] E.H. Feilchenfeld, *The International Economic Law of Belligerent Occupation* 89 (1942).
[680] P. Spoerri, 'The Law of Occupation', *The Oxford Handbook of International Law in Armed Conflict* 182, 195 (A. Clapham and P. Gaeta eds., 2014).

III. Article 64 of Geneva Convention (IV)

336. The terse provision of Hague Regulation 43 is considerably augmented by Article 64 of Geneva Convention (IV):

> The penal laws of the occupied territory shall remain in force, with the exception that they may be repealed or suspended by the Occupying Power in cases where they constitute a threat to its security or an obstacle to the application of the present Convention. Subject to the latter consideration and to the necessity for ensuring the effective administration of justice, the tribunals of the occupied territory shall continue to function in respect of all offences covered by the said laws.
>
> The Occupying Power may, however, subject the population of the occupied territory to provisions which are essential to enable the Occupying Power to fulfil its obligations under the present Convention, to maintain the orderly government of the territory, and to ensure the security of the Occupying Power, of the members and property of the occupying forces or administration, and likewise of the establishments and lines of communication used by them.[681]

337. The structure and language of Article 64 call for a number of observations. First and foremost, Article 64 ought to be deemed 'an amplification and clarification' of Hague Regulation 43.[682] That is to say, 'Article 64 expresses, in a more precise and detailed form, the terms of Article 43 of the Hague Regulations'.[683] The authors of Article 64 did not intend to expand 'the traditional scope of occupation legislation'.[684]

338. Secondly, Article 64 (first paragraph) refers to the repeal or suspension of existing penal laws. Granting that a permanent repeal of these laws would usually exceed the authority of the Occupying Power, we shall see (*infra* 344, 347) that sometimes this is required by the Convention. Nevertheless, suspension of the laws – for the period of the occupation – is the common option open to the Occupying Power. Such suspension will routinely be accompanied by a new text (modifying the original version), in force during the occupation. Irrespective of existing legislation, there are valid reasons for additional legislation for the period of occupation (as outlined in the second paragraph of Article 64).

339. Thirdly, Article 64 (first paragraph) – dealing with existing legislation – speaks solely of penal laws. The second paragraph (bringing up the issue of new legislation) seems to address the law in more general terms. Yet, in Article 66 (quoted *infra* 419), there is a limitative mention of 'the penal provisions promulgated by it by virtue of the second paragraph of Article 64'. Based on the text (and an interpretation of its *travaux préparatoires*), it

[681] Geneva Convention (IV), *supra* note 29, at 598–9.
[682] J.A.C. Gutteridge, 'The Geneva Conventions of 1949', 26 *BYBIL* 294, 324 (1949).
[683] *Commentary, IV Geneva Convention*, *supra* note 31, at 335.
[684] Schwarzenberger, *supra* note 204, at 194.

has been argued that Article 64 as a whole must be construed as confined to penal laws and inapplicable to, say, commercial legislation.[685] But the argument has been rebutted.[686] Indeed, the general view in the legal literature is that – despite the exclusive reference to penal laws in Article 64 – 'the entire legal system of the occupied territories is actually meant by this rule'.[687] Logic dictates that Article 64 should be construed as applicable to every type of law, including civil or administrative legislation. This affects both respect for the existing civil law of the occupied territory and the competence of the Occupying Power to suspend and modify it (in the same manner as it would penal law).[688]

340. Fourthly, Article 64 (first paragraph) mentions two types of exceptional situations – threats to the security of the Occupying Power and obstacles to the application of the Geneva Convention – whereas three exceptional situations are adverted to in Article 64 (second paragraph): the same two plus the need to maintain the orderly government of the territory. If that is not enough, the first paragraph speaks of not repealing or suspending existing legislation, while the second paragraph uses the phraseology of subjecting the population to – i.e., enacting[689] – provisions meeting certain criteria. For all the apparent lack of linguistic correspondence, the two paragraphs of Article 64 must be read in unison. Whether the Occupying Power merely suspends old statutes or introduces new legislation, the old and the new must mesh within a single, coherent, legal system. If an 'absurd result' is to be avoided, all new legislation must be viewed as altering contradictory old statutes as long as the occupation lasts.[690]

IV. The Specific Categories of Permissible Legislation

341. The main advantage of Geneva Article 64 over Hague Regulation 43 is that, instead of a mere reiteration of the original Hague phrase 'empêchement absolu' – or even an alternative use of the portmanteau expression 'necessity' – we find in the Geneva text an elucidation of the circumstances in which the Occupying Power may have recourse to legislation. Such legislation comes under the following headings.

685 See J.A. Carballo Leyda, 'The Laws of Occupation and Commercial Law Reform in Occupied Territories: Clarifying a Widespread Misunderstanding', 23 *EJIL* 179, 183–4 (2012).

686 See E. Benvenisti, 'The Laws of Occupation and Commercial Law Reform: A Reply to Jose Alejandro Carballo Leyda', 23 *EJIL* 199, 201–10 (2012).

687 Gasser and Dörmann, *supra* note 196, at 284.

688 See Greenspan, *supra* note 383, at 243.

689 See R. Wolfrum, 'The Adequacy of International Humanitarian Law Rules on Belligerent Occupation: To What Extent May Security Council Resolution 1483 Be Considered a Model for Adjustment?', *International Law and Armed Conflict: Exploring the Faultlines, supra* note 194, at 497, 502.

690 Sassòli, *supra* note 575, at 670.

A. *Security Legislation*

342. The paramount manifestation of permissible new legislation in an occupied territory is embedded in the rudimentary need of the Occupying Power to remove any direct threat to its security (including what is known as force protection: the security of members of its armed forces or administrative staff, as well as installations and property of the military government) and to maintain safe lines of communication. This must be considered against the background of Article 27 (fourth paragraph) of the Geneva Convention (quoted *supra* 286), authorizing the Occupying Power to take the necessary measures of control and security.

343. Much is left here to the discretion of the Occupying Power. The ICRC Commentary enumerates a number of admissible security measures, such as the requirement to carry identity cards; a ban on possession of firearms; prohibitions of access to certain areas; restrictions of movement; assigned residence; and internment.[691] It is noteworthy that one of the first Orders issued by the Coalition Provisional Authority in Iraq, in 2003, was to ban the unauthorized possession of arms.[692] Other recurrent permissible measures include the imposition of curfew at night;[693] censorship curbing freedom of expression;[694] control of means of communication (such as telephones);[695] restraints of freedom of association;[696] and curtailment of freedom of assembly and demonstrations.[697] Some of these measures will be dealt with separately, and it must be appreciated that the listing is by no means exhaustive.

B. *Repeal of Legislation Inconsistent with Geneva Convention (IV)*

(a) ***Fundamental Rights and Elimination of Discrimination***

344. The Occupying Power is entitled to enact legislation in the occupied territory in order to implement the Geneva Convention (and, by extension of this principle, also any other binding norms of international law, whether customary or conventional). This is designed to protect the basic rights of the

[691] *Commentary, IV Geneva Convention*, *supra* note 31, at 207.

[692] Coalition Provisional Authority Order Number 3, II *The Occupation of Iraq: The Official Documents*, *supra* note 78, at 60, 61.

[693] See von Glahn, *supra* note 339, at 141. See also *infra* 474–5.

[694] See US Department of Defense, *Law of War Manual*, *supra* note 1, at 778; *UK Manual of the Law of Armed Conflict*, *supra* note 230, at 286.

[695] See HCJ 270/88, *LSM (Law in the Service of Man)* et al. *v. IDF Commander of Judea and Samaria*, 42(3) *PD* 260, 263–4 (per President Shamgar). (The Judgment is excerpted in English in 23 *IYHR* 293 (1993)).

[696] See Greenwood, *supra* note 582, at 247–8.

[697] See, e.g., Coalition Provisional Authority Order Number 19, II *The Occupation of Iraq: The Official Documents*, *supra* note 78, at 141, 143.

inhabitants of the occupied territory under the Convention: such rights trump the laws of the displaced sovereign.[698]

345. Above all, the Occupying Power is allowed to expunge by law 'any adverse distinction based, in particular, on race, religion or political opinion', since discrimination of this nature runs counter to Article 27 (third paragraph) of the Geneva Convention.[699] A good example of eliminating adverse distinctions can be found in British legislation – during the belligerent occupation of the Dodecanese Islands, prior to the adoption of the Geneva Convention – abolishing all existing discriminatory statutes passed when the Islands belonged to Fascist Italy.[700]

346. There is little disagreement today with the postulate that the Occupying Power is also entitled to enact legislation that is 'genuinely necessary to protect human rights law'.[701] Along these lines, in 2004 – during the occupation of Iraq – the Coalition Provisional Authority amended Iraq's Labour Code, with a view to the prohibition of child labour, in line with International Labour Conventions to which Iraq was a Contracting Party.[702]

(b) Right or Duty?

347. Article 64 is couched in language of right ('may'), rather than duty, when conferring on the Occupying Power the authority to repeal or suspend the existing legislation.[703] But, like all Contracting Parties of the Geneva Convention, the Occupying Power has unconditionally undertaken (in Article 1) 'to respect and to ensure respect' for the Convention 'in all circumstances'.[704] The Occupying Power is barred from introducing (in the name of necessity) new legislation that clashes with the Geneva Convention or with the Hague Regulations (see *infra* 389). Moreover, it cannot leave in place – let alone implement – domestic legislation that collides with them.

348. Article 146 (first paragraph) of the Geneva Convention obligates Contracting Parties to enact any enabling domestic legislation that is required to give effect to the Convention (in connection with effective penal sanctions against persons committing grave breaches of the Convention).[705] The obligation devolves on Occupying Powers no less than on other Contracting Parties.

[698] See K. Boon, 'Legislative Reform in Post-Conflict Zones: *Jus Post Bellum* and the Contemporary Occupant's Law-Making Powers', 50 *McG.LJ* 285, 303 (2005).
[699] Geneva Convention (IV), *supra* note 29, at 589.
[700] See Chrysanthopoulos, *supra* note 48, at 228–9.
[701] See G. Giacca, 'Economic, Social, and Cultural Rights in Occupied Territories', *The 1949 Geneva Conventions: A Commentary*, *supra* note 309, at 1485, 1492.
[702] Coalition Provisional Authority Order Number 89, II *The Occupation of Iraq: The Official Documents*, *supra* note 78, at 539, 540.
[703] The point is emphasized by J. Stone, *No Peace – No War in the Middle East* 15 (1969).
[704] Geneva Convention (IV), *supra* note 29, at 580.
[705] *Ibid.*, 624.

(c) Prevalence over Conflicting Domestic Law

349. Article 27 of the 1969 of the Vienna Convention on the Law of Treaties confirms the overarching principle that a Contracting Party to a valid treaty 'may not invoke the provisions of its internal law as justification for its failure to perform a treaty'.[706] This is true of the Occupying Power's legislation in its own country, and the same rule should apply *a fortiori* to the domestic laws in force in an occupied territory.

350. The Geneva Convention must take precedence whenever it is incompatible with any existing legislation in or out of an occupied territory: 'when the penal legislation of the occupied territory conflicts with the provisions of the Convention, the Convention must prevail'.[707] It is impossible to argue with the proposition that '[a]n occupying power cannot rely upon the fact that national law already in force in the occupied territory permits the imposition of a particular sanction in order to justify taking action which is contrary to a provision of the Hague Regulations or the Fourth Geneva Convention'.[708] The *travaux préparatoires* of the Geneva Convention strengthen this interpretation of Article 64.[709]

351. The primacy of the Geneva Convention must be recalled when the Occupying Power is pleased with – and more than willing to enforce in the occupied territory – some legislation inherited from the displaced sovereign, which is in conflict with the Convention. The leading illustration is the Israeli reliance on Section 119(1) of the (British Mandatory) 1945 Defence (Emergency) Regulations, left intact in the West Bank and the Gaza Strip on the eve of the occupation (see *infra* 620). Section 119(1) permits the authorities to destroy private property as a punitive measure, and not merely 'where such destruction is rendered absolutely necessary by military operations' (as prescribed in Article 53 of the subsequently adopted Geneva Convention quoted *infra* 598).

352. Section 119(1) served as the legal bedrock for a prodigious number of demolitions of houses from which attacks had been launched by saboteurs in the territories occupied by Israel. A spate of petitions to the Israel Supreme Court, challenging the validity of Section 119(1), did not deflect the policy from its course. The Court – especially in the *Jaber* case – pronounced (per President Shamgar) that Section 119(1) represents legislation which was in force prior to the occupation, and it remains in force by dint of the provisions

[706] Vienna Convention on the Law of Treaties, 1969, [1969] *UNJY* 140, 148.

[707] *Commentary, IV Geneva Convention*, *supra* note 31, at 336.

[708] Greenwood, *supra* note 582, at 249.

[709] See M.B. Carroll, 'The Israeli Demolition of Palestinian Houses in the Occupied Territories: An Analysis of Its Legality in International Law', 11 *Mich.JIL* 1195, 1206 (1989–90).

of Hague Regulation 43 and Geneva Article 64.[710] This dictum is a glaring example of approbation and reprobation. The Hague Regulations and the Geneva Convention are summoned as a buttress for keeping a piece of domestic legislation in place, and yet the same instruments are brushed aside when they expressly curb the latitude allowed to the Occupying Power in the matter of destruction of property. How can it be argued that the existing law in an occupied territory, maintained in force thanks to the Geneva Convention and the Hague Regulations, outweighs the same instruments when it is irreconcilable with their edicts?[711] The notion that the Occupying Power can fulfil selectively some obligations crafted by the Convention and the Regulations – while disregarding others – is simply untenable.

C. *Legislation Geared to the Needs of the Civilian Population*

353. Under Article 64, there is a need to ensure the smooth operation of the 'orderly government' of the occupied territory. What does this phrase signify? Generally speaking, the *jus in bello* is based on a delicate balance between two magnetic poles: military necessity, on the one hand, and humanitarian considerations, on the other.[712] The tension between military necessity and humanitarian considerations pervades also the law of belligerent occupation. There are acute needs of the Occupying Power (constituting military necessity), but they coexist with counterpart needs of the population under occupation (reinvigorated by humanitarian considerations). The legislative power vested in the Occupying Power is sufficiently broad to cover action taken on behalf of the local inhabitants.[713] Practice sustains many types of legislation by the Occupying Power advancing the interests of the local population. A case in point is the introduction of rationing of foodstuffs and other commodities (ranging from clothing to gasoline or heating oil), in order to cope with chronic wartime shortages.[714] Another example is the 2003 Regulatory Code enacted by the Coalition Provisional Authority in Iraq, in order to

[710] HCJ 897/86, *Jaber v. Commander of the Central Region*, 41(2) *PD* 522, 525–6. (The Judgment is excerpted in English in 18 *IYHR* 252 (1988)).

[711] See M. Qupty, 'The Application of International Law in the Occupied Territories as Reflected in the Judgments of the High Court of Justice in Israel', *International Law and the Administration of Occupied Territories, supra* note 582, at 87, 107.

[712] See Dinstein, *supra* note 14, at 8–10. The statement made by the present writer (in several publications) on the need for such a balance has been frequently cited by the Israel Supreme Court. See, e.g., HCJ 2056/04, *Beit Sourik* et al. *v. Government of Israel* et al., 58(5) *PD* 807, 833. (The Judgment is excerpted in English in 35 *IYHR* 340 (2005). A full translation is available in 43 *ILM* 1099 (2004)).

[713] See Schwenk, *supra* note 570, at 400–1.

[714] See von Glahn, *supra* note 339, at 145–8.

thwart acts of theft and smuggling of oil 'that affect the wellbeing and future of all Iraqis'.[715]

354. The welfare of the civilian population may invite legislative measures having a spin-off beyond the temporal horizons of the occupation. This is especially true under conditions of prolonged occupation (see *infra* 357 *et seq.*). Law is a living organism, and life cannot come to a standstill: *tempora mutantur*. If the Occupying Power is to maintain the 'orderly government' of the occupied territory, it must possess the right to revise and even reform legislation in consonance with new developments. As a classic mundane illustration, one may cite the duty to install safety belts in all motor vehicles, introduced by the military government in the territories occupied by Israel.[716] When the displaced sovereign regains effective control of the occupied territory, it is obviously free to repeal any legislation enacted by the Occupying Power. Yet, the likelihood of rescinding legislation about the use of safety belts – already installed in cars – is not high.

D. Other Legislation

355. The categories of legislation that an Occupying Power may enact, as enumerated in Article 64, cannot be regarded as exhaustive. The concept of necessity, embedded in Hague Regulation 43 (as construed in practice), is elastic enough to go beyond the text of Article 64. As a result, the Occupying Power will be allowed to adopt other types of legislation if they are reasonably required by the conditions of occupation. For instance, nobody can question an amendment of the laws in force in an occupied territory, which is designed to sever any subordination of the local courts to appellate bodies operating in a non-occupied region retained by the displaced sovereign (see *infra* 414).

356. In the next section, we shall deal with further legislative needs that are generated by a prolonged occupation. On the face of it, there is also the precedent of the occupation of Iraq that – albeit far from prolonged, lasting technically less than fourteen months (from May 2003 through June 2004) – produced a torrent of Orders and other legislative measures issued by the Coalition Provisional Authority (see *supra* 38). But the sole excuse for the overabundant legislation in such a brief period is that the Occupying Powers set their sights on transforming post-occupation Iraq, relying in part on Security Council resolutions (see *supra* 40). The profusion of the Iraqi promulgations should

[715] Coalition Provisional Authority Order Number 36, II *The Occupation of Iraq: The Official Documents*, *supra* note 78, at 191, *id.*

[716] See *The Rule of Law in the Areas Administered by Israel* 9 (Israel National Section of the International Commission of Jurists, 1981).

definitely not be regarded as a model for similarly brief occupations in the future.

V. Prolonged Occupation

357. The highest watermark of a prolonged belligerent occupation in modern times is that of the Israeli occupation of Arab territories, which has been going on since 1967. A period exceeding half a century is exceptionally long.[717] It would simply be inconceivable for the legal system in Israel's occupied territories to have remained frozen in a time capsule. But occupation for a number of years (rather than decades) – in the order of magnitude of longevity of the occupations instigated by WWI and WWII (see *supra* 24–5) – must also be considered at least semi-prolonged. If left unchanged in such cases, the legal system is imperilled with stagnation: serious modifications may then become indispensable.[718] The longer the occupation lasts, the more compelling the need to weigh the merits of a whole gamut of novel legislative measures designed to ensure that societal needs in the occupied territory do not remain too long in a legal limbo.[719]

358. A semi-prolonged occupation of some note took place in the Ottoman province of Palestine, which was conquered by the British during WWI and remained occupied thereafter, pending the entry into force of the Mandate. The British military authorities decided that the situation called for a stream of legislative enactments. They preserved in principle the (Ottoman) laws in force, but issued Orders concerning the carrying of firearms, communication with the enemy, currency, food prices, public health and sanitation, cruelty to animals, cutting down trees, rent control, and protection of antiquities; introducing changes also in court procedure, in order to shift it somewhat from European-continental to Anglo-Saxon patterns.[720] Unmistakably, whereas the Orders pertaining to the carrying of firearms and communication with the enemy were geared to the needs of the Occupying Power, Orders apropos subject-matters such as rent control were passed to serve the interests of the inhabitants of the occupied territory.

717 Although it must be remembered that the Turkish occupation of Northern Cyprus (commencing in 1974) is not much shorter. As well, after Germany's unconditional surrender (thus taking place post-hostilities), 'the military occupation of West Berlin by the Allied Powers that exercised military authority there continued from 1945 until 1990'. W.H. Boothby and W. Heintschel von Heinegg, *The Law of War: A Detailed Assessment of the US Department of Defense Law of War Manual* 279 (2018).

718 See N. Lubell, 'Human Rights Obligations in Military Occupation', 885 *IRRC* 317, 329 (2012).

719 See Roberts, *supra* note 319, at 52.

720 See Bentwich, *supra* note 52, at 145–6.

359. Similarly, in Singapore, where the Japanese occupation in WWII lasted for more than three years, it was held – in the *Chartered Bank* case of 1956 – that, given the length of the occupation, '[i]t was a practical necessity, and within their legal power and duty under Article 43, for the Japanese to provide for and regulate matters of currency and banking so that the population could live orderly lives'.[721]

360. The sweep of legislation that can be adopted in the course of a prolonged occupation was debated in proceedings before the Israel Supreme Court in the *Jamait Askan* case.[722] A concise recital of the facts may be useful.[723] The petitioner was a cooperative association for the housing of West Bank teachers. The association purchased land north of Jerusalem and submitted for approval an outline of a housing project for its members. The scheme was rejected by the military government, owing to a conflict with an ambitious engineering blueprint for a large clover-leaf connecting two high-speed motorways. Subsequently, building permits already issued were revoked, and some of the real estate of the association was seized (compensation being offered), with a view to putting in effect the traffic layout. The priority given by the military government to the traffic upgrade venture – over the establishment of a housing project on the land owned by the association – was contested by the petitioner. The primary argument pitched was that the Occupying Power had no right to press through with grandiose plans of action having permanent fallout (enduring beyond the end of the occupation).[724] The respondents maintained that, after fifteen years of occupation (the period that had elapsed when the proceedings started), the Occupying Power could not confine itself to the conservation of an outdated road system.[725]

361. The Supreme Court (per Justice Barak), delivering its Judgment on the basis of both parts of Regulation 43, stressed the need to balance the interests of the Occupying Power and those of the civilian population.[726] Justice Barak noted that the construction of high-speed motorways, facilitating the swift movement of troops across occupied territories, was in the military and strategic interest of the Occupying Power.[727] But, in the main, the Judgment turned around the axis of a large engineering enterprise – for the benefit of the civilian population in the occupied territory – having permanent implications

[721] *Public Trustee v. Chartered Bank of India, Australia and China* (Singapore, Original Civil Jurisdiction, 1956), 23 *ILR* 687, 693–4.
[722] HCJ 393/82, *supra* note 158, at 785 *et seq.*
[723] *Ibid.*, 788–90.
[724] *Ibid.*, 791.
[725] *Ibid.*
[726] *Ibid.*, 794, 797 *et seq.*
[727] *Ibid.*, 795–6.

beyond the horizon of the occupation.[728] Justice Barak observed that the same legislative measures which may be unacceptable in a short-lived occupation may become palatable in a prolonged occupation.[729] He pointed out that the Occupying Power cannot ignore the fact that the life of the civilian population is in a constant flux: steps have to be taken to guarantee growth, including the development of industry, commerce, agriculture, education, health, etc.[730] This includes an investment in infrastructure that will only bear fruit in the long term, and the Occupying Power is entitled to make such an investment when it is deemed reasonably necessary for the prosperity of the civilian population.[731]

362. Justice Barak was not unaware of the problem intrinsic in a factual constellation in which the military government – albeit temporary by nature – undertakes long-range capital expenditures that bring about change-overs likely to endure beyond the end of the occupation.[732] He quoted an earlier decision delivered in the first *Jerusalem District Electricity Co.* case (per Justice Landau):

> Supplying the electricity required for the needs of the local population is, undoubtedly, one of the tasks imposed on the military rule, so as to ensure the orderly life of the population. We have seen that the present supply of electricity to the city of Hebron stands on a weak foundation requiring early improvements, and nobody disputes the fact that such improvement can come only by connecting the city to one of the grids out of the region. This need exists at the present time and has to be fulfilled. Mr. Shimron argues that the construction of the high voltage line required for that purpose determines facts for a long period, whereas a military government is not allowed to take measures beyond what is required for its own duration. But there is no reasonable way to provide for the existing needs today without infrastructure investments, including the construction of the high voltage line. Anyhow, nobody knows today how long the existing situation in this region will last and what final status arrangements will come into effect when the military rule is over. If necessary, these arrangements may include agreed terms adjusting the facts created now to the situation that will prevail at the end, either by acquisition in return for compensation or in some other way. The action of the military government regarding the subject of this petition is not, therefore, in breach of Hague Regulation 43. On the contrary, this action fulfils the obligation of the government to look after the economic welfare of the area's population.[733]

[728] *Ibid.*, 799–800.
[729] *Ibid.*, 800–1.
[730] *Ibid.*, 804–6.
[731] *Ibid.*, 805.
[732] *Ibid.*
[733] HCJ 256/72, *Jerusalem District Electricity Co. Ltd. v. Minister of Defence* et al., 27(1) *PD* 124, 138. (The Judgment is excerpted in English in 5 *IYHR* 381 (1975)).

363. Having quoted with approval this extract from the Judgment in the first *Jerusalem District Electricity Co.* case,[734] Justice Barak proceeded to quote from a later Judgment rendered by the Court (per Justice I. Kahan) in the second *Jerusalem District Electricity Co.* case.[735] Here, basing himself on Hague Regulation 43, Justice Kahan reasoned:

> From the nature of a military government in an occupied area ... it is clear that basically such a government is temporary, and its principal task – taking into account the needs of war and security – is to act, as far as possible, to maintain public order and security. It is true that the 'temporariness' of the possession of the area is relative, and the example of Judea and Samaria will prove that, since so far the possession of the area as a region subject to the rule of a military commander continues for almost 14 years. From the provision about respect for the existing law one can learn that, absent special considerations, the region's commander must not – as a rule – initiate such changes in the region that, even if they do not alter the existing law, they will still have far-reaching and long-term influence on the situation in the region, transcending the period in which its possession as a military region will end one way or another, unless these are acts for the benefit of the inhabitants of the region.[736]

364. Not surprisingly, perhaps, D. Kretzmer is of the opinion that the Judgments in the two *Jerusalem District Electricity Co.* cases represent completely disparate models of judicial thinking.[737] In the *Jamait Askan* case, Justice Barak was mindful of the dissonance between the two quoted passages; but, as he saw it, there is a minimal standard and a maximal standard of ensuring the public order and life of the local population under Regulation 43.[738] The Occupying Power cannot go below the minimal standard or above the maximal standard, yet – as long as it is acting within this margin of appreciation – it has freedom of choice.[739]

365. Not everybody will agree with the *Jamait Askan* Judgment on the specific merits of the case. However, in more universal terms, it must be perceived that pressures for departures from the legal *status quo* in occupied territories proliferate over time and there comes a moment when they cannot be put off. The present writer takes it as almost axiomatic that, to avoid inertia that is liable to cause grievous social woes, the military government must be given more leeway in the application of its law-making power if the occupation

734 HCJ 393/82, *supra* note 158, at 805.
735 *Ibid.*, 805–6.
736 HCJ 351/80 etc., *Jerusalem District Electricity Co. Ltd. v. Minister of Energy and Infrastructure* et al., 35(2) *PD* 673, 690. (The Judgment is excerpted in English in 11 *IYHR* 354 (1981)).
737 Kretzmer, *supra* note 167, at 66–8.
738 HCJ 393/82, *supra* note 158, at 806–7.
739 *Ibid.*

endures for many years. While drawing attention to the risk of 'according too much leeway to the Occupying Power', V. Koutroulis points out that:

> The main danger in such [prolonged] occupations is that IHL rules applicable to occupations may be applied in an overly rigid manner, resulting in the 'freezing' of the life of the occupied population and impeding evolution.[740]

In circumstances of a really drawn-out occupation, most commentators admit that legal stasis is not a viable option.[741] A. Roberts even comes up with the notion that prolonged occupation should be regarded as a distinct and special category within the law of belligerent occupation.[742]

VI. The Litmus Test

366. When the Occupying Power shows solicitude for the welfare of the population in the occupied territory, this posture is not above suspicion. A professed humanitarian concern may camouflage a hidden political agenda, and it may be prudent to guard the inhabitants from the bear's hug of the Occupying Power. For that reason, the question of whether or not there is a genuine necessity for each new piece of legislation by an Occupying Power deserves to be fully fathomed.

367. The dilemma can best be appreciated against the silhouette of a Judgment delivered by the Israel Supreme Court in the 1972 *Christian Association* case.[743] The case related to a labour dispute between the Christian Association for the Holy Places, running several charitable institutions in the city of Bethlehem, and hospital workers employed by it who went on strike. The Officer in Charge of Labour Affairs in the Israeli military government of the area initiated proceedings for settling the dispute, in accordance with a local Jordanian Labour Law predating the occupation. This statute decreed that at a certain stage of a labour dispute – after other means for its settlement have foundered – a procedure of compulsory arbitration could be set in motion. The trouble was that some of the arbitrators were supposed to have represented employers' and employees' associations, whereas such associations did not in fact exist in Jordan. To overcome the difficulty, the military government issued an Order amending the Jordanian statute, making it possible for the arbitrators

[740] V. Koutroulis, 'The Application of International Humanitarian Law and International Human Rights Law in Situation of Prolonged Occupation: Only a Matter of Time', 885 *IRRC* 165, 205 (2012).

[741] For instance, see A. Cassese, 'Powers and Duties of an Occupant in Relation to Land and Natural Resources', *International Law and the Administration of Occupied Territories*, *supra* note 582, at 420, 426–7.

[742] See Roberts, *supra* note 319, at 47, 51–3.

[743] HCJ 337/71, *supra* note 180, at 577–9.

to be appointed either by the employers and employees parties to the concrete dispute or by the Officer in Charge of Labour Affairs. The core of the controversy before the Supreme Court was whether the amending Order was in conformity with Hague Regulation 43. The majority opinion (per President J. Sussman) confirmed the validity of the Order, holding that the Occupying Power was obligated to look after the welfare of the civilian population, and – when the occupation lasts for a long time – the military government is entitled to revise the local law in a manner consistent with the changing social needs.[744]

368. Was the majority of the Court on the right track? The present writer believes (and has so stated at the time in a law review article[745]) that a litmus test for distinguishing between genuine and contrived concern for the welfare of the civilian population – under Regulation 43 – lies in the Occupying Power's show of similar concern for the welfare of its own population. In other words, if the Occupying Power enacts a law – say, introducing an obligation to install safety belts in motor vehicles in an occupied territory (see *supra* 354) – the decisive factor should be the existence of a parallel statute back home. In the absence of parallel legislation, the ostensible concern for the interests of the civilian population in the occupied territory loses credibility. Parallel does not mean identical. Variations in the details of the legislative measures adopted are not of major import. What counts is the legal nucleus of the legislation.

369. This is sometimes called a 'sincerity test'.[746] Of course, as a yardstick for assessing the motives of the Occupying Power, it cannot provide a fail-safe read-out in every instance.[747] The principal reason, in Meron's words, is that the test can be conclusive 'only in the negative sense', i.e. when the required corresponding legislation does not exist: it is then clear that the measures enacted by the Occupying Power are invalid.[748] If the correspondence in legislation does exist, all that can be said is that *prima facie* the Occupying Power ought to enjoy the benefit of doubt. Other considerations may militate in the opposite direction. Thus, if the disparities in the socio-economic conditions between the Occupying Power's own State and the occupied territory are so radical that 'what may amount to sensible economic management in one may be ruinously detrimental to the other',[749] there is no justification for the Occupying Power to emulate in the occupied territory a legal architecture that is alien to

744 *Ibid.*, 581–2.

745 See Y. Dinstein, 'The Legislative Power in the Administered Territories', 2 *TAULR* 505, 511–12 (1972).

746 R. Buchan, 'International Community and the Occupation of Iraq', 12 *JCSL* 37, 55 (2007).

747 See Benvenisti, *supra* note 50, at 92–3.

748 T. Meron, 'Applicability of Multilateral Conventions to Occupied Territories', 72 *AJIL* 542, 549–50 (1978).

749 C. McCarthy, 'The Paradox of the International Law of Military Occupation: Sovereignty and the Reformation of Iraq', 10 *JCSL* 43, 63 (2005).

the social landscape. As we are also reminded in this context by A. Pellet, the Occupying Power is not the sovereign and it cannot legislate for the population within the occupied territory in exactly the same fashion that it does within its own boundaries.[750] Still, barring extreme circumstances revealing clearly that a similar legislation in both jurisdictions would be inappropriate – or even insinuating ulterior motives on the part of the Occupying Power – the present writer is confident that the litmus test ought to prove quite efficacious.

370. Had the litmus test been resorted to in the resolution of the dispute in the *Christian Association* case, the Court should have ruled against the Occupying Power. The point is that compulsory arbitration in labour disputes has not yet been introduced in Israel itself, and the Jordanian Labour Law – although not perfected – is still more advanced than the Israeli legislation in the same sphere.[751] Occupied territories are not a laboratory for experiments in law reform, and an Occupying Power must realize that any legislative step taken by it is beheld with suspicion by the population in the occupied territory and perhaps also by outsiders.

371. In the special circumstances of the *Christian Association* case, the Occupying Power might have acted completely within the purview of its authority, had it issued an Order prohibiting strikes and lock-outs in hospitals in the West Bank. Such a hypothetical Order would have made the grade, in light of the duty devolving on the Occupying Power to ensure and maintain hospital services in the occupied territory (see *infra* 567). But in hoisting the banner of improving the legal mechanism for coping with labour disputes, and in attempting to provide the inhabitants of Bethlehem with a remedy unavailable in Tel Aviv, the actual Order exceeded the bounds of necessity.

VII. Institutional Changes

372. When (under the *cachet* of necessity) the Occupying Power is authorized to modify or suspend existing legislation in the occupied territory (for the duration of the occupation), it may act in disregard even of provisions entrenched in the local constitution or basic laws (for an example relating to the modus of appointment of local judges, see *infra* 410). But how far can the Occupying Power go tampering, in the name of necessity, with the governmental institutions of the occupied territory?

373. Assuredly, should institutional changes be introduced by the Occupying Power, they must not deprive the civilian population in the occupied territory

[750] A. Pellet, 'The Destruction of Troy Will Not Take Place', *International Law and the Administration of Occupied Territories, supra* note 582, at 169, 201.

[751] See the Dissenting Opinion of Justice Cohn, HCJ 337/71, *supra* note 180, at 588.

of any benefits bestowed on them by the law of belligerent occupation. Article 47 of Geneva Convention (IV) states:

Protected persons who are in occupied territory shall not be deprived, in any case or in any manner whatsoever, of the benefits of the present Convention by any change introduced, as the result of the occupation of a territory, into the institutions or government of the said territory, nor by any agreement concluded between the authorities of the occupied territories and the Occupying Power, nor by any annexation by the latter of the whole or part of the occupied territory.[752]

The tenor of this clause is that the Occupying Power may not circumvent its obligations towards protected persons through cosmetic surgery that appears to reconstruct the outer face of the occupied territory. This includes the creation of a puppet (Quisling-like) Government, which is at the beck and call of the Occupying Power, albeit endowed with the trappings of office.[753] As the European Court of Human Rights put it, in the *Loizidou* case, the obligation to secure human rights in an area under effective control outside the national territory – taken by military action – 'derives from the fact of such control whether it be exercised directly, through its armed forces, or through a subordinate local administration'.[754]

374. A caveat must be added. Article 47 does not preclude agreements freely arrived at, epitomized by the 'Oslo Accords' between Israel and the Palestinians (see *supra* 54). The 'Oslo Accords' did create Palestinian institutions not previously existing in the occupied territories, introducing new measures of (autonomous) governance. However, despite some doctrinal reservations,[755] it would be incongruous to find fault with a peace process by invoking Article 47 to undermine it.[756] What Article 47 bans is an agreement reducing protection of the inhabitants of occupied territories and evading the responsibilities of the Occupying Power under the Geneva Convention. Nothing of the kind has happened as a result of the inauguration of qualified Palestinian self-government in the 'Oslo Accords'.

375. Agreements aside, can the Occupying Power radically transform the political institutions of government in an occupied territory when such action does not detrimentally affect the benefits granted to the civilian population by the Convention? The problem is that, as the ICRC Commentary concedes, the

[752] Geneva Convention (IV), *supra* note 29, at 594.

[753] See R.T. Yingling and R.W. Ginnane, 'The Geneva Conventions of 1949', 46 *AJIL* 393, 418 (1952).

[754] *Loizidou v. Turkey* (Merits), *supra* note 66, at 453.

[755] See R. Kolb, 'Etude sur l'Occupation et sur l'Article 47 de la IVème Convention de Genève du 12 Août 1949 Relative à la Protection des Personnes Civiles en Temps de Guerre: Le Degré d'Intangibilité des Droits en Territoire Occupé', 10 *AYIL* 267, 305–21 (2002).

[756] See P. Malanczuk, 'Some Basic Aspects of the Agreements between Israel and the PLO from the Perspective of International Law', 7 *EJIL* 485, 498 (1996).

only object of Article 47 is 'to safeguard human beings and not to protect the political institutions and government machinery of the State as such'.[757]

376. On the other hand, as long as there is no head-on collision between the exigencies of the occupation and the political institutions existing in the occupied territory, there is no genuine necessity for the Occupying Power to tinker with the latter. The Occupying Power is not allowed to shake the pillars of government in the occupied territory.[758] Thus, it cannot validly transform a unitary system in the occupied territory into a federal one (or vice versa), even if the metamorphosis would allegedly be in force only during the period of occupation.[759] Changing the configuration of political institutions is an activity that exceeds the powers of the military government. This is due to the disquieting possibility that profound structural innovations – once the population gets used to them (especially in the course of a prolonged occupation) – may prove hard to eradicate when the occupation is terminated.

377. Unfortunately, a translation of this undisputed general principle into the specifics of a concrete occupation is a rather murky undertaking. When the Germans divided occupied Belgium during WWI into two separate administrative districts (one Flemish and one Walloon), the move was met with a blizzard of protest as a breach of Hague Regulation 43; yet, when the British divided occupied Libya during WWII into two separate administrative districts (Cyrenaica in the east and Tripolitania in the west), the measure was accepted without demur.[760] State practice does not draw any clear line in the sand that must not be crossed by the Occupying Power in this respect.

VIII. Taxation

378. Taxation in occupied territories is the subject of Hague Regulations 48 and 49:

> 48. If, in the territory occupied, the occupant collects the taxes, dues, and tolls imposed for the benefit of the State, he shall do it, as far as possible, in accordance with the rules in existence and the assessment in force, and will in consequence be bound to defray the expenses of the administration of the occupied territory on the same scale as that to which the legitimate Government was bound.
>
> 49. If, besides the taxes referred to in the preceding Article, the occupant levies other money contributions in the occupied territory, this can only be for military necessities or the administration of such territory.[761]

[757] *Commentary, IV Geneva Convention*, *supra* note 31, at 274.
[758] See McDougal and Feliciano, *supra* note 238, at 767–8.
[759] See *ibid.*
[760] See Watts, *supra* note 53, at 72–3.
[761] Hague Regulations, *supra* note 22, at 246–7.

379. The term 'taxes', as employed in Regulation 48, appears to cover all direct and indirect compulsory payments, including customs duties, excises and tolls of whatever kind. Still, the provision is confined to governmental taxes owed to the treasury of the State. As for taxes owed to local authorities (such as municipalities), the Occupying Power is not entitled to levy them for itself, although it may assist in – or supervise – their collection.[762] Money contributions, under Regulation 49, are additional to taxes dealt with in Regulation 48.

380. When Hague Regulations 48 and 49 are perused jointly, they appear to create a neat distinction between existing and new taxes. Regulation 48 is restricted to the collection of existing taxes. The contraction of its scope to such taxes can be deduced in particular from the allusion in the text to rates of assessment already in force, which the Occupying Power is bound to observe as far as possible. New taxes then fall within the range of Regulation 49, dealing with contributions. The two Hague Regulations thus present the Occupying Power with a stark choice. If it desires to collect existing taxes – on the basis of legislation enacted by the displaced sovereign prior to the occupation – this has to be done in line with Regulation 48. Should new taxes be required, the Occupying Power must resort to levying money contributions in compliance with Regulation 49.

381. When necessary, the Occupying Power is authorized to increase the rates of assessment of existing taxes. Especially in a prolonged occupation, with the passage of time, there are likely to be perfect reasons for the Occupying Power to raise the rates.[763] But there may be valid reasons to ratchet up the rates even after a relatively short period of occupation. After all, Regulation 48 obligates the Occupying Power to cover the expenses of the administration of the occupied territory to the same extent as was originally done by the displaced sovereign. If – owing, e.g., to inflation – the costs of the administration have upsurged, the Occupying Power may have no alternative but to offset them by revising existing rates of taxation.

382. Money contributions, in tandem with Regulation 49, may be exacted in order either to cover the needs of the army of occupation or to defray the costs of the administration of the occupied territory. A good illustration for the latter alternative can be found in the case of Iraq, when the Coalition Provisional Authority imposed a 'Reconstruction Levy' for the purpose of funding improvements in infrastructure and capital public investments.[764]

[762] See von Glahn, *supra* note 339, at 152.
[763] See Feilchenfeld, *supra* note 679, at 49.
[764] Coalition Provisional Authority Order Number 38, II *The Occupation of Iraq: The Official Documents*, *supra* note 78, at 197, 198.

383. Money contributions cannot be demanded for purposes extraneous to the needs of the army of occupation and the administration of the occupied territory. It is illegal to use this mode of revenue-raising in order to enrich the Occupying Power, alleviate the costs of the general war effort (outside the occupied territory) or impose fines on the civilian population under the guise of contributions.[765]

384. Hague Regulation 51 proclaims:

> No contribution shall be collected except under a written order and on the responsibility of a Commander-in-chief.
>
> The levy shall only take place, as far as possible, in accordance with the rules in existence and the assessment in force for taxes.
>
> For every contribution a receipt shall be given to the payer.[766]

The first two paragraphs speak for themselves. As for the third, money contributions – mentioned here – must not be confounded with contributions (or requisitions) in kind referred to in Regulation 52 (quoted *infra* 699). In both instances the term 'contributions' is a euphemism (considering the involuntary nature of the exaction), but there is a big difference between the two. Contributions in kind, which can only be insisted upon for the needs of the army of occupation, have to be paid for in cash. If no payment is made on the spot, a receipt must be given. Such a receipt is redeemable in cash at a later date. By contrast, a receipt for money contribution under Regulation 51 is only intended as evidence of payment, and the Occupying Power does not have to redeem it in cash.[767] The reason is that a money contribution is tantamount to an extraordinary tax rather than a compulsory loan.

385. Money contributions usually constitute a surtax (namely, an additional levy), but they can also replace all existing taxes in the occupied territory. The Occupying Power is entitled to impose a money contribution in order to finance requisitions in kind.[768] It follows that a property requisitioned in kind from an individual owner can be paid for in full by the Occupying Power out of funds drawn from the entire civilian population through the introduction of money contributions. The reasoning underlying this circular manoeuvre is that it allows for the economic burden to be distributed more equitably among all the inhabitants of the occupied territory (in lieu of falling in its plenitude on the shoulders of the individual owner of the requisitioned property).[769]

[765] See J.W. Garner, 'Contributions, Requisitions, and Compulsory Service in Occupied Territory', 11 *AJIL* 74, 80 (1917).

[766] Hague Regulations, *supra* note 22, at 248–9.

[767] See T.E. Holland, *The Laws of War on Land (Written and Unwritten)* 55 (1908).

[768] See Oppenheim, *supra* note 201, at 410, 412.

[769] See Holland, *supra* note 767, at 55.

386. An Occupying Power is not precluded from remitting or reducing existing taxes that it considers ill-conceived or unfair.[770] Nor is it obligated to levy money contributions. In fact, '[t]he practice of recent occupations indicates that occupants make little use of the right to levy contributions and tend to fill deficits in the military's budget for administering the occupied territory with payments from their own treasury'.[771] This has certainly been the policy of Israel, which (over a period of more than half a century) has avoided altogether the mechanism of money contributions. Shortfalls in the budget of the military government have been habitually covered by financial subsidies from the Occupying Power's treasury.[772]

387. In 1976, Orders were enacted by the military government in the Israeli occupied territories, instituting a new excise on products and services patterned after legislation introducing (in 1975) a value added tax (VAT) within the boundaries of Israel. The purpose of the VAT in the occupied territories was to serve as an equalizing device, so as to augment the free flow of goods and services between them and Israel. The legality of the measure – which was a new tax but not a money contribution (inasmuch as it was not levied for the needs of the army of occupation or the administration of the occupied territories) – was challenged before the Supreme Court, in the *VAT* case, on the ground of incompatibility with Hague Regulations 48 and 49.[773]

388. The Court (per Deputy President Shamgar) dismissed the petitions, sidestepping the constraints imposed by Regulations 48 and 49, pronouncing that tax legislation is no different from any other legislation: the Occupying Power could impose VAT as a new tax on the ground of necessity (in accordance with Regulation 43).[774] The way the Court saw it – relying on State practice and scholarly doctrine that it dissected[775] – the saving clause in Regulation 43 could be grafted onto the texts of Regulations 48 and 49, thus subordinating the prohibition of new taxes (not constituting money contributions) to the necessity exception. This proposition – which, in truth, has little or no direct backing either in State practice or in the legal literature[776] – is certainly innovative. Yet, notwithstanding some doctrinal criticism,[777] it is by no means incongruous.[778]

[770] See Greenspan, *supra* note 383, at 229.

[771] See I. Venzke, 'Contributions', II *MPEPIL* 766, 767.

[772] See D. Shefi, 'Taxation in the Administered Territories', 1 *IYHR* 290, 294 (1971).

[773] HCJ 69/81 etc, *supra* note 175, at 209.

[774] *Ibid.*, 273–4.

[775] *Ibid.*, 274 *et seq.*

[776] But cf. US, Department of the Army, *Field Manual: The Law of Land Warfare*, *supra* note 233, at 157; US Department of Defense, *Law of War Manual*, *supra* note 1, at 826.

[777] See Venzke, *supra* note 771, at 768.

[778] See Y. Dinstein, 'Taxation under Belligerent Occupation', *Des Menschen Recht zwischen Freiheit und Verantwortung* 115, 122–3 (*Festschrift für J. Partsch*, 1989).

IX. Limitations of the Legislative Power

389. When the Occupying Power introduces new laws in harmony with Hague Regulation 43 and Article 64 of Geneva Convention (IV), the new legislation must interface with all the injunctions appearing in the Regulations and the Convention. To single out the most rudimentary application of this requirement, one may cite the prohibition to compel the inhabitants of the occupied territory to swear allegiance to the Occupying Power. Manifestly, the Occupying Power cannot release itself from this interdiction (laid down in Hague Regulation 45 quoted *supra* 176) by enacting inconsistent legislation in the name of necessity (ostensibly in line with Hague Regulation 43).

390. Apart from this substantive limitation on the legislative capacity of the Occupying Power, there are also procedural conditions set out by Article 65 of the Geneva Convention:

> The penal provisions enacted by the Occupying Power shall not come into force before they have been published and brought to the knowledge of the inhabitants in their own language. The effect of these penal provisions shall not be retroactive.[779]

391. Two restraints emerge for the Occupying Power. First of all, the legislation passed must be published. It does not enter into force until the text is printed in full, and circulated, in the local language of the population of the occupied territory. Mere broadcasting or posting of a condensed version of the legislation on bulletin boards will not be enough.[780]

392. More significantly, perhaps, penal legislation must not have a retroactive effect. This terse provision is complemented by Article 67 (first sentence) of the Convention, pertaining to military courts established by the Occupying Power (see *infra* 419):

> The courts shall apply only those provisions of law which were applicable prior to the offence, and which are in accordance with general principles of law, in particular the principle that the penalty shall be proportionate to the offence.[781]

Of the general principles of law adumbrated generically in Article 67 (first sentence) – apart from the *nullum crimen sine lege* postulate and the injunction that the penalty must be proportionate to the offence – the ICRC Commentary adduces in particular the rule that 'nobody may be punished for an offence committed by someone else'[782] (in tune with the first paragraph of Article 33 of the Convention quoted *infra* 470).

[779] Geneva Convention (IV), *supra* note 29, at 599.
[780] See *Commentary, IV Geneva Convention*, *supra* note 31, at 338.
[781] Geneva Convention (IV), *supra* note 29, at 599.
[782] *Commentary, IV Geneva Convention*, *supra* note 31, at 342.

X. Settlers

393. We shall address in some detail (*infra* 734 *et seq.*) the issue of the legality of settlements in occupied territories. The geographic proximity of Israeli settlers and local inhabitants in the West Bank has led to friction between them, triggering countless problems for the military government in terms of the maintenance of law and order.[783] But it is important to recall that (unlike the local inhabitants) Israeli nationals, including settlers, do not benefit from the status of protected persons under Geneva Convention (IV) (see *supra* 197). This fundamental truth – with all its attendant consequences – had to be faced head-on by Israeli settlers when, by Knesset legislation, they were evacuated against their will from the Gaza Strip (as part of the unilateral withdrawal of September 2005; see *supra* 49). When their petition to the Supreme Court was dismissed, in the *Gaza Coast Local Council* case, a special panel of eleven Justices (*per curiam*) expressly underscored the absence of protection pursuant to the Convention.[784]

394. While settlers are therefore not to be treated on a basis of equivalence with the local inhabitants, it is impossible to ignore their presence in the occupied territory. The Supreme Court felt that the needs of settlers have to be taken into account by the military government in diverse ways. For example, in the first *Jerusalem District Electricity Co.* case, the Court (per Justice Landau) said that – when drawing the contours of the obligation of the military government to look after the welfare of the civilian population – the settlers of Kiryat Arba must be deemed part of the population, and they too are entitled to get a regular supply of electric power.[785]

395. Settlers, like other nationals of the Occupying Power present in an occupied territory, benefit from the premise that – when there is a gap in protection afforded by the law of belligerent occupation – irreducible human rights law may step in (see *supra* 259). These rights are vested in them – as in other human beings – irrespective of their status as settlers. As noted (*supra* 248), the Court decided in the *Rachel's Tomb* case that freedom of religion must be respected not only where protected persons are concerned but also with respect to nationals of the Occupying Power (whether or not settlers). Above all, settlers are entitled to security of their lives (to be ensured by the military government). This approach was affirmed by the Supreme Court in

[783] Indeed, at the point of maximum friction – in the urban area of Hebron – a multinational observer unit (the TIPH) was created by agreement for monitoring purposes. See *supra* note 317.

[784] HCJ 1661/05 etc., *supra* note 159, at 517. The single Justice who dissented from the decision did not address this point.

[785] HCJ 256/72, *supra* note 733, at 138.

multiple cases, particularly *Tzalum* of 1987 (per Justice Barak),[786] *Kawasmi* of 2005 (per Justice Beinisch),[787] and *Beit Sira* of 2009 (see *infra* 397). The application of human rights law naturally works to 'equalize the playing field' between protected and non-protected persons under the Geneva Convention.[788] Not a few commentators frown upon this outcome,[789] advancing the argument that the human rights factor of the security of settlers (and other nationals of the Occupying Power) may be corrosive of the *jus in bello* rights of protected persons in the occupied territory.[790] But the two sets of rights can actually be harmonized in sundry sets of circumstances. As we shall see (*infra ibid.*), while upholding the security concerns of settlers and commuters, the Supreme Court invalidated an order of the military commander that unduly restricted the freedom of movement of protected persons.

396. Undeniably, the presence of settlers in an occupied territory must not unduly override the rights of protected persons. In the *Yanun* case of 2006, the Court (per Justice Beinisch) disallowed denial of access by Palestinian farmers to their agricultural lands (through declarations of 'closed areas' by the military government) – thus infringing on their freedom of movement and right to property – on the pretext that the measures were designed to protect them from harassment by settlers.[791] The Judgment elucidated that the declaration of a 'closed area' may be admissible if required in order to safeguard the lives of settlers (although they do not come within the category of protected persons) against terrorist attacks.[792] But when the tables are turned and what is anticipated is harassment of protected persons by the settlers, the duty of the military government is to direct its powers against the prospective troublemakers and not against the prospective victims.[793]

397. A balancing act, between settlers (as well as other nationals of the Occupying Power) and protected persons, was also the subject of the *Beit Sira* case (see *supra* 251, 395). Here the Court encountered discrimination in favour

[786] HCJ 72/86 etc., *Tzalum* et al. *v. Military Commander of Judea and Samaria* et al., 41(1) *PD* 528, 532. (The Judgment is excerpted in English in 19 *IYHR* 371 (1989)).

[787] HCJ 7007/03, *Kawasmi v. Military Commander of Judea and Samaria* et al., para. 5. (The Judgment is excerpted in English in 37 *IYHR* 327 (2007)).

[788] D. Mennie, 'The Role of the International Covenant on Civil and Political Rights in the Israeli-Palestinian Conflict: Should Israel's Obligations under the Covenant Extend to Gaza and the Other Occupied Palestinian Territories?', 21 *TLCP* 511, 543–4 (2012–13).

[789] See *ibid.*; A.M. Gross, 'Human Proportions: Are Human Rights the Emperor's New Clothes of the International Law of Occupation?', 18 *EJIL* 1, 7–9 (2007).

[790] See G. Harpaz and Y. Shany, 'The Israeli Supreme Court and the Incremental Expansion of the Scope of Discretion under Belligerent Occupation Law', 43 *Is.LR* 514, 528–50 (2010).

[791] HCJ 9593/04, *Yanun* et al. *v. IDF Commander of Judea and Samaria* et al., 61(1) *PD* 844, 869–71. (The Judgment is excerpted in English in 39 *IYHR* 387 (2009)).

[792] *Ibid.*, 866–7.

[793] *Ibid.*, 871.

of the settlers and other Israelis travelling through the West Bank, at the expense of protected persons. The case related to a decision by the military government, after the second *intifada*, to exclude Palestinian vehicles from a major artery of communication (open to Israelis), which was the site of numerous acts of violence.[794] The highway was originally constructed by the Occupying Power for the benefit of the local population and in part this was even done on land seized from private owners.[795] The Court (per Justice U. Vogelman) stressed the need to ensure the safety of the settlers and even of ordinary Israeli commuters using the thoroughfare, suggesting that rigorous security screenings of local vehicles joining it would be proper.[796] Yet, the Judgment held that an absolute ban of local traffic on a main road is disproportionate, and the military government must take other measures to cope with the problem of security.[797]

398. Israeli settlers have been subjected to a whole spectrum of extra-territorial legislation, passed by the Knesset, with 'personal' – rather than territorial – application.[798] However, as residents of the occupied territory, the settlers have not been exempted from the jurisdictional powers of the military government. In the *Shaer* case, the Supreme Court (per Justice Matza) concluded that settlers may be interned by the military government, just like other inhabitants of the occupied territories (see *infra* 519).[799] In some respects, the military government was even allowed to discriminate against the settlers: thus, supplementary land taxes – not levied from the Palestinians – were imposed on them.[800] The Court also endorsed a decision by the military government to demolish a monument to a fanatic who had died killing Arabs in the contested holy site of the Machpela Cave;[801] it permitted the military government to remove squatters who had settled down in the West Bank in defiance of Government policy;[802] and it gave a green light to the closure by the military government of an abandoned hotel used by settlers protesting their forced evacuation from the Gaza Strip.[803]

[794] HCJ 2150/07, *supra* note 517, at 340–3.
[795] *Ibid.*, 363.
[796] *Ibid.*, 364–7, 378
[797] *Ibid.*, 381.
[798] See, especially, HCJ 5808/93, *Economic Corporation for Jerusalem Ltd. v. IDF Commander of Judea and Samaria* et al., 49(1) *PD* 89, 97 (per Justice Goldberg). (The Judgment is excerpted in English in 30 *IYHR* 322 (2000)).
[799] HCJ 2612/94, *Shaer v. IDF Commander of Judea and Samaria* et al., 48(3) *PD* 675, 679–82. (The Judgment is excerpted in English in 30 *IYHR* 314 (2000)).
[800] See *ibid.*, 97–8.
[801] HCJ 6195/98, *Goldstein* et al. *v. Commander of the Central Region* et al., 53(5) *PD* 317, 334–5 (per Justice Cheshin).
[802] HCJ 548/04 etc., *Amana – Settlement Movement of Gush Emunim* et al. *v. IDF Commander in Judea and Samaria* et al., 58(3) *PD* 373, 379 (per Justice Dorner).
[803] HCJ 6339/05, *Matar* et al. *v. IDF Commander of the Gaza Strip*, 59(2) *PD* 846, 852 (per President Barak).

399. Some courts for local affairs were established, in two of the larger Israeli settlements, by order of the military government.[804] In the past, the Supreme Court has recognized the authority of the military courts in the occupied territories to exercise their criminal jurisdiction over settlers.[805] But more recent practice has been to subject settlers to the jurisdiction of Israeli civil courts.[806]

[804] On the powers of these courts, see HCJ 336/99, *Delta v. Court for Local Affairs in Ariel* et al., 55(3) *PD* 246, 250–1 (per Justice Zamir).

[805] See, especially, HCJ 61/80, *Haetzni v. Minister of Defence* et al., 34(3) *PD* 595, 596–7 (per President Landau). (The Judgment is excerpted in English in 11 *IYHR* 358 (1981)).

[806] See Y. Ronen, 'Blind in Their Own Cause: The Military Courts in the West Bank', 2 *CJICL* 738, 744 (2013).

6 The Judicial System in Occupied Territories

I. The Double-Tiered System of Courts

400. The civilian population of an occupied territory is subject to a judicial system comprising two different layers: local courts (existing on the brink of the occupation) and military courts (established by the Occupying Power).

A. *Local Courts*

401. Local courts in an occupied territory – predating the occupation – continue to have jurisdiction over civil and criminal cases emanating from the domestic laws. An express reference to the 'tribunals of the occupied territory', carrying on with their functions in penal matters, appears in Article 64 (first paragraph) of Geneva Convention (IV) (quoted *supra* 336). Evidently, an uninterrupted judicial functioning is also to be expected in civil affairs. The operation of local courts raises a lot of issues in practice.

(a) Judicial Review of New Legislation by the Occupying Power

402. When the existing (penal or civil) laws are amended by the Occupying Power – in accordance with Article 64 and Hague Regulation 43 (quoted *supra* 269) – the local courts hardly have any choice but to apply the modified version. Experience demonstrates that local courts under occupation 'have been reluctant to inquire whether legislative measures which prima facie could be intended to safeguard public order, and thus to satisfy the requirements of Article 43 of the Hague Regulations, were in fact necessary'.[807] Even if a local court under occupation might theoretically be inclined to invalidate legislative acts enacted by the Occupying Power, it would usually recoil from exercising such proactive judicial review in practice.[808] After all, the Occupying Power can always remove local judges from their posts (see *infra* 409); and dismissal

[807] F. Morgenstern, 'Validity of the Acts of the Belligerent Occupant', 28 *BYBIL* 291, 306 (1951).
[808] See Arai-Takahashi, *supra* note 149, at 157 n. 89.

may well be anticipated once local judges exercise their judicial authority in a manner deemed obstructive to the Occupying Power.[809]

403. Interestingly, the Ramallah Court of Appeal for the West Bank held – in the 1968 *Al-Ja'bari* case – that (i) generally speaking, the local courts in an occupied territory 'are not competent to consider whether or not an imperative need exists that requires additional or amending legislation' by the Occupying Power as per Hague Regulation 43; but (ii) in the specific instance of a concerted decision by advocates in the West Bank to deny their professional services to local inhabitants (see *infra* 412), the Occupying Power was certainly right to issue an Order (a legislative enactment) granting Israeli advocates the right to appear before the local courts.[810]

(b) New Local Courts

404. The general presupposition is that the local courts were in existence prior to the occupation. However, there are extraordinary situations in which – due to the fact that the local population is sparse or nomadic – no courts were operating in the occupied territory when the displaced sovereign lost effective control.[811] In that case, the Occupying Power is not compelled to set them up.

405. Exceptionally, the Occupying Power may create new local courts tasked with hitherto unaddressed issues. Thus, in 2004, the Coalition Provisional Authority in Iraq established a new Central Criminal Court with discretionary jurisdiction over terrorism; organized crimes; governmental corruption; acts intended to destabilize democratic institutions or processes; violence based on race, nationality, ethnicity or religion; and instances in which a criminal defendant may not be able to obtain a fair trial in ordinary courts.[812]

406. In the West Bank, the military government empowered the construction of a new network of municipal courts – vested with limited penal jurisdiction over subject-matters arising from municipal by-laws (such as infringements of town planning ordinances) – on condition that each court is to function solely if requested to do so by the respective municipality, which remains in control of prosecutions.[813]

[809] See T. Ferraro, 'Enforcement of Occupation Law in Domestic Courts: Issues and Opportunities', 41 *Is.LR* 331, 350 (2008).

[810] *Al-Ja'bari v. Al-'Awiwi* (Ramallah Court of Appeal, 1968), 42 *ILR* 484, 486–7.

[811] Apparently, there were no local courts (as distinct from Egyptian military courts) in the Sinai Peninsula before the Israeli occupation. See Shamgar, *supra* note 141, at 269.

[812] Coalition Provisional Authority Order Number 13, II *The Occupation of Iraq: The Official Documents*, *supra* note 78, at 93, 97.

[813] See M. Drori, 'The Legal System in Judea and Samaria: A Review of the Previous Decade with a Glance at the Future', 8 *IYHR* 144, 152–3 (1978).

(c) Judges in the Local Courts

407. It goes without saying that if a new local court is set up by the Occupying Power, new judges have to be appointed to them. If (as is commonly the case) the local courts do exist, the expectation is that local judges will continue to serve in them. Yet, two complementary stipulations calibrate this norm.

408. On the one hand, Article 54 (first paragraph) of the Geneva Convention disallows the Occupying Power to take measures of coercion against any local judges who refuse to fulfil their functions under the occupation for reasons of conscience (see *supra* 192). Local judges are mentioned explicitly in the text, together with public officials.

409. On the other hand, Article 54 (second paragraph) recognizes the right of the Occupying Power to remove from their posts public officials (see *supra ibid.*), and the expression definitely covers judges in local courts.[814] In Iraq, the Coalition Provisional Authority established a Judicial Review Committee, which was empowered to 'investigate and gather information on the suitability of Judges and Prosecutors to hold office'.[815] The Israel Supreme Court (per Justice Barak) pronounced, in the *Hassan* case, that the Occupying Power – on the basis of its own legislation (and regardless of local laws) – can arrest a local judge, not only when he is accused of a breach of security but, e.g., for taking a bribe.[816]

410. Should local judges resign from service, leave the occupied territory or die, the Occupying Power has to replace them, in order to ensure the continuous functioning of the local courts. In a prolonged occupation, the Occupying Power faces the further need of appointing successors to judges who retire. Inescapably, the pre-existing process of appointment or election of new judges (which will normally require input by central organs of the displaced sovereign) will not correspond to the new realities of occupation, and the Occupying Power will have to amend the law in this respect.[817]

411. Where required – in the absence of competent persons available, willing and able to serve as local judges under conditions of occupation – the Occupying Power may have no option other than to bring from outside the occupied territory judges of its own choosing, to fill the slots vacated in the local courts.[818] If all the local judges are replaced, State practice suggests that the Occupying Power may even introduce changes in judicial procedures and structures, so

[814] *Commentary, IV Geneva Convention*, *supra* note 31, at 308.

[815] Coalition Provisional Authority Order Number 15, II *The Occupation of Iraq: The Official Documents*, *supra* note 78, at 100, 101 (Section 4).

[816] HCJ 174/85, *Hassan v. IDF Commander of Judea and Samaria* et al., 39(3) *PD* 245, 248–9.

[817] See *Israel, the 'Intifada' and the Rule of Law* 87 (D. Yahav *et al.* eds., 1993).

[818] See A.V. Freeman, 'War Crimes by Enemy Nationals Administering Justice in Occupied Territory', 41 *AJIL* 579, 589 (1947).

that they will be more familiar or user-friendly to the judges whom it imports.[819] However, even when (there being no other choice) officers of the Occupying Power serve as local judges – and even when the entire organizational chart of the judiciary is redrawn – the identity of the local courts (applying domestic law) must be maintained, and they are not to be commingled with the military courts, to be discussed *infra* 419 *et seq.*[820]

(d) Members of the Bar

412. The functioning of the local courts in the West Bank almost came to a standstill at the outset of the Israeli occupation, inasmuch as the vast majority of local advocates – having been warned off by the Jordanian Bar Council not to 'collaborate' with the Occupying Power – declined to engage in any professional activity, boycotting all courts.[821] In the almost total absence from the courts of legal counsel from the West Bank, the military government enacted an Order allowing Israeli advocates to appear in proceedings before the local courts on behalf of Palestinian inhabitants.[822] As mentioned (*supra* 403), the Ramallah Court of Appeal gave its seal of approval to that legislation.

413. Gradually, many of the Palestinian advocates resumed professional activities in the West Bank, but then their licences were revoked by the Jordanian Bar Council in Amman.[823] On the initiative of the disbarred advocates, as well as other inhabitants of the West Bank who in the meantime had become qualified to practice law, the military government established – by a legislative Order – a separate West Bank Bar Council, severing the new body from the Jordanian Bar Council.[824] A petition to the Israel Supreme Court was filed by some West Bank advocates who wanted the new Bar Council to enjoy more independence than was countenanced by the Order.[825] The Court (per Justice E. Goldberg) determined in the *Tamimi* case that – in view of what had transpired previously – the military government was plainly empowered under Regulation 43 to establish the West Bank Bar Council and to retain some control over it; although the Court instructed the military government to reexamine some aspects of the Order, with a view to affording the Council a greater degree of autonomy.[826]

[819] See Bentwich, *supra* note 52, at 141–3.

[820] See E. Wolff, 'Municipal Courts of Justice in Enemy Occupied Territory', 29 *TGS* 99, 113–14 (1943).

[821] See Y.Z. Blum, 'The Missing Reversioner: Reflections on the Status of Judea and Samaria', 3 *Is.LR* 279, 296 (1968).

[822] See T.S. Kuttner, 'Israel and the West Bank: Aspects of the Law of Belligerent Occupation', 7 *IYHR* 166, 190 (1977).

[823] HCJ 507/85, *Tamimi* et al. *v. Minister of Defence* et al., 41(4) *PD* 57, 60. (The Judgment is excerpted in English in 18 *IYHR* 248 (1988)).

[824] *Ibid.*

[825] *Ibid.*, 60–2.

[826] *Ibid.*, 62.

(e) Appeals

414. When an occupied territory consists of only a portion of the land of the displaced sovereign, it frequently happens that (under the existing legal system) an appeal from local courts – either in criminal or civil proceedings (or both) – has to be lodged with an appellate body whose seat is established in the non-occupied remnant of the country. In such circumstances, the Occupying Power need not preserve this umbilical cord to the displaced sovereign. The military government can suspend the nexus to the higher tribunal, transferring the authority to hear appeals from the local courts to a (new or extant) judicial instance operating within the occupied territory.[827]

415. In the West Bank, where (under Jordanian law) recourse from the local courts was possible to a Court of Cassation in Amman, the military government shifted all such applications to a local Court of Appeal sitting in Ramallah.[828] In the *Arjoub* case, the Israel Supreme Court (per President Shamgar) gave its approval to the new arrangement – which it regarded as entirely in compliance with Hague Regulation 43 – since an Occupying Power cannot tolerate appeals to a judicial instance located within an area controlled by the enemy.[829]

(f) Jurisdiction

416. It must be emphasized that '[m]ilitary and civilian personnel of the occupying forces and occupation administration and persons accompanying them are not subject to the local law or to the jurisdiction of the local civil or criminal courts of the occupied territory'.[830] Naturally, the Occupying Power is expected to ensure that other 'tribunals are in existence to deal with civil litigation to which they are parties and with offenses committed by them'.[831]

417. Apart from the local courts of general jurisdiction (in civil and criminal matters), special courts and tribunals may also function in an occupied territory pursuant to existing legislation. These may have limited jurisdiction over labour disputes, traffic violations and so on. In the West Bank (and the Gaza Strip), religious tribunals – of diverse religious communities – have been operating, with jurisdiction confined to personal status disputes.[832]

[827] See C. Fairman, 'Asserted Jurisdiction of the Italian Court of Cassation over the Court of Appeal of the Free Territory of Trieste', 45 *AJIL* 541, 548 (1951).

[828] See M. Drori, *supra* note 813, at 150.

[829] HCJ 87/85, *Arjoub* et al. *v. IDF Commander of Judea and Samaria* et al., 42(1) *PD* 353, 365. (The Judgment is excerpted in English in 18 *IYHR* 255 (1988)).

[830] US Department of Defense, *Law of War Manual*, *supra* note 1, at 780.

[831] *Ibid.*, 781.

[832] See Y. Meron, 'The Religious Courts in the Administered Territories', I *Military Government in the Territories Administered by Israel 1967–1980, supra* note 99, at 353–66.

(g) Rights of Action

418. As pointed out (*supra* 401), the local courts have jurisdiction – in conformity with the existing laws of the occupied territory (as amended) – in both criminal and civil affairs. Under the first paragraph of Hague Regulation 23(h), it is forbidden:

> To declare extinguished, suspended, or unenforceable in a court of law the rights and rights of action of the nationals of the adverse party.[833]

This is also a war crime under Article 8(2)(b)(xiv) of the Rome Statute of the International Criminal Court.[834] While the overall span of the prohibition in Hague Regulation 23(h) has been questioned, it is uniformly accepted as applicable in occupied territories.[835] The centre of gravity of the provision is that the imprint of the occupation on acquired rights (and rights of action) in civil matters should be minimal, subject to supervening security considerations. Thus, a military commander would be barred from 'arbitrarily annulling the results of civil proceedings between private parties'.[836]

B. Military Courts

(a) The Nature of the Military Courts

419. Military courts, set up by the military government, try and punish offenders against the security legislation enacted by the Occupying Power (consistent with its authority under Hague Regulation 43 and Geneva Article 64). Article 66 of the Geneva Convention prescribes:

> In case of a breach of the penal provisions promulgated by it by virtue of the second paragraph of Article 64, the Occupying Power may hand over the accused to its properly constituted, non-political military courts, on condition that the said courts sit in the occupied territory. Courts of appeal shall preferably sit in the occupied country.[837]

420. Belligerent occupation is 'a special situation in which civilians may be tried by a military legal system'.[838] However, as highlighted in Article 66, the military courts in an occupied territory must be non-political and properly constituted. This would patently exclude summary trials conducted by military commanders in the field. As stressed in the text, the military courts must sit in the occupied territory.

833 Hague Regulations, *supra* note 22, at 234–5.
834 Rome Statute of the International Criminal Court, *supra* note 350, at 1318.
835 See T.E. Holland, 'Article 23(h)', 28 *LQR* 94–8 (1912).
836 US Department of Defense, *Law of War Manual*, *supra* note 1, at 787.
837 Geneva Convention (IV), *supra* note 29, at 599.
838 S. Weill, 'The Judicial Arm of the Occupation: The Israeli Military Courts in the Occupied Territories', 866 *IRRC* 395, 403 (2007).

421. The ICRC Commentary defines 'military courts' as 'courts whose members have military status and are subordinate to the military authorities'.[839] The Commentary goes on to say that these are the same courts that deal with offences committed by members of the army of occupation.[840] In practice, members of the armed forces of the Occupying Power are frequently 'tried by courts-martial and not by the military courts set up by the occupant to deal with offenses by the civilian population'.[841] Thus, in the Israeli system, the military courts – properly constituted for the prosecution of the inhabitants of the occupied territories who have acted in breach of the security legislation enacted by the Occupying Power – are delinked from ordinary military tribunals. As a matter of policy, IDF soldiers are court-martialed by separate military tribunals.[842]

(b) Appeals

422. Is there an obligation to establish military courts of appeal? Article 66 of the Geneva Convention (quoted *supra* 419) says, in its second sentence, that military courts of appeal shall preferably sit in the occupied territory (military courts of first instance must do so under the first sentence). What are the implications of the text? The Israel Supreme Court (per President Shamgar) opined, in the *Arjoub* case, that the provision relates solely to the venue of courts of appeal – assuming that they are installed – and it does not signify that there is a duty to set them up.[843]

423. The *Arjoub* conclusion is backed up by scholars,[844] as well as by the language of Article 73 of the Convention:

> A convicted person shall have the right of appeal provided for by the laws applied by the court. He shall be fully informed of his right to appeal or petition and of the time limit within which he may do so.
>
> The penal procedure provided in the present Section shall apply, as far as it is applicable, to appeals. Where the laws applied by the Court make no provision for appeals, the convicted person shall have the right to petition against the finding and sentence to the competent authority of the Occupying Power.[845]

It is quite evident that Article 73 speaks of the right of appeal merely as an option that is open to the Occupying Power, to be resolved as it deems fit in the legislation applicable in the occupied territory. The text tacitly acknowledges the possible unavailability of appeal (in which case the only channel accessible

[839] *Commentary, IV Geneva Convention, supra* note 31, at 340.
[840] See *ibid.*
[841] Greenspan, *supra* note 383, at 255.
[842] See Z. Hadar, 'The Military Courts', I *Military Government in the Territories Administered by Israel 1967–1980, supra* note 99, at 171, 197–8.
[843] HCJ 87/85, *supra* note 829, at 365–6.
[844] See von Glahn, *supra* note 339, at 117.
[845] Geneva Convention (IV), *supra* note 29, at 601.

to a convicted person is a petition to a competent authority, i.e. a non-judicial echelon).[846]

424. Despite the absence of a legal obligation to institute a right of appeal, the Supreme Court strongly urged the establishment of a military instance of appeal – as a matter of policy and preference – in light of the prolonged Israeli occupation.[847] A system of military courts of appeal in the West Bank (and the Gaza Strip) was accordingly set up in 1989.[848]

425. To avoid confusion, it ought to be added that the Supreme Court does not sit as an instance of further appeal from the military courts in the Israeli occupied territories. This was stressed by the Court (per President Shamgar) in the *Matar* case: the Court would only put its foot down – acting as a High Court of Justice – if a military court were to exceed the lawful exercise of its functions.[849] In actuality, although the Supreme Court has examined a number of petitions against the military courts of appeals, it has steadfastly declined to intervene.[850]

(c) Special Cases

426. The military courts system of the Occupying Power may include specialized courts for particular sets of offenders. Thus, in 2009, Israel established in the West Bank a Military Youth Court.[851] In addition to military courts, the Occupying Power may also set up – as Israel did – quasi-judicial appeal boards dealing with civilian or administrative claims against the military government, for instance as regards appraisal of custom duties.[852]

427. An unanticipated issue arose before the Supreme Court in the *Alla* case, where an inhabitant of the West Bank charged with murder and other crimes committed in the occupied territory was extradited to Israel from the US on condition that he would be tried by a civil – rather than a military – court.[853] The Court (per Justice T. Or) concluded that, in these singular circumstances, there was no bar to the exercise of jurisdiction by the Jerusalem District Court.[854] The case was examined purely through the lens of the Israeli domestic legal system: the Court did not mention Article 66 of the Geneva Convention or the

[846] See HCJ 87/85, *supra* note 829, at 367–70.
[847] *Ibid.*, 375–9.
[848] See *Israel, the 'Intifada' and the Rules of Law, supra* note 817, at 97–8.
[849] HCJ 460/86, *Matar v. The Military Court in Shchem* et al., 40(3) *PD* 817, 818–19.
[850] See HCJ 765/89, *Alatrash* et al. *v. President of the Military Court of Appeals, Ramallah*, 43(4) *PD* 127, 132 (per Justice Goldberg).
[851] See H. Moodrick-Even Khen, 'Juvenile Justice in Belligerent Occupation Regimes: Comparing the Coalition Provisional Authority Administration in Iraq with the Israeli Military Government in the Territories Administered by Israel', 42 *DJILP* 119, 151 *et seq.* (2013–14).
[852] See Kuttner, *supra* note 822, at 220.
[853] VAC 75/91, *Alla v. State of Israel*, 45(1) *PD* 710, 711.
[854] *Ibid.*, 711–13.

requirement of prosecuting the accused before a military court sitting in the occupied territory. Still, the question that arises is whether the strings attached to an extradition order can be sturdy enough to overcome the ordinary application of the law of belligerent occupation. The case laid bare two interlocked problems pertaining to the transfer of a criminal trial of a protected person: (i) from a military court to a civil court; and (ii) from occupied to non-occupied territory.

C. Concurrent Jurisdiction

428. In view of the existence of two parallel criminal jurisdictions over the inhabitants of an occupied territory – the local courts and the military courts – there is a potential problem of concurrent exercise of jurisdiction and double jeopardy.

429. Concurrent jurisdiction has the advantage of flexibility, opening opportunities for switching cases between different courts, as and when necessary. The Israel Supreme Court (per President Sussman) held, in the *Liftawi* case, that the military government in the West Bank was entitled to transfer penal proceedings – based on a charge of murder (under the local Jordanian law) – from the local courts to the military courts, if there was cause to believe that the accused would fail to get a fair trial in the local courts owing to his close commercial and other contacts with Israel.[855] This was an isolated instance. But, after the outbreak of the first *intifada* – in the course of which hundreds of Palestinians were murdered by other Palestinians on suspicion of being 'collaborators' with Israel, and the judges of the local courts were subject to intimidation – the prosecution of a large number of alleged offenders, charged with infractions of the local law in force in the occupied territories, was transferred by the military government from the local courts to the military courts.[856]

430. Can a protected person be prosecuted twice for offences engendered by the same set of facts, once by a local court and then by a military court (or vice versa)? At first sight, this may appear to run counter to 'general principles of law' mentioned in Geneva Article 67 (first sentence) (quoted *supra* 392), specifically, the principle of *ne bis in idem*. However, in point of fact, 'a single act may give rise to a mixed offence' against both the ordinary criminal law and the security legislation of the Occupying Power; and, in such circumstances, an accused may be prosecuted separately by a local court (for the ordinary offence) and by a military court (for the security offence).[857]

[855] HCJ 481/76, *Liftawi v. Minister of Defence* et al., 31(1) *PD* 266, 267–9.
[856] See *Israel, the 'Intifada' and the Rules of Law*, *supra* note 817, at 89–92.
[857] Kuttner, *supra* note 822, at 194.

431. Article 75(4)(h) of Additional Protocol I states:

no one shall be prosecuted or punished by the same Party for an offence in respect of which a final judgement acquitting or convicting that person has been previously pronounced under the same law and judicial procedure.[858]

The qualifying words 'by the same Party', as well as 'under the same law and judicial procedure', leave no doubt that the principle of *ne bis in idem* does not bar consecutive trials by a local court and a military court in an occupied territory. These courts belong to two different Parties – the displaced sovereign and the Occupying Power – and the laws and judicial procedure are not identical. The solution offered by human rights law coincides with that of the *jus in bello*. Protocol No. 7 to the European Convention, which turns freedom from double jeopardy into a non-derogable human right (see *supra* 238), circumscribes it to 'criminal proceedings under the jurisdiction of the same State'.[859] The Human Rights Committee, too, came to the conclusion that the principle of *ne bis in idem* is not applicable 'with regard to the national jurisdictions of two or more States'.[860]

432. For exactly the same reason, a judgment of a military court of the Occupying Power will not bar – on the ground of double jeopardy – penal proceedings for the same offence from being conducted by the restored sovereign after the end of the occupation.[861]

II. The Right to a Fair Trial

433. Article 67 (first sentence) of Geneva Convention (IV) (quoted *supra* 392) enunciates that the military courts must apply only those legal provisions which were applicable prior to the commission of the offence and are in keeping with general principles of law, in particular the precept that the penalty must be proportionate to the offence. Under Article 68 (first paragraph), when protected persons in an occupied territory commit an offence intended to harm the Occupying Power – but not coming within the ambit of offences justifying capital punishment – a sentence of imprisonment may be meted out to them by a military court in proportion to the severity of the act perpetrated.[862] Article 69 requires that any period in which a protected person

[858] Additional Protocol I, *supra* note 33, at 749.

[859] Protocol No. 7 to the European Convention for the Protection of Human Rights and Fundamental Freedoms, *supra* note 482, at 110 (Article 4(1)).

[860] *A.P. v. Italy* (Human Rights Committee, Communication No. 204/1986), 2 *Selected Decisions of the Human Rights Committee under the Optional Protocol* 67, 68 (1990).

[861] Cf. *Double Jeopardy* case (Germany, Supreme Court, 1954), 21 *ILR* 480.

[862] Geneva Convention (IV), *supra* note 29, at 599.

is under arrest awaiting trial or punishment be deducted from the duration of the imprisonment.[863]

434. Article 70 (first paragraph) of the Convention sets forth:

Protected persons shall not be arrested, prosecuted or convicted by the Occupying Power for acts committed or for opinions expressed before the occupation, or during a temporary interruption thereof, with the exception of breaches of the laws and customs of war.[864]

This clause deals (*inter alia*) with the plight of protected persons who – during a brief interlude in the course of belligerent occupation but under the wrong impression that the occupation is over – resort to actions or express opinions that run counter to the Occupying Power's security legislation. Once the occupation is resumed, the text safeguards them from legal proceedings relating to what they did or said when they rashly thought that the occupation was over (unless a breach of the *jus in bello* was involved). The protection from legal proceedings covers not only private individuals but also local judges or officials.[865] However, the latter may of course be removed from office by the returning Occupying Power (see *supra* 191, 409).

435. Article 71 (first paragraph) of the Convention lays down:

No sentence shall be pronounced by the competent courts of the Occupying Power except after a regular trial.[866]

The idea of a 'regular trial' by 'competent courts' is of fundamental import. Under Article 147, 'willfully depriving a protected person of the rights of fair and regular trial prescribed in the present Convention' constitutes a grave breach.[867] As such, it is a war crime in accordance with Article 8(2)(a)(vi) of the Rome Statute of the International Criminal Court.[868] This has its origins in the post-WWII case law, especially the *Justice* trial.[869]

436. Article 71 (second paragraph) provides that an accused person prosecuted by the Occupying Power must be promptly informed in writing, in a language that he understands, of the charges preferred against him.[870] In keeping with Article 72, an accused has the right to submit evidence necessary to his defence (and, in particular, call witnesses), as well as to be assisted by

[863] *Ibid.*, 600.
[864] *Ibid.*
[865] See *Commentary, IV Geneva Convention*, *supra* note 31, at 349.
[866] Geneva Convention (IV), *supra* note 29, at 600.
[867] *Ibid.*, 624.
[868] Rome Statute of the International Criminal Court, *supra* note 350, at 1317.
[869] *Justice* trial, *supra* note 54, at 102–3.
[870] Geneva Convention (IV), *supra* note 29, at 600.

qualified counsel of his choice (enjoying the necessary facilities for the preparation of the defence) and an interpreter.[871]

437. Consonant with Article 73 (quoted *supra* 423), a convicted person is entitled to lodge an appeal or at least a petition to the competent authority of the Occupying Power. If there is a Protecting Power (see *supra* 214), it has important supervisory duties to discharge under Articles 71 *et seq.*[872]

438. Detailed strictures ensuring a fair trial also appear in Article 75(4) of Additional Protocol I:[873] (i) no sentence may be passed and no penalty executed except pursuant to a conviction by an impartial and regularly constituted court; (ii) the accused must be informed without delay of the particulars of the charge against him; (iii) he must be afforded all rights and means of defence; (iv) the basis of penal responsibility must be individual (and not collective); (v) no one can be convicted of an act or omission which did not constitute a criminal offence at the time when it was committed, nor can a heavier penalty be imposed than that which was permissible at the time of the commission of the offence; (vi) anyone charged with an offence is presumed innocent until proved guilty; (vii) an accused must be tried in his presence; (viii) no one can be compelled to testify against himself or to confess guilt; (ix) an accused has the right to examine witnesses against him; (x) there is freedom from double jeopardy (see *supra* 431); (xi) judgment must be pronounced publicly; and (xii) a convicted person must be advised of any judicial or other remedies available to him (including time limits).

439. Article 75(4) safeguards the rights of all persons charged with offences related to the armed conflict, and it is not limited to protected persons in the sense of Geneva Convention (IV).[874] Indeed, the judicial guarantees enumerated in this clause are universally applicable, being declaratory of customary international law.[875] Essentially the same guarantees are also articulated in Articles 14–15 of the Civil and Political Rights Covenant.[876] The difference between the *jus in bello* judicial guarantees in occupied territories and general human rights law in this domain is that the former cannot be suspended (see *supra* 254). As for the latter, while Article 15 of the Covenant (dealing with *ex post facto* penalization) is listed as non-derogable in Article 4(2) of the Covenant (see *supra* 238), that is not the case with respect to Article 14 (concerning all the other aspects of due process

[871] *Ibid.*, 601.
[872] *Ibid.*, 600–2.
[873] Additional Protocol I, *supra* note 33, at 749–50.
[874] See Y. Arai-Takahashi, 'Law-Making and the Judicial Guarantees in Occupied territories', *The 1949 Geneva Conventions: A Commentary*, *supra* note 309, at 1421, 1439.
[875] See I *Customary International Humanitarian Law, supra* note 40, at 352 *et seq.*
[876] International Covenant on Civil and Political Rights, *supra* note 335, at 47–9.

of law).[877] Still, *vide* the non-binding position on the subject taken by the Human Rights Committee (*supra* 240).

III. Capital Punishment

440. There is no need to dwell on the point that the inhabitants of an occupied territory must not be executed without a fair trial. The cardinal issue is whether a death sentence passed by a military court of the Occupying Power, meeting all the standards of a fair trial, is permissible. The Hague Regulations do not address the question and do not imply any limitation of the Occupying Power's freedom of action in this regard. For its part, Article 68 (second paragraph) of Geneva Convention (IV) stipulates:

> The penal provisions promulgated by the Occupying Power in accordance with Articles 64 and 65 may impose the death penalty on a protected person only in cases where the person is guilty of espionage, of serious acts of sabotage against the military installations of the Occupying Power or of intentional offences which have caused the death of one or more persons, provided that such offences were punishable by death under the law of the occupied territory in force before the occupation began.[878]

Thus, capital punishment is explicitly acknowledged as admissible in extreme instances of sabotage or espionage. All the same, there is a clear-cut condition precedent: the death penalty must have been in force in the occupied territory before the occupation. If the death sentence had existed in the past but was abolished prior to the occupation, the Occupying Power is not entitled to reinstate it.

441. Under Article 68 (third and fourth paragraphs), (i) a death penalty must not be pronounced unless the attention of the court has been particularly called to the fact that, since the accused is not a national of the Occupying Power, he does not owe it allegiance (see *supra* 175); and (ii) it is prohibited to sentence to death a person who was under eighteen years of age at the time of the commission of the offence.[879]

442. Article 76(3) of Additional Protocol I provides:

> To the maximum extent feasible, the Parties to the conflict shall endeavour to avoid the pronouncement of the death penalty on pregnant women or mothers having dependent infants, for an offence related to the armed conflict. The death penalty for such offences shall not be executed on such women.[880]

[877] *Ibid.*, 45.

[878] Curiously, this paragraph is missing from the text of Geneva Convention (IV) as published, *supra* note 29, at 600. But see the full text in *Commentary, IV Geneva Convention*, *supra* note 31, at 343.

[879] Geneva Convention (IV), *supra* note 29, at 600.

[880] Additional Protocol I, *supra* note 33, at 750.

Since the sentencing to death of pregnant women and mothers having dependent infants is not ruled out in the first limb of this clause, the thrust of the second limb is not self-evident. It might be construed as a mere requirement to postpone the execution of pregnant women and mothers of young babies until after the birth and weaning of their children. But the ICRC Commentary takes the high ground, expressing the uncompromising view that a mother 'should in no event be executed, even when the child is no longer dependent'.[881]

443. According to Article 75 (first paragraph) of the Geneva Convention, persons condemned to death have a right to petition for pardon or reprieve.[882] When there is a Protecting Power, it must be notified of the sentence and its grounds under Article 74 (second paragraph).[883] Article 75 (second and third paragraphs) adds that the sentence must not be carried out before the expiration of six months from the date of the receipt of the notification by the Protecting Power, except in circumstances of grave emergency involving an organized threat to the security of the Occupying Power, and even then the Protecting Power has to be given an opportunity to make representations to the competent authorities in respect of the sentence.[884]

444. Capital punishment (if it has not been abolished in the occupied territory in advance of the occupation) may be imposed not only by military courts operating under the security legislation of the Occupying Powers, but also by the local courts dealing with felonies not related to the occupation. Saddam Hussein was tried by an Iraqi Special Tribunal under a Statute promulgated by the Coalition Provisional Authority (in tune with Security Council resolutions seeking accountability for international crimes).[885] In the event, the trial commenced immediately after the formal end of the belligerent occupation of Iraq (see *supra* 41), and Saddam was sentenced to death in 2006.[886]

445. The competence of courts to impose a death sentence may be impacted upon by a human rights treaty in which the Occupying Power undertakes to abolish capital punishment. Thus, the Second Optional Protocol of 1989 to the International Covenant on Civil and Political Rights ordains that no one within the jurisdiction of a Contracting Party is to be executed.[887] Parallel provisions exist under regional instruments: both in Europe – where it was done in two stages, first with an option for States to maintain the death penalty

[881] C. Pilloud and J. Pictet, 'Article 76', *Commentary on the Additional Protocols, supra* note 327, at 891, 895.
[882] Geneva Convention (IV), *supra* note 29, at 602.
[883] *Ibid.*, 601–2.
[884] *Ibid.*, 602.
[885] Coalition Provisional Authority Order Number 48, II *The Occupation of Iraq: The Official Documents, supra* note 78, at 70, 70–1.
[886] See 66 *Facts on File* 862–863, 989–91 (2006).
[887] Second Optional Protocol to the International Covenant on Civil and Political Rights, *supra* note 481, at 65 (Article 1).

in wartime,[888] and then excluding this possibility[889] – and in the American continent.[890] If the Occupying Power is a Contracting Party to such a treaty, its military courts would be barred from sentencing a person to death.

446. Assuming that the Occupying Power is a Contracting Party to a treaty abolishing capital punishment, the question arises whether it is obligated to interfere in the imposition of a death sentence by the local courts where the displaced sovereign has not given its consent (anteceding the occupation) to be bound by such a treaty. The *UK Manual of the Law of Armed Conflict* states that UK service personnel or officials may not assist in any way in the imposition of death sentences by local courts in an occupied territory, but the Manual does not deny that such sentences may be carried out subject to the limitations set out in the Geneva Convention.[891]

[888] Protocol No. 6 to the European Convention for the Protection of Human Rights and Fundamental Freedoms Concerning the Abolition of the Death Penalty, *supra* note 481, at 105 (Articles 1–2).

[889] Protocol No. 13 to the European Convention for the Protection of Human Rights and Fundamental Freedoms Concerning the Abolition of the Death Penalty in All Circumstances, *supra* note 481, at 515 (Article 1).

[890] Protocol to the American Convention on Human Rights to Abolish the Death Penalty, 1990, *Raoul Wallenberg Compilation of Human Rights Instruments, supra* note 335, at 189.

[891] *UK Manual of the Law of Armed Conflict, supra* note 230, at 298.

7 Protection of the Civilian Population under Belligerent Occupation

I. Freedom from Genocide and the Right to Life

A. *The Prohibition of Genocide*

447. Every national group – including the civilian population of an occupied territory – has a basic right to existence (i.e. to life) protecting it from genocide.[892] This right is enshrined in Article I of the 1948 Convention on the Prevention and Punishment of the Crime of Genocide:

> The Contracting Parties confirm that genocide, whether committed in time of peace or in time of war, is a crime under international law which they undertake to prevent or to punish.[893]

The wording appears at first sight to relate to acts perpetrated by actors other than the Contracting Parties themselves. But in the 2007 *Genocide Convention* case (Bosnia/Serbia), the International Court of Justice held that – although '[t]he article does not *expressis verbis* require States to refrain from themselves committing genocide' – such a prohibition follows from the obligation to prevent the commission of genocide.[894] As the Court put it, '[i]t would be paradoxical' if States 'were not forbidden to commit such acts through their organs' while they are under obligation to prevent genocide.[895] The Judgment added that the obligation not to commit genocide applies 'to a State wherever it may be acting or may be able to act', in a manner that is not limited by territorial bounds.[896] This patently covers occupied territories.

[892] See W.A. Schabas, *Genocide in International Law: The Crimes of Crimes* 6 (2000).
[893] Convention on the Prevention and Punishment of the Crime of Genocide, 1948, *The Laws of Armed Conflicts, supra* note 29, at 839, 840.
[894] *Case Concerning the Application of the Convention on the Prevention and Punishment of the Crime of Genocide* (Bosnia and Herzegovina, Serbia and Montenegro), 2007, 46 *ILM* 188, 232 (2007).
[895] *Ibid.*
[896] *Ibid.*, 236.

448. The term 'genocide' is defined as follows in Article II of the Genocide Convention:

In the present Convention, genocide means any of the following acts committed with intent to destroy, in whole or in part, a national, ethnical, racial or religious group, as such:

(a) Killing members of the group;
(b) Causing serious bodily or mental harm to members of the group;
(c) Deliberately inflicting on the group conditions of life calculated to bring about its physical destruction in whole or in part;
(d) Imposing measures intended to prevent births within the group;
(e) Forcibly transferring children of the group to another group.[897]

449. In the *Genocide Convention* case, the International Court accentuated the following elements in the definition: (i) the protected group ('a collection of people who have a particular group identity') must have 'particular positive characteristics': national, ethnical, racial or religious; (ii) the intent of the genocider must be to destroy the group 'as such'; (iii) the intent to destroy the group 'in whole or in part' means that the target may be confined to 'at least a substantial part of the particular group'; (iv) the approach to assessing what constitutes 'a substantial part' does not have to be quantitative, but can be also qualitative (e.g., if a specific part of the group is essential to its survival); (v) the intent may be limited to destroying the group 'within a geographically limited area' rather than everywhere.[898]

450. Already in 1951, the Court – in its Advisory Opinion on *Reservations to the Genocide Convention* – stated that 'the principles underlying the Convention are principles which are recognized by civilized nations as binding on States, even without any conventional obligation'.[899] In 2006, in the *Case Concerning Armed Activities on the Territory of the Congo* (Congo v. Rwanda), the Court pronounced that the prohibition of genocide is 'assuredly' a norm of *jus cogens*.[900]

[897] Convention on the Prevention and Punishment of the Crime of Genocide, *supra* note 893, at 840.

[898] *Case Concerning the Application of the Convention on the Prevention and Punishment of the Crime of Genocide*, *supra* note 894, at 238–40.

[899] Advisory Opinion on *Reservations to the Convention on the Prevention and Punishment of the Crime of Genocide*, [1951] *ICJ Rep.* 15, 23.

[900] *Case Concerning Armed Activities on the Territory of the Congo* (Jurisdiction of the Court and Admissibility of the Application) (Congo v. Rwanda), [2006] *ICJ Rep.* 6, 32 (2006).

B. *The Individual Right to Life*

451. The right to life is not only a collective right of the civilian population in an occupied territory *qua* a group. Every inhabitant of an occupied territory benefits from Hague Regulation 46 (first paragraph):

> Family honour and rights, the lives of individuals and private property, as well as religious convictions and liberty of worship, must be respected.[901]

The sequence of the values to be respected, as inscribed in Regulation 46 (first paragraph), is somewhat quaint: it would have made more sense to refer to the preservation of life ahead of family honour. But – whatever the order in which they appear – the obligations are clear, and they prominently include respect for 'the lives of individuals' in an occupied territory. An attempt to make this provision subject to overriding dictates of military necessity was aborted at the inception of the Hague Regulations.[902]

452. Article 32 of the Geneva Convention (quoted *supra* 250) proscribes murder of protected persons. Article 147 marks out 'wilful killing' of protected persons as a grave breach of the Convention.[903] This turns it also into a war crime under Article 8(2)(a)(i) of the Rome Statute of the International Criminal Court.[904]

II. Ensuring the Survival of the Civilian Population

A. *The Prohibition of Starvation of Civilians*

453. Article 54(1) of Additional Protocol I prohibits '[s]tarvation of civilians as a method of warfare'.[905] According to Article 54(2), it is forbidden to destroy, remove or render useless objects indispensable to the survival of the civilian population, such as foodstuffs, crops, livestock, drinking water installations and irrigation works, in order to starve out civilians, to cause them to move away, or for any other motive.[906] Intentionally using the starvation of civilians as a method of warfare, by depriving them of objects indispensable to their survival, is a war crime under Article 8(2)(b)(xxv) of the Rome Statute.[907]

454. Although these injunctions are not directed specifically at occupied territories, they have special resonance there (in particular, as regards the removal

[901] Hague Regulations, *supra* note 22, at 246–7.
[902] See Graber, *supra* note 264, at 207–8.
[903] Geneva Convention (IV), *supra* note 29, at 624.
[904] Rome Statute of the International Criminal Court, *supra* note 350, at 1317.
[905] Additional Protocol I, *supra* note 33, at 737.
[906] *Ibid.*
[907] Rome Statute of the International Criminal Court, *supra* note 350, at 1319.

of foodstuffs and the desire to cause civilians to drift away). Under Article 54(5) of Additional Protocol I, a derogation from the prohibitions contained in Article 54(2) is permitted to a Belligerent Party – 'in defence of its national territory against invasion' – as long as the territory is under its own control and this is 'required by imperative military necessity'.[908] Such a derogation enables a Belligerent Party to initiate 'scorched earth' tactics, within the national territory that it controls, when withdrawing in the face of invading enemy forces. But the derogation is not available to an Occupying Power. An Occupying Power, retreating from an occupied territory, cannot resort to a 'scorched earth' policy by destroying objects indispensable to the survival of the civilian population.[909]

B. Sieges

455. The prohibition of starvation of civilians has complex connotations regarding siege warfare.[910] Siege warfare may seem to have only scant bearing on belligerent occupation. Yet, the Israeli experience shows otherwise. In 2002, during the second *intifada*, armed Palestinians took control of the Church of the Nativity in Bethlehem. The IDF wisely decided not to storm the Church but to besiege it. This raised the issue of supplies of food, water, medications etc. to non-combatants present in the Church compound. Although some clergymen left the Church, others chose to remain there and they were then joined by civilians (actually, voluntary 'human shields'; see *supra* 326).

456. The matter came before the Supreme Court twice in the *Church of the Nativity* cases. In the first case, where the petitioner was the Catholic *Custodia*, the Court (per Justice Strasberg-Cohen) rendered an interim decision,[911] the outcome of which was that dead bodies were allowed to be removed from the Church and relief supplies were delivered to the clergymen.[912] In the second case, new petitioners asked for delivery of supplies to the other persons ensconced in the Church. The Court (per President Barak) rejected the petition, holding that (i) there was no breach of international law in denying supplies to combatants: they always have the option of coming out and surrendering; and

[908] Additional Protocol I, *supra* note 33, at 738.

[909] See C. Pilloud and J. Pictet, 'Article 54', *Commentary on the Additional Protocols, supra* note 327, at 651, 659.

[910] See Y. Dinstein, 'Siege Warfare and the Starvation of Civilians', *Humanitarian Law of Armed Conflict Challenges Ahead: Essays in Honour of Frits Kalshoven* 145, 148–52 (A.J.M. Delissen and G.T. Tanja eds., 1991).

[911] HCJ 3436/02, *Custodia Internazionale de Terra Santa v. Government of Israel* et al., 56(3) *PD* 22. (The Judgment is excerpted in English in 32 *IYHR* 370 (2002)).

[912] HCJ 3451/02, *Almadni* et al. *v. Minister of Defence* et al., 56(3) *PD* 30, 33. (The Judgment is excerpted in English in 32 *IYHR* 373 (2002)).

(ii) as far as civilians were concerned, since there was a well in the compound with some water available, in addition to minimal foodstuffs – and inasmuch as the IDF was prepared to allow the civilians to come out, get food for their own needs and then return to the compound – the IDF had met its obligations under the *jus in bello*.[913]

C. Ensuring Essential Supplies

457. Article 55 (first paragraph) of Geneva Convention (IV) declares:

> To the fullest extent of the means available to it, the Occupying Power has the duty of ensuring the food and medical supplies of the population; it should, in particular, bring in the necessary foodstuffs, medical stores and other articles if the resources of the occupied territory are inadequate.[914]

Article 55 (first paragraph) is confined, in substance, to foodstuffs and medicines. However, Article 69(1) of Additional Protocol I goes much further:

> In addition to the duties specified in Article 55 of the Fourth Convention concerning food and medical supplies, the Occupying Power shall, to the fullest extent of the means available to it and without any adverse distinction, also ensure the provision of clothing, bedding, means of shelter, other supplies essential to the survival of the civilian population of the occupied territory and objects necessary for religious worship.[915]

458. There is no need to give an elaborate explanation for the Additional Protocol's extension of the menu of indispensable supplies that the Occupying Power is obligated (to the fullest extent of the means available to it) to ensure to the civilian population of an occupied territory. It is manifestly clear that not only foodstuffs and medicines but also clothing, bedding and means of shelter may be vital for the survival of the civilian population. In adverse climate conditions, extreme heat or cold may be no less dangerous than lack of food or medicines.[916]

459. The phrase '[t]o the fullest extent of the means available to it', used both in Article 55 (first paragraph) of the Geneva Convention and in Article 69(1) of the Additional Protocol, leaves 'a small loophole' in the protection guaranteed to the civilian population.[917] But this is unavoidable. The framers of the two instruments were fully aware of the predicament in which the Occupying Power is liable to find itself for reasons that may well be beyond its control. The same explanation accounts for the weak 'should' language employed

[913] *Ibid.*, 35–6.
[914] Geneva Convention (IV), *supra* note 29, at 596.
[915] Additional Protocol I, *supra* note 33, at 746.
[916] See Y. Sandoz, 'Article 69', *Commentary on the Additional Protocols, supra* note 327, at 811, 812.
[917] See D. Marcus, 'Famine Crimes in International Law', 97 *AJIL* 245, 267 (2003).

in Article 55 (first paragraph) as regards the Occupying Power bringing in foodstuffs and medications into the occupied territory. After all, the population of the Occupying Power – within its own territory – may be exposed to similar hardships and privations, e.g., as a result of a blockade imposed by an enemy country. The sole effective remedy to a paucity of essential supplies in an occupied territory may, therefore, be the provision of humanitarian relief from the outside (see *infra* 582).

III. Respect for the Rights of Protected Persons

460. A core right of protected persons in occupied territories is elucidated in Article 27 (first paragraph) of Geneva Convention (IV):

> Protected persons are entitled, in all circumstances, to respect for their persons, their honour, their family rights, their religious convictions and practices, and their manners and customs. They shall at all times be humanely treated, and shall be protected especially against all acts of violence or threats thereof and against insults and public curiosity.[918]

461. According to the ICRC Commentary, this is 'the basis of the Convention, proclaiming as it does the principles on which the whole of 'Geneva Law' is founded'.[919] Six principles are enumerated, and they relate to respect for: (i) person; (ii) honour; (iii) family rights; (iv) religious convictions and practices; (v) manners and customs; as well as (vi) an obligation to grant humane treatment.[920] '[W]illfully causing great suffering or serious injury to body or health' of protected persons constitutes a grave breach of the Convention pursuant to Article 147.[921] As such, it constitutes a war crime under Article 8(2)(a)(iii) of the Rome Statute of the International Criminal Court.[922] In the words of the ICTY Trial Chamber in the *Delalić* case of 1998, 'the suffering incurred can be mental or physical'.[923]

IV. The Prohibition of Hostage-Taking

462. Hostage-taking, as defined in Article 1 of the 1979 International Convention against the Taking of Hostages,[924] is an international offence.

[918] Geneva Convention (IV), *supra* note 29, at 589.
[919] *Commentary, IV Geneva Convention*, *supra* note 31, at 199–200.
[920] On the meaning of these principles, see *ibid.*, 201–5.
[921] Geneva Convention (IV), *supra* note 29, at 624.
[922] Rome Statute of the International Criminal Court, *supra* note 350, at 1317.
[923] *Prosecutor v. Delalić* et al. (ICTY, Trial Chamber, 1998), para. 509. See also *Prosecutor v. Blaškić*, *supra* note 64, at para. 186.
[924] International Convention against the Taking of Hostages, 1979, [1979] *UNJY* 124, *id.*

It is generally viewed as a symptom of the wider syndrome of terrorism.[925] However, in occupied territories hostage-taking assumes a different dimension. Historically, Occupying Powers have indulged in the taking of inhabitants as hostages, with a view to intimidating the civilian population at large. The practice of taking hostages by an Occupying Power has been applied in a variety of situational dimensions. Mainly, hostages have been put behind bars, with the sword of execution dangling over their heads as a potential reaction to the misconduct of other inhabitants of the occupied territory: through acts of commission (sabotage) or even omission (say, non-payment of a 'contribution' levied on a particular community).[926]

463. In 1948, the American Military Tribunal, in the *Hostages* trial, concluded that the taking and shooting of hostages are in conformity with the customary laws of war if certain conditions are fulfilled, especially: (i) an advance warning is issued to the civilian population; (ii) there is a connection between the civilian population from which the hostages are taken and the acts prompting their shooting; (iii) the actual perpetrators are not found; (iv) there is a proportion between the number of the hostages shot and the gravity of those acts; (v) a judicial finding (as distinct from an administrative determination by a military commander) is made that the preceding conditions have been satisfied.[927] This alarming decision (steeped with tradition but not attuned to a new *Zeitgeist*) stunned public opinion and was repudiated by many detractors.[928] The backlash paved the way to an antithetical solution in Geneva Convention (IV) of 1949.

464. Article 34 of the Convention now decrees *tout court* that '[t]he taking of hostages is prohibited'.[929] Hostage-taking (of protected persons) is also a grave breach of the Convention, as per Article 147.[930] As such, it is branded as a war crime by Article 8(2)(a)(viii) of the Rome Statute of the International Criminal Court.[931]

465. Hostage-taking is now forbidden without any conditions or qualifications: it is linked to the interdiction of collective penalties and reprisals against protected persons in Article 33 (first paragraph) (see *infra* 470). While hostage-taking is usually linked also to an unlawful detention, there is no reason to exclude the possibility that the person seized is lawfully

[925] See J. L. Lambert, *Terrorism and Hostages in International Law: A Commentary on the Hostages Convention of 1979* 46–61 (1990).
[926] See E. Hammer and M. Salvin, 'The Taking of Hostages in Theory and Practice', 38 *AJIL* 20, 27–9 (1944).
[927] *Hostages* trial, *supra* note 11, at 78–9.
[928] See Lord Wright, 'The Killing of Hostages as a War Crime', 25 *BYBIL* 296, 299–310 (1948).
[929] Geneva Convention (IV), *supra* note 29, at 590.
[930] *Ibid.*, 624.
[931] Rome Statute of the International Criminal Court, *supra* note 350, at 1317.

interned (see *infra* 519) but is then subjected to a threat turning him into a hostage.[932]

466. The banning of hostage-taking is comprehensive enough to go beyond any prospective execution of the hostages. This was made clear by the 2004 Judgment of the ICTY Appeals Chamber in the *Blaškić* case, which – borrowing from the definition appearing in Article 1 of the 1979 Hostages Convention (cited *supra* 462) – stated that 'a situation of hostage-taking exists when a person seizes or detains and threatens to kill, injure or continue to detain another person in order to compel a third party to do or to abstain from doing something as a condition for the release of that person'.[933] The emphasis is on the words 'injure or continue to detain', complementing the threat of death. The Elements of Crime, appended to the Rome Statute, repeat the same phrase.[934] Thus, while the threat of impending death is particularly odious, it is not the exclusive scenario: the alternative of non-lethal injury or continued detention must not be downplayed.

467. In the proceedings of the Special Court for Sierra Leone, the question arose (not in the context of occupied territories) whether threats against hostages must be communicated to a third party. The Trial Chamber in the *Sesay* case of 2009 held that 'threats made to the captives do not suffice', inasmuch as 'the offence of hostage taking requires the threat to be communicated to a third party, with the intent of compelling the third party to act or refrain from acting as a condition for the safety or release of the captives'.[935] Yet, the Appeals Chamber – in a Judgment delivered the same year – reversed the lower tier's decision on this point, pronouncing that 'the Trial Chamber erred in introducing into the elements of the crime a requirement that the threat must have been communicated to a third party'.[936]

468. Another issue came up in the Israeli experience (although, again, not in the setting of occupied territories) with respect to hostages taken as 'bargaining chips'. The case related to Lebanese nationals who were brought to Israel and detained as 'bargaining chips' vis-à-vis Hezbollah, in the hope of facilitating the release of captured Israeli personnel. Initially, the detention was approved by the majority of a regular panel of the Supreme Court (2:1) (per President Barak) in an *Anonymous* case.[937] Yet, on review, the Court – sitting in a special panel of nine Justices, also by majority vote (this time, 6:3) and

[932] See D. Tuck, 'Taking of Hostages', *The 1949 Geneva Conventions: A Commentary*, *supra* note 309, at 300, 309–10.

[933] *Prosecutor v. Blaškić* (ICTY, Appeals Chamber, 2004), para. 639.

[934] See Dörmann, *supra* note 355, at 124.

[935] *Prosecutor v. Sesay* et al. (Special Court for Sierra Leone, Trial Chamber, 2009), para. 1964.

[936] *Prosecutor v. Sesay* et al. (Special Court for Sierra Leone, Appeals Chamber, 2009), para. 586.

[937] ADA 10/94, *Anonymous v. Minister of Defence*, 53(1) *PD* 97. (The Judgment is excerpted in English in 30 *IYHR* 335 (2000)).

per President Barak (who had changed his mind in the interval) – reversed itself on the ground that a human being can only be detained if he personally poses a danger to security.[938] Although the Judgment was anchored in Israeli domestic law, President Barak expressly mentioned that the holding of a person as a 'bargaining chip' constitutes hostage-taking, which is prohibited by international law.[939] He cited both Article 34 of the Geneva Convention and Article 1 of the Hostages Convention, pronouncing that – even if, *arguendo*, the prohibition of hostage-taking does not reflect customary international law – there is a 'presumption of correspondence' between international law (in this instance, treaty law) and domestic law.[940] It should also be observed that, in occupied territories, internment of such nature runs afoul of Article 78 of the Geneva Convention (see *infra* 519).

V. Collective Penalties and Reprisals

A. Collective Penalties

469. By writ of Hague Regulation 50:

> No general penalty, pecuniary or otherwise, shall be inflicted on the population on account of the acts of individuals for which it cannot be regarded as collectively responsible.[941]

The provision, originally intended to exclude only collective fines, has been made applicable to all collective penalties.[942] However, the text is rather elliptical: it does not flesh out the conditions under which the population in an occupied territory can be considered collectively responsible for individual acts,[943] nor does it answer the question whether vicarious individual responsibility of one person for the acts of another (usually a member of the family) is admissible.[944]

470. Article 33 (first paragraph) of Geneva Convention (IV) is more transparent:

938 CFH 7048/97, *Anonymous v. Minister of Defence*, 54(1) *PD* 721, 742. (The Judgment is excerpted in English in 30 *IYHR* 340 (2000)).

939 *Ibid.*

940 *Ibid.*, 742–3.

941 Hague Regulations, *supra* note 22, at 246–7.

942 See *Rauter* trial (Netherlands, Special Court of Cassation, 1949), 14 *LRTWC* 89, 135–6.

943 See J.W. Garner, 'Community Fines and Collective Responsibility', 11 *AJIL* 511, 528–31 (1917).

944 See Freeman, *supra* note 818, at 607.

No protected person may be punished for an offence he or she has not personally committed. Collective penalties and likewise all measures of intimidation or of terrorism are prohibited.[945]

471. As for the first sentence of this clause, its most important ramification is that communities (such as villages or towns) cannot be held 'collectively responsible for acts committed by one or more individuals in their midst'.[946] In the words of the ICRC Commentary, '[r]esponsibility is personal and it will no longer be possible to inflict penalties on persons who have themselves not committed the acts complained of'.[947]

472. The second sentence in Article 33 (first paragraph) prompts the reader to enquire what constitutes 'collective penalties'. The generally accepted answer is: 'a form of sanction imposed on persons or a group of persons in response to a crime committed by one of them or a member of the group'.[948] Furthermore, the term 'penalties' should be perceived in a broad sense: it does not matter if they are inflicted by sentence of a court of law or as an administrative measure.[949]

473. During the first *intifada*, when minors committed acts harmful to military security or public safety – for which they could not be prosecuted because they had not yet reached the age of criminal responsibility – the Israel Supreme Court, in the *Taha* case, ruled that the Occupying Power was entitled to impose on their parents an obligation to deposit a pecuniary bail (to be forfeited if new offences were to be perpetrated by the minors within the bail period).[950] The Court (per Justice D. Levin) rejected the argument that the measure was inconsistent with either Hague Regulation 50 or Geneva Article 33 (first paragraph), since the deposit was paid individually by parents who had been remiss in their duty to supervise their minor children and not by other persons.[951]

B. Prolonged Curfews

474. The subject-matter of collective penalties came up before the Israel Supreme Court, more than once, in the context of prolonged night curfews. In the *Shua* case, a night curfew – imposed on the Gaza Strip for a cumulative period of two years – was challenged.[952] The Court (per Justice G. Bach)

[945] Geneva Convention (IV), *supra* note 29, at 590.
[946] Kalshoven and Zegveld, *supra* note 649, at 78.
[947] *Commentary, IV Geneva Convention*, *supra* note 31, at 225.
[948] P. Rabbat and S. Mehring, 'Collective Punishment', II *MPEPIL* 311, *id.*
[949] See S. Darcy, 'Punitive House Demolitions, the Prohibition of Collective Punishment, and the Supreme Court of Israel', 21 *PSILR* 477, 488 (2002–3).
[950] HCJ 591/88, *supra* note 578, at 48–51.
[951] *Ibid.*, 54–5.
[952] HCJ 1113/90, *Shua* et al. *v. IDF Commander of the Gaza Strip*, 44(4) *PD* 590, 591. (The Judgment is excerpted in English in 23 *IYHR* 332 (1993)).

conceded that, ordinarily, such a protracted curfew might appear to amount to an improper collective penalty; but it reached the conclusion that this was not so, given the special circumstances of the *intifada*.[953] The ruling was confirmed by the Court (per Justice I. Zamir) in the *Sruzberg* case.[954]

475. Evidently, a drawn-out night curfew seriously upsets the life of the civilian population in an occupied territory. The legality of a curfew therefore depends on its purpose in the concrete circumstances. The real aim of the military government, in imposing the measure, is liable to contravene the Geneva prohibition of collective penalties in an occupied territory.[955] Yet, as long as a curfew is directly associated with the exigencies of a specific security situation, there is nothing legally wrong with it (see *supra* 343).[956]

C. *Demolition or Sealing Off of Houses*

476. The main setting for raising the problem of collective penalties in the territories occupied by Israel has been the practice of demolition and sealing off of houses as an administrative penalty under Section 119(1) of the Defence (Emergency) Regulations (mentioned *supra* 351 and discussed *infra* 619 *et seq.*). As we shall see (*infra* 627), post-combat demolition of houses is incompatible with the law of belligerent occupation. Independently, the demolition or even sealing off of a house may well constitute a breach of the interdiction of collective penalties.

477. Not all cases of demolition or sealing off of buildings are necessarily germane to the prohibition of collective penalties. Thus, a saboteur may be the sole resident in the premises demolished or sealed off (with no side effects on adjacent dwellings).[957] Alternatively, only a segment of a house (e.g., a single room) – in which a saboteur resides – may be demolished or sealed off, while other portions are left undamaged.[958] However, in a host of instances, the demolition or sealing off of a place of habitation causes the uprooting from their homes of relatives and neighbours who live with or next door to the saboteur. Here a distinction must be made between family members and neighbours who may have been accomplices – so that they can be held accountable together

[953] *Ibid.*

[954] HCJ 1759/94, *Sruzberg* et al. *v. Minister of Defence*, 55(1) *PD* 625, 628.

[955] See C.V. Reicin, 'Preventive Detention, Curfews, Demolition of Houses, and Deportations: an Analysis of Measures Employed by Israel in the Administered Territories', 8 *Car.LR* 515, 544 (1986–7).

[956] See M. Greenspan, 'Human Rights in the Territories Occupied by Israel', 12 *SCL* 377, 389 (1972).

[957] This was the factual setting, e.g., in HCJ 572/82, *Muslah v. Minister of Defence*, 36(4) *PD* 610. (The Judgment is excerpted in English in 29 *IYHR* 255 (1999)).

[958] This was the factual setting, e.g., in HCJ 22/81, *Hamed* et al. *v. Commander of Judea and Samaria*, 35(3) *PD* 223. (The Judgment is excerpted in English in 11 *IYHR* 365 (1981)).

with the saboteur – and individuals who had no inkling of, or connection to, the act of sabotage.[959] It is in the latter instances that the demolition or sealing off would be in violation of Article 33 (first paragraph) of the Geneva Convention.

478. The case law of the Israel Supreme Court is rife with decisions voicing the need to apply Section 119(1) of the Defence (Emergency) Regulations with a yardstick of proportion in mind, so that the harm done to persons other than the saboteur would not be excessive.[960] But the concern evinced by the Court was largely circumscribed to undue distress befalling neighbours (in or near the unit condemned to be demolished),[961] and especially harm done to persons who knew nothing of the saboteur's intentions.[962] There is, for instance, a dictum of the Court that it would not allow the military government to destroy an entire high-rise building only because a saboteur lived in a single room in a row of apartments.[963]

479. The Court showed much less empathy towards members of the immediate family of a saboteur sharing the same accommodation with him, even when they could not be considered accomplices. In the *Dajalis* case, the Court (per Justice M. Ben Dror) was not impressed by the argument that this would form a collective penalty, taking the position that (i) if the deterrent effect of Section 119(1) is to carry weight, a saboteur must know that his criminal acts will not only harm himself but in all likelihood will expose members of his family to a great deal of anguish; and (ii) the suffering of the immediate members of the family (such as small children) – ensuing from the demolition of a house – is no different from what they would go through when an ordinary sentence is passed by a criminal court, resulting in the imprisonment of the bread-earner.[964]

480. These words do not sit well with the prohibition of collective penalties. As for the deterrent effect of Section 119(1) – no matter how efficacious it is in the suppression of sabotage – the outcome boils down to a sanction barred by the Geneva Convention. The comparison between the demolition of a house and an imprisonment sentence is not persuasive. Beside the fact that demolition is an administrative measure whereas imprisonment is imposed by

[959] See B. Farrell, 'Israeli Demolition of Palestinian Houses as a Punitive Measure: Application of International Law to Regulation 119', 28 *Brook.JIL* 871, 909 (2002–3).

[960] See, e.g., HCJ 5510/92, *Turkman v. Minister of Defence* et al., 48(1) *PD* 217, 219–20. (The Judgment is excerpted in English in 25 *IYHR* 345 (1995)).

[961] See, e.g., HCJ 5740/90 etc., *Hajba* et al. *v. IDF Commander of Judea and Samaria*, 45(3) *PD* 254, 257–8. (The Judgment is excerpted in English in 23 *IYHR* 336 (1993)).

[962] See, e.g., HCJ 2722/92, *Almarin v. IDF Commander of the Gaza Strip*, 46(3) *PD* 694, 700. (The Judgment is excerpted in English in 25 *IYHR* 337 (1995)).

[963] *Ibid.*, 699.

[964] See e.g., HCJ 698/85, *Dajalis* et al. *v. IDF Commander of Judea and Samaria*, 40(2) *PD* 42, 44. (The Judgment is excerpted in English in 17 *IYHR* 315 (1987)).

a court of law, it must be taken into account that the children of a felon behind bars do not themselves go to jail, although they are distressed by their father's enforced absence. Conversely, the children of a saboteur who are left roofless may suffer as much as the offender himself, and – when the offender is in jail or dead – they may be the only ones to sustain this specific injury. Surely, their plight comes within the compass of the definition of unlawful collective penalties. 'A convicted terrorist should be punished according to the Law, but his family should not become homeless'.[965]

481. The implacable stand taken by the Court must be seen against the backdrop of a relentless increase in the incidence of acts of terrorism, with 'suicide bombers' setting off their lethal devices to explode amidst innocent bystanders. The Court had to dispose of a string of petitions following the demolition of houses goaded by a wave of 'suicide bombs'. In the principal proceedings, concerning *A. Nazal*, the Court – sitting in a special panel of five Justices (and deciding the case by a majority of 4:1) – approved (per Justice Matza) the demolition of the house of a 'suicide bomber', despite pernicious consequences for the members of his family.[966] A minority of one (Justice M. Cheshin) dissented. Justice Cheshin did not question the demolition per se,[967] but in his opinion it should have been restricted to just the room of the 'suicide bomber'; the demolition of other sections of the house amounted to an unacceptable collective penalty.[968]

482. Leaving aside considerations of compatibility with the Geneva Convention, the deterrence argument advanced by the majority of the Court seems paradoxically to lose its footing where 'suicide bombers' are concerned. After all, for deterrence to be effective, a prospective perpetrator must flinch from the counter-measures likely to be taken against him by the military government. An ordinary saboteur may therefore be deterred by the threat of demolition of his house, which he would desire to repossess upon being released from custody. However, a 'suicide bomber' plans to inflict death on himself, as well as on the innocent victims who happen to be present in the wrong place at the wrong time. Why would he look at the demolition of his house as condign punishment when he is not going to be around to suffer the consequences?

483. The out-of-kilter calculus of deterrence of 'suicide bombers' has not eluded the Court, which noted the complexity of the issue.[969] Still, the majority

[965] Meron, *supra* note 154, at 119.

[966] HCJ 6026/94, *A. Nazal* et al. *v. IDF Commander of Judea and Samaria*, 48(5) *PD* 338, 349–50. (The Judgment is excerpted in English in 29 *IYHR* 264 (1999)).

[967] For a more detailed explanation of Justice Cheshin's dissent on the same issue in this and in other cases, see Y. Dinstein, 'The Israel Supreme Court and the Law of Belligerent Occupation: Demolitions and Sealing Off of Houses', 29 *IYHR* 285, 299–300 (1999).

[968] HCJ 6026/94, *supra* note 966, at 351–2.

[969] See HCJ 8084/02 etc., *Abassi* et al. *v. Commander of the Home Front*, 57(2) *PD* 55, 60 (per President Barak). (The Judgment is excerpted in English in 35 *IYHR* 315 (2005)).

thought that deterrence may play a role when the demolition of a house affects kith and kin of the 'suicide bomber'. The Court was impressed by military experts who have come to the conclusion (on the basis of evaluation of intelligence data) that – in a raft of instances – live-in relatives had in fact dissuaded would-be 'suicide bombers' from proceeding with the execution of their lethal scheme, in order not to put at risk the family residence.[970] In the *Jenimat* case, Justice Goldberg observed that, while no scientific research had been (or could be) conducted – demonstrating how many 'suicide bombings' have actually been averted as a result of this deterrent effect of demolition of family abodes – suffice it that the military authorities have faith in the efficacy of the measure, for the Court to not interfere in the exercise of their discretionary power.[971] For more about the expediency of the practice of demolition of family houses, see *infra* 629. But pondering questions of expediency must not diffuse the main point, which is that the practice is not reconcilable with the Geneva prohibition of collective penalties (see *supra* 470).

D. Reprisals

484. Article 33 (third paragraph) of the Geneva Convention prohibits '[r]eprisals against protected persons and their property'.[972] What is the extent of this prohibition? G. von Glahn contends that demolition of houses – as practised by Israel – is in breach of Article 33 (third paragraph).[973] Yet, the application of the construct of reprisals to this subject-matter is wrong (see *infra* 485). What is more, since destruction of private property unrelated to military operations is anyhow banned by the law of belligerent occupation (see *infra* 598), there does not seem to be any value added in attaching to the legal analysis a component that can only obfuscate an otherwise lucid injunction.

485. As put by the ICRC Commentary, '[r]eprisals are measures contrary to law, but which, when taken by one State with regard to another State to ensure the cessation of certain acts ... are considered as lawful in the particular conditions under which they are carried out'.[974] Illicit reprisals under Article 33 (third paragraph) take the form of counteracts directed against protected persons and their property. But there is a preliminary question: whose original acts

[970] See HCJ 8262/03, *Abu Salim* et al. *v. IDF Commander of the West Bank*, 57(6) *PD* 569, 574–5 (per Justice Beinisch). (The Judgment is excerpted in English in 35 *IYHR* 320 (2005)).

[971] HCJ 2006/97, *Jenimat* et al. *v. Commander of the Central Region*, 51(2) *PD* 651, 655. (The Judgment is excerpted in English in 30 *IYHR* 333 (2000)).

[972] Geneva Convention (IV), *supra* note 29, at 590.

[973] G. von Glahn, *Law among Nations* 677 (7th edn, 1996).

[974] *Commentary, IV Geneva Convention*, *supra* note 31, at 227.

can lead to this response? The answer was given by the Netherlands Special Court of Cassation in the *Rauter* trial:

In the proper sense one can speak of reprisals only when a State resorts, by means of its organs, to measures at variance with International Law, on account of the fact that its *opponent* – in this case the State with which it is at war – had begun, by means of one or more of its organs, to commit acts contrary to International Law.[975]

Reprisals, therefore, consist only of retaliatory acts taken as a reaction to antecedent breaches of the *jus in bello* by the enemy State. When a saboteur perpetrates a security offence, his action is not necessarily imputable to any Belligerent Party. Counter-measures against him may not then be subsumed under the heading of reprisals.[976]

VI. Deportations and Transfer

A. *Voluntary Departure, Deportation and Relocation*

486. If a person present in an occupied territory wishes to leave the area voluntarily, and the Occupying Power is prepared to let him go, there is obviously nothing to preclude such a move. Under Article 48 of Geneva Convention (IV):

Protected persons who are not nationals of the Power whose territory is occupied, may avail themselves of a right to leave the territory subject to the provisions of Article 35, and decisions thereon shall be taken according to the procedure which the Occupying Power shall establish in accordance with the said Article.[977]

It is principally nationals of neutral countries who can capitalize on this clause. However, as Article 48 itself stipulates, the text is subject to Article 35, which introduces (in its first paragraph) the proviso that departure from the territory may be prevented if it is 'contrary to the national interests of the State' (in this case, the Occupying Power).[978] The phrase 'national interests' is broader than security considerations and covers also economic reasons (such as obviating a manpower shortage that may be a major handicap in wartime).[979]

487. So much for voluntary departure. The central issue, of course, is that of non-voluntary expulsion of protected persons from an occupied territory. The topic is governed by Article 49 (first paragraph) of the Geneva Convention:

[975] *Rauter* trial, *supra* note 942, at 132. Emphasis in the original.
[976] The term 'quasi-reprisals' has been offered for dealing with such situations in occupied territories. F. Kalshoven, *Belligerent Reprisals* 38 (1971).
[977] Geneva Convention (IV), *supra* note 29, at 594.
[978] *Ibid.*, 590.
[979] *Commentary, IV Geneva Convention*, *supra* note 31, at 236.

Individual or mass forcible transfers, as well as deportations of protected persons from occupied territory to the territory of the Occupying Power or to that of any other country, occupied or not, are prohibited, regardless of their motive.[980]

It is striking that security considerations – playing a meaningful role under the second paragraph of Article 49 (quoted *infra* 512) with respect to evacuation – are erased from the canvas of the first paragraph. The words 'regardless of their motive' are important, since they imply that even the most compelling security considerations cannot vindicate the deportation of a protected person from an occupied territory (although such considerations may justify some other rigorous measures, e.g., internment; see *infra* 519).

488. Unlawful deportations or transfer (of protected persons) constitute a grave breach of the Convention in accordance with Article 147[981] and Article 85(4)(a) of Additional Protocol I.[982] The Rome Statute of the International Criminal Court brands deportations and transfers twice as war crimes: both in Article 8(2)(a)(vii) and in Article 8(2)(b)(viii).[983]

489. What is the difference between deportation and transfer? The case law of the ICTY has quite consistently[984] adhered to the view that – in the words of a Trial Chamber in the *Krnojelac* case of 2002 – '[d]eportation requires the displacement of persons across a national border, to be distinguished from forcible transfer which may take place within national boundaries'.[985] The last few words indicate that an unlawful transfer (unlike a deportation) may also dislocate people from one place to another within an occupied territory. This approach is strengthened by Article 8(2)(b)(viii) of the Rome Statute, which refers to the 'deportation or transfer of all or parts of the population of the occupied territory within or outside this territory':[986] the preposition 'within' should be highlighted. In an even more transparent fashion, the Elements of Crime attached to Article 8(2)(a)(vii) of the Rome Statute advert to deportation or transfer 'to another State or to another location'.[987] The binary formula denotes that an unlawful transfer to 'another location' (differentiated from 'another State') may take place within an occupied territory.[988] It must be observed, however, that in the Geneva vocabulary a relocation within an

[980] Geneva Convention (IV), *supra* note 29, at 594.
[981] *Ibid.*, 624.
[982] Additional Protocol I, *supra* note 33, at 754.
[983] Rome Statute of the International Criminal Court, *supra* note 350, at 1317–18.
[984] See, e.g., *Prosecutor v. Krstić* (ICTY, Trial Chamber, 2001), para. 521; *Prosecutor v. Simić* et al. (ICTY, Trial Chamber, 2003), para. 122.
[985] *Prosecutor v. Krnojelac* (ICTY, Trial Chamber, 2002), para. 474.
[986] Rome Statute of the International Criminal Court, *supra* note 350, at 1318.
[987] Dörmann, *supra* note 355, at 106.
[988] See *ibid.*

occupied territory is actually pigeonholed as either evacuation (see *infra* 512) or assigned residence (see *infra* 532).

B. *The Israeli Practice*

490. Deportations from occupied territories – as a security measure – became a *cause célèbre* as a result of an unabashed Israeli policy, discontinued in principle only in 1993. In some instances, these deportations were carried out *ab initio* on a temporary basis. On other occasions, the authorities ultimately reneged and the deportees were permitted to return. But, whatever the time frame, the fact is that protected persons were deported from the occupied territories.

491. The Israeli deportations were based on powers originally vested in the High Commissioner of British Mandatory Palestine, in Section 112 of the Defence (Emergency) Regulations enacted in 1945.[989] Section 112 remained in force in all parts of Palestine at the point of termination of the British Mandate (1948). In Israel, the Section was repealed only in 1979, under the Emergency Powers (Detention) Law.[990] As for the occupied territories, it is necessary to distinguish between the West Bank and the Gaza Strip. In the Gaza Strip, there is no question that Section 112 was left intact when Egypt took over in 1948, although an argument has been presented that the Section was abrogated implicitly by the Egyptians at a later stage (either in 1955 or in 1962).[991] The Israel Supreme Court (per Justice Goldberg) rejected this contention, in the *Maslam* case, pronouncing that – in the absence of an express repeal – Section 112 remained in force in Gaza until 1967 (the time of the Israeli occupation) and thereafter.[992] As regards the West Bank, the Court (per President Sussman) initially took a similar position in the *Abu Awad* case.[993] But, since the Jordanian Constitution of 1952 declares that '[n]o Jordanian shall be exiled from the territory of the Kingdom', the majority of the Court (President Landau and Justice Kahan) – in the second *Kawasme* case – preferred to rely on an Order issued by the Israeli military government, whereby the Emergency Regulations which had been in force at the termination of the British Mandate were reinstated.[994]

[989] Defence (Emergency) Regulations, 1945, [1945] *PG* (No. 1442), Supp. No. 2, 1055, 1085.

[990] Emergency Powers (Detention) Law, 1979, 33 *LSI* 89, 92 (1978–9).

[991] See HCJ 1361/91 etc., *Maslam* et al. *v. IDF Commander of the Gaza Strip*, 45(3) *PD* 444, 455–6. (The Judgment is excerpted in English in 23 *IYHR* 342 (1993)).

[992] *Ibid.*

[993] HCJ 97/79, *Abu Awad v. Commander of Judea and Samaria*, 33(3) *PD* 309, 314–15. (The Judgment is excerpted in English in 9 *IYHR* 343 (1979)).

[994] HCJ 698/80, *Kawasme* et al. *v. Minister of Defence* et al., 35(1) *PD* 617, 623–6, 647. (The Judgment is excerpted in English in 11 *IYHR* 349 (1981)).

The same path was followed by the Court (per President Shamgar) in the *W. Nazal* case.[995]

492. In the *Abu Awad* case, President Sussman had already averred that the application of Section 112 is not incompatible with Article 49 (first paragraph) of the Geneva Convention.[996] The Judgment explained that the purpose of the Geneva provision was to prevent a repetition of the hideous atrocities perpetrated by the Nazis in WWII – in the course of which millions of people were deported as part of an extermination scheme or a slave labour programme, condemning them to annihilation or to immense suffering in concentration camps – and, therefore, the prohibition had nothing to do with the specific deportations under review.[997] This reasoning was endorsed by a majority of the Court in the second *Kawasme* case, which accentuated that – whatever the correct reading of Article 49 (first paragraph) – the Convention is constitutive in character and therefore it is not part of the domestic law of Israel (see *supra* 89–90).[998]

493. The main decision on deportations was rendered by a special panel of five Justices in the *Afu* case, where the Court was split 4:1. The majority (per President Shamgar) reinforced the earlier judicial opinions in minute detail, restricting the range of application of Article 49 (first paragraph) to Nazi-style mass deportations, in contradistinction to ordinary individual deportations (the subject of the proceedings).[999] The sole dissenter (Justice Bach) insisted on the need to construe Article 49 (first paragraph) as an unbridled prohibition of all deportations, regardless of their character and circumstances.[1000]

494. An analysis of the Israeli case law on this topic requires a careful dissection of several sub-questions, commencing with the attempt to differentiate between individual and mass deportations.

C. Individual versus Mass Deportations

495. Evidently, Article 49 (first paragraph) – like other provisions of the Geneva Conventions – was formulated in 1949 under the shadow cast by the bitter experience of WWII and the barbarous behaviour of the Nazis.[1001] Nevertheless, the outlook of the Conventions – including Article 49 (first paragraph) – is prospective and not retrospective. Article 49 (first paragraph) was

[995] HCJ 513/85 etc., *W. Nazal* et al. *v. IDF Commander of Judea and Samaria*, 39(3) *PD* 645, 649–52. (The Judgment is excerpted in English in 16 *IYHR* 329 (1986)).

[996] HCJ 97/79, *supra* note 993, at 316.

[997] *Ibid.*

[998] HCJ 698/80, *supra* note 994, at 627.

[999] HCJ 785/87 etc., *supra* note 176, at 24–33, 66–7.

[1000] *Ibid.*, 68–76.

[1001] See, especially, *Commentary, IV Geneva Convention, supra* note 31, at 278–9.

plainly designed to ensure that, in future, any deportation of protected persons from occupied territories would be unlawful.

496. The ordinary mode of deportation, as perceived also in Section 112 of the Defence (Emergency) Regulations, is individual. Surely, if Article 49 (first paragraph) was intended to exclude this elementary form of deportation from the scope of the Geneva prohibition, the text would have said so explicitly. As a matter of fact, the language chosen conveys the opposite. The two adjectives '[i]ndividual or mass', opening the text of Article 49 (first paragraph), are linked not only to the immediately following phrase 'forcible transfers' but also to 'deportations' (appearing after the conjunctive 'as well as'). Had it not been for the interjection of the words 'forcible transfers, as well as' between '[i]ndividual or mass' and 'deportations' in the text, it is hard to imagine that anyone would have hesitated in fathoming the noun 'deportations' as encompassing both individual and mass expulsions.

497. In conformity with the ordinary meaning of the words of Article 49 (first paragraph) in their context, every deportation of a protected person from an occupied territory is proscribed, regardless of the individual or collective nature of the act or its motive. In order to evade the ordinary meaning of the words, President Shamgar enlarged upon the need to factor in the object and purpose of the treaty.[1002] What he actually proceeded to do was search for an original intent that he ascribed to the authors of the instrument, whereby solely mass deportations were allegedly in their minds. However, even had they been animated by such an intent (and there is no evidence whatever that such was the case), this is not articulated in the text.

498. President Shamgar's reading of Article 49, to quote Meron, is 'contrary to the rules of treaty-interpretation stated in the Vienna Convention on the Law of Treaties'.[1003] President Shamgar completely ignored the textual approach to the interpretation of treaties, which won the day in the Vienna Conference of 1969.[1004] While citing Articles 31 and 32 of the Vienna Convention,[1005] President Shamgar actually believed that he was not bound by a literal and 'simplistic' meaning of the language employed in a treaty.[1006] He failed to notice that, in international law, 'the cardinal rule for any interpretation' is the 'primacy of the text', and it is therefore necessary to submit to 'the *expression* of the parties' intention'.[1007]

[1002] HCJ 785/87 etc., *supra* note 176, at 32–3.
[1003] Meron, *supra* note 436, at 49.
[1004] See R.D. Kearney and R.E. Dalton, 'The Treaty on Treaties', 64 *AJIL* 495, 519–20 (1970).
[1005] Vienna Convention on the Law of Treaties, *supra* note 706, at 149.
[1006] HCJ 785/87 etc., *supra* note 176, at 32–3.
[1007] P. Reuter, *Introduction to the Law of Treaties* 74–5 (1989). Emphasis in the original.

499. President Shamgar surveyed the international legal literature, seeking authorities that corroborate his position. There is admittedly one commentator who has been receptive to the idea that 'the sweeping literal words of Article 49' should be limited to 'situations at least remotely similar to those contemplated by the draftsmen, namely the Nazi World War II practices'.[1008] But, generally speaking, scholars dealing with Article 49 either refer to an 'absolute prohibition' of deportations[1009] or say that deportations are 'strictly prohibited'.[1010] In Resolution 607 (1988), the Security Council called upon Israel 'to refrain from deporting any Palestinian civilians from the occupied territories'.[1011] The (non-binding) call was repeated several times.[1012]

500. Fortunately, one member of the Court's panel in the *Afu* case – Justice Bach – did not share the legal misconceptions of the majority. In his dissenting opinion, Justice Bach animadverted on the Court's Judgment:

> The language of Article 49 is unequivocal and plain. [The text] leaves … no room for doubt that the Article applies not only to mass deportation but also to deportation of individuals, and that the prohibition is designed to be total, sweeping and unqualified – 'regardless of their motive'.[1013]

501. The artificiality of the distinction between individual and mass deportations came to the fore in a dramatic fashion in the setting of the Court's (politically) most celebrated and (legally) most disappointing decision, delivered unanimously by a special panel of seven Justices (*per curiam*) in the *Hamas and Islamic Jihad Deportations* case.[1014] The proceedings related to the deportation in December 1992 (following a wave of assassinations and other crimes) of no less than 415 persons active in the two Moslem fundamentalist organizations deemed responsible. While the deportation orders were confined to a prescribed period (18 to 24 months), their mass dimension appears to be incontestable. Not only were the deportation orders issued simultaneously, but they included several persons who were erroneously expelled and subsequently allowed to return. Yet, the Court declined to invalidate the deportation

[1008] Stone, *supra* note 703, at 17.

[1009] See, for example, J.L. Kunz, 'The Geneva Conventions of August 12, 1949', *Law and Politics in the World Community* 279, 302 (G.A. Lipsky ed., 1953).

[1010] See, by way of illustration, J.S. Pictet, 'The New Geneva Conventions for the Protection of War Victims', 45 *AJIL* 462, 474 (1951).

[1011] Security Council Resolution 607 (1988), *Resolutions and Statements of the United Nations Security Council, supra* note 60, at 729, *id.*

[1012] See Security Council Resolutions 608 (1988), 636 (1989), 641 (1989), 694 (1991), 726 (1992), *Resolutions and Statements of the United Nations Security Council, supra* note 60, at 729–30, 733–4.

[1013] HCJ 785/87 etc., *supra* note 176, at 70.

[1014] HCJ 5973/92 etc., *Association for Civil Rights in Israel* et al. *v. Minister of Defence* et al., 47(1) *PD* 267. (The Judgment is excerpted in English in 23 *IYHR* 353 (1993)).

orders, closing its eyes to their exceptional scale. In a quite perfunctory way, the Judgment stuck to the fiction that the case concerned a large cluster of individual deportations.[1015] The failure by the Court to seriously compartmentalize mass and individual deportations shows that it did not attach much significance to this dichotomy per se. The real faultline lay elsewhere: whereas Nazi-style deportations (with the end result of extermination or slave labour) were utterly repudiated, the Court was prepared to tolerate mere banishment not detrimental to the life or health of the expellees. Whatever the logic of this position *in abstracto*, accepting it would unstitch the fabric of the text of Article 49 (first paragraph).[1016]

D. *'Exclusion' versus Deportation*

502. In striving to show that a rendering of Article 49 (first paragraph) as an all-inclusive prohibition of deportations would be unreasonable, President Shamgar raised the spectre of protection afforded to infiltrators and spies.[1017] Actually, infiltrators and spies cannot be treated interchangeably. The fate of spies is determined by the definition of protected persons in Article 4 (first paragraph) of the Geneva Convention (quoted *supra* 72). As pointed out by the ICRC Commentary, the protection of the Convention is spread over spies (as well as saboteurs) in occupied territories.[1018] This is attested by the fact that Article 5 (second paragraph) (quoted *supra* 206) permits only denial of 'rights of communication' to 'a spy or saboteur'.

503. Infiltrators pose a separate problem. It is necessary to sort persons who arrive lawfully in an occupied territory (after the occupation has begun) from those who do not. Those who do (e.g., tourists) are not different from other protected persons (see *supra* 204). However, this is not true of infiltrators who gain entrance into an occupied territory unlawfully.

504. No provision in the Geneva Convention bars the 'exclusion'[1019] – as distinct from deportation – of infiltrators who have entered an occupied territory unlawfully. There is no resemblance between an infiltrator and a tourist (who enters the territory by permission). As President Shamgar emphasized already in the *Kasarawi* case, whatever the ken of Article 49 (first paragraph),

[1015] *Ibid.*, 281.

[1016] See B. Dayanim, 'The Israeli Supreme Court and the Deportations of Palestinians: The Interaction of Law and Legitimacy', 30 *SJIL* 115, 157–65 (1994).

[1017] HCJ 785/87 etc., *supra* note 176, at 32.

[1018] *Commentary, IV Geneva Convention*, *supra* note 31, at 47.

[1019] On the conceptual distinction between exclusion and deportation (in a peacetime context), see I.A. Shearer, *Extradition in International Law* 76 (1971).

it has never been suggested that infiltrators come within its fold.[1020] Infiltrators are simply not shielded by the Convention as protected persons. Their non-entitlement to protection is of particular significance in the context of an occupied territory like Iraq, where the ranks of local saboteurs were swollen by foreigners who had infiltrated Iraq unlawfully in order to take part in a *jihad* against infidel Occupying Powers.

505. Even insofar as a tourist is concerned, if his permit of stay in an occupied territory expires after a time limit – and he declines to leave – the Occupying Power may compel him to do so. In the *El-Tin* case, the Supreme Court (per Justice M. Etzioni) rightly pronounced that – when a person is allowed to enter an occupied territory for a finite period – exclusion upon expiration of that period does not constitute a deportation, and neither Article 4 (first paragraph) nor Article 49 (first paragraph) of the Convention applies.[1021]

E. The State of Nationality versus Other Countries

506. For the most part, deportations from the territories occupied by Israel were carried out into Lebanon. But what would have happened if inhabitants of the West Bank – possessing Jordanian nationality – had been expelled into the (unoccupied) East Bank? In the *Abu Awad* case, the Court posed a question to counsel for the petitioner, whether he would prefer to be expelled to Jordan (the country of nationality) instead of Lebanon, but the response was negative.[1022] Then the Court was seized with a petition by the mayors of Hebron and Halhul, both Jordanian nationals who had been deported to Lebanon and moved from there to Jordan. Since the deportation took place without first enabling the two mayors to have the decision reviewed by an Advisory Committee (as provided by Section 112), the majority of the Court (President Landau and Justice Kahan), in the first *Kawasme* case, allowed the deportees to return in order to appear before the Committee (Deputy President H. Cohn dissented, inasmuch as he would have preferred to quash the deportation altogether).[1023] The two mayors were consequently allowed to cross the Jordan River: they appeared before the Advisory Committee, which, however, gave its seal of approval to the deportation. The petition was revisited

[1020] HCJ 454/85 etc., *Kasarawi* et al. *v. Minister of Defence* et al., 39(3) *PD* 401, 410. (The Judgment is excerpted in English in 16 *IYHR* 332 (1986)).

[1021] HCJ 500/72, *El-Tin v. Minister of Defence* et al., 27(1) *PD* 481, 486. (The Judgment is excerpted in English in 5 *IYHR* 376 (1975)).

[1022] HCJ 97/79, *supra* note 993, at 315.

[1023] HCJ 320/80, *Kawasme* et al. *v. Minister of Defence* et al., 35(3) *PD* 113, 124–5, 132, 136–7. (The Judgment is excerpted in English in 11 *IYHR* 344 (1981)).

by the same three Justices of the Supreme Court in the second *Kawasme* case, and the result was an identical split of 2:1.[1024] An interesting exchange took place here between Justice Kahan (of the majority) and Deputy President Cohn (the dissenter). Deputy President Cohn floated the peculiar idea that, for purposes of deportation, the occupied West Bank and the rest of the Kingdom of Jordan should be deemed to be separate States.[1025] Justice Kahan (speaking for the majority) contradicted him, suggesting that – since the petitioners were Jordanian nationals – had they been expelled to the East Bank, Jordan would have had no choice but to admit them within its boundaries.[1026] The issue, in any event, was moot.

507. The exchange between Deputy President Cohn and Justice Kahan glossed over the text of Article 49 (first paragraph) of the Geneva Convention, which is the fulcrum of the ban on deportations from occupied territories. Article 49 (first paragraph) covers only deportations of protected persons 'from occupied territory to the territory of the Occupying Power' (e.g., from the West Bank into Israel) 'or to that of any other country, occupied or not'. The latter phrase covers a neighbouring country (like Lebanon) as much as distant lands. But does it cover Jordan when that is the State of nationality and the displaced sovereign? Surely, Jordan is not 'any other country' in the context of the law belligerent occupation, and Deputy President Cohn went astray when he suggested that the West Bank and the East Bank may be considered separate States because of the occupation. As long as Jordan was the displaced sovereign (see *supra* 51–2), an expulsion of protected persons of Jordanian nationality from the West Bank to the (unoccupied) East Bank could not be typecast as a deportation forbidden by Article 49 (first paragraph). This legal proposition, originally advanced by Shamgar in a published essay (at a time when he served as Attorney General),[1027] was reiterated by him as President of the Court in the *W. Nazal* case.[1028]

508. Admittedly, if one follows the trail blazed by the ICTY and the Rome Statute of the International Criminal Court (especially the Elements of Crime; see *supra* 489) – whereby any forcible relocation within an occupied territory constitutes an unlawful transfer – the conclusion to be reached, with even more convincing force, is that no such relocation can take place from an occupied territory into the unoccupied land of the displaced sovereign.

[1024] HCJ 698/80, *supra* note 994, at 635, 649.

[1025] *Ibid.*, 646. For an analysis of Deputy President Cohn's views in this case, see Y. Dinstein, 'The Israel Supreme Court and the Law of Belligerent Occupation: Deportations', 23 *IYHR* 1, 3–12 (1993).

[1026] HCJ 698/80, *supra* note 994, at 649.

[1027] Shamgar, *supra* note 141, at 274.

[1028] HCJ 513/85 etc., *supra* note 995, at 654.

F. *Occupying versus Occupied Territory*

509. In the *Ketziot* case, the Supreme Court was faced with a new aspect of the application of Article 49 (first paragraph): internment of large numbers of inhabitants of the West Bank and the Gaza Strip in a facility located within Israel proper (outside the occupied territories), as a direct result of the first *intifada*.[1029] The petitioners[1030] propped up their application by citing the ICRC Commentary, which states that protected persons subject to internment under Article 78 (first paragraph) of the Geneva Convention (see *infra* 519) enjoy the benefits of Article 49 (first paragraph): 'they can therefore only be interned ... within the frontiers of the occupied country itself'.[1031] The majority of the Court (per President Shamgar) was unwilling to reexamine Article 49 (first paragraph) and simply relied on the decision in the *Afu* case, but it also disagreed with the Commentary's construction of the Convention.[1032]

510. The petitioners drew an analogy from Article 76 (first paragraph) of the Convention – dealing with protected persons accused or convicted of crimes (i.e. not those who are interned) – which enjoins that they be detained 'in the occupied country'.[1033] President Shamgar rejected the analogy, finding sustenance in an *argumentum a contrario*: Article 79 of the Convention says that '[t]he Parties to the conflict shall not intern protected persons, except in accordance with the provisions of Articles 41, 42, 43, 68 and 78',[1034] thus citing Article 78 but omitting Article 76.[1035]

511. Justice Bach dissented again, pointing out that the comprehensive prohibition of deportations of protected persons under Article 49 (first paragraph) does not differentiate between the territory of the Occupying Power and that of any other country.[1036] To his mind, the fact that the deportation in the *Ketziot* proceedings was for the purpose of internment did not reshuffle the cards: indeed, if protected persons convicted of criminal offences must be detained in the occupied territory – as required by Article 76 (first paragraph) of the Convention – the same rule should apply *a fortiori* in case of those subject to mere internment (since internees are not brought to trial before a competent court).[1037] In the opinion of the present writer, once more, Justice

[1029] HCJ 253/88 etc., *Sajdia* et al. *v. Minister of Defence*, 42(3) *PD* 801. (The Judgment is excerpted in English in 23 *IYHR* 288 (1993)).

[1030] For the arguments of the petitioners, see *ibid.*, 806–7.

[1031] *Commentary, IV Geneva Convention*, *supra* note 31, at 368.

[1032] HCJ 253/88 etc., *supra* note 1029, at 811–12.

[1033] Geneva Convention (IV), *supra* note 29, at 602.

[1034] *Ibid.*, 603.

[1035] HCJ 253/88 etc., *supra* note 1029, at 812.

[1036] *Ibid.*, 826.

[1037] *Ibid.*, 829.

Bach's interpretation of Article 49 was accurate and unimpeachable. The view that the scope of Article 78 is 'delimited' by Article 49 is supported also by scholars.[1038]

VII. Evacuation

512. Article 49 of Geneva Convention (IV) distinguishes between deportation (the subject of the first paragraph) and evacuation, which is brought up in the second paragraph:

> Nevertheless, the Occupying Power may undertake total or partial evacuation of a given area if the security of the population or imperative military reasons so demand. Such evacuation may not involve the displacement of protected persons outside the bounds of the occupied territory except when for material reasons it is impossible to avoid such displacement. Persons thus evacuated shall be transferred back to their homes as soon as hostilities in the area in question have ceased.[1039]

513. Evacuation is linked to a specific geographic region from which it is undertaken. Generally speaking, evacuation must be carried out – from one area to another – within the bounds of the occupied territory. But, if there are unavoidable 'material reasons', the evacuees (the entire community living in the area or only a fraction of it) may be relocated temporarily outside that territory.

514. What unavoidable 'material reasons' justify evacuation outside the bounds of the occupied territory? The Eritrea Ethiopia Claims Commission – citing Article 49 – expressly dismissed, in 2004, an Ethiopian objection to the evacuation into Eritrean territory of the inhabitants of an occupied territory in Ethiopia who were at risk because of Ethiopian artillery fire.[1040] There is little room for doubt that, when hostilities are raging, a valid reason exists for the evacuation of the civilian population from a combat zone.

515. Safeguarding the inhabitants of occupied territories from the hazards of fighting, which threatens to engulf them, is not the only admissible reason for their temporary evacuation into the territory of the Occupying Power. Another valid ground is a military need for the Occupying Power to deploy its armed forces, due to a military necessity, without having to worry about civilians clogging the roads and being in the way. Evacuation may usually be based by the Occupying Power on a combination of both motives: protective and military. Still, absent either one of them, evacuation will be considered an unlawful banishment of protected persons from their homes.[1041]

[1038] See L.M. Olson, 'Admissibility of and Procedure for Internment', *The 1949 Geneva Conventions: A Commentary*, *supra* note 309, at 1327, 1334.

[1039] Geneva Convention (IV), *supra* note 29, at 594.

[1040] Eritrea Ethiopia Claims Commission, Partial Award (Central Front), *supra* note 65, at 1289.

[1041] See *Prosecutor v. Krstić*, *supra* note 984, at para. 527.

516. The argument of military necessity in this context may be stretched further. In the *Pithat Rafiah Case*, the Israel Supreme Court denied a petition challenging evacuation of nomadic Bedouins from an area lying between the Sinai Peninsula and the Gaza Strip (with the Occupying Power paying compensation for the compulsory move), in order to create a closed security buffer zone between the two regions.[1042] Assertions have also been made in the legal literature that an Occupying Power is allowed to relocate to safe hamlets villagers living in guerrilla-infested districts, demolishing their original abodes so as to preclude the use of the structures as shelters for enemy combatants planning attacks.[1043]

517. Under Article 49 (third paragraph), the Occupying Power must see to it that evacuation is carried out in satisfactory conditions of safety, health, nutrition and accommodation.[1044] Evacuation as such does not entail internment (see *infra* 519). Most significantly, the dislocation of civilians has to be temporary in nature:[1045] once the underlying causes of the evacuation melt away, the evacuees must be allowed to return to their homes. The precise duration of the evacuation has to be determined by the circumstances prevailing at the time.

518. Article 78(1) of Additional Protocol I provides for a possible temporary evacuation of children to a foreign country; but in occupied territories this is permitted only for compelling reasons of health or medical treatment, and not for reasons of safety.[1046] The text gives vent to a 'deep-seated concern' for the contingency of abuse by the Occupying Power of the discretion granted to it in the matter.[1047] However, Article 78(1) merely applies to temporary evacuation of children as such (individually or in groups): it does not prevent a temporary evacuation of entire families – accompanied by children – for reasons of security (in keeping with Article 49 (second paragraph) of the Geneva Convention).[1048]

VIII. Internment (Administrative Detention)

A. *Internment as a Safety Measure*

519. Under Article 78 (first paragraph) of Geneva Convention (IV):

If the Occupying Power considers it necessary, for imperative reasons of security, to take safety measures concerning protected persons, it may, at the most, subject them to assigned residence or to internment.[1049]

[1042] See HCJ 302/72, *supra* note 165, at 184.
[1043] See Greenspan, *supra* note 956, at 391.
[1044] Geneva Convention (IV), *supra* note 29, at 594.
[1045] See Dörmann, *supra* note 355, at 213.
[1046] Additional Protocol I, *supra* note 33, at 751.
[1047] C. Pilloud and J. Pictet, 'Article 78', *Commentary on the Additional Protocols, supra* note 327, at 907, 912.
[1048] See W.A. Solf, 'Article 78', *New Rules for Victims of Armed Conflicts, supra* note 400, at 538, 542.
[1049] Geneva Convention (IV), *supra* note 29, at 602–3.

We shall deal here with internment (assigned residence will be addressed *infra* 532 *et seq.*).

520. To begin with, two remarks are called for regarding the key words 'imperative reasons of security':

(a) The purport of the adjective 'imperative' – appearing also in other settings, e.g., Article 49 (second paragraph) (quoted *supra* 512) with respect to evacuation – is not translucent, especially when compared to other adjectives, such as 'absolute' or 'urgent', which are common in the Hague Regulations and in the Geneva Convention (cf. *infra* 599). This point was stressed by the Israel Supreme Court (per Justice Shamgar) in the *Ben Zion* case.[1050]

(b) As observed by the UK Supreme Court, in the *Al-Waheed* Judgment of 2017, the expression 'reasons of security' is broader than 'the security of the Detaining Power'[1051] (a phrase appearing in Article 42 (first paragraph) of the Geneva Convention, in connection with the internment of protected persons in non-occupied territories[1052]). Thus, the Occupying Power may be motivated by reasons concerning the overall security of the civilian population in the occupied territories. Indeed, according to the UK Supreme Court, 'internment in an occupied territory may be necessary for the security of those interned'.[1053]

521. In the *Al-Jedda* case of 2011, the Grand Chamber of the European Court of Human Rights commented that 'it would appear from the provisions of the Fourth Geneva Convention that under international humanitarian law internment is to be viewed not as an obligation on the Occupying Power but as a measure of last resort'.[1054] Of course, the Occupying Power is not obligated in Article 78 (first paragraph) – but only authorized – to resort to internment as a security measure. The reference to 'last resort' is somewhat imprecise in this connection: what the text of the Convention conveys is that internment is the most severe administrative measure short of a criminal trial.[1055]

522. As explained in the Preface to this book, we shall not delve into conditions of internment, but *vide supra* 509–11 about incarceration outside the occupied territory. It should also be observed that, under Article 81 (third paragraph) of the Geneva Convention, if detainees have dependents who are

[1050] HCJ 369/79, *Ben Zion v. IDF Commander of Judea and Samaria* et al., 34(1) *PD* 145, 150–1. (The Judgment is excerpted in English in 10 *IYHR* 342 (1980)).

[1051] *Al-Waheed* et al. v. *Ministry of Defence* (UK Supreme Court, 2017), para. 58 (Lord Sumption).

[1052] Geneva Convention (IV), *supra* note 29, at 592.

[1053] *Al-Waheed* et al. v. *Ministry of Defence*, *supra* note 1051, at para. 58.

[1054] *Al-Jedda v. United Kingdom* (European Court of Human Rights, Grand Chamber, 2011), 50 *ILM* 950, 991 (2011).

[1055] See Pejic, *supra* note 562, at 847–9.

without adequate means of support or are unable to earn a living, the Occupying Power must provide for them.[1056]

B. *The Difference between Internment and Imprisonment*

523. Internment in conformity with Article 78 (first paragraph) must be set apart from a sentence of imprisonment imposed by a competent court on a person convicted after a fair trial. The essence of internment under Article 78 (first paragraph) is that it is an administrative measure of a preventive rather than punitive nature. In the *L. Salame* case, the Israel Supreme Court (per President Barak) said that (i) if prosecution of a person for his actions is feasible, it has to be preferred to administrative detention, one reason being that in judicial proceedings the accused can address the evidence (which is often withheld from him in the process of internment); (ii) however, a penal prosecution is not always possible, due to the need to protect intelligence sources; (iii) it must not be forgotten that penal proceedings and administrative detention operate on different levels:

> The point of departure is that administrative detention is designed to thwart a future danger to the security of the State or public safety. Administrative detention is not a punitive measure for what has happened in the past nor is it a substitute for criminal proceedings.[1057]

All the same, the Court (per Justice A. Grunis) stressed in the *Federman* case – concerning a settler administratively detained under Israeli legislation – that a prognosis regarding the future may be predicated on past activities.[1058] Justice Grunis added that speculations about prospective behaviour must be based on probable cause rather than on a mere possibility of an indeterminate security risk.[1059]

524. In revoking an extension of a detention order, the Court (per Justice Zamir) – in the *Al Amla* case – commented that the deprivation of liberty through internment is a particularly harsh measure, since (i) the decision to detain is taken not by a court of law but by an administrative body; (ii) the decision is often based on classified material, as distinct from overt evidence that can be challenged; and (iii) the internment is not restricted in time (although it is subject to periodic review) so that a person may languish in detention indefinitely.[1060] No wonder that Article 78 (first paragraph) underscores that this is

[1056] Geneva Convention (IV), *supra* note 29, at 603.

[1057] HCJ 5784/03 etc., *L. Salame* et al. *v. IDF Commander of Judea and Samaria* et al., 57(6) *PD* 721, 726. (The Judgment is excerpted in English in 36 *IYHR* 289 (2006)).

[1058] ADA 8788/03, *Federman v. Minister of Defence,* 58(1) *PD* 176, 185.

[1059] *Ibid.*, 188.

[1060] HCJ 2320/98, *Al Amla* et al. *v. IDF Commander of Judea and Samaria* et al., 52(3) *PD* 346, 349. (The Judgment is excerpted in English in 32 *IYHR* 341 (2002)).

the administrative measure that can be taken by the Occupying Power 'at the most' (short of a criminal trial) against a protected person.

525. In the *Mar'ab* case, the Court (per President Barak) stated that a justification for internment must be individual, and that mass internment is prohibited (although it is possible that a number of persons will be detained simultaneously, each on his individual account).[1061] President Barak was emphatic that there were only two lawful types of detention (any other type being arbitrary and unlawful): (i) detention for the purpose of interrogation on suspicion of having committed criminal activities, prefatory to penal prosecution for an offence against the security legislation; and (ii) (administrative) internment pursuant to Article 78.[1062] Of course, speaking empirically, the two lawful types of detention are not hermetically sealed from each other. Detention may initially be undertaken with penal prosecution in mind, yet – upon further reflection – the military government may switch gears and (instead of either charging the suspect or releasing him) opt to have recourse to internment consistent with Article 78.

C. Appeal and Periodic Review

526. It cannot be contradicted that, under Article 78 (first paragraph) of the Geneva Convention, '[t]he decision whether an internment is justified "by imperative reasons of security" rests with the occupying power itself'.[1063] Still, the Occupying Power is required by Article 78 (second paragraph) to establish a regular procedure including the right of appeal (with the least possible delay), as well as a 'periodical review, if possible every six months, by a competent body' (to be set up by the Occupying Power).[1064] '[U]nlawful confinement of a protected person' constitutes a grave breach of the Convention pursuant to Article 147.[1065] As such, Article 8(2)(a)(vii) of the Rome Statute of the International Criminal Court brands it as a war crime.[1066]

527. The ICTY Trial Chamber stated in the *Delalić* case – admittedly in an *obiter dictum* (since the case did not relate to an occupied territory) – that the right of appeal and periodic review are of fundamental importance and, if not respected, an initially lawful internment would be tainted with illegality.[1067]

1061 HCJ 3239/02, *Mar'ab* et al. *v. IDF Commander of Judea and Samaria* et al., 57(2) *PD* 349, 367 (per President Barak). (The Judgment is excerpted in English in 34 *IYHR* 307 (2004)).

1062 *Ibid.*, 365–6.

1063 A. Eide, 'The Laws of War and Human Rights – Differences and Convergences', *Studies and Essays on International Humanitarian Law and Red Cross Principles in Honour of Jean Pictet* 675, 689 (ICRC, C. Swinarski ed., 1984).

1064 Geneva Convention (IV), *supra* note 29, at 603.

1065 *Ibid.*, 624.

1066 Rome Statute of the International Criminal Court, *supra* note 350, at 1317.

1067 *Prosecutor v. Delalić* et al., *supra* note 923, at paras. 578, 582–3.

528. The question is: appeal and periodic review conducted by whom? Article 78 (second paragraph) uses the expression 'competent body', and the procedure is expressly left in the hands of the Occupying Power. In the *Hassan* case of 2014, the Grand Chamber of the European Court of Human Rights conceded that the 'competent body' mentioned in Article 78 need not be a 'court' – in the usual sense – but (to pass muster from a human rights perspective) it 'should provide sufficient guarantees of impartiality and fair procedure to protect against arbitrariness'.[1068]

529. The ICRC Commentary argues that the 'competent body' has to be either a 'court' (a judicial organ) or a 'board' (an administrative body), so that the decision will not be made by a single individual.[1069] Hence, when the Israeli military government altered a previous procedure and entrusted the appeal and reviewing authority to one legally qualified judge (in lieu of a three-member board, chaired by a legally qualified judge), the measure was stridently criticized by some commentators.[1070] However, as far as the plain text of Article 78 goes, the criticism is unwarranted. President Shamgar suggested, in the *Ketziot* case, that the legally qualified judge even had a built-in advantage over the previously functioning three-member board in that the sole judge was actually empowered to overrule the order of detention or shorten its duration, whereas the three-member board had a purely advisory capacity.[1071] Indeed, the whole point about the impartial 'competent body' is vesting it with an authority to bring about the release of the internee.[1072]

530. The legal structure, created by the Israeli military government, almost burst at the seams under the hectic pressures of events following the eruption of the second *intifada*. In the *Mar'ab* case, the Court (per President Barak) considered the maximum lapse of time permissible, prior to bringing a detainee before a legally qualified judge. Although Article 78 does not give an answer to the question, President Barak instructed the military government (on the footing of general human rights criteria) that this must be done 'promptly', insisting that a period of twelve or eighteen days is too long.[1073] He showed less concern about delays in enabling the detainee access to counsel, but quashed attempts to hold detainees incommunicado: the Judgment mentioned

[1068] *Hassan v. United Kingdom*, *supra* note 261, at para. 106.
[1069] See *Commentary, IV Geneva Convention*, *supra* note 31, at 369.
[1070] See A.A. Pacheco, 'Occupying an Uprising: The Geneva Law and Israeli Administrative Detention Policy during the First Year of the Palestinian Uprising', 21 *CHRLR* 515, 547 (1989–90).
[1071] HCJ 253/88 etc., *supra* note 1029, at 818.
[1072] See J. Pejic, 'Procedural Principles and Safeguards for Internment/Administrative Detention in Armed Conflict and Other Situations of Violence', 858 *IRRC* 375, 387 (2005).
[1073] HCJ 3239/02, *supra* note 1061, at 371–5.

in particular the right to be visited by the ICRC.[1074] In the *Ouda* case, the Court (per Deputy President M. Elon) underlined that notice of the internment must be promptly given to the family of the detainee and to the ICRC.[1075]

531. In the *Abu Bakr* case, the Court (per Justice Shamgar) determined that – when a periodic review takes place – the onus of persuading the legally qualified judge that the grounds of the internment are still cogent lies on the shoulders of the military government; and the internee is not burdened with a need to show that the circumstances leading to the original internment have changed.[1076] In the *Braham* case, the Court (per Justice Or) also ruled that the legally qualified judge must have access to all the evidence available (including evidence that is inadmissible before a court of law).[1077]

IX. Assigned Residence

532. Assigned residence is explicitly permitted in Article 78 (first paragraph) of the Geneva Convention (quoted *supra* 519), subject to the same conditions as internment (as outlined in Article 78 (second paragraph) cited *ibid.*). Under Article 78 (third paragraph), if – as a result of assigned residence – a protected person is required to leave his home, he 'shall enjoy the full benefit of Article 39'.[1078] Article 39 (second paragraph) stipulates that, should a protected person not be gainfully employed due to measures taken against him by a Party to the conflict, the latter 'shall ensure his support and that of his dependents'.[1079]

533. In the Israeli practice, the issue of assigned residence arose principally in connection with members of families of 'suicide bombers'. In the *Ajuri* case, a special panel of nine Justices of the Supreme Court conceded that the dislocation of a person from his home is a harsh measure, and, in revoking an order of assignment of residence against one of the petitioners, held (per President Barak) that the sanction cannot be used against a member of the family of a 'suicide bomber' (who did not himself pose any threat to security) on the sole ground of deterrence to others.[1080] President Barak said that the military

[1074] *Ibid.*, 378–82. See also HCJ 6302/92, *Rumhia v. Israel Police* et al., 47(1) *PD* 209, 211–13 (per Justice Barak). (The Judgment is excerpted in English in 30 *IYHR* 308 (2000)).

[1075] HCJ 670/89, *Ouda* et al. *v. IDF Commander of Judea and Samaria* et al., 43(4) *PD* 515, 517–20. (The Judgment is excerpted in English in 23 *IYHR* 326 (1993)). See also HCJ 3412/91, *Sufian v. IDF Commander of the Gaza Strip* et al., 47(2) *PD* 843, 853.

[1076] HCJ 466/86, *Abu Bakr v. Judge of the Military Court in Shchem*, 40(3) *PD* 649, 650–1.

[1077] HCJ 4400/98, *Braham v. Legally Qualified Judge* et al., 52(5) *PD* 337, 341–2. (The Judgment is excerpted in English in 32 *IYHR* 345 (2002)).

[1078] Geneva Convention (IV), *supra* note 29, at 603.

[1079] *Ibid.*, 591.

[1080] HCJ 7015/02 etc., *supra* note 173, at 365, 381.

government can only resort to assigned residence for 'imperative reasons of security', construing the phrase as indicative that the person whose freedom is curtailed must himself present a danger to security that the assigned residence is aimed at staving off.[1081]

534. For some reason, President Barak characterized his decision as 'a dynamic interpretative approach' to Article 78, to which he gravitated owing to the new reality of 'suicide bombers'.[1082] The expression 'a dynamic interpretative approach' has been disparaged by some commentators.[1083] Other scholars have expressed admiration for the 'meticulous and courageous way' in which the Court approached its task.[1084] Yet, the conclusions of the Court do not call for any departure from a straightforward interpretation of Article 78.

535. In using the veiled language of 'a dynamic interpretative approach', President Barak may have been thinking of the Judgment's ruling that the West Bank and the Gaza Strip form two parts of a single occupied territory (see *infra* 847), leading to the conclusion that a protected person from one part of the territory (the West Bank) may be assigned residence in the other (the Gaza Strip).[1085] Admittedly, a displacement from the West Bank to the Gaza Strip (two regions detached from each other geographically) strenuously disrupts ordinary life.[1086] But, as long as both regions are combined in a single occupied territory (and this has been a basic tenet with the Palestinians themselves), there is no need to search for 'a dynamic interpretative approach' to Article 78.

536. In the *G. Salame* case, the Court (per Justice E. Hayut) noted the importance of the provision of Article 39 (see *supra* 532) in attenuating the harm done to a protected person whose residence is assigned.[1087] As Justice Hayut saw it, the main dissimilarity between assigned residence and internment is that internment results in total abrogation of freedom of movement, whereas the person whose residence is assigned can still get around within a prescribed area.[1088] The ICRC Commentary, too, rates assigned residence as a less severe measure compared to internment.[1089]

1081 *Ibid.*, 370–5.
1082 *Ibid.*, 382.
1083 See R. Ziegler, 'The 'Assigned Residence' Case: H.C. 7015, 7019/02 *Kipah Ajuri* et al. *v. IDF Commander in the West Bank* et al.', 36 *Is.LR* 179, 194 (2002).
1084 D.F. Vagts, 'Case Note', 97 *AJIL* 173, 175 (2003).
1085 See D. Barak-Erez, 'Assigned Residence in Israel's Administered Territories: The Judicial Review of Security Measures', 33 *IYHR* 303, 312 (2003).
1086 See Kretzmer, *supra* note 171, at 408–9.
1087 HCJ 9586/03 etc., *G. Salame* et al. *v. IDF Commander of Judea and Samaria* et al., 58(2) *PD* 342, 347. (The Judgment is excerpted in English in 37 *IYHR* 329 (2007)).
1088 *Ibid.*
1089 *Commentary, IV Geneva Convention, supra* note 31, at 256.

X. Compulsory Work

537. Hague Regulation 52 (quoted *infra* 699) authorizes the Occupying Power to requisition services from the inhabitants of an occupied territory under certain conditions (mainly, that the services must not involve taking part in military operations against the inhabitants' own country). The outrages of the Nazi slave labour policy in occupied Europe during WWII were held by the International Military Tribunal at Nuremberg to be 'in flagrant violation of the terms' of Regulation 52.[1090] But the Hague provision proved to be too diluted in view of the enormity of what transpired. The law of belligerent occupation was therefore considerably advanced in Geneva Convention (IV).

538. Article 51 (first paragraph) of the Convention (quoted *supra* 178) forbids the Occupying Power to compel civilians in an occupied territory to serve in its armed forces (although voluntary enlistment in such forces is allowed). More significantly, the second, third and fourth paragraphs of Article 51 set ten cumulative conditions that must be met if the Occupying Power wishes to compel protected persons to work: (i) the labourers are over eighteen years of age; (ii) the work is required either for the needs of the army of occupation or 'for the public utility services, or for the feeding, sheltering, clothing, transportation or health of the population of the occupied country'; (iii) the work does not involve participation in military operations; (iv) the labourers do not have to employ force to ensure the security of the installations where they are doing their compulsory work; (v) the labour is carried out exclusively in the occupied territory; (vi) as far as possible, each labourer is kept in his usual place of employment; (vii) the labourers are paid fair wages; (viii) the work is proportionate to the physical and intellectual capabilities of the labourers; (ix) the legislation in the occupied territory concerning working conditions and safeguards (in particular, as regards wages, hours of work and compensation for occupational hazards) remains in force; and (x) the labourers are not mobilized in an organization of a military or semi-military character.[1091]

539. On the whole, Geneva Convention Article 51 – with its ten strictures – goes a long way beyond Hague Regulation 52 in putting brakes on the requisition of services by the Occupying Power. Only in the Geneva text are there references to fair wages, to the actual capabilities of the labourer, and so forth. However, whereas Hague Regulation 52 permits requisition of such services only 'for the necessities of the army of occupation' (*infra* 699), Geneva Article 51 allows also compulsory work 'for the public utility services, or for the feeding, sheltering, clothing, transportation or health of the population of the

[1090] International Military Tribunal (Nuremberg), *supra* note 5, at 239.
[1091] Geneva Convention (IV), *supra* note 29, at 595.

occupied country'. The ICRC Commentary explains that the purpose of this clause is to enable the Occupying Power 'to ensure continuity in industrial production and also in agricultural production and mining'.[1092]

540. The Hague and Geneva stipulations relate to compulsory work. They do not preclude voluntary work for remuneration in the service of the Occupying Power.[1093] For that very reason, Article 52 (second paragraph) of the Geneva Convention forbids measures 'aiming at creating unemployment' in an occupied territory, in order to induce the inhabitants to work for the Occupying Power.[1094]

541. In the context of the occupation of Iraq, the question has been posed whether the Occupying Powers were allowed to create massive unemployment by dissolving all Ba'athist entities.[1095] But the dissolution of these entities – under a Coalition Provisional Authority Order[1096] – was surely not designed to induce those affected to work for the Occupying Powers.[1097] Hence, while the Order could be (and was) challenged on policy grounds,[1098] it was not incompatible with Article 52 (second paragraph).

542. Of course, unemployment may cripple the economy of an occupied territory through no fault of the Occupying Power. In such circumstances, the tables are turned and the question is what the Occupying Power can do to alleviate unemployment by offering those looking for work opportunities to find it. In the Israeli experience, until the outbreak of the first *intifada*, the Government went out of its way to enable scores of thousands of Palestinian labourers from the West Bank and the Gaza Strip – on a purely voluntary basis – to get gainful employment within Israeli farms and towns (at higher wages than those available in the occupied territories).[1099] This proactive policy began to grind to a halt as a result of the first *intifada* and virtually ended in the wake of the second.

[1092] *Commentary, IV Geneva Convention*, *supra* note 31, at 296.
[1093] See US Department of Defense, *Law of War Manual*, *supra* note 1, at 822.
[1094] Geneva Convention (IV), *supra* note 29, at 596.
[1095] See Giacca, *supra* note 701, at 1499.
[1096] Coalition Provisional Authority Order Number 2, II *The Occupation of Iraq: The Official Documents*, *supra* note 78, at 15.
[1097] As conceded by Giacca, *supra* note 701, at 1499.
[1098] H. Zahawi, 'Redefining the Laws of Occupation in the Wake of Operation Iraqi "Freedom"', 95 *Cal.LR* 2295, 2326 (2007).
[1099] See M.S. Perry, 'Worker and Trade Union Rights of Palestinian Arabs from the Occupied Territories', 23 *IYHR* 27, 34–6 (1993).

8 Special Protection in Occupied Territories

543. Special protection in occupied territories is conferred on (i) certain classes of persons, owing to their vulnerability (refugees, women and children); as well as on (ii) certain indispensable services that must be performed for humanitarian purposes (medical services, civil defence and humanitarian relief). Special protection merely adds to – and never detracts from – the ordinary protection enjoyed by the inhabitants of an occupied territory.

I. Refugees

544. Although nationals of the Occupying Power are not protected persons under Geneva Convention (IV) (see *supra* 197), there is a *sui generis* extension of protection in favour of refugees. The Convention tackles this knotty problem in Article 70 (second paragraph):

> Nationals of the Occupying Power who, before the outbreak of hostilities, have sought refuge in the territory of the occupied State, shall not be arrested, prosecuted, convicted or deported from the occupied territory, except for offences committed after the outbreak of hostilities, or for offences under common law committed before the outbreak of hostilities which, according to the law of the occupied State, would have justified extradition in time of peace.[1100]

545. The idea underlying Article 70 (second paragraph) is that the right to asylum, enjoyed by refugees before the outbreak of hostilities, 'must continue to be respected by their home country, when it takes over control as Occupying Power in the territory of the country of asylum'.[1101] The paradigmatic example is that of German Jews who, on the eve of WWII, sought asylum in countries like France or the Netherlands while retaining their German nationality: when the countries of refuge were later overrun by the Nazis, these refugees ought to have continued to benefit from protection.[1102]

[1100] Geneva Convention (IV), *supra* note 29, at 600.
[1101] *Commentary, IV Geneva Convention*, *supra* note 31, at 351.
[1102] See Kunz, *supra* note 1009, at 310.

546. The protection of refugees under Article 70 (second paragraph) is only from arrest, prosecution, conviction and deportation. That is to say, other measures which may be taken by the Occupying Power against refugees (e.g., deprivation of property) are not affected. Even insofar as arrest, prosecution, conviction and deportation are concerned, the protection accorded to refugees is circumscribed in three important respects.

547. First, Article 70 (second paragraph) applies only to refugees who sought asylum in an occupied territory before the start of the war. If a refugee flees from his country of nationality after the outbreak of hostilities – albeit prior to the beginning of the occupation – he does not benefit from the protection.[1103]

548. Secondly, the arrest, prosecution, conviction or deportation of pre-war refugees is permissible if they commit acts of treason against their country of origin during hostilities.[1104] Refugees seeking asylum in a foreign country in peacetime are entitled to a certain degree of political agitation against their country of origin as long as peace reigns.[1105] However, once the two countries plunge into war, refugees must be on their guard: they must abstain from any further activity which may be construed as treasonable against their country of origin. If they persist, Article 70 (second paragraph) will not protect them from that country should it become the Occupying Power.

549. Thirdly, the arrest, prosecution, conviction or deportation of pre-war refugees is permissible for ordinary common law offences, committed before the war, if they are extraditable under the law of the occupied State. This exception is designed to ensure that ordinary fugitives from justice will not benefit from the immunity of genuine refugees. The usual touchstone is the political or non-political aspect of the alleged crime. If a crime committed before the war by a refugee is imbued with a political colour, extradition will normally be excluded under the law of the occupied State, and the refugee will thus be protected from the Occupying Power.[1106] Conversely, if the crime is an ordinary (non-political) crime – and extradition would have been possible in peacetime – the Occupying Power may arrest the refugee, take him back to its own land and prosecute him there.[1107] But the definition of a 'political crime' will be determined under the law in force in the occupied territory, and any procedural safeguards guaranteed by that law will have to be respected.[1108] Moreover, under Article 45 (fourth

1103 See Solf, *supra* note 400, at 504.
1104 *Commentary, IV Geneva Convention, supra* note 31, at 351.
1105 *Ibid.*
1106 *Ibid.*, 352.
1107 *Ibid.*, 351–2.
1108 *Ibid.*, 352.

paragraph) of the Convention, a protected person cannot be transferred to a country where he may have reason to fear persecution for his political opinions or religious belief.[1109]

550. With a view to expanding the ambit of protection bestowed on refugees in occupied territories under the Geneva Convention, Article 73 of Additional Protocol I stipulates

> Persons who, before the beginning of hostilities, were considered as stateless persons or refugees under the relevant international instruments accepted by the Parties concerned or under the national legislation of the State of refuge or State of residence shall be protected persons within the meaning of Parts I and III of the Fourth Convention, in all circumstances and without any adverse distinction.[1110]

551. Like Article 70 (second paragraph) of the Geneva Convention, Article 73 of the Additional Protocol is also confined to refugees who reached the occupied territory before the outbreak of hostilities. Those who entered the State of refuge after the start of the war, although prior to the occupation, are still left out of the ambit of protection. Contrastingly, pre-war refugees are brought by Article 73 of the Protocol under the canopy of protected persons, even though they are nationals of the Occupying Power. In effect, the definition of protected persons in Article 4 (first paragraph) of the Geneva Convention (quoted *supra* 72) – which excludes, in general, nationals of the Occupying Power (see *supra* 197) – is amended (among Contracting Parties to the Additional Protocol) by adding the new category of pre-war refugees.[1111]

552. As protected persons, pre-war refugees are entitled to the full gamut of rights conferred by the Convention. They are protected not only from arrest, prosecution, conviction and deportation, but also in innumerable other ways. If they are subjected to compulsory work, this must be done with all the required safeguards guaranteed by Article 51 of the Convention (see *supra* 538); they are allowed to receive individual relief consignments (Article 62 referred to *infra* 590); they benefit from certain limitations relating to the imposition of capital punishment (Article 68 (second paragraph) quoted *supra* 440); and so on. Furthermore – although they still owe allegiance to the Occupying Power – they are covered by Article 51 (first paragraph) (quoted *supra* 178), which does not allow compelling protected persons to serve in its armed forces.

[1109] Geneva Convention (IV), *supra* note 29, at 593.
[1110] Additional Protocol I, *supra* note 33, at 748.
[1111] See Wenger, *supra* note 399, at 854.

II. Women and Children

A. *Women*

553. Article 27 (second paragraph) of Geneva Convention (IV) enunciates:

Women shall be especially protected against any attack on their honour, in particular against rape, enforced prostitution, or any form of indecent assault.[1112]

This clause must be read together with the first paragraph of Article 27 (quoted *supra* 460), which protects everybody – male or female – 'against all acts of violence'. The second paragraph 'aims to strengthen this protection by highlighting sexual violence'.[1113] Article 76(1) of Additional Protocol I reiterates the obligation to afford women special protection against rape, forced prostitution and any other form of indecent assault.[1114] The Additional Protocol's language is broad enough to cover all women, whether or not they are protected persons under the Geneva Convention.[1115] Rape, sexual slavery, enforced prostitution and other forms of sexual violence are branded as war crimes by Article 8(2)(b)(xxii) of the Rome Statute of the International Criminal Court.[1116]

554. As for enforced prostitution, its most notorious manifestation occurred in WWII, when Imperial Japan systematically coerced women in occupied territories – and elsewhere – to serve as 'comfort women' to soldiers (a practice formally acknowledged by modern Japan only in the 1990s).[1117] Unfortunately, this nefarious conduct was not confined to Imperial Japan and has not disappeared in more recent armed conflicts.

B. *Children*

(a) ***Protection and Respect***

555. The Geneva Convention, as noted, includes some specific protections of children in connection with evacuation from occupied territories (see *supra* 512) and compulsory work (see *supra* 538). Children are also referred to expressly in the particular settings of safety zones and besieged areas, in Articles 14 (first paragraph) and 17; but, curiously enough – where it comes to general protection – Article 16 (first paragraph), while listing 'expectant

[1112] Geneva Convention (IV), *supra* note 29, at 589.
[1113] C. Lindsay, 'Women and War', 839 *IRRC* 561, 577 (2000).
[1114] Additional Protocol I, *supra* note 33, at 750.
[1115] See Pilloud and Pictet, *supra* note 881, at 892.
[1116] Rome Statute of the International Criminal Court, *supra* note 350, at 1319.
[1117] See Arai-Takahashi, *supra* note 149, at 379–80.

mothers' among those who are to be 'the object of particular protection and respect', fails to mention children.[1118] This is a 'strange lacuna',[1119] which is only partially compensated for in an obligation not to leave to their own resources children who are orphaned or separated from their families (Article 24 (first paragraph)).[1120] There is also the general duty of respect for 'family rights' in Article 27 (first paragraph) of the Convention (quoted *supra* 460). The preservation of the family is of particular resonance where children are concerned, inasmuch as – given their inability to fend for themselves – the dissolution of the family may prove no less traumatic for children than the surrounding violence.[1121]

556. The gap in the Geneva Convention is filled by Article 77(1) of Additional Protocol I, which states:

> Children shall be the object of special respect and shall be protected against any form of indecent assault. The Parties to the conflict shall provide them with the care and aid they require, whether because of their age or for any other reason.[1122]

By safeguarding children against indecent assault, this clause also supplements the text of Article 27 (second paragraph) of the Convention, which – as noted (*supra* 553) – is focused on women.[1123]

557. Article 38(4) of the 1989 Convention on the Rights of the Child declares:

> In accordance with their obligations under international humanitarian law to protect the civilian population in armed conflicts, States Parties shall take all feasible measures to ensure protection and care of children who are affected by an armed conflict.[1124]

An amendment to replace the adjective 'feasible' with the stronger word 'necessary' failed in the process of the drafting of the Convention.[1125] The decision has been the subject of some trenchant criticism.[1126] But, in any event, it cannot diminish from the more robust language of Additional Protocol I, which is the *lex specialis* (see *supra* 261).[1127]

1118 Geneva Convention (IV), *supra* note 29, at 584–5.
1119 H. Mann, 'International Law and the Child Soldier', 36 *ICLQ* 32, 34 (1986).
1120 Geneva Convention (IV), *supra* note 29, at 588.
1121 See R.C. Hingorani, 'Protection of Children during Armed Conflicts', *Humanitarian Law: A Felicitation Volume in Honour of Professor Jovica Patrnogic* 150, 154 (2nd edn, 1987).
1122 Additional Protocol I, *supra* note 33, at 750.
1123 See C. Pilloud and J. Pictet, 'Article 77', *Commentary on the Additional Protocols, supra* note 327, at 897, 900.
1124 Convention on the Rights of the Child, *supra* note 443, at 291–2.
1125 See *The United Nations Convention on the Rights of the Child: A Guide to the* 'Travaux Préparatoires' 516–17 (S. Detrick ed., 1992).
1126 See G. Van Bueren, 'The International Legal Protection of Children in Armed Conflicts', 43 *ICLQ* 809, 820 (1994).
1127 See E. David, *Principes de Droit des Conflits Armés* 421 (1994).

(b) Care and Education

558. Article 50 (first paragraph) of the Geneva Convention requires that the Occupying Power – 'with the cooperation' of local authorities – facilitate the proper functioning of all institutions devoted to the care and education of children.[1128] 'Cooperation' presupposes some sort of 'mutual agreement' between the Occupying Power and the local authorities,[1129] and it is not clear what happens if that agreement cannot be arrived at.[1130] Although no age limit is set by the Convention, the ICRC Commentary suggests that the term 'children' here should be construed as applying up to the age of fifteen.[1131]

559. Article 50 (third paragraph) of the Convention adds that, if the local institutions are inadequate for the purpose, the Occupying Power must make arrangements for the maintenance and education of children who are orphaned or separated from their parents and cannot be adequately cared for by near relatives or friends (if possible, this has to be done by persons of the children's own nationality, language and religion).[1132] The limitation of the provision to orphaned and separated children might imply that the Occupying Power is not obliged to provide free primary education to other children if they did not benefit from it prior to the occupation.[1133] But this would be in dissonance with the general prescript – embodied in Article 13(2)(a) of the 1966 International Covenant on Economic, Social and Cultural Rights – that '[p]rimary education shall be compulsory and available free to all'.[1134]

560. The Occupying Power is entitled to ascertain that teachers in educational institutions for children (or, for that matter, youth and even adults) do not indulge in subversive activities under the guise of education; it may also examine textbooks and, if necessary, expunge from them hostile materials.[1135] In the *Insh El Usra Association* case, the Israel Supreme Court (per Justice Bach) upheld an order to temporarily close down institutions, supposedly devoted to vocational training and other educational purposes, when it turned out that their prime concern was incitement to violence at the time of the first *intifada*.[1136]

561. In the *Taha* case, the Israel Supreme Court (per Justice D. Levin) decided that, by obligating parents to exercise care where the conduct of their

1128 Geneva Convention (IV), *supra* note 29, at 594.

1129 *Ibid.*, 286.

1130 See J.T. Horowitz, 'The Right to Education in Occupied Territories: Making More Room for Human Rights in Occupation Law', 7 *YIHL* 233, 247 (2004).

1131 *Commentary, IV Geneva Convention*, *supra* note 31, at 285.

1132 Geneva Convention (IV), *supra* note 29, at 595.

1133 See J. Horowitz, 'Human Rights, Positive Obligations, and Armed Conflict: Implementing the Right to Education in Occupied Territories', 1 *JIHLS* 304, 315 (2010).

1134 International Covenant on Economic, Social and Cultural Rights, *supra* note 335, at 37.

1135 See Greenspan, *supra* note 383, at 234.

1136 HCJ 660/88, *Insh El Usra Association* et al. *v. IDF Commander in Judea and Samaria*, 43(3) *PD* 673, 677–8. (The Judgment is excerpted in English in 23 *IYHR* 307 (1993)).

minor children is concerned, the Occupying Power does not do anything that clashes with the special protection of children under the Geneva Convention and Additional Protocol I: on the contrary, parental care would protect the children from penalties that might otherwise be imposed on them directly (cf. *supra* 473).[1137]

(c) Identification

562. Under Article 50 (second paragraph, first sentence, as well as fourth paragraph) of the Convention, the Occupying Power must take all necessary steps to facilitate the identification of children and the registration of their parentage.[1138] This is a matter of great practical importance, especially in respect of infants, in view of the dispersion of many families in consequence of war and occupation.[1139] There is a nexus between identification and the general human right to a name (a right that is non-derogable under the American Convention on Human Rights; see *supra* 238).

(d) Preferential Treatment

563. Article 50 (fifth paragraph) prescribes that the Occupying Power must not hinder the application of any preferential measures in favour of children (in addition to expectant mothers and mothers of young children) – as regards food, medical care and protection against the effects of war – that may have been adopted prior to the occupation.[1140] Two comments are called for:

(a) A preferential treatment constitutes, *ex hypothesi* a discriminatory measure. Nevertheless, it is fully endorsed by the Convention, in contradistinction to other discriminatory measures (see *supra* 345).
(b) The preferential treatment is derived not from the Convention itself, but from legislative measures enacted by the displaced sovereign, and the provision of Article 50 (fifth paragraph) forms a limitation on the Occupying Power's authority to change legislation in force in accordance with Article 64 (quoted *supra* 336).[1141]

(e) Enlistment and Recruitment

564. Article 50 (second paragraph, second sentence) disallows the Occupying Power to enlist children in 'formations or organizations subordinated to it'.[1142]

[1137] HCJ 591/88, *supra* note 578, at 56.
[1138] Geneva Convention (IV), *supra* note 29, at 595.
[1139] See D. Plattner, 'Protection of Children in International Humanitarian Law', 24 *IRRC* 140, 145 (1984).
[1140] Geneva Convention (IV), *supra* note 29, at 595.
[1141] See *Commentary, IV Geneva Convention*, *supra* note 31, at 290.
[1142] Geneva Convention (IV), *supra* note 29, at 595.

The allusion is to forcing young people to join political youth movements and suchlike organizations, as distinct from recruitment to the armed forces.[1143]

565. Article 77(2) of Additional Protocol I establishes that Belligerent Parties must refrain from recruiting children under the age of fifteen into their armed forces.[1144] Pursuant to Article 8(2)(b)(xxvi) of the Rome Statute of the International Criminal Court, conscripting or enlisting children under the age of fifteen or using them to participate actively in hostilities is a war crime.[1145] It ought to be recalled that, in occupied territories, the forced recruitment of protected persons to serve in the armed forces of the Occupying Power is generally forbidden under Article 51 (first paragraph) (quoted *supra* 178), and this covers of course children. What is new in the Rome Statute is that, when dealing with children, even voluntary enlistment (which is allowed in the case of adults; see *supra* 181) is impermissible.[1146] The point was accentuated by a Pre-Trial Chamber of the International Criminal Court in the *Lubanga* case.[1147]

566. Article 38(3) of the Convention on the Rights of the Child reiterates the duty to refrain from recruiting children who have not attained the age of fifteen.[1148] In an Optional Protocol to the Convention, formulated in 2000, the age bar of compulsory recruitment of children is raised from fifteen to eighteen.[1149] As for voluntary enlistment of children under eighteen, it is still permissible (subject to some safeguards), provided that they do not take a direct part in hostilities.[1150]

III. Medical Services

A. *Medical Needs and Hospitals*

567. As noted (*supra* 457), Article 55 (first paragraph) of Geneva Convention (IV) mandates that – to the fullest extent of the means available to it – the Occupying Power is required to ensure the medical supplies of the population. This provision is complemented by Article 56 (first paragraph) of the Convention:

> To the fullest extent of the means available to it, the Occupying Power has the duty of ensuring and maintaining, with the cooperation of national and local authorities,

1143 See *Commentary, IV Geneva Convention*, *supra* note 31, at 288.

1144 Additional Protocol I, Protocol I, *supra* note 33, at 750.

1145 Rome Statute of the International Criminal Court, *supra* note 350, at 1319.

1146 See T. Webster, 'Babes with Arms: International Law and Child Soldiers', 39 *GWILR* 227, 240 (2007).

1147 *Prosecutor v. Lubanga Dyilo*, *supra* note 63, at 844.

1148 Convention on the Rights of the Child, *supra* note 443, at 291.

1149 Optional Protocol to the Convention on the Rights of the Child on the Involvement of Children in Armed Conflict, 2000, 39 *ILM* 1286, 1287 (2000) (Article 2).

1150 *Ibid.*, 1287–8 (Article 3).

the medical and hospital establishments and services, public health and hygiene in the occupied territory, with particular reference to the adoption and application of the prophylactic and preventive measures necessary to combat the spread of contagious diseases and epidemics. Medical personnel of all categories shall be allowed to carry out their duties.[1151]

568. Article 14(1) of Additional Protocol I also requires the Occupying Power, in general terms, 'to ensure that the medical needs of the civilian population in occupied territory continue to be satisfied'.[1152] The ICRC Commentary sharpens the two principal interlinked differences between this clause and Articles 55–6 of the Convention: (i) on the one hand, in Article 14(1) of the Additional Protocol, the qualifying words '[t]o the fullest extent of the means available to it' do not appear; but (ii) on the other hand, the duty of the Occupying Power in Article 14(1) is not simply 'to ensure that the medical needs of the civilian population *are* satisfied but that they *continue* to be satisfied'.[1153] It follows that the obligation imposed on the Occupying Power is more ironclad in its nature, but it is less extensive: if medical conditions in the occupied territory prior to the occupation were deplorable, the Occupying Power is not expected to rectify the situation rapidly.[1154]

569. If new hospitals are set up in the occupied territory, they must be granted recognition under Article 56 (second paragraph).[1155] When the Occupying Power adopts measures of health and hygiene, it has to take into consideration the sensitivity of the civilian population in the occupied territory in matters of ethics (Article 56 (third paragraph)).[1156]

B. *Medical Personnel*

570. Article 20 (first paragraph) of the Geneva Convention proclaims:

Persons regularly and solely engaged in the operation and administration of civilian hospitals, including the personnel engaged in the search for, removal and transporting of and caring for wounded and sick civilians, the infirm and maternity cases, shall be respected and protected.[1157]

This protection has a particular meaning in occupied territories, where – according to Article 20 (second paragraph) – the above personnel have to be

[1151] Geneva Convention (IV), *supra* note 29, at 596–7.
[1152] Additional Protocol I, *supra* note 33, at 721.
[1153] Y. Sandoz, 'Article 14', *Commentary on the Additional Protocols, supra* note 327, at 181, 182–3. Emphasis in the original.
[1154] See *ibid.*, 183.
[1155] Geneva Convention (IV), *supra* note 29, at 597.
[1156] *Ibid.*
[1157] *Ibid.*, 586.

recognizable by means of identity cards and armlets carrying the Red Cross emblem (or its equivalents).[1158]

571. The range of Article 20 of the Convention is limited to civilian hospital staff, thus excluding from special protection civilian medical personnel not associated with hospitals, and this lacuna was filled only in Additional Protocol I.[1159] Article 18(3) of the Additional Protocol reiterates the requirement for all civilian medical personnel in occupied territories to identify themselves by the distinctive emblem.[1160] Medical personnel are defined in Article 8(c) of the Protocol in a manner inclusive of the personnel of National Red Cross Societies and similar recognized voluntary aid societies.[1161]

572. Article 15(3) of the Additional Protocol lays down:

> The Occupying Power shall afford civilian medical personnel in occupied territories every assistance to enable them to perform, to the best of their ability, their humanitarian functions. The Occupying Power may not require that, in the performance of those functions, such personnel shall give priority to the treatment of any person except on medical grounds. They shall not be compelled to carry out tasks which are not compatible with their humanitarian mission.[1162]

The gravamen of the text is that the Occupying Power may not order civilian medical personnel to give priority to its own wounded and sick. Yet, this is not a one-way street. For their part, the civilian medical personnel 'cannot leave without care the wounded and sick of the Occupying Power taken to them in emergencies'.[1163]

573. In the *Association of Israeli-Palestinian Physicians for Human Rights* case, the Israel Supreme Court (per President Shamgar) was emphatic that – even when permissible restrictions on freedom of movement are imposed in an occupied territory (e.g., during curfew) – all medical services must be operable and ambulances must be allowed to move around when there is a call for help.[1164]

C. *Medical Care by the Civilian Population and Red Cross Societies*

574. Article 17(1) of Additional Protocol I ordains that the civilian population must respect – and commit no act of violence against – the wounded, sick

---

1158 *Ibid.*

1159 See M. Torrelli, 'La Protection du Médecin dans les Conflits Armés', *Studies and Essays, supra* note 1063, at 581, 598.

1160 Additional Protocol I, *supra* note 33, at 723.

1161 *Ibid.*, 718.

1162 *Ibid.*, 722.

1163 Y. Sandoz, 'Article 15', *Commentary on the Additional Protocols, supra* note 327, at 189, 193.

1164 HCJ 477/91, *Association of Israeli-Palestinian Physicians for Human Rights v. Minister of Defence* et al., 45(2) *PD* 832, 834–6. (The Judgment is excerpted in English in 23 *IYHR* 341 (1993)).

and shipwrecked, even when they belong to the enemy.[1165] This is the only place in the Additional Protocol where an obligation devolves explicitly on the civilian population.[1166] At the same time, Article 17(1) gives the civilian population in occupied territories permission to collect and care for wounded, sick and shipwrecked on their own initiative, with the aid of National Red Cross Societies or their counterparts (the latter provision is rooted in Article 18 (second paragraph) of Geneva Convention (I)[1167]).

575. Article 63 of Geneva Convention (IV) sets forth that, subject to temporary and exceptional measures which the Occupying Power may introduce for urgent reasons of security, recognized National Red Cross Societies must be permitted to pursue their activities in occupied territories in accordance with the Red Cross principles.[1168] Other relief societies must also be permitted to continue their humanitarian activities under similar conditions, and the Occupying Power may not require changes in the personnel or the structure of these societies that would be prejudicial to their work.[1169]

IV. Civil Defence

576. Civil defence organizations fulfil diverse humanitarian tasks enumerated in Article 61(a) of Additional Protocol I, such as rescue, fire-fighting, management of shelters and various emergency assistance missions.[1170] Under Article 63(1)–(2) of the Protocol, civilian civil defence organizations in occupied territories must receive from the Occupying Power the 'facilities necessary for the performance of their tasks'; and the Occupying Power may not (i) compel their personnel to carry out activities which would interfere with the proper implementation of those tasks; (ii) change their structure or personnel in a way that would prejudice the efficient accomplishment of their mission; (iii) require them to give priority to its own nationals or interests; or (iv) compel or induce them to discharge their duties in a manner prejudicial to the interests of the civilian population.[1171] The Occupying Power is only required to assist the operation of existing

[1165] Additional Protocol I, *supra* note 33, at 722–3.
[1166] Y. Sandoz, 'Article 17', *Commentary on the Additional Protocols*, *supra* note 327, at 209, 211.
[1167] Geneva Convention (I), *supra* note 397, at 468.
[1168] Geneva Convention (IV), *supra* note 29, at 598.
[1169] *Ibid.*
[1170] Additional Protocol I, *supra* note 33, at 742–3.
[1171] *Ibid.*, 743.

organizations, rather than create a new civil defence organization where none was functioning prior to the occupation.[1172]

577. What 'facilities' are deemed necessary for the performance of the tasks of civil defence organizations (and must therefore be provided by the Occupying Power)? The ICRC Commentary leans in the direction of procurement of *materiel,* such as essential equipment for fire-fighting.[1173] In case of deficiencies, the Occupying Power may authorize relief shipments from the outside.[1174]

578. Article 63(3) of the Protocol authorizes the Occupying Power to disarm civil defence personnel for reasons of security.[1175] Under Article 65(1), the protection which they enjoy ceases (after due warning) if acts harmful to the Occupying Power are committed outside the proper tasks of civil defence organizations.[1176] Two cumulative conditions are combined here. Protection is lost only if (i) the personnel of a civil defence organization act in excess of the tasks listed in Article 61(a), and, on top of that, (ii) these acts are harmful to the Occupying Power.[1177]

579. According to Article 66(3) of the Protocol, where fighting is taking or likely to take place in occupied territories, civil defence personnel should be recognizable by wearing a distinctive special sign and carrying appropriate identity cards.[1178]

580. Article 67(2) of the Protocol sets forth that, when military personnel serving within civil defence organizations fall into the hands of the enemy, they become prisoners of war; still, an Occupying Power may continue to employ them on civil defence missions in the occupied territory, in the interest of the local population (provided that, if the work is dangerous, they can only be employed on a voluntary basis).[1179]

581. As per Article 64(3) of the Protocol, when civil defence organizations of neutral countries operate in an occupied territory, the Occupying Power may not exclude them from the territory, or hobble their activities, unless it can ensure the adequate performance of civil defence tasks from its own resources or those of the territory.[1180]

[1172] See M.J. Kelly, *Peace Operations: Tackling the Military Legal and Policy Challenges* 5–17 (1997).
[1173] See Y. Sandoz, 'Article 63', *Commentary on the Additional Protocols, supra* note 327, at 745, 748.
[1174] See *ibid.*, 749.
[1175] Additional Protocol I, *supra* note 33, at 743.
[1176] *Ibid.*, 744.
[1177] See R.W. Gehring, 'Loss of Civilian Protections under the Fourth Geneva Convention and Protocol I', 90 *Mil.LR* 49, 77–8 (1980).
[1178] Additional Protocol I, *supra* note 33, at 745.
[1179] *Ibid.*, 746.
[1180] *Ibid.*, 744.

V. Humanitarian Relief

A. *Relief Consignments*

582. As indicated (*supra* 457), under Article 55 (first paragraph) of Geneva Convention (IV), the Occupying Power is in duty bound (to the fullest extent of the means available to it) to ensure the supplies of foodstuffs, medications, etc., to the civilian population in an occupied territory. However, meeting this obligation may be beyond the means available to the Occupying Power. Article 59 (first and second paragraphs) of the Convention addresses the problem:

> If the whole or part of the population of an occupied territory is inadequately supplied, the Occupying Power shall agree to relief schemes on behalf of the said population, and shall facilitate them by all the means at its disposal.
>
> Such schemes, which may be undertaken either by States or by impartial humanitarian organizations such as the International Committee of the Red Cross, shall consist, in particular, of the provision of consignments of foodstuffs, medical supplies and clothing.[1181]

583. The causes of the inadequacy of essential supplies in an occupied territory are immaterial: they may be due to natural disasters (drought, floods, etc.);[1182] poor administrative policies; or difficulties in transportation (especially in an area recently ravaged by hostilities). It does not matter whether scarcities are the fault of the Occupying Power or its adversary (which may have imposed a blockade on imports). What counts is the bottom line of inadequate supplies to the population of the occupied territory.

584. Whereas in Article 55 (first paragraph) the obligation incumbent on the Occupying Power is qualified by the words '[t]o the fullest extent of the means available to it', no similar reservation is used in Article 59. The expression 'shall agree' in Article 59 (first paragraph) connotes an unqualified obligation. When the predicament of the civilian population in the occupied territory is not in dispute, the Occupying Power 'may not withhold consent to offers to conduct humanitarian relief operations that are exclusively humanitarian and impartial in character'.[1183] In other words, once supplies to the civilian population in an occupied territory are inadequate, the obligation of the Occupying Power to allow relief consignments from the outside is cemented in an unconditional

[1181] Geneva Convention (IV), *supra* note 29, at 597.

[1182] See D. Gavshon, 'The Applicability of IHL in Mixed Situations of Disaster and Conflict', 14 *JCSL* 243, 253–4 (2009).

[1183] *Oxford Guidance on the Law Relating to Humanitarian Relief Operations in Situations of Armed Conflict: Conclusions* 7 (United Nations Office for the Coordination of Humanitarian Affairs, 2016).

fashion.[1184] The only problem is that Article 59 (first paragraph) does not set any criteria for establishing when 'the whole or part of the population of an occupied territory is inadequately supplied'. Even if one does not accept the contention that 'this inadequacy is left entirely open-ended',[1185] it cannot be denied that there are borderline situations in which there may be a reasonable difference of opinion as to whether or not the civilian population of an occupied territory is 'inadequately supplied'.

585. While obligated to allow humanitarian relief from the outside to the civilian population of an occupied territory when it is 'inadequately supplied', the Occupying Power may select the specific provider of humanitarian relief (assuming that more than one offer of relief is on the table). The potential providers of relief mentioned in the text of Article 59 (second paragraph) are States – presumably those that are neutral in the specific armed conflict[1186] – and impartial humanitarian (non-governmental) organizations such as the ICRC. But, of course, inter-governmental organizations (e.g., the United Nations or the European Union) can qualify as well.

586. A violation of Article 59 is not listed as one of the grave breaches enumerated in Article 147 of the Convention.[1187] However, 'wilfully impeding relief supplies as provided for under the Geneva Conventions' is categorized as a war crime in Article 8(2)(b)(xxv) of the Rome Statute of the International Criminal Court.[1188]

587. In conformity with Article 60 of the Convention, relief consignments do not by themselves discharge the Occupying Power of its responsibilities under Article 55; nor is the Occupying Power allowed to divert relief consignments from their intended purpose, except in case of urgent necessity in the interest of the civilian population in the occupied territory (and with the consent of the Protecting Power).[1189] The idea behind the exceptional permission of diversion of relief consignments is that, e.g., an epidemic may stop in one town and start in another; or the destination originally chosen for the delivery of foodstuffs has become inaccessible.[1190]

588. Under Article 59 (third paragraph), all Contracting Parties to the Convention – that is to say, whether they are Belligerent Parties or neutrals in the armed conflict – must permit the free passage of relief consignments en route to

[1184] See *Commentary, IV Geneva Convention*, *supra* note 31, at 320.

[1185] E.E. Kuijt, 'A Humanitarian Crisis: Reframing the Legal Framework on Humanitarian Assistance', *Humanitarian Action: Global, Regional and Domestic Legal Responses* 54, 67 (A. Zwitter, C.K. Lamont, H.-J. Heintze and J. Herman eds., 2015).

[1186] See *HPCR Manual on International Law Applicable to Air and Missile Warfare* 282 (2013).

[1187] Geneva Convention (IV), *supra* note 29, at 624–5.

[1188] Rome Statute of the International Criminal Court, *supra* note 350, at 1319.

[1189] Geneva Convention (IV), *supra* note 29, at 598.

[1190] *Commentary, IV Geneva Convention*, *supra* note 31, at 324.

an occupied territory and guarantee their protection.[1191] This includes an obligation for a blockading State to allow relief consignments to cross a blockade line when they are destined for the civilian population of an occupied territory.[1192] Nevertheless, under Article 59 (fourth paragraph), an enemy State – whose territory (or blockade line) has to be crossed – has the right to search the relief consignments, to regulate their passage by insisting on timetables and routes, and to be reasonably satisfied through the Protecting Power that they are really to be used for the welfare of the needy civilian population in the occupied territory (rather than for the benefit of the army of occupation).[1193] The inspecting State is also entitled to verify that the relief supplies are genuine and that they do not contain any weapons, munitions or other items susceptible of military purposes.[1194] All these qualifications indicate that the issuance of a safe conduct pass through a blockade line – to a vessel carrying relief consignments for occupied territories – has to be granted for each specific voyage and, albeit obligatory under Article 59, has to be based on a modicum of prior agreement.[1195]

589. Article 61 (second paragraph) of the Convention exempts relief consignments from all taxes, charges or customs in the occupied territory, unless these are necessary in the interests of the economy of the territory.[1196] The exception to the exemption is peculiar, and the circumstances in which it becomes applicable are rather obscure.[1197] In any event, all Contracting Parties must endeavour (under Article 61 (third paragraph)) to permit the transit of relief consignments free of charge on their way to the occupied territory.[1198]

590. Subject to imperative reasons of security, Article 62 permits protected persons in an occupied territory to receive also individual relief parcels (which do not detract from collective relief schemes).[1199]

B. *Relief Personnel*

591. Article 71(1) of Additional Protocol I promulgates that, where necessary, relief personnel may form part of the assistance rendered (especially for purposes of transportation, administration and distribution of relief consignments), but the participation of such personnel depends on the approval of the Party in whose territory they are to perform their tasks.[1200] Article 69(2)

[1191] Geneva Convention (IV), *supra* note 29, at 597.
[1192] *Commentary, IV Geneva Convention*, *supra* note 31, at 322.
[1193] Geneva Convention (IV), *supra* note 29, at 597.
[1194] See *Commentary, IV Geneva Convention*, *supra* note 31, at 322.
[1195] See R.W. Tucker, *The Law of War and Neutrality at Sea* 97 n.12 (50 ILS, 1955).
[1196] Geneva Convention (IV), *supra* note 29, at 598.
[1197] See *Commentary, IV Geneva Convention*, *supra* note 31, at 327.
[1198] Geneva Convention (IV), *supra* note 29, at 598.
[1199] *Ibid.*
[1200] Additional Protocol I, *supra* note 33, at 747.

emphasizes that the provision of Article 71 applies *inter alia* to occupied territories.[1201] Yet, by a *lapsus linguae*, Article 71 refers to the approval of the Party 'in whose territory' the personnel will discharge their duties. An occupied territory belongs to the displaced sovereign 'whose territory' it therefore is (see *supra* 161), but the bidding of common sense is that the required approval must be obtained from the Occupying Power (who is in effective control of the area in which the relief personnel would function). This is indeed the interpretation given to the clause by the ICRC Commentary.[1202]

592. Article 71(2) goes on to enjoin that '[s]uch personnel' – namely, relief personnel that has been approved by the Occupying Power – must be 'respected and protected'.[1203] Under Article 8(2)(b)(iii) of the Rome Statute of the International Criminal Court, intentionally directing attacks against personnel involved in a humanitarian assistance mission constitutes a war crime.[1204]

593. Article 71(3) of the Additional Protocol states that the Party receiving the relief consignments must, to the fullest extent practicable, assist the relief personnel in carrying out their mission: only imperative military necessity may warrant curtailing the freedom of movement of the personnel, and even that can be done only temporarily.[1205]

594. The flip side of the coin is that, under Article 71(4), relief personnel may not exceed the terms of their mission – in particular, they must take into account the security requirements of the Party 'in whose territory' (the same inelegant expression again) they are operating – and, should they fail to do so, their mission may be terminated.[1206]

1201 *Ibid.*, 746.

1202 See Y. Sandoz, 'Article 71', *Commentary on the Additional Protocols, supra* note 327, at 831, 833.

1203 Additional Protocol I, *supra* note 33, at 747.

1204 Rome Statute of the International Criminal Court, *supra* note 350, at 1318.

1205 Additional Protocol I, *supra* note 33, at 747.

1206 *Ibid.*

9 Destruction, Spoliation and Pillage of Property in Occupied Territories

I. Destruction of Property

A. *The General* Jus in Bello *Rule*

595. When hostilities take place – in or out of occupied territories – the destruction of some civilian property is an almost inevitable result of the fighting. This will happen for any number of reasons. Shell fire may be directed against enemy combatants holding out in an urban or rural locality – wrecking buildings and torching crops – or a line of fire may be cleared in cultivated lands.[1207] Potential enemy fortifications may be pulverized, trenches and dugouts may have to be shovelled in tilled soil, tanks may have to ride over farmlands, and so forth.[1208] The quintessential rule of the *jus in bello* is that enemy property (and in this context there is no distinction between movable or immovable, private or public, property) must not be destroyed, except for reasons of military necessity. Hague Regulation 23(g) formulates the general prohibition:

> To destroy or seize the enemy's property, unless such destruction or seizure be imperatively demanded by the necessities of war.[1209]

This is also a war crime under Article 8(2)(b)(xiii) of the Rome Statute of the International Criminal Court.[1210] But it is clear that, when 'imperatively demanded by the necessities of war', enemy property may be destroyed.

596. The International Court of Justice expressed the view, in the Advisory Opinion on the *Wall*, that – since Hague Regulation 23(g) appears in the section of the text devoted to hostilities, rather than belligerent occupation – it is not 'pertinent' to occupied territories.[1211] This dictum is inexplicable, inasmuch

[1207] See P.C. Jessup, 'A Belligerent Occupying Power's Power over Property', 38 *AJIL* 457, 458 (1944).
[1208] See Oppenheim, *supra* note 201, at 413–14.
[1209] Hague Regulations, *supra* note 22, at 234–5.
[1210] Rome Statute of the International Criminal Court, *supra* note 350, at 1318.
[1211] Advisory Opinion on *Legal Consequences of the Construction of a Wall in the Occupied Palestinian Territory*, *supra* note 25, at 185.

as the next paragraph (appearing, of course, in the same section) – Regulation 23(h) – is generally conceded to be applicable to occupied territories (see *supra* 177, 418). The Court's assertion is also inconsistent with the interpretation of Regulation 23(g) in previous case law[1212] and with current doctrinal treatment of the subject.[1213]

597. The real polarity in the relevant norms of the *jus in bello* is not between occupied and non-occupied territories, but between destruction of property 'when imperatively demanded by the necessities of war' and destruction of property in other sets of circumstances. When hostilities are conducted in an occupied territory, they are no different from hostilities elsewhere, and there can be no possible impediment to the application of Regulation 23(g).[1214] Thus, in the *Gusin* case, the Israel Supreme Court (per President Barak) saw this provision as the proper legal basis for the demolition of a factory used for ambushes during hostilities that were raging in the Gaza Strip.[1215] President Barak reverted to the issue in the *Alfei Menashe* case (see *infra* 785).

B. Article 53 of Geneva Convention (IV)

598. The theme of destruction of property in occupied territories is specifically addressed in Article 53 of Geneva Convention (IV):

> Any destruction by the Occupying Power of real or personal property belonging individually or collectively to private persons, or to the State, or to other public authorities, or to social or cooperative organizations, is prohibited, except where such destruction is rendered absolutely necessary by military operations.[1216]

By protecting from destruction not only private but also public (and specifically State) property, Article 53 covers all types of property in occupied territories irrespective of ownership.[1217] This holistic feature of Article 53 'does not really fit with the rest of the scope of the Convention', which is otherwise confined to protections granted to civilians.[1218] However, arguably, the purpose

[1212] See, e.g., *Krupp* trial (*Krupp* et al.) (US Military Tribunal, Nuremberg, 1948), 10 *LRTWC* 69, 136.

[1213] Y. Arai-Takahashi, 'Protection of Private Property', *The 1949 Geneva Conventions: A Commentary*, *supra* note 309, at 1515, 1519–20.

[1214] See N. Lubell, 'The ICJ Advisory Opinion and the Separation Barrier: A Troublesome Route', 35 *IYHR* 283, 294–9 (2005).

[1215] HCJ 4219/02, *Gusin v. IDF Commander of the Gaza Strip*, 56(4) *PD* 608, 610–11. (The Judgment is excerpted in English in 32 *IYHR* 379 (2002)).

[1216] Geneva Convention (IV), *supra* note 29, at 596.

[1217] See A. Van Engeland, 'Protection of Public Property', *The 1949 Geneva Conventions: A Commentary*, *supra* note 309, at 1535, 1537.

[1218] *Ibid.*; *Commentary, IV Geneva Convention*, *supra* note 31, at 301.

of the framers was to obviate civilian suffering that may be due to destruction of any type of property.[1219]

599. The Geneva phrase 'absolutely necessary by military operations' – on which the exception to the prohibition of the destruction of property in Article 53 is predicated – is sometimes viewed as narrower than the parallel language of Hague Regulation 23(g) ('imperatively demanded by the necessities of war').[1220] Yet, the discrepancy (if any) is not abundantly clear. In any event, the distinction between 'absolute' and 'imperative' – in this as in other contexts (see *supra* 519) – seems to be nominal.[1221] The two adjectives are frequently employed interchangeably.[1222]

600. The phrase 'military operations' in occupied territories must be understood as spreading a wide net. Military operations embrace not only engaging in hostilities against the enemy, but also action taken by the Occupying Power in order to quell violence by organized armed groups and individual saboteurs. Experience – especially in the West Bank and in Iraq – shows that military operations, even against non-State actors in occupied territories (if they have to be dislodged from fortified positions), may entail much destruction of property.

C. Extensive and Wanton Destruction

601. An 'extensive destruction and appropriation of property, not justified by military necessity and carried out unlawfully and wantonly', is defined as a grave breach by Article 147 of the Convention.[1223] As such, it is a war crime under Article 8(2)(a)(iv) of the Rome Statute of the International Criminal Court,[1224] which overlaps to some extent Article 8(2)(b)(xiii) (see *supra* 595).[1225]

602. The grave breach, as defined in Article 147 of the Geneva Convention, is clearly linked to destruction of property in occupied territories (proscribed in Article 53).[1226] The qualifying adjective 'extensive' is incorporated only in Article 147 and not in Article 53, where the subject-matter is '[a]ny destruction'. 'Extensive' destruction would therefore be a constituent element of a grave breach (or a war crime) but not of an ordinary breach of Article 53, which may be non-extensive. When is destruction considered 'extensive'? The ICRC

1219 See L. Brilmayer and G. Chepiga, 'Ownership or Use? Civilian Property Interests in International Humanitarian Law', 49 *Har.ILJ* 413, 426 (2008).

1220 See Arai-Takahashi, *supra* note 1213, at 1518.

1221 See H. McCoubrey, *International Humanitarian Law: Modern Developments in the Limitation of Warfare* 200 (2nd edn, 2000).

1222 For an example, see *Prosecutor v. Brdanin* (ICTY, Trial Chamber, 2004), para. 588.

1223 Geneva Convention (IV), *supra* note 29, at 624–5.

1224 Rome Statute of the International Criminal Court, *supra* note 350, at 1317.

1225 See Dörmann, *supra* note 355, at 251.

1226 *Commentary, IV Geneva Convention*, *supra* note 31, at 601.

Commentary opines that 'an isolated incident would not be enough'.[1227] Still, the Trial Chamber of the ICTY, in the *Blaškić* case, held that '[t]he notion of 'extensive' is evaluated according to the facts of the case – a single act, such as the destruction of a hospital, may suffice to characterise an offence under this count'.[1228]

603. The adverb 'wantonly' in Article 147 is borrowed from the classical definition of war crimes – appearing in Article 6(b) of the 1945 Charter of the International Military Tribunal – which includes 'wanton destruction of cities, towns or villages, or devastation not justified by military necessity'.[1229] Wanton destruction is the antonym of destruction stemming from military necessity: it connotes the lack of military-operational rhyme or reason.[1230] A good illustration of wanton destruction of property in an occupied territory – without any genuine military necessity – is that of Iraq systematically setting fire to hundreds of oil wells in occupied Kuwait, in 1991, upon being forced by Coalition forces to evacuate the country.[1231] As noted (*supra* 454), a 'scorched earth' policy cannot be undertaken by a retreating Occupying Power. The Eritrea Ethiopia Claims Commission made the following comment on the destruction of civilian infrastructure by Ethiopian troops retreating from an occupied territory:

> The Commission does not agree that denial of potential future use of properties like these, which are not directly usable for military operations as are, for example, bridges or railways, could ever be justified under Article 53.[1232]

D. *The Discretion of the Occupying Power*

604. It may be debatable whether 'imperative military requirements' justify the destruction of a particular property, in a given set of circumstances, in an occupied territory. Who is to make the determination that these requirements have been met? The ICRC Commentary states that 'it will be for the Occupying Power to judge the importance of such military requirements', while softening the effect of the statement by adding that 'the occupying authorities must try to keep a sense of proportion in comparing the military advantages to be gained with the damage done'.[1233]

[1227] *Ibid.*

[1228] *Prosecutor v. Blaškić*, *supra* note 64, at 157.

[1229] Charter of the International Military Tribunal (Annexed to London Agreement for the Prosecution and Punishment of the Major War Criminals of the European Axis), 1945, *The Laws of Armed Conflicts, supra* note 29, at 1253, 1255, 1256.

[1230] It has been suggested that 'wanton' should be considered in the sense of 'reckless' (see Arai-Takahashi, *supra* note 1213, at 1531). But the two terms are actually disparate.

[1231] See Dinstein, *supra* note 14, at 245–6.

[1232] Eritrea Ethiopia Claims Commission, Partial Award (Central Front), *supra* note 250, at 1265.

[1233] *Commentary, IV Geneva Convention*, *supra* note 31, at 302.

605. Weighing military advantages against the damage contemplated is a judgment call. The Israel Supreme Court (per President Shamgar), in the *Timraz* case, held that – generally speaking – a military-operational necessity prevails over the duty to protect property in an occupied territory, if compensation is paid for the property destroyed (although such payment is not required by Article 53).[1234] In the *Abu Daher* case, the petitioner challenged a decision by the military government to cut off (as a precautionary measure) privately owned olive trees in the West Bank, adjacent to the border with Israel, where the home of a new Israeli Minister of Defence happened to be located.[1235] The Court (per Justice A. Procaccia), applying the proportionality criterion advocated by the ICRC Commentary mentioned *supra* 604, allowed pruning the trees (to improve visibility) but prohibited cutting them off.[1236]

606. Although left a great deal of discretion in the matter, the Occupying Power is not the final arbiter. As the Eritrea Ethiopia Claims Commission pointed out in 2004, when there is a recurrent pattern of destruction of property 'ascribable to deliberate action' by an Occupying Power – including the widespread use of bulldozers – the Occupying Power bears the onus of proof that there was a military necessity for the destruction (in conformity with Article 53).[1237] Breaches of Article 53 were established by the International Court of Justice both in the *Armed Activities* case (of 2005)[1238] and in the *Wall* Advisory Opinion (see *infra* 778).

E. *Special Protection*

(a) ***Civilian Hospitals***

607. Under Article 18 (first paragraph) of the Geneva Convention, civilian hospitals must 'at all times be respected and protected by the Parties to the conflict'.[1239] The message is clear: '[t]he Fourth Convention forbids the destruction of civilian hospitals and their property'.[1240]

[1234] HCJ 24/91, *Timraz* et al. *v. IDF Commander of the Gaza Strip*, 45(2) *PD* 325, 335. (The Judgment is excerpted in English in 23 *IYHR* 337 (1993)).

[1235] HCJ 7862/04, *Abu Daher v. IDF Commander of Judea and Samaria*, 59(5) *PD* 368, 371–2. (The Judgment is excerpted in English in 37 *IYHR* 339 (2007)).

[1236] *Ibid.*, 377, 384.

[1237] Eritrea Ethiopia Claims Commission, Partial Award (Central Front), Ethiopia's Claim 2, *supra* note 65, at 1290.

[1238] *Case Concerning Armed Activities on the Territory of the Congo* (Congo v. Uganda), *supra* note 26, at 244.

[1239] Geneva Convention (IV), *supra* note 29, at 585.

[1240] *Commentary, IV Geneva Convention*, *supra* note 31, at 601.

(b) Cultural Property

608. Hague Regulation 56 (second paragraph) affirms:

> All seizure of, and destruction, or intentional damage done to such institutions [institutions dedicated to religious worship, charity, education, art and science], historical monuments, works of art or science, is forbidden, and should be made the subject of legal proceedings.[1241]

As the Eritrea Ethiopia Commission observed, the principle embodied here relates to the destruction of all historic monuments, not necessarily the most famous.[1242]

609. Regulation 56 (second paragraph) is the sole Hague provision referring 'explicitly to the legal responsibility of individuals who violate it, although it does not specify whether the proceedings in question should be penal or merely disciplinary'.[1243] It is therefore noteworthy that, in the *Lingenfelder* trial of 1947, a French Military Tribunal decided that a partial destruction – under German occupation – of a war monument to the dead of WWI constituted not just a breach of Regulation 56 (second paragraph) but also a crime.[1244]

610. Although Regulation 56 (second paragraph) is couched in absolute terms, it has to be seen as subject to the escape valve in Regulation 23(g), so that destruction of the property is not forbidden if it is 'imperatively demanded by the necessities of war'.[1245]

611. The 1954 Hague Convention for the Protection of Cultural Property in the Event of Armed Conflict (adopted under the aegis of UNESCO) defines 'cultural property' broadly in Article 1, covering movables and immovables of great importance to the cultural heritage of every people, such as architectural or historical monuments, archaeological sites, museums, libraries, works of art, manuscripts, books, scientific collections and archives.[1246] An obligation to respect cultural property in the event of an armed conflict, by refraining from any act of hostility directed against it, is included in Article 4(1) of the Convention.[1247] Article 4 applies 'as much to belligerent occupation as to active hostilities'.[1248] That said, the 1954 text's protection is non-absolute in nature, inasmuch as (under Article 4(2)) it may be waived 'where military necessity

[1241] Hague Regulations, *supra* note 22, at 252–3. The words within square brackets are taken from the first paragraph of Regulation 56 (quoted *infra* 677).

[1242] Eritrea Ethiopia Claims Commission, Partial Award (Central Front), Eritrea's Claims, *supra* note 250, at 1270.

[1243] O'Keefe, *supra* note 199, at 31.

[1244] *Lingenfelder* trial (Permanent Military Tribunal, Lyon, 1947), 9 *LRTWC* 67, 67–8.

[1245] See O'Keefe, *supra* note 199, at 31–2.

[1246] Hague Convention for the Protection of Cultural Property in the Event of Armed Conflict, *supra* note 144, at 1001.

[1247] *Ibid*., 1001–2.

[1248] O'Keefe, *supra* note 199, at 120.

imperatively requires such a waiver'.[1249] The waiver right is an exceptional measure that cannot be used too liberally. It is significantly modulated in Article 6 of a Second Protocol to the Convention adopted in 1999.[1250]

612. A few words about institutions dedicated to education. In the 2001 *Kordić* case, the Trial Chamber of the ICTY maintained that 'educational institutions are undoubtedly immovable property of great importance to the cultural heritage of peoples in that they are without exception centres of learning, arts, and sciences, with their valuable collections of books and works of art and science'.[1251] The Appeals Chamber (in 2004) found that the Trial Chamber had erred in its sweeping reference to all educational institutions, 'without exception', as important to the cultural heritage of peoples.[1252] Yet, even when educational buildings are shorn of such exaggerated pretensions, the Appeals Chamber agreed that their destruction constitutes a crime under customary international law.[1253]

613. 'Cultural property is particularly exposed to destruction or damage during occupation' even in the absence of any bad intentions on the part of the Occupying Power.[1254] Article 5(1) of the 1954 Convention ordains that the Occupying Power 'shall as far as possible support the competent national authorities of the occupied country in safeguarding and preserving its cultural property'.[1255] Article 5(2) adverts in particular to the preservation of cultural property that has been damaged by military operations, if the competent local authorities in the occupied territory are unable to cope with the situation.[1256] The Occupying Power is required, as far as possible, to take measures designed to prevent the further deterioration of the damaged cultural property, but this must be done in collaboration with the competent local authorities (always assuming that the latter are not capable of handling the matter by themselves).[1257]

614. The need to safeguard archaeological sites in an occupied territory was accentuated more than once by the Israel Supreme Court. In the *Kandu* case, the Court (per Justice Barak) held that the Occupying Power is bound under customary international law to protect and preserve archaeological

[1249] Hague Convention for the Protection of Cultural Property in the Event of Armed Conflict, *supra* note 144, at 1002.

[1250] Second Protocol to the Hague Convention of 1954 for the Protection of Cultural Property in the Event of Armed Conflict, 1999, *The Laws of Armed Conflicts*, *supra* note 29, at 1039, 1040.

[1251] *Prosecutor v. Kordić* et al. (ICTY, Trial Chamber, 2001), para. 360.

[1252] See *Prosecutor v. Kordić* et al. (ICTY, Appeals Chamber, 2004), para. 92.

[1253] See *ibid.*

[1254] R. Wolfrum, 'Protection of Cultural Property in Armed Conflict', 32 *IYHR* 305, 331 (2002).

[1255] Hague Convention for the Protection of Cultural Property in the Event of Armed Conflict, *supra* note 144, at 1002.

[1256] *Ibid.*

[1257] O'Keefe, *supra* note 199, at 120.

treasures.[1258] This ruling was repeated in the *Hass* case, where the Court (per Justice Procaccia) relied also on the 1954 Convention.[1259] in the *Shahrur* case, the Court (per President Shamgar) – citing the duty imposed on an Occupying Power by Regulation 56 – even approved the prosecution before military courts of offenders under the Jordanian Antiquities Law, when it became apparent that the local courts did not treat such offences with sufficient gravity.[1260]

615. Extensive archaeological excavations – carried out by Israeli scholars in the Old City of Jerusalem and in the West Bank – drew stern rebuke in UNESCO deliberations.[1261] Article 9 of the 1999 Second Protocol to the 1954 Convention permits archaeological excavations in occupied territories only when strictly required to safeguard, record or preserve cultural property, and subject to close cooperation with the competent national authorities of the occupied territory.[1262] This limitation of archaeological digs to rescue excavations is not free of controversy under conditions of a prolonged occupation.

(c) Submarine Cables

616. Hague Regulation 54 (which was introduced in the Hague text only in 1907) raises an offbeat theme:

> Submarine cables connecting a territory occupied with a neutral territory shall not be seized or destroyed except in the case of absolute necessity. They also must be restored and indemnities for them regulated at the peace.[1263]

617. The usual interpretation is that 'this provision affects only the landing end of the cable in occupied territory (within the territorial waters of the territory)', rather than the high seas.[1264] However, the San Remo Manual on Sea Warfare propounds that damage to cables laid on the seabed – not exclusively serving Belligerent Parties – must be avoided.[1265] As clarified in Article 54 (fourth paragraph) of the 1913 Oxford Manual, 'no distinction is to be made between [submarine] cables, according to whether they belong to the State or to individuals'.[1266]

[1258] HCJ 270/87, *Kandu v. Minister of Defence* et al., 43(1) *PD* 738, 742. (The Judgment is excerpted in English in 23 *IYHR* 286 (1993)).

[1259] HCJ 10356/02 etc., *Hass* et al. *v. IDF Commander of the West Bank* et al., 58(3) *PD* 443, 464. (The Judgment is excerpted in English in 36 *IYHR* 308 (2006)).

[1260] HCJ 560/88, *Shahrur v. Military Commander of Judea and Samaria* et al., 44(2) *PD* 233, 234. (The Judgment is excerpted in English in 23 *IYHR* 298 (1993)).

[1261] See O'Keefe, *supra* note 199, at 138–9.

[1262] Second Protocol to the Hague Convention, *supra* note 1250, at 1041.

[1263] Hague Regulations, *supra* note 22, at 250–1.

[1264] Von Glahn, *supra* note 339, at 215. See also US Department of Defense, *Law of War Manual*, *supra* note 1, at 807.

[1265] *San Remo Manual on International Law Applicable to Armed Conflicts at Sea* 111 (L. Doswald-Beck ed., 1995).

[1266] *Oxford Manual of Naval War*, *supra* note 306, at 1131.

618. In the past, submarine cables were of special relevance to telegraphic communications. Nowadays, they are particularly important in the context of cyber communications.[1267]

F. *Demolition of Houses as a Sanction*

(a) ***The Israeli Case Law***

619. The main problem that has arisen in the Israeli occupied territories in the context of destruction of property relates to the policy of demolishing houses as an administrative sanction against saboteurs. We have already examined a spin-off of the same subject in connection with collective penalties (see *supra* 476 *et seq.*). But the demolition penalty invites consideration irrespective of whether it is collective in nature.

620. The Israeli demolition policy is predicated on Section 119(1) of the Defence (Emergency) Regulations, enacted in 1945 in British Mandatory Palestine.[1268] This provision of the Defence Regulations (as amended) remained in force in all parts of Palestine at the time of termination of the British Mandate (1948) and thereafter: in the West Bank (incorporated in the Hashemite Kingdom of Jordan), in the Gaza Strip (occupied by Egypt) and even in Israel.[1269]

621. Section 119(1) authorizes a military commander to forfeit – and then destroy – any structure from which (i) a firearm has been illegally discharged, or any explosive thrown or detonated, or (ii) some of the inhabitants have committed (or attempted to commit, abetted or were accessories after the fact to the commission of) any offence against the Defence Regulations involving violence. The range of Section 119(1) is very extensive, but 'IDF guidelines require a direct link between the building and either the offense (as in cases where shots were fired or hand-grenades thrown therefrom) or the offender (such as the house in which the offender resided during the period in which the offenses occurred)'.[1270] Ownership of the dwelling place is immaterial: the acid test is use of the premises for the commission (including preparation) of the offence or residence therein by the offender.

622. The forfeiture of property – lying at the root of Section 119(1) – is at loggerheads with the prohibition of the confiscation of private property contained in Hague Regulation 46 (second paragraph) (see *infra* 689).

[1267] See *Talinn Manual on the International Law Applicable to Cyber Warfare* 247 (M.N. Schmitt ed., 2013).

[1268] Defence (Emergency) Regulations, *supra* note 989, at 1089.

[1269] See especially HCJ 358/88, *Association for Civil Rights in Israel* et al. *v. Commander of the Central Region* et al., 43(2) *PD* 529, 532–3. (The Judgment is excerpted in English in 23 *IYHR* 294 (1993)).

[1270] *Israel, the 'Intifada' and the Rule of Law, supra* note 817, at 142.

However, the principal pitfall in Section 119(1) is not forfeiture as such: it is the demolition of a house. In practice, the military government has developed an alternative for demolition: the sealing off of a place of habitation. Although sealing off is not mentioned *expressis verbis* in Section 119(1), it has been inferred by analogy: if the more draconian measure (demolition) is allowed, the more lenient measure (sealing off) should be permissible *a fortiori*.[1271]

623. Section 119(1) does not provide for a lapse of time enabling the persons affected to appeal or challenge the decision. All the same, the Israel Supreme Court (per President Shamgar) ruled, in one of several *Association for Civil Rights* cases, that – in the absence of military-operational reasons requiring instantaneous action – the demolition of a house on the basis of Section 119(1) (being irreversible) must be postponed, to enable judicial review, whereas sealing off (which is reversible) can be carried out immediately.[1272] The importance of judicial review surfaced in the *Nasman* case, where the majority of the Court (per Justice Or) determined that – should there be a factual error in the demolition order (in this instance, a wrongly stated charge that the petitioner was an accomplice to the burning down of an Income Tax office) – the order would be quashed.[1273]

624. In the *Hamri* case, the Court (per Justice Barak) remarked that, under Section 119(1), there are different gradations of measures, starting with mere forfeiture, going through sealing off, and reaching a peak with demolition.[1274] Justice Barak openly recognized that the demolition of a house impelled by Section 119(1) is a 'harsh and severe measure' in three respects: (i) it denies the inhabitants a place of living; (ii) it precludes the possibility of *restitutio in integrum*; and (iii) it may sometimes be harmful to neighbours.[1275] Sealing off, therefore, became the preferred practice, profiting also from the extra-added benefit of reversibility. Since the property was left undamaged, the possibility remained open that eventually it would be made available (perhaps under certain conditions) for repossession by the former inhabitants or members of their family. Section 119(1) itself raises the possibility of a remission of the forfeiture of a house and the restoration of the rights of the inhabitants. In the *Zakik* case, the Court (per Deputy President Elon) developed the concept of remission, observing that it can be explored at any time on the ground of

[1271] See *ibid.*, 143.

[1272] HCJ 358/88, *supra* note 1269, at 540–2.

[1273] HCJ 802/89, *Nasman* et al. *v. IDF Commander of the Gaza Strip*, 44(2) *PD* 601, 606–7. (The Judgment is excerpted in English in 23 *IYHR* 327 (1993)).

[1274] HCJ 361/82, *Hamri v. Commander of Judea and Samaria*, 36(3) *PD* 439, 443. (The Judgment is excerpted in English in 17 *IYHR* 314 (1987)).

[1275] *Ibid.*

(i) the gravity of the offence; (ii) the circumstances prevailing when remission is requested; (iii) the rehabilitation of the offender; or (iv) humanitarian considerations.[1276]

625. Over the years, the Court shifted the fulcrum of demolition of houses from the punitive to the deterrent dimension. The Court stressed time and again – as it did (*per curiam*) in the *Sahwil* case – that the power of the military commander is 'an unusual punitive action, whose main objective is to deter the performance of similar acts'.[1277] Of course, the distinction between the punitive and the deterrent aspects of demolition is not always easily discernible.[1278]

626. In quite a few instances in the Israeli experience, the two different strands of demolition of a house as a punitive-deterrent measure and the destruction of property due to imperative military necessity – i.e. for operational reasons – have been harnessed together in a rather baffling manner. Thus, in the *El Boreij Refugee Camp* case, the Court (per Deputy President Elon) confirmed the urgency of the demolition of a cluster of houses and shops, along a narrow road in a refugee camp, in the aftermath of the killing of a soldier.[1279] The military commander informed the Court that he was going to both (i) widen the road for general security purposes (while paying compensation to persons losing a place to live in or to ply their trade), and (ii) exercise his authority under Section 119(1) as a punitive-deterrent measure against those implicated in the homicide.[1280] Deputy President Elon (citing Hague Regulations 23(g) and 43, and especially Article 53 of the Geneva Convention) concluded that, despite the general prohibition of the destruction of property situated in occupied territories, such destruction is permissible when rendered absolutely necessary by military requirements.[1281]

627. Although the Judgment's summary of the law of belligerent occupation with respect to destruction of property – when standing by itself – is accurate, it must be delinked from the preceding argumentation. The pivotal point is that destruction of property brought about by actual military operations is not the same as demolition of a house as a punitive-deterrent sanction. Unlike the former, the latter measure is not compatible with the *jus in bello*. As for the widening of an artery of communication – accompanied by the payment of compensation – it actually falls neither in one rubric nor in the other. It must

[1276] HCJ 5139/91, *Zakik v. Commander of IDF Forces in the West Bank*, 46(4) *PD* 260, 263. (The Judgment is excerpted in English in 25 *IYHR* 334 (1995)).

[1277] HCJ 434/79, *Sahwil* et al. *v. Commander of Judea and Samaria*, 34(1) *PD* 464, 466. (The Judgment is excerpted in English in 10 *IYHR* 345 (1980)).

[1278] See Farrell, *supra* note 959, at 927–8.

[1279] HCJ 4112/90, *Association for Civil Rights in Israel v. Commanding Officer of the Southern Region*, 44(4) *PD* 626, 629–32. (The Judgment is excerpted in English in 23 *IYHR* 333 (1993)).

[1280] *Ibid.*, 633–4.

[1281] *Ibid.*, 636.

be seen in terms of expropriation of property for public purposes, based on the local law in force in the occupied territory (see *infra* 693).

628. The Court consistently declined to draw a dividing line between destruction of property as a measure taken during military operations and as a punitive-deterrent sanction. The tendency to amalgamate the two disparate types of activities by the Occupying Power is particularly noticeable in more recent Judgments, e.g., in the *Amer* case (per President Barak).[1282] But the trend goes back as far as 1971, when – in a seminal article on the occupied territories – the future President of the Supreme Court, Shamgar (then Attorney-General), maintained that when hand-grenades are thrown out of a house, that house becomes a military base and there is no difference between immediate military reaction leading to its destruction and later demolition as a punitive act.[1283] This curious concept seems to have had a subliminal influence on the ensuing policy of the military government and, more directly, on the thinking of the Court. If correct, the Shamgar approach would have reconciled the demolition practice predicated on Section 119(1) with the provisions of the Geneva Convention and the Hague Regulations. No wonder that the Court steadfastly denied that Section 119(1) is contradicted by either the Geneva Convention[1284] or the Hague Regulations.[1285] Nevertheless, the notion that military-operational needs can be lumped together with punitive-deterrent measures is spurious. The Court's outlook was occluded by its failure to notice that, once the fighting is over, lawful options affecting private property – available to the Occupying Power up to that point – are dramatically reduced. In the post-combat stage, the law governing the situation undergoes a profound transformation, and a house surviving combat is no longer susceptible of deliberate destruction.

629. In 2005, the policy of demolition of houses (or parts thereof) as an administrative sanction was generally suspended by the Minister of Defence, although still allowed in some extraordinary circumstances. In the *Abu Dheim* Judgment of 2009, the Supreme Court (per Justice M. Naor) took note of the general suspension but declined to intervene when it was decided by the competent authority to proceed to demolition in an exceptional instance.[1286] But the overall suspension came to an end in 2014, and this led to several unsuccessful attempts to reopen the entire topic before the Court on the ground that the

[1282] HCJ 6696/02 etc., *Amer* et al. *v. IDF Commander of the West Bank*, 56(6) *PD* 110, 115. (The Judgment is excerpted in English in 32 *IYHR* 381 (2002)).

[1283] Shamgar, *supra* note 141, at 276.

[1284] See, e.g., HCJ 434/79, *supra* note 1277, at 466 (*per curiam*); HCJ 2977/91 etc., *Taj* et al. *v. Minister of Defence* et al. 46(5) *PD* 467, 473 (per Justice D. Levin). (The Judgment is excerpted in English in 25 *IYHR* 330 (1995)).

[1285] See HCJ 2977/91 etc., *ibid.*

[1286] HCJ 9353/08, *Abu Dheim* et al. v. *Commander of the Home Front Command*, paras. 9–11. (The Judgment is excerpted in English in 39 *IYHR* 400 (2009)).

previous string of Judgments was outdated. Interestingly, in a new *Kawasme* case, the Court (per Justice Y. Danziger) held that the demolition practice based on Section 119(1) is consistent with the provision of Article XII(1) of the 1995 Israeli-Palestinian Interim Agreement (quoted *infra* 788).[1287] In the *Centre for the Defence of the Individual* case, the Court (per Justice E. Rubinstein) dismissed the petition – not without some misgivings – by applying here, as in so many other instances (see *infra* 768), the criterion of proportionality.[1288] Challenges to the effectivity of demolitions of houses as a deterrent measure received much attention in this Judgment (especially in the separate opinions of Justices N. Sohlberg[1289] and Hayut[1290]), yet the Court was not swayed by them.

(b) A Trade-Off of Sanctions?

630. In a Symposium convened by Tel Aviv University in 1971, A. Dershowitz came up with the following justification of the Israeli demolition policy:

> the destruction of houses in the occupied territories in Israel. Let us assume that such destruction would be a technical violation of some Convention. On the other hand, looked at realistically, what is it? It is a monetary punishment. Surely everybody would agree that, in terms of human values, it is better to destroy somebody's house than to destroy somebody's person; it is better to destroy his house than to detain him.[1291]

To paraphrase the argument, an Occupying Power has the discretion to trade off the imposition of capital punishment or internment – expressly permitted under the Geneva Convention, subject to certain qualifications (see *supra* 440, 519) – in favour of the more humane measure of demolition of houses (indefensible under the Convention). This view has been endorsed by a number of Israeli officials exonerating the application of Section 119(1). Thus, D. Shefi, giving prominence to the fact that Israel does not execute saboteurs, went on to say:

> It can hardly be claimed that, from the humanitarian point of view, a system which prefers a punishment that involves the demolition of the property of an individual to the taking of his life (which, under international law, it was empowered to) is lacking in sensitivity to humanitarian reactions.[1292]

631. Indubitably, a death sentence is the ultimate penalty. However, since it must be embodied in a judicial verdict and is contingent on criminal guilt

[1287] HCJ 5290/14 etc., *Kawasme* et al. v. *Military Commander of the West Bank Area* et al., para. 28.
[1288] HCJ 8091/14, *Centre for the Defence of the Individual* et al. v. *Minister of Defence* et al., paras. 21–8. (The Judgment is excerpted in English in 45 *IYHR* 229 (2015)).
[1289] *Ibid.*, paras. 4–14.
[1290] *Ibid.*, paras. 4–5.
[1291] Symposium on Human Rights in Time of War, Discussion Extracts, Comments by A. Dershowitz, 1 *IYHR* 361, 376 (1971).
[1292] D. Shefi, 'The Protection of Human Rights in Areas Administered by Israel: United Nations Findings and Reality', 3 *IYHR* 337, 347 (1973).

being established beyond reasonable doubt (following a fair trial), it cannot be put on the same level with an administrative decision taken by the military government to raze a saboteur's home.[1293] Moreover, the perception of a discretionary power vested (as it were) in an Occupying Power, to weigh human values on a sliding scale – and to barter binding obligations for seemingly more humane entitlements – verges on the bizarre. When the framers of an international treaty negotiate its strictures, they have an opportunity to mull over competing interests and values. Once the text is finalized, a Contracting Party must abide by it to the letter (unless, at the critical time of expressing consent to be bound by the treaty, the State concerned has made a valid reservation excluding or modifying the legal effect of certain provisions in their application to itself[1294]). If every Occupying Power were given leave to determine unilaterally whether or not to absolve itself of an unpalatable treaty obligation – by sacrificing a counterpart right that it is willing to discard – this would wreak havoc with the *jus in bello*.[1295] The danger inherent in the Dershowitz thesis is aggravated by his confident assertion that 'detention is a much more serious violation than economic punishment – specifically, the destroying of houses'.[1296] Many victims of the pair of sanctions would beg to differ.

G. Demolitions of Houses on Other Grounds

632. M. Bothe maintains that 'at least in the case of a long-term occupation, it could be argued that there are other legitimate reasons for demolitions, for example demolitions to allow infrastructure developments for the benefit of the population' (although 'only in extreme circumstances under limited conditions').[1297] While this is no doubt correct, such demolitions will have to be based on lawful expropriation coupled with compensation: a subject-matter that will be discussed *infra* 693.

II. Spoliation

633. One of the fundamental principles of belligerent occupation is the prohibition of spoliation (or plunder) of an occupied territory by the Occupying Power. As formulated by the International Military Tribunal at Nuremberg:

[1293] See E.R. Cohen, *Human Rights in the Israeli-Occupied Territories 1967–1982* 103 (1985).

[1294] See Articles 2(d) and 19 of the Vienna Convention on the Law of Treaties, *supra* note 706, at 141, 145.

[1295] See D. Simon, 'The Demolition of Homes in the Israeli Occupied Territories', 19 *YJIL* 1, 58 (1994).

[1296] Symposium, *supra* note 1291, at 377.

[1297] Bothe, *supra* note 589, at 1472.

under the rules of war, the economy of an occupied country can only be required to bear the expense[s] of the occupation, and these should not be greater than the economy of the country can reasonably be expected to bear.[1298]

634. In the *I.G. Farben* trial (part of the 'Subsequent Proceedings' at Nuremberg), an American Military Tribunal stated in 1948 that the Nazi occupation had entailed unlawful spoliation of both public and private property in occupied Europe.[1299] The Tribunal noted that the Hague Regulations do not explicitly employ the term 'spoliation', but this is a term of convenience – synonymous with 'plunder' – embracing widespread and systematic acts of dispossession of property in occupied territories in violation of the *jus in bello*.[1300]

635. In the *Krupp* trial, another American Military Tribunal pronounced:

The Articles of the Hague Regulations … are clear and unequivocal. Their essence is: if, as a result of war action, a belligerent occupies territory of the adversary, he does not, thereby, acquire the right to dispose of property in that territory, except according to the strict rules laid down in the Regulations.[1301]

It then added:

Spoliation of private property … is forbidden under two aspects: firstly, the individual private owner of property must not be deprived of it; secondly, the economic substance of the belligerently occupied territory must not be taken over by the occupant or put to the service of his war effort – always with the proviso that there are exemptions from this rule which are strictly limited to the needs of the army of occupation insofar as such needs do not exceed the economic strength of the occupied territory.[1302]

636. The ICTY Judgment of the Trial Chamber in the *Kordić* case summed up the law as regards spoliation in saying:

The offence of plunder or spoliation has long been known to international law, and it is prohibited as a matter of both conventional and customary law.[1303]

III. Pillage

A. *The General Prohibition*

637. Pillage (or looting) is sometimes merged with plunder (or spoliation),[1304] but it is better to examine the two categories of unlawful activities separately.

[1298] International Military Tribunal (Nuremberg), *supra* note 5, at 235.
[1299] *I.G. Farben* trial (*Krauch* et al.) (US Military Tribunal, Nuremberg, 1948), 10 *LRTWC* 1, 44–5.
[1300] *Ibid.*
[1301] *Krupp* trial, *supra* note 1212, at 133–4.
[1302] *Ibid.*, 135.
[1303] *Prosecutor v. Kordić* et al., *supra* note 1251, at para. 351.
[1304] See *Prosecutor v. Delalić* et al., *supra* note 923, at para 591.

The prohibition of pillage is incorporated in Hague Regulation 47[1305] and in Article 33 (second paragraph) of Geneva Convention (IV).[1306] Pillage is a war crime under Article 8(2)(b)(xvi) of the Rome Statute of the International Criminal Court.[1307]

638. As defined by the Trial Chamber of the ICTY in the *Delalić* case (not in the context of occupied territories), pillage consists of an unlawful appropriation of public or private property by individual soldiers motivated by personal greed.[1308] The Elements of Crime appended to Article 8(2)(b)(xvi) of the Rome Statute refer to appropriation 'for private or personal use'.[1309]

639. In the *Delalić* Judgment, it was taken for granted that pillaged property must have a 'sufficient monetary value'.[1310] But, to the victim, the property looted may have a sentimental value that far outstrips financial considerations.[1311] In any event, the *jus in bello* prohibition of pillage (as distinct, perhaps, from the felony that is the subject of a war crime prosecution) is by no means tied to any monetary threshold. Unlawful trophy-taking is a form of pillage, too.

640. The Eritrea Ethiopia Claims Commission, in 2004, found Ethiopia liable for losses resulting from looting by its soldiers that occurred in a town occupied by it for more than half a year.[1312] The International Court of Justice held in the *Armed Activities* (Congo v. Uganda) case that, in or out of an occupied territory, every Belligerent Party has a 'duty of vigilance' to take adequate measures ensuring that its military forces do not engage in pillage.[1313] The Court said that an Occupying Power's obligation in an occupied territory goes further: it must take appropriate measures to prevent looting not only by undisciplined members of its own armed forces, but even by private persons.[1314] This holding is apposite to the fact-finding report of widespread looting of Georgian property by Ossetian civilians in a 'buffer zone' that was under Russian occupation for several months in 2008 (see *supra* 35).[1315]

1305 Hague Regulations, *supra* note 22, at 246–7. See also Hague Regulation 28, *ibid.*, 236–7.

1306 Geneva Convention (IV), *supra* note 29, at 590.

1307 Rome Statute of the International Criminal Court, *supra* note 350, at 1318.

1308 *Prosecutor v. Delalić* et al, *supra* note 923, at paras. 590–1.

1309 Dörmann, *supra* note 355, at 272.

1310 *Prosecutor v. Delalić* et al., *supra* note 923, at para. 1154.

1311 See A. Zahar and G. Sluiter, *International Criminal Law* 146–7 (2008).

1312 Eritrea Ethiopia Claims Commission, Partial Award (Central Front), Eritrea's Claims, *supra* note 250, at 1264–5.

1313 *Case Concerning Armed Activities on the Territory of the Congo* (Congo v. Uganda), *supra* note 26, at 252.

1314 See *ibid.*, 253.

1315 See II *Report of the Independent International Fact-Finding Mission on the Conflict in Georgia*, *supra* note 72, at 365.

641. When the evidence leaves room for doubt whether goods in an occupied territory were pillaged for private ends by members of the armed forces of the Occupying Power or unlawfully taken for public purposes (in the absence of payment in cash or redeemable receipt; see *infra* 699), the Arbitrators in the *German Responsibility* case of 1930 (R. Fazy, R. Guex and A. de Meuron) stated that there should be a presumption in favour of the latter interpretation of the events.[1316]

B. *Cultural Property*

642. It is important to highlight the first sentence of Article 4(3) of the 1954 Hague Convention for the Protection of Cultural Property in the Event of Armed Conflict, in which the Contracting Parties undertake:

> to prohibit, prevent and, if necessary, put a stop to any form of theft, pillage or misappropriation of, and any acts of vandalism directed against, cultural property.[1317]

643. Occupied territories are not mentioned in this clause, and there is some disagreement as to whether it applies to them.[1318] But, assuming that it does (and the present author firmly believes that such is the case), one should keep in mind that any special protection of cultural property would be supplementary to the general 'duty of vigilance' that obligates an Occupying Power to prevent pillage by private persons in occupied territories (see *supra* 640).

644. Allegations of failure to meet acceptable standards of prevention of pillage were much debated following the ransacking of the Iraqi National Museum (and other sites) at the point of entry of US forces into Baghdad in April 2003. The looting was perpetrated not by American armed forces but by local mobs. Yet, it was contended that the US Command, as the Occupying Power, fell short of taking the necessary precautionary steps to secure the museum from potentially irretrievable losses.[1319] The argument rested on the assumption that, at the time the looters went on the rampage, the US was already the Occupying Power in Baghdad.[1320] However, the meltdown of

[1316] *Responsabilité de l'Allemagne à Raison des Actes Commis Postérieurement au 31 Juillet 1914 et avant que le Portugal Ne Participât à la Guerre* (Portugal, Germany), 1930, 2 *RIAA* 1035, 1046.

[1317] Hague Convention for the Protection of Cultural Property in the Event of Armed Conflict, *supra* note 144, at 1002.

[1318] See E. Varner, 'The Art of Armed Conflicts: An Analysis of the United States' Legal Requirements towards Cultural Property under the 1954 Hague Convention', 44 *Cre.LR* 1185, 1227–9 (2010–11).

[1319] See C. Phuong, 'The Protection of Iraqi Cultural Property', 53 *ICLQ* 985, 986–7 (2004).

[1320] For a day-by-day analysis of the situation on the ground in Baghdad during the relevant time frame, see J.C. Johnson, 'Under New Management: The Obligation to Protect Cultural Property during Military Occupation', 190–1 *Mil.LR* 111, 149–52 (2006–7).

the Saddam Hussein regime brought about a 'transition period between war fighting and effective occupation',[1321] and it stands to reason that the looting took place during an hiatus between the invasion stage and the consolidation of belligerent occupation in Iraq (see *supra* 134). In realistic terms, the US could be taken to task only if the looting occurred after the onset of belligerent occupation in Baghdad. In the thick of battle, it may prove practically impossible for a Belligerent Party to detach from the fighting formations special units tasked with the prevention of looting of cultural (or any other) property by civilians. Only when the situation has stabilized does the Belligerent Party – as an Occupying Power – incur the responsibility of taking strident measures against such occurrences.

[1321] A.P.V. Rogers, *Law on the Battlefield* 202 (3rd edn, 2012).

10 Seizure and Requisition of Property in Occupied Territories

I. General Observations

A. Definitions

645. Since diverse terms are often used for the taking of property in occupied territories, it is useful to define them carefully:
(a) 'Seizure' is a comprehensive term for the taking of any property (movable or immovable) by an Occupying Power, for whatever use, irrespective of the type of ownership (public or private) and regardless of indemnity or restoration.
(b) 'Requisition' is embedded in the *jus in bello* and it must be distinguished from 'confiscation'. In both instances, the Occupying Power seizes property, but – unlike confiscation – requisition is associated with payment, compensation or restoration.
(c) 'Expropriation' relates to property taken from an owner for public purposes – subject to compensation – in accordance with the local law of the occupied territory, as distinct from the *jus in bello*.

646. Destruction and seizure of property in occupied territories are frequently conflated in treaty texts (see *supra* 595, 608, 616). Yet, objectively speaking, there is a profound distinction between these two modes of action: after all, destruction is irreversible whereas seizure is not. Of course, if seizure of property causes possession to be divested indefinitely in a prolonged occupation, destruction and seizure may have the same traumatic effect from the subjective perspective of the aggrieved owner.[1322]

B. Challenging the Validity of Seizure

647. The validity of the seizure of property by the Occupying Power in an occupied territory – and any resultant transfer of title over the real estate

[1322] See Brilmayer and Chepiga, *supra* note 1219, at 423–4.

or goods – can be challenged *a posteriori*, in domestic or international proceedings that may take place many years after the event[1323] (see, e.g., the *Lighthouses* case *infra* 651). Litigations before international courts or arbitral tribunals are not likely to mature over a relevant case while an occupation is in progress (unless the occupation is prolonged). Domestic proceedings have a greater chance of arising during the occupation. Domestic courts may belong to (i) the Occupying Power itself; (ii) the displaced sovereign, sitting outside the occupied territory; or (iii) neutral or allied countries. However, local courts within the occupied territory are not generally disposed to investigate in real time the legal pros and cons of the seizure of property by the Occupying Power. This is due to the fact that local judges will normally do their utmost not to be impaled on the horns of the dilemma of validating or invalidating the legislation of the Occupying Power while the occupation is ongoing (see *supra* 402).

C. The Distinction between Public and Private Property

648. Insofar as seizure of property in occupied territories is concerned, a critical distinction has to be drawn between private and public (or State) property, with a preferential treatment granted to private property. The purpose of the distinction – as observed by the Arbitrator W.D. Hines in the 1921 Award in the *Cession of Vessels and Tugs for Navigation on the Danube* case – is to place the burdens of war on the Belligerent Party whose territory is under occupation, rather than on private individuals.[1324] It is evident, all the same, that the advantageous position of private over public property can be manipulated to the detriment of countries in which the economy is nationalized.[1325]

649. A segregation between private and public property is sometimes fraught with difficulty:

(a) There may be joint (public and private) ownership of the same property.
(b) Property may belong to public bodies which are only quasi-governmental in character.[1326]
(c) There is an issue as regards 'common lands' that are neither private nor owned by the State (or by local communities). These are usually incorporated in the category of public property.[1327]

1323 See J.H.W. Verzijl, IX *International Law in Historical Perspective,* 185–8 (1978).
1324 *Cession of Vessels and Tugs for Navigation on the Danube* case (Allied Powers, Germany, Austria, Hungary and Bulgaria), 1921, 1 *RIAA* 97, 107.
1325 See J. Robinson, 'Transfer of Property in Enemy Occupied Territory', 39 *AJIL* 216, 218 (1945).
1326 See von Glahn, *supra* note 339, at 179.
1327 See Gasser and Dörmann, *supra* note 196, at 293.

650. Title to property may be transferred from the displaced sovereign to private individuals. The Occupying Power need not recognize such transactions as valid unless they were effected well before the commencement of the occupation.[1328]

651. The legal position is further tangled by concessions issued by the State to private individuals or corporations. A good example can be found in the *Lighthouses* arbitration of 1956, relating to the belligerent occupation of Salonika by the Greeks in the first Balkan War of 1912.[1329] The proceedings concerned lighthouses dues collected by a French company operating a concession granted by the Ottoman Empire (the displaced sovereign). Greece wished to seize the cash as State funds. The Arbitral Tribunal (headed by J.H.W. Verzijl) did not deny that, had the lighthouses dues been collected directly by the Ottoman Government, they would indeed have constituted State funds (in which eventuality they would have been susceptible of seizure by the Occupying Power; see *infra* 670).[1330] However, since the concession conferred on the French company the right to collect the dues (concurrently with the costly obligation of maintaining the lighthouses), the cash in hand – albeit collected in the name of the Government – had to be labelled as private property and, in consequence, could not be seized.[1331]

652. The Israel Supreme Court, in the *El Nazer* case, decided (per Justice Shamgar) that, when doubt arises as to whether property is publicly or privately owned, it will be treated as public property until the issue of ownership is settled.[1332] This position was reconfirmed by the Court in other instances, e.g., in the *Al Nawar* case (per President Shamgar).[1333] Admittedly, there is a controversy here: some authorities shore up the Court's approach,[1334] whereas others deny the existence of any presumption in favour of the public character of property.[1335] The foremost argument against the existence of a presumption, in the words of A. Cassese, is that it means 'in fact broaden[ing] the powers of the occupant'.[1336] Yet, the *UK Manual of the Law of Armed Conflict* throws its weight behind the counter-view that, in case of doubt, property (e.g., stores and supplies) 'must be considered to be public property unless and until its private

[1328] See Van Engeland, *supra* note 1217, at 1538.

[1329] *Affaire Relative à la Concession des Phares de l'Empire Ottomane* (Greece, France), 1956, 12 *RIAA* 157, 161.

[1330] *Ibid.*, 201.

[1331] *Ibid.*, 201–2.

[1332] HCJ 285/81, *El Nazer* et al. *v. Commander of Judea and Samaria* et al., 36(1) *PD* 701, 704–5. (The Judgment is excerpted in English in 13 *IYHR* 368 (1983)).

[1333] HCJ 574/82, *Al Nawar v. Minister of Defence* et al., 39(3) *PD* 449, 470. (The Judgment is excerpted in English in 16 *IYHR* 321 (1986)).

[1334] See von Glahn, *supra* note 339, at 179.

[1335] See Schwarzenberger, *supra* note 204, at 309.

[1336] Cassese, *supra* note 741, at 437–8.

character is clearly shown'.[1337] In a similar vein, the US Department of Defense *Law of War Manual* states that '[i]f it is unknown whether certain property is public or private, it should be treated as public property until its ownership is ascertained'.[1338]

II. Public Property

653. An Occupying Power may seize public property belonging to the displaced sovereign and use it in accordance with its needs. But the degree of permissible use hinges on a distinction between movable and immovable property.

A. Immovable Property

(a) The Rights of Usufruct

654. The law governing the seizure of immovable property is laid down in Hague Regulation 55:

> The occupying State shall regard itself only as administrator and usufructuary of the public buildings, immovable property, forests and agricultural undertakings belonging to the hostile State, and situated in the occupied country. It must protect the capital of these properties, and administer it according to the rules of usufruct.[1339]

The emphasis in Regulation 55 on 'forests and agricultural undertakings' must not detract from the general reference to public immovable property. There is no question, for instance, that an Occupying Power can seize and use airfields, naval dockyards, military barracks, etc., in occupied territories.[1340]

655. In the *El Nazer* case, the Israel Supreme Court (per Justice Shamgar) picked out the following elements in Regulation 55: (i) ownership over State immovable property does not pass from the displaced sovereign to the Occupying Power; (ii) the Occupying Power is entitled to administer the property and reap its fruits; but, as against this right, there is an obligation: (iii) the Occupying Power has to preserve the property and ensure its continued existence.[1341]

656. The Occupying Power must keep the capital of immovable State property unharmed (subject to ordinary wear and tear, depending on the type of property), and its position is that of an 'administrator and usufructuary'. As is

[1337] *UK Manual of the Law of Armed Conflict, supra* note 230, at 304.
[1338] US Department of Defense, *Law of War Manual, supra* note 1, at 810.
[1339] Hague Regulations, *supra* note 22, at 250–1.
[1340] See *UK Manual of the Law of Armed Conflict, supra* note 230, at 303.
[1341] HCJ 285/81, *supra* note 1332, at 704.

common in a usufruct, entitlements are limited to the rights of use (*jus utendi*) and consumption of fruits (*jus fruendi*).[1342] Administration and usufruct denote the exclusion of an entitlement to sell the property (in the absence of ownership by the Occupying Power), while lease, utilization or cultivation of land is permitted.[1343] Most significantly, the Occupying Power is disallowed to do anything amounting to unlawful spoliation of the land (see *supra* 633 *et seq*.).[1344] Thus, the Occupying Power can operate public railways (owned by the displaced sovereign or seized by it, in turn, prior to the occupation).[1345] Still, as a mere usufructuary, the Occupying Power cannot remove the tracks of a public railroad and transport them elsewhere for the construction of new rail lines in support of its military operations.[1346]

657. A very important aspect of its rights as a usufructuary is that an Occupying Power may billet units of the army of occupation and the military government in public buildings owned by the displaced sovereign.[1347] As the case of Iraq shows, the Occupying Power may establish a security zone (the so-called 'Green Zone' in Baghdad) from which it would control the occupied territory.[1348]

658. The Occupying Power is also entitled to collect rents due from tenants in public buildings, provided that these mature during the occupation (the corollary is that the displaced sovereign cannot demand repayment of the same rents upon being restored to the occupied territory; see *infra* 879).[1349]

659. The Occupying Power may assume ownership of crops growing in public agricultural lands (as distinct from the lands themselves). But that will not happen automatically. If the Occupying Power desires to exercise its rights over such crops, it cannot remain passive: some overt action must be taken displaying intention. In the *Affaire du Guano* arbitration of 1901, the Arbitral Tribunal (presided over by H. Hafner) decided that, as long as this is not done, the proprietary right over the crops – or their counterpart (in this case, guano) – is not transferred from the displaced sovereign to the Occupying Power.[1350]

660. Usufruct rights denote that 'the product or proceeds' arising out of the capital of immovable public property may be used by the Occupying Power at its discretion – not necessarily within the occupied territory – and it may

[1342] See von Glahn, *supra* note 339, at 176–7.
[1343] See HCJ 285/81, *supra* note 1332, at 704.
[1344] See *Ministries* trial, *supra* note 357, at 361.
[1345] For an interesting example, see S. Rosenne, 'The Jaffa-Jerusalem Railway Arbitration (1922)', 28 *IYHR* 239, 243 (1998).
[1346] See A.V. Freeman, 'General Note on the Law of War Booty', 40 *AJIL* 795, 801 (1946).
[1347] See W.E. Hall, *A Treatise on International Law* 504 (8th edn, A.P. Higgins ed., 1924).
[1348] See A. McDonald and H. Brollowski, 'Security Zones', IX *MPEPIL* 90, 92–3.
[1349] See II *Wheaton's International Law* 258 (7th edn, A.B. Keith ed., 1944).
[1350] *Affaire de Guano* (Chili, France), 1901, 15 *RIAA* 77, 367.

even be sold.[1351] This view, while not shared by everybody,[1352] is sustained by the tenor of Regulation 55. The prohibition of sale implicit in Regulation 55 is limited to the (immovable) public property as such, i.e. the capital: it does not extend to the yield harvested from public lands.[1353]

(b) Mining Rights

661. In general, fruit consumption by the Occupying Power must not encroach upon the capital. Nevertheless, it is acknowledged that – in the words of the *UK Manual of the Law of Armed Conflict* – the Occupying Power may not only sell crops, but also 'cut and sell timber, and work mines', notwithstanding the fact that the process depletes the capital that is left to be exploited.[1354] With timber the logic is latent in the situation: the expectation is that the trees will grow again and thus the capital is renewable. That is not the case with mines: ores and other minerals extracted are obviously not renewable. There is, however, a good practical reason for allowing the Occupying Power to work mines: non-maintenance is liable to lead to long-term system decline, thereby endangering resumption of operations under the restored sovereign.[1355]

662. As far as existing State-owned mines are concerned, it is by and large agreed that – as a rule of thumb – any ongoing mining in the occupied territory must not exceed average production levels previously established.[1356] In other words, the Occupying Power is not allowed to exploit mineral deposits at an unreasonably accelerated rate, exhausting a lode in an untimely fashion.[1357] But it is doubtful whether this means that the Occupying Power is barred (especially in a prolonged occupation) from installing new and more efficient technologies increasing output.[1358]

(c) New Mines and Quarries

663. A separate issue is whether the Occupying Power (in the course of a prolonged occupation) may explore and operate new mines, not in use prior

[1351] See von Glahn, *supra* note 339, at 177.

[1352] See S. Vité, 'The Interrelation of the Law of Occupation and Economic, Social and Cultural Rights: The Examples of Food, Health and Property', 871 *IRRC* 629, 648 (2008).

[1353] See von Glahn, *supra* note 339, at 177–8.

[1354] *UK Manual of the Law of Armed Conflict, supra* note 230, at 303.

[1355] See I. Scobbie, 'Natural Resources and Belligerent Occupation: Mutation through Permanent Sovereignty', *Human Rights, Self-Determination and Political Change in the Occupied Palestinian Territories* 221, 238 (S. Bowen ed., 1997).

[1356] See *UK Manual of the Law of Armed Conflict, supra* note 230, at 303.

[1357] See M. Leigh, 'Department of State Memorandum of Law on Israel's Right to Develop New Oil Fields in Sinai and the Gulf of Suez', 16 *ILM* 733, 740 (1977).

[1358] See R.D. Langenkamp and R.D. Zedalis, 'What Happens to the Iraqi Oil?: Thoughts on Some Significant, Unexamined International Legal Questions Regarding Occupation of Oil Fields', 14 *EJIL* 417, 429 (2003).

to the occupation. There is a school of thought denying that such action is permissible, despite the enhanced value of the property when it is eventually handed back to the restored sovereign.[1359] Yet, as a minimum, one cannot ignore the burgeoning needs of the local inhabitants. Thus, the Israel Supreme Court (per Justice Grunis), in a brief Judgment in the *Na'ale* case, decided that the opening of a new quarry in the West Bank was consistent with Regulation 55 since its product would be used for local works in the territory.[1360] The same rationale applies to coal required for heating in the occupied territory and other, analogous, situations.

664. A much more detailed analysis of the status of quarries (and mines) in occupied territories has been undertaken in the *Yesh Din* case of 2011, where the Court (per President Beinisch) had to address a general challenge to their operation in the West Bank.[1361] The Judgment cited Article 31 of Annex I to the 1995 Interim Agreement between Israel and the PLO,[1362] whereby powers and responsibilities relating to quarries and mines in the West Bank and the Gaza Strip will be transferred gradually to the Palestinians and in the meantime operating quarries shall not be adversely affected.[1363] As for the application of Hague Regulation 55, the Court cited the view (expressed by the present author and others) that the usufruct rights of the Occupying Power include an entitlement to operate quarries and to sell their product (as distinct from the capital) outside the occupied territory.[1364] President Beinisch found nothing wrong in a reasonable operation of new quarries by private concessionaires.[1365] She fully endorsed the position of the respondents that the development of such quarries enhances the welfare of the local population, since – even if their product is sold outside the occupied territory – hundreds of local inhabitants benefit from gainful employment, and substantial revenues from quarries' concession fees are spent for the administration of the area.[1366] The Judgment tied this to earlier decisions (especially in the *Jamait Askan* case, *supra* 360 *et seq.*) on the special nature of prolonged occupation, saying:

[1359] See B.M. Clagett and O.T. Johnson, Jr., 'May Israel as a Belligerent Occupant Lawfully Exploit Previously Unexploited Oil Resources of the Gulf of Suez?', 72 *AJIL* 558, 574–5 (1978).

[1360] HCJ 9717/03, *Na'ale – Association for Settlement in Samaria of Employees of the Israel Aircraft Industry v. Higher Planning Council in Judea and Samaria,* 58(6) *PD* 97, 102–3. (The Judgment is excerpted in English in 37 *IYHR* 332 (2007)).

[1361] HCJ 2164/09, *Yesh Din v. Commander of the IDF Forces in the West Bank* et al., paras. 6–13.

[1362] Protocol Concerning Redeployment and Security Arrangements, Annex I to Israel-Palestine Liberation Organization, Interim Agreement on the West Bank and the Gaza Strip, *supra* note 116, at 619.

[1363] HCJ 2164/09, *supra* note 1361, at paras. 6–7.

[1364] *Ibid.*, para. 7.

[1365] *Ibid.*, para. 8.

[1366] *Ibid.*, paras. 9–13.

the belligerent occupation by Israel of the area has unique characteristics, the most important of which is the duration of the occupation period, which requires the adjustment of the laws to the reality on the ground; imposing on Israel an obligation to administer normal life for a period that – even if it is legally temporary – is certainly long-range. Hence, the traditional occupation laws require adjustment to the prolongation of the occupation, to the continuation of normal life in the area and to the existence of the economic relations between the two authorities: the occupying and the occupied.[1367]

The *Yesh Din* decision has been criticized on several grounds.[1368] But the express provision of the Israel-PLO Interim Agreement seems to override most of them.

(d) New Oil Wells

665. The paramount issue in this context is whether the Occupying Power can prospect for oil (petroleum) in the occupied territory, including its continental shelf. Again, some commentators propound that the Occupying Power is forbidden to deplete oil reserves, which must be left untouched.[1369] The better view, in the opinion of the present writer, is that '[e]xploration for resources by an occupant (including exploration in lawfully delimited offshore areas) normally cannot be considered a prohibited activity'.[1370] The controversy came to a head in the concrete circumstances of Israel drilling new oil wells in the continental shelf of the Sinai Peninsula, in the Gulf of Suez, in the 1970s.[1371]

666. A preliminary question presents itself, whether crude underground oil should be classified as movable or immovable property. The matter was deliberated by the Court of Appeal in Singapore, in 1956, in the *Bataafsche* case,[1372] the facts of which will be narrated *infra* 722. The majority of the Court pronounced that crude oil remaining underground constitutes immovable property.[1373] Withal, the position is not so simple.[1374] It is undeniable that crude oil already pumped into artificial reservoirs above ground forms movable property. If so, what is the difference between man-made storage of pumped oil above ground and natural reservoirs of crude oil underground? It ought to be borne in mind that strategic reserves of oil are often stored by States subterraneously. Is there a good reason for setting pumped oil apart from untapped oil? After all, coal must be carved out of rock. Oil, contrariwise, is in a liquid

1367 *Ibid.*, para. 10.
1368 See D. Kretzmer, 'The Law of Belligerent Occupation in the Supreme Court of Israel', 885 *IRRC* 207, 220–2 (2012)
1369 See Clagett and Johnson, *supra* note 1359, at 575.
1370 Von Glahn, *supra* note 973, at 687–8.
1371 See Gerson, *supra* note 267, at 730–2.
1372 *N.V. de Bataafsche Petroleum Maatschappij* et al. *v. The War Damage Commission* (Singapore, Court of Appeal, 1956), 23 *ILR* 810.
1373 *Ibid.*, 823–4 (per Whyatt, C.J.). See also *ibid.*, 835 (per Mathew, J.).
1374 See Anonymous, 'Note', 71 *HLR* 568, 570 (1957–8).

state within a natural pocket underground, and drilling for it merely means that the oil can gush out – or be drawn up – onto the surface. If underground oil is to be viewed as movable property, Regulation 55 is no longer applicable and the matter is resolved by rules that will be discussed *infra* 717 *et seq*. For sure, even if underground oil is deemed to be movable property, this does not affect the status of the oil drilling installations which may be categorized as immovables.[1375]

(e) Permanent Sovereignty over Natural Resources

667. In the *Armed Activities* (Congo v. Uganda) case, the International Court of Justice brought up – in the context of exploitation of the natural resources of an occupied territory – the peacetime principle of permanent sovereignty over natural resources (developed mainly in a series of General Assembly resolutions).[1376] The Court did not actually consider the topic relevant to the proceedings, which pertained to individual looting (see *supra* 640), rather than to a governmental policy of the Occupying Power in draining natural resources.[1377] Yet, the Court held that the principle of permanent sovereignty over natural resources is part and parcel of customary international law.[1378]

668. This conclusion is subscribed to by some scholars.[1379] But others have objected that – bearing in mind the vagueness of the principle of permanent sovereignty over natural resources – its elevation by the Court to customary status is 'very questionable'.[1380] All the more so, given the ambiguities abounding in the texts of the relevant resolutions with respect to the central issue whether permanent sovereignty over natural resources is vested in States (Governments) or in peoples.[1381]

669. Even if the principle of permanent sovereignty over natural resources is binding as custom in peacetime, a controversy exists regarding its applicability under belligerent occupation. There are those who take that applicability for granted.[1382] According to another school of thought, the principle – as a *lex*

[1375] See 'B', 'The Case of the Singapore Oil Stocks', 5 *ICLQ* 85, 94–5 (1956).
[1376] *Case Concerning Armed Activities on the Territory of the Congo* (Congo v. Uganda), *supra* note 26, at 251.
[1377] See *ibid.*, 251–2.
[1378] See *ibid.*, 251.
[1379] See N.J. Schrijver, 'Natural Resources, Permanent Sovereignty over', VII *MPEPIL* 535, 542–3.
[1380] J. D'Aspremont, 'Towards an International Law of Brigandage: Interpretative Engineering for the Regulation of Natural Resources Exploitation', 3 *As.JIL* 1, 13 (2013).
[1381] See E. Duruigbo, 'Permanent Sovereignty and Peoples' Ownership of Natural Resources in International Law', 38 *GWILR* 33, 43–50 (2006).
[1382] See M. Longobardo, 'State Responsibility for International Humanitarian Law Violations by Private Actors in Occupied Territories and the Exploitation of Natural Resources', 63 *NILR* 251, 256 (2016).

generalis – has to be subordinated to the *lex specialis* of the elaborate provisions of the *jus in bello* on seizure of property by an Occupying Power.[1383]

B. *Movable Property*

670. Hague Regulation 53 (first paragraph) stipulates:

An army of occupation can only take possession of the cash, funds and realizable securities which are strictly the property of the State, depôts of arms, means of transport, stores and supplies, and, generally, all movable property of the State which may be used for operations of war.[1384]

The clause relates only to State movable property, 'which may be used for operations of war'. But the spectrum of items listed, including cash and realizable securities, is conspicuously wide.

671. In the *Al Nawar* case, the Israel Supreme Court (per President Shamgar) pointed out that, with the exception of movables that are entirely unsuitable for military use – and are not catalogued expressly in Regulation 53 (first paragraph) – the status of State movable property in an occupied territory is not materially different from that of similar property captured on the battlefield: it constitutes booty of war.[1385] In theory, there is a marked distinction between State movables in an occupied territory and booty of war captured on the battlefield: whereas the stamp of booty of war is affixed to all types of movables belonging to the enemy State,[1386] Regulation 53 (first paragraph) covers only those State movables that 'may be used for military operations'.[1387] However, the practical gap between State movables in occupied territories and booty of war on the battlefield shrinks when one ponders the implications of the broad span of items explicitly listed in Regulation 53 (first paragraph) that encompasses cash, etc.

672. Means of transport – also enumerated in Regulation 53 (first paragraph) – range from bicycles, cars and railroad rolling stock to ships and aircraft. They include even ambulances, if they are the property of the State and are used for the conveyance of the wounded and sick in military operations.[1388] As for stores and supplies, a French Court of Appeal pronounced in 1948, in

1383 See P.N. Okowa, 'Natural Resources in Situations of Armed Conflict: Is There a Coherent Framework for Protection?', 9 *ICLR* 237, 256 (2007).

1384 Hague Regulations, *supra* note 22, at 248–51.

1385 HCJ 574/82, *supra* note 1333, at 467.

1386 See Y. Dinstein, 'Booty in Warfare', I *MPEPIL* 990, *id.*

1387 See K. Skubiszewski, 'Use of Force by States. Collective Security. Law of War and Neutrality', *Manual of Public International Law* 739, 833–4 (M. Sørensen ed., 1968).

1388 See *Mestre Hospital v. Defence Administration* (Italy, Court of Cassation, 1954), 22 *ILR* 991, 993.

the *Monmousseau* case, that wine vats – owned by the French Army supply department and used for the provisioning of troops – were 'used for military operations'.[1389]

673. Under conditions of modern warfare, most movables are susceptible – directly or indirectly – of military use.[1390] If cloth is taken as an illustration, it can easily be turned into military uniforms.[1391] Nevertheless, certain items are entirely beyond military use. This is patently the case with cultural property, such as works of art or books, the seizure of which is forbidden by Regulation 56 (second paragraph) (quoted *supra* 608).

674. In the *Flick* trial of 1947 (part of the 'Subsequent Proceedings' at Nuremberg), an American Military Tribunal enunciated that Regulation 53 (first paragraph) 'is not applicable to such properties as means of production'.[1392] Standing by itself, the phrase 'means of production' is not exceedingly helpful. There is a difference between a plough furrowing the soil and a lathe serving as a tool in the manufacture of rifles. Even a tractor, a veritable means of agricultural production, can lend itself to manifold military uses.

675. When an Occupying Power takes possession of State movables – in conformity with Regulation 53 (first paragraph) – it acquires title in them. Hence, the ultimate disposition of the property (e.g., by sale) 'is not a question for international but for domestic law'.[1393] There is admittedly a view that movable State property seized by an Occupying Power must serve military purposes (as distinct from commercial ends).[1394] But this approach is not borne out by the language of Regulation 53 (first paragraph).

676. It may be inferred from the very listing of 'realizable securities' in Hague Regulation 53 (first paragraph) that the Occupying Power is allowed to realize (i.e. cash in) State movables, and – since there is no limitation on the use of the money obtained – it follows that it can be earmarked to easing the financial strain on resources characteristic of wartime.[1395] Admittedly, the exact scope of the expression 'realizable securities' is controversial, the main question being whether or not they include debts of all types owed to the treasury of the occupied territory and maturing within the period of

[1389] *French State v. Etablissements Monmousseau* (Court of Appeal, Orleans, 1948), 15 *ILR* 596, 597.

[1390] See *ibid.*, 468–9.

[1391] See Oppenheim, *supra* note 201, at 400.

[1392] *Flick* trial (*Flick* et al.) (US Military Tribunal, Nuremberg, 1947), 9 *LRTWC* 1, 42.

[1393] W.G. Downey, 'Captured Enemy Property: Booty of War and Seized Enemy Property', 44 *AJIL* 488, 499 (1950).

[1394] See E. Cummings, 'Oil Resources in Occupied Arab Territories under the Law of Belligerent Occupation', 9 *JILE* 533, 576–7 (1974).

[1395] The present writer's view on this subject was endorsed by the Israel Supreme Court (per President Shamgar) in HCJ 574/82, *supra* note 1333, at 467.

occupation.[1396] Still, it is impossible to deny that – as a minimum – the phrase embraces interest-bearing bonds.

III. Extraordinary Property

A. *Communal Property*

677. Hague Regulation 56 (first paragraph) declares:

> The property of the communes, that of institutions dedicated to religious worship, charity, education, art and science, even when belonging to the State, shall be treated as private property.[1397]

The interpretation of the term 'property of the communes' is not free of complications. It appears that what was meant by the framers was communal property dedicated to public purposes – e.g., archives, public records or land registry – irrespective of ownership.[1398] Such property must not be confused with ordinary property of communes – namely, municipalities or other local authorities – which is no different from other private property (this is corroborated by the fact that communes are explicitly mentioned in the context of requisitions in kind in Regulation 52, discussed *infra* 699 *et seq.*).[1399] With regard to State archives, it is necessary to add a caveat – brought to the fore by the *UK Manual of the Law of Armed Conflict* – that '[o]fficial documents and papers connected with the armed conflict may be seized, even if they are part of official archives, because they will be of military significance'.[1400]

B. *Cultural Property*

678. Hague Regulation 56 (second paragraph) (quoted *supra* 608) forbids seizure – no less than destruction or damage – of cultural property in occupied territories. The second sentence of Article 4(3) of the 1954 Convention prohibits 'requisitioning movable cultural property situated in the territory of another High Contracting Party'.[1401] Books and paintings – already adduced as an exception to the application of Hague Regulation 53 (first paragraph) (see *supra* 670) – will evidently come within the ambit of this prohibition. The

[1396] See von Glahn, *supra* note 339, at 156–9.
[1397] Hague Regulations, *supra* note 22, at 250–1.
[1398] See W.M. Franklin, 'Municipal Property under Belligerent Occupation', 38 *AJIL* 383, 390–2, 395–6 (1944).
[1399] See *ibid.*, 395–6.
[1400] *UK Manual of the Law of Armed Conflict, supra* note 230, at 304.
[1401] Hague Convention for the Protection of Cultural Property in the Event of Armed Conflict, *supra* note 144, at 1002.

waiver clause on the ground of imperative military necessity (see *supra* 611) will not apply where the ban of requisition of cultural property is concerned.[1402] It does not matter whether the cultural property is publicly or privately owned.

679. Pursuant to both the First and the Second Protocols appended to the 1954 Convention, exports of cultural property from occupied territories are proscribed and must be prevented.[1403] If exported despite the prohibition, the cultural property must be returned at the close of the hostilities to the competent authorities of the territory previously occupied.[1404] Any indemnity to holders in good faith of the cultural property, which has to be returned, will be paid for by the Occupying Power whose duty it was to prevent the exportation.[1405] This is an important provision, since a leading inducement to the seizure of cultural property in occupied territories is the prospective world market in which they may fetch a very high price from museums or private collectors.[1406]

C. *Medical Property*

680. In principle, unlike cultural property, medical property is not protected from seizure under the Hague Regulations. However, Article 34 of Geneva Convention (I) protects the 'real and personal property of aid societies' (like National Red Cross Societies), proclaiming that they shall be regarded as private property and adding that the right of requisition – recognized for Belligerent Parties under the laws and customs of war – must not be exercised except in case of urgent necessity and after the welfare of the wounded and sick has been ensured.[1407] Occupied territories are not explicitly mentioned here, but there is no doubt that the authors of the provision set their sights on them.[1408]

681. Article 57 of Geneva Convention (IV) extends this partial protection from requisition to civilian hospitals and their supplies:

> The Occupying Power may requisition civilian hospitals only temporarily and only in cases of urgent necessity for the care of military wounded and sick, and then on condition that suitable arrangements are made in due time for the care and treatment of the patients and for the needs of the civilian population for hospital accommodation.

1402 See J. Toman, *The Protection of Cultural Property in the Event of Armed Conflict* 70, 79 (UNESCO, 1996).

1403 (First) Protocol for the Protection of Cultural Property in the Event of Armed Conflict, 1954, *The Laws of Armed Conflicts*, *supra* note 29, at 1027, *id.* (Article 1); Second Protocol for the Protection of Cultural Property in the Event of Armed Conflict, *supra* note 1250, at 1041 (Article 9(1)).

1404 (First) Protocol for the Protection of Cultural Property in the Event of Armed Conflict, *ibid.* (Article 3).

1405 *Ibid.* (Article 4).

1406 See F. Francioni, 'Au-delà des Traités: L'Emergence d'un Nouveau Droit Coutumier pour la Protection du Patrimonie Culturel', 111 *RGDIP* 19, 27 (2007).

1407 Geneva Convention (I), *supra* note 397, at 472.

1408 See *Commentary, I Geneva Convention* 278–9 (ICRC, J.S. Pictet ed., 1952).

The material and stores of civilian hospitals cannot be requisitioned so long as they are necessary for the needs of the civilian population.[1409]

682. It is clear from the text of Article 57 that requisition of a civilian hospital may take place only in radical circumstances (when the urgent care of military wounded and sick trumps the needs of civilians) and on a temporary basis: as soon as the military needs subside, the civilian hospital must be restored to its normal use.[1410] In any event, the Occupying Power is required to make arrangements 'in due time' for the treatment of civilian patients. Moreover, 'the needs of the civilian population for hospital accommodation' must be met. That is to say, the Occupying Power must cope not only with the needs of the specific patients affected by the requisition but also with those of the civilian population as a whole. This is a 'logical inference' from Article 56 (first paragraph) (quoted *supra* 567), whereby hospital services in occupied territories must be maintained.[1411]

683. Article 14(2) of Additional Protocol I goes further:

The Occupying Power shall not, therefore, requisition civilian medical units, their equipment, their *matériel* or the services of their personnel, so long as these resources are necessary for the provision of adequate medical services for the civilian population and for the continuing medical care of any wounded and sick already under treatment.[1412]

684. Medical units are defined in Article 8(e) of the Additional Protocol as including hospitals, first-aid stations, blood transfusion centres, preventive medicine institutes, medical depots and their pharmaceutical stores, etc.[1413] *Matériel*, listed here separately from equipment, covers a wide array of items from medications to linen.[1414] As for 'the services of ... personnel', they relate not only to the treatment of patients (medical personnel) but also to the overall functioning of hospitals (so that the service personnel range from cooks to laundry staff).[1415]

685. Requisitions of medical units and other resources, although restricted, are definitely not ruled out by the Additional Protocol. Three conditions are set out in Article 14(3):

Provided that the general rule in paragraph 2 continues to be observed, the Occupying Power may requisition the said resources, subject to the following particular conditions:

(a) that the resources are necessary for the adequate and immediate medical treatment of the wounded and sick members of the armed forces of the Occupying Power or of prisoners of war;

[1409] Geneva Convention (IV), *supra* note 29, at 597.
[1410] See Giacca, *supra* note 701, at 1497.
[1411] *Commentary, IV Geneva Convention*, *supra* note 31, at 317.
[1412] Additional Protocol I, *supra* note 33, at 721.
[1413] *Ibid.*, 719.
[1414] See Sandoz, *supra* note 1153, at 183.
[1415] See *ibid.*, 183–4.

(b) that the requisition continues only while such necessity exists; and
(c) that immediate arrangements are made to ensure that the medical needs of the civilian population, as well as those of any wounded and sick under treatment who are affected by the requisition, continue to be satisfied.[1416]

Particular attention must be paid to the adjective 'immediate' in the first condition. What it conveys is that requisition is not allowed 'for future needs, even if these are genuinely predictable'.[1417]

D. Civil Defence Matériel

686. Article 63(4) of Additional Protocol I states:

> The Occupying Power shall neither divert from their proper use nor requisition buildings or *matériel* belonging to or used by civil defence organizations if such diversion or requisition would be harmful to the civilian population.[1418]

Under Article 61(d) of the Protocol, *matériel* of civil defence organizations means equipment, supplies and transports used by civil defence organizations for the performance of their tasks.[1419]

687. When requisition or diversion of civil defence buildings or *matériel* is admissible, the Occupying Power may carry it out under Article 63(5) only subject to the following two conditions:
(a) that the buildings or *matériel* are necessary for other needs of the civilian population; and
(b) that the requisition or diversion continues only while such necessity exists.[1420]

It follows that the limits imposed on the requisition of civil defence *matériel* are more stringent than those affecting the requisition of medical supplies: requisition of civil defence *materiel* is permissible solely when it is designed to meet other needs of the local population, whereas the requisition of medical supplies is allowed also for the benefit of the Occupying Power when certain strictures are satisfied (see Article 14(3) of the Additional Protocol quoted *supra* 685).[1421]

688. Article 63(6) forbids, under any circumstances, to divert or requisition shelters needed for the use of the civilian population.[1422] Moreover, according to Article 67(4):

[1416] Additional Protocol I, *supra* note 33, at 722.
[1417] Sandoz, *supra* note 1153, at 186.
[1418] Additional Protocol I, *supra* note 33, at 743.
[1419] *Ibid.*
[1420] *Ibid.*, 743–4.
[1421] See M. Bothe, 'Article 63', *New Rules for Victims of Armed Conflicts, supra* note 400, at 449, 451.
[1422] Additional Protocol I, *supra* note 33, at 744.

The *matériel* and buildings of military units permanently assigned to civil defence organizations and exclusively devoted to the performance of civil defence tasks shall, if they fall into the hands of an adverse Party, remain subject to the laws of war. They may not be diverted from their civil defence purpose so long as they are required for the performance of civil defence tasks, except in case of imperative military necessity, unless previous arrangements have been made for adequate provision for the needs of the civilian population.[1423]

The reference to the laws of war is tied to the relevant provisions of the Hague Regulations: what it means is that the property may be requisitioned by the Occupying Power, provided that the civilian population does not suffer as a result.[1424]

IV. Private Property

A. The Prohibition of Confiscation

689. The status of private property in an occupied territory is unlike that of public property belonging to the displaced sovereign. Hague Regulation 46 (first paragraph) (quoted *supra* 451) lays down in its first sentence that 'private property' must be respected, and complements this in its second paragraph:

Private property cannot be confiscated.[1425]

As expounded in the Judgment in the *Krupp* trial, respect for private property under this provision does not mean merely protection from loss of ownership: for a breach to occur it is enough if the owner is actually prevented from exercising his rightful prerogatives.[1426] Similarly, in the *Loizidou* case, the European Court of Human Rights held that continuous denial of access to land means effective loss of ownership rights over it.[1427]

690. An important insight gained from the *I.G. Farben* Judgment is that the payment of money in consideration for private property does not per se relieve an act of confiscation of its unlawfulness, if it is carried out against the will of the owner.[1428] Every act of seizure of property has to be appraised on the basis of all its circumstances, in light of the system of checks and balances created by the *jus in bello*.

[1423] *Ibid.*, 746.
[1424] See Y. Sandoz, 'Article 67', *Commentary on the Additional Protocols, supra* note 327, at 791, 803–4.
[1425] Hague Regulations, *supra* note 22, at 246–7.
[1426] *Krupp* trial, *supra* note 1212, at 137–8.
[1427] *Loizidou v. Turkey* (Merits), *supra* note 66, at 455.
[1428] *I.G. Farben* trial, *supra* note 1299, at 44.

691. The *I.G. Farben* Judgment also signalled that the obligation of respect for private property shields not only tangible-physical possessions, but also an intangible asset ('such as is involved in the acquisition of stock ownership').[1429] Intellectual property will come into the fold as well.

692. Hague Regulation 46 (second paragraph) is not qualified in a manner akin to that of Regulation 23(g) (quoted *supra* 595), which forbids seizing the enemy's property in the course of hostilities subject to the imperative demands of the necessities of war. Still, it would be wrong to assume that the prohibition of confiscation of private property in an occupied territory is a catch-all formula. Apart from taxation and money contributions (*supra* 378 *et seq.*), the sweeping injunction against confiscation of private property does not trawl in its net (i) expropriations under the local law; (ii) penalties imposed for breaches of security legislation; (iii) temporary possession of immovable property; (iv) requisition in kind of movable property; or (v) seizure (and in extreme cases even confiscation) of *munitions de guerre* and related items

B. Expropriation under the Local Law

693. An expropriation of private property may be carried out by the Occupying Power – for public purposes and subject to compensation – in a manner compatible with the local law in force.[1430] The Occupying Power 'remains free to make use for its purposes of the expropriation legislation in force in the occupied enemy territory prior to the occupation', provided that this is done for reasons of public interest with adequate compensation.[1431] In the *Tabib* case, the Israel Supreme Court (per Justice I. Shilo) said that an Occupying Power is free to use local expropriation legislation in order to construct roads, even if the main purpose of these roads is military (facilitating the movement of troops, etc.).[1432]

694. In the first *Jerusalem District Electricity Co.* case, the Court (per Justice Landau) pronounced that the Occupying Power's obligations under Regulation 46 (second paragraph) (quoted *supra* 689) incorporate recognition of 'vested rights', such as a concession.[1433] However, there may be friction between the parties regarding the scope of the concession. The question that arose in these proceedings was whether the concession of the Jerusalem District Electricity Co. Ltd. – originally going back to the British Mandatory period and extended by Jordan to prescribed zones in the West Bank – included also the city of

[1429] *Ibid.*, 45–6.
[1430] See Feilchenfeld, *supra* note 679, at 50.
[1431] Schwarzenberger, *supra* note 204, at 245.
[1432] HCJ 202/81, *Tabib* et al. *v. Minister of Defence* et al., 36(2) *PD* 622, 631. (The Judgment is excerpted in English in 13 *IYHR* 364 (1983)).
[1433] HCJ 256/72, *supra* note 733, at 138–9.

Hebron, and the Court gave a negative answer.[1434] Since the petitioner had no concessionary vested right to supply electricity to the city of Hebron, the military government was entitled to allow another contender to do so.[1435]

695. The proceedings had an interesting sequel years later. In the second *Jerusalem District Electricity Co.* case, the Court had to examine an attempt by the Occupying Power to take advantage of an option available under a Mandatory Ordinance – lying at the root of the concession – to purchase the undertaking.[1436] The Court (per Justice Kahan) upheld the company's petition, basing itself on Hague Regulation 43 (quoted *supra* 269) and arriving at the conclusion that there was no justification for the exercise of the option.[1437]

C. *Penalties Imposed by Security Legislation*

696. Breaches of the security legislation of the Occupying Power may lead to the forfeiture without compensation of private property. An example given by Von Glahn,[1438] and endorsed by the US Department of Defense *Law of War Manual*,[1439] is that of forfeiture of unauthorized private vehicles found on a road closed to traffic by security legislation.

D. *Temporary Possession of Immovable Property*

697. Even though the Hague Regulations do not refer to the subject, it is undeniable that – pursuant to customary law – the Occupying Power is entitled to take temporary possession of privately owned immovable property (buildings and lands) for diverse military uses, including in particular the quartering of troops.[1440] The Israel Supreme Court decided (per Justice S. Levin), in the *Abu Rian* case, that the Hague Regulations permit the temporary seizure of private immovables for military purposes (in this instance, the establishment of a military outpost) subject to compensation.[1441]

698. In the *Juha* case, the Court (per President Shamgar) laid down three cumulative conditions to such seizure: (i) it must be for a fixed time, although the period may subsequently be extended; (ii) the owner is 'automatically' entitled to payment of compensation for the use of the property; and (iii) should

1434 *Ibid.*, 131–3.
1435 *Ibid.*, 139–40.
1436 HCJ 351/80 etc., *supra* note 736, at 676–9.
1437 *Ibid.*, 690–1.
1438 Von Glahn, *supra* note 339, at 188.
1439 US Department of Defense, *Law of War Manual*, *supra* note 1, at 812.
1440 See *UK Manual of the Law of Armed Conflict*, *supra* note 230, at 300.
1441 HCJ 401/88, *Abu Rian* et al. *v. IDF Commander of Judea and Samaria*, 42(2) *PD* 767, 770. (The Judgment is excerpted in English in 23 *IYHR* 296 (1993)).

any damage be caused to the property (for instance, by cutting off trees), this is also subject to compensation.[1442] It ought to be remarked that, if compensation is paid solely for use and damage, the Occupying Power does not acquire title to the property and cannot sell it.[1443]

E. Requisitions in Kind of Movable Property

(a) Hague Regulation 52

699. A compendious provision regarding movable property appears in Hague Regulation 52:

> Neither requisitions in kind nor services can be demanded from communes or inhabitants except for the necessities of the army of occupation. They must be in proportion to the resources of the country, and of such a nature as not to imply for the population any obligation to take part in military operations against their country.
>
> These requisitions and services shall only be demanded on the authority of the Commander in the locality occupied.
>
> Supplies in kind shall, as far as possible, be paid for in ready money; if not, their receipt shall be acknowledged and the payment of the amount due shall be made as soon as possible.[1444]

700. The property of communes has already been mentioned (see *supra* 677). Although requisitions in kind and in services can be demanded from communes under Regulation 52, communal property is protected by Regulation 56 (first paragraph) (quoted *ibid.*).

701. The main thrust of Regulation 52 is the movable property of the inhabitants, i.e. private property. Requisitions in kind will deprive the affected individual of the movable property. Requisitions of services relate primarily to compulsory work by the inhabitants (see *supra* 537), but they may also be construed as extending to a temporary compulsory use of movable property (such as a vehicle), to be returned to the owner after the service has ended.

702. Requisition in kind and services may be demanded only 'for the necessities of the army of occupation'. A rundown of some of these necessities was given in the Judgment in the *Krupp* trial:

> All authorities are again in agreement that the requisitions in kind and services referred to in Article 52, concern such matters as billets for the occupying troops and the occupation authorities, garages for their vehicles, stables for their horses, urgently needed

[1442] HCJ 290/89, *Juha v. Military Commander of Judea and Samaria*, 43(2) *PD* 116, 120. (The Judgment is excerpted in English in 23 *IYHR* 323 (1993)).

[1443] See Lord McNair and A.D. Watts, *The Legal Effects of War* 394 (4th edn, 1966).

[1444] Hague Regulations, *supra* note 22, at 248–9.

equipment and supplies for the proper functioning of the occupation authorities, food for the Army of Occupation, and the like.[1445]

703. As the passage accentuates, the billeting of troops (and related activities) is permissible under Regulation 52, possibly under the rubric of requisition of services. This is curious, inasmuch as billeting takes place in immovable property. However, despite the absence of any mention of the subject in the text, Regulation 52 has always been construed as allowing billeting of troops of the Occupying Power (as well as administrative units of the military government) in private houses, provided that compensation is paid as soon as possible for the use of the property.[1446] Cf. *supra* 697–8.

704. Some commentators would like to go beyond billeting of troops, looking upon requisitions in Regulation 52 as generally applicable to 'possession in immovables'.[1447] Schwarzenberger, a leading exponent of this view, found confirmation in Article 57 (first paragraph) of Geneva Convention (IV) (quoted *supra* 681), which states that '[t]he Occupying Power may requisition civilian hospitals' under certain provisos.[1448] The desire to bring private immovables under the aegis of Regulation 52 is natural – since this would subject their seizure to perspicuous conditions – but, when carried to extremes, it is inconsistent with the plain meaning of the text.

705. Considering that requisitioning is permissible only for 'the necessities of the army of occupation', it cannot be a tool of satisfying the demands of the Occupying Power's industry or feeding its population at home.[1449] Indeed, the Occupying Power is not allowed to divert requisitioned property even in order to meet shortages in its own army, if they arise outside the occupied territory. Thus, a Dutch Court concluded in 1947, in the *Gusto* case, that the German authorities in occupied Netherlands could not demand from a shipyard – by way of requisitioning – the construction of sand dredgers earmarked for deepening rivers in occupied Russia.[1450]

706. Requisitions in kind and services must not involve the inhabitants in military operations – or operations of war – against their own country (see *supra* 177). The banned activities encompass also preparations for such operations. Thus, in the 1947 *Bouquet* case, a Dutch Court of Appeal interpreted the prohibition as covering the construction of fortifications, building of warships, etc.[1451]

1445 *Krupp* trial, *supra* note 1212, at 137.
1446 See Oppenheim, *supra* note 201, at 411.
1447 Schwarzenberger, *supra* note 204, at 288. See also von Glahn, *supra* note 339, at 165, 167.
1448 G. Schwarzenberger, 'The Protection of Private Property in the Law of Belligerent Occupation', 1 *IJIL* 193, 198 n. 31 (1960–1).
1449 See *Krupp* trial, *supra* note 1212, at 135–7; *Ministries* trial, *supra* note 357, at 360.
1450 In *Re Shipbuilding Yard 'Gusto'* (Netherlands, Special Criminal Court, 1947), 14 *ILR* 309, *id.*
1451 *Bouquet* et al. *v. Slom* (Netherlands, Court of Appeal, 1947), 14 *ILR* 308, *id.*

707. Some doubt has arisen about the status of requisitioned perishable goods that have a short lifespan. Following WWI, contrasting opinions have been expressed in the case law as to whether the German Occupying Power was entitled to ship such goods to units deployed outside the occupied territory, as an alternative to letting them get stale.[1452] But there seems to be no doubt today that, in the words of the Judgment in the *Krupp* trial:

> Just as the inhabitants of the occupied territory must not be forced to help the enemy in waging the war against their own country or their own country's allies, so must the economic assets of the occupied territory not be used in such a manner.[1453]

708. Regulation 52 imposes a condition of proportionality to the resources of 'the country'. Some doubt exists whether the proportion is linked to the resources of the entire occupied territory or, as is argued by certain scholars, only to those of the specific locality affected by the requisition.[1454] Either way, the benchmark is collective and not individual. As long as the requisition is 'in proportion to the resources of the country' in the aggregate, it cannot be faulted only because it impoverishes a single person.[1455] The upshot is that the random impact of the requisition may be flagrantly iniquitous, and it hardly needs saying that there is no consolation for the impoverished individual to be told that proportionality has been respected in an impersonal manner.

709. On the other hand, when collective resources are surveyed, assessment should take into account not only extant conditions and privations but also prospective exigencies based on reasonable projections for the future.[1456] Otherwise, the population is liable to be unlawfully denuded of essentials that may prove indispensable for its ultimate survival (see *supra* 453–4).

710. The decision to requisition a certain property or service must be taken by a local commander, not necessarily the highest echelon in the occupied territory. The pith of the rule is that not every private soldier in the army of occupation is qualified to decide on such requisition.[1457] But there is no requirement in Regulation 52 of any particular formality in the decision-making process.[1458]

[1452] See B. Cheng, *General Principles of Law as Applied by International Courts and Tribunals* 41–2 n. 41 (1953).

[1453] *Krupp* trial, *supra* note 1212, at 134.

[1454] See McDougal and Feliciano, *supra* note 238, at 820.

[1455] See H. Dichter, 'The Legal Status of Israel's Water Policies in the Occupied Territories', 35 *Har.ILJ* 565, 576 (1994).

[1456] See J. Stone, *Legal Controls of International Conflict: A Treatise on the Dynamics of Disputes – and War – Law* 709 (Rev. edn, 1959).

[1457] See McDougal and Feliciano, *supra* note 238, at 821.

[1458] See Rousseau, *supra* note 301, at 167.

(b) Payment for Requisitioned Goods

711. The hallmark of requisition in kind (as distinct from confiscation) is that requisitioned goods must be paid for in cash or exchanged for a redeemable receipt. How much should be paid for the goods? Regulation 52 is silent on this crucial issue, leaving open the possibility of the Occupying Power paying a mere pittance for expensive items. Article 55 (second paragraph) of the Geneva Convention (quoted *infra* 715) employs the phrase 'fair value' for requisitioned goods. In an Arbitral Award in the *Goldenberg* case of 1928 (two decades prior to the Geneva Convention), the term used (by the Arbitrator Fazy) was 'indemnité equitable'.[1459] When fair or equitable value is actually paid, a requisition in kind is 'not necessarily an evil', since in some circumstances the 'Occupying Power may be a welcome, and perhaps the only available, buyer for a product of the occupied territory'.[1460]

712. Whether or not a requisition in kind is objectively an evil, there may be resistance to it (especially when there is a bone of contention as to what constitutes fair or equitable value). It must therefore be perceived that, to secure a requisition, the military government is allowed to resort to the use of reasonable coercive measures.[1461]

713. When a receipt is given for a requisition in kind, it must be redeemed as soon as possible. This requirement did not appear in the 1899 text of Regulation 52 and was supplemented in 1907.[1462] The intention of the drafters was to make sure that payment is not postponed until the end of the war.[1463] As explained by the Arbitrator Fazy, in the *Goldenberg* case, a requisition in kind may initially be lawful, but – in order to remain lawful – payment must be made without unreasonable delay.[1464] The ruling was confirmed by a panel of three Arbitrators (Fazy, Guex and Meuron), in 1930, in the *German Responsibility* case.[1465]

714. A requisition in kind under Regulation 52, if carried out lawfully, transfers to the Occupying Power title to the requisitioned property (for which compensation has been paid).[1466] Consequently, even if the Occupying Power does not use the property, there is no need to return it to the original owner.[1467]

[1459] *Affaire Goldenberg* (Germany, Roumania), 1928, 2 *RIAA* 901, 909.

[1460] M. Bothe, 'Article 14', *New Rules for Victims of Armed Conflicts, supra* note 400, at 132. 133.

[1461] See US Department of Defense, *Law of War Manual, supra* note 1, at 816.

[1462] Compare the two texts: Hague Regulations, *supra* note 22, at 248–9.

[1463] See Graber, *supra* note 264, at 245.

[1464] *Affaire Goldenberg, supra* note 1459, at 909.

[1465] *Responsabilité de l'Allemagne à Raison des Actes Commis Postérieurement au 31 Juillet 1914 et avant que le Portugal Ne Participât à la Guerre, supra* note 1316, at 1039.

[1466] See McNair and Watts, *supra* note 1443, at 394.

[1467] See Schwarzenberger, *supra* note 204, at 274–6.

(c) Foodstuffs and Medical Supplies

715. Article 55 (second paragraph) of the Geneva Convention prescribes:

> The Occupying Power may not requisition foodstuffs, articles or medical supplies available in the occupied territory, except for use by the occupation forces and administration personnel, and then only if the requirements of the civilian population have been taken into account. Subject to the provisions of other international Conventions, the Occupying Power shall make arrangements to ensure that fair value is paid for any requisitioned goods.[1468]

This stipulation must be read in conjunction with the first paragraph of Article 55 (quoted *supra* 457), whereby the Occupying Power – to the fullest extent of the means available to it – must ensure the medical supplies of the population in an occupied territory. The needs of the population take precedence over those of the Occupying Power itself. The reference to other Conventions should be construed as a *renvoi* to the conditions spelt out in Hague Regulation 52.[1469]

716. Since the saving clause of Article 55 (second paragraph) mentions only 'use by the occupation forces and administration personnel', a problem arises in the not uncommon situation in which the general population is afflicted by scarcities of certain foodstuffs at the same time that stockpiles are hoarded by private speculators. The text would not allow the Occupying Power to requisition the hoarded foodstuffs from the speculators for the direct benefit of the population at large. What the Occupying Power can do, however, is act circuitously. It can release foodstuffs from its own resources 'in sufficient quantities for the needs of the civilian population and then to requisition from private ownership the hoarded stores for the needs of the army'.[1470]

F. Seizure of Munitions de Guerre *and Related Items*

(a) The Scope of the Special Category

717. A special category of movable private property in occupied territories is that of *munitions de guerre* and related items. Hague Regulation 53 (second paragraph) reads:

> All appliances, whether on land, at sea, or in the air, adapted for the transmission of news or for the transport of persons or goods apart from cases governed by maritime law, depôts of arms, and, generally, all kinds of war material may be seized, even though belonging to private persons, but they must be restored and indemnities for them regulated at the peace.[1471]

1468 Geneva Convention (IV), *supra* note 29, at 596.

1469 See *Commentary, IV Geneva Convention, supra* note 31, at 311.

1470 *UK Military Manual* quoted in X *Digest of International Law* 585 (M.M. Whiteman ed., 1968).

1471 Hague Regulations, *supra* note 22, at 250–1.

718. The English expression 'war material' is a translation of the common French term *munitions de guerre* used in the authentic text of Regulation 53 (second paragraph).[1472] The language employed is a progeny of two paragraphs in Article VI of the 1874 Brussels Project, which dealt separately with the diverse items listed and confined the duty of ultimate restoration and compensation to '[r]ailway plant, land telegraphs, steamers and other ships'.[1473]

719. Appliances for the transmission of news or transport cover telephones, telegraph, aircraft, trucks, buses, cars, railway rolling stock, barges, etc.[1474] The exception concerning naval law is due to the law of prize, which permits condemnation of private property without compensation.[1475] Schwarzenberger maintained that Regulation 53 (second paragraph) should be applicable not only to movables but to some immovable as well (cf. also *supra* 704), arguing that there can be no difference between the seizure of rolling stock and that of the whole railway plant.[1476] However, the contention is incompatible with the plain language of the text. It is noteworthy that the expression '[r]ailway plant' (which had originated in the Brussels Project) appeared in the 1899 version,[1477] yet was omitted from the 1907 text where the reference is to '[a]ll appliances'.

720. The key phrase in Regulation 53 (second paragraph) is *munitions de guerre*. Some scholars construe this phrase in a way which is comprehensive to the point of incongruity; encompassing, for example, bank accounts.[1478] A narrower rendering of *munitions de guerre* is that they consist of 'all movable articles for which a modern army can find any normal use', including food and tobacco.[1479] But even this definition is too pliable. The correct interpretation of *munitions de guerre* is that they are applicable to military equipment and similar items that may be used in warfare.[1480] In the *Esau* case of 1949, a Dutch Court of Cassation held that boring machines, lathes, lamps, tubes and gold – which may be important for scientific/technical research – are not *munitions de guerre*.[1481] But is it so self-evident that lathes and drills cannot be used in warfare?

[1472] *Ibid.*,

[1473] Brussels Project, *supra* note 45, at 23.

[1474] See *UK Manual of the Law of Armed Conflict*, *supra* note 230, at 301.

[1475] See Schwarzenberger, *supra* note 1448, at 221–3.

[1476] *Ibid.*, 219–20.

[1477] Hague Regulations, *supra* note 22, at 250–1.

[1478] See C.A. Farleigh, 'The Validity of Acts of Enemy Occupation Authorities Affecting Property Rights', 35 *CLQ* 89, 107 (1949–50).

[1479] H.A. Smith, 'Booty of War', 23 *BYBIL* 227, 228–9 (1946).

[1480] See E. Lauterpacht, 'The Hague Regulations and the Seizure of *Munitions de Guerre*', 32 *BYBIL* 218, 242 (1955–6).

[1481] In *Re Esau* (Netherlands, Special Court of Cassation, 1949), 16 *ILR* 482, 483.

721. Seizure pursuant to Regulation 53 (second paragraph) must be distinguished from requisition in kind under Regulation 52 (quoted *supra* 699). In the opinion of the present writer, items such as food and clothing should come within the confines of Regulation 52: they would, therefore, be subject only to requisition in kind and not to seizure per Regulation 53 (second paragraph). The difference lies not in semantics but in the disparate legal regimes created by Regulations 52 and 53 (second paragraph). The nub of the matter is that Regulation 53 (second paragraph) does not contain the safeguards built into Regulation 52. This means that *munitions de guerre* – as well as other items falling within Regulation 53 (second paragraph) – can be seized regardless of any proportionality to the resources of the country; their use is not limited to the army of occupation; and there is no obligation of payment in cash on the spot or within a short stretch of time (compensation is to be fixed only when peace is concluded).[1482]

(b) Crude Oil

722. An item which palpably comes within the orbit of *munitions de guerre* is oil (petroleum). Still, the question arises whether the term *munitions de guerre* applies only to pumped oil or also to oil remaining underground. The issue was joined before the Singapore Court of Appeal, in 1956, in the abovementioned *Bataafsche* case (see *supra* 666). These proceedings related to Dutch companies, which produced oil in Sumatra (present-day Indonesia). When the Japanese occupied Sumatra during WWII, they captured the companies' installations. Later, they pumped oil and kept it in storage tanks in occupied Singapore. When the British returned to Singapore, they seized the oil found there as booty of war. The Dutch companies claimed that the oil was their property and demanded indemnity for the seizure. The majority of the Court of Appeal (per Whyatt, C.J.) did not consider a raw material such as oil – while still underground – as coming within the parameters of *munitions de guerre*, both because it is immovable property and due to the fact that it is not susceptible of direct military use without pumping and refining in elaborate installations.[1483] Hence, it was decided that the seizure of the crude oil by the Japanese contravened the *jus in bello*.[1484] But the minority Judgment (per Whitton, J.) pointed out that, had the Japanese found the oil ready for immediate use, they would have been entitled to seize it as *munitions de guerre*.[1485] The minority reached the conclusion that, by the same token, oil must be viewed as *munitions de guerre* even before it is pumped and when still underground.[1486]

[1482] See Schwarzenberger, *supra* note 1448, at 212–13.
[1483] *Bataafsche* case, *supra* note 1372, at 822–4.
[1484] *Ibid.*, 822.
[1485] *Ibid.*, 847.
[1486] *Ibid.*

723. It is noteworthy that the *UK Manual of the Law of Armed Conflict* rejects the majority view by stating that the category of *munitions de guerre* 'includes raw materials such as crude oil'.[1487] There is support in the legal literature, too, for the view that 'crude oil, whether in the ground or pumped, may be treated as any other war munition'.[1488] It has been aptly remarked that the *Bataafsche* case's majority focus on the length and complexity of the process of extraction of raw materials is 'unrealistic, since even uranium ore would not qualify as munitions de guerre under this approach'.[1489]

(c) Restoration and Compensation

724. The Occupying Power is not restricted in its use of *munitions de guerre* or of the other items enumerated in Regulation 53 (second paragraph). Thus, the Occupying Power may move seized vehicles from the occupied territory and take them to its own country, to relieve a dearth of transport there.[1490] On the other hand, as can be inferred from the duty of restitution at the end of the war, the Occupying Power does not acquire title to such property and, therefore, may not sell it.[1491] As pronounced by the Supreme Court of Austria in 1951, in the *Requisitioned Property* case:

> The seizure of property referred to in Article 53(2) of the Hague Regulations and belonging to private individuals, including property used for the transport of persons and goods, does not result in a change of ownership, because such property has to be returned upon the conclusion of peace.[1492]

725. The conjunctive obligation of both restoring and fixing compensation for the goods when peace comes is quite odd. It was intelligible in the original Brussels limited context of '[r]ailway plant, land telegraphs, steamers and other ships' (see *supra* 718), since these assets raise an issue not only of their capital value but also of loss of profits while in use by the Occupying Power; yet, if goods like *munitions de guerre* are restored, why is compensation to be fixed in addition to restitution?[1493] It makes more sense, in such cases, to look at the obligation of compensation as an alternative to restitution. Indeed, compensation may prove the sole effectual redress when restitution of the goods is not feasible owing to wear and tear caused by extensive use in wartime.[1494]

1487 *UK Manual of the Law of Armed Conflict*, *supra* note 230, at 301.

1488 E.J. Wallach, 'The Use of Crude Oil by an Occupying Belligerent State as a *Munition de Guerre*', 41 *ICLQ* 287, 309 (1992).

1489 M. Paparinskis, 'Singapore Oil Stocks Case', IX *MPEPIL* 213, 215.

1490 See Jessup, *supra* note 1207, at 459.

1491 See *ibid.*

1492 *Requisitioned Property* case (Austria, Supreme Court, 1951), 18 *ILR* 696, *id.*

1493 See P. Bordwell, *The Law of War between Belligerents: A History and Commentary* 326 (1908).

1494 See A.P. Higgins, *War and the Private Citizen: Studies in International Law* 60 (1912).

726. The obligation to restore and/or compensate when peace comes segregates the two paragraphs of Regulation 53: the duty appears only in the second paragraph (relating to private property) and not in the first (pertaining to public property; see *supra* 670).[1495] Since the requirement of restitution of the property under the second paragraph materializes only upon the arrival of peace, in the interval – which, in a prolonged occupation, may mean years or even decades – this is 'merely a question of accountancy'.[1496] Still, sooner or later, the day of financial reckoning will arrive. Although the second paragraph does not mention an obligation to issue a receipt when the property is seized, this is the only practical way to keep an orderly ledger for the moment of restoration and/or compensation.[1497]

(d) Confiscation

727. Regulation 53 (second paragraph) is based on a hidden assumption that the items of private property with which it deals – especially *munitions de guerre* – have not actually been used in warfare against the Occupying Power. In the Arbitral Award in the *Cession of Vessels and Tugs for Navigation on the Danube* case, the Arbitrator Hines said:

> Article 53, which speaks of restoration of, and compensation for, privately owned means of transport and privately owned ammunition of war, does not contemplate war material in actual hostile use at the time of seizure, and no one seriously contends that the Article has so been applied as to require restitution of, and compensation for, war material in actual use as such.[1498]

The Arbitrator added that, in the event of actual use of privately owned *munitions de guerre* against the Occupying Power, they can be confiscated, notwithstanding the general principle – expressed in Regulation 46 (second paragraph) (quoted *supra* 689) – prohibiting the confiscation of private property.[1499]

728. Thus, if we are talking about a privately owned gun, it is necessary to establish whether the gun (i) forms part of a private weapon collection, (ii) is in normal non-combatant use by a civilian, especially where there is reasonable trepidation of domestic banditry, or (iii) is taken off the hands of a saboteur. In all three instances, the Occupying Power is entitled to seize the gun. But, in instances (i) or (ii), the gun must be restored to the owner at the end of the war; whereas in instance (iii) it may be confiscated. One can say that, in instance (iii), the gun loses its private nature and acquires a status akin to that of a publicly owned gun.

[1495] See Feilchenfeld, *supra* note 679, at 54.
[1496] Smith, *supra* note 1479, at 231.
[1497] See Oppenheim, *supra* note 201, at 404.
[1498] *Cession of Vessels and Tugs for Navigation on the Danube Case*, *supra* note 1324, at 105–6.
[1499] *Ibid.*, 105.

G. *The Right of Angary*

729. Nationals of neutral States are protected persons in an occupied territory under Geneva Convention (IV) (see *supra* 198–9). Hague Regulation 53 (second paragraph) (quoted *supra* 717) governs seizure of property belonging to 'private individuals', a category that includes inhabitants who are nationals of neutral countries. However, there is a special type of neutral property – owned by neutral non-inhabitants – that, by happenstance, passes through a territory at the very point of its occupation (ships lying at anchor in ports or roadsteads, aircraft parked in airports, rolling stock in railroad marshalling yards, trucks and cars on the roads, barges in rivers and canals, etc.). Regulation 53 (second paragraph) could in theory apply in these cases too, but then restitution and compensation would have to await the advent of peace (see *supra* 726).

730. A special normative arrangement has therefore evolved. It is based on the customary right of angary, whereby seizure of neutral merchant ships – albeit permissible in case of dire necessity – is contingent on the payment of full compensation.[1500] Notwithstanding deprecation by some commentators,[1501] the general view is that the right of angary (whether or not this term of art is actually resorted to) may be exercised in an occupied territory.[1502] Angary superficially resembles ordinary requisition. Yet, there is a material difference between the two, reflected in the need to pay full compensation for neutral property, without waiting for the arrival of peace (as per Regulation 53 (second paragraph)).[1503]

731. Although the right of angary was originally linked in customary international law to neutral merchant vessels, it has fanned out to other means of transport. There is a specific provision in Article 19 of Hague Convention (V) of 1907 as regards railway material – which, in the context, means primarily rolling stock (whether public or private) – coming from the territory of a neutral State and recognizable as such: it can only be requisitioned when absolutely necessary, and compensation must be paid in proportion to actual usage.[1504] This provision is expository of the right of angary,[1505] and it is applicable to occupied territories.[1506]

[1500] See Schwarzenberger, *supra* note 204, at 636.

[1501] See C.L. Bullock, 'Angary', 3 *BYBIL* 99, 122–5 (1922–3).

[1502] See Harvard Research in International Law, Rights and Duties of Neutral States in Naval and Aerial War, 33 *AJIL*, Supp., 1, 359 *et seq.* (1939) (Article 21 and Comment).

[1503] See H. Lauterpacht, 'Angary and Requisition of Neutral Property', 27 *BYBIL* 455, *id.* (1950).

[1504] Hague Convention (V) Respecting the Rights and Duties of Neutral Powers and Persons in Case of War on Land, 1907, *The Hague Peace Conferences*, *supra* note 22, at 281, 286–7.

[1505] See J.E. Harley, 'The Law of Angary', 13 *AJIL* 267, 283–4 (1919).

[1506] See von Glahn, *supra* note 339, at 220.

732. Article 31 of the non-binding 1923 Hague Rules of Air Warfare allows requisition of private neutral aircraft found in an occupied territory on condition of payment of full indemnity.[1507] The text refers to the principles of Hague Regulation 53, but an explanatory note clarifies that the indemnity to neutrals should be paid promptly, without waiting for peace to be concluded.[1508]

733. The US Department of Defense *Law of War Manual* (which expressly refers to the right of angary in terms of neutral ships and railway materials) states broadly that '[t]he right of angary recognizes the right of belligerents to requisition (upon payment of just compensation) neutral property transiently within their territory, or in territory that they have occupied, where the property is urgently required for the conduct of the war'.[1509] Indeed, there is no reason to confine the reach of the right of angary to vessels, rolling stock and aircraft. It should equally extend to other types of neutral property transiently present in the occupied territory, especially trucks, cars, barges and other means of transport.[1510]

[1507] Hague Rules of Air Warfare, 1923, *The Laws of Armed Conflicts*, *supra* note 29, at 317, 321.

[1508] Commission of Jurists to Consider and Report upon the Revision of the Rules of Warfare, Rules of Aerial Warfare, 32 *AJIL*, Supp. 1, 12, 29–30 (1938).

[1509] US Department of Defense, *Law of War Manual*, *supra* note 1, at 982–3.

[1510] See Bullock, *supra* note 1501, at 126–8 (but note that the author did not speak about occupied territories).

11 Other Major Issues Relating to Belligerent Occupation

I. Settlements

A. *Geneva Convention (IV)*

734. Article 49 (sixth paragraph) of Geneva Convention (IV) promulgates:

The Occupying Power shall not deport or transfer parts of its own civilian population into the territory it occupies.[1511]

735. Although this prohibition is not enumerated as a grave breach in the Convention itself, Article 85(4)(a) of Additional Protocol I appends it to the list of grave breaches.[1512] Article 8(2)(b)(viii) of the Rome Statute of the International Criminal Court stigmatizes as a war crime the 'transfer, directly or indirectly, by the Occupying Power of parts of its own civilian population into the territory it occupies'.[1513] The words 'directly or indirectly' appear neither in the original Geneva text nor in the Additional Protocol. They were inserted in the Rome Statute as a reminder that not only a compulsory transfer into the occupied territories counts, but also one based on acts of 'inducement and facilitation'.[1514] The reminder was intended 'as a snub to Israel'.[1515] In the Elements of Crime, a footnote was appended, whereby '[t]he term "transfer" needs to be interpreted in accordance with the relevant provisions of international humanitarian law'.[1516]

736. The key verbs 'deport' and 'transfer' are used both in the first and in the sixth paragraphs of Article 49, except that in the first paragraph of the Article (quoted *supra* 487) they refer to protected persons in an occupied territory, whereas in the sixth paragraph they are employed in relation to the Occupying Power's own population. This may cause some confusion. It must,

[1511] Geneva Convention (IV), *supra* note 29, at 594.
[1512] Additional Protocol I, *supra* note 33, at 754.
[1513] Rome Statute of the International Criminal Court, *supra* note 350, at 1318.
[1514] Dörmann, *supra* note 355, at 211.
[1515] R. Cryer, *Prosecuting International Crimes: Selectivity and the International Criminal Law Regime* 274 (2005).
[1516] Dörmann, *supra* note 355, at 208.

therefore, be emphasized that the sixth paragraph is not aimed at protecting the nationals of the Occupying Power from any coercive measures taken by their own Government, since nationals of the Occupying Power are not protected persons under the Geneva Convention (see *supra* 197).[1517] The goal of the sixth paragraph is to enhance the protection of the civilian population of the occupied territory by disenabling the Occupying Power to bring about – through transfer – a fundamental demographic change in the area. In Resolution 2334 (2016), the Security Council condemned 'all measures aimed at altering the demographic composition, character and status of the Palestinian Territory occupied since 1967, including East Jerusalem'.[1518] It must also be fully appreciated that the injunction against transfer applies irrespective of any displacement of the local inhabitants.[1519]

737. There is a *lacuna* in Article 49 (sixth paragraph) in that the text is limited to the transfer into the occupied territory of civilian nationals of the Occupying Power, without any consideration given to the possibility of a similar transfer of the civilian nationals of a co-belligerent or neutral State. Logically, any attempt by the Occupying Power to effect a major demographic change in the occupied territory – whether with its own or with any other nationals – should be equally barred. In principle, all such transfers ought to be treated alike. However, the text does not explicitly say so.

738. By definition, a deportation is carried out in a compulsory manner, against the wishes of the person concerned: if he elects to leave a territory of his own free will, he cannot be regarded as a deportee. The word 'transfer' is more malleable. It is noteworthy that, whereas the first paragraph of Article 49 refers to 'forcible transfers' (see *supra* 487), the sixth paragraph speaks about transfer without attaching the qualification of its being 'forcible'.[1520] The Rome Statute makes this even clearer (see *supra* 735).

739. Indeed, nationals of an Occupying Power who are transferring into an occupied territory may be more than willing to participate in the process (whether on ideological grounds, in return for economic inducements, or for personal reasons). Their voluntary cooperation in the transfer does not diminish from its illicit character, pursuant to the sixth paragraph of Article 49, as long as the Occupying Power stands behind the project.

[1517] See J.-M. Henckaerts, 'Deportation and Transfer of Civilians in Time of War', 26 *VJTL* 469, 478 (1993–4).

[1518] Security Council Resolution 2334 (2016), 56 *ILM* 648 *id.* (2017) (Preamble). See also Security Council Resolution 465 (1980), *Resolutions and Statements of the United Nations Security Council, supra* note 60, at 720, 721.

[1519] The reference to displacement (which appears in Oppenheim, *supra* note 201, at 452) is wrong: see [1978] *Digest of United States Practice in International Law* 1577 (M.L. Nash ed.).

[1520] See T. Meron, 'The West Bank and International Humanitarian Law on the Eve of the Fiftieth Anniversary of the Six-Day war', 111 *AJIL* 357, 373 (2017).

740. A transfer entails organized movement of persons into an occupied territory with a view to settling there. The prohibition of transfer obviously does not embrace civil servants or officials brought by an Occupying Power into the occupied territory – on a temporary as well as functional basis – with a view to assisting in running the military government (see *supra* 183).

741. It is habitually glossed over that Article 49 (sixth paragraph) does not forbid individual nationals of the Occupying Power from privately settling (on their own initiative) in the occupied territory, if and when this is done without any direct or indirect intervention of their Government. In the opinion of the present writer, such voluntary settlement, not precipitated or organized by the Occupying Power (and taking place on land purchased in a valid manner), does not amount to 'transfer' and is not proscribed by Article 49 (sixth paragraph). Those who object to this distinction[1521] utterly ignore the plain meaning of the word 'transfer'. More about this important issue *infra* 744.

B. *The Israeli Settlements*

742. The settlement of nationals of an Occupying Power in an occupied territory is by no means a rare phenomenon. Thus, 'Turkish settlers were brought in large numbers from the Turkish mainland' to Northern Cyprus.[1522] But, no doubt, settlements have become emblematic of the Israeli occupation in the West Bank. In the Advisory Opinion on the *Wall*, the International Court of Justice pronounced (in a non-binding text) that these settlements were in violation of Article 49 (sixth paragraph): the Court declared that the prohibition of Article 49 covers not only forcible transfers, 'but also any measures taken by an occupying Power in order to organize or encourage transfers of parts of its own population into the occupied territory'.[1523] In Resolution 2334 (2016), the Security Council reaffirmed that 'the establishment by Israel of settlements in the Palestinian territory occupied since 1967, including East Jerusalem, has no legal validity and constitutes a flagrant violation under international law'.[1524] Although a non-binding resolution,[1525] the message conveyed was clear.

[1521] See, e.g., C.J. Drew, 'Self-Determination, Population Transfer and the Middle East Peace Accord', *Human Rights, Self-Determination and Political Change in the Occupied Palestinian Territories*, *supra* note 1355, at 119, 144–6.

[1522] C. Tomuschat, 'Prohibition of Settlements', *The 1949 Geneva Conventions: A Commentary*, *supra* note 309, at 1551, 1558.

[1523] Advisory Opinion on *Legal Consequences of the Construction of a Wall in the Occupied Palestinian Territory*, *supra* note 25, at 183.

[1524] Security Council Resolution 2334 (2016), *supra* note 1518, at 649 (para. 1).

[1525] See P. Sharvit Baruch, 'UN Security Council Resolution 2334 (2016) – An Analysis', 48 *IYHR* 275, 282–6 (2018).

743. Legally speaking, the dicta of the Court and the Council are unassailable as far as they relate to transfer. Their weak spot is treating the Israeli settlements in the West Bank in monochromatic terms, without any attempt to assay whether the Occupying Power is poised behind them (organizing or encouraging the transfer in the words of the Court) or whether they constitute purely private enterprises. The non-discriminating approach is typical. It underlies also previous Security Council Resolutions, like Resolution 465 (1980) that calls upon Israel 'to dismantle the existing settlements'.[1526]

744. In reality, as noted (*supra* 741), the crucial reference to 'transfer' in the text of Article 49 (sixth paragraph) requires some calibration where the Occupying Power gives the settlements no backing at all. The 'one-size-fits-all' panoramic view of settlements in the West Bank is incompatible with the Geneva limitation of the prohibition to those settlements that can be subsumed under the heading of a 'transfer'. It is easy to understand the condemnation of settlers who come to live in an occupied territory under the cloak of a Government-coordinated (and subsidized) scheme, by dint of official organization or institutional inducement (the paramount manifestation of which is the offer of public land by the military government for the purposes of the settlement and the building of supportive infrastructure). However, the chorus of recriminations against Israeli settlements disregards two (by no means trivial) categories of settlements in the West Bank:

(a) So-called 'outposts', set up by private Israeli individuals acting without official support, and frequently against the policy of the Government of the day, having purchased the land for full market value from those vested with valid title to it (provided that the purchase transaction is not fictitious); and

(b) Israeli nationals who repossess private land owned by their (Jewish) families and registered in their names since the days of the British Mandate or even the Ottoman Empire (or persons who have purchased such land from the rightful owners). Jewish access to these lands was denied between 1948 and 1967, and the property was in the hands of a Jordanian Custodian of Enemy Property.[1527]

745. As far as the Hague Regulations are concerned, this is what the *I.G. Farben* Judgment had to say about private consensual transactions relating to the purchase of land in an occupied territory:

We look in vain for any provision in the Hague Regulations which would justify the broad assertion that private citizens of the nation of the military occupant may not enter

[1526] Security Council Resolution 465, *supra* note 1518, at 721.

[1527] See HCJ 277/84, *Ahreib v. Appeals Commission* et al., 40(2) *PD* 57, 60–1 (per President Shamgar).

into agreements respecting property in occupied territories when consent of the owner is, in fact, freely given.[1528]

From the perspective of the Geneva Convention, when settlers act entirely on their own initiative; when they do not arrogate to themselves land belonging to others or requisitioned from its rightful owners; and when they do not benefit from any overt or covert governmental backing (other than protecting their basic human rights; see *supra* 395), neither the letter nor the spirit of Article 49 (sixth paragraph) comes into play.

746. If individual Israeli settlers have gained ownership of real estate in the West Bank, their private transaction should not have any impact on any final status agreement regarding the future of the area. Once the occupation is over, these settlers – if they choose to remain in the formerly occupied territory (and if the final status agreement allows them to do so) – may have to live under a new flag. 'In principle, there should be a symmetry between Israel and its neighbours. Israel has a large Arab minority which enjoys civil rights within it. Why shouldn't Jews be allowed to live in neighbouring Arab countries?'[1529]

C. *The Judgments of the Supreme Court of Israel*

(a) ***The Salient Decisions***

747. The principal judicial decisions of the Israel Supreme Court on this topic were delivered unanimously by the same special panel of five Justices – within a short span of time – in the *Beth El* case (in March 1979) and in the *Elon Moreh* case (in October 1979). In both instances, the Court refused to address Article 49 (sixth paragraph) of the Geneva Convention on the ground that – as a constitutive treaty provision – the text could not govern the proceedings (see *supra* 89–90).[1530] In the *Beth El* case, the Court (per Deputy President Landau) emphasized that this is particularly true of Article 49 (sixth paragraph), which – even according to the ICRC Commentary – was adopted 'after some hesitation',[1531] thus showing that it was innovative and not part of customary international law.[1532]

748. Nevertheless, the Court agreed to examine the petitions – filed by inhabitants of the West Bank whose private lands had been seized (with an

[1528] *I.G. Farben* trial, *supra* note 1299, at 44.

[1529] R. Gavison, 'Legal Systems and Public Attitudes during Negotiations towards Transition from Conflict to Reconciliation: The Middle East, 1992–1994', *The Arab-Israeli Accords: Legal Perspectives, supra* note 122, at 21, 41–2.

[1530] See HCJ 606/78 etc., *supra* note 177, at 122 (per Justice Witkon), 127 (per Deputy President Landau); HCJ 390/79, *supra* note 179, at 29 (per Justice Witkon).

[1531] *Commentary, IV Geneva Convention, supra* note 31, at 283.

[1532] HCJ 606/78 etc., *supra* note 177, at 127.

offer to pay compensation) for the purpose of the construction of civilian settlements – on the basis of customary international law, as mirrored in Hague Regulations 46 (second paragraph) (quoted *supra* 689) (prohibiting confiscation of private property) and 52 (first paragraph) (quoted *supra* 699) (dealing with requisitions in kind and services, construed as applicable also to possession of land; see *supra* 703).

749. In the *Beth El* case, relating to a settlement adjacent to major military facilities constructed earlier on the same lands, the Court rejected the petition.[1533] Applying the Hague Regulations, the Court (per Justice Witkon) differentiated between an impermissible confiscation of private property (done without consideration or for an unlawful purpose) and a permissible requisition, which it deemed applicable to a temporary seizure of immovable private property – without deprivation of ownership – for use by the army of occupation and against consideration.[1534] The Court (on this issue, mainly per Deputy President Landau) considered the seizure of the disputed land to be a genuine instance of permissible requisition, inasmuch as the settlement was established in a strategic location, fulfilling 'the needs of the army of occupation' as required by Regulation 52 (first paragraph).[1535] Deputy President Landau ruled that such needs include anticipation of acts of sabotage originating from either within or without the occupied territory.[1536] He was persuaded by the respondents that the settlement fulfilled an important military function as part of an in-depth 'spatial defence' belt created by the Occupying Power.[1537] In answer to the question as to how the settlement could be built on land seized only for temporary use, Deputy President Landau said that the settlement would last solely as long as the area is occupied by the IDF and its fate may be resolved by international negotiations.[1538]

750. The pivotal issue is whether the seizure of private lands by an Occupying Power is permitted for the purpose of the construction of a civil settlement. The rationale used by Deputy President Landau – that a civilian settlement can constitute an integral part of a military 'spatial defence' belt – is quite problematic. He did not advert to *Nahal* (a Hebrew acronym for Pioneering Combatant Youth) settlements in which soldiers, doing their army service, used to be engaged (on a part-time basis) in agriculture. The *Nahal* settlements – quite common in the early days of occupation (although subsequently civilianized) – were clearly army bases, even if the *Nahal* soldiers

[1533] *Ibid.*, 134.
[1534] *Ibid.*, 123.
[1535] *Ibid.*, 130–1.
[1536] *Ibid.*, 131.
[1537] *Ibid.*, 127.
[1538] *Ibid.*, 131.

devoted some of their efforts to tilling the land.[1539] But the Judgment took a much broader view, seeing no difficulty in painting a purely civilian settlement with military colours in light of its potential contribution to long-term military planning. Deputy President Landau mentioned that Israeli men and women of military age serve as reservists in the IDF,[1540] although he did not address two queries: (i) what is the status of these reservists before and after they are called up for active duty (which, after all, affects only a fraction of their time)?; and (ii) what about the presence in a civilian settlement of children and their mothers, the elderly and other civilians exempt from military service in Israel on various grounds of disability?

751. In the *Matityahu* case (decided by a regular panel of the Court, consisting of three Justices, in August 1979), the Judgment (per Deputy President Landau) drew attention to the fact that the settlement in question was located in the heights commanding Israel's International (Ben Gurion) Airport, and was therefore a potential look-out post facilitating military protection of this sensitive strategic point.[1541] By portraying such a civilian settlement in terms of a military outpost, Deputy President Landau's rationale (as expressed both in *Beth El* and in *Matityahu*) is an object lesson in the danger of unintended consequences. After all, the most fundamental principle of the *jus in bello* is distinction between combatants and civilians.[1542] In application of this principle, lawful attacks – in the course of hostilities – must be confined to military objectives, to the exclusion of civilian objects (see Article 52 of Additional Protocol I[1543]). Obviously, if a civilian settlement acquires a military dimension, that would corrode its civilian status and expose it to lawful attacks as a military objective.

752. Half a year after delivering the decision on *Beth El*, the same special panel of five Justices had to retread familiar ground in the *Elon Moreh* case, except that here the Judgment went in favour of the petitioners.[1544] The Court (per Deputy President Landau and Justice Witkon) restated its position on the law, but underscored that the security considerations motivating the establishment of each civilian settlement must be gauged on their merits, and, in the specific circumstances of Elon Moreh, it emerged that the main reason for the seizure of private property on which the settlement was to be built was not

[1539] See N.M. Kerber, *Les Droits de l'Homme dans les Territoires Administrés par Israël* 91 n. 104 (1978).

[1540] HCJ 606/78 etc., *supra* note 177, at 127.

[1541] HCJ 258/79, *Amira* et al. *v. Minister of Defence* et al., 34(1) *PD* 90, 92–3. (The Judgment is excerpted in English in 10 *IYHR* 331 (1980). A full translation is available in I *Military Government in the Territories Administered by Israel 1967*–1980, *supra* note 99, at 398).

[1542] See Dinstein, *supra* note 14, at 12–13.

[1543] Additional Protocol I, *supra* note 33, at 737.

[1544] HCJ 390/79, *supra* note 179, at 31.

security-oriented; hence unlawful.[1545] Justice Witkon in particular brought to the fore the fact that there was no 'military purpose' behind the construction of the settlement.[1546] Deputy President Landau found fault with an open admission by the settlers that they intended to remain in Elon Moreh permanently:

> The decision to establish a permanent settlement designed in advance to stay in its place perpetually – even beyond the duration of the military government established in Judea and Samaria – encounters an insurmountable legal obstacle, for a military government cannot create facts in its area for its military needs, designed in advance to exist even after the end of the military rule in that area, when we do not yet know what will be the fate of the area after the termination of military rule.[1547]

753. The Elon Moreh settlement was dismantled, although it was reconstructed not far from the original site.[1548] The military government learned a valuable lesson from the judicial message relayed: instead of seizing private land for the establishment of future civilian settlements, it started to allocate public lands with the same objective in mind.[1549]

(b) The More Recent Cases

754. Over the years, multiple disputes have surfaced concerning attempts made by settlers (especially in 'outposts') to encroach onto land privately owned by Palestinian inhabitants in the West Bank, where title to the land has been in some sort of dispute. Generally speaking, disputes of this nature can only be resolved by the judiciary and they tend to be time-consuming. Whenever local inhabitants' claims to ownership could be verified, the military commander was invariably instructed by the Supreme Court to evict the trespassers – if necessary by force – and to dismantle any buildings or appurtenances constructed by them. There were a number of cases that caused a lot of political controversy in Israel – particularly, the dismantling of a new neighbourhood in Beth El in 2012[1550] and the entire settlement of Amona in 2017[1551] – but, after a number of delays, the settlers were evicted in both of these instances (as in many others).

[1545] *Ibid.*, 22 (per Deputy President Landau), 23 (per Justice Witkon).
[1546] *Ibid.*, 23.
[1547] *Ibid.*, 22.
[1548] See Kretzmer, *supra* note 167, at 89.
[1549] See *ibid.*, 89–91.
[1550] For the final Judgment in the case (per President Grunis), see HCJ 9060/08, *Abdallah* et al. *v. Minister of Defence* et al., 65(2) *PD* 667, 676.
[1551] The complex history of the *Amona* case is narrated in English in 48 *IYHR* 345–50 (2018). The original Judgment (per President Grunis) to vacate and dismantle Amona (with a two-year grace period) was delivered at the end of 2014: HCJ 9949/08, *Hamad* et al. *v. Minister of Defence* et al., para. 18. When the grace period expired at the end of 2016, a request for its extension was denied by the Court. The settlement was forcibly demolished by the military government in early 2017 (although the settlers were promised future relocation to public land).

755. Admittedly, even in recent years, there has been some seizure (accompanied by compensation) of ordinary private property from inhabitants of the West Bank, but this was not linked to settlements. It related either to infrastructure works (see *supra* 360) or to the construction of the security barrier (see *infra* 763).

756. Although in recent times the Supreme Court has been increasingly willing to apply the Geneva Convention, the Court exhibited no inclination to put settlements to the test of Article 49 (sixth paragraph). A sweeping attack against the Government's settlement policy in the West Bank and the Gaza Strip was launched in 1991, in the *'Peace Now' Movement* case: the petition related to all civilian settlements (past and present), insisting that they must be justified solely by security reasons and that all settlers must be willing to commit themselves to evacuate their places of habitation once those security reasons expired.[1552] The petition cited both the Hague Regulations and the non-transfer clause in the Geneva Convention.[1553] But the very magnitude of the challenge to governmental policy led the Supreme Court (per President Shamgar) to decline to adjudicate the case, on the ground of injusticiability, explaining that the Court was ready to deal with specific disputes but not to engage itself in abstract political controversies.[1554]

757. In the subsequent *Ma'ale Adumim* case – flowing from the use of public land for a large urban settlement to the east of Jerusalem – the Court (in three separate but concurring opinions) dismissed the petition.[1555] Justice Matza observed that, once a final status agreement is reached between Israel and the Palestinian Authority, it will resolve the fate of the contested land.[1556] Justice Strasberg-Cohen was more concrete:

> The issue of Israeli settlement is one of the topics to be found on the negotiating table between Israel and the PLO, within the framework of negotiations on a permanent agreement. The status of the Israeli settlements in the region will be determined within the framework of the political arrangements. This Court is not supposed to address the issue in the midst of political contacts and to meddle indirectly in the drawing up of maps. This is the clear task of the various arms of the government.[1557]

Justice Cheshin came back to the argument of injusticiability: in his opinion, the State should speak with one voice on such a sensitive topic, and it would be highly improper for the Court to vent its view in a matter that ought to be

[1552] HCJ 4481/91 etc., *Bargil, Director-General of the 'Peace Now' Movement* et al. *v. Government of Israel* et al., 47(4) *PD* 210, 213.

[1553] *Ibid.*, 214.

[1554] *Ibid.*, 215–17.

[1555] HCJ 3125/98, *Ayad* et al. *v. IDF Commander of Judea and Samaria* et al., 55(1) *PD* 913, 915.

[1556] *Ibid.*, 917.

[1557] *Ibid.*, 918.

resolved by negotiations conducted by the Government.[1558] None of the three Justices mentioned the Geneva Convention.

758. As will be seen (see *infra* 786), in the *Alfei Menashe* case, the Court – sitting in a special panel of nine Justices (per President Barak) – desisted from disposing of the issue of the legality of the settlements, without denying the possibility of their being unlawful.

(c) The Impermanent Nature of the Settlements

759. In the final analysis, the greatest contribution of the Court to the legal discourse about settlements has been the recurrent emphasis on their impermanent nature. In the *Beth El* case, Deputy President Landau was adamant that a civilian settlement built in an occupied territory cannot be permanent in the full sense of the word (see *supra* 749). True, large factions of settlers (inspired by the fervour of religious convictions rooted in the Bible) zealously regard their homes in the West Bank as permanent. But, as another member of the bench in the *Beth El* case – Justice M. Ben Porat – phrased it, 'permanent' in this setting is a 'purely *relative* term'.[1559]

760. Naturally, when an occupation is as prolonged as the Israeli occupation (and the Beth El settlement – like most other settlements in the West Bank – is still standing and flourishing at the time of writing), a sceptic is entitled to doubt the degree to which the permanence of the settlements is relative. Nevertheless, it must be kept in mind that the Israeli occupation is associated not only with building long-lasting settlements in droves, but also with dismantling clusters of others after years of existence. Over the decades of occupation, Israel has evicted (at times, by force) tens of thousands of settlers from the Sinai Peninsula, the Gaza Strip, and even the West Bank (see *supra* 754). In Gaza, this required special legislation by the Knesset, which was challenged before the Supreme Court (sitting in an exceptional panel of eleven Justices), but the petition was denied by a lopsided majority in the *Gaza Coast Local Council* case (10:1).[1560]

761. The joint Judgment of the majority in the last case highlighted the transitory dimension of settlement:

> Most Israelis do not have ownership in the land on which they built their homes and businesses in the evacuated area. They acquired their rights from the military commander or from those acting on his behalf. These are not the owners of the property, and they cannot transfer more rights than they have. To the extent that the Israelis built their

[1558] *Ibid.*, 919.

[1559] HCJ 606/78 etc., *supra* note 177, at 134. Emphasis in the original. These words have been cited with approval in subsequent Judgments of the Court. See, e.g., HCJ 4400/92 etc., *Local Council Kiryat Arba Hebron* et al. *v. Prime Minister* et al., 48(5) *PD* 597, 607 (per Justice D. Levin).

[1560] HCJ 1661/05 etc., *supra* note 159, at 814.

homes and assets on land that is not private ('State land'), it is not owned by the military commander. His powers are established in Hague Regulation 55, and they reflect customary international law.[1561]

In a follow-up Judgment on the same subject, in the *Nango* case, the Court (per Justice Beinisch) reverted to the theme that – since belligerent occupation is temporary in nature – the status of the Israeli settlements in the Gaza Strip could not be other than temporary.[1562]

II. Israel's Security Barrier

A. *The Setting*

762. From 1967 until the flare-up of the second *intifada*, the Green Line – separating Israel from the West Bank (see *supra* 45) – was a porous border, in many respects a notional line, marked on maps but not on the ground: although there were some roadblocks, access between the two territories was fairly facile. However, the increased frequency of 'suicide bombers' launched from the West Bank into Israel during the second *intifada* actuated a decision by the Israeli Government (in 2002) to start constructing a security barrier that – albeit not impermeable – would impede the crossing. In view of the almost instant success of the measure (which was conducive to the number of 'suicide bomber' attacks plummeting dramatically), it was decided to extend the barrier further, and ultimately it has been planned to cover the entire border between Israel and the West Bank.

763. The security barrier largely consists of a 'smart' fence with electronic sensors, a paved patrol road, a strip of sand for detecting footprints, a ditch and barbed wire (usually reaching a width of between 50 and 70 metres). In urban areas (e.g., Jerusalem), such an elaborate construction is impossible, and in consequence the wider barrier has been replaced by a mere line of tall concrete slabs (the so-called 'wall'). The land needed for the construction of the barrier was either public or private (in which case compensation was offered to the owners).

764. There is a profusion of fenced borders all over the globe, and it is apodeictic that Israel was and is at liberty to build a security barrier on its own side of the Green Line. In some sectors, this is what happened. The crunch is that, for most of the route, the security barrier has been constructed within the West Bank, in some instances encompassing also settlements located near the Green Line. This has prompted a number of objections to the project: (i)

[1561] *Ibid.*, 584.

[1562] HCJ 7918/05, *Nango* et al. *v. Government of Israel* et al., 59(2) *PD* 856, 859.

politically, the construction of the barrier looked like a unilateral attempt on the part of Israel to set a final status border, encroaching on the West Bank; (ii) the seizure of private property for the construction of parts of the barrier was challenged (notwithstanding the offer of compensation); (iii) while the private land needed for construction per se may have been negligible, the barrier split apart multifarious tracts of private land. In particular, throngs of Palestinian farmers living to the east of the barrier found it difficult to reach their lands located to the west of it (despite the availability of dozens of access gates).

B. *The* Beit Sourik *Case*

765. Shortly after the construction of the security barrier commenced, a spate of petitions (each dealing with a specific sector) poured into the docket of the Israel Supreme Court. The most important petition – against a 40-kilometre stretch of the barrier north-west of Jerusalem – reached the Court in the *Beit Sourik* case.[1563] The Court (per President Barak) arrived at the following conclusions on what it called the 'separation fence':

(a) The 'fence' cannot be designed to delineate a political border: the powers of the military government are in essence transient (since the belligerent occupation itself is temporary in its character), and final status arrangements do not come within the lawful authority of the military government.[1564] However, the petitioners failed to convince the Court that (i) the decision to build the 'fence' was based on political rather than security considerations, or that (ii) the construction was permanent in nature.[1565]

(b) The military government is authorized by Hague Regulations 23(g) and 52, as well as Article 53 of Geneva Convention (IV) (quoted *supra* 595, 598 and 699), to seize lands as required for military needs (subject to payment of compensation for their use).[1566] As long as the construction of the 'fence' comes within the framework of military requirements, it preempts the right to private property.[1567]

(c) The main question is not the issue of principle but the concrete demarcation on the ground of the route of the 'fence', which must be based on the canon of proportionality – deemed by the Court a general principle of international law – striking a proper (and objective) balance between

[1563] HCJ 2056/04, *supra* note 712, at 846.
[1564] *Ibid.*, 829–30.
[1565] *Ibid.*, 830–1.
[1566] *Ibid.*, 831–2.
[1567] *Ibid.*, 832.

military necessity and humanitarian considerations.[1568] The delineation of the 'fence' must therefore minimize the harm inflicted on local inhabitants.[1569]

766. Having painstakingly sifted the evidence regarding the 40-kilometre stretch of the 'fence' before it, and having weighed the plight of farmers separated from their lands, the Court rescinded on the footing of disproportionality no less than six out of seven orders of seizure of private lands assailed in the *Beit Sourik* case.[1570]

767. The Judgment in the *Beit Sourik* case is not perfect. Moreover, the citing of specific Hague and Geneva clauses is occasionally inapt. Thus, the provision of Geneva Article 53 is only about destruction – and not seizure – of private property (the sole issue before the Court). Hague Regulation 52, notwithstanding attempts to widen its range, is devoted to requisitions in kind and services: it has no bearing on immovable property, save for the quartering of troops and officials (see *supra* 703). Hague Regulation 23(g) is confined to 'the necessities of war' (*supra* 595), and its relevance to the construction of a 'fence' is not self-evident.[1571] Having said that, the Judgment is of immense significance, and it seems to have found an equitable solution to a thorny problem. The Court's decision certainly compelled the military government to redemarcate the entire route of the security barrier.

768. A special comment is called for as regards the criterion of proportionality. This is not the first time that the Court (and especially President Barak) underlined proportionality as a major consideration in the solution of problems pertaining to belligerent occupation. Notably, in the *Ajouri* case (decided by a panel of nine Justices in 2002), President Barak emphasized the importance of proportionality in the context of assigned residence.[1572] But in *Beit Sourik* proportionality became a central theme. Incontrovertibly, President Barak was carried away in presenting it as 'a principle underlying the whole body of international law'.[1573] Still, subsequent to rendering the *Beit Sourik* Judgment, proportionality has become an omnipresent beacon guiding the Court in navigating its way through the often uncharted waters of disputes emanating from the West Bank.[1574]

[1568] *Ibid.*, 832–8.
[1569] *Ibid.*
[1570] *Ibid.*, 862.
[1571] See Lubell, *supra* note 1214, at 298.
[1572] HCJ 7015/02, *supra* note 173, at 373.
[1573] M. Pertile, '*Beit Sourik Village Council v. The Government of Israel*: A Matter of Principle (and Neglected Rules)', 65 *Heid.JIL* 677, 697 (2005).
[1574] See G. Harpaz, 'Being Unfaithful to One's Own Principles: The Israeli Supreme Court and House Demolitions in the Occupied Palestinian Territories', 47 *Is.LR* 401, 405 (2014).

C. *The Advisory Opinion of the International Court of Justice*

769. On 9 July 2004, a little more than a week after the delivery of the Supreme Court's Judgment in the *Beit Sourik* case (on 30 June 2004), the International Court of Justice rendered its own Advisory Opinion on *Legal Consequences of the Construction of a Wall in the Occupied Palestinian Territory,* in which it found (14:1) that the construction of the 'wall' was contrary to international law.[1575] Surely, the writing of the Advisory Opinion had been completed before the release of the Supreme Court's Judgment. But, bearing in mind that Israel abstained from making submissions on the merits before the International Court (having challenged the jurisdiction and propriety of the proceedings), one might have hoped that the International Court would wish to peruse the Supreme Court's Judgment prior to coming out with the Advisory Opinion.[1576] Had the International Court done that, it might have realized that many facts and figures pertaining to the potential repercussions of the construction of the 'wall' – as stated in the Advisory Opinion on the basis of inaccurate information imparted to the Court by the UN – were grossly inflated (e.g., the false claim that almost 17 per cent of the West Bank would lie between the Green Line and the 'wall';[1577] for the accurate percentage see *infra* 782–3).

770. The Advisory Opinion was requested from the International Court by the UN General Assembly, and this is where the misleading terminology relating to a 'wall' came from.[1578] In actuality, as admitted by the Court, out of about 180 kilometres of the barrier constructed up to that time, only some 8.5 kilometres (less than 5 per cent) consisted of a concrete wall[1579] (for an update, see *infra ibid.*).

771. The Advisory Opinion endorsed all the key objections to the construction of the 'wall', and then some. The trouble with the Advisory Opinion, in the words of Roberts, is that 'it is so definite, so wide-ranging in its scope, and so controversial'.[1580] About the security motivation leading to the construction of the 'wall', the Court had this to say:

> Whilst the Court notes the assurance given by Israel that the construction of the wall does not amount to annexation and that the wall is of a temporary nature ..., it nevertheless cannot remain indifferent to certain fears expressed to it that the route of the

[1575] Advisory Opinion on *Legal Consequences of the Construction of a Wall in the Occupied Palestinian Territory*, *supra* note 25, at 201.

[1576] See Y. Shany, 'Capacities and Inadequacies: A Look at the Two Separation Barrier Cases', 38 *Is.LR* 230, 246 (2005).

[1577] Advisory Opinion on *Legal Consequences of the Construction of a Wall in the Occupied Palestinian Territory*, *supra* note 25, at 170.

[1578] *Ibid.*, 164.

[1579] *Ibid.*, 170.

[1580] Roberts, *supra* note 194, at 462.

wall will prejudge the future frontier between Israel and Palestine, and the fear that Israel may integrate the settlements and their means of access. The Court considers that the construction of the wall and its associated régime create a 'fait accompli' on the ground that could well become permanent, in which case, and notwithstanding the formal characterization of the wall by Israel, it would be tantamount to *de facto* annexation.[1581]

772. Although the Court conceded elsewhere in the Advisory Opinion that an 8-kilometre section near the town of Baqa al-Sharqiya had already been demolished by Israel,[1582] it obviously discredited Israel's professed readiness to consider redrawing other sections of the 'wall'.[1583] Had the International Court opted to study the Supreme Court's Judgment in the *Beit Sourik* case – and, even more significantly perhaps, had the International Court given itself the opportunity to consider the aftermath of the Supreme Court's decision – it would have perceived that the so-called 'fait accompli' could be, and was, easily overturned: the route of the security barrier has been radically altered without any apparent difficulty and within a short space of time.

773. The International Court was keenly critical of the creation of enclaves between the Green Line and the 'wall', surprisingly finding that the harm is 'most marked in urban areas',[1584] while in fact the principal complaint related to hard-to-reach agricultural lands. The Court also determined that there were inimical effects for the population regarding the exercise of a bundle of human rights.[1585] As already pointed out (see *supra* 265), the Court put a misplaced emphasis on freedom of movement in occupied territories. Even more surprisingly, perhaps, the Court dilated on the denial of freedom of access to Holy Places located on Mount Zion (situated within Israel proper, to the west of the Green Line).[1586] There are some legal issues relating to the sources and scope of this freedom of access, which were not addressed in depth by the Court.[1587] But the most dismaying aspects are factual. First, freedom of access to Holy Places can be fully guaranteed by the multiple gates interspersing the 'wall'. Secondly, how can the very existence of the 'wall' run afoul of freedom of access to these Holy Places when exactly the same barrier would have passed muster had it been constructed entirely on the Israeli side of the Green Line

[1581] Advisory Opinion on *Legal Consequences of the Construction of a Wall in the Occupied Palestinian Territory*, *supra* note 25, at 184.

[1582] *Ibid.*, 169–70.

[1583] See Lubell, *supra* note 1214, at 288.

[1584] Advisory Opinion on *Legal Consequences of the Construction of a Wall in the Occupied Palestinian Territory*, *supra* note 25, at 190.

[1585] *Ibid.*, 187–92.

[1586] *Ibid.*, 189.

[1587] See M. Hirsch, 'The Legal Status of Jerusalem Following the ICJ Advisory Opinion on the Separation Barrier', 38 *Is.LR* 298, 311–13 (2005).

(still to the east of Mount Zion), notwithstanding the consequent possible inconveniences to pilgrims?

774. There is even a 'stranger' reference ('stranger' is a phrase used by Judge R. Higgins in her Separate Opinion[1588]) to the exercise of the vaguely defined rights to work, to the protection of children, to an adequate standard of living, to health and to education,[1589] enunciated in the Economic, Social and Cultural Rights Covenant,[1590] and in the Convention on the Rights of the Child.[1591] The linkage between these human rights and the security barrier is, to say the least, tenuous.

775. To cap it all, the Court expressed the view that, by contributing to the alteration of the demographic composition of the West Bank, the construction of the 'wall' constituted a breach of Israel's obligation to respect the Palestinian people's right to self-determination (see *supra* 170).[1592] As Judge P.H. Kooijmans commented in his Separate Opinion, it would have been better if the Court had left issues of self-determination to the political process.[1593] Judge Higgins was 'puzzled' by the application of self-determination to the present case, stating that it was 'both unrealistic and unbalanced' for the Court to find that the 'wall' (rather than larger issues) was a serious obstacle to self-determination.[1594]

776. The Advisory Opinion also raised (somewhat indirectly) the question of proportionality.[1595] But – unlike the Israel Supreme Court – the International Court preferred to tar the entire 'wall' with the brush of a blanket condemnation, without allowing for the possibility that a section-by-section examination of the route might show that in part it could meet standards of proportionality. The Court's core conclusion was that the 'wall' – by infringing numerous rights of the Palestinian inhabitants of the occupied territory – could not 'be justified by military exigencies or by the requirement of national security or public order'.[1596]

777. The International Court pronounced that the Geneva Convention was fully applicable in the West Bank (see also *supra* 71).[1597] Accordingly, it ruled that settlements were in violation of Article 49 (sixth paragraph) of

[1588] Advisory Opinion on *Legal Consequences of the Construction of a Wall in the Occupied Palestinian Territory*, *supra* note 25, at 213.

[1589] *Ibid.*, 189.

[1590] International Covenant on Economic, Social and Cultural Rights, *supra* note 335, at 35–8 (Articles 6–7, 10–14).

[1591] Convention on the Rights of the Child, *supra* note 443, at 284, 287–9 (Articles 16, 24, 27–8).

[1592] Advisory Opinion on *Legal Consequences of the Construction of a Wall in the Occupied Palestinian Territory*, *supra* note 25, at 184.

[1593] *Ibid.*, 228.

[1594] *Ibid.*, 214.

[1595] *Ibid.*, 193.

[1596] *Ibid.*, 193.

[1597] *Ibid.*, 177.

the Geneva Convention (quoted *supra* 734).[1598] As seen by the Court, this provision was apposite in that 'the route chosen for the wall gives expression *in loco* to the illegal measures taken by Israel with regard to Jerusalem and the settlements'.[1599]

778. The International Court also stated that the destruction or requisition of properties for the purpose of the construction of the 'wall' was in breach of Geneva Article 53, as well as Hague Regulations 46 and 52 (quoted *supra* 451, 598, 689 and 699).[1600] The references to Geneva Article 53 and Hague Regulation 52, curiously enough, were also made by the Israel Supreme Court (see *supra* 765). The citation of Article 53 by the International Court was stimulated by its acceptance of charges that the construction of the 'wall' entailed destruction of property, and the fact that it was 'not convinced that the destruction carried out contrary to the prohibition in Article 53 of the Fourth Geneva Convention were rendered absolutely necessary by military operations'.[1601] The allusion to Regulation 52 was made by the International Court without asking whether that clause actually deals with immovables (other than in the context of billeting of troops), nor did it try to parse the qualifying words 'except for the necessities of the army of occupation'.[1602] Regulation 46 (insisting on respect for – and non-confiscation of – private property) was mentioned blandly: not even a hint was given to the issue of compensation offered for the non-consensual use of property.[1603]

779. The cardinal weakness of the Advisory Opinion – accentuated by the sole Dissenting Judge (T. Buergenthal[1604]), but acknowledged also by three of the majority Judges in their respective Separate Opinions (Judges Higgins,[1605] Kooijmans[1606] and H. Owada[1607]) – is that it did not approach the subject in a balanced way, putting blinkers on its eyes in the face of the violence that had preceded the construction of the security barrier.[1608] There is no mention in the Advisory Opinion of 'suicide bombers'. Indeed, to quote Judge Buergenthal:

all we have from the Court is a description of the harm the wall is causing and a discussion of various provisions of international humanitarian law and human rights

[1598] *Ibid.*, 183–4. Even the sole dissenter, Judge Buergenthal, agreed on this point, *ibid.*, 244.
[1599] *Ibid.*, 184.
[1600] *Ibid.*, 189.
[1601] *Ibid.*, 192.
[1602] See N. Keidar, 'An Examination of the Authority of the Military Commander to Requisition Privately Owned Land for the Construction of the Separation Barrier', 38 *Is.LR* 247, 251–3 (2005).
[1603] The point was underlined by Judge Buergenthal, in his Dissenting Opinion, Advisory Opinion on *Legal Consequences of the Construction of a Wall in the Occupied Palestinian Territory*, *supra* note 25, at 244.
[1604] *Ibid.*, 243–4.
[1605] *Ibid.*, 211–12.
[1606] *Ibid.*, 221–2.
[1607] *Ibid.*, 270–1.
[1608] See M. Pomerance, 'A Court of "UN Law"', 38 *Is.LR* 134, 147–50 (2005).

instruments followed by the conclusion that this law has been violated. Lacking is an examination of the facts that might show why the alleged defences of military exigencies, national security or public order are not applicable to the wall as a whole or to the individual segments of its route. The Court says that 'it is not convinced' but it fails to demonstrate why it is not convinced, and that is why these conclusions are not convincing.[1609]

Elsewhere, Judge Buergenthal remarked that the Advisory Opinion lacked 'credibility'.[1610] Typically, when the Court ruled that Hague Regulation 23(g) (quoted *supra* 595) – which relates to 'the necessities of war' – does not pertain to occupied territories (see *supra* 596), the Court neglected to examine 'the question whether the situation on the West Bank is not only a situation of occupation, but also one of active hostilities'.[1611]

780. 'It follows from the concept of advisory opinions that they are not binding ... for any State'.[1612] The Court itself has emphasized the point in an earlier Advisory Opinion: 'The Court's reply is only of an advisory character: as such, it has no binding force'.[1613] In the event, Israel has largely ignored the Advisory Opinion on the *Wall*. On the other hand, the route of the security barrier has been thoroughly recast, with a view to meeting the yardsticks of proportionality imposed by the Supreme Court.

D. *The* Alfei Menashe *Case*

781. The Israel Supreme Court had to redirect its attention to the 'fence' on several occasions, each relating to a separate sector, and it has consistently followed in the footsteps of the *Beit Sourik* Judgment.[1614] The Court was also given ample opportunity to examine the Advisory Opinion of the International Court. This happened in the *Alfei Menashe* case, before a special panel of nine Justices. The facts related to a sector of the security barrier protecting a settlement with 5,650 residents located approximately 4 kilometres from the

[1609] Advisory Opinion on *Legal Consequences of the Construction of a Wall in the Occupied Palestinian Territory*, *supra* note 25, at 244.

[1610] *Ibid.*, 241.

[1611] See D. Kretzmer, 'The Advisory Opinion: The Light Treatment of International Humanitarian Law', 99 *AJIL* 88, 96 (2005).

[1612] K. Oellers-Frahm, 'Article 96 UN Charter', *The Statute of the International Court of Justice: A Commentary* 181, 182 (A. Zimmermann, C. Tomuschat and K. Oellers-Frahm eds., 2006).

[1613] Advisory Opinion on *Interpretation of Peace Treaties with Bulgaria, Hungary and Romania* (First Phase), [1950] *ICJ Rep.* 65, 71. The passage was quoted in the Advisory Opinion on *Legal Consequences of the Construction of a Wall in the Occupied Palestinian Territory*, *supra* note 25, at 157.

[1614] See, e.g., HCJ 940/04, *Abu Tir* et al. *v. Military Commander of Judea and Samaria* et al., 59(2) *PD* 320, 328 (per Justice Proccacia). (The Judgment is excerpted in English in 37 *IYHR* 333 (2007)).

Green Line.[1615] Since the barrier also covered a road connecting the settlement to Israel, several Palestinian villages (with altogether 1,200 inhabitants) were stranded in an enclave on the west side of the barrier (with several access gates). The villagers petitioned the Court on the basis of both the *Beit Sourik* precedent and the Advisory Opinion. The Court instructed the military government to reconsider the demarcation of the contentious sector, in order to minimize the injury to the petitioners.[1616]

782. By the time that the *Alfei Menashe* decision was delivered in 2005, the construction of some 242 kilometres of the barrier had been completed, and 157 additional kilometres were under construction (out of a total of 763 kilometres then projected); the actual wall component of the built-up barrier rising to 28 kilometres, i.e. 11 per cent.[1617] The overall plan called for a maximum of 7.8 per cent of the West Bank to be west of the barrier, but more than half of this assessment was in a nebulous study stage not likely to materialize (anyhow, even in the worst-case scenario, less than half the estimate by the International Court; see *supra* 769).[1618]

783. By 2018, approximately 525 kilometres of the barrier have been built, with less than 200 kilometres still under construction (the original projected length having been reduced in scale). The actual wall component is less than 70 kilometres, and the portion of the West Bank to the west of the security barrier is under 5 per cent.

784. In the *Alfei Menashe* case, the Supreme Court (again, per President Barak) analysed the Advisory Opinion in detail.[1619] It noted that the Advisory Opinion is not legally binding, but acknowledged that the International Court is the top judicial body in the international community and its interpretation of international law must be given full weight.[1620] President Barak compared the Judgment in the *Beit Sourik* case with the Advisory Opinion and expressed the view that they need not be regarded as polarized. In fact, he said, there is much common ground: there is no dispute that the West Bank is under belligerent occupation, that it cannot be annexed, and that the Hague Regulations apply.[1621] As for the Advisory Opinion's ruling on the applicability of the Geneva Convention to the West Bank (*supra* 777), President Barak felt that – in light of the Government's oft-stated stance that it follows all the humanitarian

1615 For the facts, see HCJ 7957/04, *Mara'abe* et al. v. *Prime Minister of Israel* et al., 60(2) *PD* 477, 489 *et seq*. (The Judgment is excerpted in English in 37 *IYHR* 345 (2007). A full translation is available in 45 *ILM* 202 (2006)).

1616 *Ibid*., 555.

1617 *Ibid*., 487.

1618 *Ibid*., 488.

1619 *Ibid*., 511–22.

1620 *Ibid*., 522–3.

1621 *Ibid*., 523.

provisions of the instrument (see *supra* 76–7) – there was no need to get into the issue, which is essentially moot.[1622] Human rights treaties were cited in the Advisory Opinion, and not in the *Beit Sourik* case, but President Barak did not question their applicability (see *supra* 226), although he stressed that human rights – for instance, freedom of movement – are subject to intrinsic limitations (see *supra* 241–2).[1623]

785. According to President Barak, both Courts were also in agreement that the legality of the construction of the 'fence' (the 'wall' in the parlance of the Advisory Opinion) had to be resolved on the basis of Hague Regulations 43 and 52, and Article 53 of the Geneva Convention (quoted *supra* 269, 598 and 699).[1624] There were, of course blatant dissimilarities. President Barak did not see the reliance on Regulation 46 (quoted *supra* 689) – with respect to the prohibition of confiscation – as apposite, since the seizure of land was accompanied by an offer of compensation and it was temporary in nature.[1625] He also objected to the Advisory Opinion's refusal to apply to the 'fence' Hague Regulation 23(g) (about destruction and seizure of property) (quoted *supra* 595), finding in the legal literature support for the Supreme Court's position and underscoring that one cannot overlook the actual incidence of hostilities inside an occupied area (see *supra* 597).[1626]

786. President Barak maintained that the Occupying Power's obligation to ensure public order in an occupied territory is not restricted to protected persons, but is spread over all those who are present in the area.[1627] He relied on the Supreme Court's previous case law where – with the object of imposing law and order on unruly settlers – the authority of the military government over all those present in the occupied territories (whether or not protected persons) was established (see *supra* 398).[1628] He now turned around the cutting edge of the argument, emphasizing that the settlers had a right to life as human beings, even if they are not protected persons.[1629] His conclusion was that the construction of the 'fence' to protect settlers is lawful even if *arguendo* – as held in the Advisory Opinion – the settlements are unlawful, a matter that the Supreme Court declined to delve into.[1630]

[1622] *Ibid.*
[1623] *Ibid*, 503–4, 523.
[1624] *Ibid.*, 495, 523.
[1625] *Ibid.*, 494–5. See on this issue, F. Domb, 'The Separation Fence in the International Court of Justice and the High Court of Justice: Commonalities, Differences and Specifics', *International Law and Armed Conflict: Exploring the Faultlines, supra* note 194, at 509, 522–3, 540.
[1626] HCJ 7957/04, *supra* note 1615, at 495–6.
[1627] *Ibid.*, 496–8.
[1628] *Ibid.*
[1629] *Ibid.*, 498–9
[1630] *Ibid.*, 499.

787. There is not a little discomfort among commentators about the protection of settlers who should not have been residing in the West Bank in the first place.[1631] Indeed, there is an inexorable vicious circle here. On the one hand, the human rights argument about the need to protect the lives of settlers is irreproachable. On the other hand, it is impossible to ignore the reality that 'any settlement sets in motion a chain of events which then requires a continuous increase in security devices' in order to ensure the settlers' safety.[1632]

788. However, there is an additional factor to consider. As President Barak mentioned,[1633] the 1995 Interim Agreement between Israel and the PLO expressly leaves the issue of settlements to the final status negotiations (Article XVII(1)(a)) as well as Article XXXI(5)).[1634] It was even agreed that Israel shall carry 'the responsibility for overall security of Israelis and Settlements, for the purpose of safeguarding their internal security and public order, and will have all the powers to take the steps necessary to meet this responsibility' (Article XII(1)).[1635] For reasons explained (*supra* 56), the 'Oslo Accords' – of which the Interim Agreement is the centrepiece – can be deemed to be somewhat analogous to agreements with the displaced sovereign.

789. It has been argued that – since, under Articles 7 and 47 of Geneva Convention (IV) (see *supra* 255, 373), even the displaced sovereign cannot deprive protected persons of the benefits of the Convention – the PLO was unable to waive in the Interim Agreement the humanitarian right enshrined in Article 49 (sixth paragraph) as regards transfer into the occupied territory of the civilian population of the Occupying Power.[1636] Yet, it is doubtful whether transfers *eo ipso* deprive the vested rights of protected persons who are not displaced (cf. *supra* 736). In pragmatic terms, one cannot overlook the likelihood that a final status agreement concerning the West Bank will conserve clusters of settlements through land swaps with Israel (see *supra* 58), and the Interim Agreement may be reckoned as a marker in that direction pending completion of lengthy negotiations.

790. President Barak was convinced that the main difference between the perspectives of the two Courts lay in the Advisory Opinion's assertion that the infringement of the Palestinian inhabitants' rights could not 'be justified by military exigencies or by the requirement of national security or public order' (see *supra* 776).[1637] The orientation of the Supreme Court was diametrically

[1631] See Gross, *supra* note 789, at 13–26.
[1632] See Tomuschat, *supra* note 1522, at 1565.
[1633] HCJ 7957/04, *supra* note 1615, at 499.
[1634] Israel-Palestine Liberation Organization, Interim Agreement on the West Bank and the Gaza Strip, *supra* note 116, at 564, 567.
[1635] *Ibid.*, 562.
[1636] See A. Gross, *The Writing on the Wall: Rethinking the International Law of Occupation* 296 (2017).
[1637] HCJ 7957/04, *supra* note 1615, at 524–5.

opposed. It fully recognized the military necessity of constructing the 'fence', subject to the need to ensure that there be no disproportionate injury to the rights of the Palestinian inhabitants.[1638] Security reasons have to be counterweighed as against humanitarian considerations, and the balance must rest on proportionality (see *supra* 768).[1639]

791. President Barak was under the impression that the divergent conclusions of the two Courts were primarily impelled by the disparate background materials available to them.[1640] He dwelt on the data provided to the International Court by the UN – which in essence ignored the security needs prompting the construction of the 'fence' – and noted that they affected the thrust of the Advisory Opinion (citing also Judge Buergenthal, as well as Judges Koojimans and Owada).[1641] President Barak called the result 'a grave omission', adding that it does not matter who was to blame: the International Court or Israel (by refusing to offer submissions on the merits), but either way the outcome was that the Advisory Opinion had been based on feeble factual foundations.[1642] Thus, the extent of the damage inflicted on the Palestinian inhabitants was highly exaggerated in the UN background materials and in the Advisory Opinion.[1643] In consequence, the Advisory Opinion was tilted, not providing proper equilibrium between military needs and the rights of the inhabitants.[1644] It ought to be recorded in this context that President Barak went out of his way to use relatively mild terms of reproof. In a concurring opinion, one of the other members of the Court's panel, Deputy President Cheshin, minced no words to express his dim view of the Advisory Opinion, which to his mind had no factual foundation whatever.[1645]

792. President Barak regretted that the Advisory Opinion had addressed the entire 'fence' as a single unit, whereas the Supreme Court dissected it sector-by-sector, thus being able to weigh carefully preponderant local circumstances.[1646] He calculated that 153 kilometres out of 763 kilometres planned (some 20 per cent) are on or near the Green Line, and 135 additional kilometres (some 17.7 per cent) are within less than 2 kilometres from it (without any Palestinian habitation or agricultural lands being affected).[1647] How can it be contended, asked President Barak, that the construction of these sectors of the 'fence'

[1638] *Ibid.*, 525.
[1639] *Ibid.*, 506–7.
[1640] *Ibid.*, 525.
[1641] *Ibid.*, 527–9.
[1642] *Ibid.*, 530.
[1643] *Ibid.*, 531–2.
[1644] *Ibid.*, 532–3.
[1645] *Ibid.*, 557–8.
[1646] *Ibid.*, 534.
[1647] *Ibid.*

are in breach of international law?[1648] In some other sectors, there were few agricultural lands west of the barrier, and access gates installed, so the injury to the local farmers was minimal.[1649] Of course, there were sectors in which disproportionate injury was indeed brought upon the Palestinian inhabitants, and – as the Court had shown in the *Beit Sourik* case, no less than in the present proceedings – it was prepared to strike them down.[1650] Finally, President Barak detected no factual underpinning for the suspicion evinced in the Advisory Opinion about the real motivation for the construction of the 'fence' (i.e. the alleged calculated intent to annex parts of the West Bank situated to the west of the barrier; see *supra* 771).[1651]

*E. Post-*Alfei Menashe *Cases*

793. Since its delivery, the *Alfei Menashe* Judgment has been reaffirmed and followed in multiple decisions of the Israel Supreme Court reviewing additional petitions filed against other sectors of the security barrier. Time and again, proceedings before the Court led to the redrawing of the routes of large segments of the security barrier, in some instances more than once. An extreme example is the *Modi'in Ilit* case, which involved no less than five consecutive – and profoundly different – routes until gaining approval by the Court (per President Beinisch) in 2007.[1652] That said, the Judgments constantly hark back to the proposition that – regardless of the legality of settlements – the military government has a duty to protect settlers in the West Bank.[1653]

794. The Supreme Court did not permit criss-crossing the West Bank with additional security barriers. In the *Dahariya* case of 2006, the Court (per President Barak) ordered the military commander to dismantle a concrete barricade, more than 40 kilometres long, designed to protect traffic travelling on roads transecting the Hebron Mountain, north of the security barrier under construction (routed there on a West–East axis).[1654] The Court arrived at the conclusion that the creation of an enclave in the West Bank – blocked to the south by the security barrier and to the north by the concrete barricade (albeit

[1648] *Ibid.*
[1649] *Ibid.*
[1650] *Ibid.*
[1651] *Ibid*, 534–5.
[1652] For the last round, see *Modi'in Ilit* case (HCJ 2645/04 etc., *Nasser* et al. v. *Prime Minister* et al., paras. 3–7, 40).
[1653] See, especially, two Judgments of the Court delivered by President Beinisch: in the *Efrat* case (HCJ 834/07, *Tekatka* et al. *v. Government of Israel* et al., para. 8) and in a previous *Modi'in Ilit* case (HCJ 8414/05, *Bil'in v. Government of Israel* et al., 62(2) *PD* 822, 844).
[1654] HCJ 1748/06 etc., *Dahariya* et al. *v. IDF Commander in the West Bank* et al., para. 22. (The Judgment is excerpted in English in 41 *IYHR* 281 (2011)).

with some gates) – had harmful effects on the fabric of life of the Palestinian inhabitants, in breach of their human rights, and did not meet the standard of proportionality (see *supra* 768).[1655] The Court did approve an alternative possibility (proposed by the petitioners) of replacing the concrete barricade with a low metal rail – common on divided highways – that would impede the passage of cars but not present an obstacle to pedestrians or livestock.[1656]

795. The construction of the security barrier has led to a complication regarding the Palestinian inhabitants living in areas between the barrier and the Green Line. These areas came to be known as a 'seam space', inasmuch as there is no physical buffer between them and Israeli territory. To alleviate security concerns, the military commander declared the 'seam space' to be a 'closed area' where residence and presence require permits. In response to petitions lodged against this policy, the Supreme Court in 2011 (per President Beinisch) – in a *Centre for the Defence of the Individual* case – upheld the general closure of the area on security grounds.[1657] Still, the Judgment emphasized the need to respect the human rights of the local inhabitants (especially, farmers cultivating agricultural lands) by enabling them to exercise freedom of movement in and out of the 'seam space'.[1658]

III. Reunion of Families

A. *Admission to an Occupied Territory*

796. Specious arguments have been made to the effect that permanent residents of an occupied territory who are absent at the outset of the occupation are entitled to return to their homes thereafter.[1659] Nothing in Geneva Convention (IV) sustains that view.

797. In the *El-Tin* case, the Israel Supreme Court (per Deputy President Sussman and Justice E. Manny) decided that an Occupying Power is clearly allowed to restrict entry from the outside into an occupied territory by declaring it a closed area and making admission contingent on obtaining a permit from the military government.[1660] Here the petitioner – who had been a permanent resident of the West Bank but had moved to Kuwait – returned on a tourist visa and upon its expiry strove to remain in the area. The Court was divided

[1655] *Ibid.*, paras. 16–19.
[1656] *Ibid.*, para. 20.
[1657] HCJ 9961/03 etc., *Centre for the Defence of the Individual* et al. v. *Government of Israel*, paras. 16–18.
[1658] *Ibid.*, paras. 24–7.
[1659] See J. Quigley, 'Mass Displacement and the Individual Right of Return', 68 *BYBIL* 65, 71 (1997).
[1660] HCJ 500/72, *supra* note 1021, at 484–5.

on whether it should apply the Geneva Convention domestically.[1661] However, the petition was rejected unanimously (Justice Etzioni joining his brethren): it was agreed that, once the petitioner had voluntarily left the occupied territory and changed her domicile (so that her standing was merely that of a non-resident tourist), the military government had a right to dismiss her application to remain in the area when her permit of entry expired.[1662] The petitioner also relied on the Jordanian Constitution, which grants every Jordanian national (such as herself) the right to establish residence anywhere within the realm. But the Court pronounced that, in such matters, the Occupying Power is not bound by the Constitution of the displaced sovereign.[1663]

B. Dispersed Families and Their Reunion

798. According to the ICRC Commentary, Article 27 (first paragraph) of the Geneva Convention – which guarantees in a vague way respect for the 'family rights' of protected persons (see full quote *supra* 460) – 'implies not only that family ties must be maintained, but further that they must be restored should they have been broken as a result of wartime events'.[1664] Yet, the only clause in the Convention addressing directly the issue of reunion of families is Article 26:

> Each Party to the conflict shall facilitate enquiries made by members of families dispersed owing to the war, with the object of renewing contact with one another and of meeting, if possible. It shall encourage, in particular, the work of organizations engaged on this task provided they are acceptable to it and conform to its security regulations.[1665]

Article 25 (first paragraph) of the Convention states that all persons in occupied territories must be allowed to give and receive news of a strictly personal nature to and from members of their families, wherever they may be.[1666]

799. Assistance to renewing contacts and arranging meetings between members of families dispersed as a result of war is a necessary step towards reunion of such families. Still, Article 26 imposes no obligation on the Occupying Power to implement the reunion, either through emigration out of the occupied territory or through immigration into it. The lack of any obligation under the Convention to enable reunion of families was highlighted by the Israel Supreme Court (per President Shamgar) in the *Shaeen* case.[1667]

[1661] *Ibid.*, 485–6.
[1662] *Ibid.*, 484–6.
[1663] *Ibid.*, 484.
[1664] *Commentary, IV Geneva Convention*, *supra* note 31, at 202–3.
[1665] Geneva Convention (IV), *supra* note 29, at 589.
[1666] *Ibid.*, 588.
[1667] HCJ 13/86 etc., *supra* note 161, at 208–10.

800. Article 74 of Additional Protocol I goes beyond the limits of the Convention:

> The High Contracting Parties and the Parties to the conflict shall facilitate in every possible way the reunion of families dispersed as a result of armed conflict and shall encourage in particular the work of the humanitarian organizations engaged in this task in accordance with the provisions of the Conventions and of this Protocol and in conformity with their respective security regulations.[1668]

This innovative duty of facilitating reunion of families is couched in unambiguous 'shall' language, and it is imposed on all Contracting Parties (not only Parties to the conflict – i.e. Belligerent Parties – but also neutrals).[1669]

801. Article 74 deals only with 'the reunion of families dispersed as a result of armed conflict' (as does Article 26 of the Convention). Occupied territories as such are not mentioned in Article 74, although there is every reason to believe that it applies to them too. However, the text avoids an issue of great significance under conditions of a prolonged occupation, namely, a marriage contracted by an inhabitant of an occupied territory with a non-inhabitant subsequent to the beginning of the occupation (so that the family is not really dispersed as a result of the armed conflict). Do post-occupation weddings forge a right for spouses to live together as a family, especially when they have children?

802. It is noteworthy that Article 74 does not say that reunion of every dispersed family must invariably be carried out inside the occupied territory. Members of a dispersed family certainly do not have an acquired right to be reunited within an occupied territory, as distinct from outside it. The Occupying Power may, therefore, insist on the departure of one part of the family from the occupied territory in lieu of the entry into it by the other part.

C. 'Macro' and 'Micro' Considerations

803. There is extensive case law of the Israel Supreme Court on the subject of reunion of families (independently of Article 74 that is not binding on Israel), and interestingly it treats post-occupation marriages on a par with other grounds for reunion of families.[1670] The Court (per President Shamgar) pointed out, in the *I. Awad* case, that permission for a family to reunite inside the West Bank is an *ex gratia* act, based on humanitarian considerations, within the

[1668] Additional Protocol I, *supra* note 33, at 748.

[1669] See C. Pilloud and J. Pictet, 'Article 74', *Commentary on the Additional Protocols, supra* note 327, at 857, 859.

[1670] See Y. Dinstein, 'The Israel Supreme Court and the Law of Belligerent Occupation: Reunification of Families', 18 *IYHR* 173–88 (1988).

discretionary power of the military government.[1671] Hence, the military government is entitled to adopt a general policy regulating the matter, subject to alteration from time to time (keeping pace with changing circumstances).[1672] The petition was dismissed, notwithstanding the fact that the original application for reunion of the family had been submitted at a time when a more liberal policy had been in force. It was the misfortune of the petitioners that – due only to a heavy bureaucratic load – their application came to be considered several years later, when a new (more rigid) policy was in effect. President Shamgar said that, inasmuch as this was a matter of discretion rather than right, the determinant policy is the one reigning at the time of decision-making.[1673] Thus, the Court's ruling was wedded to 'macro' (impersonal) considerations, completely divorced from the 'micro' (individual) circumstances of the specific petitioners.

804. The inclination to follow a 'macro' approach was carried to even greater lengths in the *Shaeen* case, where the Court (again per President Shamgar) concentrated on the high-level policy of the military government.[1674] The Court held that, since the number of applications for reunion of families (based on an earlier, more lenient, policy) had increased exponentially, the military government was entitled to apply new strict criteria that were called for by the security, political and economic implications of the phenomenon of thousands upon thousands of people knocking at the gates of the occupied territories in the name of reunion of families.[1675]

805. It appears to the present writer that the Court in these cases was all too willing to sacrifice an individual scrutiny of concrete applications for reunion of families at the altar of a 'macro' scheme designed to avert an influx of new residents into the occupied territories. It stands to reason that, if the Occupying Power is swamped by applications for permits of entry, it may wish to keep the floodgates closely monitored. The military government may also entertain the suspicion that the reunion of a family in a certain circumstantial setting is merely a convenient ruse for attempted immigration into the occupied territory. But, even so, the optimal response would be a rigorous screening of every single file. The predominant consideration must remain humanitarian, and as

[1671] HCJ 263/85 etc., *I. Awad* et al. *v. Commander of the Civil Administration, Ramallah District* et al., 40(2) *PD* 281, 285. (The Judgment is excerpted in English in 17 *IYHR* 305 (1987)).

[1672] *Ibid.*

[1673] *Ibid.*

[1674] HCJ 13/86 etc., *supra* note 161, at 214–15.

[1675] *Ibid.* In another case, the Court (per President Shamgar) observed that the overwhelming majority of the tens of thousands of applications for reunion of families were filed by spouses. HCJ 673/86, *El Saudi* et al. *v. Head of the Civil Administration in the Gaza Strip*, 41(3) *PD* 138, 140. (The Judgment is excerpted in English in 18 *IYHR* 246 (1988)).

such it cannot be discharged in a 'macro' fashion. Each application has to be evaluated individually.

806. Evidently, post-occupation marriages can be fictitious: the sole purpose of the ceremony may be paving the road for a foreigner to gain access to the occupied territory. The Occupying Power cannot be faulted if it is prudently looking into the possibility of a fraudulent marriage compact. But if a husband and wife consummate their marriage, and the family bond produces issue, parents and children should be allowed to live together.

807. The central question, nevertheless, is the best-suited modus for the reunion of a family to be effected. There may be impeccable reasons why a dispersed family may justifiably be denied the right to be live together inside the occupied territory. In particular, if the presence of a member of the family in the occupied territory is determined to pose a threat to security, down-to-earth military concerns need not flinch because of lofty humanitarian considerations. Similarly, when there is lack of visible means of support for the reunited family in the occupied territory, and there is scant prospect of any member of the family finding remunerative employment there, the Occupying Power may balk at adding a social welfare burden to the expenses of the occupation. There are other, equally compelling, rationales for turning a cold shoulder to an application for the reunion of a family which is directed inwards instead of outwards. In such circumstances, the Occupying Power meets its obligation to facilitate the reunion of a dispersed family by permitting the departure of a particular family member from the occupied territory, rather than the entry by another (see *supra* 802). Still, when the reunion of a specific family is fully justified on compassionate grounds, and there are no weighty countervailing reasons on the 'micro' level, the present writer believes that it is improper – and certainly non-humanitarian – to disqualify the application only because of a problem existing on the 'macro' level, for which the applicant bears no responsibility.

808. It is, therefore, interesting to note that, in the *Samara* case, the Court (per Justice Barak who was also on the bench in the *Shaeen* case) pronounced that reunion of a family in the West Bank should be permitted on the following cumulative grounds, all related to the 'micro' level: (i) the need to respect, on humanitarian grounds, the nuclear family unit (in this instance, husband and wife – with children – in contrast to other instances in which family ties proved more remote); (ii) the fact that the alternative for the family in question was to reunite in Germany where the husband was working, but the culture and customs were alien to them; (iii) the actual absence of security reasons for withholding the permit in the concrete circumstances.[1676] These are salutary

[1676] HCJ 802/79, *Samara* et al. *v. Commander of Judea and Samaria*, 34(4) *PD* 1. (The Judgment is excerpted in English in 11 *IYHR* 362 (1981)).

guidelines and – although the Court did not cite Article 74 of Additional Protocol I – the Judgment is a good precedent for the application of that provision as well.

IV. Political Activities and Elections

809. In general, as decided by the Israel Supreme Court (per Deputy President Sussman) in the *Arnon* case, the Occupying Power is entitled 'to curb, or even to prohibit entirely, political activity' in an occupied territory.[1677] Obviously, a lot depends on the concrete manifestation of the political activity. Thus, while the military government may ban political parades in an occupied territory, it is necessary to perceive that – should such a parade take place without a permit – civilians marching in a non-violent manner cannot be treated as if they were directly participating in hostilities (a separate issue examined *supra* 315 *et seq.*). In the *Rafiah* case, the Supreme Court of Israel (per President Barak) emphasized that caution must be exercised not to harm the civilian population, even if it is protesting against the Occupying Power.[1678] The legal outlook undergoes a radical change if a political demonstration degenerates into a riot (see *supra* 302–3).

810. As far as elections are concerned, the underlying question is whether they are national or local in character. Needless to say, the Occupying Power cannot be expected to allow the inhabitants of the occupied territory to participate in national elections conducted by the displaced sovereign.[1679] On the other hand, after lapse of time, local elections (on the municipal or regional level) are normally given leave to take place, and – in such a case – the inhabitants must be permitted an unimpeded exercise of their right to vote.[1680]

811. Israel granted its approval for local elections in the West Bank in 1972 and in 1976, but the four-year cycle was halted in 1980.[1681] In the *Amar* case, the Supreme Court (per Deputy President Ben Porat) was of the opinion that the Occupying Power is at liberty to suspend new local elections and in the meantime to appoint committees to run municipal affairs.[1682]

812. Article II of the 1995 Israel-PLO Interim Agreement provided for political elections to be held in the West Bank and the Gaza Strip, in order that the

[1677] HCJ 507/72, *Arnon* et al. *v. Attorney-General* et al., 27(1) *PD* 233, 237. (The Judgment is excerpted in English in 9 *IYHR* 334 (1979)).

[1678] HCJ 4764/04, *supra* note 630, at 405.

[1679] See von Glahn, *supra* note 339, at 98.

[1680] See *ibid.*

[1681] See J. Singer, 'The Emerging Palestinian Democracy under the West Bank and Gaza Strip Self-Government Arrangements', 26 *IYHR* 313, 317–18 (1996).

[1682] HCJ 774/83, *Amar* et al. *v. Minister of Defence* et al., 38(4) *PD* 645, 648–52. (The Judgment is excerpted in English in 15 *IYHR* 274 (1985)).

Palestinian people may govern themselves.[1683] Such elections for the Palestinian Council were conducted (after redeployment of Israeli forces, but still under belligerent occupation) in January 1996.[1684] Another round of elections for the Palestinian Council – in 2006 (after the unilateral Israeli pull-out from Gaza) – gave Hamas a majority of the votes cast.[1685] No further elections have been held since then.

V. Freedom of Expression and Censorship

813. There is no full freedom of expression under belligerent occupation (see *supra* 343). Interestingly, Article 70 (first paragraph) of Geneva Convention (IV) (quoted *supra* 434) forbids prosecution of protected persons 'for opinions expressed before the occupation, or during a temporary interruption thereof'. The *a contrario* inference that clearly follows is that an Occupying Power may punish hostile opinions expressed when the occupation is going on.[1686] Moreover, the Occupying Power is entitled to impose censorship on the media in an occupied territory (see *supra* 343). Indeed, all local newspapers, radio and television broadcasts can be fully controlled – and even shut down or suspended – by the military government.[1687]

814. As regards the printed press, censorship can be effectively accomplished either directly or indirectly. Directly, a newspaper may be exposed to a prior restraint order or its distribution may be forbidden. In the *Al Talia* case, the Israel Supreme Court (per Justice Shamgar) ruled that the military government was allowed to prohibit the distribution in the West Bank of a newspaper published outside the area by a group engaged in acts of violence against the Occupying Power.[1688] But censorship can also be imposed on a newspaper indirectly. Considering that in wartime there is usually a shortage of pulp for printing purposes, the military government – by allocating the paper available to selected applicants, taking into account their record – may muzzle other (more hostile) newspapers.[1689]

1683 Israel-Palestine Liberation Organization, Interim Agreement on the West Bank and the Gaza Strip, *supra* note 116, at 559.

1684 See G.S. Goodwin-Gill, 'The West Bank and Gaza: Free and Fair Elections, Human Rights and the Transition to Democracy', *Human Rights, Self-Determination and Political Change in the Occupied Palestinian Territories, supra* note 1355, at 47, 59–64.

1685 See 66 *Facts on File* 41–3 (2006).

1686 See O. Hathaway *et al.*, 'Which Law Governs during Armed Conflict? The Relationship between International Humanitarian Law and Human Rights Law', 96 *Minn.LR* 1883, 1940 (2011–12).

1687 See von Glahn, *supra* note 339, at 139.

1688 HCJ 619/78, *Al Talia Weekly Magazine* et al. *v. Minister of Defence* et al., 33(3) *PD* 505, 510–13. (The Judgment is excerpted in English in 10 *IYHR* 333 (1980)).

1689 See C. Fairman, 'Some Observations on Military Occupation', 32 *Minn.LR* 319, 329 (1947–8).

815. Censorship of local newspapers is not the same as insulating an occupied territory from coverage by the world media. The media today – especially, the electronic media – are globalized, and it is virtually impossible to seal off an occupied territory from the scrutiny of world public opinion. Any attempt to deny access to the world media is anyhow likely to be viewed as a disproportionate infringement of freedom of the press.[1690] Yet, free access does not mean free rein. The Coalition Provisional Authority in Iraq, in 2003, prohibited certain activities – even when conducted by international media organizations – such as inciting to violence against Coalition forces or advocating the return to power of the Ba'ath Party.[1691]

816. At the time of the final evacuation of the Sinai Peninsula (in 1982), the IDF initially tried to bar all media coverage of the event, lest the presence of reporters and their cameras would inflame violent resistance by settlers.[1692] In proceedings before the Supreme Court, in the *Association of Foreign Correspondents in Israel* case, the IDF reassessed its position: it agreed to allow sixteen journalists (including TV crews) selected by their peers – estimated at 200 foreign correspondents – to cover the evacuation on a pool basis.[1693] The petitioners were not satisfied with the compromise, but the Supreme Court rendered Judgment (*per curiam*) that (i) in view of the sensitivity of the event, the presence of hundreds of journalists might have a negative impact on the process of evacuation, perhaps even imperilling lives; while (ii) the compromise arrangement strikes a fair balance between freedom of the press and the proper discharge by the authorities of their duties.[1694] At bottom, the decision must be construed as confirming freedom of the press.[1695]

VI. Freedom of Religion

817. In addition to clauses relating to the protection of institutions dedicated to religious worship (see *supra* 608, 677), Hague Regulation 46 (first paragraph) (quoted *supra* 451) proclaims that the Occupying Power must respect 'religious convictions and practices' in the occupied territory. The obligation,

[1690] See I. Zamir, 'Media Coverage of Military Operations', 18 *IYHR* 61, 64 (1988).

[1691] Coalition Provisional Authority Order Number 14, II *The Occupation of Iraq: The Official Documents*, *supra* note 78, at 98, 99.

[1692] See Zamir, *supra* note 1690, at 65.

[1693] HCJ 236/82, *Association of Foreign Correspondents in Israel* et al. *v. Government of Israel* et al., 36(2) *PD* 637, 638.

[1694] *Ibid.*, 638–9.

[1695] See Zamir, *supra* note 1690, at 68.

as regards protected persons, is reiterated in Article 27 (first paragraph) of Geneva Convention (IV) (quoted *supra* 460). Article 58 (first paragraph) of the Convention adds:

> The Occupying Power shall permit ministers of religion to give spiritual assistance to the members of their religious communities.[1696]

This language covers, e.g., 'offering the last rites to a dying member of a resistance group'.[1697] However, as underscored by the ICRC Commentary, 'religious assistance must in no case serve as a pretext for political agitation against the Occupying Power'.[1698]

818. Article 58 (second paragraph) of the Geneva Convention has this to say:

> The Occupying Power shall also accept consignments of books and articles required for religious needs and shall facilitate their distribution in occupied territory.[1699]

As noted, Article 69(1) of Additional Protocol I (quoted *supra* 457) stipulates that the Occupying Power must ensure, to the fullest extent of the means available to it and without any adverse distinction, the provision of objects necessary for religious worship.

819. In the Israeli experience, religious worship became a major issue in the occupied territories because of competing claims between Moslems, Christians and Jews to the same (or adjacent) holy sites. The leading case is that of the Machpela Cave in Hebron, an important shrine for both Jews and Moslems (see *supra* 248). Following a number of deadly attacks, the military government seized private property (and demolished two abandoned houses), in order to enlarge and protect an existing 'worshippers' path' (730 metres long) leading to the site from a nearby Jewish settlement. The Supreme Court (per Justice Procaccia) held that freedom of religious worship is vested in all the inhabitants of the West Bank, Moslems and Jews alike, and it must be implemented by guaranteeing safe passage to holy sites.[1700] Of course, the owners of any seized or destroyed property are entitled to compensation (see *supra* 698).[1701]

820. The same reasoning was adduced by the Court (per Justice Beinisch), in the *Rachel's Tomb* case, as regards a site holy only to Jews.[1702] As the Court

[1696] Geneva Convention (IV), *supra* note 29, at 597.
[1697] H. MacCoubrey, 'The Protection of Creed and Opinion in the Laws of Armed Conflict', 5 *JCSL* 135, 150 (2000).
[1698] *Commentary, IV Geneva Convention*, *supra* note 31, at 318.
[1699] Geneva Convention (IV), *supra* note 29, at 597.
[1700] HCJ 10356/02 etc., *supra* note 1259, at 461–2.
[1701] *Ibid.*, 468.
[1702] HCJ 1890/03, *supra* note 508, at 751–2.

noted here,[1703] security arrangements concerning Rachel's Tomb are expressly provided for in a Protocol annexed to the Israel-PLO Interim Agreement (which mainly placed the City of Bethlehem under Palestinian jurisdiction).[1704]

VII. Human Dignity

821. Article 27 of Geneva Convention (IV) (first paragraph) (quoted *supra* 460) safeguards the 'honour' of protected persons in occupied territories. 'Family honour' is also mentioned in Hague Regulation 46 (first paragraph) (quoted *supra* 451). As a minimum, respect for honour excludes acts of humiliation.[1705] Article 8(2)(b)(xxi) of the Rome Statute of the International Criminal Court brands as a war crime the commission of outrages upon personal dignity, in particular humiliating and degrading treatment.[1706] In the Elements of Crime, a footnote was appended to clarify that the victim may be a dead person and that his cultural background must be taken into account.[1707]

822. The issue of the treatment of the dead, in the context of the need to protect human dignity, elicited a lot of attention in the case law of the Israel Supreme Court. In the *Rafiah* case, the Court (per President Barak) saw it as the point of departure that the protection of 'honour' – enshrined in Article 27 – cloaks not only the living inhabitants of an occupied territory but also the dead.[1708] In a *Jenin* case, the Court (also per President Barak) pronounced that the burial of the dead must be performed properly, in accordance with religious rites and in a manner showing respect for the dignity of the deceased.[1709] In the earlier *Barkat* case, the Court (once more per Justice Barak) – while stressing the need for a decent burial – made a concession to security considerations: they may drive the military government to insist on a funeral being conducted at night, in order to avoid riots and disturbances.[1710]

[1703] *Ibid.*, 752.

[1704] Protocol Concerning Redeployment and Security Arrangements, Annex I to Israel-Palestine Liberation Organization. Interim Agreement on the West Bank and the Gaza Strip, *supra* note 116, at 569, 576 (Article V(7)).

[1705] See *Commentary, IV Geneva Convention*, *supra* note 31, at 202.

[1706] Rome Statute of the International Criminal Court, *supra* note 350, at 1319.

[1707] See Dörmann, *supra* note 355, at 314.

[1708] HCJ 4764/04, *supra* note 630, at 403.

[1709] HCJ 3114/02, *Barake* et al. *v. Minister of Defence* et al., 56(3) *PD* 11, 15. (The Judgment is excerpted in English in 32 *IYHR* 364 (2002)).

[1710] HCJ 3933/92, *Barkat* et al. *v. Commander of Central Region*, 46(5) *PD* 1, 6–7. (The Judgment is excerpted in English in 25 *IYHR* 341 (1995)).

12 The Termination of Belligerent Occupation

I. The Complete End of Belligerent Occupation

A. *Treaty of Peace*

823. Belligerent occupation goes on as long as the Occupying Power continues to exercise effective control in an occupied territory, and the war (which may manifest itself exclusively in the ongoing occupation) is not over. Normally, the end of the occupation and of the war will coincide and occur following the conclusion of a treaty of peace. The displaced sovereign will then retrieve possession of the occupied territory (in whole or in part) and restore its control there. However, it is possible that the treaty of peace (or a related agreement) will allow – for a period of time – the uninterrupted presence of foreign troops in the formerly occupied territory, notwithstanding the reversion of the area to the restored sovereign (see the example of the Rhineland *supra* 109).

824. The treaty of peace may permit the future return of armed forces of the (formerly) Occupying Power to at least a portion of what used to be an occupied territory, in response to a material breach by the restored sovereign of the provisions agreed upon. Article 430 of the Treaty of Versailles allowed such reoccupation as a counter-measure against Germany's possible failure to observe its obligations in the sphere of reparations.[1711] In the event, France and Belgium actually reoccupied the Ruhr Valley on that basis in 1923.[1712] Since the renewed occupation in such circumstances is implanted in an agreement (the treaty of peace), it cannot be regarded as belligerent in nature (see *supra* 106).

825. In a treaty of peace – terminating the war and the belligerent occupation – the restored sovereign (the rightful owner) may cede title over the occupied territory (or part thereof) to the Occupying Power or to a third State. The most famous cession of territory to an Occupying Power was that of Alsace and Lorraine by France to Germany in the 1871 Versailles Preliminary Treaty of

[1711] Versailles Treaty of Peace, *supra* note 208, at 330.
[1712] See I. Brownlie, *International Law and the Use of Force by States* 342–3 (1963).

Peace.[1713] The two provinces were recovered by France in the 1919 Versailles Treaty of Peace (following WWI),[1714] occupied again by Germany in WWII and then liberated by Allied troops. Another signal case in point was that of the double cession of the Dodecanese Islands in two treaties of peace following WWI and WWII: first from Turkey to Italy, and then from Italy to Greece (see *supra* 23).

826. In the past, a treaty of cession could have the function of rubber-stamping the successful results of a war of aggression.[1715] But nowadays the validity of cession is contingent on its being actuated from the aggressor State to the victim of aggression, and not vice versa: an aggressor State cannot reap the fruits of aggression in a treaty transferring to it title to occupied territories.[1716] Any treaty of peace forcing cession to the aggressor will be void under Article 52 of the 1969 Vienna Convention on the Law of Treaties.[1717] However, pursuant to Article 75 of the Vienna Convention, this is without prejudice to treaty obligations arising for an aggressor State in consequence of its aggression.[1718] It follows that '(peace) treaties forced upon an aggressor State are not *eo ipso* invalid'.[1719]

B. Prescription

827. It is theoretically possible that war is terminated (either by a treaty of peace, which neglects to advert to the fate of the occupied territory, or otherwise); hostilities are long over; yet, the actual occupation continues as before, without the displaced sovereign or anybody else challenging this reality. Under such conditions, there may ultimately be 'continuous and peaceful display of State authority during a long period of time', in the words of the Arbitrator M. Huber, in 1928, in the *Island of Palmas* case.[1720] If so, title may be acquired by the State in charge through prescription, although that would be contingent on a peaceful and uncontested possession over a protracted period of time through presumed acquiescence.[1721]

828. The Arab reaction to the Israeli belligerent occupation is a stark example of the very opposite of acquiescence, showing that even a very

[1713] France-Germany, Versailles Preliminary Treaty of Peace, 1871, I *Major Peace Treaties of Modern History 1648–1967*, *supra* note 47, at 645, 645–6 (Article I).

[1714] Versailles Treaty of Peace, *supra* note 208, at 143 (Article 51).

[1715] See H. Kelsen, *General Theory of Law and State* 215 (1961).

[1716] See Dinstein, *supra* note 3, at 40–1.

[1717] Vienna Convention on the Law of Treaties, *supra* note 706, at 153.

[1718] *Ibid.*, 159.

[1719] O. Dörr, 'Use of Force, Prohibition of', X *MPEPIL* 607, 614 (2015).

[1720] *Island of Palmas* case (Netherlands, USA), 1928, 2 *RIAA* 829, 869.

[1721] See M.N. Shaw, *International Law* 364 (7th edn, 2014).

prolonged occupation per se does not by itself produce prescription. In any event, any Occupying Power harbouring the thought of prescription must today take into account the right of self-determination vested in the people inhabiting the occupied territory (see *supra* 170).

C. *Withdrawal from an Occupied Territory*

829. Nothing stands in the way of the termination of belligerent occupation even before the end of the war. It often happens that the Occupying Power winds up its effective control in an occupied territory by withdrawing from it.

830. Such withdrawal may be sparked by an interim agreement – short of a treaty of peace – reached between the Occupying Power and the displaced sovereign, making the termination of the belligerent occupation a consensual process without leading to peace (as yet).

831. More frequently, the end of belligerent occupation is spurred by the fortunes of war. The displaced sovereign (directly or through its allies) may unleash a victorious counter-offensive, which would cause the Occupying Power to be reeling back, losing effective control over the occupied territory. But the Occupying Power may be deprived of effective control not only as a result of pitched battles with the enemy. A successful rebellion of the inhabitants (provided that this is not a fleeting or partial success; see *supra* 149) may bring about the termination of occupation.[1722]

832. Naturally, 'the law of belligerent occupation ceases to apply whenever an Occupying Power loses effective control over the occupied territory'.[1723] Nevertheless, the loss of effective control as a result of defeat in the field need not last long, inasmuch as the pendulum of military ascendancy in war may swing again in the opposite direction. Article 70 (first paragraph) of Geneva Convention (IV) (quoted *supra* 434) recognizes the possibility of 'a temporary interruption' in belligerent occupation. A definitive close of the occupation can only follow upon a durable shift of effective control in the territory from the Occupying Power to the restored sovereign (or its allies).

833. The Occupying Power may unilaterally decide to withdraw from the occupied territory for reasons of its own that are not connected to any agreement or crushing defeat at the hands of the displaced sovereign (or insurgents). This may be due to political or strategic reasons, such as military pressure in other theatres of conflict. Whatever the reason, the Occupying Power 'is free to depart at any time of its own pleasing', and – assuming that it does so – the belligerent occupation will automatically be over.[1724]

[1722] See *UK Manual of the Law of Armed Conflict*, *supra* note 230, at 277.
[1723] Schwarzenberger, *supra* note 204, at 317.
[1724] Kelly, *supra* note 1172, at 4–14.

D. *Binding Decision by the UN Security Council*

834. The situation in Iraq has shown that belligerent occupation can also be terminated by fiat of the Security Council. As noted (*supra* 41), in Resolution 1546 (2004), the Council welcomed the fact that the occupation was to end by the end of June 2004, when Iraq would reassert its full sovereignty. Whether or not the Security Council was right in confirming the reassertion of Iraqi sovereignty at that time,[1725] the point is that this was done in a binding resolution adopted under Chapter VII of the United Nations Charter.[1726] The cessation of occupation meant that the continued presence of Coalition forces in Iraq had to be legally based on an invitation by the new interim Iraqi Government.[1727] Admittedly, in practice, there was little change on the ground following the formal termination of the occupation.[1728] For several years subsequent to June 2004, Coalition forces were still engaged in (occasionally heavy) combat – against insurgents representing both remnants of the overthrown Ba'athist regime and *Al-Qeida* in Mesopotamia – and, while doing so, actually retained effective control over large tracts of Iraq. As long as that went on, it is arguable that the occupation of Iraq ended only 'notionally'.[1729]

835. In Resolution 1790 (2007) – another binding resolution adopted under Chapter VII of the Charter – the Security Council noted 'that the presence of the multinational force in Iraq is at the request of the Government of Iraq'.[1730] An Agreement on the withdrawal of US forces from Iraq was concluded between the two countries late in 2008, with complete withdrawal envisaged by the end of 2011.[1731] In the event, some US military presence in Iraq has continued to the time of writing.

836. A number of scholars contend that the Security Council did not have the power, in Resolution 1546, to derogate from Hague Regulation 42 (quoted *supra* 117) by setting up an artificial date for the end of occupation in Iraq.[1732] However, binding decisions of the Security Council prevail over the obligations of Member States under any other international agreement (or customary rules): this is the combined effect[1733] of Articles 25 and 103 of

[1725] For an argument that the Council misread ('intentionally or otherwise') the factual situation in Iraq at the time, see A. Carcano, *The Transformation of Occupied Territory in International Law* 369 (2015).

[1726] Security Council Resolution 1546 (2004), *supra* note 91, at 1460 (Preamble).

[1727] See A. Roberts, 'The End of Occupation: Iraq 2004', 54 *ICLQ* 27, 43 (2005).

[1728] See P.J. Walker, 'Iraq and Occupation', *New Wars, New Laws, supra* note 641, at 259, 283.

[1729] Roberts, *supra* note 194, at 488.

[1730] Security Council Resolution 1790 (2007), para. 1.

[1731] On the Agreement and the protracted negotiations leading to it, see C. Bassiouni, 'Legal Status of US Forces in Iraq from 2003–2008', 11 *Chi.JIL* 1, 9–20 (2010).

[1732] See Kolb and Vité, *supra* note 239, at 292–3.

[1733] On the combined effect of Articles 25 and 103 of the Charter as regards Security Council resolutions, see Dinstein, *supra* note 3, at 322–4.

the United Nations Charter.[1734] As a binding decision of the Security Council, Resolution 1546 must be seen as 'overriding' ordinary rules of the *jus in bello* concerning belligerent occupation.[1735]

837. The present author cannot accept the purely doctrinal view[1736] that the Security Council is not empowered to derogate from the law of belligerent occupation. It is true that the Council cannot simply override *jus cogens*,[1737] but there is no plausible ground for any allegation that the norms concerning the end of belligerent occupation have a peremptory character.

II. Partial End of Belligerent Occupation

838. Belligerent occupation may come to a partial end in the sense that it is finished in one segment of an occupied territory but continues in others. This may happen in one of three ways: (i) by agreement between the Parties; (ii) by the tidal waves of hostilities; or (iii) by unilateral decision of the Occupying Power. Whatever the mode of the partial expiry of occupation, it is important to note that the consequences of full termination (see *infra* 872 *et seq.*) do not come into effect (unless otherwise agreed upon by the Parties; see *infra* 839).

A. Agreement between the Parties

839. A partial withdrawal from an occupied territory may result from agreement between the Parties, notably (but not necessarily) a treaty of peace. A good illustration is the 1979 Treaty of Peace with Egypt, whereby Israel vacated the Sinai Peninsula in two phases over a period of three years.[1738] Agreed Minutes relating to the phased withdrawal expressly stated:

> Egypt's resumption of the exercise of full sovereignty over the Sinai provided for in paragraph 2 of Article I shall occur with regard to each area upon Israel's withdrawal from that area.[1739]

Thus, even prior to the completion of the Israeli withdrawal from the whole of Sinai in 1982 (and *stricto sensu* only in 1989, subsequent to the *Taba* Arbitration; see *supra* 47), the withdrawal that took place – although partial in its geographic scope – was full in its substantive implications within the confines of the vacated area.

[1734] Charter of the United Nations, *supra* note 19, at 339, 361.
[1735] See Sassòli, *supra* note 575, at 684.
[1736] See, e.g., R. Kolb, 'Occupation in Iraq since 2003 and the Powers of the UN Security Council', 869 *IRRC* 29–50 (2008); Koutroulis, *supra* note 228, at 242–53 (2010).
[1737] See Dinstein, *supra* note 3, at 376.
[1738] Israel-Egypt, Treaty of Peace, *supra* note 101, at 363, 367 (Article I(2); Annex I, Article I(2)).
[1739] *Ibid.*, 392, *id.* (Agreed Minutes, Article I).

840. In the 1990s – by virtue of the 'Oslo Accords' (see *supra* 54) – the Israeli military government redeployed its forces in the West Bank and the Gaza Strip, transferring to the Palestinians most (albeit not all) powers and responsibilities over designated areas in the occupied territories. These powers and responsibilities were acquired by the Palestinian Council and Authority from Israel (as the Occupying Power), and Israel continued to exercise other 'powers and responsibilities not so transferred' (see *supra* 190). The very existence of Israel's residual powers unmistakably indicates that the belligerent occupation was not over. The Israeli redeployment may be deemed a partial withdrawal in terms of both geography and content. All the same, as emphasized by the International Court of Justice in the *Wall* Advisory Opinion, 'Israel has continued to have the status of occupying Power' despite the partial transfer of limited powers to the Palestinians.[1740]

841. A partial withdrawal by an agreement of this type is bound to raise practical problems in its implementation. Indeed, a question came up before the Israel Supreme Court, in the *Wafa* case, with respect to the seizure of private land (accompanied by an offer of compensation) for the purpose of constructing a road in the West Bank that – according to the petitioners – lay outside the zone where the military government had retained its previous powers.[1741] The Court (per Justice Zamir) observed that in the occupied West Bank – just like in Israel proper (see *supra* 89) – an international agreement is not directly applicable, unless and until it is incorporated there by order of the military government.[1742] Even when such incorporation of an international agreement does take place (as it was, in this instance, by a Proclamation issued by the military commander), it is not the Interim Agreement but the Proclamation that governs the situation:

> the Proclamation is the law. It determines who is vested with authority and what the authority is for a particular purpose in this or that area. The Proclamation, and not the Interim Agreement. The Interim Agreement is the historical source of the Proclamation, but it is not the source of the validity of the Proclamation. Hence, even if there is a discrepancy between the provisions of the Proclamation and the provisions of the Interim Agreement, and even if there is a contradiction between them, the provisions of the Proclamation prevail. The provisions of the Interim Agreement are part of the law applicable in Judea and Samaria only if adopted, and to the extent adopted, by the Proclamation.[1743]

[1740] Advisory Opinion on *Legal Consequences of the Construction of a Wall in the Occupied Palestinian Territory*, *supra* note 25, at 167.

[1741] HCJ 2717/96, *Wafa* et al. *v. Minister of Defence* et al., 50(2) *PD* 848, 850–1. (The Judgment is excerpted in English in 30 *IYHR* 330 (2000)).

[1742] *Ibid.*, 851–2.

[1743] *Ibid.*, 853.

842. As long as the Occupying Power does not relinquish *in toto* its effective control in a particular segment of an occupied territory, the occupation there is not really over. This is a moral that may have to be inculcated by experience. The Israeli redeployment resulting from the 'Oslo Accords' (see *supra* 54–5) created for a while the mirage of an occupation in the process of waning. Yet, in response to the staggering blow of the second *intifada* of 2000, the IDF went back into many of the populated areas in Palestinian territories from which it had formerly withdrawn (see *supra* 57). The rising cycle of violence has led Israel to reassert a revived authority as an Occupying Power.[1744]

B. *The Tide of Hostilities*

843. In the course of war, the front line between the two Belligerent Parties may crest and recede alternately. The extent of the area subject to belligerent occupation may be affected by military setbacks or gains. The loss of effective control over a distinct portion of the occupied territory denotes the end of occupation there, regardless of the position elsewhere.

844. The French Permanent Military Tribunal had this to say in the *Bauer* trial in 1945:

> Any part of territory in which the occupant has been deprived of *actual* means for carrying out *normal* administration by the presence of opposing military forces, would not have the status of 'occupied' territory within the terms of Articles 2 and 42 of the Hague Regulations. The fact that other parts of the occupied country, as a whole, are under effective enemy occupation, would not affect this situation.[1745]

Although the statement predates the Geneva Convention (IV) and Additional Protocol I, it is quoted with approval in the ICRC Commentary on the Protocol.[1746]

C. *Israel's Unilateral Withdrawal from the Gaza Strip*

845. In September 2005, Israel withdrew unilaterally from the whole of the Gaza Strip, dismantling in the process all settlements and military installations there. In consequence, Israel has claimed that its status as Occupying Power in the Strip has come to an end. This is not merely a matter of political atmospherics. Legally, the operation of the Gaza military court has been discontinued.[1747] Detainees brought to Israel from the Gaza Strip since the unilateral withdrawal

[1744] See K.A. Cavanaugh, 'Rewriting Law: The Case of Israel and the Occupied Territories', *New Wars, New Laws?, supra* note 641, at 227, 247.

[1745] *Bauer* et al. trial, *supra* note 609, at 18. Emphasis in the original.

[1746] J. de Preux, 'Article 44', *Commentary on the Additional Protocols, supra* note 327, at 519, 531.

[1747] The Knesset even enacted a special law dealing with transition issues generated by imprisonment sentences imposed in the past by the Gaza military court: 2090 *SH* 158 (2007).

have been prosecuted in accordance with the Israeli Internment of Unlawful Combatants Law of 2002;[1748] a practice authorized by the Supreme Court (per President Beinisch) in the *Anonymous* case of 2007.[1749]

846. The proposition that the Israeli occupation in the Gaza Strip is over has gained some support by commentators.[1750] Yet, that is not the prevalent opinion,[1751] and the present writer cannot possibly accept it. The non-termination of the Israeli occupation is borne out by a number of considerations.

(a) The Gaza Strip and the West Bank as a Single Unit

847. The first point to be examined is whether the Gaza Strip and the West Bank (where Israel has undeniably remained as Occupying Power) are two separate occupied territories. Despite their geographic detachment and their original occupation from two different countries (Egypt and Jordan, respectively) – not to mention the fact that they were governed by Israel through two separate structures of military government – a special panel of nine Justices of the Supreme Court (per President Barak) held, in the *Ajuri* case, that the Gaza Strip and the West Bank must be viewed as a single occupied territory (see *supra* 535).[1752]

848. This is not just a matter of a decision by the Israel Supreme Court: it is staunchly embedded in the Interim Agreement between Israel and the PLO. Article XI(1) of the Agreement clearly declares: 'The two sides view the West Bank and the Gaza Strip as a single territorial unit, the integrity and status of which will be preserved during the interim period'.[1753] Article XXXI(8) reiterates this formula word for word, superseding 'sides' by 'Parties'.[1754] If that twice-repeated proclamation is not enough, Article XXXI(7) adds: 'Neither side shall initiate or take any step that will change the status of the West Bank or the Gaza Strip pending the outcome of the permanent status negotiations'.[1755] The latter clause was initially aimed at preventing either a unilateral annexation of the Palestinian occupied territory by Israel or a unilateral declaration of independence by the PLO.[1756] But surely it applies to any attempt – in

[1748] 1834 *SH* 192 (2002). The Law has been translated into English in 32 *IYHR* 389 (2002).

[1749] Criminal Appeal 6659/06 *etc.*, *Anonymous v. State of Israel*, 62(4) *PD* 329. The Judgment has been translated into English in 47 *ILM* 768 (2008).

[1750] See N. Rostow, 'Gaza, Iraq, Lebanon: Three Occupations under International Law', 37 *IYHR* 205, 217–19 (2007).

[1751] See K. Cavanaugh, 'The Israeli Military Court System in the West Bank and Gaza', 12 *JCSL* 197, 199 (2007).

[1752] HCJ 7015/02, *supra* note 173, at 369.

[1753] Israel-Palestine Liberation Organization, Interim Agreement on the West Bank and the Gaza Strip, *supra* note 116, at 561.

[1754] *Ibid.*, 568.

[1755] *Ibid.*

[1756] See B. Rubin, 'Disengagement from the Gaza Strip and Post-Occupation Duties', 42 *Is.LR* 528, 547 (2009).

whatever form – to alter the status of occupation in a unilateral form.[1757] To satisfy the requirements of the Interim Agreement, the Israeli pull-out from the Gaza Strip (although covering the entire Strip) must be seen as another redeployment within the single Palestinian occupied territory.

849. The change in the political environment, caused by the violent assumption of power in the Gaza Strip by Hamas in June 2007 (thereby fracturing Palestinian unity), does not impugn this legal analysis. In the *Hamdan* case, the Supreme Court (per Justice Rubinstein) pronounced – subsequent to the Hamas takeover – that the concept of unity between the Gaza Strip and the West Bank in the overall Palestinian context is still valid in principle, even though it does not express itself in actuality due to the fact that the Palestinian Authority had lost control over Gaza.[1758] In Resolution 1860 (2009), the Security Council stressed that 'the Gaza Strip constitutes an integral part of the territory occupied in 1967 and will be a part of the Palestinian state'.[1759]

850. Despite their constant feuds, neither Hamas nor the Palestinian Authority has ever regarded Palestinian unity – stretching over the West Bank and Gaza – as severed. The loss of control over the Gaza Strip did not induce the Palestinian Authority to recognize a permanent split between the Gaza Strip and the West Bank (over which it has retained uninterrupted power, subject to the limitations imposed by the provisions of the 'Oslo Accords' and the realities of Israeli occupation). Indeed, over the years, the Palestinian Authority has actually continued to pay for many services and salaries in Gaza, notwithstanding the fact that it had been deprived of actual power there. Attempts to seal the breach between Hamas and the Palestinian Authority have been made repeatedly, and the latest reconciliation agreement was concluded in 2017, when some marginal functions were ostensibly handed back to the Palestinian Authority. But soon relations soured again, and the rupture has remained unhealed at the time of writing.

(b) Israel's Continuing Links to the Gaza Strip

851. It must be registered that, despite the unilateral withdrawal, Israel has not washed its hands of the situation in the Gaza Strip. Notwithstanding the unilateral withdrawal and the handover of the administration of the Gaza Strip to the Palestinians, Israel has not lost or relinquished diverse core ingredients of effective control.[1760] As noted (*supra* 50), the Gaza Strip has been subjected

[1757] See N. Stephanopoulos, 'Israel's Legal Obligations to Gaza after the Pullout', 31 *YJIL* 524, 525–6 (2006).

[1758] HCJ 11120/05 etc., *Hamdan* et al. *v. Commander of Southern Region* et al., para. 14.

[1759] Security Council Resolution 1860 (2009) (Preamble).

[1760] See S. Darcy and J. Reynolds, 'An Enduring Occupation: The Status of the Gaza Strip from the Perspective of International Humanitarian Law', 15 *JCSL* 211, 241–2 (2010).

by Israel to a regime of relative 'closure', which is analogous – albeit not identical – to a partial state of siege.[1761] The land borders with Israel are fenced off: large-scale violent attempts by Gazans (led or prompted by Hamas personnel) to breach the fence in 2018 were repulsed by the use of lethal force.[1762] There is careful continuous modulation of the transit of persons and goods to and from Israel at specific crossing points. There are fluctuating quantitative caps on some commodities and a contraband list of material that cannot go into Gaza at all. The number of persons allowed in and out varies periodically. The crossing points are closed now and again, the closure being tightened or loosened in tune with the protean changes in circumstances. Of course, the Gaza Strip also abuts Egypt (the Sinai Peninsula). Yet, as a general rule, Egypt does not enable uninterrupted free passage of persons and goods through this border either.

852. In the air, the Gaza Strip is completely disconnected from the outside world, since Israel does not permit the construction of an airport. It is useful to cite the strictly-observed Article XIII(4) of Annex I (Protocol Concerning Redeployment and Security Arrangements) of the Interim Agreement: 'All aviation activity or use of the airspace by any aerial vehicle in the West Bank and the Gaza Strip shall require prior approval of Israel'.[1763]

853. At sea, some fishing off the Gaza Strip is permitted within prescribed limits. Other maritime activities are severely restricted under Article XIV of the same instrument (Security along the Coastline to the Sea of Gaza),[1764] Moreover, in 2009, Israel imposed a naval blockade on the Gaza coastline.[1765] In 2010, the blockade led to a lethal boarding incident by Israeli forces on the high seas of a blockade-running flotilla of Turkish private vessels (known as the *Marmara* incident). A 2011 Report of a United Nations Secretary-General's Panel of Inquiry into the incident (the Palmer Report) confirmed Israel's right to impose a blockade under the *jus in bello,* but insisted on a proportionate

[1761] Obviously, the 'closure' differs from an ordinary siege in that it is aimed not at engineering a new take-over of the Gaza Strip by Israeli ground troops (see S. Solomon, 'Occupied or Not: The Question of Gaza's Legal Status after the Israeli Disengagement', 19 *Car.JICL* 59, 80–1 (2011)), but at bringing an end to the Hamas menace of missile/rocket attacks.

[1762] It must be borne in mind that (i) attempts to breach a security fence are not to be confused with a mere riot (see *supra* 302); and (ii) civilians taking a direct part in hostilities risk their lives (just like combatants) and are exposed to lethal attack (see *supra* 323). A petition against the IDF Rules of Engagement enabling the use of lethal force against those trying to violently breach the fence was rejected by the Supreme Court in HCJ 3003/16, *Yesh Din* et al. v. *Chief of the General Staff of the IDF* et al.

[1763] Protocol Concerning Redeployment and Security Arrangements, Annex I to Israel-Palestine Liberation Organization, Interim Agreement on the West Bank and the Gaza Strip, *supra* note 116, at 586.

[1764] *Ibid.*, 587.

[1765] On the meaning and scope of a naval blockade, see Dinstein, *supra* note 14, at 257–9.

level of force in enforcing the blockade where civilians are concerned.[1766] The dispute was settled in 2016 when Israel paid compensation to Turkey for the application of excessive force.

854. Despite its declaration that the Gaza Strip constitutes 'hostile territory' (*supra* 50), Israel has not abdicated its responsibilities as regards access of humanitarian relief into the Gaza Strip. In its Judgment in the *Fuel and Electricity* case (rendered in January 2008), the Supreme Court (per President Beinisch) accepted the Government's contention that – since September 2005 (the unilateral withdrawal) – Israel is no longer in effective control of the Gaza Strip and it is therefore no longer bound by the obligations of an Occupying Power.[1767] However, considering the dependence of the Gaza Strip on Israel insofar as the supply of electricity is concerned, President Beinisch ruled that Israel has certain humanitarian obligations vis-à-vis the civilian population in Gaza.[1768] This was not contested by the Government,[1769] which conceded its duty to allow the passage of humanitarian relief consignments to enemy civilians in unoccupied territories, in conformity with the rather narrow obligation under Article 23 of Geneva Convention (IV),[1770] and the broader one in accordance with 70 of Additional Protocol I[1771] (not binding on Israel as treaty law, but accepted by the Government as customary international law). Article 54 of the Additional Protocol prohibiting the starvation of civilians as a method of warfare (see *supra* 453) was also mentioned. Curiously enough, both the Government and the Court made an extrapolation from relief consignments of foodstuffs, medications, etc., to the supply of electricity and fuel. The Court allowed a reduction in such supplies only to a level that would safeguard the basic humanitarian needs of the civilian population in the Gaza Strip.[1772]

855. The artificiality of the Government's claim – endorsed by the Court – that the Israeli belligerent occupation of the Gaza Strip has ended is only highlighted by this Judgment. The notion that a Belligerent Party in wartime is in duty bound to supply electricity and fuel to its enemy is plainly absurd. Even those who support the view that the occupation of Gaza is over are forced to admit that the Court's conclusion about these supplies cannot be premised on the *jus in bello*.[1773] From the *jus in bello*'s perspective, the sole rationale for the

[1766] Excerpts from the Report of the United Nations Secretary-General's Panel of Inquiry on the 31 May 2010 Flotilla Incident (the Palmer Report), 2011, are published in a Special Supplement to 42 *IYHR* (2012). For the summary of conclusions, see *ibid.*, 33–4.

[1767] HCJ 9132/07, *supra* note 39, at para. 12.

[1768] *Ibid.*

[1769] For the Government's position, see *ibid.*, paras. 12–15.

[1770] Geneva Convention (IV), *supra* note 29, at 587–8.

[1771] Additional Protocol I, *supra* note 33, at 747.

[1772] HCJ 9132/07, *supra* note 39, paras. 21–2.

[1773] See Y. Shany, 'The Law Applicable to Non-Occupied Gaza: A Comment on *Bassiouni v. The Prime Minister of Israel*', 42 *Is.LR* 101, 107–8 (2009).

existence of an obligation to ensure such supplies for the benefit of the civilian population – even at a minimal level – is that the occupation is not over.

(c) Use of Force

856. The crux of the matter, perhaps, is that – despite the unilateral withdrawal from the Gaza Strip – Israel still believes that it is free (on an equally unilateral basis) to send back its armed forces into the area whenever this is deemed vital to its security. In point of fact, occasional small-scale Israeli military land incursions into various parts of the Gaza Strip – and, more frequently, air strikes (augmented by occasional naval assaults) – have occurred relentlessly subsequent to the unilateral withdrawal. In response to intermittent missiles and rocket fire, several large-scale military operations were also undertaken (see *supra* 50) and went on for weeks at a time until the restoration of some sort of quiescence.

(d) Effective Control

857. It is necessary to weigh the extent of effective control wielded by Israel in the Gaza Strip in light of two apposite considerations: (i) the small size of the Gaza Strip (365 square kilometres); and (ii) the fact that it is only one district within the overall Palestinian occupied territory which includes the West Bank.

858. Although belligerent occupation cannot be established in the first place without some 'boots on the ground' (see *supra* 140), it is necessary to recall (see *supra* 139) that the occupation is not contingent on maintaining a fixed garrison throughout the occupied territory. As long as an occupation is strictly maintained in some crucial respects, it is imprudent to look at the removal of 'boots on the ground' from one district as conclusive evidence of the total disappearance of effective control there and the complete abandonment of the Occupying Power's responsibility. The present author cannot accept the view that '[t]he tests for determining the end of occupation represent a mirror image of the tests for determining its beginning'.[1774] Once belligerent occupation commences, the degree of effective control can wane or wax. P.M.R. Stirk is right in suggesting that 'military occupation has to be considered not as a fixed condition, requiring the deployment of a quantifiable force, or even involving the assumption of a specified number of functions and offices, but as a continuum'.[1775] One should not unduly rush to the conclusion that the continuum is broken. Consequently, although effective control cannot initially be established by air or sea alone (see *supra* 140), when an Occupying Power

[1774] Shany, *supra* note 123, at 378.
[1775] Stirk, *supra* note 321, at 53.

withdraws its land forces from part of an occupied territory but retains control over the airspace and the maritime areas, effective control need not automatically be looked upon as relinquished.[1776]

(e) The Impact of the 'Oslo Accords'

859. Undeniably, by virtue of the unilateral withdrawal, Israel's responsibilities in Gaza have shrunk dramatically. But the shrinkage started even prior to the unilateral withdrawal and it is tied to the 'Oslo Accords'. Once it was mutually agreed upon that the exercise of certain functions of government – both in Gaza and in the West Bank – would be performed by the Palestinian powers-that-be, Israel has not borne the brunt of responsibility for them. The withdrawal from the Gaza Strip meant that even more functions of government are laid at the door of the Palestinians.

860. From the very beginning of the exercise of Palestinian self-government under the 'Oslo Accords', problems have arisen regarding arbitrary decisions and patterns of behaviour.[1777] The situation has been significantly aggravated by the Hamas takeover of Gaza. Surely, blame for glaring symptoms of dysfunction of the internal Palestinian administration cannot be pinned on Israel.

861. In accordance with the Protocol Concerning Legal Matters, constituting Annex IV to the 1995 Interim Agreement, the Palestinian Council gained criminal jurisdiction over all offences committed by Palestinians in the Gaza Strip.[1778] Hence, to take a hypothetical example, should a Palestinian criminal court in Gaza fail to respect the general principle whereby the penalty has to be proportional to the offence – in breach of Article 67 (first sentence) of the Geneva Convention (quoted *supra* 392) – it would be incongruous to maintain that Israel is still accountable for what transpires beyond its reach within the Palestinian judicial system. This is not due (as is sometimes suggested[1779]) to the fact that Israel lacks overall effective control: it is due to the consensual transfer by Israel to the Palestinians of specific government functions.

862. The exercise of self-government by the inhabitants within a part of an occupied territory does not, by itself, negate continued effective control by the Occupying Power. Although its grip on the area is not as firm as it used to be

[1776] See S. Wills, 'Occupation Law and Multi-National Operations: Problems and Perspectives', 77 *BYBIL* 256, 289 (2006).

[1777] See M. Rishmawi, 'Judicial Independence under Palestinian Rule', *The Arab-Israeli Accords: Legal Perspectives*, *supra* note 122, at 259, 264–5.

[1778] Protocol Concerning Legal Matters, Annex IV to Israel-Palestine Liberation Organization, Interim Agreement on the West Bank and the Gaza Strip, *supra* note 116, at 635, *id.* (Article I(1)).

[1779] See E. Benvenisti, 'Responsibility for the Protection of Human Rights under the Interim Israeli-Palestinian Agreements', 28 *Is.LR* 297, 313 (1994).

at earlier stages of the occupation, Israel remains the Occupying Power in the Gaza Strip until all the existing fastened locks of effective control are unbolted.

III. Post-Hostilities Belligerent Occupation

A. *Belligerent or Pacific Occupation?*

863. Quite frequently, hostilities actually come to an end but the formal state of war goes on, and so does the occupation. This is a case of post-hostilities occupation, which is still belligerent occupation, although it is ordinarily expected to continue only during a transition period pending the conclusion of a treaty of peace. The occupation is not 'pacific', since it is not consensual (see *supra* 106). The end of hostilities may prove ephemeral and, in any event, it cannot erase the belligerent antecedents of the occupation.

B. *Article 6 of Geneva Convention (IV)*

(a) ***The Special Legal Regime***

864. In a post-hostilities belligerent occupation, there is a marked change in the legal regime by dint of Article 6 (third paragraph) of Geneva Convention (IV):

> In the case of occupied territory, the application of the present Convention shall cease one year after the general close of military operations; however, the Occupying Power shall be bound, for the duration of the occupation, to the extent that such Power exercises the functions of government in such territory, by the provisions of the following Articles of the present Convention: 1 to 12, 27, 29 to 34, 47, 49, 51, 52, 53, 59, 61 to 77, 143.[1780]

865. It is true that Article 3(b) of Additional Protocol I states that 'the application of the Conventions and of this Protocol shall cease, … in the case of occupied territories, on the termination of the occupation'.[1781] That is to say, the temporal application of Geneva Convention (IV) in its entirety is extended until the actual termination of the occupation. However, this innovative provision is applicable only to Contracting Parties to the Additional Protocol, and not to a country such as Israel, which is not.[1782] An allegation that Article 6 (third paragraph) has fallen into desuetude and that the Protocol's provision now reflects customary international law is insupportable.[1783]

[1780] Geneva Convention (IV), *supra* note 29, at 582.

[1781] Additional Protocol I, *supra* note 33, at 716.

[1782] See R. Wolfrum, 'The Attack of September 11, 2001, the Wars against the Taliban and Iraq: Is There a Need to Reconsider International Law on the Recourse to Force and the Rules in Armed Conflict?', 7 *MPYUNL* 1, 64 (2003).

[1783] See J. Grignon, 'The Geneva Conventions and the End of Occupation', *The 1949 Geneva Conventions: A Commentary*, *supra* note 309, at 1575, 1582–4.

(b) *The Meaning of the Special Regime*

866. What does the text of Article 6 (third paragraph) of the Geneva Convention denote? As long as the occupation is in progress – and to the extent that the Occupying Power still exercises functions of government – only those provisions of the Convention which are enumerated in the text remain operative. In contradistinction to the clauses expressly listed in Article 6 (third paragraph), all other stipulations of the instrument become dormant. The upshot of Article 6 (third paragraph) is a partial application of the Convention. Only 'a hard core of provisions' of the Geneva Convention endures during the remainder of the occupation.[1784]

867. By and large, the list of clauses of the Convention that outlast the general close of military operations – congruent with Article 6 (third paragraph) – covers the more important provisions of the instrument. But that is not a hard and fast rule. Curiously, Article 78 (dealing with internment; see *supra* 519) is not enumerated. What is the import of the omission? Surely, it does not mean that the Occupying Power gains a free hand to detain civilians administratively (without trial), unencumbered by the strictures that are of fundamental importance in Article 78 (see *supra* 527). When the Convention ceases to apply, human rights law takes over. Consistent with that law, detainees must be brought promptly before a judicial authority, and they are entitled to trial within a reasonable time or release.[1785] Alas, this human right is derogable and, if a derogation is duly made, a purely administrative detention becomes possible (see the *Lawless* case *supra* 257). The drafters of the Geneva Convention apparently assumed that, subsequent to the general close of the hostilities, 'stringent measures against the civilian population will no longer be justified'.[1786] In other words, they must have intuited that non-judicial internment will have lost its *raison d'être*. However, reality has a tendency to develop in a counter-intuitive fashion.

(c) *When Is the Special Regime Applicable?*

868. Article 6 (third paragraph) employs the phrase 'after the general close of military operations'. The coinage, which is not unequivocal, ought to be juxtaposed with the language used in Article 118 of Geneva Convention (III): 'after the cessation of active hostilities'.[1787] It is not clear whether the use of two different formulas in Geneva Conventions (III) and (IV) 'was

[1784] Gasser and Dörmann, *supra* note 196, at 281.

[1785] See Article 9(3) of the International Covenant on Civil and Political Rights, *supra* note 335, at 46.

[1786] *Commentary, IV Geneva Convention*, *supra* note 31, at 63.

[1787] Geneva Convention (III), *supra* note 397, at 551.

deliberate or was the consequence of uncoordinated drafting'.[1788] Some commentators maintain that the time frames adduced by the two expressions were meant to coincide.[1789] Another view is that '[t]he general close of military operations may occur after the "cessation of active hostilities"'.[1790] In any event, there is no doubt that the cessation of active hostilities can precede a treaty of peace,[1791] and this must be true also of the general close of military operations.

869. Whatever the exact meaning of the phraseology employed – as long as no final treaty of peace has entered into force – three points must be borne in mind:

(a) A general close of military operations must be (in the words of the Trial Chamber of the ICTY in the 2011 *Gotovina* Judgment) 'sufficiently general, definitive and effective'.[1792]
(b) This being the case, it may take a while before one may reach the safe conclusion that military operations have actually come to a general close.
(c) Even if military operations are deemed closed at a specific point of time, they may reopen at a later date and they will then trigger the renewed operation of Geneva Convention (IV) *in toto*.[1793]

870. In the Advisory Opinion on the *Wall*, the International Court of Justice took the position that '[s]ince the military operations leading to the occupation of the West Bank in 1967 ended a long time ago, only those Articles of the Fourth Geneva Convention referred to in Article 6, paragraph 3, remain applicable in that occupied territory'.[1794] This is a bewildering statement, which suggests that the clock of the one-year rule of Article 6 (third paragraph) started ticking as soon as the Israeli occupation began, in June 1967. As rightly protested by A. Imseis:

> The problem with the Court's interpretation of Article 6 is its misguided focus on 'military operations leading to occupation'. Article 6 in fact provides that insofar as occupied

[1788] M. Milanovic, 'The End of Application of International Humanitarian Law', 893 *IRRC* 893 163, 172–3 (2014).
[1789] See B. Scholdan, '"The End of Active Hostilities": The Obligation to Release Conflict Internees under International Law', 38 *Hous.JIL* 99, 161–2 (2016).
[1790] B. Zimmermann, 'Article 3', *Commentary on the Additional Protocols*, *supra* note 327, at 65, 68.
[1791] See Y. Dinstein, 'The Release of Prisoners of War', *Studies and Essays*, *supra* note 1063, at 37, 44–5.
[1792] *Prosecutor v. Gotovina* et al. (ICTY, Trial Chamber, 2011), para. 1697.
[1793] See Roberts, *supra* note 319, at 55.
[1794] Advisory Opinion on *Legal Consequences of the Construction of a Wall in the Occupied Palestinian Territory*, *supra* note 25, at 185.

territories are concerned, application of the Convention 'shall cease one year after the general close of military operations', not on the 'general close of military operations *leading to the occupation*', as asserted by the Court.[1795]

A premature celebration of the general close of military operations poses a danger to the civilian population, inasmuch as it reduces the scope of protection that the population enjoys under the Convention.

871. The historical record shows that, over more than five decades since June 1967, there were several surges of hostilities in the West Bank and in the Gaza Strip (particularly during two *intifadas* and three major incursions of Israel into Gaza). At several junctures during the prolonged Israeli occupation, Article 6 (third paragraph) should have come into play.[1796] Still, as hopes and dreams of an early peace dimmed time and again, and as hostilities resumed, the entire Convention must be acknowledged to have been fully reactivated. In conformity with Article 6 (third paragraph), the Convention – like an accordion – may be compressed (one year after the general close of military operations), stretched out in full (if and when hostilities resume), recompressed, restretched, and so on.

IV. The Consequences of the Termination of Occupation

872. With the actual termination of belligerent occupation, the occupied territory (in whole or in part) is usually restored to the displaced sovereign. There are, of course, prominent exceptions (like Jordan detaching itself from the West Bank in favour of the Palestinians; see *supra* 52). But the ensuing discussion will be based on the assumption that it is the displaced sovereign to whom possession of the occupied territory is restored.

A. *Legislation and Official Appointments*

873. Upon the termination of belligerent occupation, the authority of the Occupying Power in the occupied territory lapses. Hence, in principle, any special legislation enacted by the military government in pursuit of Hague Regulation 43 and Geneva Article 64 (quoted *supra* 269, 336) ceases to be valid as soon as the occupation has ended, unless the restored sovereign opts to keep that legislation intact.[1797]

[1795] See A. Imseis, 'Critical Reflections on the International Humanitarian Aspects of the ICJ *Wall* Advisory Opinion', 99 *AJIL* 102, 106 (2005). Emphasis in the original.

[1796] See Y. Dinstein, 'Autonomy and Legal Status: A Rejoinder', 26 *Security Dialogue* 185, 187–8 (1995); 'The International Legal Status of the West Bank and the Gaza Strip – 1998', 28 *IYHR* 37, 42–4 (1998).

[1797] See McNair and Watts, *supra* note 1443, at 388–9.

874. Obviously, there are strong prosaic reasons militating in favour of the restored sovereign not rushing to abrogate the legislation passed by the Occupying Power (which may consequently have a 'successional' effect).[1798] There is also an interstitial space of time before any meaningful change can occur. But, even beyond a transition period, it may prove difficult (if not impossible) to go back in time, all the more so when certain legislation introduced by the Occupying Power gains staunch popular support. Realistically, 'any lengthy military occupation brings about certain changes in legal and other spheres which cannot be completely wiped out after the return of the legitimate sovereign'.[1799] A sedimentary deposit of legislation by the Occupying Power is therefore likely to remain in place for a long time, even if overlaid by new statutes passed by the restored sovereign.

875. Appointments conferred by the Occupying Power on local judges and other public officials expire at the end of the occupation: no such appointees can claim security of tenure.[1800] Yet, for the sake of stability, the restored sovereign may deem it expedient to keep or reinstate some judges or officials in their positions.

B. Prisoners and Detainees

876. Article 77 of Geneva Convention (IV) lays down:

> Protected persons who have been accused of offences or convicted by the courts in occupied territory, shall be handed over at the close of occupation, with the relevant records, to the authorities of the liberated territory.[1801]

Thus, upon rolling back at the close of the occupation, the Occupying Power is not allowed to take with it convicted prisoners or persons under indictment.[1802] The text does not throw light on the question whether, following the transfer, prisoners must remain in jail or they may be released.[1803] Apparently, this is up to the restored sovereign.

877. As for internees, they must all be released, and, under Article 134 of the Convention, every effort should be made by the Contracting Parties to enable their return to their last place of residence.[1804] In accordance with Article 135 (first paragraph), the costs of sending internees back to their homes must be borne by the Detaining (Occupying) Power.[1805]

[1798] Verzijl, *supra* note 1323, at 160.
[1799] Von Glahn, *supra* note 339, at 257.
[1800] See Kelsen, *supra* note 4, at 74 n. 39.
[1801] Geneva Convention (IV), *supra* note 29, at 602.
[1802] *Commentary, IV Geneva Convention*, *supra* note 31, at 366.
[1803] See Gasser and Dörmann, *supra* note 196, at 308.
[1804] Geneva Convention (IV), *supra* note 29, at 620.
[1805] *Ibid.*

C. *Postliminium and Acquired Rights*

878. A state of affairs in which the displaced sovereign is restored in the formerly occupied territory is called in Latin *postliminium*.[1806] As stated by the Arbitrator G. Sauser-Hall, in the 1953 Award in the *Albanian Gold* case, a *postliminium* entails the invalidation of all acts committed by the Occupying Power in breach of international law.[1807] The legal ramifications of the nullification of the Occupying Power's acts may be quite extensive, although they would vary from one domestic legal system to another.[1808] A case in point is that of private property confiscated by the Occupying Power in contravention of the Hague Regulations and sold in open market to a buyer in good faith. While the confiscation itself is void, the original owner will not automatically be entitled to restitution from the new one: everything depends on the domestic law of the State concerned.[1809]

879. The legal effects of acts duly performed by the Occupying Power, in harmony with the law of belligerent occupation, cannot be denied. The restored sovereign must recognize the validity of rights acquired under valid legislation, judicial pronouncements and administrative activities of the Occupying Power. Thus, the restored sovereign must acknowledge the lawful collection of ordinary taxes by the Occupying Power, and it cannot object to the sale (and corresponding purchase) of fruits from State immovables.[1810]

1806 On the origins of the idiom, see J.-C. Woltag, 'Postliminium', VIII *MPEPIL* 389, 389–90 (2009).

1807 *Affaire Relative à l'Or de la Banque Nationale d'Albanie* (US, France, Italy, UK), 1953, 12 *RIAA* 13, 40.

1808 See G.N. Barrie, 'The International Law Relating to Belligerent Occupation at the Advent of the Twenty-First Century', [2012] *JSAL* 433, 457.

1809 See Morgenstern, *supra* note 807, at 309.

1810 See Oppenheim, *supra* note 201, at 618.

Conclusion

880. If there is a lodestar guiding the law of belligerent occupation, it is the principle that the civilian population of an occupied territory must benefit from maximal safeguards feasible in the circumstances. The protection of the civilian population is the key concern of relevant international legal norms, whether they are engendered by custom or by treaty. This means that life and order in the occupied territory must not be destabilized, let alone reach a vanishing point. The authority of the Occupying Power is not untrammelled. Primarily, apart from its elementary obligation to preserve life and order, the Occupying Power is barred from three d's: it is not allowed to despoil resources, destroy property (in a context that exceeds military operations) or deport the local inhabitants.

881. All the same, it would be wrong to think that the interests of the Occupying Power are ignored or trampled over by the law of belligerent occupation. As in other branches of the *jus in bello*, humanitarian considerations (while of the utmost importance) are liable to be trumped by countervailing requirements of military necessity. In particular, although the Occupying Power fails to acquire sovereignty over the occupied territory, it need not brook forcible opposition to its continued effective control over the area. The military government can mobilize and employ all the power available to it (within the limits imposed by the *jus in bello*) in order to quell organized resistance or individual acts of sabotage.

882. Belligerent occupation bristles with tantalizing problems derived from a combustible situation that is in many respects unique. The nostrum that these problems may be resolved through cross-pollination of precepts grown in the different culture of human rights appears to the present writer to be deluded. The extraordinary requirements of belligerent occupation strenuously challenge the practicality of subjecting it to ordinary human rights. Whatever their allure in general, human rights – whether because they are derogable in wartime or because they contain built-in limitations – may too often be relegated to irrelevance under conditions of belligerent occupation. International law has no choice but to come up with *lex specialis* solutions. Only such solutions can be tailor-made to the specific exigencies spawned in occupied territories.

883. Largely, this *lex specialis* already exists: in the main, it was formed at The Hague in 1899/1907 and then recast in Geneva in 1949. Only relatively minor modifications have been made (in a non-systematic fashion) since then. The law as it stands has not lost its vitality and it has much merit. Yet, experience accumulated in recent decades shows that existing norms have to be stretched to the limit when belligerent occupation is unduly prolonged. The welfare of the civilian population requires the legal system to keep abreast of the times. To achieve that, the scope of authority vested in the Occupying Powers must be commensurate with the objective need – accelerating the longer the occupation lasts – to enact new legislation, to introduce new development projects, and to consider new schemes of socio-economic reform. The interests of the international community would be well served if some aspects of the law of belligerent occupation in force would be reassessed in terms of their adaptability to a prolonged occupation. Despite a current reluctance to tinker with a normative system that on the whole functions well, it is crucial to ensure that the law is not outstripped by the march of events.

Index of Persons

Index of Subjects